From Modernization to Globalization

BLACKWELL READERS IN SOCIOLOGY

Each volume in this authoritative series aims to provide students and scholars with comprehensive collections of classic and contemporary readings for all the major sub-fields of sociology. They are designed to complement single-authored works, or to be used as stand-alone textbooks for courses. The selected readings sample the most important works that students should read and are framed by informed editorial introductions. The series aims to reflect the state of the discipline by providing collections not only on standard topics but also on cutting-edge subjects in sociology to provide future directions in teaching and research.

J. Timmons Roberts and Amy Hite: *From Modernization to Globalization: Perspectives on Development and Social Change*

Forthcoming:
Anne Branaman: *Self and Society*
Jaber Gubrium and James Holstein: *Aging and Everyday Life*
C. Lee Harrington and Denise Bielby: *Cultural Production and Consumption*
Darin Weinberg: *Qualitative Methods*
Lynn Spillman: *Cultural Sociology*
Craig Calhoun: *Classic Sociological Theory*
Craig Calhoun: *Contemporary Sociological Theory*

From Modernization to
Globalization
Perspectives on Development and Social Change

Edited by

J. Timmons Roberts
and
Amy Hite

BLACKWELL
Publishers

Copyright © Blackwell Publishers Ltd 2000; editorial introductions and arrangement copyright ©
J. Timmons Roberts and Amy Hite 2000

First published 2000

2 4 6 8 10 9 7 5 3 1

Blackwell Publishers Inc.
350 Main Street
Malden, Massachusetts 02148
USA

Blackwell Publishers Ltd
108 Cowley Road
Oxford OX4 1JF
UK

Library of Congress Cataloging-in-Publication Data

From modernization to globalization : perspectives on development and
  social change / edited by J. Timmons Roberts and Amy Hite.
     p. cm.—(Blackwell readers in sociology)
   Includes bibliographical references and index.
   ISBN 0–631–21096–2 (hardcover : alk. paper).—ISBN 0–631–21097–0
(pbk. : alk. paper)
    1. Community development—developing countries. 2. Economic development—Social aspects—
Developing countries. 3. Social change—Developing countries. 4. International economic integra-
tion—Social aspects—Developing countries. 5. Developing countries—Social conditions. I. Roberts,
J. Timmons. II. Hite, Amy. III. Series.
HN981.C6F76 1999
307.1′4′091724—dc21   99–16942
                                                      CIP

British Library Cataloguing in Publication Data

A CIP catalogue record for this book is available from the British Library.

Typeset Sabon in 10 on 12 pt
by Kolam Information Services Pvt. Ltd., Pondicherry, India

Printed in Great Britain by TJ International, Padstow, Cornwall

This book is printed on acid-free paper.

Contents

About the Editors

J. Timmons Roberts is Associate Professor in Sociology and Latin American Studies at Tulane University. His research examines the social and environmental impacts of globalization. He is conducting work in four areas. First, he is utilizing world-system techniques to examine the relation between paths of development and national environmental performance. Second, he is studying how global environmental standards and treaties are affecting firms' behaviors, focusing on the chemical industry in the USA, Mexico, and Brazil. Third, he is completing a book on environmental struggles in Louisiana, USA (*Chronicles from the Environmental Justice Frontlines*, forthcoming from Cambridge University Press). Finally, he continues his work on urbanization and globalization in the Brazilian Amazon. His articles have appeared in *World Development*, *Social Problems*, *Economic Development and Cultural Change*, *Geographical Review*, the *Journal of Developing Societies*, *Political Research Quarterly*, *Sociological Inquiry*, and *Current Sociology*.

Amy Hite is a doctoral candidate and Visiting Instructor at the Center for Latin American Studies at Tulane University. Her primary research interest is how Latin American cities have managed concurrent processes of urban growth, decentralization, and economic restructuring, and how these development processes have affected both the material conditions of residents and their views about citizenship and the government's role in providing basic urban services. Of particular interest to her are secondary cities such as Santa Cruz, Bolivia and Ciudad Guayana, Venezuela, where she has conducted field research. She has also researched the coca/cocaine industry from a commodity chain perspective, which appeared in the Greenwood volume *Latin America in the World Economy*.

Preface and Acknowledgments

Why are poor countries poor? What should they do to turn their situation around? What happens to countries and individuals when they move from being "backward" to being "modern"? What does it mean to "develop" and be "modern," anyway? What are the social effects of the process of worldwide economic, cultural, and political integration called globalization?

In spite of renewed interest in processes of social change and development in the "Third World," we found no satisfactory books to use in our classes which combine excerpts of original classic and contemporary thought on the key issues. Many such edited volumes seem to have long since gone out of print or seem to cover just one region or perspective. All the readers with any of the classic development debates lack any discussion of the transition to post-industrial or "postmodern" societies as the result of economic restructuring and globalization. In attempting to fill some of this gap, this book seeks to provide a primer for scholars wishing to get quickly up to speed and for students of Sociology, Globalization, Regional Studies, Geography, Political Science, Economics, or other courses on modernization, development, or social change.

The book is organized into four parts. Part I reviews formative ideas on the transition to modern society, with brief readings from Marx and Engels, Durkheim, and Weber. These fundamental works echo through a century and a half of thought about development. The Modernizationists' influential discussion of how development changes people is sampled in Part II, with selections from Parsons, Rostow, Lewis, Lerner, Inkeles, and Huntington. The response from dependency and world-system theorists is reviewed in Part III with readings from Frank, Cardoso, de Janvry and Garramón, Wallerstein, Chase-Dunn, and Gereffi. The final section offers a diverse sampling of how eight different theorists conceptualize the social effects of the current general trend of globalization. This section includes works by Fröbel, Heinrichs, and Kreye, McMichael, Harvey, Rodrik, Ward and Pyle, Sutcliffe, Sklair, and Portes.

We hope the book can serve as a companion to a number of core texts in upper-level undergraduate and graduate courses on development. Examples of such core texts are P. W. Preston's *Development Theory: An Introduction* or John Brohman's *Popular Development* (both Blackwell, 1996). We believe it would complement several other books: Phil McMichael's *Development and Social Change* (Pine Forge Press, 1996), David Harrison's *The Sociology of Modernization and Development* (Routledge, 1998), Leslie Sklair's *Sociology of the Global System* (Johns Hopkins University Press, 1991), or Anton L. Allahar's *Sociology and the Periphery* (Garamond, 1995). There are many others.

Finally, we would like to take a moment to thank those who made this volume possible. Susan Rabinowitz at Blackwell has been an encouraging and understanding editor and Ken Provencher provided us with much needed logistical support. Ginnie Stroud-Lewis did the laborious task of securing copyrights from the dozens of publishers whose work is included here. Juanita Bullough oversaw the process of editing and proofreading the full manuscript. As Acting Director of the Tulane University Stone Center for Latin American Studies, Gener Yeager provided summer support that got us through most of the excerpting work. Quinn Roberts, Holly Flood, and Jim and Gann Roberts provided the core support team for the first author, and I am ever and deeply grateful to them. The second author is, as always, forever grateful for the support of John Hite and other family members, especially Ellen and Jules Bellone. Gratitude for participation in this project goes solely to longtime mentor, first author Timmons Roberts. Our hope is that this volume serves to keep alive what we believe are vitally important debates about the nature of development and social change.

Acknowledgments to Sources

The editors and publishers gratefully acknowledge permission to reproduce copyright material. Every effort has been made to trace the copyright holders, but if any have been inadvertently overlooked the publishers will be pleased to make the necessary arrangements at the first opportunity.

Cardoso, Fernando Henrique, "Dependency and Development in Latin America," *New Left Review*, 74 (July/August 1972).

Chase-Dunn, Christopher, "The Effects of International Economic Dependence on Development and Inequality: A Cross-National Study," *American Sociological Review*, 40 (December 1975), reprinted by permission of the American Sociological Association.

de Janvry, Alain and Carlos Garramón, "The Dynamics of Rural Poverty in Latin America," *Journal of Peasant Studies*, 4:3 (1977).

Durkheim, Emile, selections from *The Division of Labor in Society* (1893).

Frank, Andre Gunder, "The Development of Underdevelopment," *Monthly Review*, 18:4 (1969). Copyright © 1966 by Monthly Review Press, reprinted by permission of Monthly Review Foundation.

Fröbel, Folker, Jürgen Heinrichs, and Otto Kreye, "The new international division of labor in the world economy," from *The New International Division of Labour* (Cambridge University Press, 1980).

Gereffi, Gary, "Rethinking Development Theory: Insights from East Asia and Latin America," from A. Douglas Kincaid and Alejandro Portes (eds.), *Comparative National Development: Society and Economy in the New Global Order*. Copyright © 1994 by the University of North Carolina Press. Used by permission of the publisher.

Harvey, David, "Capitalism: The Factory of Fragmentation," *New Perspectives Quarterly*, 9 (Spring 1992).

Huntington, Samuel, "The Change to Change: Modernization, Development and Politics," *Comparative Politics*, 3 (April 1971).

Huntington, Samuel, *Political Order in Changing Societies* (Yale University Press, New Haven, 1968).

Inkeles, Alex, "Making Men Modern: On the Causes and Consequences of Individual Change in Six Developing Countries," *American Journal of Sociology*, 75 (1969).

Lerner, Daniel, *The Passing of Traditional Society* (Free Press, Glencoe, 1958).

Lewis, Oscar, *A Study of Slum Culture: Backgrounds for La Vida* (Random House, New York and David Higham Associates, London, 1968).

Marx, Karl, and Engels, Friedrich, "Manifesto of the Communist Party" (1848) and "Alienated Labor" (1844).

McMichael, Philip, "Globalization: Myths and Realities," *Rural Sociology*, 61:1 (1996).

Parsons, Talcott, "Evolutionary Universals in Society," *American Sociological Review*, 29 (June 1964), reprinted by permission of American Sociological Association, Washington, DC.

Portes, Alejandro, "Neoliberalism and the Sociology of Development: Emerging Trends and Unanticipated Facts," *Population and Development Review*, 23:2 (1997).

Rodrik, Dani, "Introduction," from *Has Globalization Gone Too Far?* (Institute for International Economics, Washington, DC 1997).

Rostow, W. W., "The Five Stages-of-Growth – A Summary," from *The Stages of Economic Growth: A Non-Communist Manifesto* (2nd ed.) (Cambridge University Press, New York, 1971).

Sklair, Leslie, "Social Movements and Global Capitalism," *Sociology*, 29:3 (1995).

Sutcliffe, Bob, "Development after Ecology," from *The North, the South and the Environment: Ecological Constraints and the Global Economy* (St. Martin's Press, New York, 1995).

Wallerstein, Immanuel, "The Rise and Future Demise of the World Capitalist System: Concepts for Comparative Analysis," from *The Capitalist World-Economy* (Cambridge University Press, 1979).

Ward, Kathryn B., and Jean Larson Pyle, "Gender, Industrialization, Transnational Corporations and Development: An Overview of Trends and Patterns," from Christine E. Bose and Edna Acosta-Belen (eds.), *Women in the Latin American Development Process* (Temple University Press, Philadelphia, 1995). Reprinted by permission of Temple University Press. Copyright © 1995 by Sociologists for Women in Society. All Rights Reserved.

Weber, Max, *The Protestant Ethic and the Spirit of Capitalism*, 1930.

Editors' Introduction

A luxury cruise ship the size of a small city steams into a tropical harbor where residents live in dirt-floored shacks equipped only with pit toilets. An Islamic woman doctor is veiled as she carries out her work. Massive hydroelectric dams inundate vast fields to fuel export factories and modern city life; their power lines pass directly over the heads of rural poor in darkened hamlets. Asian businesspeople visit a Buddhist temple on their way to tour a factory that produces athletic shoes for a major US brand name. Street children without shoes polish a new Mercedes that stands outside government and corporate high-rises.

Throughout the world, the unevenness of economic development and social change presents us with stark paradoxes and contrasts.[1] While these visual contrasts seem sometimes irreconcilable, they are just microcosms of inequality between the two worlds that exist on our one planet: the so-called "developed" and the "underdeveloped" worlds, the "First World" and the "Third World,"[2] the poor and the rich nations. Within each poor nation the great divide is more startling because the contrasts are so close together.

Why care about these poorer countries and their economic and social development? A hundred people would give as many answers. Many would have several reasons for their concern. Some people in the wealthier nations are excited about economic opportunities in what might be a booming market for export products in the "undeveloped South"; some see a source of cheap imports to keep inflation down and of products to market here. Others want to know about development because they worry about the loss of jobs to those same new industries in the South and sense a loss of European and US control over the world's political and economic scenarios. Some experts worry about political instability or extremism in developing countries threatening the safety of travelers, government personnel, or business interests abroad – or even security at home. There is grave concern in some places about large-scale illegal immigration from poorer areas of the world. Others still are troubled about the global environment and are aware of the crucial role poorer nations play in problems as diverse as global warming, biodiversity in rainforests, or the preservation of individual, treasured species such as elephants, macaws, and mountain gorillas. Others care about developing countries because they have experienced their warm beaches, jungles, mountains, pyramids, and temples. These are some concrete reasons for caring.

Some people's concern springs from very different places, based in moral, religious, or purely academic roots. Some specialists who have devoted their lives to "development studies" or who work in development agencies are aware that of the world's six billion people, almost five billion live in countries where the average income is less than $3 a day.[3] At the same time, on average, the people in the high-income countries get to live on 23 times that much, and the gap between the two groups is widening.[4] About one out of four people in the world today lives in absolute poverty, defined as "too poor to afford an adequate diet and other necessities." Malnutrition is said to stunt the growth and development of 40 percent of all two-year-olds in poorer countries.[5]

Many religious groups have targeted these billions as the greatest potential growth areas for their churches, sending missionaries, money and material aid. Some are concerned to convert all the world's major population groups to hasten the Second Coming of Christ.[6] Other religious groups might be concerned with studying and documenting gaps in development, so that their populations might live without the daily indignities of poverty. Some people want to understand the roots and potential cures of the problems that cause the desperate poverty we are reminded of on television advertisements for groups who bring aid.

Finally, a few people point out that in countries which our economic and social system have not fully penetrated there remains a possible alternative to the development model followed in the wealthy countries. Beyond the material level, many authors are now proposing that we can learn from aboriginal cultures not just their medicinal uses of plants and land-use, but also their cosmology and non-materialist values. More concretely, education and health techniques have "trickled up" from Brazil and Central America to wider application in the rich nations. Under duress from the collapse of the Soviet Empire and an embargo from the USA, for example, Cuban agriculture has conducted the largest experiment ever in organic farming. At the other end of the political and economic spectrum, worldwide austerity programs, in which government services and spending are cut, have taken a leaf from the book of Chile's experiences in the 1980s and early 1990s.

People, then, have diverse and often multiple reasons for caring about what happens to the poor nations, and it is critical to grasp the roots of their interest to understand the approach they take and the conclusions they reach. The aim of this Introduction is to provide some context for new readers and some framework for old hands. It begins with a discussion of the deep divide in our society about who is to blame for the poverty of poor nations. This divide runs through the decades of debate about international development, which this reader attempts to chronicle. We then introduce the readings in the four sections of the book by briefly discussing their contexts, main questions, and approaches. The first section introduces excerpts from the three "dead white men," or "classical" thinkers, on these questions of how societies change: Karl Marx, Max Weber and Emile Durkheim. The limitations of culling excerpts is perhaps most apparent in their cases, since each left a lifetime of intricate, elaborate, and evolving ideas. The three sections that follow them introduce and discuss the works categorized as "modernization theory," "dependency and world-system theories," and the still-emerging literature on the relationship between globalization and development. This Introduction, then, can be read as a whole, or the latter three sections can be referred to as one approaches each set of selections in the book.

In these latter sections we have included selections that demonstrate how theorists of varied disciplines explored central themes. We hope that this introductory material will provide a simple but useful framework of the most basic ideas of each group, upon which readers can build the nuance they deserve. In turn, we hope that readers will someday explore the original works more fully to avoid being potentially misled by oversimplifying the bodies of literature from the few small excerpts we were able to accommodate in this volume.[7]

Why Are the Poor Countries Poor? Diverging Opinions

Why are the poor countries poor? There are extremely polarized opinions about this seemingly simple question. Debates about developing countries reflect a similar chasm within our society between those who believe poor *individuals* are poor because of factors that are either in, or out of, their control. Who is to blame: the poor or their society? This debate runs through the classics of philosophy and religion, but is not limited to intellectuals: it cuts through discourse amongst politicians, theologians, business groups, labor unions, and advocates for the poor. In both Britain and the USA, the division often seems to split us along party lines. On one side are those who believe that poor people are lazy and will only improve their lot if they "pull themselves up by their own bootstraps," finding ways to make themselves rich by their own inventiveness. On the other side are those who see poor people as victims of their birth into bad conditions, of bad times and economic disruptions such as mass layoffs in "restructured" industries, as victims of discrimination on the basis of skin color, gender, or cultural differences. There is a similarly deep disagreement among social scientists about the ability of individuals to change things. It is difficult to overstate how profound this split's implications are for the role of government. Should "the state" step in and try to overcome some of the structural barriers that create poverty? Or should states get out of the way and let ingenuity and the market solve the problem?

There are surprising parallels between these acrimonious national debates and those over why poor countries are poor and what should be done about them. This book seeks to introduce readers to some of the many complex theories that have been advanced to explain national poverty, development, and wealth. But through the complexity it is often useful to weigh whether authors believe national poverty or "backwardness" is due to *internal* or *external* factors. That is, whether nations are poor because their society lacks key elements, or whether their situation is the product of centuries of colonial exploitation and continuing political and economic domination by more powerful imperialist nations like the Netherlands, Spain, Great Britain, the USA and Japan. As you will see in the following section, the earliest social theorists disagreed about the causes of development. This debate has "raged" ever since. The "modernization theorists" put their emphasis on *internal* factors while the authors presented in the third section of the volume stress the importance of external factors in the development process. By no means is this debate settled.

Social Turmoil and the Classical Thinkers

To understand the startling contrasts and rapid changes going on in developing countries, contemporary "development" thinkers look back to earlier changes their own societies experienced during the age of industrialization. And to do so, they draw on three of the most influential social thinkers: Marx, Weber, and Durkheim. Political, economic, scientific, and social turmoil served as the backdrop for the work of nineteenth-century German theorists Karl Marx (1818–83), Friedrich Engels (1820–95) and Max Weber (1864–1920), and the Frenchman Emile Durkheim (1858–1917).

While factories, railroads, and cities were proliferating, centuries-old institutions such as religion, intimate communities, and the authority of traditional rulers like kings and lords were unraveling before everyone's eyes. As the Industrial Revolution rocked Europe, fear of its disruptions spread. Poor peasants lost their land to "enclosures" by capitalist ranchers. Old, moneyed, landowning classes saw their power to control government weaken as urban-based businesspeople gained influence in first economic, and then political, circles. But most frightening to many people were the masses of urban unemployed and industrial workers hired by the sprawling new factories. These workers' brusque, unrefined ways offended many "proper" urbanites; and as living conditions were often tight and unsanitary, disease (both physical and social), promiscuity, and unrest were seen as inevitable. Factory work and city life were changing peasants into a new type of proletarian laborer. Controlling them and planning for the future required understanding the fundamental but unknown implications of this enormous class.

To all three authors discussed here, one thing was apparent: modern Western society was fundamentally different from anything that had come before. For the team of Karl Marx and Friedrich Engels, this difference signaled a precursor to a future revolutionary stage of history, where a new type of social structure that would end class struggle would eclipse capitalism. For Max Weber and Emile Durkheim, modern society was unique because even though it grew out of European history, it required a fundamentally different way of thinking, working, and organizing as a society.

All of these theorists observed similar trends. They saw a sharp shift from "traditional" to "modern" ways of life. They documented a breakdown of the ties and institutions governing those "traditional" societies. These theorists observed and documented a process of *increased division of labor*. That is, they saw different members of a society increasingly specializing in specific tasks (such as selling, carpentry, fishing, etc.). Perhaps most importantly, Marx, Weber, and Durkheim all observed that society was changing from one where authority and beliefs stemmed from traditions, superstitions, fatalism, or emotions, to one dominated by the application of reason and practicality, an appreciation of efficiency and the ability to explain the world scientifically. This new complex of beliefs – that nature could be understood and controlled and that life should be organized with a goal of efficiency – they termed "rationalization."

In general, all of these classic social theorists saw this shift to modernity in terms of increased complexity. In other words, what people do and how they do it, how people relate to one another, how people envision their universe, how individuals organize as a group, and how people make decisions all become more specialized, segmented, and complex. For example, someone working in a modern factory and living in a city might specialize in creating one thing in exchange for a daily wage and would use new technologies in production. This "modern" person might not know his or her neighbors. Instead of believing in natural forces they would base faith and decisions on science, law, and accounting. And instead of knowing only a few people intimately, they might have daily but superficial contact with hundreds of individuals very different from themselves. Their interactions with these near-strangers would be based on their survival needs of making an exchange of money, or goods, or services, or work.

Alongside evidence that this new economic system – capitalism – was an incredibly powerful one came contradictory evidence that despite its ability to generate wealth, it also created dire poverty, social inequalities, and political crises. It was working to understand the roots of these contradictions that drove Marx and Engels. Marx thought that people and their history could only be understood in relation to what they produce: his historical analyses hinged on studying the relationships among workers, the tools they use to produce, and the owners of these tools (the capitalists). Marx saw these *relations of production* as the most important explanations of why society is as it is and how it changes. In short, for Marx and Engels the root of any social situation or conflict lies in economic relationships. This type of analysis is known as *historical materialism*. Marx differed from the other authors in this section and the next in that his work is essentially a critique of capitalism. According to Marx and Engels, capitalism was merely a historical stage, albeit a crucial one, in which all relationships are mediated by the exchange of things that can be bought and sold.

Marx's greatest legacy is probably his contention that all history is a story of struggles between those who own factories and tools to produce goods (the *bourgeoisie*), and those who must sell their labor in order to purchase the goods they need to survive (the *proletariat*). This separation of society into workers and owners means that in capitalist society there is a constant struggle over the difference between what workers are paid and the final price of what they create. For example, using modern production techniques workers might create 100 shoes per day, each of which might sell for $1, yet each worker might only earn $3 a day. In capitalism there is a constant struggle between workers and owners over the difference between the cost of production and the price that products command on the market. As long as workers are unable to capture the surplus value of what they produce (the difference between the cost of producing 100 shoes and the $100 the shoes sell for), conflict permeates economic and social relationships. It is conflict in the form of exploitation of labor that both characterizes capitalism as a system and will, according to Marx and Engels, lead to its demise.

Marx once said something along the lines of "men make their own history but not in situations of their own making." For Marx, the point in studying history was not just memorizing the deeds of individuals or their actions, but understanding the evolving *structure* of things. He saw the capitalist system of wage labor and exchange for profit as an overarching, all-encompassing structure that breeds exploitative economic relationships among individuals, classes, and regions. These economic relationships, in turn determine how people think – they influence prevailing ideologies and behaviors. Confronted with what they saw as a dehumanizing and seemingly overwhelming force of capitalism, Marx and Engels were nonetheless hopeful that because of its structure capitalism would inevitably undermine itself, making way for a new society. One hundred and fifty years after its publication, many of the predictions of the *Communist Manifesto* (i.e., that socialist revolutions would come in the most industrial countries) seem to have been proven wrong. Still, as we see in piece after piece in this book, the ideas in the clear, strident, and political *Manifesto* are incorporated, expanded, refuted, and directly critiqued by social scientists of all stripes who followed. They were clear, testable hypotheses, but more than that, the ideas resonated with billions of citizens around the world.

Writing about a half-century after Marx and Engels, Max Weber was less interested in presenting a political agenda and more interested in explaining the underlying forces that allowed the new society around him to develop. For centuries, European society was dominated by sources of traditional authority – the Church, the Crown, or the landed elite. As society urbanized and industrialized, the power of these institutions eroded quickly as an almost scientific pursuit of moneymaking emerged as the dominating force of the era. People were more interested in investing their surplus in productive investments than in spending it on luxury goods (as they had in the past). Weber noted that this new approach to work and money brought with it profound attitudinal and behavioral changes, a veritable "Spirit of Capitalism." For example, instead of the old system of people placing trust and esteem in a family name or age-old tradition, in the new system they were more likely to trust a written contract, a title bestowed on someone because of ability or expertise, or formal accounting procedures. Instead of basing government hierarchy on tradition or wealth, bureaucratic hierarchy came to be based on special criteria for different positions. Instead of personal relationships leading to rewards, people were increasingly treated in accordance with objective standards. In short, society had come to value rational procedures.

Weber's writings explained how society went from valuing tradition to one dominated by new, more objective practices and values such as the written contract, merit, expertise, universal standards, and established methods and procedures for completing tasks. Weber asks: How did written rules, limited jurisdictions, limited powers, record-keeping, separation of public and private life, and the following of documented, comprehensive procedures come to almost replace religion and lineage as a source of authority? His answer is that the ideas accompanying the emergence of Protestantism and rational bureaucratic organization spilled over and even dominated an economic system, modern capitalism. In this sense Weber differs greatly from Marx: where Marx believed economic arrangements determined ideology (ideas) and nearly everything else, Weber believed in the possibility that the ideas of men could lead the process of economic development. In this case, Protestant ideas helped shape the rise of capitalism in its modern form.

Weber is not saying that in order to be capitalist and productive a society must be Protestant! Instead, he argues that the initial development of Protestantism in Europe and North America contributed to economic arrangements of that specific era; capitalism is no longer imbued with Protestantism but is an independent force. Specifically, Weber argued that certain Protestant religious practices had become secularized and developed into a new type of authority. For example, Protestants advocated devoting one's life to a calling to demonstrate one's desire to obey God's will. Therefore, hard work in a specific area was a virtue, and laziness or idleness considered sinful. This devotion to a calling, coupled with the belief in the sinfulness of an unproductive accumulation of wealth (as it was evidence of a lack of grace), led to vocational specialization and the reinvestment of capital. It was only the Protestant attitude towards wealth, argued Weber, which resulted in capital being viewed as something to reinvest judiciously. Similarly, specialization according to one's calling infused work with religious meaning and made hard work, efficiency, and asceticism inherently virtuous, as the accumulation of wisely invested wealth demonstrated a state of grace. This change following the Protestant reformation was a profound one. Previously, it was thought that work was not for "proper" people and that showing God's glory should be done through art, poetry, or music. Gentlemen and ladies focused on these fineries and a pursuit of courtly love. Nowhere was concern over one's vocation or even excelling in that area considered virtuous.

The influence of Weber's observations cannot be overstated: the works you will read by modernization theorists written many decades later all have the implicit assumption that there is something inherently morally superior in the investment of wealth, harder work, efficiency, and strict bureaucratic structures. They called these traits in a society "modern" and "rational," labeling the others as leftovers of previous social structures, as "irrational," or as impediments to progress. Many other ideas have been carried forward from Weber's work. For example, some authors included in the final section of this volume take up Weber's assertion that power is based not just on relations of production (i.e., on money), but on factors like access to information, cultural identification, and organizational potential. Likewise, his attention to social status and the role of the state (the government) has informed a new generation of scholarship on social change and development.

Like the other classic social theorists, Emile Durkheim's interest in social change was closely linked to his observations on the process of a division of labor. In a traditional society, instead of specializing in one thing, each individual replicates the same range of activities and roles. In other words, people in a traditional society are very similar to one another: they know fewer people, they do fewer things, and they do not venture far from home. As a consequence, their worldview is limited to what is familiar or passed on through tradition. For Durkheim, a society that has low levels of differentiation and specialization gets by on the basis of this sameness. He termed this *mechanical solidarity*. Once a division of labor occurs and becomes more complex, people become increasingly exposed to new requirements, experiences, and values. The further this process of specialization and division of labor progresses, the more different people become and the more a society is able to produce. Instead of having many roles and doing many things, individuals specialize to varying degrees. Somewhat confusingly, Durkheim said that this specialized, interdependent type of society was based on *organic* solidarity. Like an organism, the division of labor and the heterogeneity of its parts allow it to function on the basis of interdependencies. Since Durkheim, Talcott Parsons and the other authors you will read in the following section have employed similar traditional-modern dichotomies and the concept of division of labor to understand how poor countries differed from wealthy ones and where they might be going.

Along with a shift to this new kind of solidarity, people needed to deal with a world of greater diversity and a faster pace of change. In order to do this they needed to change their worldview from the narrow and particularistic to a broader, less rigid, and more universal one. Theorists such as Durkheim and Parsons suggested that this process was not only inevitable but also *necessary*. Because traditional societies operate on a smaller scale, because parts of the whole operate relatively independently, and because every member of the society is basically the same, there is no real social need to develop abstract rules that organize society in the present and attempt to deal with the future. Therefore, Durkheim was interested in studying how the division of labor changed social institutions, ranging from religion to legal systems. Parsons and a group of thinkers later labeled the "modernizationists" picked up Durkheim's central ideas and applied them to developing countries.

As the decades pass, there seem to be fewer direct references to these three great classical theorists. Talcott Parsons, writing in the 1960s, cited Durkheim and Weber on nearly every page. By contrast, Portes and the other writers in the final section on globalization, writing in the 1990s, nearly never explicitly refer to them. However, the lack of direct references to arguments pioneered by Marx and Engels, Weber, and Durkheim does not mean that they are not profoundly influential. The debate over what drives social change is one that is alive and well and very evident throughout this volume's excerpts: even the newest theories of development have elements which can be considered "Marxian," "Weberian," or "Durkheimian" in origin.

Becoming Modern

Why do some countries remain poor and "backward" despite exposure to capitalism and other aspects of modern life? What can be done to make capitalism develop further in these countries? These were the questions addressed by a group of theorists whose ideas heavily influenced US efforts to foster capitalist development in poorer nations, then called the "Third World."[8]

After World War Two, the USA found itself alone at the top of the world power structure. It was the only nation on either side of the war that had its infrastructure of roads, bridges, buildings, and banks intact. It had a near-monopoly on new technology and the industry in place to produce goods that would sell for a high price around the world. But without functioning economies to buy these products, the growth of the US economy was limited. Aiding the recovery of Europe and Asia was the right moral thing to do, and failing to do so might risk allowing communism to spread, so the Marshall Plan was set up to help them rebuild.

Coupled with a concern for the wellbeing of obvious trading and military partners in Europe was one about what was to become of the billions of people living in the poor, sometimes newly independent nations in the Southern Hemisphere. On the one hand there was a fear among people in wealthier countries of the kind of social unrest that could result from such widespread poverty in a world of modernity and late-twentieth-century prosperity. On the other hand was an even larger, more evident threat: the Soviet Union. The Soviet Union offered a solution to development that had a strong mass appeal and also had something of a proven track record. Politicians, development experts, academicians, and the public were afraid of people in Latin America and Africa deciding that communism was a surer path to development than capitalism. In response, theories about development that were generated in the 1950s and 1960s in the USA provided an explicitly non-communist solution to poverty and underdevelopment.

A group of influential development experts saw three obvious problems holding back the industrialization of the poor countries. First, companies there simply were not big enough to construct the modern factories needed to compete with the huge corporations of the big powers of Europe and North America. Second, access to great amounts of capital allowed corporations in these "developed" nations to continually develop and adapt new technologies, which was sorely lacking in the poor nations. Third, and most important for our discussion here, they saw the cultural, institutional, and organizational features of poorer countries as roadblocks in their attempts to develop and democratize. Therefore, according to this group of "modernization theorists," poorer nations are poor because they lack big capital, technology, and modern social organization and values.[9] This group of theorists set out to explain the reasons for these absences and laid out policy recommendations to overcome them.

The analyses this body of theorists produced carried weight in US policy toward development in foreign countries. W. W. Rostow, for example, served in both the Kennedy and Johnson administrations. The US Agency for International Development programs based policies on the concepts of modernization theory (e.g., the Alliance for Progress, the Peace Corps). And the ideas are still very much alive: many of the policy programs stemming from this era are still influential in policy-making circles today, including among planners in many poorer nations.

To understand the gap between wealthier and poorer nations, modernization theorists explored the *process* of development and offered a composite portrait of what it means to be "modern." In modernization theory's dualistic schema, societies go from being one type of society (traditional, or *un*developed) to another type of society (modern, or developed). Samuel Huntington, a noted "modernization theorist" whose work ends this section of the reader, explained that modernization is an *evolutionary* process that changes societies in a *revolutionary* manner.[10]

Although different disciplines produced their own species of these theories, they all set up dichotomies and perceived development as progressing from point A to point B along a *single* trajectory. Different theorists saw varied "motors" as the key to movement from traditional to modern. This section of readings demonstrates the nuances and anecdotal and quantitative support those modernization theorists offered for their generalizations: note among the six authors the wide variety of indicators of modernization and the level of importance they accord to each. Some modernization theorists, such as Rostow, thought that an increased accumulation of capital would lead a modernization process that would then affect other elements of a society such as politics and values. Others considered non-economic factors the most important in explaining why poorer countries are poor and why some countries have been unable to generate sufficient capital and technology to "modernize." Bert Hoselitz, for example, perceived entrepreneurs as key figures in a society's shift in attitude from traditional to modern.[11] In a traditional society the entrepreneur is a social deviant because he is doing something new and different; in a modern society change is routine, innovation is valued, and the entrepreneur esteemed. D. C. McClelland saw the "need for achievement" as a key factor in distinguishing "modern" individuals.[12] For Daniel Lerner it was "projection" – the individual believing that others are like them, and "introjection" – an enlarged sense of oneself that includes new ideas and habits. Hagen's theory was also psychological – he said what motivates modern individuals were creativity and anxiety, the latter due to an uneasy feeling when they weren't being productive, a product of their mother's insatiable demands.[13]

All these authors saw modernization as a *process*: a social, psychological, economic, cultural, political, and even a biological sequence of changes. Modernization involves the adoption of new ways of material life – such as how work and community are organized, or how technology or governments are dealt with – and it also changes our education system and our most basic values and attitudes. For example, it was widely believed that one of the most powerful forces that would modernize people was living in cities. According to modernization theorists, urban life necessitates interdependencies, a complex division of labor, and a worldview that can accommodate differences and rapid change. For children living in cities it exposed them to formal schools (McClelland made much of this); for parents it was assumed that the workplace would be formal, contractual, and meritocratic (Inkeles considered the workplace a key agent of people's socialization).

However, the evidence could not always support the hypothesis that there is a relationship between levels of urbanization and whether residents are modern. That people lived in big cities but remained "backward" was a puzzle to modernization theorists (as one gathers from readings by Lewis and Lerner). When poorer countries underwent urbanization, experienced higher rates of literacy, etc., it was seen as paradoxical that they did not resemble people in the nations of Europe and North America that developed earlier. Finally, political structures were seen as important elements of a modernization process. Huntington, for example, argues that urbanization and the adoption of democratic processes force people to become more modern in their values, because political participation forces abstract and critical thinking.

So what does modernization theory suggest nations should do to become more "developed"? Although the major thrust of modernization implied that nations should focus on changing their internal society by rationalizing it, many also believed that "developed" countries could play a pivotal role assisting and guiding the modernization of later developers. Rostow, for example, argued that investments and the transfer of technology by wealthier countries would allow "backward" societies to become modern at a faster rate than earlier developers. Lerner suggested that the media would act as an accelerator of change because it would expose people to abstract situations and force them to think beyond their own lives. Gino Germani thought that a process of diffusion and demonstration of innovations would accelerate the development in late modernizers.[14]

For these late modernizers the prescription was the same: borrow, import, imitate, and rationalize. To get investments flowing, to break the nation out of the cycle of poverty and lack of investment, nations should allow large firms from wealthy countries free access to their national markets, labor, and resources. Some of this production would be for local and some for export markets, but at least money would finally be flowing where before it was lacking entirely, or was locked up in the overly cautious and fragmented hands of wealthy landed elites who had no experience in industry. This lack of concentrated industrial capital also suggested that borrowing money might be necessary to jump-start an economy.

After two decades of dominance in development circles, modernization theory came under attack from several angles. First, it was seen to be ahistorical: modernization theory failed to make distinctions between countries, regions, structural conditions, or specific historical experiences. For example, modernization theorists did not address the fact that these poorer regions exhibited not one situation of poverty or one type of society, but multiple "pre-modernities." Many of the countries that would be classified as "undeveloped" in fact already had "modern" industries, educational systems, or the other "precursors" that were thought necessary for modernity. A critique was increasingly lodged that the term "modernization" was only a euphemism for "Americanization," a point supported by a closer reading of several early authors in the lineage. The field was therefore labeled ethnocentric and pro-capitalist, an explicit tool of the American Cold War anti-communist effort. And by emphasizing nations' internal problems as the cause of underdevelopment, modernization theory seemed to blame the victims themselves for their poverty. Critics claimed that important external causes of poverty and underdevelopment are ignored.

Alejandro Portes and William Canak said nearly two decades ago that while heavily critiqued by later "dependency" theorists, these modernization theories were at least sociological (in the classical sense of the word).[15] That is, the importance of development sociology was clear in that someone was needed to theorize and document cultural change by studying how individuals' attitudes and behaviors are modified by living in cities, working in factories, and attending formal schools. It must also be said that some of these ideas are coming back into fashion both on what is called the Right, and from some surprising quarters of the Left.[16] For example, some postmodernists hold that culture has now become more important than economics in driving social change, and that in fact it probably always was so. As argued below, analyses of development which entirely ignore internal "cultural" variables between and even within nations will fail to provide complete answers to the question of why the different parts of the world are diverging.

Dependency and World Systems Theories

Were modernizationists "blaming the victims"? Beginning in the late 1950s, harsh refutation of the modernizationists' ideas came from a steadily growing group of scholars and planners in Latin America. The earliest ideas came from a group of economists working in Santiago, Chile at the Economic Commission for Latin America (ECLA), a United Nations agency that analyzed how development could be achieved in the region.[17] When Raúl Prebisch led ECLA in the 1950s there emerged a theory that as a result of colonial and later neocolonial relationships, the "Third World" had been kept in a subordinate position to Europe, serving merely as a source for cheap raw materials and as a market for its more expensive manufactures.[18] The problem with this arrangement was that while the value of manufactures has a tendency to rise steadily over time, the value of raw materials and primary foodstuffs generally declines. ECLA identified this trend of *declining terms of trade* as a key reason Latin America remained less developed than wealthier nations: poor countries had to sell more and more goods to get less in return.

Exports of raw materials and sale of cheap labor tended to lead to "enclaves of modernity" in a sea of backwardness, such as those suggested by some of the contrasting scenes at the beginning of this Introduction. In cases of export enclaves, the internal market was unimportant for producers: the tiny class of wealthy people desired products not produced locally; the masses were too poor to buy more than the very bare necessities. Samir Amin, Alain de Janvry and Carlos Garramón called these "disarticulated" economies because there was no connection between local producers and consumers, and because there often were no "multiplier" effects created by supplying the export enclaves with locally produced component parts.[19] Both Amin and de Janvry also made much of the "rural labor reserves," subsistence farming areas where workers could return when sick, old, or unemployed, to recover and survive more cheaply than possible in cities where employers might have to fully cover the costs of their workers' long-term survival. These rural reserves were believed to provide a crucial invisible subsidy for businesses operating in poor nations and to consumers of their products in the rich nations. Later authors have pointed out that households that share survival expenses – and the urban informal sector – work without a formal contract or sales/services without licenses, and also provide similar subsidies.

Dependency theorists paid special attention to explaining the savage inequalities in poor nations, tying them to colonial histories of those regions and to current economic and political systems of exclusion and repression of the masses. Dependency theorists thought that ignoring colonial legacies by arguing that later industrialization should be as easy as early industrialization was blatantly self-serving for the rich nations. Dependency theorists did not put all the blame for the poorer nations' poverty outside the nations, however. Cardoso, de Janvry, and several others identified local elites as critical actors who profit by paving the way for transnational corporations and unfavorable trade and banking arrangements.

By the 1960s, the fusion of elements of ECLA's work with that of neo-Marxist theory emerged as a serious theoretical challenge to the US-led modernization theory.[20] Some members of this new "dependency school" were ECLA economists; others were academics; some were members of a vibrant Latin American leftist movement. While dependency theory was already influencing policy in Latin America in the 1950s, it was not until the late 1960s that authors like André Gunder Frank "popularized" the theory and development scholars in the rich nations began to take note. Frank simplified many of the dependency group's ideas and was the first author to be widely published in English.[21] In the era of Vietnam and other military interventions by the US around the world, the ideas dependency theory presented were a welcome alternative approach that profoundly questioned the mainstream social science of the day.

Dependency theory presented the world as consisting of two poles: wealthy countries are the "center" of the global capitalist system, and poor countries are its "satellite" or "periphery." Peripheral countries have low wages, enforced by coercive regimes that undermine independent labor unions and social movements. The center exploits them for cheap labor, cheap minerals, and fertile tropical soils. Therefore the poor and wealthy countries are parts of the same whole (that whole being the global capitalist system), not similar entities at different stages of development (as modernizationists would have had us believe). For dependency theorists, underdevelopment in the periphery is the direct result of development in the center, and vice versa. The center-periphery hierarchy and its exploitation was repeated along a chain, from wealthy nations to capital cities in poor nations, to their regional cities, and then to the hinterlands. Flowing up the chain of unequal relations were power and "surplus value" from labor; flowing down were control, ideology, and expensive products.

Dependency implies that center nations need access to raw materials and larger markets for their goods in order to increase their wealth. Class conflict in the center nations is temporarily resolved by their (imperialistic) ability to exploit the periphery. At the same time, peripheral areas are kept in a dependent relationship on the center for a market for their cheap, primary exports as well as a source of more expensive goods. This whole process highlights not only the global character of capitalism, but also the fact that its expansion is the result of not just economic growth but specific relationships of economic development. Furthermore, the center-periphery analogy emphasizes the inherently hierarchical nature of capitalist relationships, both on a global and national scale. While previous development theories treated capitalism as a homogeneous force, dependency and world-systems theorists focus on the inequalities created by this set of international economic relationships.

Dependency theorists identified several key agents that promote and thrive on a situation of dependency. Obvious sources of "core" power within the "periphery" are foreign capital, such as multinational corporations. In the excerpt in this volume, Chase-Dunn presents quantitative analysis that showed the (negative overall) impact these corporations have on poverty and inequality in poorer host nations. Another key group many dependency theorists cite as structuring relations of dependency is elites within nations of the periphery. The Brazilian sociologist Fernando Henrique Cardoso paid especially close attention to the ways in which groups of elites in Latin American countries organized external trade relations so that they and their allies profited at the expense of the masses within the periphery. According to Cardoso, situations of dependency can only exist where a local "host" facilitates the economic ties. Finally, national governments were seen by many dependency theorists as crucial links in dependent relationships with center countries. In some cases the state serves to assure cooperation by the masses. Gereffi's excerpt in this volume clearly demonstrates that the different paths Latin American and East Asian nations took to achieve development are substantially attributable to differences in how these peripheral nations were governed.

How can this situation of dependency be "fixed"? Here, dependency theories can be divided into two schools. One argues that underdevelopment is not a phase but a permanent, inescapable condition. In other words, the only way this situation of dependency can be escaped is to escape from the entire capitalist system. In this camp are authors such as Paul Baran, Andre Gunder Frank, Theotonio Dos Santos, and Samir Amin. These authors believe that the capitalist system is not a competitive one, but one based on monopolies. Therefore, poorer countries can not expect to change their situation through competition. For example, Baran argues that places like Latin America are not engaged in a process of becoming more capitalistic. Instead, their historical experience resulted in their being stuck in what he calls an "imperialist" stage of capitalism.[22] For these authors, the clear solution to the development dilemma is to reject capitalism. These theorists have been widely criticized on the basis that they do not really offer any feasible solutions. This strain of dependency theory also seemed to lack mechanisms for analyzing change (especially the upward mobility experienced by some peripheral countries), for recognizing heterogeneity within the periphery, or for acknowledging any vulnerability on the part of center areas. For example, when dependency theory suggests that capitalism produces permanent unalterable relationships, it fails to explain why there appear to be greater levels of exploitation over time or why there are significant differences among poorer countries. Instead, this camp of dependency theory may be more useful in furthering specific political agendas than actually explaining processes of development or underdevelopment.

Another school of dependency theory acknowledges the crucial impacts of situations of dependency, but envisions a *possibility* for some degree of development within this relationship. In other words, these authors attempt to visualize processes of *associated development* and *dependent development*.[23] These are circumstances where poorer countries are subject to a situation of dependency yet manage to develop to some extent. Through a set of policies known as Import Substitution Industrialization, ECLA advocated the development of domestic industries as a way to develop a comparative advantage in products with higher values and reduce Latin American countries' *dependency* on center countries. This type of policy was an effort to acknowledge dependency, but attempts to ameliorate its effects by developing in only relative isolation from the damaging relations with the wealthy nations.

These "structuralist" theories are most useful in the factors they use to explain how this partial development occurred. Some of these factors include the actions of elites within the periphery (e.g., Cardoso and Faletto) and specific state policies designed to achieve development within a context of dependency (e.g., Gereffi and Evans). These "structuralist" dependency theorists paid a lot of attention to differences among nations of the periphery, both in terms of historical experiences and internal factors (i.e., economic resource bases, elite actions, types of governance, and relationships among actors in the periphery). Instead of simply describing a situation of dependency, many asked what mechanisms (both economic and non-economic) perpetuated these relationships. For example, by describing the historical roles of elites in the periphery they demonstrated that the influence of the core has not been uniform and that differences among elites in the periphery can help explain different political regimes, economies, and class relationships within the periphery. Evans even goes further in his perceptions of possibilities for autonomous action by asking what challenges to the situation of dependency have arisen, especially from peripheral economies (specifically, Brazil).[24]

Perhaps the most serious critique lodged at the more radical dependency theory is that it failed as a theory of development. Why did some countries (such as the "Asian Tigers" of Singapore, Taiwan, Korea, and Hong Kong) successfully overcome many of the conditions of a disease expected to be fatal for all patients? This critique, of course, applies nearly equally to the others reviewed in this volume. In other words, if a theory's role is at least in part to predict what might happen, then the highly descriptive nature of dependency theory does not have much explanatory power. As you will see as you read through this section, later authors like Chase-Dunn and Gereffi who employ comparative and quantitative research methods avoid dependency theory's overly descriptive nature; they are now actively expanding the boundaries of what is called World Systems theory.

Because it emerged from structuralist dependency theories, World Systems theory is both a distinct theory as well as a variant of dependency; the groundwork for it is rooted in the second structuralist variant of dependency theory described above. Authors such as Christopher Chase-Dunn, Peter Evans, and Gary Gereffi did early work that could have been classified as dependency theory, and later became key contributors to World Systems theory. The theory is also a response to the many critiques that were made of dependency theory. These criticisms centered on dependency theory's difficulty in generating testable hypotheses and lack of explanatory power. Furthermore, after dependency theory's initial splash in the development theory arena, many analysts sought to move beyond the rather crude dichotomy of core–periphery (as outsiders often mistakenly portrayed it) and to engage in more rigorous attention to the impact of historical contexts. The result of this splitting-off from dependency theory (especially its initial variants) was an attempt to analyze development in a manner more comprehensive than ever before (perhaps with the exception of Weber's work). It also was the "Americanization" of dependency theory, where World Systems research became increasingly cross-sectional (using data for only one time) and quantitative.[25] This was not always the case, as the historical works of Fernand Braudel and Immanuel Wallerstein attest.[26] World Systems theory, then, attempted this comprehensive analysis of the development process not only from a historical perspective, but also through systematic analyses of the operation of capitalism and the global economic system.

It was Immanuel Wallerstein's three-volume *The Modern World System* – the first volume of which was published in 1974 – that marked the birth of the subdiscipline in the USA. Wallerstein's work (and others who followed, such as Chase-Dunn in 1984 and 1989) describes four core postulates of World Systems theory. First, that there is one single underlying set of processes in the world system, to which all economies are subject. Any history of a location must include an understanding of that history of the whole. Therefore, the nation-state, although an important variable in development, is not the only level of analysis in understanding processes of development. Instead, there are worldwide processes that serve as key determinants of development and change. Second, and elaborating on the work of the dependency theorists, this worldwide system consists of three zones: the core, semi-periphery, and periphery. The semi-peripheral zone includes nations like Brazil and South Africa which have features of both the rich and poor countries, and which act as intermediaries in the processes of exploitation of the periphery by the core. It is important to note that unlike the crudest forms of dependency theory, World Systems theory allows for the possibility of mobility in the hierarchy of this single global system, though most countries have not been able to move up. Third, the processes by which wealth is extracted from the periphery are similar to those described by the dependency theorists: unequal exchange, active or subtle repression, and the control of marketing and the high-value ends of commodity chains (see Gereffi). Finally, World Systems theory proposes that in addition to cycles, capitalism has some crucial secular trends. These included the broadening of the areas of the world participating in capitalist exchange, and the deepening which goes on by attaching a price to everything (commodification), making everyone a wage-worker (proletarianization), mechanization, and the polarization of social classes.

In his useful book *An Introduction to the World System Perspective* (1989), Thomas Shannon reviews these tenets and generalizations of World Systems theory writing, cataloging a series of critiques that have been leveled against this group of scholars. (To soften his critique, he also notes that the field is extremely young and that it has already begun to respond to several of them.) Three bear special mention. Most profoundly, the field is too economistic. That is, like other Marxian writings, the economy is assumed to be driving all other realms of the system. World Systems theorists have responded by incorporating the state more directly in their theorizing; but have yet to do much with culture as causation. Second, much World Systems argumentation borders on teleology – assuming that the capitalist world system is driving toward some end, and has agency and functionalist needs of its own. Third, the theory is imprecise and many of its propositions cannot be tested. In the final piece in this volume, Portes also levels a harsh critique of World Systems theory for often remaining at high levels of abstraction and failing to capitalize on the burgeoning awareness that the economy had indeed gone global. World Systems theorists had been saying this for years.[27]

From Development to Globalization

From the earliest social theorists all the way through the dependency theorists of the 1950s and 1960s, the literature on social change and development was largely associated with industrialization and the gaps between wealthier and poorer nations. Marx, Weber, and Durkheim wrote about and analyzed the Industrial Revolution; modernization theorists thought an urban, industrial milieu was a sort of school for modernity; and many dependency theorists thought that if Latin America wished to become part of the "developed world," it would need to have more national industries. Since then, all that has been questioned. Contributions to this final section of the volume perceive development differently. First, it is no longer a given that building factories and infrastructure means raising wellbeing for a nation or its people. Rather, power in the world is increasingly linked to control over information, technology, and international banking institutions. Second, the new literature on globalization moves beyond the poor versus rich nations as if there were two or three "worlds." Instead, this literature often argues how interdependent and integrated the world has become: the same rules seem to apply everywhere.

Like most relatively new concepts still being hashed out among theorists and used widely in the popular press, the term "globalization" is often used without clarification. First and most broadly, globalization refers to a set of processes that increasingly make the parts of the world interdependently integrated.[28] Although the world has long had important international linkages, globalization refers to integration where firms are interdependent, production is linked on a global scale, there is a dramatic increase in visible and invisible trade and national economies are linked. Beyond this increase in trade and globally organized production, for some authors globalization means also the control of decision-making by a new "largely unaccountable political and economic elite," or more explicitly, the "Wall Street-US Treasury-IMF/World Bank Complex."[29] For these authors globalization is not just economic integration, but centralized, homogenized control. There is debate about both these dimensions.

Writing at the Max Planck Institute in the late 1970s, Germans Folker Fröbel, Jurgen Heinrichs and Otto Kreye described what was emerging as a "New International Division of Labour" (NIDL). They described a pattern of firms shutting down manufacturing plants in the developed countries and investing in the poor countries. The social effects they saw in wealthy nations were devastating: "more and more workers are losing not only their jobs but also their acquired profession ... they are thrown on to the labour market where . . . they are obliged to sell their labour-power as unskilled or semiskilled workers at considerably worse terms than before."[30] They describe these adjustments by individual workers as "rapid and psychologically exhausting," while the government suffers a "long-term fiscal crisis" (p. 4). These governments were caught between a shrinking tax base and employment on the one hand, and rising demands for unemployment and retirement benefits on the other.

Meanwhile, the cities of the world's poor nations were "overcrowded with [millions of] landless rural immigrants . . . forced to seek employment regardless of the level of remuneration and under the most inhuman conditions merely to ensure their sheer physical survival" (p. 5). They and a series of other researchers documented how employers selected those workers according to age, sex, and skill, most frequently choosing to exploit young women because they worked hard and tended not to quit or unionize. In contrast to the optimism of the modernizationists, Fröbel, Heinrichs, and Kreye saw no likely improvement of living conditions as a result of the industrial work by these people in factories set up for producing exports. Like dependency theorists Frank and Cardoso, they saw complicity by local elites as largely to blame for dependency on world markets and widespread poverty. *The New International Division of Labour* echoed the alarm of once-protected workers and observers in the developed world, that something had changed and that their security was gone: they could no longer act without concern for the poor nations.

Phillip McMichael argues here that we cannot simply describe globalization in terms of economic integration. Rather, "a qualitative shift in the mode of social organization that marks an historic transition in the capitalist world order" is occurring. Speculative financial capital uses globally uniform indicators of "credit-worthiness" to decide which firms and even governments can borrow money and on what terms. This global uniformity puts tremendous power in the hands of a new "global ruling class." In this new elite McMichael puts three groups of managers: bureaucrats and politicians willing to cut government spending and play by the new global rules of relentless efficiency; owners and executives of transnational corporations and international banks; and those who run the multilateral organizations like the IMF, World Bank, and World Trade Organization.[31] Nowadays, firms and states cannot make policy without always considering how their decisions will be seen by global creditors who could quickly make their lives miserable with poor credit ratings, disinvestment, or savage speculation on the demise of their currency. These are increasingly the central issues of our day. With globalization individual actors are certainly important, but it is often hard to tell who is involved or in charge because everything has become so extensively integrated. This situation is made all the more acute because the proliferation of information and the rate at which it can be exchanged makes the pace of economic change and financial markets faster than ever.

Debt has played an important part in the globalization process, as McMichael states very explicitly. The poorer nations took on heavy debts in the 1960s and 1970s to try to build their industrial sectors and infrastructures to catch up with the core nations. Loans allowed these poor nations to finally do some development planning – building roads, airports, new capitals, dams, and oil refineries. But the rates for their loans were often adjustable, and like a credit-card or house-mortgage debt with an adjustable rate, an increase in US interest rates exponentially increased the total debt burden of these countries. In 1982 Mexico and then Brazil said they could not pay their debts, and soon the list of defaulting nations grew. To continue to get the money they needed to pay even just the interest they owed, these nations had to secure more loans, and usually it was only multinational agencies like the World Bank and IMF that agreed to lend to them. In exchange for these loans, the heavily indebted nations had to submit to a sweeping program of cuts in food, housing, and transport subsidies, privatization of state-run companies, and lowering tariff barriers to force local industries to face global competition.[32] These sweeping reforms (called Structural Adjustment Programs by the banks), have been the subject of two decades of bitter debate, protests, riots, and even rebellions across the Third World.[33] Cutting government intervention in the economy, changing political and economic structures, and acting to stabilize macroeconomic indicators are more broadly called "neoliberalism." As Portes describes in his piece, the term "neoliberalism" revives early beliefs in the ability of "free trade" and laissez-faire capitalism to solve economic and social problems.

Parallel to the economic arguments that some profound change is occurring in the world, postmodernist thought has emerged. Modernism held that there was a concrete reality and progress that could be described with the scientific and rational approaches of Western society. Postmodernism responded that other cultures were equally valid and that scientific/linear thought was not the only way to truth, because no single truth exists. This brought into question the idea that the development process is dependent on increased rationalization (a fundamental hypothesis of both the classic and modernization theorists). Furthermore, this means that no single form of social organization can provide a template of what it means to be "developed" or even "rational." Another way in which postmodernists confronted the conventional wisdom of development theory was by their argument that in our age it is not the economy that determines culture, but that culture drives economic change.

David Harvey, in his book *The Condition of Postmodernity* (1989) and in the small piece reproduced here, refuted many of the claims of postmodernists and argued that we need to pay attention to capitalism and its functioning. Harvey argues that the shift of capitalism from large-scale and rigid arrangements to smaller-scale more flexible types of production was the precise transition that led to the explosion of postmodernist thinking. Improved transportation and communication compress space and time. In searching for a viable "radical politics," Harvey dismisses the focus on culture and local exclusiveness as much as do free-traders, but he is interested in turning our gaze towards addressing exploitation of nature and humans. In this way Harvey continues the explicit project of the dependency theorists: to imagine a social system after capitalism.

In an excerpt from his provocatively titled book *Has Globalization Gone Too Far?* (1997), Dani Rodrik raises the question on many people's minds. He argues that the stark differences in opinions out there about globalization simply reveal the deep fault line between the winners and losers in that process. The divide, he says, is between those who "have the skills and mobility to flourish in global markets and those who either don't have these advantages or perceive the expansion of unregulated markets as inimical to social stability and deeply held norms." In that latter group Rodrik puts "workers, pensioners, and environmentalists." He warns economists about taking these critiques too lightly, saying their "unease" could disrupt the drive to global free trade and bring back the isolationism and protection-ism of the period between World Wars One and Two. Rodrik appears ambivalent about the importance of traditions and norms (which sociologists define as unwritten rules and expectations), at least those norms and traditions that lead people to question the value of free trade. Rodrik's goal is to acknowledge the arguments of both globalization's proponents and its detractors, and to create a dialogue and develop policy that can address the social tensions without limiting free trade.

Following these general theories about development in the era of globalization are pieces that address more specific responses to and effects of globalization: regarding gender, environment, and social movements. The details in these readings might explain why Rodrik's "losers" are uneasy about globalization. For example, Kathryn Ward and Jean Pyle document that one effect of global assembly is that young women increasingly work for transnational corporations who set up factories in assembly zones in poor nations, especially in industries shifting to the use of sub-contracting and home-based "outputting." This type of work in the factories can be dangerous, stressful, and extremely poorly paid. On the other hand, the experience of meeting other women may empower women, and the pay they receive may increase their power within the household. The feminization of the labor force has had important social impacts, as noted by Ward and Pyle in their review of the substantial literature on women and development. What has emerged is an under-standing that exploitation is complex and increasingly based on irregular (that is, without a formal contract) work arrangements, and that gender, race, and ethnicity combine with class in different ways to shape exploitation in different cultural settings. Women's unpaid work in the home supporting other laborers provides a massive subsidy to the expansion of capitalism by lowering wages around the world.

The modernizationists and dependency theorists agreed on far more than they might admit, says Bob Sutcliffe in his piece "Development after Ecology." He argues that both Left and Right shared the view "that development was desirable" (that it would solve human welfare needs of the majority), that whole nations develop or do not, and that any obstacles were human: social, economic, or political. While other critics were chiseling away at modernity and development, profound environmental concerns surfaced about the desire for nations to rise from poverty. The most uncomfortable point for many of us is the realization that "the globalization of the characteristics of developed countries would surely make the planet uninhabitable." Sutcliffe states flatly that "the development of underdevelopment has also been the development of unsustainability." This suggests simply that development is going in the wrong direction. It is the underdeveloped countries, he asserts, which provide better models for sustainable societies than do developed ones. Even as development agencies and firms have hijacked the term "sustainability" to their own ends and then moved on to the next fad, the profound ecological critique put forward by Sutcliffe is the 500-pound gorilla which is essentially ignored by virtually all social studies of development.

In "Social Movements and Global Capitalism," Leslie Sklair ties questions of globalization to the rise of the much-discussed New Social Movements, such as those that have brought together women, ethnic and racial groups, lesbian and gay groups, and the peace and environmental movements. In reviewing that literature, Sklair endorses the view that any Marxian analysis focused only on labor is inadequate, that what is needed is "an historical materialism of all oppressed groups." His argument is partly based on the observation that "globalising capitalism has all but defeated labour." These new social movements have arisen precisely as labor movements have weakened, and they simultaneously contribute to its demise by siphoning off potential activists and fragmenting popular classes. Sklair identifies the three main institutions moving globalization: transnational corporations, a still-emerging transnational capitalist class, and the culture-ideology of consumerism. Underlying Sklair's argument is the point that all three tend to be profoundly "anti-social," undermining the conditions of life for the majority.

Echoing McMichael, Sklair says that increasingly, groups under the heel of global capitalism "find difficulty in identifying their adversaries," making what used to work as resistance difficult. Sklair argues that the only successful opposition movements are those that actively disrupt and do not get co-opted into the system, and which do so with local organizations and targets. Looking back, the success of "modernization" can be seen in the spread of the consumerist belief that products will make us happy and give our life meaning. Sklair calls this a "social change of truly global proportions." For this reason he sees anti-consumerist social movements as the most "subversive" in the lot: they are anti-modernizing.

Finally, Alejandro Portes concludes this volume with a critical look at social analysis of development, where it has been, and where it is going. The work reflects Portes's view that the surest ground for social sciences of development is in revealing "unintended consequences" of development theories and policies. He begins with what he considers a great surprise, that development discussions are no longer about reducing inequality, but that development seems to now be only concerned with making nations efficient participants in the global market. Portes considers this an unintended consequence of the current development paradigm, which is neoliberalism. He finds some value in neoliberal economic theories, especially that they provide a series of testable hypotheses. However, he faults the theory for being based on the idea that people act as individuals, and that they make decisions based on economic rationality. Portes says that such an approach is blind to the complex historical and social context in which people make decisions. Each decision we make, he argues, depends on issues of politics, demography, class, and on our networks of family and friends. His critique does not end with neoliberals (free-traders) and planners. He takes World Systems theorists to task for marginalizing sociology in development by staying in the realm of abstraction and outside of policy debates. Portes argues that we need to get beyond the old modernization versus dependency arguments and make social perspectives on development more concrete.

Marx and Rostow both assumed that countries would go through a series of stages leading to greater industrialization. Inkeles's work suggested that working in factories would change peoples' outlook to a modern one; Marx imagined they would gain a consciousness of their exploitation. Portes suggests they all may have been wrong, that to most everyone's surprise people are turning away from factories to informal work that is based on networks of family and friends, and is often done in the home. To compete with other havens of cheap labor, governments in countries around the world have done away with even the weak protections they offered their workers. This "informalization" of the state in its effort to compete has driven a movement of workers back to the household. Portes also reports that not only corporations, but also individuals, have also "gone global" with transnational communities and transnational enterprises. These groups may not have the muscle of Sklair's Transnational Capitalist Class, but they do drive globalization forward while providing a new strategy for survival by trading across borders.

We believe that social scientists working in the area of development need to be aware of the debates that preceded them so that they can glean insights and avoid repeating old mistakes. We hope this volume provides readers with the opportunity to begin to examine this crucial debate over the past century and a half. Though helping the poor nations should be enough reason to care, social sciences of development are no longer only about helping the poor nations. The emerging work on globalization and on the environmental consequences of development has taken away any doubt from the proposition that our fate is intricately linked to those of the other six billion souls with whom we share the planet.

Having lost ground to economics in discussions of what should be done, Portes argued that the sociology of development must produce "fine-tuned descriptions of the political, demographic, and social conditions limiting the application of models of development and of the likely reactions of different sectors of the population." This work must minutely examine current societies but must be built on the century and a half of thought sampled here. However, we would expand Portes's claim beyond sociology to propose that a broader interdisciplinary development of global studies is needed which incorporates the vision of a fuller range of social, natural, and applied scientists, plus activist-practitioners and citizen-scholars. Natural scientists and environmentalists are needed to alert us to another category of "unintended consequences": natural disasters and chronic human suffering being driven by our overtaxing the land, sea, and air. The roots of an ever-lengthening list of natural disasters lie in development models applied by nations and encouraged by pressures from the world economy.

The decisions of development planners are based in part on the theories debated on these pages. But so are they based on the pressures of a globalizing economy that is being successfully harnessed by a relatively small number of actors: the transnational capitalist class identified by Sklair and McMichael. Our work must be suggested by the conditions of life of citizens and their ideas and serve their interests: and the delicate balance is in keeping the big questions in mind while examining the minutia of social organization. Why are the poor countries poor? What happens to people when they become modern? Who's to blame for the unintended consequences of development? And what can be done? Should states step in and try to overcome some of the structural barriers that create poverty, or should they get out of the way and let ingenuity and the market solve the problem? These audacious questions – those of the wellbeing and survival of five or perhaps all six billion of the world's population – are the ones that the readings in this volume explicitly attempt to address.

NOTES

1. Many of the terms used here are highly debated, perhaps none so much as the term "development" itself. Rather than enter into that debate here, we follow Kincaid and Portes in conceptualizing national development as change in economic growth, social welfare, and citizenship (political rights). A. Douglas Kincaid and Alejandro Portes, *Comparative National Development: Society and Economy in the New Global Order*, Chapel Hill, NC: University of North Carolina Press, 1994, p. 2.
2. In what is now outdated, Cold-War terminology, the First World consisted of Western Europe, the USA and Canada, while the Second World was the communist bloc of the Soviet Union and its allies. The rest was the Third World.
3. World Bank, *World Development Report 1997*, Oxford: Oxford University Press, 1997, pp. 214–15.
4. The World Bank recently admitted: "on average, countries that started rich grew faster...poor countries tend to grow more slowly." World Bank, *World Development Report 1995*, Oxford: Oxford University Press, 1995, p. 53.
5. UNRISD, *States of Disarray: The Social Effects of Globalization*, Geneva: UNRISD, 1997, p. 24; CARE Development Facts, 2 Sept. 1996: http://www.care.org/world/dev-fact.html. 6 billion people total; 1/3 of 5 billion = 1.5 billion, which = 1 in 4.
6. We suggest readers visit the websites of major evangelical Christian groups.
7. Our goal in excerpting has been to maintain the central points of each reading while shortening them enough to fit the variety of authors in this volume. We regret the possible confusion and lost arguments that such excerpting requires; we also removed most of the footnotes with more nuanced arguments.
8. See note 2.
9. We acknowledge the excellent framework from lectures by the geographer Maria Patricia Fernandez-Kelly.
10. "The Change to Change: Modernization, Development and Politics," *Comparative Politics*, 3 (April 1971).
11. Bert F. Hoselitz, *Sociological Aspects of Economic Growth*, Chicago: Free Press, 1964.
12. D. C. McClelland, *The Achieving Society*, New York: Free Press, 1961.
13. E. Hagen, *On the Theory of Social Change*, Homewood: Dorsey Press, 1962.
14. Gino Germani, "Stages in Modernization in Latin America," *Studies in Comparative International Development*, 5:8 (1969–70).
15. Alejandro Portes and William Canak, "Latin America: Social Structures and Sociology," *Annual Review of Sociology*, 7 (1981), 225–48.
16. Two 1998 pieces serve as examples. On the right, Landes's monumental book *The Wealth and Poverty of Nations* (New York: Norton) concludes that "Some people [respond to markets] better than others, and culture can make all the difference" (p. 522). On the other side of the spectrum, Cristobal Kay endorses Sunkel's 1993 opinion that "The heart of development lies in the supply side: quality, flexibility, the efficient combination and utilization of productive resources, the adoption of technological development, an innovative spirit, creativity, the capacity for organization and social discipline" ("Relevance of Structuralist and Dependency Theories in the Neoliberal Period: A Latin American Perspective," The Hague: Institute of Social Sciences, Working Paper Series No. 281, 1998, p. 18).
17. The group's Spanish acronym is CEPAL. "And the Caribbean" was later added to its English name: it is now named ECLAC.
18. African theorist Samir Amin called this "unequal exchange."

19. For de Janvry's and Garramón's discussion of disarticulation see Chapter 12 in this volume. For Samir Amin's, see "Accumulation and Development: a Theoretical Model," *Review of African Political Economy*, 1: 9–26.

20. Peter F. Klarén, "Lost Promise: Explaining Latin American Underdevelopment," in *Promise of Development: Theories of Change in Latin America*, Boulder: Westview, 1986, p. 14.

21. By contrast, Fernando Henrique Cardoso's more subtle analysis excerpted here was initially published in 1971 but was not published in English until 1979.

22. Klarén, "Lost Promise," p. 17.

23. See Chapter 11; and Peter Evans, *Dependent Development: The Alliance of Multinational, State and Local Capital in Brazil*, Princeton: Princeton University Press, 1979. Cristobal Kay reminds us that this line is "Structuralism", while the more radical line is true "dependency" theory (*Latin American Theories of Development and Underdevelopment*, New York, Routledge, 1989, and "Relevance of Structuralist and Dependency Theories").

24. Evans, *Dependent Development*.

25. Instead of one or two cases, some World Systems theory analyzes used statistics to examine patterns among samples of dozens or over one hundred countries.

26. See Fernand Braudel, *Civilization and Capitalism, 15th–18th Century*, vols. I–III, New York: Harper & Row, 1982.

27. The field of World Systems theory remains alive in sociology and political science in the USA, but its growth was curtailed by the postmodernist critique that no overarching theory of development could be possible (J. Timmons Roberts and Peter E. Grimes, "Extending the World-system to the Whole System: Towards a Political Economy of the Biosphere," in *The Global Environment and the World-System*, eds Walter Goldfrank, David Goodman, and Andrew Szasz, Westport, CT, Greenwood Press, 1999, pp. 59–83). It should be pointed out that several of the authors presented under the section on globalization are in fact active in networks of World Systems scholars; they are here attempting to explain globalization from World Systems perspectives.

28. Peter Dicken, Global Shift, 3rd edn, New York, Guilford, 1998, p. 5.

29. The first quote is paraphrased from McMichael's excerpt in this volume (p. 274ff). The second phrase is an adaptation of a coinage by Wade and Veneroso 1998, cited in Kay, "Relevance of Structuralist and Dependency Theories in the Neoliberal Period." IMF = International Monetary Fund.

30. Fröbel, Heinrichs, and Kreye 1980, p. 3.

31. McMichael, 1996, p. 32. In his later piece in this volume, Sklair calls this the new transnational capitalist class.

32. McMichael, 1996, pp. 36–7.

33. See, e.g., John Walton, "Debt, Protest, and the State in Latin America," in *Power and Popular Protest*, ed. Susan Eckstein, Berkeley, CA: University of California Press, 1989, pp. 298–328.

Part I

Formative Ideas on the Transition to Modern Society

1 Manifesto of the Communist Party (1848) and Alienated Labor (1844)

Karl Marx and Friedrich Engels

Billions of lives have been influenced by the revolutionary content of *The Communist Manifesto*, penned by Germans Karl Marx (1818–83) and his sometime co-author and friend Friedrich Engels (1820–95). "The Manifesto" was written as a program for a new socialist league of German journeymen living in Paris, Brussels and London. As with all of Marx's work, it is a critique of modern (to him that was "capitalist") society. While much debated and sometimes off in its predictions, the forcefully written manifesto has inspired social scientists and citizens by hypothesizing that contradictions within capitalism will cause it to inevitably be replaced by a new social order. In one of Marx's earlier works, "Alienated Labor," he argues that one of the ways capitalist production exploits workers is that it makes them feel estranged from the products of their own hands. Capitalism's negative effects go well beyond the workplace. They pervade money markets, politics, and even household relationships. When the systems of social relationships created by a system out of our control dominate us, this is referred to as alienation. Marx's critiques of capitalism share one central idea: the human relationships capitalism requires do not allow people to reach their full, creative potentials or exercise free will, which he conceives as fundamental parts of human nature.

Manifesto of the Communist Party

Bourgeois and Proletarians

The history of all hitherto existing society is the history of class struggles.

Freeman and slave, patrician and plebeian, lord and serf, guild-master and journeyman, in a word, oppressor and oppressed, stood in constant opposition to one another, carried on an uninterrupted, now hidden, now open fight, a fight that each time ended, either in a revolutionary reconstitution of society at large, or in the common ruin of the contending classes.

In the earlier epochs of history, we find almost everywhere a complicated arrangement of society into various orders, a manifold gradation of social rank. In ancient Rome we have patricians, knights, plebeians, slaves; in the Middle Ages, feudal lords, vassals, guild-masters, journeymen, apprentices, serfs; in almost all of these classes, again, subordinate gradations.

The modern bourgeois society that has sprouted from the ruins of feudal society, has not done away with class antagonisms. It has but established new classes, new conditions of oppression, new forms of struggle in place of the old ones.

Our epoch, the epoch of the bourgeoisie, possesses, however, this distinctive feature; it has simplified the class antagonisms. Society as a whole is more and more splitting up into two great hostile camps, into two great classes directly facing each other: Bourgeoisie and Proletariat.

From the serfs of the Middle Ages sprang the chartered burghers of the earliest towns. From these burgesses the first elements of the bourgeoisie were developed.

The discovery of America, the rounding of the Cape, opened up fresh ground for the rising bourgeoisie. The East Indian and Chinese markets, the [colonization] of America, trade with the colonies, the increase in the means of exchange and in commodities generally, gave to commerce, to navigation, to industry, an impulse never before known, and thereby, to the revolutionary element in the tottering feudal society, a rapid development.

The feudal system of industry, under which industrial production was mono-polized by close guilds, now no longer sufficed for the growing wants of the new markets. The manufacturing system took its place. The guild-masters were pushed on one side by the manufacturing middle class; division of labor between the different corporate guilds vanished in the face of division of labor in each single workshop.

Meantime the markets kept ever growing, the demand, ever rising. Even manu-facture no longer sufficed. Thereupon, steam and machinery revolutionized indus-trial production. The place of manufacture was taken by the giant, Modern Industry, the place of the industrial middle class, by industrial millionaires, the leaders of whole industrial armies, the modern bourgeois.

Modern industry has established the world-market, for which the discovery of America paved the way. This market has given an immense development to com-merce, to navigation, to communication by land. This development has, in its turn, reacted on the extension of industry; and in proportion as industry, commerce, navigation, railways extended, in the same proportion the bourgeoisie developed, increased its capital, and pushed into the background every class handed down from the Middle Ages.

We see, therefore, how the modern bourgeoisie is itself the product of a long course of development, of a series of revolutions in the modes of production and of exchange.

Each step in the development of the bourgeoisie was accompanied by a cor-responding political advance of that class. An oppressed class under the sway of the feudal nobility, an armed and self-governing association in the mediaeval commune, here independent urban republic (as in Italy and Germany), there taxable "third estate" of the monarchy (as in France), afterwards, in the period of manufacture proper, serving either the semi-feudal or the absolute monarchy as a counterpoise against the nobility, and, in fact, cornerstone of the great monarchies in general, the bourgeoisie has at last, since the establishment of Modern Industry and of the world-market, conquered for itself, in the modern representative State, exclusive political sway. The executive of the modern State is but a committee for managing the common affairs of the whole bourgeoisie.

The bourgeoisie, historically, has played a most revolutionary part.

The bourgeoisie, wherever it has got the upper hand, has put an end to all feudal, patriarchal, idyllic relations. It has pitilessly torn asunder the motley feudal ties that bound man to his "natural superiors," and has left remaining no other nexus between man and man than naked self-interest, than callous "cash payment." It has drowned the most heavenly ecstasies of religious fervour, of chivalrous enthusiasm, of philistine sentimentalism, in the icy water of egotistical calculation. It has resolved personal worth into exchange value, and in place of the numberless indefensible chartered freedoms, has set up that single, unconscionable freedom – Free Trade. In one word, for exploitation, veiled by religious and political illusions, it has substituted naked, shameless, direct, brutal exploitation.

The bourgeoisie has stripped of its halo every occupation hitherto honoured and looked up to with reverent awe. It has converted the physician, the lawyer, the priest, the poet, the man of science, into its paid [wage-laborers].

The bourgeoisie has torn away from the family its sentimental veil, and has reduced the family relation to a mere money relation.

The bourgeoisie has disclosed how it came to pass that the brutal display of vigour in the Middle Ages, which Reactionists so much admire, found its fitting complement in the most slothful indolence. It has been the first to show what man's activity can bring about. It has accomplished wonders far surpassing Egyptian pyramids, Roman aqueducts, and Gothic cathedrals; it has conducted expeditions that put in the shade all former Exoduses of nations and crusades.

The bourgeoisie cannot exist without constantly revolutionizing the instruments of production, and thereby the relations of production, and with them the whole relations of society. Conservation of the old modes of production in unaltered form, was, on the contrary, the first condition of existence for all earlier industrial classes. Constant revolutionizing of production, uninterrupted disturbance of all social conditions, everlasting uncertainty and agitation distinguish the bourgeois epoch from all earlier ones. All fixed, fast-frozen relations, with their train of ancient and venerable prejudices and opinions, are swept away, all new-formed ones become antiquated before they can ossify. All that is solid melts into air, all that is holy is profaned, and man is at last compelled to face with sober senses, his real conditions of life, and his relations with his kind.

The need of a constantly expanding market for its products chases the bourgeoisie over the whole surface of the globe. It must nestle everywhere, settle everywhere, establish [connections] everywhere.

The bourgeoisie has through its exploitation of the world-market given a cosmopolitan character to production and consumption in every country. To the great chagrin of Re-actionists, it has drawn from under the feet of industry the national ground on which it stood. All old-established national industries have been destroyed or are daily being destroyed. They are dislodged by new industries, whose introduction becomes a life and death question for all civilized nations, by industries that no longer work up indigenous raw material, but raw material drawn from the remotest zones; industries whose products are consumed, not only at home, but in every quarter of the globe. In place of the old wants, satisfied by the productions of the country, we find new wants, requiring for their satisfaction the products of distant lands and climes. In place of the old local and national seclusion and self-sufficiency, we have intercourse in every direction, universal interdependence of nations. And as in material, so also in intellectual production. The intellectual creations of individual nations become common property. National one-sidedness and narrowmindedness become more and more impossible, and from the numerous national and local literatures there arises a world-literature.

The bourgeoisie, by the rapid improvement of all instruments of production, by the immensely facilitated means of communication, draws all, even the most barbarian, nations into civilization. The cheap prices of its commodities are the heavy artillery with which it batters down all Chinese walls, with which it forces the barbarians' intensely obstinate hatred of foreigners to capitulate. It compels all nations, on pain of extinction, to adopt the bourgeois mode of production; it compels them to introduce what it calls civilization into their midst, i.e., to become bourgeois themselves. In a word, it creates a world after its own image.

The bourgeoisie has subjected the country to the rule of the towns. It has created enormous cities, has greatly increased the urban population as compared with the rural, and has thus rescued a considerable part of the population from the idiocy of rural life. Just as it has made the country dependent on the towns, so it has made barbarian and semi-barbarian countries dependent on the civilized ones, nations of peasants on nations of bourgeois, the East on the West.

The bourgeoisie keeps more and more doing away with the scattered state of the population, of the means of production, and of property. It has agglomerated population, centralized means of production, and has concentrated property in a few hands. The necessary consequence of this was political centralization. Independent, or but loosely connected provinces, with separate interests, laws, governments and systems of taxation, became lumped together in one nation, with one government, one code of laws, one national class-interest, one frontier and one customs-tariff.

The bourgeoisie, during its rule of scarce one hundred years, has created more massive and more colossal productive forces than have all preceding generations together. Subjection of Nature's forces to man, machinery, application of chemistry to industry and agriculture, steam-navigation, railways, electric telegraphs, clearing of whole continents for cultivation, canalization of rivers, whole populations conjured out of the ground – what earlier century had even a presentiment that such productive forces slumbered in the lap of social labor?

We see then: The means of production and of exchange on whose foundation the bourgeoisie built itself up, were generated in feudal society. At a certain stage in the development of these means of production and of exchange, the conditions under which feudal society produced and exchanged, the feudal organization of agriculture and manufacturing industry, in one word, the feudal relations of property became no longer compatible with the already developed productive forces; they became so many fetters. They had to burst asunder; they were burst asunder.

Into their places stepped free competition, accompanied by a social and political constitution adapted to it, and by the economical and political sway of the bourgeois class.

A similar movement is going on before our own eyes. Modern bourgeois society with its relations of production, of exchange and of property, a society that has conjured up such gigantic means of production and of exchange, is like the sorcerer, who is no longer able to control the powers of the nether world whom he has called up by his spells. For many a decade past the history of industry and commerce is but the history of the revolt of modern productive forces against modern conditions of production, against the property relations that are the conditions for the existence of the bourgeoisie and of its rule. It is enough to mention the commercial crises that by their periodical return put on its trial, each time more threateningly, the existence of the entire bourgeois society. In these crises a great part not only of the existing products, but also of the previously created productive forces, are periodically destroyed. In these crises there breaks out an epidemic that, in all earlier epochs, would have seemed an absurdity – the epidemic of overproduction. Society suddenly finds itself put back into a state of momentary barbarism; it appears as if a famine, a universal war of devastation had cut off the supply of every means of subsistence; industry and commerce seem to be destroyed; and why? Because there is too much civilization, too much means of subsistence, too much industry, too much commerce. The productive forces at the disposal of society no longer tend to further the development of the conditions of bourgeois property; on the contrary, they have become too powerful for these conditions, by which they are fettered, and so soon as they overcome these fetters, they bring disorder into the whole of bourgeois society, endanger the existence of bourgeois property. The conditions of bourgeois society are too narrow to comprise the wealth created by them. And how does the bourgeoisie get over these crises? On the one hand by enforced destruction of a mass of productive forces; on the other, by the conquest of new markets, and by the more thorough exploitation of the old ones. That is to say, by paving the way for more extensive and more destructive crises, and by diminishing the means whereby crises are prevented.

The weapons with which the bourgeoisie felled feudalism to the ground are now turned against the bourgeoisie itself.

But not only has the bourgeoisie forged the weapons that bring death to itself; it has also called into existence the men who are to wield those weapons – the modern working class – the proletarians.

In proportion as the bourgeoisie, i.e., capital, is developed, in the same proportion is the proletariat, the modern working class, developed, a class of laborers, who live only so long as they find work, and who find work only so long as their labor increases capital. These laborers, who must sell themselves piecemeal, are a commodity, like every other article of commerce, and are consequently exposed to all the vicissitudes of competition, to all the fluctuations of the market.

Owing to the extensive use of machinery and to division of labor, the work of the proletarians has lost all individual character, and, consequently, all charm for the workman. He becomes an appendage of the machine, and it is only the most simple, most monotonous, and most easily acquired knack that is required of him. Hence, the cost of production of a workman is restricted, almost entirely, to the means of subsistence that he requires for his maintenance, and for the propagation of his race. But the price of a commodity, and also of labor, is equal to its cost of production. In proportion, therefore, as the repulsiveness of the work increases, the wage decreases. Nay more, in proportion as the use of machinery and division of labor increases, in the same proportion the burden of toil also increases, whether by prolongation of the working hours, by increase of the work enacted a given time, or by increased speed of the machinery, etc.

Modern industry has converted the little workshop of the patriarchal master into the great factory of the industrial capitalist. Masses of laborers, crowded into the factory, are organized like soldiers. As privates of the industrial army they are placed under the command of a perfect hierarchy of officers and sergeants. Not only are they the slaves of the bourgeois class, and of the bourgeois State, they are daily and hourly enslaved by the machine, by the over-looker, and, above all, by the individual bourgeois manufacturer himself. The more openly this despotism proclaims gain to be its end aim, the more petty, the more hateful and the more embittering it is.

The less the skill and exertion or strength implied in manual labor, in other words, the more modern industry becomes developed, the more is the labor of men super-seded by that of women. Differences of age and sex have no longer any distinctive social validity for the working class. All are instruments of labor, more or less expensive to use, according to their age and sex.

No sooner is the exploitation of the laborer by the manufacturer, so far, at an end, that he receives his wages in cash, than he is set upon by the other portions of the bourgeoisie, the landlord, the shopkeeper, the pawnbroker, etc.

The lower strata of the middle class – the small tradespeople, shopkeepers, and retired tradesmen generally, the handicraftsmen and peasants – all these sink gradu-ally into the proletariat, partly because their diminutive capital does not suffice for the scale on which Modern Industry is carried on, and is swamped in the competition with the large capitalists, partly because their specialised skill is rendered worthless by new methods of production. Thus the proletariat is recruited from all classes of the population.

The proletariat goes through various stages of development. With its birth begins its struggle with the bourgeoisie. At first the contest is carried on by individual laborers, then by the work-people of a factory, then by the operatives of one trade, in one locality, against the individual bourgeois who directly exploits them. They direct their attacks not against the bourgeois conditions of production, but against the instruments of production themselves; they destroy imported wares that compete with their labor, they set factories ablaze, they seek to restore by force the vanished status of the workman of the Middle Ages.

At this stage the laborers still form an incoherent mass scattered over the whole country, and broken up by their mutual competition. If anywhere they unite to form more compact bodies, this is not yet the consequence of their own active union, but of the union of the bourgeoisie, which class, in order to attain its own political ends, is compelled to set the whole proletariat in motion, and is moreover yet, for a time, able to do so. At this stage, therefore, the proletarians do not fight their enemies, but the enemies of their enemies, the remnants of absolute monarchy, the landowners, the non-industrial bourgeois, the petty bourgeoisie. Thus the whole historical move-ment is concentrated in the hands of the bourgeoisie; every victory so obtained is a victory for the bourgeoisie.

But with the development of industry the proletariat not only increases in number; it becomes concentrated in greater masses, its strength grows, and it feels that strength more. The various interests and conditions of life with the ranks of the proletariat are more and more equalized, in proportion as machinery obliterates all distinctions of labor, and nearly everywhere reduces wages to the same low level. The growing competition among the bourgeois, and the resulting commercial crises, make the wages of the workers ever more fluctuating. The unceasing improvement of machinery, ever more rapidly developing, makes their livelihood more and more precarious; the collisions between individual workmen and individual bourgeois take more and more the character of collisions between two classes. Thereupon the workers begin to form combinations (Trades' Unions) against the bourgeois; they club together in order to keep up the rate of wages; they found permanent associations in order to make provision beforehand for these occasional revolts. Here and there the contest breaks out into riots.

Now and then the workers are victorious, but only for a time. The real fruit of their battles lies, not in the immediate result, but in the ever expanding union of the workers. This union is helped on by the improved means of communication that are created by modern industry, and that place the workers of different localities in contact with one another. It was just this contact that was needed to centralise the numerous local struggles, all of the same character, into one national struggle between classes. But every class struggle is a political struggle. And that union, to attain which the burghers of the Middle Ages, with their miserable highways, required centuries, the modern proletarians, thanks to railways, achieve in a few years.

This organization of the proletarians into a class, and consequently into a political party, is continually being upset again by the competition between the workers themselves. But it ever rises up again, stronger, firmer, mightier. It compels legislative recognition of particular interests of the workers, by taking advantage of the divisions among the bourgeoisie itself. Thus the ten-hours'-bill in England was carried.

Altogether collisions between the classes of the old society further, in many ways, the course of development of the proletariat. The bourgeoisie finds itself involved in a constant battle. At first with the aristocracy; later on, with those portions of the bourgeoisie itself, whose interests have become antagonistic to the progress of industry; at all times, with the bourgeoisie of foreign countries. In all these battles it sees itself compelled to appeal to the proletariat, to ask for its help, and thus, to drag it into the political arena. The bourgeoisie itself, therefore, supplies the proletariat with its own elements of political and general education, in other words, it furnishes the proletariat with weapons for fighting the bourgeoisie.

Further, as we have already seen, entire sections of the ruling classes are, by the advance of industry, precipitated into the proletariat, or are at least threatened in their conditions of existence. These also supply the proletariat with fresh elements of enlightenment and progress.

Finally, in times when the class-struggle nears the decisive hour, the process of dissolution going on within the ruling class, in fact with the whole range of old society, assumes such a violent, glaring character, that a small section of the ruling class cuts itself adrift, and joins the revolutionary class, the class that holds the future in its hands. Just as, therefore, at an earlier period, a section of the nobility went over to the bourgeoisie, so now a portion of the bourgeoisie goes over to the proletariat, and in particular, a portion of the bourgeois ideologists, who have raised themselves to the level of comprehending theoretically the historical movements as a whole.

Of all the classes that stand face to face with the bourgeoisie today, the proletariat alone is a really revolutionary class. The other classes decay and finally disappear in the face of modern industry; the proletariat is its special and essential product.

The lower-middle class, the small manufacturer, the shopkeeper, the artisan, the peasant, all these fight against the bourgeoisie, to save from extinction their existence as fractions of the middle class. They are therefore not revolutionary, but conservative. Nay more, they are reactionary, for they try to roll back the wheel of history. If by chance they are revolutionary, they are so, only in view of their impending transfer into the proletariat, they thus defend not their present, but their future interests, they desert their own standpoint to place themselves at that of the proletariat.

The "dangerous class," the social scum, that passively rotting mass thrown off by the lowest layers of old society, may, here and there, be swept into the movement by a proletarian revolution; its conditions of life, however, prepare it far more for the part of a bribed tool of reactionary intrigue.

In the conditions of the proletariat, those of old society at large are already virtually swamped. The proletarian is without property; his relation to his wife and children has no longer anything in common with the bourgeois family-relations; modern industrial labor, modern subjection to capital, the same in England as in France, in America as in Germany, has stripped him of every trace of national character. Law, morality, religion, are to him so many bourgeois prejudices, behind which lurk in ambush just as many bourgeois interests.

All the preceding classes that got the upper hand, sought to fortify their already acquired status by subjecting society at large to their conditions of appropriation. The proletarians cannot become masters of the productive forces of society, except by abolishing their own previous mode of appropriation, and thereby also every other previous mode of appropriation. They have nothing of their own to secure and to fortify; their mission is to destroy all previous securities for, and insurances of, individual property.

All previous historical movements were movements of minorities, or in the interest of minorities. The proletarian movement is the self-conscious, independent movement of the immense majority, in the interest of the immense majority. The proletariat, the lowest stratum of our present society, cannot stir, cannot raise itself up, without the whole superincumbent strata of official society being sprung into the air.

Though not in substance, yet in form, the struggle of the proletariat with the bourgeoisie is at first a national struggle. The proletariat of each country must, of course, first of all settle matters with its own bourgeoisie.

In depicting the most general phases of the development of the proletariat, we traced the more or less veiled civil war, raging within existing society, up to the point where that war breaks out into open revolution, and where the violent overthrow of the bourgeoisie, lays the foundation for the sway of the proletariat.

Hitherto, every form of society has been based, as we have already seen, on the antagonism of oppressing and oppressed classes. But in order to oppress a class, certain conditions must be assured to it under which it can, at least, continue its slavish existence. The serf, in the period of serfdom, raised himself to membership in the commune, just as the petty bourgeois, under the yoke of feudal absolutism, managed to develop into a bourgeois. The modern laborer, on the contrary, instead of rising with the progress of industry, sinks deeper and deeper below the conditions of existence of his own class. He becomes a pauper, and pauperism develops more rapidly than population and wealth. And here it becomes evident, that the bourgeoisie is unfit any longer to be the ruling class in society, and to impose its conditions of existence upon society as an overriding law. It is unfit to rule, because it is incompetent to assure an existence to its slave within his slavery, because it cannot help letting him sink into such a state, that it has to feed him, instead of being fed by him. Society can no longer live under this bourgeoisie, in other words, its existence is no longer compatible with society.

The essential condition for the existence, and for the sway of the bourgeois class, is the formation and augmentation of capital; the condition for capital is wage-labor. Wage-labor rests exclusively on competition between the laborers. The advance of industry, whose involuntary promoter is the bourgeoisie, replaces the isolation of the laborers, due to competition, by their involuntary combination, due to association. The development of Modern Industry, therefore, cuts from under its feet the very foundation on which the bourgeoisie produces and appropriates products. What the bourgeoisie therefore produces, above all, are its own grave-diggers. Its fall and the victory of the proletariat are equally inevitable.

Alienated Labor

We shall begin from a *contemporary* economic fact. The worker becomes poorer the more wealth he produces and the more his production increases in power and extent. The worker becomes an ever cheaper commodity the more goods he creates. The *devaluation* of the human world increases in direct relation with the *increase in value* of the world of things. Labor does not only create goods; it also produces itself and the worker as a *commodity*, and indeed in the same proportion as it produces goods.

This fact simply implies that the object produced by labor, its product, now stands opposed to it as an *alien being*, as a *power independent* of the producer. The product of labor is labor which has been embodied in an object and turned into a physical thing; this product is an *objectification* of labor. The performance of work is at the same time its objectification. The performance of work appears in the sphere of political economy as a *vitiation* [debasement] of the worker, objectification as a *loss* and as *servitude to the object*, and appropriation as *alienation*.

So much does the performance of work appear as vitiation that the worker is vitiated to the point of starvation. So much does objectification appear as loss of the object that the worker is deprived of the most essential things not only of life but also of work. Labor itself becomes an object which he can acquire only by the greatest effort and with unpredictable interruptions. So much does the appropriation of the object appear as alienation that the more objects the worker produces the fewer he can possess and the more he falls under the domination of his product, of capital.

All these consequences follow from the fact that the worker is related to the *product of his labor* as to an *alien* object. For it is clear on this presupposition that the more the worker expends himself in work the more powerful becomes the world of objects which he creates in face of himself, the poorer he becomes in his inner life, and the less he belongs to himself. It is just the same as in religion. The more of himself man attributes to God the less he has left in himself. The worker puts his life into the object, and his life then belongs no longer to himself but to the object. The greater his activity, therefore, the less he possesses. What is embodied in the product of his labor is no longer his own. The greater this product is, therefore, the more he is diminished. The *alienation* of the worker in his product means not only that his labor becomes an object, assumes an *external* existence, but that it exists independently, *outside himself*, and alien to him, and that it stands opposed to him as an autonomous power. The life which he has given to the object sets itself against him as an alien and hostile force...

(The alienation of the worker in his object is expressed as follows in the laws of political economy: The more the worker produces the less he has to consume; the more value he creates the more worthless he becomes; the more refined his product the more crude and misshapen the worker; the more civilized the product the more barbarous the worker; the more powerful the work the more feeble the worker; the more the work manifests intelligence the more the worker declines in intelligence and becomes a slave of nature.)

Political economy conceals the alienation in the nature of labor insofar as it does not examine the direct relationship between the worker (work) and production. Labor certainly produces marvels for the rich but it produces privation for the worker. It produces palaces, but hovels for the worker. It produces beauty, but deformity for the worker. It replaces labor by machinery, but it casts some of the workers back into a barbarous kind of work and turns the others into machines. It produces intelligence, but also stupidity and cretinism for the workers.

The direct relationship of labor to its products is the relationship of the worker to the objects of his production. The relationship of property owners to the objects of production and to production itself is merely a *consequence* of this first relationship and confirms it. We shall consider this second aspect later.

2 The Division of Labor in Society (1893)

Emile Durkheim

French sociologist Emile Durkheim (1864–1920) saw industrialization changing society from simplicity and uniformity to specialization and differences. Unlike Marx, who focused on the negative effects of alienation and rationality that accompanied the rise of capitalism, Durkheim did not view the transition from tradition to modernity with alarm or as a moral breakdown. Instead, he examined the process of the transition to modernity in an effort to show the new functions of new ways. The selection here excerpts Durkheim's doctoral dissertation which was published as *The Division of Labor in Society* in 1893. His observations and analyses are taken from the context of the industrial revolution that occurred first in England and then throughout Europe. The process of industrialization was so revolutionary, in part, because many traditional jobs were replaced by machines that could mass-produce goods at a lower price and required the coordination of the efforts of many people doing specialized tasks. Durkheim was not the first to document these changes, but he was the first to investigate the consequences of the division of labor that caused these changes. In the world of increasing interdependencies, how would people bond together as a society, yet maintain their sense of individuality that allows modern society to function? What are the consequences of not bonding with a society or of losing individual control?

Introduction

The Problem

Although the division of labour is not of recent origin, it was only at the end of the last century that societies began to become aware of this law, to which up to then they had submitted almost unwittingly. Undoubtedly even from antiquity several thinkers had perceived its importance. Yet Adam Smith was the first to attempt to elaborate the theory of it. Moreover, it was he who first coined the term, which social science later lent to biology.

Nowadays the phenomenon has become so widespread that it catches everyone's attention. We can no longer be under any illusion about the trends in modern industry. It involves increasingly powerful mechanisms, large-scale groupings of power and capital, and consequently an extreme division of labour. Inside factories, not only are jobs demarcated, becoming extremely specialised, but each product is itself a speciality entailing the existence of others . . . . Although this evolution occurs spontaneously and unthinkingly, those economists who study its causes and evaluate its results, far from condemning such diversification or attacking it, proclaim its necessity. They perceive in it the higher law of human societies and the condition for progress.

Yet the division of labour is not peculiar to economic life. We can observe its increasing influence in the most diverse sectors of society. Functions, whether political, administrative or judicial, are becoming more and more specialised. The same is true in the arts and sciences. The time lies far behind us when philosophy constituted the sole science. It has become fragmented into a host of special disciplines, each having its purpose, method and ethos. "From one half-century to another the men who have left their mark upon the sciences have become more specialized." . . .

Not only is the scientist no longer immersed in different sciences at the same time, but he can no longer encompass the whole field of one science. The range of his research is limited to a finite category of problems or even to a single one of them. Likewise, the functions of the scientist which formerly were almost always exercised alongside another more lucrative one, such as that of doctor, priest, magistrate or soldier, are increasingly sufficient by themselves. . . . [T]he law of the division of labour applies to organisms as well as to societies. It may even be stated that an organism occupies the more exalted a place in the animal hierarchy the more specialised its functions are. This discovery has had the result of not only enlarging enormously the field of action of the division of labour, but also of setting its origins back into an infinitely distant past, since it becomes almost contemporaneous with the coming of life upon earth. It is no longer a mere social institution whose roots lie in the intelligence and the will of men, but a general biological phenomenon, the conditions for which must seemingly be sought in the essential properties of organised matter. The division of labour in society appears no more than a special form of this general development. In conforming to this law societies apparently yield to a movement that arose long before they existed and which sweeps along in the same direction the whole of the living world.

Such a fact clearly cannot manifest itself without affecting profoundly our moral constitution, for the evolution of mankind will develop in two utterly opposing directions, depending on whether we abandon ourselves to this tendency or whether we resist it. Yet, then, one question poses itself urgently: of these two directions, which one should we choose? Is it our duty to seek to become a rounded, complete creature, a whole sufficient unto itself or, on the contrary, to be only a part of the whole, the organ of an organism? In short, whilst the division of labour is a law of nature, is it also a moral rule for human conduct and, if it possesses this last characteristic, through what causes and to what extent? There is no need to demonstrate the serious nature of this practical problem: whatever assessment we make of the division of labour, we all sense that it is, and increasingly so, one of the fundamental bases of the social order. . . . The time is past when the perfect man seemed to us the one who, capable of being interested in everything but attaching himself exclusively to nothing, able to savour everything and understand everything, found the means to combine and epitomise within himself the finest aspects of civilisation. Today that general culture, once so highly extolled, no longer impresses us save as a flabby, lax form of discipline. To struggle against nature we need to possess more vigorous faculties, deploy more productive energies. We desire our activity to be concentrated, instead of being scattered over a wide area, gaining in intensity what it has lost in breadth. We are wary of those too volatile men of talent, who, lending themselves equally to all forms of employment, refuse to choose for themselves a special role and to adhere to it. We feel a coolness towards those men whose sole preoccupation is to organise their faculties, limbering them up, but without putting them to any special use or sacrificing a single one, as if each man among them ought to be self-sufficient, constituting his own independent world. It appears to us that such a state of detachment and indeterminateness is somewhat antisocial. The man of parts, as he once was, is for us no more than a dilettante, and we accord no moral value to dilettantism. Rather, do we perceive perfection in the competent man, one who seeks not to be complete but to be productive, one who has a well-defined job to which he devotes himself, and carries out his task, ploughing his single furrow. "To perfect oneself," says Secrétant, "is to learn one's role, to make oneself fit to fulfil one's function . . . . The yardstick for our perfection is no longer to be found in satisfaction with ourselves, in the plaudits of the crowd or the approving smile of an affected dilettantism, but in the sum total of services rendered, and in our ability to continue to render them." Thus the moral ideal, from being the sole one, simple and impersonal, has become increasingly diversified. We no longer think that the exclusive duty of man is to realise within himself the qualities of man in general, but we believe that he is no less obliged to have those qualities that relate to his employment. One fact, among others, reflects this view: this is the increasingly specialist character assumed by education. More and more we deem it necessary not to subject all children to a uniform culture, as if all were destined to lead the same life, but to train them differently according to the varying functions they will be called upon to fulfil. In short, in one of its aspects the categorical imperative of the moral consciousness is coming to assume the following form: *Equip yourself to fulfil usefully a specific function.*

. . . If public opinion recognises the rule of the division of labour, it is not without some anxiety and hesitation. Whilst commanding men to specialise, it has always seemingly the fear that they will do so to excess. Side by side with maxims extolling intensive labour are others, no less widely current, which alert us to its dangers. "It is," declares Jean-Baptiste Say, "sad to have to confess that one has never produced more than the eighteenth part of a pin; and do not let us imagine that it is solely the workman who all his life wields a file and hammer, who demeans the dignity of his nature in this way. It is also the man who, through his status, exercises the most subtle faculties of his mind." . . . Nor is de Tocqueville any less severe. "As the principle of the division of labour is ever increasingly applied," he states, "art makes progress but the artisan regresses." Generally speaking, the maxim that decrees that we should specialise is as if refuted everywhere by its opposite, which bids us all realise the same ideal, one that is far from having lost all authority. In principle this conflict of ideas is certainly not surprising. Moral life, like that of body and mind, responds to different needs which may even be contradictory. Thus it is natural for it to be made up in part of opposing elements, which have a mutually limiting and balancing effect. Nevertheless, there is truly something about so marked an antimony which should trouble the moral consciousness of nations. It needs indeed to be able to explain how such a contradiction can arise.

We shall first investigate the function of the division of labour, that is, the social need to which it corresponds.

Next, we shall determine the causes and conditions upon which it depends.

Finally, as it would not have been the subject of such serious charges against it did it not in reality deviate more or less frequently from the normal state, we shall aim to classify the principal abnormal forms that it assumes, in order to avoid confusing them with the rest . . . .

BOOK I

Chapter I

The Method of Determining This Function

I

At first sight nothing appears easier than to determine the role of the division of labour. Are not its efforts known to everybody? Since it increases both the productive capacity and skill of the workman, it is the necessary condition for the intellectual and material development of societies; it is the source of civilisation. Moreover, since we ascribe somewhat glibly an absolute value to civilisation, it does not even occur to us to seek out any different function for the division of labour.

We cannot conceive it necessary to argue that it does in reality have such a result. But if it had no other result and served no other purpose, there would be no reason for attributing any moral character to it.

[. . .]

. . . But the field of ethics is far from being so indeterminate. It comprises all the rules of action that are imposed categorically upon behaviour and to which a punishment is attached, but goes no further than this. Consequently, since civilisation comprises nothing that displays this criterion of morality, it is morally neutral. Thus if the role of the division of labour were solely to make civilisation possible, it would share this same moral neutrality.

Something else must be said: if the division of labour fulfils no other role, not only does it possess no moral character, but no reason for its existence can be perceived. Indeed we shall see that of itself civilisation has no intrinsic and absolute value. What confers value upon it is the fact that it meets certain needs.

Everything therefore impels us to search for some other function for the division of labour. A few commonly observed facts will set us on the path to a solution.

II

Everybody knows that we like what resembles us, those who think and feel as we do. But the opposite phenomenon is no less frequently encountered. Very often we happen to feel drawn to people who do not resemble us, precisely because they do *not* do so. . . .

What demonstrates these opposing doctrines is the fact that both forms of friendship exist in nature. Dissimilarity, just like resemblance, can be a cause of mutual attraction. However, not every kind of dissimilarity is sufficient to bring this about. We find no pleasure in meeting others whose nature is merely different from our own. Prodigals do not seek the company of the miserly, nor upright and frank characters that of the hypocritical and underhand. Kind and gentle spirits feel no attraction for those of harsh and evil disposition. Thus only differences of a certain kind incline us towards one another. These are those which, instead of mutually opposing and excluding one another, complement one another. . . .

Thus the theorist with a reasoning and subtle mind has often a very special sympathy for practical men who are direct and whose intuition is swift. The fearful are attracted to those who are decisive and resolute, the weak to the strong, and vice versa. However richly endowed we may be, we always lack something, and the best among us feel our own inadequacy. This is why we seek in our friends those qualities we lack, because in uniting with them we share in some way in their nature, feeling ourselves then less incomplete. In this way small groups of friends grow up in which each individual plays a role in keeping with his character, in which a veritable exchange of services occurs. The one protects, the other consoles; one advises, the other executes, and it is this distribution of functions or, to use the common expression, this division of labour, that determines these relations of friendship.

We are therefore led to consider the division of labour in a new light. In this case, indeed, the economic services that it can render are insignificant compared with the moral effect that it produces, and its true function is to create between two or more people a feeling of solidarity. However this result is accomplished, it is this that gives rise to these associations of friends and sets its mark upon them.

The history of marital relationships affords an even more striking example of the same phenomenon.

Doubtless, sexual attraction is never felt save between individuals of the same species, and fairly generally love presumes a certain harmony of thought and feeling. It is nevertheless true that what imparts its specific character to this tendency and generates its specific force is not the similarity but the dissimilarity of the natures that it links together. It is because men and women differ from one another that they seek out one another with such passion. . . . it is the sexual division of labour which is the source of conjugal solidarity, and this is why psychologists have very aptly remarked that the separation of the sexes was an event of prime importance in the evolution of the sentiments . . . .

. . . . The division of labour between the sexes is capable of being more, and capable of being less. It can relate only to the sexual organs and some secondary traits that depend on them, or, on the contrary, can extend to all organic and social functions. It can be seen historically as having developed precisely along the same lines and in the same way as marital solidarity.

The further we go back into the past, the more we see that the division of labour between the sexes is reduced to very little. . . . Labour became increasingly divided up as between the sexes. At first limited to the sexual functions alone, it gradually extended to many other functions. The woman had long withdrawn from warfare and public affairs, and had centred her existence entirely round the family. Since then her role has become even more specialised. Nowadays, among civilised peoples the woman leads an existence entirely different from the man's. It might be said that the two great functions of psychological life had become as if dissociated from each other, one sex having taken over the affective, the other the intellectual function. Noticing how, among certain social classes the women are taken up with art and literature, just as are the men, one might, it is true, believe that the activities of both sexes are tending once more to become homogeneous. But even in this sphere of activity, the woman brings to bear her own nature, and her role remains very special, one very different from that of the man. What is more, if art and letters are beginning to become matters that occupy women, the other sex appears to be abandoning them so as to devote itself more especially to science. Thus it might well happen that this apparent reversion to a primeval homogeneity is no more than the beginning of a fresh differentiation. Moreover, these functional differences are made perceptible physically by the morphological differences they have brought about. Not only are size, weight and general shape very dissimilar as between a man and a woman, but Dr Lebon has shown, as we have seen, that with the advance of civilisation the brain of the two sexes has increasingly developed differently. According to this observer, this progressive gap between the two may be due both to the considerable development of the male skull and to a cessation and even a regression in the growth of the female skull. He states: "Whilst the average size of the skulls of male Parisians places them among the largest known skulls, the average size of those of female Parisians places them among the smallest skulls observed, very much below those of Chinese women and scarcely above those of the women of New Caledonia."

In all these examples the most notable effect of the division of labour is not that it increases the productivity of the functions that are divided in this way, but that it links them very closely together. In all these cases its role is not simply to embellish or improve existing societies, but to make possible societies which, without these functions, would not exist . . . . If indeed the sexes had not separated off from each other at all, a whole style of social living would not have arisen. It is possible that the economic usefulness of the division of labour has had some bearing upon the outcome. In any case, however, it goes very considerably beyond the sphere of purely economic interests, for it constitutes the establishment of a social and moral order *sui generis*. Individuals are linked to one another who would otherwise be independent; instead of developing separately, they concert their efforts. They are solidly tied to one another and the links between them function not only in the brief moments when they engage in an exchange of services, but extend considerably beyond. . . .

If exchange alone has often been held to constitute the social relationships that arise from the division of labour, it is because we have failed to recognise what exchange implies and what results from it. It presumes that two beings are mutually dependent upon each other because they are both incomplete, and it does no more than interpret externally this mutual dependence. . . .

Despite the brevity of this analysis, it is sufficient to show that this mechanism is not identical to the one on which are founded those feelings of empathy that spring from similarity. There can certainly never be solidarity between ourselves and another person unless the image of the other person is united with our own. But when union derives from the similarity between two images, it consists in an agglutination. The two representations become solidly bonded together because, being indistinct from each other either wholly or in part, they fuse completely, becoming one. They are only solid with one another in so far as they are fused in this way. On the contrary, in the case of the division of labour, they remain outside each other and are linked only because they are distinct. The feelings that arise cannot therefore be the same in both cases, nor can the social relationships that derive from them.

Thus we are led to ask whether the division of labour might not play the same role in more extensive groupings – whether, in contemporary societies where it has developed in the way that we know, it might not fulfil the function of integrating the body social and of ensuring its unity. It is perfectly legitimate to suppose that the facts we have just observed are replicated here also, but on a broader scale; that these great political societies also cannot sustain their equilibrium save by the specialisation of tasks; and that the division of labour is the source – if not the sole, at least the main one – of social solidarity. Comte had already taken this view....

> it leads one immediately to look not only at individuals and classes but also, in many respects, at different peoples, as participating at one and the same time, each following in its own fashion and to its own special, determined degree, in a vast common enterprise. It is one whose inevitable and gradual development links, moreover, those co-operating together at the present time with the line of their predecessors, whoever these may have been, and even to the line of their various successors. Thus it is the continuous distribution of different human tasks which constitutes the principal element in social solidarity and which becomes the primary cause of the scale and growing complexity of the social organism.

If this hypothesis were proved, the division of labour may play a much more important role than is normally attached to it. It would serve not only to endow societies with luxury, perhaps enviable but nevertheless superfluous. It would be a condition for their existence. It is through the division of labour, or at least mainly through it, that the cohesion of societies would be ensured. It would determine the essential characteristics that constitute them. By this very fact, although we are not yet in a position to resolve the question with any rigour, already we can nevertheless vaguely perceive that, if this is the real function of the division of labour, it must possess a moral character, since needs for order, harmony and social solidarity are generally reckoned to be moral ones.

[...]

III

To state the position precisely, at the point we have now reached it is not easy to say whether it is social solidarity that produces these phenomena or, on the contrary, whether it is the result of them. Likewise it is a moot point whether men draw closer to one another because of the strong effects of social solidarity, or whether it is strong because men *have* come closer together. However, for the moment we need not concern ourselves with clarifying this question. It is enough to state that these two orders of facts are linked, varying with each other simultaneously and directly. The more closely knit the members of a society, the more they maintain various relationships either with one another or with the group collectively. For if they met together rarely, they would not be mutually dependent, except sporadically and somewhat weakly. Moreover, the number of these relationships is necessarily proportional to that of the legal rules that determine them. In fact, social life, wherever it becomes lasting, inevitably tends to assume a definite form and become organised. Law is nothing more than this very organisation in its most stable and precise form. Life in general within a society cannot enlarge in scope without legal activity simultaneously increasing in proportion. Thus we may be sure to find reflected in the law all the essential varieties of social solidarity.

It may certainly be objected that social relationships can be forged without necessarily taking on a legal form. Some do exist where the process of regulation does not attain such a level of consolidation and precision. This does not mean that they remain indeterminate; instead of being regulated by law they are merely regulated by custom. Thus law mirrors only a part of social life and consequently provides us with only incomplete data with which to resolve the problem. What is more, it is often the case that custom is out of step with the law. It is repeatedly stated that custom tempers the harshness of the law, corrects the excesses that arise from its formal nature, and is even occasionally inspired with a very different ethos. Might then custom display other kinds of social solidarity than those expressed in positive law?

But such an antithesis only occurs in wholly exceptional circumstances. For it to occur law must have ceased to correspond to the present state of society and yet, although lacking any reason to exist, is sustained through force of habit. In that event, the new relationships that are established in spite of it will become organised, for they cannot subsist without seeking to consolidate themselves. Yet, being at odds with the old law, which persists, and not succeeding in penetrating the legal domain proper, they do not rise beyond the level of custom. Thus opposition breaks out. But this can only happen in rare, pathological cases, and cannot even continue without becoming dangerous. Normally custom is not opposed to law; on the contrary, it forms the basis for it. It is true that sometimes nothing further is built upon this basis. There may exist social relationships governed only by that diffuse form of regulation arising from custom. But this is because they lack importance and continuity, excepting naturally those abnormal cases just mentioned. Thus if types of social solidarity chance to exist which custom alone renders apparent, these are assuredly of a very secondary order. On the other hand the law reproduces all those types that are essential, and it is about these alone that we need to know.

Should we go further and assert that social solidarity does not consist entirely in its visible manifestations; that these express it only partially and imperfectly; that beyond law and custom there exists an inner state from which solidarity derives; and that to know it in reality we must penetrate to its heart, without any intermediary?

[...]

Thus our method is clearly traced out for us. Since law reproduces the main forms of social solidarity, we have only to classify the different types of law in order to be able to investigate which types of social solidarity correspond to them. It is already likely that one species of law exists which symbolises the special solidarity engendered by the division of labour. Once we have made this investigation, in order to judge what part the division of labour plays it will be enough to compare the number of legal rules which give it expression with the total volume of law.

To undertake this study we cannot use the habitual distinctions made by jurisprudents. Conceived for the practice of law, from this viewpoint they can be very convenient, but science cannot be satisfied with such empirical classifications and approximations. The most widespread classification is that which divides law into public and private law. Public law is held to regulate the relationships of the individual with the state, private law those of individuals with one another. Yet when we attempt to define these terms closely, the dividing line, which appeared at first sight to be so clear-cut, disappears. All law is private, in the sense that always and everywhere individuals are concerned and are its actors. Above all, however, all law is public, in the sense that it is a social function, and all individuals are, although in different respects, functionaries of society. The functions of marriage and parenthood, etc., are not spelt out or organised any differently from those of ministers or legislators. Not without reason did Roman law term guardianship a *munus publicum*. Moreover, what is the state? Where does it begin, where does it end? The controversial nature of this question is well known. It is unscientific to base such a fundamental classification on such an obscure and inadequately analysed idea.

In order to proceed methodically, we have to discover some characteristic which, whilst essential to juridical phenomena, is capable of varying as they vary. Now, every legal precept may be defined as a rule of behaviour to which sanctions apply. Moreover, it is clear that the sanctions change according to the degree of seriousness attached to the precepts, the place they occupy in the public consciousness, and the role they play in society. Thus it is appropriate to classify legal rules according to the different sanctions that are attached to them.

These are of two kinds. The first consist essentially in some injury, or at least some disadvantage imposed upon the perpetrator of a crime. Their purpose is to do harm to him through his fortune, his honour, his life, his liberty, or to deprive him of some object whose possession he enjoys. These are said to be repressive sanctions, such as those laid down in the penal code. It is true that those that appertain to purely moral rules are of the same character. Yet such sanctions are administered in a diffuse way by everybody without distinction, whilst those of the penal code are applied only through the mediation of a definite body – they are organised. As for the other kind of sanctions, they do not necessarily imply any suffering on the part of the perpetrator, but merely consist in *restoring the previous state of affairs*, re-establishing relationships that have been disturbed from their normal form. This is done either by forcibly redressing the action impugned, restoring it to the type from which it has deviated, or by annulling it, that is depriving it of all social value. Thus legal rules must be divided into two main species, according to whether they relate to repressive, organised sanctions, or to ones that are purely restitutory. The first group covers all penal law; the second, civil law, commercial law, procedural law, administrative and constitutional law, when any penal rules which may be attached to them have been removed.

Let us now investigate what kind of social solidarity corresponds to each of these species.

Chapter III

Solidarity Arising From the Division of Labour, or Organic Solidarity

IV

Since negative solidarity on its own brings about no integration, and since, moreover, there is nothing specific in it, we shall identify only two kinds of positive solidarity, distinguished by the following characteristics:

(1) The first kind links the individual directly to society without any intermediary. With the second kind he depends upon society because he depends upon the parts that go to constitute it.

(2) In the two cases, society is not viewed from the same perspective. In the first, the term is used to denote a more or less organised society composed of beliefs and sentiments common to all the members of the group: this is the collective type. On the contrary, in the second case the society to which we are solidly joined is a system of different and special functions united by definite relationships. Moreover, these two societies are really one. They are two facets of one and the same reality, but which none the less need to be distinguished from each other.

(3) From this second difference there arises another which will serve to allow us to characterise and delineate the features of these two kinds of solidarity.

The first kind can only be strong to the extent that the ideas and tendencies common to all members of the society exceed in number and intensity those that appertain personally to each one of those members. The greater this excess, the more active this kind of society is. Now what constitutes our personality is that which each one of us possesses that is peculiar and characteristic, what distinguishes it from others. This solidarity can therefore only increase in inverse relationship to the personality. As we have said, there is in the consciousness of each one of us two consciousnesses: one that we share in common with our group in its entirety, which is consequently not ourselves, but society living and acting within us; the other that, on the contrary, represents us alone in what is personal and distinctive about us, what makes us an individual. The solidarity that derives from similarities is at its *maximum* when the collective consciousness completely envelops our total consciousness, coinciding with it at every point. At that moment our individuality is zero. That individuality cannot arise until the community fills us less completely. Here there are two opposing forces, the one centripetal, the other centrifugal, which cannot increase at the same time. We cannot ourselves develop simultaneously in two so opposing directions. If we have a strong inclination to think and act for ourselves we cannot be strongly inclined to think and act like other people. If the ideal is to create for ourselves a special, personal image, this cannot mean to be like everyone else. Moreover, at the very moment when this solidarity exerts its effect, our personality, it may be said by definition, disappears, for we are no longer ourselves, but a collective being.

The social molecules that can only cohere in this one manner cannot therefore move as a unit save in so far as they lack any movement of their own, as do the molecules of inorganic bodies. This is why we suggest that this kind of solidarity should be called mechanical. The word does not mean that the solidarity is produced by mechanical and artificial means. We only use this term for it by analogy with the cohesion that links together the elements of raw materials, in contrast to that which encompasses the unity of living organisms. What finally justifies the use of this term is the fact that the bond that thus unites the individual with society is completely analogous to that which links the thing to the person. The individual consciousness, considered from this viewpoint, is simply a dependency of the collective type, and follows all its motions, just as the object possessed follows those which its owner imposes upon it. In societies where this solidarity is highly developed the individual, as we shall see later, does not belong to himself; he is literally a thing at the disposal of society. Thus, in these same social types, personal rights are still not yet distinguished from "real" rights.

The situation is entirely different in the case of solidarity that brings about the division of labour. Whereas the other solidarity implies that individuals resemble one another, the latter assumes that they are different from one another. The former type is only possible in so far as the individual personality is absorbed into the collective personality; the latter is only possible if each one of us has a sphere of action that is peculiarly our own, and consequently a personality. Thus the collective conscious-ness leaves uncovered a part of the individual consciousness, so that there may be established in it those special functions that it cannot regulate. The more extensive this free area is, the stronger the cohesion that arises from this solidarity. Indeed, on the one hand each one of us depends more intimately upon society the more labour is divided up, and on the other, the activity of each one of us is correspondingly more specialised, the more personal it is. Doubtless, however circumscribed that activity may be, it is never completely original. Even in the exercise of our profession we conform to usages and practices that are common to us all within our corporation. Yet even in this case, the burden that we bear is in a different way less heavy than when the whole of society bears down upon us, and this leaves much more room for the free play of our initiative. Here, then, the individuality of the whole grows at the same time as that of the parts. Society becomes more effective in moving in concert, at the same time as each of its elements has more movements that are peculiarly its own. This solidarity resembles that observed in the higher animals. In fact each organ has its own special characteristics and autonomy, yet the greater the unity of the organism, the more marked the individualisation of the parts. Using this analogy, we propose to call "organic" the solidarity that is due to the division of labour.

BOOK 2

Chapter II

The Causes

[...]

The increase in the division of labour is therefore due to the fact that the social segments lose their individuality, that the partitions dividing them become more permeable. In short, there occurs between them a coalescence that renders the social substance free to enter upon new combinations.

But the disappearance of this type can only bring about this result for the following reason. It is because there occurs a drawing together of individuals who were separated from one another, or at least they draw more closely together than they had been. Hence movements take place between the parts of the social mass which up to then had no reciprocal effect upon one another. The more the alveolar system is developed, the more the relationships in which each one of us is involved become enclosed within the limits of the alveola to which we belong. There are, as it were, moral vacuums between the various segments. On the other hand these vacuums fill up as the system levels off. Social life, instead of concentrating itself in innumerable small foci that are distinct but alike, becomes general. Social relationships – more exactly we should say intrasocial relationships – consequently become more numerous, since they push out beyond their original boundaries on all sides. Thus the division of labour progresses the more individuals there are who are sufficiently in contact with one another to be able mutually to act and react upon one another. If we agree to call dynamic or moral density this drawing together and the active exchanges that result from it, we can say that the progress of the division of labour is in direct proportion to the moral or dynamic density of society.

But this act of drawing together morally can only bear fruit if the real distance between individuals has itself diminished, in whatever manner. Moral density cannot therefore increase without physical density increasing at the same time, and the latter can serve to measure the extent of the former. Moreover, it is useless to investigate which of the two has influenced the other; it suffices to realise that they are inseparable.

The progressive increase in density of societies in the course of their historical development occurs in three main ways:

(1) Whilst lower societies spread themselves over areas that are relatively vast in comparison with the number of individuals that constitute them, amongst more advanced peoples the population is continually becoming more concentrated . . . .

The activity of nomadic tribes, whether hunters or shepherds, entails in fact the absence of any kind of concentration and dispersion over as wide an area as possible. Agriculture, because it is of necessity a settled existence, already presumes a certain drawing together of the social tissues, but one still very incomplete, since between each family tracts of land are interposed. In the city, although the condensation process was greater, yet houses did not adjoin one another, for joined building was not known in Roman law. This was invented on our own soil and demonstrates that the social ties have become tighter. Moreover, from their origins European societies have seen their density increase continuously in spite of a few cases of temporary regression.

(2) The formation and development of towns are a further symptom, even more characteristic, of the same phenomenon. The increase in average density can be due solely to the physical increase in the birth rate and can consequently be reconciled with a very weak concentration of people, and the very marked maintenance of the segmentary type of society. But towns always result from the need that drives individuals to keep constantly in the closest possible contact with one another. They are like so many points where the social mass is contracting more strongly

than elsewhere. They cannot therefore multiply and spread out unless the moral density increases. Moreover, we shall see that towns recruit their numbers through migration to them, which is only possible to the extent that the fusion of social segments is far advanced.

[...]

(3) Finally, there is the number and speed of the means of communication and transmission. By abolishing or lessening the vacuums separating social segments, these means increase the density of society. Moreover, there is no need to demonstrate that they are the more numerous and perfect the higher the type of society.

Since this visible and measurable symbol reflects the variations in what we have termed moral density, we can substitute this symbol for the latter in the formula that we have put forward. We must, moreover, repeat here what we were saying earlier. If society, in concentrating itself, determines the development of the division of labour, the latter in its turn increases the concentration of society. But this is of no consequence, for the division of labour remains the derived action, and consequently the advances it makes are due to a parallel progress in social density, whatever may be the cause of this progress. This all we wished to establish.

But this factor is not the only one.

If the concentration of society produces this result, it is because it multiplies intra-social relationships. But these will be even more numerous if the total number of members in a society also becomes larger. If it includes more individuals, as well as their being in closer contact, the effect will necessarily be reinforced. Social volume has therefore the same influence over the division of labour as density.

In fact, societies are generally more voluminous the more advanced they are and consequently labour is more divided up in them.

[...]

Yet there are exceptions. The Jewish nation, before the conquest, was probably more voluminous than the Roman city of the fourth century; yet it was of a lower species. China and Russia are much more populous than the most civilised nations of Europe. Consequently among these same peoples the division of labour did not develop in proportion to the social volume. This is because the growth in volume is not necessarily a mark of superiority if the density does not grow at the same time and in the same proportion. A society can reach very large dimensions because it contains a very large number of segments, whatever may be the nature of these. If therefore the largest of them only reproduces societies of a very inferior type, the segmentary structure will remain very pronounced, and in consequence the social organisation will be little advanced. An aggregate of clans, even if immense, ranks below the smallest society that is organised, since the latter has already gone through those stages of evolution below which the aggregate has remained. Likewise if the number of social units has some influence over the division of labour, it is not through itself and of necessity, but because the number of social relationships increases generally with the number of individuals. To obtain this result it is not enough for the society to comprise a large number of persons, but they must be in fairly intimate contact so as to act and react upon one another. If on the other hand they are separated by environments that are mutually impenetrable, only very rarely, and with difficulty, can they establish relationships, and everything occurs as if the number of people was small. An increase in social volume therefore does not always speed up the progress of the division of labour, but only when the mass condenses at the same time and to the same degree. Consequently it is, one may say, only an additional factor. Yet, when joined to the first factor, it extends the effects by an action peculiarly its own, and thus requires to be distinguished from it.

We can therefore formulate the following proposition:

> *The division of labour varies in direct proportion to the volume and density of societies and if it progresses in a continuous manner over the course of social development it is because societies become regularly more dense and generally more voluminous.*

We state, not that the growth and condensation of societies *permit* a greater division of labour, but that they *necessitate* it. It is not the instrument whereby that division is brought about; but it is its determining cause.

III

If labour becomes increasingly divided as societies become more voluminous and concentrated, it is not because the external circumstances are more varied, it is because the struggle for existence becomes more strenuous.

In the same town different occupations can coexist without being forced into a position where they harm one another, for they are pursuing different objectives. The soldier seeks military glory, the priest moral authority, the statesman power, the industrialist wealth, the scientist professional fame. Each one of them can therefore reach his goal without preventing others from reaching theirs . . . .

However, the closer the functions are to one another, the more points of contact there are between them, and, as a result, the more they tend to conflict. As in this case they satisfy similar needs by different means, it is inevitable that they should seek, more or less, to encroach upon others. The magistrate is never in competition with the industrialist. But the brewer and the winegrower, the draper and the maker of silks, the poet and the musician often attempt mutually to supplant each other. As for those that discharge exactly the same function, they cannot prosper save to the detriment of their fellows. . . . This is the case not only within each town but over society as a whole. Similar occupations located at different sites over an area enter into fiercer rivalry the more alike they are, provided that difficulties of communications and transport do not constrain their sphere of action.

This having been said, it is easy to understand that any concentration in the social mass, particularly if accompanied by a growth in population, necessarily determines the progress of the division of labour.

[. . .]

In other words, to the extent that the social constitution is a segmentary one, each segment has its own organs that are, so to speak, protected and kept at a distance from similar organs by the partitions separating the different segments. But, as these partitions disappear, it is inevitable that organs similar to one another come into contact, embark upon a struggle and try to substitute themselves for one another.

However, in whatever way this substitution occurs, some advance along the road to specialisation cannot fail to be the outcome. For on the one hand, the segmentary organ that triumphs, if we may speak in those terms, cannot be sufficient to undertake the larger task that now falls to it in the future save by a greater division of labour. On the other hand, the vanquished can only continue to exist by concentrating upon one part only of the total function that they fulfilled up to that time. The small employer becomes a foreman, the small shopkeeper an employee, etc. This share can moreover be of greater or lesser size depending on whether their inferiority is more or less glaring. It can even happen that the original function simply becomes split into two parts of equal importance. Instead of entering into competition, or remaining so, two similar undertakings find their equilibrium again by sharing their common task: instead of one becoming subordinate to the other, they co-ordinate their activities. But in every case new specialities appear.

Although the above examples are especially taken from economic life, this explanation is applicable to all social functions without distinction. Work, whether scientific, artistic, or otherwise, does not divide up in any other way or for any other reasons. It is still because of these same causes that, as we have seen, the central regulatory mechanism absorbs to itself the local regulatory organs, reducing them to the role of specialised auxiliary ones.

[...]

The division of labour is therefore one result of the struggle for existence: but it is a gentle dénouement. Thanks to it, rivals are not obliged to eliminate one another completely, but can coexist side by side. Moreover, as it develops, it provides a greater number of individuals, who in more homogeneous societies would be condemned to extinction, with the means of sustaining themselves and surviving. Among many lower peoples, any ill-formed organism was fatally doomed to perish, for it was not usable for any function at all. Sometimes the law, anticipating and in some way sanctioning the results of natural selection, condemned to death the sickly and weak newborn babies, and Aristotle himself found this practice natural. Things are completely different in more advanced societies. A puny individual can find within the complex cadres of our social organisation a niche in which he can render a service. If he is only weak bodily and his mind is healthy, he will devote himself to the labour of the study, to the speculative functions. If it is his brain that is defective "he will undoubtedly have to renounce taking on great intellectual competition; but society has, in the secondary cells of the hive, places small enough which will prevent him from being eliminated".

[...]

An industry can only live if it corresponds to some necessity. A function can only become specialised if that specialisation corresponds to some need in society. Every new specialisation has as a result an increase and improvement in production. If this advantage is not the reason for the existence of the division of labour, it is its necessary consequence. As a result, lasting progress cannot be established unless individuals really feel the need for more abundant or better-quality products. ... Yet from where may such new demands spring?

They are an effect of the same cause that determines the progress of the division of labour. ... in order for life to continue the reward must always be proportionate to the effort; ...

Moreover, it is above all the central nervous system that bears the whole brunt of this. This is because one must be inventive in finding the means of sustaining the struggle, to create new specialities, and make them known. Generally the more the environment is subject to change, the greater the part played by intelligence in life. It alone can discover the new conditions necessary for an equilibrium which is constantly being broken, and can restore it. Thus the activity of the brain develops at the same time as competition becomes fiercer, and to the same extent. This parallel advance can be noted not only among the elite, but in all classes of society. On this point we need only compare once more the industrial worker with the agricultural worker. It is an acknowledged fact that the former is much the more intelligent, in spite of the mechanical character of the tasks to which he is often tied. Moreover, it is not without reason that mental illnesses go hand in hand with civilisation, nor that they break out in towns rather than the countryside, and in large rather than small towns. Now a more capacious and delicate brain has different needs from an encephalon which is of a coarser nature. Troubles and privations that the latter would not even feel wrack the former with pain. For the same reason more complex stimuli are necessary to give pleasure to the brain organ, once it has become refined, and more are needed because at the same time it has developed. Finally, more than all other needs, specifically intellectual needs increase. Vulgar explanations can no longer satisfy more practised minds. New enlightenment is sought, and science nurtures these aspirations at the same time as it assuages them.

All these changes are therefore wrought automatically by necessary causes. If our intelligence and sensibility develop, becoming more acute, it is because we exercise them more. And if we do so, it is because we are constrained by the greater violence of the struggle we have to sustain. This is how, without having willed it, humanity finds itself prepared to accept a more intense and varied culture. . . .

Even when we are drawn towards an object because of a very strong inherited disposition towards it, we can only desire it after having come into contact with it. . . . But at the very moment when man is in a position to taste these new joys and summons them up even unconsciously, he finds them within his grasp, because the division of labour has at the same time developed and has provided them for him. Without there being the slightest pre-established harmony in this, the two orders of facts meet, quite simply because they are effects of the same cause.

This is how we might conceive such an encounter to come about. The attraction of novelty would already be enough to induce man to taste these pleasures. He is even more naturally inclined to do so because the greater richness and complexity of these stimuli make him esteem to be of a more mediocre quality those with which he had contented himself up to that point. He can moreover adapt himself mentally to them before he has ever tried them out. As in reality they correspond to changes that have taken place in his constitution, he feels in advance that he will find them agreeable. Experience then comes to confirm this presentiment. Needs that were dormant are awakened, become precise, acquire an awareness of themselves and begin to be organised. However this does not signify that in each case this adjustment is equally perfect, or that every new product that is due to further advances in the division of labour, always corresponds to some real need in our nature. On the contrary, it is very likely that fairly often the needs take shape because we have acquired a habit for the object to which they relate. This object was neither necessary nor useful. Yet we have happened to experience it several times and have grown so accustomed to it that we can no longer do without it. Harmonies arising from wholly automatic causes can never be other than imperfect and approximate, but they are sufficient to maintain order generally. This is what happens with the division of labour. The progress that it makes is generally – but not in all cases – in harmony with the changes that occur in man, and this it is that makes them lasting.

[...]

We see how different our view of the division of labour appears from that of the economists. For them it consists essentially in producing more. For us this greater productivity is merely a necessary consequence, a side-effect of the phenomenon. If we specialise it is not so as to produce more, but to enable us to live in the new conditions of existence created for us.

IV

A corollary of everything that has gone before is that the division of labour cannot be carried out save between the members of a society already constituted.

[...]

It consists in the sharing out of functions that up till then were common to all. But such an allocation cannot be effected according to any preconceived plan. We cannot say beforehand where the line of demarcation is drawn between tasks, once they have been separated. In the nature of things that line is not marked out so self-evidently, but on the contrary depends upon a great number of circumstances. The division must therefore come about of itself, and progressively. Consequently, in these conditions for a function to be capable of being shared out in two exactly complementary fractions, as the nature of the division of labour requires, it is indispensable that the two parties specialising should be in constant communication over the whole period that this dissociation is occurring. There is no other way for one part to take over from the other the whole operation that the latter is surrendering, and for them to adapt to each other. Now, just as an animal colony, the tissue of whose members is a continuum, constitutes an individual, so every aggregate of individuals in continuous contact forms a society. The division of labour can therefore only occur within the framework of an already existing society. By this we do not just simply mean that individuals must cling materially to one another, but moral ties must also exist between them. Firstly, material continuity alone gives rise to links of this kind, provided that it is lasting. Moreover, they are directly necessary. If the relationships beginning to be established during the period of uncertainty were not subject to any rule, if no power moderated the clash of individual interests, chaos would ensue from which no new order could emerge. It is true that we imagine that everything occurs by means of private agreements freely argued over. All social action therefore seems to be absent. But we forget that contracts are only possible where a legal form of regulation, and consequently a society, already exists.

Thus it has been wrong sometimes to see in the division of labour the basic fact of all social life. Work is not shared out between independent individuals who are already differentiated from one another, who meet and associate together in order to pool their different abilities. It would be a miracle if these differences, arising from chance circumstances, could be so accurately harmonised as to form a coherent whole. Far from their preceding collective life, they derive from it. They can only occur within a society, under the pressure of social sentiments and needs. This is what makes them essentially capable of being harmonised. Thus there is a social life outside of any division of labour, but one that the latter assumes. This is in fact what we have directly established by demonstrating that there are societies whose cohesion is due essentially to a community of beliefs and sentiments, and that it is from these societies that others have emerged whose unity is ensured by the division of labour.

[...]

What draws men together are mechanical forces and instinctive forces such as the affinity of blood, attachment to the same soil, the cult of their ancestors, a commonality of habits, etc. It is only when the group has been formed on these bases that co-operation becomes organised.

[...]

Collective life did not arise from individual life; on the contrary, it is the latter that emerged from the former. On this condition alone can we explain how the personal individuality of social units was able to form and grow without causing society to disintegrate. Indeed, since in this case it developed from within a pre-existing social environment, it necessarily bears its stamp. It is constituted in such a way as not to ruin that collective order to which it is solidly linked. It remains adapted to it, whilst detaching itself from it. There is nothing antisocial about it, because it is a product of society. It is not the absolute personality of the monad, sufficient unto itself, and able to do without the rest of the world, but that of an organ or part of an organ that has its own definite function, but that cannot, without running a mortal risk, separate itself from the rest of the organism. In these conditions co-operation not only becomes possible, but necessary.

[...]

The argument concerning the international division of labour will be adduced. It seems clear, in this case at least, that the individuals who share the work do not belong to the same society. But we should remember that a group, whilst it retains its individuality, can be enveloped within another larger one, which comprises others of the same kind. We may even affirm that a function, whether of an economic or any other kind, can only be divided up between two societies if these share in some respects in the same common life and, consequently, belong to the same society. Let us indeed suppose that these two collective consciousnesses are not in some respects intermingled together. Then we would not be able to see how the two aggregates might have the continuous contact that is necessary nor, in consequence, how one of them could abandon one of its functions to the other. For a people to allow itself to be penetrated by another, it must have ceased to shut itself up in an exclusive form of patriotism, and must have learned another that is more all-embracing.

However, we can observe directly this relationship of fact in the most striking example of the international division of labour that history offers us. We may indeed say that it has never really occurred save in Europe and in our own day. It was at the end of the last century and the beginning of our own that a common consciousness began to form in European societies . . . .

Chapter III
Secondary Factors

The Progressive Indeterminacy of the Common Consciousness and its Causes

I

In a small society, since everybody is roughly placed in the same conditions of existence, the collective environment is essentially concrete. It is made up of human beings of every kind who people the social horizon. The states of consciousness that represent it are therefore of the same character. At first they relate to precise objects, such as a particular animal, tree, plant, or natural force, etc. Then, since everyone is similarly placed in relation to these things, they affect every individual consciousness in the same way. The whole tribe, provided it is not too extensive, enjoys or suffers equally the advantages and inconveniences of sun and rain, heat and cold, or of a particular river or spring, etc. The collective impressions resulting from the fusion of all these individual impressions are thus determinate in their form as in their objects. Consequently the common consciousness has a definite character. But this consciousness alters in nature as societies grow more immense. Because they are spread over a much vaster area, the common consciousness is itself forced to rise above all local diversities, to dominate more the space available, and consequently to become more abstract. For few save general things can be common to all these various environments. There is no longer question of such and such an animal, but of such and such a species; not this spring, but these springs; not this forest, but forest *in abstracto*.

Moreover, because living conditions are not the same everywhere, these common objects, whatever they may be, can no longer determine everywhere feelings so completely identical. The results for the collectivity thus lack the same distinctness, and this is even more the case because the component elements are more dissimilar. The more differences between the individual portraits that have served to make a composite portrait, the more imprecise the latter is. It is true that local collective consciousness can retain their individuality within the general collective consciousness and that, since they encompass narrower horizons, they can more easily remain concrete. But we know that gradually they vanish into the general consciousness as the different social segments to which they correspond fade away.

Perhaps the fact that best demonstrates this increasing tendency of the common consciousness is the parallel transcendence of the most vital of all its elements – I refer to the notion of divinity. Originally the gods were not apart from the universe, or rather there were no gods, but only sacred beings, without the sacred character with which they were invested being related to some external entity as its source. The animals or plants of the species that serve as the clan totem are the object of worship.

... But gradually the religious forces become detached from the things of which they were at first only the attributes, and are reified. In this way is formed the notion of spirits or gods who, whilst preferring this or that location, nevertheless exist outside the particular objects to which they are more especially attached. This fact alone renders them less concrete. However, whether they are many or have been reduced to a certain unity, they are still immanent in the world. Partly separated from things, they still exist in space. Thus they remain very close to us, continually intermingling with our life. Greco-Roman polytheism, which is a higher and better organised form of animism, marks a new step towards transcendence. The dwelling-place of the gods becomes more clearly distinct from that of man. Having withdrawn to the mysterious heights of Olympus or to the depths of the earth, except intermittently they no longer intervene personally in human affairs. But it is only with Christianity that God finally goes beyond space; His Kingdom is no longer of this world. The dissociation of nature and the divine becomes so complete that it even degenerates into hostility. At the same time the notion of divinity becomes more general and abstract, for it is formed not from sensations, as it was in the beginning, but from ideas. The God of humanity is necessarily not so comprehensible as those of a city or clan.

Moreover, at the same time as religion, legal rules become universalised, as do those of morality. First bound to local circumstances, to racial or climatic peculiarities, etc., they gradually free themselves from these and simultaneously become more general. What makes this increase in generality more apparent is the unbroken decline in formalism. In lower societies the form of behaviour – even its external form – is predetermined even down to the detail. The way in which men must take food or dress in every situation, the gestures they must perform, the formulas they must pronounce, are precisely laid down. On the other hand, the more distant the point of departure, the more moral and legal prescriptions lose clarity and preciseness. They no longer regulate any save the most general forms of behaviour, and these only in a very general way, stating what should be done, but not how it should be done. Now everything definite is expressed in a definite form. If collective sentiments were as determinate as once they were, they would be expressed in no less determinate a fashion. If the concrete details of action and thought were as uniform, they would be as obligatory.

The fact has often been remarked upon that civilisation has tended to become more rational and logical. We can now see the cause of this. That alone is rational that is universal. What defies the understanding is the particular and the concrete. We can only ponder effectively upon the general. ... Thus it is the growth in the size of societies and their greater density that explains this great transformation.

The more general the common consciousness becomes, the more scope it leaves for individual variations. When God is remote from things and men, His action does not extend to every moment of time and to every thing. Only abstract rules are fixed, and these can be freely applied in very different ways. ... once reflective thinking has been stimulated, it is not easy to set bounds to it. When it has gathered strength, it spontaneously develops beyond the limits assigned to it. At the beginning certain articles of faith are stipulated to be beyond discussion, but later the discussion extends to them. There is a desire to account for them, the reason for their existence is questioned, and however they fare in this examination, they relinquish some part of their strength. For ideas arising from reflection have never the same constraining power as instincts. Thus actions that have been deliberated upon have not the instant immediacy of involuntary acts. Because the collective consciousness becomes more rational, it therefore becomes less categorical and, for this reason again, is less irksome to the free development of individual variations.

II

... What constitutes the strength of the collective states of consciousness is not only that they are common to the present generation, but particularly that they are for the most part a legacy of generations that have gone before. The common consciousness is in fact formed only very slowly and modified in the same way. Time is needed for a form of behaviour or a belief to attain that degree of generality and crystallisation, and time also for it to lose it. Thus it is almost entirely a product of the past. But what springs from the past is generally an object of very special respect. A practice to which everyone unanimously conforms has without doubt great prestige. But if it is also strong because it bears the mark of ancestral approval, one dares even less to depart from it. The authority of the collective consciousness is therefore made up in large part of the authority of tradition. ...

III

Finally as society spreads out and becomes denser, it envelops the individual less tightly, and in consequence can restrain less efficiently the diverging tendencies that appear.

To confirm that this is the case it is sufficient to compare large and small towns. With the latter, the person who seeks to emancipate himself from accepted customs comes up against resistances that are on occasion very fierce. Any bid for independence is a subject of public scandal, and the general opprobrium attached to it is such as to discourage imitators. On the contrary, in large towns the individual is much more liberated from the yoke of the collectivity; this is indisputably a fact of experience. It is because we depend more closely upon public opinion the more narrowly it supervises all our activities. When everyone's attention is constantly fixed upon what everyone else is doing, the slightest deviation is remarked upon and immediately repressed. Conversely, the greater freedom each individual has to follow his own bent, the easier it is for him to escape surveillance.

[...]

Collective curiosity is therefore stronger when personal relations between individuals are more continuous and frequent. On the other hand, it is evident that they are rarer and briefer when each separate individual is in contact with a larger number of other people.

This is why the pressure of opinion is felt with less force in large population centres. It is because the attention of each individual is distracted in too many different directions. Moreover, we do not know one another so well. Even neighbours and members of the same family are in contact less often and less regularly, separated as they are at every moment by a host of matters and other people who come between them. Undoubtedly if the population is larger in number than it is concentrated in density, it can happen that the business of living, scattered over a wider area, is less intense at any and every point. The large town then splits up into a certain number of smaller ones and consequently the preceding remarks do not apply exactly. Yet wherever the density of the conurbation is proportionate to its volume, personal ties are few and weak. We lose sight of others more easily, even those very close to us physically. And to the same extent we lose interest in them. Since this mutual indifference has the effect of relaxing the supervision of the collectivity, the range of freedom of individual action is enlarged *de facto*, and gradually this situation of fact becomes one *de jure*. Indeed we know that the common consciousness only retains its strength if it countenances no contradiction. As a result of this decrease in social control, acts are committed daily that infringe it, without however its reacting. If therefore some acts are repeated sufficiently frequently and consistently, they end up by enfeebling the collective sentiment that they offend. A rule no longer appears as respectable when it ceases to be respected, and this without incurring punishment. One does not find so self-evident an article of faith that has been allowed to be challenged unduly. Moreover, once we have enjoyed a liberty, we acquire a need for it. It becomes as necessary and as sacred to us as all the others. We deem intolerable a control we are no longer accustomed to. An acquired right to a greater autonomy is set up. Thus encroachments committed by the individual personality, when that personality is less forcibly constrained externally, end up by receiving the consecration of custom.

If this fact is more apparent in large towns, it is not peculiar to them. It happens also in the others, depending upon their importance. Thus since the disappearance of the segmentary type of society entails an ever-increasing development of urban centres, this is a prime reason for causing this phenomenon to become more general. But, in addition, as the moral density of a society is raised, so it becomes itself like a large city, which would contain within its walls the whole population.

Indeed, as the material and moral distance between different regions tends to vanish, they are placed in relation to one another in a situation still more analogous to that of different quarters of the same city. The cause that in large towns determines the weakening of the common consciousness must therefore produce its effect over the whole expanse of society. So long as the various segments, retaining their individuality, remain sealed off from one another, each narrowly restricts the social horizon of individuals. Separated from the rest of society by barriers more or less difficult to surmount, there is nothing to turn us away from the life of the neighbourhood, and in consequence our entire activity is concentrated upon it. But as the fusion of segments becomes more complete, perspectives broaden out – all the more because at the same time society itself becomes generally more extensive. From then onwards even the inhabitant of a small town lives less exclusively upon the life of the small group immediately around him. He enters into relationships with distant localities that are all the more numerous as the movement towards concentration advances. His more frequent journeys, the more active communications that he exchanges, the affairs with which he busies himself outside his own locality, etc., divert his gaze from what is taking place around him. The centre of his life and concerns is no longer to be found wholly in the place where he lives. Thus he takes less interest in his neighbours, because they occupy a more minor place in his life. Moreover, the small town has less hold upon him, by the very fact that his life has broken out beyond its narrow framework and his interests and affections stretch well beyond it. For all these reasons local opinion weighs less heavily with each one of us, and as public opinion in society generally is not capable of replacing it, because it cannot supervise closely the behaviour of all its citizens, collective surveillance is irrevocably relaxed, the common consciousness loses its authority, and individual variability increases. In short, for social control to be rigorous and for the common consciousness to be maintained, society must be split up into moderately small compartments that enclose completely the individual. By contrast, both social control and the common consciousness grow weaker as such divisions fade.

Yet it will be objected that the crimes and offences to which are attached organised punishments never leave indifferent the organs charged with their repression. Whether the town be large or small, or the density of society be concentrated or not, the magistrates do not let go unpunished the criminal and the delinquent. It would therefore appear that the particular process of weakening, the cause of which we have just indicated, must be located in that part of the collective consciousness that determines only diffuse reactions and is incapable of extending further. Yet in reality so specific a location is impossible, for the two areas are so closely linked to each other that the one cannot be affected without the other being disturbed also. The actions that morality alone represses are no different in nature from those the law punishes; they are merely less serious. Thus if one action loses its serious character, the corresponding graduation in seriousness of the others is upset at the same time. They diminish in gravity by one or several degrees and appear less abhorrent. If one is no longer sensitive to small failings, one is even less so to major ones. When no great importance any longer attaches to simple neglect of religious observances, blasphemous or sacrilegious acts are no longer inveighed against with such indignation. When we have grown accustomed to suffering free unions complacently, adultery becomes less scandalous. When the weakest sentiments lose their potency the stronger ones of the same kind, which serve the same purpose, cannot retain intact their own potency. Thus the disturbance is gradually transmitted to the common consciousness in its entirety.

IV

Now we can explain how it happens that mechanical solidarity is linked to the existence of the segmentary type of society, as we established in the preceding book. It is because this particular structure enables society to hold the individual more tightly in its grip, making him more strongly attached to his domestic environment, and consequently to tradition. Finally, by helping to limit his social horizon, the structure also helps in making the latter concrete and definite. Thus it is entirely mechanical causes which ensure that the individual personality is absorbed into the collective personality, and it is causes of the same nature which ensure that the same individual personality can free itself. Undoubtedly this emancipation is useful, or at least is used. It makes advances in the division of labour possible. More generally, it imparts more flexibility and elasticity to the social organism. Yet it is not because it is useful that it occurs. It is because things cannot be otherwise. The experience of the services that it renders can only consolidate it once it exists.

However, we may ask if, within organised societies, the organ does not play the same role as the segment, and whether the corporate and professional spirit does not bid fair to replace local parochialism and exert the same pressure upon individuals. In that case individuals would have gained nothing from the change. This doubt is all the more legitimate, since the class ethos has certainly had this effect, and class is a social organ. We know also how greatly the organisation of trade guilds for a long time impeded the development of individual variations. We have cited some examples of this above.

It is certain that organised societies are not possible without a developed system of rules laying down in advance the functioning of each organ. As work becomes divided up many professional moralities and legal prescriptions are constituted. Yet this regulatory process does not leave the individual with a scope for action any less enlarged.

Firstly, the professional spirit can only have influence upon professional life. Beyond this sphere the individual enjoys that larger liberty whose origin we have just demonstrated. It is true that social class enlarges its action ever further, but it is not properly an organ. It is a segment transformed into an organ. It therefore partakes of the nature of both. At the same time as it is entrusted with special functions, it constitutes a distinctive society within the total aggregate. It is a "society-cum-organ", analogous to those "individuals-cum-organ" observable within certain organisms. It is this that allows class to embrace the individual in a way more exclusive than do the ordinary corporations.

In the second place, as these rules have roots only in a small number of consciousnesses, leaving society as a whole indifferent, their authority is less because of this lesser universality. Thus they offer less resistance to change. It is for this reason that in general faults that may properly be termed professional are not of the same degree of seriousness as the others.

On the other hand, the same causes that in general lighten the collective yoke produce their liberating effect within the corporation as they do outside it. To the extent that the segmentary organs fuse together each social organ becomes larger in volume, and this all the more so because in principle the overall volume of society increases simultaneously. Practices common to the professional group thus become more general and abstract, as do those common to society as a whole, and consequently leave the field more open for particular divergences. Likewise the greater independence enjoyed by the later generations in comparison with their elders cannot fail to weaken the traditionalism of the profession, and this makes the individual still freer to innovate.

Thus not only does professional regulation, by its very nature, hinder less than any other form of regulation the free development of individual variation, but moreover it hinders it less and less.

[...]

The necessities of our subject have in fact obliged us to classify moral rules and to review the main species among them. ... We have split them into two kinds: rules with a repressive sanction, which is either diffuse or organised, and rules with a restitutory sanction. We have seen that the former express the conditions of that solidarity *sui generis* which derives from resemblances, and to which we have given the name mechanical solidarity. The latter, those of negative solidarity, we have termed organic solidarity. Thus we may state generally that the characteristic of moral rules is that they enunciate the basic conditions of social solidarity. Law and morality represent the totality of bonds that bind us to one another and to society, which shape the mass of individuals into a cohesive aggregate. We may say that what is moral is everything that is a source of solidarity, everything that forces man to take account of other people, to regulate his actions by something other than the promptings of his own egoism, and the more numerous and strong these ties are, the more solid is the morality. We can see how inaccurate it is to define it, as has often been done, in terms of freedom. It rather consists much more in a state of dependence. Far from it serving to emancipate the individual, disengaging him from the surrounding environment, its essential function, on the contrary, is to be the integrating element in a whole, and in consequence it removes from the individual some of his freedom of movement.

... Thus society is not, as has often been believed, some happening that is a stranger to morality, or which has only secondary repercussions upon it. It is not a mere juxtaposition of individuals who, upon entering into it, bring with them an intrinsic morality. Man is only a moral being because he lives in society, since morality consists in solidarity with the group, and varies according to that solidarity. Cause all social life to vanish, and moral life would vanish at the same time, having no object to cling to.

[...]

Not only does the division of labour exhibit that character by which we define morality, but it increasingly tends to become the essential condition for social solidarity. As evolution advances, the bonds that attach the individual to his family, to his native heath, to the traditions that the past has bequeathed him, to the collective practices of the group – all these become loosened. Being more mobile, the individual changes his environment more easily, leaves his own people to go and live a more autonomous life elsewhere, works out for himself his ideas and sentiments. Doubtless all trace of common consciousness does not vanish because of this. At the very least there will always subsist that cult of the person and individual dignity about which we have just spoken, which today is already the unique rallying-point for so many minds. But how insignificant this is if we consider the ever-increasing scope of social life and, consequently, of the individual consciousness! As the latter becomes more expansive, as the intelligence becomes even better equipped, and activity more varied, for morality to remain unchanged, that is, for the individual to be bound to the group even so strongly as once he was, the ties that bind him must be reinforced, becoming more numerous. Thus if only those ties were forged that were based on similarities, the disappearance of the segmentary type of society would be accompanied by a steady decline in morality. Man would no longer be held adequately under control. He would no longer feel around him and above him that salutary pressure of society that moderates his egoism, making of him a moral creature. This it is that constitutes the moral value of the division of labour. Through it the individual is once more made aware of his dependent state *vis-à-vis* society. It is from society that proceed those forces that hold him in check and keep him within bounds. In short, since the division of labour becomes the predominant source of social solidarity, at the same time it becomes the foundation of the moral order.

We may thus state literally that in higher societies our duty lies not in extending the range of our activity but in concentrating it, in making it more specialised. We must limit our horizons, select a definite task, and involve ourselves utterly, instead of making ourselves, so to speak, a finished work of art, one that derives all its value from itself rather than from the services it renders. Finally, this specialisation must be carried the farther the more society is of a higher species. No other limits can be placed upon it. Undoubtedly we must also work towards realising within ourselves the collective type, in so far as it exists. There are common sentiments and ideas without which, as one says, one is not a man. The rule prescribing that we should specialise remains limited by the opposite rule. We conclude that it is not good to push specialisation as far as possible, but only as far as necessary. The weight to be given to these two opposing necessities is determined by experience and cannot be calculated *a priori*. It suffices for us to have shown that the latter is no different in nature from the former, but that it is also moral and that, moreover, this duty becomes ever more important and urgent, because the general qualities we have discussed suffice less and less to socialise the individual.

Thus it is not without reason that public sentiment is continually distancing itself even more markedly from the dilettante, and even from those who, too much absorbed with a culture that is exclusively general, shrink from allowing themselves to be wholly caught up with the professional organisation. This is in fact because they do not adhere closely enough to society or, if one likes, society does not hold on to them closely enough. They elude it, and precisely because they do not feel it with the sense of vividness and continuity needed, they are unaware of all the obligations laid upon them by their condition as social beings. The general idea to which they are attached being, for reasons we have given, formal and fluctuating, it cannot draw them very much outside themselves. Without a determinate goal one does not cling to very much, so that one can scarcely lift oneself out of a more or less refined egoism. On the other hand, he who has dedicated himself to a definite task is reminded at every moment of the common sentiment of solidarity through the thousand and one duties of professional morality.

II

Yet does not the division of labour, by rendering each one of us an incomplete being, not entail some curtailment of the individual personality? This criticism has often been made.

Firstly, let us note that it is difficult to see why it might be more in accord with the logic of human nature to develop more superficially rather than in depth. Why should a more extensive activity, one that is more dispersed, be superior to one more concentrated and circumscribed? Why should more dignity attach to being complete and mediocre than in leading a more specialised kind of life but one more intense, particularly if we can recapture in this way what we have lost, through our association with others who possess what we lack and who make us complete beings? We start from the principle that man must realise his nature as man – as

Aristotle said, accomplish his οἰχέίον έργον . But at different moments in history this nature does not remain constant; it is modified with societies. Among lower peoples, the act that connotes a man is to resemble his fellows, to realise within himself all the characteristics of the collective type which, even more than today, was then confused with the human type. In more advanced societies man's nature is mainly to be a part of society; consequently the act that connotes a man is for him to play his part as one organ of society.

There is something more: far from the progress of specialisation whittling away the individual personality, this develops with the division of labour.

Indeed to be a person means to be an autonomous source of action. Thus man only attains this state to the degree that there is something within him that is his and his alone, that makes him an individual, whereby he is more than the mere embodiment of the generic type of his race and group. It will in any case be objected that he is endowed with free will, and that this is sufficient upon which to base his personality. But whatever this freedom may consist of – and it is the subject of much argument – it is not this impersonal, invariable, metaphysical attribute that can serve as the sole basis for the empirical, variable and concrete personality of individuals. That personality cannot be formed by the entirely abstract capacity to choose between two opposites. This faculty must be exercised in relation to ends and motives that are peculiar to the person acting. In other words the stuff of which his consciousness is made up must have a personal character. Now we have seen in the second book of this study that is an outcome that occurs progressively as the division of labour itself progresses. The disappearance of the segmentary type of society, at the same time as it necessitates greater specialisation, frees the individual consciousness in part from the organic environment that supports it, as it does from the social environment that envelops it. This dual emancipation renders the individual more independent in his own behaviour. The division of labour itself contributes to this liberating effect. Individual natures become more complex through specialising; by this very fact they are partly shielded against the effects of the collectivity and the influences of heredity, which can scarcely enforce themselves except in simple, general matters.

Thus, as a consequence of a veritable illusion, one could occasionally believe that the personality was more whole, so long as it had not been breached by the division of labour. Doubtless, viewing from the outside the variety of occupations that the individual embarks upon, it may seem that the personality then develops more freely and completely. But in reality the activity he displays is not his own. It is society, it is the race, which act in and through him; he is only the intermediary through which they are realised. His liberty is only apparent, his personality is borrowed. Since the life of societies is in certain respects less regular, we imagine that original talents can more easily come to light, that it is easier for each individual to follow his own tastes, that greater room is left for the free play of fantasy. Yet this is to forget that personal sentiments are then very rare. If the motives governing conduct do not occur with the same regularity as they do today, they do not cease to be collective, and consequently impersonal. The same is true for the actions they inspire. We have moreover shown above how the activity becomes richer and more intense the more specialised it becomes.

Thus the advance of the individual personality and that of the division of labour depend on one and the same cause. Thus also it is impossible to will the one without willing the other. Nowadays no one questions the obligatory nature of the rule that ordains that we should exist as a person, and this increasingly so.

One final consideration will show to what extent the division of labour is linked to our whole moral life.

It has long been a dream cherished by men to succeed at last in achieving as a reality the ideal of human brotherhood. Peoples raise their voices to wish for a state of affairs where war would no longer govern international relations, where relationships between societies would be regulated peacefully as are already those between individuals, and where all men would co-operate in the common task and live the same life. Although these aspirations are partly neutralised by others that relate to the particular society of which we form part, they remain very strong and are continually gathering strength. However, they cannot be satisfied unless all men form part of one and the same society, subject to the same laws. For, just as private conflicts can only be contained by the regulatory action of a society that embraces all individuals, so inter-social conflicts can only be contained by the regulatory action of a society that embraces all societies. The only power that can serve to moderate individual egoism is that of the group; the only one that can serve to moderate the egoism of groups is that of another group that embraces them all.

Really, once the problem has been posed in these terms, we must acknowledge that this ideal is not on the verge of being realised in its entirety. Between the different types of society coexisting on earth there are too many intellectual and moral divergences to be able to live in a spirit of brotherhood in the same society. Yet what is possible is that societies of the same species should come together, and it is indeed in this direction that our society appears to be going. We have seen already that there is tending to form, above European peoples, in a spontaneous fashion, a European society that has even now some feeling of its own identity and the beginnings of an organisation. If the formation of one single human society is for ever ruled out – and this has, however, not yet been demonstrated – at least the formation of larger societies will draw us continually closer to that goal. Moreover, these facts do not at all contradict the definition we have given of morality. If we cling to humanity and ought to continue to do so, it is because it is a society in the process of realising itself in this way, one to which we are solidly bound.

Yet we know that more extensive societies cannot be formed without the development of the division of labour. Without a greater specialisation of functions not only could they not sustain their equilibrium, but the increase in the number of elements in competition would also automatically suffice to bring about that state. Even more would this be the case, for an increase in volume does not generally occur without an increase in population density. Thus we may formulate the following proposition: the ideal of human brotherhood cannot be realised unless the division of labour progresses. We must choose: either we must abandon our dream, if we refuse to limit our individual activity any further; or we can pursue the consummation of our dream, but only on the condition just stated.

III

Yet if the division of labour produces solidarity, it is not only because it makes each individual an agent of exchange, to use the language of the economists. It is because it creates between men a whole system of rights and duties joining them in a lasting way to one another. Just as social similarities give rise to a law and a morality that protect them, so the division of labour gives rise to rules ensuring peaceful and regular co-operation between the functions that have been divided up.

[...]

The division of labour does not present individuals to one another, but social functions. Society has an interest in the interplay of those functions: depending on whether they co-operate regularly or not, society will be healthy or sick. Its existence is therefore dependent upon them, all the more intimately bound up with them the more they are divided. This is why it cannot let them remain in an indeterminate state; moreover, they determine one another. It is like this that rules arise which increase in number the more labour is divided – rules whose absence makes organic solidarity either impossible or imperfect.

But the mere existence of rules is not sufficient: they must also be just. For this the external conditions of competition should be equal. If, on the other hand, we call to mind that the collective consciousness is increasingly reduced to the cult of the individual, we shall see that the characteristic of morality in organised societies, as compared to segmentary societies, is that it possesses something more human, and consequently more rational, about it. It does not cause our activity to depend upon ends that do not directly concern us. It does not make us the servants of some ideal powers completely different in nature from ourselves, powers who follow their own course without heeding the interests of men. It requires us only to be charitable and just towards our fellow-men, to fulfil our task well, to work towards a state where everyone is called to fulfil the function he performs best and will receive a just reward for his efforts. The rules constituting this morality have no constraining power preventing their being fully examined. Because they are better made for us and, in a certain sense, by us, we are freer in relation to them. We seek to understand them and are less afraid to change them.

[...]

It has been rightly stated that morality – and this must include both theory and the practice of ethics – is in the throes of an appalling crisis. What we have expounded can help us to understand the causes and nature of this sickness. Over a very short space of time very profound changes have occurred in the structure of our societies. They have liberated themselves from the segmentary model with a speed and in proportions without precedent in history. Thus the morality corresponding to this type of society has lost influence, but without its successor developing quickly enough to occupy the space left vacant in our consciousness. Our beliefs have been disturbed. Tradition has lost its sway. Individual judgement has thrown off the yoke of the collective judgement. On the other hand, the functions that have been disrupted in this period of trial have had no time to adjust to one another. The new life that all of a sudden has arisen has not been able to organise itself thoroughly. Above all, it has not been organised so as to satisfy the need for justice that has been aroused even more passionately in our hearts. If this is so, the remedy for the ill is nevertheless not to seek to revive traditions and practices that no longer correspond to present-day social conditions, and that could only subsist in a life that would be artificial, one only of appearance. We need to put a stop to this anomie, and to find ways of harmonious co-operation between those organs that still clash discordantly together. We need to introduce into their relationships a greater justice by diminishing those external inequalities that are the source of our ills. Our disease is therefore not, as occasionally we appear to believe, of an intellectual order, but linked to deeper causes. We are not suffering because we no longer know on what theoretical idea should be sustained the morality we have practised up to now. The cause is that certain elements of this morality have been irretrievably undermined, and the morality we require is only in the process of taking shape. Our anxiety does not arise because the criticism of scientists has demolished the traditional explanation handed down to us regarding our duties. Consequently it is not a new philosophical system that will ever be capable of dispelling that anxiety. Rather is it because certain of these duties no longer being grounded on reality, a loosening of ties has occurred that can only stop when a new discipline has become established and consolidated itself. In short, our first duty at the present time is to fashion a morality for ourselves. Such a task cannot be improvised in the silence of the study. It can arise only of its own volition, gradually, and under the pressure of internal causes that render it necessary. What reflection can and must do is to prescribe the goal that must be attained. That is what we have striven to accomplish.

3 The Protestant Ethic and the Spirit of Capitalism (1905); The Characteristics of Bureaucracy (1920); and Science as a Vocation (1919)

Max Weber

German sociologist Max Weber (1864–1920) was writing in response to Marx and Engels to show that changes in society involve more than just economic relationships. In his 1905 piece "The Protestant Ethic and the Spirit of Capitalism," Weber proposed that religious ideas were crucial in the development of capitalism in Europe. "The Characteristics of Bureaucracy" discusses how society is organized once capitalism has emerged, and shows why this type of organization is important for the functioning of modern capitalism and government. This type of social organization and authority is characterized by a new sense of rationality, objectivity, and efficiency. Bureaucratic management allows society to operate on the bases of specialization, merit, and limited authority. The third reading by Weber briefly suggests that rationalization, bureaucracies, and capitalist production contribute to a situation where information is so readily available yet specialized that we no longer need non-scientific explanations, our world has become "disenchanted": everything can be explained and progress and discovery will continue long after we are gone.

The Protestant Ethic and the Spirit of Capitalism

In order to understand the connection between the fundamental religious ideas of ascetic Protestantism and its maxims for everyday economic conduct, it is necessary to examine with especial care such writings as have evidently been derived from ministerial practice. For in a time in which the beyond meant everything, when the social position of the Christian depended upon his admission to the communion, the clergyman, through his ministry, Church discipline, and preaching, exercised an influence ... which we modern men are entirely unable to picture. In such a time the religious forces which express themselves through such channels are the decisive influences in the formation of national character.

For [present] purposes ... we can treat ascetic Protestantism as a single whole. But since that side of English Puritanism which was derived from Calvinism gives the most consistent religious basis for the idea of the calling, we shall ... place one of its representatives at the centre of the discussion. Richard Baxter stands out above many other writers on Puritan ethics. ...

Now, in glancing at Baxter's *Saints' Everlasting Rest*, or his *Christian Directory*, or similar works of others, one is struck at first glance by the emphasis placed, in the discussion of wealth and its acquisition, on the ebionitic elements of the New Testament. Wealth as such is a great danger; its temptations never end, and its pursuit is not only senseless as compared with the dominating importance of the Kingdom of God, but it is morally suspect. Here asceticism seems to have turned much more sharply against the acquisition of earthly goods than it did in Calvin, who saw no hindrance to the effectiveness of the clergy in their wealth, but rather a thoroughly desirable enhancement of their prestige. Hence he permitted them to employ their means profitably. Examples of the condemnation of the pursuit of money and goods may be gathered without end from Puritan writings, and may be contrasted with the late mediaeval ethical literature, which was much more open-minded on this point.

Moreover, these doubts were meant with perfect seriousness; only it is necessary to examine them somewhat more closely in order to understand their true ethical significance and implications. The real moral objection is to relaxation in the security of possession, the enjoyment of wealth with the consequence of idleness and the temptations of the flesh, above all of distraction from the pursuit of a righteous life. In fact, it is only because possession involves this danger of relaxation that it is objectionable at all. For the saints' everlasting rest is in the next world; on earth man must, to be certain of his state of grace, "do the works of him who sent him, as long as it is yet day." Not leisure and enjoyment, but only activity serves to increase the glory of God, according to the definite manifestations of His will.

Waste of time is thus the first and in principle the deadliest of sins. The span of human life is infinitely short and precious to make sure of one's own election. Loss of time through sociability, idle talk, luxury, even more sleep than is necessary for health, six to at most eight hours, is worthy of absolute moral condemnation. It does not yet hold, with [Benjamin] Franklin, that time is money, but the proposition is true in a certain spiritual sense. It is infinitely valuable because every hour lost is lost to labor for the glory of God. Thus inactive contemplation is also valueless, or even directly reprehensible if it is at the expense of one's daily work. For it is less pleasing to God than the active performance of His will in a calling. ...

Accordingly, Baxter's principal work is dominated by the continually repeated, often almost passionate preaching of hard, continuous bodily or mental labor. It is due to a combination of two different motives. Labor is, on the one hand, an approved ascetic technique, as it always has been in the Western Church, in sharp contrast not only to the Orient but to almost all monastic rules the world over. It is in particular the specific defence against all those temptations which Puritanism united under the name of the unclean life, whose role for it was by no means small. The sexual asceticism of Puritanism differs only in degree, not in fundamental principle, from that of monasticism; and on account of the Puritan conception of marriage, its practical influence is more far-reaching than that of the latter. For sexual intercourse is permitted, even within marriage, only as the means willed by God for the increase of His glory according to the commandment, "Be fruitful and multiply." Along with a moderate vegetable diet and cold baths, the same prescription is given for all sexual temptations as is used against religious doubts and a sense of moral unworthiness: "Work hard in your calling." But the most important thing was that even beyond that labor came to be considered in itself the end of life, ordained as such by God. St. Paul's "He who will not work shall not eat" holds unconditionally for everyone. Unwillingness to work is symptomatic of the lack of grace.

Here the difference from the mediaeval viewpoint becomes quite evident. Thomas Aquinas also gave an interpretation of that statement of St. Paul. But for him labor is only necessary *naturali ratione* for the maintenance of individual and community. Where this end is achieved, the precept ceases to have any meaning. Moreover, it holds only for the race, not for every individual. It does not apply to anyone who can live without labor on his possessions, and of course contemplation, as a spiritual form of action in the Kingdom of God, takes precedence over the commandment in its literal sense. Moreover, for the popular theology of the time, the highest form of monastic productivity lay in the increase of the *Thesaurus ecclesiae* through prayer and chant.

Now only do these exceptions to the duty to labor naturally no longer hold for Baxter, but he holds most emphatically that wealth does not exempt anyone from the unconditional command. Even the wealthy shall not eat without working, for even though they do not need to labor to support their own needs, there is God's commandment which they, like the poor, must obey. For everyone without exception God's Providence has prepared a calling, which he should profess and in which he should labor. And this calling is not, as it was for the Lutheran, a fate to which he must submit and which he must make the best of, but God's commandment to the individual to work for the divine glory. This seemingly subtle difference had far-reaching psychological consequences, and became connected with a further development of the providential interpretation of the economic order which had begun in scholasticism.

The phenomenon of the division of labor and occupations in society had, among others, been interpreted by Thomas Aquinas, to whom we may most conveniently refer, as a direct consequence of the divine scheme of things. But the places assigned to each man in this cosmos follow *ex causis naturalibus* and are fortuitous (contingent in the Scholastic terminology). The differentiation of men into the classes and occupations established through historical development became for Luther, as we have seen, a direct result of the divine will. The perseverance of the individual in the place and within the limits which God had assigned to him was a religious duty. ...

But in the Puritan view, the providential character of the play of private economic interests takes on a somewhat different emphasis. True to the Puritan tendency to pragmatic interpretations, the providential purpose of the division of labor is to be known by its fruits. On this point Baxter expresses himself in terms which more than once directly recall Adam Smith's well-known apotheosis of the division of labor. The specialization of occupations leads, since it makes the development of skill possible, to a quantitative and qualitative improvement in production, and thus serves the common good, which is identical with the good of the greatest possible number. So far, the motivation is purely utilitarian, and is closely related to the customary viewpoint of much of the secular literature of the time.

But the characteristic Puritan element appears when Baxter sets at the head of his discussion the statement that "outside of a well-marked calling the accomplishments of a man are only casual and irregular, and he spends more time in idleness than at work," and when he concludes it as follows: "and he [the specialized worker] will carry out his work in order while another remains in constant confusion, and his business knows neither time nor place...therefore is a certain calling the best for everyone." Irregular work, which the ordinary laborer is often forced to accept, is often unavoidable, but always an unwelcome state of transition. A man without a calling thus lacks the systematic, methodical character which is, as we have seen, demanded by worldly asceticism.

The Quaker ethic also holds that a man's life in his calling is an exercise in ascetic virtue, a proof of his state of grace through his conscientiousness, which is expressed in the care and method with which he pursues his calling. What God demands is not labor in itself, but rational labor in a calling. In the Puritan concept of the calling the emphasis is always placed on this methodical character of worldly asceticism, not, as with Luther, on the acceptance of the lot which God has irretrievably assigned to man.

Hence the question whether anyone may combine several callings is answered in the affirmative, if it is useful for the common good or one's own, and not injurious to anyone, and if it does not lead to unfaithfulness in one of the callings. Even a change of calling is by no means regarded as objectionable, if it is not thoughtless and is made for the purpose of pursuing a calling more pleasing to God, which means, on general principles, one more useful.

It is true that the usefulness of a calling, and thus its favor in the sight of God, is measured primarily in moral terms, and thus in terms of the importance of the goods produced in it for the community. But a further, and, above all, in practice the most important, criterion is found in private profitableness. For if that God, whose hand the Puritan sees in all the occurrences of life, shows one of His elect a chance of profit, he must do it with a purpose. Hence the faithful Christian must follow the call by taking advantage of the opportunity. "If God shows you a way in which you may lawfully get more than in another way (without wrong to your soul or to any other), if you refuse this, and choose the less gainful way, you cross one of the ends of your calling, and you refuse to be God's steward, and to accept His gifts and use them for Him when He requireth it: you may labor to be rich for God, though not for the flesh and sin."

Wealth is thus bad ethically only in so far as it is a temptation to idleness and sinful enjoyment of life, and its acquisition is bad only when it is with the purpose of later living merrily and without care. But as a performance of duty in a calling it is not only morally permissible, but actually enjoined. The parable of the servant who was rejected because he did not increase the talent which was entrusted to him seemed to say so directly. To wish to be poor was, it was often argued, the same as wishing to be unhealthy; it is objectionable as a glorification of works and derogatory to the glory of God. Especially begging, on the part of one able to work, is not only the sin of slothfulness, but a violation of the duty of brotherly love according to the Apostle's own word.

The emphasis on the ascetic importance of a fixed calling provided an ethical justification of the modern specialized division of labor. In a similar way the providential interpretation of profit-making justified the activities of the business man. The superior indulgence of the *seigneur* and the parvenu ostentation of the *nouveau riche* are equally detestable to asceticism. But, on the other hand, it has the highest ethical appreciation of the sober, middle-class, self-made man. "God blesseth His trade" is a stock remark about those good men who had successfully followed the divine hints. The whole power of the God of the Old Testament, who rewards His people for their obedience in this life, necessarily exercised a similar influence on the Puritan who, following Baxter's advice, compared his own state of grace with that of the heroes of the Bible, and in the process interpreted the statements of the Scriptures as the articles of a book of statutes.

...In addition to the relationships already pointed out, it is important for the general inner attitude of the Puritans, above all, that the belief that they were God's chosen people saw in them a great renaissance. Even the kindly Baxter thanked God that he was born in England, and thus in the true Church, and nowhere else. This thankfulness for one's own perfection by the grace of God penetrated the attitude toward life of the Puritan middle class, and played its part in developing that formalistic, hard, correct character which was peculiar to the men of that heroic age of capitalism.

Let us now try to clarify the points in which the Puritan idea of the calling and the premium it placed upon ascetic conduct was bound directly to influence the development of a capitalist way of life. As we have seen, this asceticism turned with all its force against one thing: The spontaneous enjoyment of life and all it had to offer. ...the Puritan aversion to sport, even for the Quakers, was by no means simply one of principle. Sport was accepted if it served a rational purpose, that of recreation necessary for physical efficiency. But as a means for the spontaneous expression of undisciplined impulses, it was under suspicion; and in so far as it became purely a means of enjoyment, or awakened pride, raw instincts or the irrational gambling instinct, it was of course strictly condemned. Impulsive enjoyment of life, which leads away both from work in a calling and from religion, was as such the enemy of rational asceticism, whether in the form of seigneurial sports, or the enjoyment of the dance-hall or the public-house of the common man. ...

Although we cannot here enter upon a discussion of the influence of Puritanism in all these directions, we should call attention to the fact that the toleration of pleasure in cultural goods, which contributed to purely aesthetic or athletic enjoyment, certainly always ran up against one characteristic limitation: they must not cost anything. Man is only a trustee of the goods which have come to him through God's grace. He must, like the servant in the parable, give an account of every penny entrusted to him, and it is at least hazardous to spend any of it for a purpose which does not serve the glory of God but only one's own enjoyment. What person, who keeps his eyes open, has not met representatives of this viewpoint even in the present? The idea of a man's duty to his possessions, to which he subordinates himself as an obedient steward, or even as an acquisitive machine, bears with chilling weight on his life. The greater the possessions the heavier, if the ascetic attitude toward life stands the test, the feeling of responsibility for them, for holding them undiminished for the glory of God and increasing them by restless effort. ...

[handwritten margin note: Sport in society became an enjoyment]

This worldly Protestant asceticism, as we may recapitulate up to this point, acted powerfully against the spontaneous enjoyment of possessions; it restricted consumption, especially of luxuries. On the other hand, it had the psychological effect of freeing the acquisition of goods from the inhibitions of traditionalistic ethics. It broke the bonds of the impulse of acquisition in that it not only legalized it, but (in the sense discussed) looked upon it as directly willed by God. The campaign against the temptations of the flesh, and the dependence on external things, was, as besides the Puritans the great Quaker apologist Barclay expressly says, not a struggle against the rational acquisition, but against the irrational use of wealth.

But this irrational use was exemplified in the outward forms of luxury which their code condemned as idolatry of the flesh, however natural they had appeared to the feudal mind. On the other hand, they approved the rational and utilitarian uses of wealth which were willed by God for the needs of the individual and the community. They did not wish to impose mortification on the man of wealth, but the use of his means for necessary and practical things. The idea of comfort characteristically limits the extent of ethically permissible expenditures. It is naturally no accident that the development of a manner of living consistent with that idea may be observed earliest and most clearly among the most consistent representatives of this whole attitude toward life. Over against the glitter and ostentation of feudal magnificence which, resting on an unsound economic basis, prefers a sordid elegance to a sober simplicity, they set the clean and solid comfort of the middle-class home as an ideal.

On the side of the production of private wealth, asceticism condemned both dishonesty and impulsive avarice. What was condemned as covetousness, Mammonism, etc., was the pursuit of riches for their own sake. For wealth in itself was a temptation. But here asceticism was the power "which ever seeks the good but ever creates evil"; what was evil in its sense was possession and its temptations. For, in conformity with the Old Testament and in analogy to the ethical valuation of good works, asceticism looked upon the pursuit of wealth as an end in itself as highly reprehensible; but the attainment of it as a fruit of labor in a calling was a sign of God's blessing. And even more important: the religious valuation of restless, continuous, systematic work in a worldly calling, as the highest means to asceticism, and at the same time the surest and most evident proof of rebirth and genuine faith, must have been the most powerful conceivable lever for the expansion of that attitude toward life which we have here called the spirit of capitalism.

When the limitation of consumption is combined with this release of acquisitive activity, the inevitable practical result is obvious: accumulation of capital through ascetic compulsion to save. The restraints which were imposed upon the consumption of wealth naturally served to increase it by making possible the productive investment of capital. ...

As far as the influence of the Puritan outlook extended, under all circumstances – and this is, of course, much more important than the mere encouragement of capital accumulation – it favoured the development of a rational bourgeois economic life; it was the most important, and above all the only consistent influence in the development of that life. It stood at the cradle of the modern economic man.

To be sure, these Puritanical ideals tended to give way under excessive pressure from the temptations of wealth, as the Puritans themselves knew very well. With great regularity we find the most genuine adherents of Puritanism among the classes which were rising from a lowly status, the small bourgeois and farmers, while the *beati possidentes*, even among Quakers, are often found tending to repudiate the old ideals. It was the same fate which again and again befell the predecessor of this worldly asceticism, the monastic asceticism of the Middle Ages. In the latter case, when rational economic activity had worked out its full effects by strict regulation of conduct and limitation of consumption, the wealth accumulated either succumbed directly to the nobility, as in the time before the Reformation, or monastic discipline threatened to break down, and one of the numerous reformations became necessary.

In fact the whole history of monasticism is in a certain sense the history of a continual struggle with the problem of the secularizing influence of wealth. The same is true on a grand scale of the worldly asceticism of Puritanism. The great revival of Methodism, which preceded the expansion of English industry toward the end of the eighteenth century, may well be compared with such a monastic reform. We may hence quote here a passage from John Wesley himself which might well serve as a motto for everything which has been said above. ... "I fear, wherever riches have increased, the essence of religion has decreased in the same proportion. Therefore I do not see how it is possible, in the nature of things, for any revival of true religion to continue long. For religion must necessarily produce both industry and frugality, and these cannot but produce riches. But as riches increase, so will pride, anger, and love of the world in all its branches. How then is it possible that Methodism, that is, a religion of the heart, though it flourishes now as a green bay tree, should continue in this state? For the Methodists in every place grow diligent and frugal; consequently they increase in goods. Hence they proportionately increase in pride, in anger, in the desire of the flesh, the desire of the eyes, and the pride of life. So, although the form of religion remains, the spirit is swiftly vanishing away. Is there no way to prevent this – this continual decay of pure religion? We ought not to prevent people from being diligent and frugal; *we must exhort all Christians to gain all they can, and to save all they can; that is, in effect, to grow rich.*" ...

As Wesley here says, the full economic effect of those great religious movements, whose significance for economic development lay above all in their ascetic educative influence, generally came only after the peak of the purely religious enthusiasm was past. Then the intensity of the search for the Kingdom of God commenced gradually to pass over into sober economic virtue; the religious roots died out slowly, giving way to utilitarian worldliness. ...

One of the fundamental elements of the spirit of modern capitalism, and not only of that but of all modern culture: rational conduct on the basis of the idea of the calling, was born – that is what this discussion has sought to demonstrate – from the spirit of Christian asceticism. One has only to [read Benjamin Franklin] in order to see that the essential elements of the attitude which was there called the spirit of capitalism are the same as what we have just shown to be the content of the Puritan worldly asceticism, only without the religious basis, which by Franklin's time had died away. ...

Since asceticism undertook to remodel the world and to work out its ideals in the world, material goods have gained an increasing and finally an inexorable power over the lives of men as at no previous period in history. Today the spirit of religious asceticism – whether finally, who knows? – has escaped from the cage. But victorious capitalism, since it rests on mechanical foundations, needs its support no longer. The rosy blush of its laughing heir, the Enlightenment, seems also to be irretrievably fading, and the idea of duty in one's calling prowls about in our lives like the ghost of dead religious beliefs. Where the fulfillment of the calling cannot directly be related to the highest spiritual and cultural values, or when, on the other hand, it need not be felt simply as economic compulsion, the individual generally abandons the attempt to justify it at all. In the field of its highest development, in the United States, the pursuit of wealth, stripped of its religious and ethical meaning, tends to become associated with purely mundane passions, which often actually give it the character of sport.

No one knows who will live in this cage in the future, or whether at the end of this tremendous development entirely new prophets will arise, or there will be a great rebirth of old ideas and ideals, or, if neither, mechanized petrification, embellished with a sort of convulsive self-importance. For of the last stage of this cultural development, it might well be truly said: "Specialists without spirit, sensualists without heart; this nullity imagines that it has attained a level of civilization never before achieved."

But this brings us to the world of judgments of value and of faith, with which this purely historical discussion need not be burdened. The next task would be rather to show the significance of ascetic rationalism, which has only been touched in the foregoing sketch, for the content of practical social ethics, thus for the types of organization and the functions of social groups from the conventicle to the State. Then its relations to humanistic rationalism, its ideals of life and cultural influence; further to the development of philosophical and scientific empiricism, to technical development and to spiritual ideals would have to be analyzed. Then its historical development from the mediaeval beginnings of worldly asceticism to its dissolution into pure utilitarianism would have to be traced out through all the areas of ascetic religion. Only then could the quantitative cultural significance of ascetic Protestant-ism in its relation to the other plastic elements of modern culture be estimated.

Here we have only attempted to trace the fact and the direction of its influence to their motives in one, though a very important point. But it would also further be necessary to investigate how Protestant Asceticism was in turn influenced in its development and its character by the totality of social conditions, especially eco-nomic. The modern man is in general, even with the best will, unable to give religious ideas a significance for culture and national character which they deserve. But it is, of course, not my aim to substitute for a one-sided materialistic an equally one-sided spiritualistic causal interpretation of culture and of history. Each is equally possible, but each, if it does not serve as the preparation, but as the conclusion of an investigation, accomplishes equally little in the interest of historical truth.

The Characteristics of Bureaucracy

Modern officialdom functions in the following specific manner:

I. There is the principle of fixed and official jurisdictional areas, which are generally ordered by rules, that is, by laws or administrative regulations. (1) The regular activities required for the purposes of the bureaucratically governed structure are distributed in a fixed way as official duties. (2) The authority to give the commands required for the discharge of these duties is distributed in a stable way and is strictly delimited by rules concerning the coercive means, physical, sacerdotal, or otherwise, which may be placed at the disposal of officials. (3) Methodical provision is made for the regular and continuous fulfillment of these duties and for the execution of the corresponding rights; only persons who have the generally regulated qualifications to serve are employed.

In public and lawful government these three elements constitute "bureaucratic authority." In private economic domination, they constitute bureaucratic "management." Bureaucracy, thus understood, is fully developed in political and ecclesiastical communities only in the modern state, and, in the private economy, only in the most advanced institutions of capitalism. Permanent and public office authority, with fixed jurisdiction, is not the historical rule but rather the exception. This is so even in large political structures such as those of the ancient Orient, the Germanic, and Mongolian empires of conquest, or of many feudal structures of state. In all these cases, the ruler executes the most important measures through personal trustees, table-companions, or court-servants. Their commissions and authority are not precisely delimited and are temporarily called into being for each case.

II. The principles of office hierarchy and of levels of graded authority mean a firmly ordered system of super- and subordination in which there is a supervision of the lower offices by the higher ones. Such a system offers the governed the possibility of appealing the decision of a lower office to its higher authority, in a definitely regulated manner. With the full development of the bureaucratic type, the office hierarchy is monocratically organized. The principle of hierarchical office authority is found in all bureaucratic structures: in state and ecclesiastical structures as well as in large party organizations and private enterprises. It does not matter for the character of bureaucracy whether its authority is called "private" or "public."

When the principle of jurisdictional "competency" is fully carried through, hierarchical subordination – at least in public office – does not mean that the "higher" authority is simply authorized to take over the business of the "lower." Indeed, the opposite is the rule. Once established and having fulfilled its task, an office tends to continue in existence and be held by another incumbent.

III. The management of the modern office is based upon written documents ("the files"), which are preserved in their original or draft form. There is, therefore, a staff of subaltern officials and scribes of all sorts. The body of officials actively engaged in a "public" office, along with the respective apparatus of material implements and the files, make up a "bureau." In private enterprise, "the bureau" is often called "the office."

In principle, the modern organization of the civil service separates the bureau from the private domicile of the official, and, in general, bureaucracy segregates official activity as something distinct from the sphere of private life. Public monies and equipment are divorced from the private property of the official. ... In principle, the executive office is separated from the household, business from private correspondence, and business assets from private fortunes. The more consistently the modern type of business management has been carried through, the more are these separations the case. The beginnings of this process are to be found as early as the Middle Ages.

It is the peculiarity of the modern entrepreneur that he conducts himself as the "first official" of his enterprise, in the very same way in which the ruler of a specifically modern bureaucratic state spoke of himself as "the first servant" of the state. The idea that the bureau activities of the state are intrinsically different in character from the management of private economic offices is a continental European notion and, by the way of contrast, is totally foreign to the American way.

IV. Office management, at least all specialized office management – and such management is distinctly modern – usually presupposes a thorough and expert training. This increasingly holds for the modern executive and employee of private enterprises, in the same manner as it holds for the state official.

V. When the office is fully developed, official activity demands the full working capacity of the official, irrespective of the fact that his obligatory time in the bureau may be firmly delimited. In the normal case, this is only the product of a long development, in the public as well as in the private office. Formerly, in all cases, the normal state of affairs was reversed: Official business was discharged as a secondary activity.

VI. The management of the office follows general rules, which are more or less stable, more or less exhaustive, and which can be learned. Knowledge of these rules represents a special technical learning which the officials possess. It involves jurisprudence, or administrative or business management.

The reduction of modern office management to rules is deeply embedded in its very nature. The theory of modern public administration, for instance, assumes that the authority to order certain matters by decree – which has been legally granted to public authorities – does not entitle the bureau to regulate the matter by commands given for each case, but only to regulate the matter abstractly. This stands in extreme contrast to the regulation of all relationships through individual privileges and bestowals of favor, which is absolutely dominant in patrimonialism, at least insofar as such relationships are not fixed by sacred tradition.

All this results in the following for the internal and external position of the official.

I. Office holding is a "vocation." This is shown, first, in the requirement of a firmly prescribed course of training, which demands the entire capacity for work for a long period of time, and in the generally prescribed and special examinations which are prerequisites of employment. Furthermore, the position of the official is in the nature of a duty. This determines the internal structure of his relations, in the following manner: Legally and actually, office holding is not considered a source to be exploited for rents or emoluments, as was normally the case during the Middle Ages and frequently up to the threshold of recent times. ... Entrances into an office, including one in the private economy, is considered an acceptance of a specific obligation of faithful management in return for a secure existence. It is decisive for the specific nature of modern loyalty to an office that, in the pure type, it does not establish a relationship to a *person*, like the vassal's or disciple's faith in feudal or in patrimonial relations and authority. Modern loyalty is devoted to impersonal and functional purposes. ...

II. The personal position of the official is patterned in the following way: (1) Whether he is in a private office or a public bureau, the modern official always strives and usually enjoys a distinct *social esteem* as compared with the governed. His social position is guaranteed by the prescriptive rules of rank order and, for the political official, by special definitions of the criminal code against "insults of officials" and "contempt" of state and church authorities.

The actual social position of the official is normally highest where, as in old civilized countries, the following conditions prevail: a strong demand for administration by trained experts; a strong and stable social differentiation, where the official predominantly derives from socially and economically privileged strata because of the social distribution of power; or where the costliness of the required training and status conventions are binding upon him. The possession of educational certificates – to be discussed elsewhere – are usually linked with qualification for office. Naturally, such certificates or patents enhance the "status element" in the social position of the official. . . .

Usually the social esteem of the officials as such is especially low where the demand for expert administration and the dominance of status conventions are weak. This is especially the case in the United States; it is often the case in new settlements by virtue of their wide fields for profit-taking and the great instability of their social stratification.

(2) The pure type of bureaucratic official is *appointed* by a superior authority. An official elected by the governed is not a purely bureaucratic figure. Of course, the formal existence of an election does not by itself mean that no appointment hides behind the election – in the state, especially, appointment by party chiefs. Whether or not this is the case does not depend upon legal statutes but upon the way in which the party mechanism functions. Once firmly organized, the parties can turn a formally free election into the mere acclamation of a candidate designated by the party chief. As a rule, however, a formally free election is turned into a fight, conducted according to definite rules, for votes in favor of one of two designated candidates. . . .

(3) Normally, the position of the official is held for life, at least in public bureaucracies; and this is increasingly the case for all similar structures. As a factual rule, *tenure for life* is presupposed, even where the giving of notice or periodic reappointment occurs. In contrast to the worker in a private enterprise, the official normally holds tenure. Legal or actual life-tenure, however, is not recognized as the official's right to the possession of office, as was the case with many structures of authority in the past. Where legal guarantees against arbitrary dismissal of transfer are developed, they merely serve to guarantee a strictly objective discharge of specific office duties free from all personal considerations. . . .

(4) The official receives the regular *pecuniary* compensation of a normally fixed *salary* and the old age security provided by a pension. The salary is not measured like a wage in terms of work done, but according to "status," that is, according to the kind of function (the "rank") and, in addition, possibly, according to the length of service. The relatively great security of the official's income, as well as the rewards of social esteem, make the office a sought-after position. . . .

(5) The official is set for a "*career*" within the hierarchical order of the public service. He moves from the lower, less important, and lower paid to the higher positions. The average official naturally desires a mechanical fixing of the conditions of promotion: if not of the offices, at least of the salary levels. He wants these conditions fixed in terms of "seniority," or possibly according to grades achieved in a developed system of expert examinations. . . .

Science as a Vocation

... Scientific progress is a fraction, the most important fraction, of the process of intellectualization which we have been undergoing for thousands of years and which nowadays is usually judged in such an extremely negative way. Let us first clarify what this intellectualist rationalization, created by science and by scientifically oriented technology, means practically.

Does it mean that we, today, for instance, everyone sitting in this hall, have a greater knowledge of the conditions of life under which we exist than has an American Indian or a Hottentot? Hardly. Unless he is a physicist, one who rides on the streetcar has no idea how the car happened to get into motion. And he does not need to know. He is satisfied that he may "count" on the behavior of the streetcar, and he orients his conduct according to this expectation; but he knows nothing about what it takes to produce such a car so that it can move. The savage knows incomparably more about his tools. When we spend money today I bet that even if there are colleagues of political economy here in the hall, almost every one of them will hold a different answer in readiness to the question: How does it happen that one can buy something for money – sometimes more and sometimes less? The savage knows what he does in order to get his daily food and which institutions serve him in this pursuit. The increasing intellectualization and rationalization do *not*, therefore, indicate an increased and general knowledge of the conditions under which one lives.

It means something else, namely, the knowledge or belief that if one but wished one *could* learn it at any time. Hence, it means that principally there are no mysterious incalculable forces that come into play, but rather that one can, in principle, master all things by calculation. This means that the world is disenchanted. One need no longer have recourse to magical means in order to master or implore the spirits, as did the savage, for whom such mysterious powers existed. Technical means and calculations perform the service. This above all is what intellectualization means.

Now, this process of disenchantment, which has continued to exist in Occidental culture for millennia, and, in general, this "progress," to which science belongs as a link and motive force, do they have any meanings that go beyond the purely practical and technical? You will find this question raised in the most principled form in the works of Leo Tolstoi. He came to raise the question in a peculiar way. All his broodings increasingly revolved around the problem of whether or not death is a meaningful phenomenon. And his answer was: for civilized man death has no meaning. It has none because the individual life of civilized man, placed into an infinite "progress," according to its own imminent meaning should never come to an end; for there is always a further step ahead of one who stands in the march of progress. And no man who comes to die stands upon the peak which lies in infinity. Abraham, or some peasant of the past, died "old and satiated with life" because he stood in the organic cycle of life; because his life, in terms of its meaning and on the eve of his days, had given to him what life had to offer; because for him there remained no puzzles he might wish to solve; and therefore he could have had "enough" of life. Whereas civilized man, placed in the midst of the continuous enrichment of culture by ideas, knowledge, and problems, may become "tired of life" but not "satiated with life." He catches only the most minute part of what the life of the spirit brings forth ever anew, and what he seizes is always something provisional and not definitive, and therefore death for him is a meaningless occurrence. And because death is meaningless, civilized life as such is meaningless; by its very "progressiveness" it gives death the imprint of meaninglessness. Throughout his late novels one meets with this thought as the keynote of the Tolstoyan art. . . .

Part II

How Does Development Change People?
Modernization Theories and the Intellectual
Roots of the Development Project

4 Evolutionary Universals in Society (1964)

Talcott Parsons

As an expert on Max Weber and as a pioneer of using Emile Durkheim's "structural functionalism" to discuss changes in the world after World War Two, American sociologist Talcott Parsons (1902–79) built many of the core ideas taken up by the "modernizationists." The ideas in this excerpt come originally from a 1963 seminar on evolution at Harvard University. Parsons believed that societies change in distinct patterns, moving from traditional to modern forms. As in biological evolution, each social adaptation either supports or inhibits further evolution. Modern societies were seen to include bureaucratic organizations, money and markets, a universalistic legal system, and the democratic association in both public and private forms. These all were ways that society adapted to disintegration. There has been tremendous debate about whether Parson's views placed European societies above others as more evolved and adapted. There is also debate about whether he was correct in suggesting there were universal patterns and stages of social evolution.

This paper is meant as a contribution to the revival and extension of evolutionary thinking in sociology. It begins with the conception that in the evolution of living systems generally, certain new developments have greatly increased the adaptive capacity of the system, so much that without them further major developmental steps would be blocked, though survival in a "niche" is possible and frequent. For organic evolution the conception is illustrated by the cases of vision and the human hands and brain. The body of the paper is devoted to six cases at the social level. The first two are differentiation on the basis of a scale of stratification and the development of patterns of cultural legitimation independent of the social structure, both of which are important in the transition from primitive social conditions to those of the "archaic" civilizations. The remaining four cases are – in order of treatment – bureaucratic organization, money and markets, a universalistic legal system, and the democratic association in both governmental and private forms. These four, taken together, are fundamental to the structure of the modern type of society, though each is highly complex and subject to a whole series of developmental stages.

Slowly and somewhat inarticulately, emphasis in both sociological and anthropological quarters is shifting from a studied disinterest in problems of social and cultural evolution to a "new relativity" that relates its universals to an evolutionary framework.

The older perspectives insisted that social and cultural systems are made up of indefinitely numerous discrete "traits," that "cultures" are totally separate, or that certain broad "human" universals, like language and the incest taboo, should be emphasized. Varied as they are, these emphases have in common the fact that they divert attention from specific *continuities* in patterns of social change, so that either traits or culture types must be treated as discretely unique and basically unconnected, and a pattern, to be considered universal, must be equally important to *all* societies and cultures. Despite their ostentatious repudiation of "culture-boundness," these perspectives have been conspicuously anthropocentric in setting off problems of man's modes of life so sharply from questions of continuity with the rest of the organic world. But the emphasis on human universals has also had a kind of "leveling" influence, tending to restrict attention to what is generally and essentially human, without considering gradations within the human category.

The "new relativity" removes this barrier and tries to consider human ways in direct continuity with the sub-human. It assumes that the watershed between sub-human and human does not mark a cessation of developmental change, but rather a stage in a long process that begins with many pre-human phases and continues through that watershed into our own time, and beyond. Granting a wide range of variability of types at all stages, it assumes that levels of evolutionary advancement may be empirically specified for the human as well as the pre-human phases.

Evolutionary Universals

I shall designate as an evolutionary universal any organizational development sufficiently important to further evolution that, rather than emerging only once, it is likely to be "hit upon" by various systems operating under different conditions.

In the organic world, vision is a good example of an evolutionary universal. Because it mediates the input of organized information from the organism's environment, and because it deals with both the most distant and the widest range of information sources, vision is the most generalized mechanism of sensory information. It therefore has the greatest potential significance for adaptation of the organism to its environment.

The evidence is that vision has not been a "one shot" invention in organic evolution, but has evolved independently in three different phyla – the molluscs, the insects, and the vertebrates. A particularly interesting feature of this case is that, while the visual organs in the three groups are anatomically quite different and present no evolutionary continuity, biochemically all use the same mechanism involving Vitamin A, though there is no evidence that it was not independently "hit upon" three times.[1] Vision, whatever its mechanisms, seems to be a genuine prerequisite of *all* the higher levels of organic evolution. It has been lost only by very particular groups like the bats, which have not subsequently given rise to important evolutionary developments.

With reference to man and his biological potential for social and cultural evolution, two familiar evolutionary universals may be cited, namely the hands and the brain. The human hand is, of course, the primordial general-purpose tool. The combination of four mobile fingers and an opposable thumb enables it to perform an enormous variety of operations – grasping, holding, and manipulating many kinds of objects. Its location at the end of an arm with mobile joints allows it to be maneuvered into many positions. Finally, the pairing of the arm–hand organs much more than doubles the capacity of each one because it permits cooperation and a complex division of labor between them.

It is worth noting that the development of the hands and arms has been bought at a heavy cost in locomotion: man on his two legs cannot compete in speed and maneuverability with the faster four-legged species. Man, however, uses his hands for such a wide range of behavior impossible for handless species that the loss is far more than compensated. He can, for instance, protect himself with weapons instead of running away.

The human brain is less nearly unique than the hand, but its advantages over the brains of even anthropoids is so great that it is man's most distinctive organ, the most important single source of human capacity. Not only is it the primary organ for controlling complex operations, notably manual skills, and coordinating visual and auditory information, but above all it is the organic basis of the capacity to learn and manipulate symbols. Hence it is the organic foundation of culture. Interestingly, this development too is bought at the sacrifice of immediate adaptive advantages. For example the brain occupies so much of the head that the jaws are much less effective than in other mammalian species – but this too is compensated for by the hands. And the large brain is partly responsible for the long period of infantile dependency because the child must learn such a large factor of its effective behavior. Hence the burden of infant care and socialization is far higher for man than for any other species.

With these organic examples in mind, the conception of an evolutionary universal may be developed more fully. It should, I suggest, be formulated with reference to the concept of adaptation, which has been so fundamental to the theory of evolution since Darwin. Clearly, adaptation should mean, not merely passive "adjustment" to environmental conditions, but rather the capacity of a living system to cope with its environment. This capacity includes an active concern with mastery, or the ability to change the environment to meet the needs of the system, as well as an ability to survive in the face of its unalterable features. Hence the capacity to cope with broad *ranges* of environmental factors, through adjustment or active control, or both, is crucial. Finally, a very critical point is the capacity to cope with unstable relations between system and environment, and hence with *uncertainty*. Instability here refers both to predictable variations, such as the cycle of the seasons, and to unpredictable variations, such as the sudden appearance of a dangerous predator.

An evolutionary universal, then, is a complex of structures and associated processes the development of which so increases the long-run adaptive capacity of living systems in a given class that only systems that develop the complex can attain certain higher levels of general adaptive capacity. This criterion, derived from the famous principle of natural selection, requires one major explicit qualification. The relatively disadvantaged system not developing a new universal need not be condemned to extinction. Thus some species representing all levels of organic evolution survive today – from the unicellular organisms up. The surviving lower types, however, stand in a variety of different relations to the higher. Some occupy special "niches" within which they live with limited scope, others stand in symbiotic relations to higher systems. They are not, by and large, major threats to the continued existence of the evolutionarily higher systems. Thus, though infectious diseases constitute a serious problem for man, bacteria are not likely to replace man as the dominant organic category, and man is symbiotically dependent on many bacterial species.

Two distinctions should be made here, because they apply most generally and throughout. The first is between the impact of an innovation when it is *first* introduced in a given species or society, and its importance as a continuing component of the system. Certain evolutionary universals in the social world, to be discussed below, initially provide their societies with major adaptive advantages over societies not developing them. Their introduction and institutionalization have, to be sure, often been attended with severe dislocations of the previous social organization, sometimes resulting in short-run losses in adaptation. Once institutionalized, however, they tend to become essential parts of later societies in the relevant lines of *development* and are seldom eliminated except by regression. But, as the system undergoes further evolution, universals are apt to generate major changes of their own, generally by developing more complex structures.

Unlike biological genes, cultural patterns are subject to "diffusion." Hence, for the cultural level, it is necessary to add a second distinction, between the conditions under which an adaptive advantage can develop for the first time, and those favoring its adoption from a source in which it is already established.

Prerequisites of the Evolution of Culture and Society

From his distinctive organic endowment and from his capacity for and ultimate dependence on generalized learning, man derives his unique ability to create and transmit *culture*. ... [I]t is not only the genetic constitution of the species that determines the "needs" confronting the environment, but this constitution *plus* the cultural tradition. A set of "normative expectations" pertaining to man's relation to his environment delineates the ways in which adaptation should be developed and extended. Within the relevant range, cultural innovations, especially definitions of what man's life *ought* to be, thus replace Darwinian variations in genetic constitution.

Cultural "patterns" or orientations, however, do not implement themselves. Properly conceived in their most fundamental aspect as "religious," they must be articulated with the environment in ways that make effective adaptation possible. I am inclined to treat the entire orientational aspect of culture itself, in the simplest, least evolved forms, as directly synonymous with *religion*.[2] But since a cultural system – never any more an individual matter than a genetic pattern – is shared among a plurality of individuals, mechanisms of *communication* must exist to mediate this sharing. The fundamental evolutionary universal here is language: no concrete human group lacks it. Neither communication nor the learning processes that make it possible, however, is conceivable without determinately organized relations among those who teach and learn and communicate.

The evolutionary origin of *social organization* seems to be kinship. In an evolutionary sense it is an extension of the mammalian system of bisexual reproduction.

The imperative of socialization is of course a central corollary of culture, as is the need to establish a viable social system to "carry" the culture. From one viewpoint, the core of the kinship system is the incest taboo, or, more generally, the rules of exogamy and endogamy structuring relations of descent, affinity, and residence. Finally, since the cultural level of action implies the use of brain, hands, and other organs in actively coping with the physical environment, we may say that culture implies the existence of technology, which is, in its most undifferentiated form, a synthesis of empirical knowledge and practical techniques.

These four features of even the simplest action system – "religion," communication with language, social organization through kinship, and technology – may be regarded as an integrated set of evolutionary universals at even the earliest human level. No known human society has existed without *all* four in relatively definite relations to each other. In fact, their presence constitutes the very minimum that may be said to mark a society as truly human.

Systematic relations exist not only among these four elements themselves, but between them and the more general framework of biological evolution. Technology clearly is the primary focus of the organization of the adaptive relations of the human system to its physical *environment*. Kinship is the social extension of the individual *organism*'s basic articulation to the species through bisexual reproduction. But, through plasticity and the importance of learning, cultural and symbolic communications are integral to the human level of individual *personality* organization. *Social* relations among personalities, to be distinctively human, must be mediated by linguistic communication. Finally, the main *cultural patterns* that regulate the social, psychological, and organic levels of the total system of action are embodied (the more primitive the system, the more exclusively so) in the religious tradition, the focus of the use of symbolization to control the variety of conditions to which a human system is exposed.

Social Stratification

Two evolutionary universals are closely interrelated in the process of "breaking out" of what may be called the "primitive" stage of societal evolution. These are the development of a well-marked system of social stratification, and that of a system of explicit cultural legitimation of differentiated societal functions, preeminently the political function, independent of kinship. The two are closely connected, but I am inclined to think that stratification comes first and is a condition of legitimation of political function.

The key to the evolutionary importance of stratification lies in the role in primitive societies of *ascription* of social status to criteria of biological relatedness. The kinship nexus of social organization is intrinsically a "seamless web" of relationships which, in and of itself, contains no principle of boundedness for the system as distinguished from certain subgroups within it. Probably the earliest and most important basis of boundedness is the political criterion of territorial jurisdiction. But the economic problem of articulation with the environment, contingent on kinship as well as other groups, is also prominent in primitive societies. In the first instance this is structured primarily through place of residence, which becomes increasingly important as technological development, notably of "settled agricul-ture," puts a premium on definiteness and permanence of location.

For present purposes, I assume that in the society we are discussing, the population occupying a territorial area is generally endogamous, with marriage of its members to those of other territorial groups being, if it occurs, somehow exceptional, and not systematically organized. Given a presumptively endogamous territorial community, comprising a plurality of purely local groups, certain general processes of internal differentiation of the society can be explained. One aspect of this tends to be a prestige difference between central or "senior" lineage groups and "cadet" groups, whether or not the differentiation is on the basis of birth. Quite generally, the latter must accept less advantageous bases of subsistence, including place of residence, than the former. At least this is apt to be the case where the residence groups become foci for the control of resources and as such are sharply differentiated from more inclusive political groupings. Thus a second aspect of an increased level of functional differentiation among the structures of the society tends to be involved.

Typically, I think, kinship status, in terms of both descent criteria and relative prestige of marriage opportunities is highly correlated with relative economic advantage and political power. This is to say that, under the conditions postulated, a tendency toward *vertical* differentiation of the society as a system overrides the pressure of the seamless web of kinship to equalize the status of all units of equi-valent *kinship* character. This tendency is the product of two converging forces.

On the one hand, relative advantages are differentiated: members of cadet lineages, the kinship units with lesser claims to preferment, are "forced" into per-ipheral positions. They move to less advantaged residential locations and accept less productive economic resources, and they are not in a position to counteract these disadvantages by the use of political power.

On the other hand, the society as a system gains functional advantages by con-centrating responsibility for certain functions. This concentration focuses in two areas, analytically, the political and the religious. First, the increased complexity of a society that has grown in population and probably territory and has become differentiated in status terms raises more difficult problems of internal order, e.g. controlling violence, upholding property and marriage rules, etc., and of defense against encroachment from outside. Second, a cultural tradition very close to both the details of everyday life and the interests and solidarities of particular groups is put under strain by increasing size and diversity. There is, then, pressure to centralize both responsibility for the symbolic systems, especially the religious, and authority in collective processes, and to redefine them in the direction of greater generality.

For the present argument, I assume that the tendencies to centralize political and religious responsibility need not be clearly differentiated in any immediate situation. The main point is that the differentiation of groups relative to an advantage–disadvantage axis tends to converge with the functional "need" for centralization of responsibility. Since responsibility and prestige seem to be inherently related in a system of institutionalized expectations, the advantaged group tends to assume, or have ascribed to it, the centralized responsibilities. It should be clear that the problem does not concern the balance between services to others and benefits accruing to the advantaged group, but the convergence of *both* sets of forces tending to the same primary structural outcome.

The development of written language can become a fundamental accelerating factor in this process, because in the nature of the case literacy cannot immediately be extended to total adult populations, and yet it confers enormous adaptive advantages. It also has a tendency to favor cultural or religious elements over the political.

The crucial step in the development of a stratification system occurs when important elements in the population assume the prerogatives and functions of higher status and, at least by implication, exclude all other elements. This creates an "upper," a "leading" or, possibly, a "ruling" class set over against the "mass" of the population. Given early, or, indeed, not so early conditions, it is inevitable that membership in this upper class is primarily if not entirely based on kinship status. Thus, an individual military or other leader may go far toward establishing an important criterion of status, but in doing so he elevates the status of his lineage. He cannot dissociate his relatives from his own success, even presuming he would wish to.

Stratification in the present sense, then, is the differentiation of the population on a prestige scale of kinship units such that the distinctions among such units, or classes of them, become hereditary to an important degree. There are reasons to assume that the early tendency, which may be repeated, leads to a *two*-class system. The most important means of consolidating such a system is upper-class endogamy. Since this repeats the primary principle which, along with territoriality, delineates the boundaries of early societies, the upper class constitutes a kind of subsociety. It is not a class, however, unless its counterpart, the lower class, is clearly included in the *same* societal community.

From this "primordial" two-class system there are various possibilities for evolutionary change. Probably the most important leads to a four-class system. This is based on the development of urban communities in which political–administrative functions, centralized religious and other cultural activities, and territorially specialized economic action are carried on. Thus, generalized "centers" of higher-order activity emerge, but the imperatives of social organization require that these centers, as local communities – including, e.g., "provincial" centers – cannot be inhabited exclusively by upper-class people. Hence the urban upper class tends to be differentiated from the rural upper class, and the urban from the rural lower class. When this occurs there is no longer a linear rank-order of classes. But so long as hereditary kinship status is a primary determinant of the individual's access to "advantages," we may speak of a stratified society; beyond the lowest level of complexity, every society is stratified.

Diffuse as its significance is, stratification is an *evolutionary* universal because the most primitive societies are not in the present sense stratified, but, beyond them, it is on two principal counts a prerequisite of a very wide range of further advances. First, what I have called a "prestige" position is a generalized prerequisite of responsible concentration of leadership. With few exceptions, those who lack a sufficiently "established" position cannot afford to "stick their necks out" in taking the responsibility for important changes. The second count concerns the availability of resources for implementing innovations. The dominance of kinship in social organization is inseparably connected with rigidity. People do what they are required to do by virtue of their kinship status. To whatever degree kinship is the basis of solidarity *within* an upper class, closure of that class by endogamy precludes kinship from being the basis of upper-class claims on the services and other resources of the lower groups. So long as the latter are genuinely within the same society, which implies solidarity across the class line, relations of mutual usefulness (e.g., patron–client relationships across class lines) on non-kin bases are possible – opening the door to universalistic definitions of merit as well as providing the upper groups with the resources to pursue their own advantages.

Social stratification in its initial development may thus be regarded as one primary condition of releasing the process of social evolution from the obstacles posed by ascription. The strong emphasis on kinship in much of the sociological literature on stratification tends to obscure the fact that the new mobility made possible by stratification is due primarily to such breaks in kinship ascription as that across class lines.

Stratification, of course, remains a major structural feature of subsequent societies and takes a wide variety of forms in their evolution. Since the general process of evolutionary change introduces a series of lines of differentiation on several bases, it is unlikely that a single simple prestige order will adequately represent the stratification system in more advanced societies. The "bourgeois" in the late European Middle Ages cannot be described simply as a "middle" class standing between the predominantly rural "feudal" classes and the peasantry. Nevertheless, stratification tends to exert a pressure to generalized hierarchization, going beyond particular bases of prestige, such as political power, special sources of wealth, etc. This is precisely because it brings these various advantages together in their relations to the diffuse status of the kinship group, and through kinship inheritance exerts pressure to continue them from generation to generation. Thus, in the transition to full modernity, stratification often becomes a predominantly conservative force in contrast to the opportunities it provides for innovation in the earlier stages.

Cultural Legitimation

Specialized cultural legitimation is, like stratification, intimately involved in the emergence from primitiveness, and certainly the two processes are related. Legitimation could, perhaps, be treated first; in certain crucial respects it is a prerequisite to the establishment of the type of prestige position referred to above. ... [W]ithout both stratification and legitimation no major advances beyond the level of primitive society can be made.

The point of reference for the development of legitimation systems is the cultural counterpart of the seamless web of the kinship nexus with its presumptive equality of units. This is the cultural definition of the social collectivity simply as "we" who are essentially human or "people" and as such are undifferentiated, even in certain concepts of time, from our ancestors – except in certain senses for the mythical "founders" – and from contemporary "others." If the others are clearly recognized to be others (in an ideal type seamless web they would not be; they would be merely special groups of kin), they are regarded as not "really human," as strange in the sense that their relation to "us" is not comprehensible.

By explicit cultural legitimation, I mean the emergence of an institutionalized cultural definition of the society of reference, namely a referent of "we" (e.g., "We, the Tikopia" in Firth's study) which is differentiated, historically or comparatively or both, from other societies, while the merit of we-ness is asserted in a normative context. This definition has to be religious in some sense, e.g., stated in terms of a particular sacred tradition of relations to gods or holy places. It may also ascribe various meritorious features to the group, e.g., physical beauty, warlike prowess, faithful trusteeship of sacred territory or tradition, etc.

This usage of the term legitimation is closely associated with Max Weber's analysis of political authority. For very important reasons the primary focus of early stages beyond the primitive is political, involving the society's capacity to carry out coordinated collective action. Stratification, therefore, is an essential condition of major advances in political effectiveness, because, as just noted, it gives the advantaged elements a secure enough position that they can accept certain risks in undertaking collective leadership.

The differentiation inherent in stratification creates new sources of strain and potential disorganization, and the use of advantaged position to undertake major innovations multiplies this strain. Especially if, as is usually the case, the authors of major social innovation are already advantaged, they require legitimation for both their actions and their positions. Thus, a dynamic inherent in the development of cultural systems[3] revolves about the cultural importance of the question *why* – why such social arrangements as prestige and authority relations, and particular attendant rewards and deprivations, come about and are structured as they are. This cultural dynamic converges with the consequences of the stratification developments already outlined. Hence the crucial problem here is distributive, that of justifying advantages and prerogatives *over against* burdens and deprivations. Back of this, however, lies the problem of the meaning of the societal enterprise as a whole. ...

The functional argument here is essentially the same as that for stratification. Over an exceedingly wide front and relatively independently of particular cultural variations, political leaders must on the long run have not only sufficient power, but also legitimation for it. Particularly when bigger implementive steps are to be legitimized, legitimation must become a relatively explicit and, in many cases, a socially differentiated function. The combination of differentiated cultural patterns of legitimation with socially differentiated agencies is the essential aspect of the evolutionary universal of legitimation.

As evolutionary universals, stratification and legitimation are associated with the developmental problems of breaking through the ascriptive nexus of kinship, on the one hand, and of "traditionalized" culture, on the other. In turn they provide the basis for differentiation of a system that has previously, in the relevant respects, been undifferentiated. Differentiation must be carefully distinguished from segmentation, i.e., from either the development of undifferentiated segmental units of any given type within the system, or the splitting off of units from the system to form new societies, a process that appears to be particularly common at primitive levels. Differentiation requires solidarity and integrity of the system as a whole, with both common loyalties and common normative definitions of the situation. Stratification as here conceived is a hierarchical status differentiation that cuts across the overall seamless web of kinship and occurs definitely within a single collectivity, a "societal community." Legitimation is the differentiation of cultural definitions of normative patterns from a completely embedded, taken-for-granted fusion with the social structure, accompanied by institutionalization of the explicit, culture-oriented, legitimizing function in subsystems of the society.

Bureaucratic Organization

A second pair of evolutionary universals develop, each with varying degrees of completeness and relative importance, in societies that have moved considerably past the primitive stage, particularly those with well-institutionalized literacy. These universals are administrative bureaucracy, which in early stages is found overwhelmingly in government, and money and markets. I shall discuss bureaucracy first because its development is likely to precede that of money and markets.

Despite the criticisms made of it, mainly in the light of the complexities of modern organizations, Weber's ideal type can serve as the primary point of reference for a discussion of bureaucracy. Its crucial feature is the institutionalization of the *authority of office*. This means that both individual incumbents and, perhaps even more importantly, the bureaucratic organization itself, may act "officially" for, or "in the name of," the organization, which could not otherwise exist. I shall call this capacity to act, or more broadly, that to make and promulgate binding decisions, *power* in a strict analytical sense.

Although backed by coercive sanctions, up to and including the use of physical force, *at the same time* power rests on the consensual solidarity of a system that includes both the users of power and the "objects" of its use. (Note that I do not say *against* whom it is used: the "against" may or may not apply.) Power in this sense is the capacity of a unit in the social system, collective or individual, to establish or activate commitments to performance that contributes to, or is in the interest of, attainment of the goals of a collectivity. It is not itself a "factor" in effectiveness, nor a "real" output of the process, but a medium of mobilization and acquisition of factors and outputs. In this respect, it is like money.

Office implies the differentiation of the role of incumbent from a person's other role-involvements, above all from his kinship roles. Hence, so far as function in the collectivity is defined by the obligations of ascriptive kinship status, the organizational status cannot be an office in the present sense. Neither of the other two types of authority that Weber discusses – traditional and charismatic – establishes this differentiation between organizational role and the "personal" status of the incumbent. Hence bureaucratic authority is always rational-legal in type. ...

Internally, a bureaucratic system is always characterized by an institutionalized hierarchy of authority, which is differentiated on two axes: *level* of authority and "sphere" of competence. Spheres of competence are defined either on segmentary bases, e.g., territorially, or on functional bases, e.g., supply vs. combat units in an army. The hierarchical aspect defines the levels at which a higher authority's decisions, in case of conflict, take precedence over those of a lower authority. It is a general bureaucratic principle that the higher the level, the smaller the relative number of decision-making agencies, whether individual or collegial, and the wider the scope of each, so that at the top, in principle, a single agency must carry responsibility for *any* problems affecting the organization. Such a hierarchy is one of "pure" authority only so far as status within it is differentiated from other components of status, e.g., social class. Even with rather clear differentiation, however, position in a stratification system is likely to be highly correlated with position in a hierarchy of authority. Seldom, if ever, are high bureaucratic officials unequivocally members of the lowest social class.

Externally, two particularly important boundaries pose difficulties for bureaucracies. The first has to do with recruiting manpower and obtaining facilities. In ideal type, a position in a bureaucratic organization constitutes an occupational role, which implies that criteria of eligibility should be defined in terms of competence and maximal responsibility to the organization, not to "private" interests independent of, and potentially in conflict with, those of the organization. ...

The second boundary problem concerns political support. An organization is bureaucratic so far as incumbents of its offices can function independently of the influence of elements having special "interests" in its output, except where such elements are properly involved in the definition of the organization's goals through its nonbureaucratic top. Insulation from such influence, for example through such crude channels as bribery, is difficult to institutionalize and, as is well known, is relatively rare.

In the optimal case, internal hierarchy and division of functions, recruitment of manpower and facilities, and exclusion of "improper" influence, are all regulated by universalistic norms. This is implicit in the proposition that bureaucratic authority belongs to Weber's rational–legal type. Of course, in many concrete instances this condition is met very imperfectly, even in the most highly developed societies.

Bureaucracy tends to develop earliest in governmental administration primarily because even a modest approximation to the essential criteria requires a considerable concentration of power, which, as noted above, depends both on prestige and on legitimation. ...

The basis on which I classify bureaucracy as an evolutionary universal is very simple. As Weber said, it is the most effective large-scale administrative organization that man has invented, and there is no direct substitute for it.[4] Where capacity to carry out large-scale organized operations is important, e.g., military operations with mass forces, water control, tax administration, policing of large and heterogeneous populations, and productive enterprise requiring large capital investment and much manpower, the unit that commands effective bureaucratic organization is inherently superior to the one that does not. It is by no means the only structural factor in the adaptive capacity of social systems, but no one can deny that it is an important one. Above all, it is built on further specializations ensuing from the broad emancipation from ascription that stratification and specialized legitimation make possible.

Money and the Market Complex

Immediate effectiveness of collective function, especially on a large scale, depends on concentration of power, as noted. Power is in part a function of the mobility of the resources available for use in the interests of the collective goals in question. Mobility of resources, however, is a direct function of access to them through the market. Though the market is the most general means of such access, it does have two principal competitors. First is requisitioning through the direct application of political power, e.g., defining a collective goal as having military significance and requisitioning manpower under it for national defense. A second type of mobilization is the activation of nonpolitical solidarities and commitments, such as those of ethnic or religious membership, local community, caste, etc. The essential theme here is, "as one of us, it is your duty..."

The political power path involves a fundamental difficulty because of the role of explicit or implied coercion – "you contribute, or else..." – while the activation of non-political commitments, a category comprising at least two others, raises the issue of alternative obligations. The man appealed to in the interest of his ethnic group, may ask, "what about the problems of my family?" In contrast, market exchange avoids three dilemmas: first, that I must do what is expected or face punishment for noncompliance; second, if I do not comply, I will be disloyal to certain larger groups, identification with which is very important to my general status; third, if I do not comply, I may betray the unit which, like my family, is the primary basis of my immediate personal security.

Market exchange makes it possible to obtain resources for future action and yet avoid such dilemmas as these, because money is a generalized resource for the consumer–recipient, who can purchase "good things" regardless of his relations to their sources in other respects. Availability through the market cannot be unlimited – one should not be able to purchase conjugal love or ultimate political loyalty – but possession of physical commodities, and by extension, control of personal services by purchase, certainly can, very generally, be legitimized in the market nexus.

As a symbolic medium, money "stands for" the economic utility of the real assets for which it is exchangeable, but it represents the concrete objects so abstractly that it is neutral among the competing claims of various other orders in which the same objects are significant. It thus directs attention away from the more consummatory and, by and large, immediate significance of these objects toward their *instrumental* significance as potential means to further ends. Thus money becomes the great mediator of the instrumental use of goods and services. ...

In the money and market system, money as a medium of exchange and property rights, including rights of alienation, must be institutionalized. In general it is a further step that institutionalizes broadly an individual's contractual right to sell his services in a labor market without seriously involving himself in diffuse dependency relationships, which at lower status levels are usually in some ways "unfree." Property in land, on a basis that provides for its alienation, presents a very important problem. Its wide extension seems, except in a very few cases, to be a late development. The institution of contract in exchange of money and goods is also a complex area of considerable variation. Finally, money itself is by no means a simple entity, and in particular the development of credit instruments, banking and the like, has many variations.

These institutional elements are to a considerable degree independently variable and are often found unevenly developed. But if the main ones are sufficiently developed and integrated, the market system provides the operating units of the society, including of course its government, with a pool of disposable resources that can be applied to any of a range of uses and, within limits, can be shifted from use to use. The importance of such a pool is shown by the serious consequences of its shrinkage for even such highly organized political systems as some of the ancient empires. . . .

A principal reason for placing money and markets after bureaucracy in the present series of evolutionary universals is that the conditions of their large-scale development are more precarious. This is particularly true in the very important areas where a generalized system of universalistic norms has not yet become firmly established. Market operations, and the monetary medium itself, are inevitably highly dependent on political "protection." The very fact that the mobilization of political power, and its implementation through bureaucratic organization, is so effective generates interests against sacrificing certain short-run advantages to favor the enhanced flexibility that market systems can provide. This has been a major field of conflict historically, and it is being repeated today in underdeveloped societies. The strong tendency for developing societies to adopt a "socialistic" pattern reflects a preference for increasing productivity through governmentally controlled bureaucratic means rather than more decentralized market-oriented means. But in general the money and market system has undoubtedly made a fundamental contribution to the adaptive capacity of the societies in which it has developed; those that restrict it too drastically are likely to suffer from severe adaptive disadvantages in the long run.

Generalized Universalistic Norms

A feature common to bureaucratic authority and the market system is that they incorporate, and are hence dependent on, universalistic norms. . . .

Although it is very difficult to pin down just what the crucial components are, how they are interrelated, and how they develop, one can identify the development of a general legal system as a crucial aspect of societal evolution. A general legal system is an integrated system of universalistic norms, applicable to the society as a whole rather than to a few functional or segmental sectors, highly generalized in terms of principles and standards, and relatively independent of both the religious agencies that legitimize the normative order of the society and vested interest groups in the operative sector, particularly in government.

The extent to which both bureaucratic organization and market systems can develop *without* a highly generalized universalistic normative order should not be underestimated. Such great Empires as the Mesopotamian, the ancient Chinese, and, perhaps the most extreme example, the Roman, including its Byzantine extension, certainly testify to this. But these societies suffered either from a static quality, failing to advance beyond certain points, or from instability leading in many cases to retrogression.[5] Although many of the elements of such a general normative order appeared in quite highly developed form in earlier societies, in my view their crystallization into a coherent system represents a distinctive new step, which more than the industrial revolution itself, ushered in the *modern* era of social evolution.[6]

The clear differentiation of secular government from religious organization has been a long and complicated process, and even in the modern world its results are unevenly developed. It has perhaps gone farthest in the sharp separation of Church and State in the United States. Bureaucracy has, of course, played an important part in this process. The secularization of government is associated with that of law, and both of these are related to the level of generality of the legal system.

Systems of law that are *directly* religiously sanctioned, treating compliance as a religious obligation, also tend to be "legalistic" in the sense of emphasizing detailed prescriptions and prohibitions, each of which is given specific Divine sanction. Preeminent examples are the Hebrew law of Leviticus, the later developments in the Talmudic tradition, and Islamic law based on the Koran and its interpretations. Legal decisions and the formulation of rules to cover new situations must then be based as directly as possible on an authoritative sacred text.

Not only does religious law as such tend to inhibit generalization of legal principle, but it also tends to favor what Weber called *substantive* over *formal* rationality.[7] The standard of legal correctness tends to be the implementation of religious precepts, not procedural propriety and consistency of general principle. ... The older systems – many of which still exist – tended to treat "justice" as a direct implementation of precepts of religious and moral conduct, in terms of what Weber called *Wertrational-ität*, without institutionalizing an independent system of *societal* norms, adapted to the function of social control at the societal level and integrated on its own terms. The most important foci of such an independent system are, first, some kind of "codification" of norms under principles not *directly* moral or religious, though they generally continue to be grounded in religion, and, second, the formalization of procedural rules, defining the situations in which judgments are to be made on a societal basis. Especially important is the establishment of courts for purposes other than permitting political and religious leaders to make pronouncements and "examples."[8] ... Common Law came to emphasize the protection of personal rights, the institution of property in private hands, and both freedom of contract and protection of contractual interests far more strongly than did the Continental law. Common Law also emphasized the development of institutions, including both the adversary system, in which parties are highly independent of the Court, and procedural protections.[9]

Significantly, these Common Law developments were integral parts of the more general development of British institutions associated with the Puritan movement, including the later establishment of the independence of Parliament and the development of physical science.

This development of English Common Law, with its adoption and further development in the overseas English-speaking world, not only constituted the most advanced case of universalistic normative order, but was probably decisive for the modern world. This general type of legal order is, in my opinion, the most important single hallmark of modern society. So much is it no accident that the Industrial Revolution occurred first in England, that I think it legitimate to regard the English type of legal system as a fundamental prerequisite of the first occurrence of the Industrial Revolution.[10]

The Democratic Association

A rather highly generalized universalistic legal order is in all likelihood a necessary prerequisite for the development of the last structural complex to be discussed as universal to social evolution, the democratic association with elective leadership and fully enfranchised membership. ...

There are four critically important components of the democratic association. First is the institutionalization of the leadership function in the form of an elective office, whether occupied by individuals, executive bodies, or collegial groups like legislatures. The second is the franchise, the institutionalized participation of members in collective decision-making through the election of officers and often through voting on specific policy issues. Third is the institutionalization of procedural rules for the voting process and the determination of its outcome and for the process of "discussion" or campaigning for votes by candidates or advocates of policies. Fourth is the institutionalization of the nearest possible approximation to the voluntary principle in regard to membership status. In the private association this is fundamental – no case where membership is ascribed or compulsory can be called a "pure" democratic association. In government, however, the coercive and compulsory elements of power, as well as the recruitment of societal communities largely by birth, modify the principle. Hence universality of franchise tends to replace the voluntary membership principle.

Formalization of definite procedural rules governing voting and the counting and evaluation of votes may be considered a case of formal rationality in Weber's sense, since it removes the consequences of the act from the control of the particular actor. It limits his control to the specific act of casting his ballot, choosing among the alternatives officially presented to him. Indirectly his vote might contribute to an outcome he did not desire, e.g., through splitting the opposition to an undesirable candidate and thus actually aiding him, but he cannot control this, except in the voting act itself.

Besides such formalization, however, Rokkan has shown in his comparative and historical study of Western electoral systems, that there is a strikingly general tendency to develop three other features of the franchise.[11] The first of these is universality, minimizing if not eliminating the overlap between membership and disenfranchisement. Thus property qualifications and, most recently, sex qualifications have been removed so that now the main Western democratic polities, with minimal exceptions, have universal adult suffrage. The second is equality, eliminating "class" systems, like the Prussian system in the German Empire, in favor of the principle, one citizen, one vote. Finally, secrecy of the ballot insulates the voting decision from pressures emanating from status superiors or peers that might interfere with the expression of the voter's personal preferences.

Certain characteristics of elective office directly complementary to those of the franchise can be formulated. Aside from the ways of achieving office and the rules of tenure in it, they are very similar to the pattern of bureaucratic office. The first, corresponding to the formalization of electoral rules, is that conduct in office must be legally regulated by universalistic norms. Second, corresponding to the universality of the franchise, is the principle of subordinating segmental or private interests to the collective interest within the sphere of competence of the office. Third, corresponding to equality of the franchise, is the principle of accountability for decisions to a total electorate. And finally, corresponding to secrecy of the ballot, is the principle of limiting the powers of office to specified spheres, in sharp contrast to the diffuseness of both traditional and charismatic authority.

The adoption of even such a relatively specific pattern as equality of the franchise may be considered a universal tendency, essentially because, under the principle that the membership rightfully chooses both the broad orientations of collective policy and the elements having leadership privileges and responsibilities, there is, among those with minimal competence, no universalistic basis for discriminating among classes of members. As a limitation on the hierarchical structure of power within collectivities, equality of franchise is the limiting or boundary condition of the democratic association, corresponding to equality of opportunity on the bureaucratic boundary of the polity.[12]

Especially, though not exclusively, in national territorial states, the stable democratic association is notoriously difficult to institutionalize. Above all this seems to be a function of the difficulty in motivating holders of immediately effective power to relinquish their opportunities voluntarily despite the seriousness of the interest at stake – relinquishment of control of governmental machinery after electoral defeat being the most striking problem. The system is also open to other serious difficulties, most notably corruption and "populist" irresponsibility, as well as *de facto* dictatorship. Furthermore, such difficulties are by no means absent in private associations, as witness the rarity of effective electoral systems in large trade unions.[13]

The basic argument for considering democratic association a universal, despite such problems, is that, the larger and more complex a society becomes, the more important is effective political organization, not only in its administrative capacity, but also, and not least, in its support of a universalistic legal order. Political effectiveness includes both the scale and operative flexibility of the organization of power. Power, however, precisely as a generalized societal medium, depends overwhelmingly on a consensual element,[14] i.e., the ordered institutionalization and exercise of influence, linking the power system to the higher-order societal consensus at the value level.[15]

No institutional form basically different from the democratic association can, *not* specifically *legitimize* authority and power in the most general sense, but *mediate consensus in its exercise* by particular persons and groups, and in the formation of particular binding policy decisions. At high levels of structural differentiation in the society itself and in its governmental system, generalized legitimation cannot fill this gap adequately. Providing structured participation in the selection of leaders and formation of basic policy, as well as in opportunities to be heard and exert influence and to have a real choice among alternatives, is the crucial function of the associational system from this point of view.

I realize that to take this position I must maintain that communist totalitarian organization will probably not fully match "democracy" in political and integrative capacity in the long run. I do indeed predict that it will prove to be unstable and will either make adjustments in the general direction of electoral democracy and a plural party system or "regress" into generally less advanced and politically less effective forms of organization, failing to advance as rapidly or as far as otherwise may be expected. ...

Conclusion

Four features of human societies at the level of culture and social organization were cited as having universal and major significance as prerequisites for socio-cultural development: technology, kinship organization based on an incest taboo, communication based on language, and religion. ...

Comparatively, the institutionalization of these four complexes and their interrelations is very uneven. In the broadest frame of reference, however, we may think of them as together constituting the main outline of the structural foundations of modern society. Clearly, such a combination, balanced relative to the exigencies of particular societal units, confers on its possessors an adaptive advantage far superior to the structural potential of societies lacking it. Surely the bearing of this proposition on problems of rapid "modernization" in present "underdeveloped" societies is extremely important. ...

NOTES

1. George Wald, "Life and Light," *Scientific American*, 201 (October, 1959), pp. 92–108.
2. Cf. Emile Durkheim, *The Elementary Forms of the Religious Life*, London: Allen and Unwin, 1915.
3. Claude Lévi-Strauss, *Totemism*, Boston: Beacon Paperbacks, 1963.
4. Max Weber, *The Theory of Social and Economic Organization*, Glencoe, IL: The Free Press, 1947.
5. S. N. Eisenstadt, *The Political Systems of Empires*, New York: The Free Press of Glencoe, 1963, pp. 349 ff.
6. Talcott Parsons, *Societies: Comparative and Evolutionary Perspectives*, Englewood, NJ: Prentice-Hall, 1964.
7. Weber, *Theory of Social and Economic Organization*, pp. 184 ff, and *Max Weber on Law in Economy and Society*, Cambridge, MA: Harvard University Press, 1954, ch. 8.
8. Weber, *Max Weber on Law in Economy and Society*.
9. See Roscoe Pound, *The Spirit of the Common Law*, Boston: Beacon Paperbacks, 1963; esp. chs 2–4.
10. It is exceedingly important here once more to distinguish the first occurrence of a social innovation from its subsequent diffusion. The latter can occur without the whole set of prerequisite societal conditions necessary for the former. Cf. Talcott Parsons, *Structure and Processes in Modern Societies*, Glencoe, IL: The Free Press, 1960, ch. 3.
11. Stein Rokkan, "Mass Suffrage, Secret Voting, and Political Participation," *European Journal of Sociology*, 2 (1961), 132–52.
12. Cf. Talcott Parsons, "On the Concept of Political Power," *Proceedings of the American Philosophical Society*, 107 (June, 1963), 232–62, and John Rawls, "Constitutional Liberty and the Concept of Justice," in C. J. Friedrich (ed.), *Justice* (Nomos VI), New York: Atherton Press, 1963.
13. Seymour Martin Lipset, Martin Trow, and James Coleman, *Union Democracy*, Glencoe, IL: The Free Press, 1956.
14. Parsons, "On the Concept of Political Power."
15. Talcott Parsons, "On the Concept of Influence," *Public Opinion Quarterly*, 27 (Spring, 1963), 37–62.

5 The Stages of Economic Growth: A Non-Communist Manifesto (1960)

W. W. Rostow

Economist Walt W. Rostow (1916–) worked in both the Kennedy and Johnson administrations, where his ideas had much currency with planners. This work is based on a 1958 series of lectures for a non-professional audience. His theory was that all nations pass through the same five stages of economic development: preconditions for take-off, take-off, the drive to maturity, the age of high mass consumption, and beyond consumption. Rostow's views were especially attractive to planners and countries who wished to increase productivity and achieve sustained economic growth. For Rostow, technology, savings, entrepreneurialism, and the correct political systems were all key motors in moving countries along this path. Another important argument he makes is that countries that begin to achieve sustained economic growth later (i.e., poorer countries) may move through the stages much faster. Rostow's work, although very influential, was also severely critiqued for making all poorer countries seem the same and for blaming only internal conditions for their lack of development.

The Five Stages-of-growth – A Summary

It is possible to identify all societies, in their economic dimensions, as lying within one of five categories: the traditional society, the preconditions for take-off, the take-off, the drive to maturity, and the age of high mass-consumption.

The Traditional Society

First, the traditional society. A traditional society is one whose structure is developed within limited production functions, based on pre-Newtonian science and technology, and on pre-Newtonian attitudes towards the physical world. Newton is here used as a symbol for that watershed in history when men came widely to believe that the external world was subject to a few knowable laws, and was systematically capable of productive manipulation.

The conception of the traditional society is, however, in no sense static; and it would not exclude increases in output. Acreage could be expanded; some *ad hoc* technical innovations, often highly productive innovations, could be introduced in trade, industry and agriculture; productivity could rise with, for example, the improvement of irrigation works or the discovery and diffusion of a new crop. But the central fact about the traditional society was that a ceiling existed on the level of attainable output per head. This ceiling resulted from the fact that the potentialities which flow from modern science and technology were either not available or not regularly and systematically applied.

Both in the longer past and in recent times the story of traditional societies was thus a story of endless change. The area and volume of trade within them and between them fluctuated, for example, with the degree of political and social turbulence, the efficiency of central rule, the upkeep of the roads. Population – and, within limits, the level of life – rose and fell not only with the sequence of the harvests, but with the incidence of war and of plague. Varying degrees of manufacture developed; but, as in agriculture, the level of productivity was limited by the inaccessibility of modern science, its applications, and its frame of mind.

Generally speaking, these societies, because of the limitation on productivity, had to devote a very high proportion of their resources to agriculture; and flowing from the agricultural system there was an hierarchical social structure, with relatively narrow scope – but some scope – for vertical mobility. Family and clan connexions played a large role in social organization. The value system of these societies was generally geared to what might be called a long-run fatalism; that is, the assumption that the range of possibilities open to one's grandchildren would be just about what it had been for one's grandparents. But this long-run fatalism by no means excluded the short-run option that, within a considerable range, it was possible and legitimate for the individual to strive to improve his lot, within his lifetime. In Chinese villages, for example, there was an endless struggle to acquire or to avoid losing land, yielding a situation where land rarely remained within the same family for a century.

Although central political rule – in one form or another – often existed in traditional societies, transcending the relatively self-sufficient regions, the centre of gravity of political power generally lay in the regions, in the hands of those who owned or controlled the land. The landowner maintained fluctuating but usually profound influence over such central political power as existed, backed by its entourage of civil servants and soldiers, imbued with attitudes and controlled by interests transcending the regions.

In terms of history then, with the phrase "traditional society" we are grouping the whole pre-Newtonian world: the dynasties in China; the civilization of the Middle East and the Mediterranean; the world of medieval Europe. And to them we add the post-Newtonian societies which, for a time, remained untouched or unmoved by man's new capability for regularly manipulating his environment to his economic advantage.

To place these infinitely various, changing societies in a single category, on the ground that they all shared a ceiling on the productivity of their economic techniques, is to say very little indeed. But we are, after all, merely clearing the way in order to get at the subject of this book; that is, the post-traditional societies, in which each of the major characteristics of the traditional society was altered in such ways as to permit regular growth: its politics, social structure, and (to a degree) its values, as well as its economy.

The Preconditions For Take-Off

The second stage of growth embraces societies in the process of transition; that is, the period when the preconditions for take-off are developed; for it takes time to transform a traditional society in the ways necessary for it to exploit the fruits of modern science, to fend off diminishing returns, and thus to enjoy the blessings and choices opened up by the march of compound interest.

The preconditions for take-off were initially developed, in a clearly marked way, in Western Europe of the late seventeenth and early eighteenth centuries as the insights of modern science began to be translated into new production functions in both agriculture and industry, in a setting given dynamism by the lateral expansion of world markets and the international competition for them. But all that lies behind the break-up of the Middle Ages is relevant to the creation of the preconditions for take-off in Western Europe. Among the Western European states, Britain, favoured by geography, natural resources, trading possibilities, social and political structure, was the first to develop fully the preconditions for take-off.

The more general case in modern history, however, saw the stage of preconditions arise not endogenously but from some external intrusion by more advanced societies. These invasions – literal or figurative – shocked the traditional society and began or hastened its undoing; but they also set in motion ideas and sentiments which initiated the process by which a modern alternative to the traditional society was constructed out of the old culture.

The idea spreads not merely that economic progress is possible, but that economic progress is a necessary condition for some other purpose, judged to be good: be it national dignity, private profit, the general welfare, or a better life for the children. Education, for some at least, broadens and changes to suit the needs of modern economic activity. New types of enterprising men come forward – in the private economy, in government, or both – willing to mobilize savings and to take risks in pursuit of profit or modernization. Banks and other institutions for mobilizing capital appear. Investment increases, notably in transport, communications, and in raw materials in which other nations may have an economic interest. The scope of commerce, internal and external, widens. And, here and there, modern manufacturing enterprise appears, using the new methods. But all this activity proceeds at a limited pace within an economy and a society still mainly characterized by traditional low-productivity methods, by the old social structure and values, and by the regionally based political institutions that developed in conjunction with them.

In many recent cases, for example, the traditional society persisted side by side with modern economic activities, conducted for limited economic purposes by a colonial or quasi-colonial power.

Although the period of transition – between the traditional society and the take-off – saw major changes in both the economy itself and in the balance of social values, a decisive feature was often political. Politically, the building of an effective centralized national state – on the basis of coalitions touched with a new nationalism, in opposition to the traditional landed regional interests, the colonial power, or both, was a decisive aspect of the preconditions period; and it was, almost universally, a necessary condition for take-off.

There is a great deal more that needs to be said about the preconditions period, but we shall leave it for chapter 3, where the anatomy of the transition from a traditional to a modern society is examined.

The Take-off

We come now to the great watershed in the life of modern societies: the third stage in this sequence, the take-off. The take-off is the interval when the old blocks and resistances to steady growth are finally overcome. The forces making for economic progress, which yielded limited bursts and enclaves of modern activity, expand and come to dominate the society. Growth becomes its normal condition. Compound interest becomes built, as it were, into its habits and institutional structure.

In Britain and the well-endowed parts of the world populated substantially from Britain (the United States, Canada, etc.) the proximate stimulus for take-off was mainly (but not wholly) technological. In the more general case, the take-off awaited not only the build-up of social overhead capital and a surge of technological development in industry and agriculture, but also the emergence to political power of a group prepared to regard the modernization of the economy as serious, high-order political business.

During the take-off, the rate of effective investment and savings may rise from, say, 5 per cent of the national income to 10 per cent or more; although where heavy social overhead capital investment was required to create the technical preconditions for take-off the investment rate in the preconditions period could be higher than 5 per cent, as, for example, in Canada before the 1890s and Argentina before 1914. In such cases capital imports usually formed a high proportion of total investment in the preconditions period and sometimes even during the take-off itself, as in Russia and Canada during their pre-1914 railway booms.

During the take-off new industries expand rapidly, yielding profits a large proportion of which are reinvested in new plant; and these new industries, in turn, stimulate, through their rapidly expanding requirement for factory workers, the services to support them, and for other manufactured goods, a further expansion in urban areas and in other modern industrial plants. The whole process of expansion in the modern sector yields an increase of income in the hands of those who not only save at high rates but place their savings at the disposal of those engaged in modern sector activities. The new class of entrepreneurs expands; and it directs the enlarging flows of investment in the private sector. The economy exploits hitherto unused natural resources and methods of production.

New techniques spread in agriculture as well as industry, as agriculture is commercialized, and increasing numbers of farmers are prepared to accept the new methods and the deep changes they bring to ways of life. The revolutionary changes in agricultural productivity are an essential condition for successful take-off; for modernization of a society increases radically its bill for agricultural products. In a decade or two both the basic structure of the economy and the social and political structure of the society are transformed in such a way that a steady rate of growth can be, thereafter, regularly sustained.

As indicated in a later chapter, one can approximately allocate the take-off of Britain to the two decades after 1783; France and the United States to the several decades preceding 1860; Germany, the third quarter of the nineteenth century; Japan, the fourth quarter of the nineteenth century; Russia and Canada the quarter-century or so preceding 1914; while during the 1950s India and China have, in quite different ways, launched their respective take-offs.

The Drive to Maturity

After take-off there follows a long interval of sustained if fluctuating progress, as the now regularly growing economy drives to extend modern technology over the whole front of its economic activity. Some 10–20 per cent of the national income is steadily invested, permitting output regularly to outstrip the increase in population. The make-up of the economy changes unceasingly as technique improves, new industries accelerate, older industries level off. The economy finds its place in the international economy: goods formerly imported are produced at home; new import requirements develop, and new export commodities to match them. The society makes such terms as it will with the requirements of modern efficient production, balancing off the new against the older values and institutions, or revising the latter in such ways as to support rather than to retard the growth process.

Some sixty years after take-off begins (say, forty years after the end of take-off) what may be called maturity is generally attained. The economy, focused during the take-off around a relatively narrow complex of industry and technology, has extended its range into more refined and technologically often more complex processes; for example, there may be a shift in focus from the coal, iron, and heavy engineering industries of the railway phase to machine-tools, chemicals, and electrical equipment. This, for example, was the transition through which Germany, Britain, France, and the United States had passed by the end of the nineteenth century or shortly thereafter. But there are other sectoral patterns which have been followed in the sequence from take-off to maturity, which are considered in a later chapter.

Formally, we can define maturity as the stage in which an economy demonstrates the capacity to move beyond the original industries which powered its take-off and to absorb and to apply efficiently over a very wide range of its resources – if not the whole range – the most advanced fruits of (then) modern technology. This is the stage in which an economy demonstrates that it has the technological and entrepreneurial skills to produce not everything, but anything that it chooses to produce. It may lack (like contemporary Sweden and Switzerland, for example) the raw materials or other supply conditions required to produce a given type of output economically; but its dependence is a matter of economic choice or political priority rather than a technological or institutional necessity.

Historically, it would appear that something like sixty years was required to move a society from the beginning of take-off to maturity. Analytically the explanation for some such interval may lie in the powerful arithmetic of compound interest applied to the capital stock, combined with the broader consequences for a society's ability to absorb modern technology of three successive generations living under a regime where growth is the normal condition. But, clearly, no dogmatism is justified about the exact length of the interval from take-off to maturity.

The Age of High Mass-Consumption

We come now to the age of high mass-consumption, where, in time, the leading sectors shift towards durable consumers' goods and services: a phase from which Americans are beginning to emerge; whose not unequivocal joys Western Europe and Japan are beginning energetically to probe; and with which Soviet society is engaged in an uneasy flirtation.

As societies achieved maturity in the twentieth century two things happened: real income per head rose to a point where a large number of persons gained a command over consumption which transcended basic food, shelter, and clothing; and the structure of the working force changed in ways which increased not only the proportion of urban to total population, but also the proportion of the population working in offices or in skilled factory jobs – aware of and anxious to acquire the consumption fruits of a mature economy.

In addition to these economic changes, the society ceased to accept the further extension of modern technology as an overriding objective. It is in this post-maturity stage, for example, that, through the political process, Western societies have chosen to allocate increased resources to social welfare and security. The emergence of the welfare state is one manifestation of a society's moving beyond technical maturity; but it is also at this stage that resources tend increasingly to be directed to the production of consumers' durables and to the diffusion of services on a mass basis, if consumers' sovereignty reigns. The sewing-machine, the bicycle, and then the various electric-powered household gadgets were gradually diffused. Historically, however, the decisive element has been the cheap mass automobile with its quite revolutionary effects – social as well as economic – on the life and expectations of society.

For the United States, the turning point was, perhaps, Henry Ford's moving assembly line of 1913–14; but it was in the 1920s, and again in the post-war decade, 1946–56, that this stage of growth was pressed to, virtually, its logical conclusion. In the 1950s Western Europe and Japan appear to have fully entered this phase, accounting substantially for a momentum in their economies quite unexpected in the immediate post-war years. The Soviet Union is technically ready for this stage, and, by every sign, its citizens hunger for it; but Communist leaders face difficult political and social problems of adjustment if this stage is launched.

Beyond Consumption

Beyond, it is impossible to predict, except perhaps to observe that Americans, at least, have behaved in the past decade as if diminishing relative marginal utility sets in, after a point, for durable consumers' goods; and they have chosen, at the margin, larger families – behaviour in the pattern of Buddenbrooks dynamics. Americans have behaved as if, having been born into a system that provided economic security and high mass-consumption, they placed a lower valuation on acquiring additional increments of real income in the conventional form as opposed to the advantages and values of an enlarged family. But even in this adventure in generalization it is a shade too soon to create – on the basis of one case – a new stage-of-growth, based on babies, in succession to the age of consumers' durables: as economists might say, the income-elasticity of demand for babies may well vary from society to society. But it is true that the implications of the baby boom along with the not wholly unrelated deficit in social overhead capital are likely to dominate the American economy over the next decade rather than the further diffusion of consumers' durables.

Here then, in an impressionistic rather than an analytic way, are the stages-of-growth which can be distinguished once a traditional society begins its modernization: the transitional period when the preconditions for take-off are created generally in response to the intrusion of a foreign power, converging with certain domestic forces making for modernization; the take-off itself; the sweep into maturity generally taking up the life of about two further generations; and then, finally, if the rise of income has matched the spread of technological virtuosity (which, as we shall see, it need not immediately do) the diversion of the fully mature economy to the provision of durable consumers' goods and services (as well as the welfare state) for its increasingly urban – and then suburban – population. Beyond lies the question of whether or not secular spiritual stagnation will arise, and, if it does, how man might fend it off: a matter considered in a later chapter.

In the four chapters that follow we shall take a harder, and more rigorous look at the preconditions, the take-off, the drive to maturity, and the processes which have led to the age of high mass-consumption. But even in this introductory chapter one characteristic of this system should be made clear.

A Dynamic Theory of Production

These stages are not merely descriptive. They are not merely a way of generalizing certain factual observations about the sequence of development of modern societies. They have an inner logic and continuity. They have an analytic bone-structure, rooted in a dynamic theory of production.

The classical theory of production is formulated under essentially static assumptions which freeze – or permit only once-over change – in the variables most relevant to the process of economic growth. As modern economists have sought to merge classical production theory with Keynesian income analysis they have introduced the dynamic variables: population, technology, entrepreneurship, etc. But they have tended to do so in forms so rigid and general that their models cannot grip the essential phenomena of growth, as they appear to an economic historian. We require a dynamic theory of production which isolates not only the distribution of income between consumption, saving, and investment (and the balance of production between consumers and capital goods) but which focuses directly and in some detail on the composition of investment and on developments within particular sectors of the economy. The argument that follows is based on such a flexible, disaggregated theory of production.

When the conventional limits on the theory of production are widened, it is possible to define theoretical equilibrium positions not only for output, investment, and consumption as a whole, but for each sector of the economy.[1]

Within the framework set by forces determining the total level of output, sectoral optimum positions are determined on the side of demand, by the levels of income and of population, and by the character of tastes; on the side of supply, by the state of technology and the quality of entrepreneurship, as the latter determines the proportion of technically available and potentially profitable innovations actually incorporated in the capital stock.[2]

In addition, one must introduce an extremely significant empirical hypothesis: namely, that deceleration is the normal optimum path of a sector, due to a variety of factors operating on it, from the side of both supply and demand.[3]

The equilibria which emerge from the application of these criteria are a set of sectoral paths, from which flows, as first derivatives, a sequence of optimum patterns of investment.

Historical patterns of investment did not, of course, exactly follow these optimum patterns. They were distorted by imperfections in the private investment process, by the policies of governments, and by the impact of wars. Wars temporarily altered the profitable directions of investment by setting up arbitrary demands and by changing the conditions of supply; they destroyed capital; and, occasionally, they accelerated the development of new technology relevant to the peacetime economy and shifted the political and social framework in ways conducive to peacetime growth.[4] The historical sequence of business-cycles and trend-periods results from these deviations of actual from optimal patterns; and such fluctuations, along with the impact of wars, yield historical paths of growth which differ from those which the optima, calculated before the event, would have yielded.

Nevertheless, the economic history of growing societies takes a part of its rude shape from the effort of societies to approximate the optimum sectoral paths.

At any period of time, the rate of growth in the sectors will vary greatly; and it is possible to isolate empirically certain leading sectors, at early stages of their evolution, whose rapid rate of expansion plays an essential direct and indirect role in maintaining the overall momentum of the economy.[5] For some purposes it is useful to characterize an economy in terms of its leading sectors; and a part of the technical basis for the stages of growth lies in the changing sequence of leading sectors. In essence it is the fact that sectors tend to have a rapid growth-phase, early in their life, that makes it possible and useful to regard economic history as a sequence of stages rather than merely as a continuum, within which nature never makes a jump.

The stages-of-growth also require, however, that elasticities of demand be taken into account, and that this familiar concept be widened; for these rapid growth phases in the sectors derive not merely from the discontinuity of production functions but also from high price- or income-elasticities of demand. Leading sectors are determined not merely by the changing flow of technology and the changing willingness of entrepreneurs to accept available innovations: they are also partially determined by those types of demand which have exhibited high elasticity with respect to price, income, or both.

The demand for resources has resulted, however, not merely from demands set up by private taste and choice, but also from social decisions and from the policies of governments – whether democratically responsive or not. It is necessary, therefore, to look at the choices made by societies in the disposition of their resources in terms which transcend conventional market processes. It is necessary to look at their welfare functions, in the widest sense, including the non-economic processes which determined them.

The course of birth-rates, for example, represents one form of welfare choice made by societies, as income has changed; and population curves reflect (in addition to changing death-rates) how the calculus about family size was made in the various stages; from the usual (but not universal) decline in birth-rates, during or soon after the take-off, as urbanization took hold and progress became a palpable possibility, to the recent rise, as Americans (and others in societies marked by high mass-consumption) have appeared to seek in larger families values beyond those afforded by economic security and by an ample supply of durable consumers' goods and services.

And there are other decisions as well that societies have made as the choices open to them have been altered by the unfolding process of economic growth; and these broad collective decisions, determined by many factors – deep in history, culture, and the active political process – outside the market-place, have interplayed with the dynamics of market demand, risk-taking, technology and entrepreneurship, to determine the specific content of the stages of growth for each society.

How, for example, should the traditional society react to the intrusion of a more advanced power: with cohesion, promptness, and vigour, like the Japanese; by making a virtue of fecklessness, like the oppressed Irish of the eighteenth century; by slowly and reluctantly altering the traditional society, like the Chinese?

When independent modern nationhood is achieved, how should the national energies be disposed: in external aggression, to right old wrongs or to exploit newly created or perceived possibilities for enlarged national power; in completing and refining the political victory of the new national government over old regional interests; or in modernizing the economy?

Once growth is under way, with the take-off, to what extent should the requirements of diffusing modern technology and maximizing the rate of growth be moderated by the desire to increase consumption *per capita* and to increase welfare?

When technological maturity is reached, and the nation has at its command a modernized and differentiated industrial machine, to what ends should it be put, and in what proportions: to increase social security, through the welfare state; to expand mass-consumption into the range of durable consumers' goods and services; to increase the nation's stature and power on the world scene; or to increase leisure?

And then the question beyond, where history offers us only fragments: what to do when the increase in real income itself loses its charm? Babies, boredom, three-day week-ends, the moon, or the creation of new inner, human frontiers in substitution for the imperatives of scarcity?

In surveying now the broad contours of each stage-of-growth, we are examining, then, not merely the sectoral structure of economies, as they transformed themselves for growth, and grew; we are also examining a succession of strategic choices made by various societies concerning the disposition of their resources, which include but transcend the income- and price-elasticities of demand.

NOTES

1. W. W. Rostow, *The Process of Economic Growth*, Oxford, 1953, esp. ch. IV. Also "Trends in the Allocation of Resources in Secular Growth", ch. 15 of Leon H. Dupriez (ed.), with the assistance of Douglas C. Hague, *Economic Progress*, Louvain, 1955.
2. In a closed model, a dynamic theory of production must account for changing stocks of basic and applied science, as sectoral aspects of investment, which is done in Rostow, *Process of Economic Growth*, esp. pp. 22–5.
3. Ibid., pp. 96–103.
4. Ibid., ch. VII, esp. pp. 164–7.
5. For a discussion of the leading sectors, their direct and indirect consequences, and the diverse routes of their impact, see Rostow, "Trends in the Allocation of Resources in Secular Growth".

6 A Study of Slum Culture: Backgrounds for La Vida (1968)

Oscar Lewis

The concept of a "culture of poverty," explained here by Oscar Lewis (1914–70), has been a subject of much debate since its introduction in the 1960s. The idea came from Lewis's observations of poor communities in Puerto Rico and Mexico. The crux of the argument is that people who live in a community where poverty is pervasive share a culture distinct from mainstream consciousness, that their values, behaviors, and views on society differ from the non-poor. This culture is characterized not only by material deprivation, but also by crime, alcoholism, and a lack of hope for mobility. These traits help the poor survive in the short term, but block them in the long run. In other words, it is not circumstances that determine behaviors of the poor so much as it is the behavior and values of the poor that seal their fate as poor. Like other modernization theorists in this section, Lewis turned attention away from structural causes of poverty like inequality, toward causes based in the individual, family, or community. Although Lewis focused on the individual in his explanation of why poor people are poor, the work bears on more "macro" development issues as well. Because his ideas were popular, and because contemporaneous theory focused on similar explanations of poverty, the concept of a culture of poverty was extended by some to refer to whole societies, and not just a subculture, as intended by Lewis. For example, some theorists have suggested Latin American countries had trouble developing because of traditional values and non-capitalistic behaviors.

The Culture of Poverty

As an anthropologist I have tried to understand poverty and its associated traits as a culture or, more accurately, as a subculture[1] with its own structure and rationale, as a way of life that is passed down from generation to generation along family lines. This view directs attention to the fact that the culture of poverty in modern nations is not only a matter of economic deprivation, of disorganization, or of the absence of something. It is also something positive and provides some rewards without which the poor could hardly carry on.

In my book *Five Families: Mexican Case Studies in the Culture of Poverty*, I suggested that the culture of poverty transcends regional, rural–urban, and national differences and shows remarkable cross-national similarities in family structure, interpersonal relations, time orientation, value systems, and spending patterns. These similarities are examples of independent invention and convergence. They are common adaptations to common problems.

The culture of poverty can come into being in a variety of historical contexts. However, it tends to grow and flourish in societies with the following set of conditions: (1) a cash economy, wage labor, and production for profit;[2] (2) a persistently high rate of unemployment and underemployment for unskilled labor; (3) low wages; (4) the failure to provide social, political, and economic organization, either on a voluntary basis or by government imposition, for the low-income population; (5) the existence of a bilateral kinship system rather than a unilateral one; and finally, (6) the existence in the dominant class of a set of values that stresses the accumulation of wealth and property, the possibility of upward mobility, and thrift and that explains low economic status as the result of personal inadequacy or inferiority.

The way of life that develops among some of the poor under these conditions is the culture of poverty. It can best be studied in urban or rural slums and can be described in terms of some seventy interrelated social, economic, and psychological traits.[3] However, the number of traits and the relationships between them may vary from society to society and from family to family. For example, in a highly literate society, illiteracy may be more diagnostic of the culture of poverty than in a society where illiteracy is widespread and where even the well-to-do may be illiterate, as in some Mexican peasant villages before the revolution.

The culture of poverty is both an adaptation and a reaction of the poor to their marginal position in a class-stratified, highly individuated, capitalistic society. It represents an effort to cope with feelings of hopelessness and despair that develop from the realization of the improbability of achieving success in terms of the values and goals of the larger society. Indeed, many of the traits of the culture of poverty can be viewed as attempts at local solutions for problems not met by existing institutions and agencies because the people are not eligible for them, cannot afford them, or are ignorant or suspicious of them. For example, unable to obtain credit from banks, they are thrown upon their own resources and organize informal credit devices without interest.

The culture of poverty, however, is not only an adaptation to a set of objective conditions of the larger society. Once it comes into existence, it tends to perpetuate itself from generation to generation because of its effect on the children. By the time slum children are age six or seven they have usually absorbed the basic values and attitudes of their subculture and are not psychologically geared to take full advantage of the changing conditions or increased opportunities that may occur in their lifetime.

Most frequently the culture of poverty develops when a stratified social and economic system is breaking down or is being replaced by another, as in the case of the transition from feudalism to capitalism or during periods of rapid technological change. Often the culture of poverty results from imperial conquest in which the native social and economic structure is smashed and the natives are maintained in a servile colonial status, sometimes for many generations. It can also occur in the process of detribalization, such as that now going on in Africa.

The most likely candidates for the culture of poverty are the people who come from the lower strata of a rapidly changing society and are already partially alienated from it. Thus, landless rural workers who migrate to the cities can be expected to develop a culture of poverty much more readily than migrants from stable peasant villages with a well-organized traditional culture. In this connection there is a striking contrast between Latin America, where the rural population has long ago made the transition from a tribal to a peasant society, and Africa, which is still close to its tribal heritage. The more corporate nature of many of the African tribal societies as compared to Latin American rural communities and the persistence of village ties tend to inhibit or delay the formation of a full-blown culture of poverty in many of the African towns and cities. The special conditions of apartheid in South Africa, where the migrants are segregated into separate "locations" and do not enjoy freedom of movement, create special problems. Here the institutionalization of repression and discrimination tends to develop a greater sense of identity and group consciousness.

The culture of poverty can be studied from various points of view: the relationship between the subculture and the larger society; the nature of the slum community; the nature of the family; and the attitudes, values, and character structure of the individual.

The lack of effective participation and integration of the poor in the major institutions of the larger society is one of the crucial characteristics of the culture of poverty. This complex matter results from a variety of factors, which may include lack of economic resources, segregation and discrimination, fear, suspicion or apathy, and the development of local solutions for problems. However, participation in some of the institutions of the larger society – for example, in the jails, the army, and the public relief system – does not per se eliminate the traits of the culture of poverty. In the case of a relief system that barely keeps people alive, both the basic poverty and the sense of hopelessness are perpetuated rather than eliminated.

Low wages and chronic unemployment and underemployment lead to low income, lack of property ownership, absence of savings, absence of food reserves in the home, and a chronic shortage of cash. These conditions reduce the possibility of effective participation in the larger economic system. And as a response to these conditions we find in the culture of poverty a high incidence of pawning of personal goods, borrowing from local moneylenders at usurious interest rates, spontaneous informal credit devices organized by neighbors, use of secondhand clothing and furniture, and the pattern of frequent buying of small quantities of food many times a day as the need arises.

People with a culture of poverty produce very little wealth and receive very little in return. They have a low level of literacy and education, do not belong to labor unions, are not members of political parties, generally do not participate in the national welfare agencies, and make very little use of banks, hospitals, department stores, museums, or art galleries. They have a critical attitude toward some of the basic institutions of the dominant classes, hatred of the police, mistrust of government and those in high position, and a cynicism that extends even to the church. These factors give the culture of poverty a high potential for protest and for being used in political movements aimed against the existing social order.

People with a culture of poverty are aware of middle-class values; they talk about them and even claim some of them as their own, but on the whole they do not live by them. Thus, it is important to distinguish between what they say and what they do. For example, many will tell you that marriage by law, by the church, or by both is the ideal form of marriage; but few marry. For men who have no steady jobs or other source of income, who do not own property and have no wealth to pass on to their children, who are present-time oriented and want to avoid the expense and legal difficulties involved in formal marriage and divorce, free unions or consensual marriages make a lot of sense. Women often turn down offers of marriage because they feel that it ties them down to men who are immature, punishing, and generally unreliable. Women feel that consensual union gives them a better break; it gives them some of the freedom and flexibility that men have. By not giving the fathers of their children legal status as husbands, the women have a stronger claim on their children if they decide to leave their men. It also gives women exclusive rights to a house or any other property they own.

In describing the culture of poverty on the local community level, we find poor housing conditions, crowding, gregariousness, and, above all, a minimum of organization beyond the level of the nuclear and extended family. Occasionally there are informal temporary groupings or voluntary associations within slums. The existence of neighborhood gangs that cut across slum settlements represents a considerable advance beyond the zero point of the continuum that I have in mind. Indeed, it is the low level of organization that gives the culture of poverty its marginal and anachronistic quality in our highly complex, specialized, organized society. Most primitive peoples have achieved a higher level of sociocultural organization than our modern urban slum dwellers.

In spite of the generally low level of organization, there may be a sense of community and esprit de corps in urban slums and in slum neighborhoods. This can vary within a single city or from region to region or country to country. The major factors that influence this variation are the size of the slum, its location and physical characteristics, length of residence, incidence of homeownership and land-ownership (versus squatter rights), rentals, ethnicity, kinship ties, and freedom or lack of freedom of movement. When slums are separated from the surrounding area by enclosing walls or other physical barriers, when rents are low and fixed and stability of residence is great (twenty or thirty years), when the population constitutes a distinct ethnic, racial, or language group or is bound by ties of kinship or compadrazgo,[4] and when there are some internal voluntary associations, then the sense of local community approaches that of a village community. In many cases this combination of favorable conditions does not exist. However, even where internal organization and esprit de corps are at a bare minimum and people move around a great deal, a sense of territoriality develops that sets off the slum neighborhoods from the rest of the city. In Mexico City and San Juan this sense of territoriality results from the unavailability of low income housing outside of the slum areas. In South Africa the sense of territoriality grows out of the segregation enforced by the government, which confines the rural migrants to specific locations.

On the family level the major traits of the culture of poverty are the absence of childhood as a specially prolonged and protected stage in the life cycle; early initiation into sex; free unions or consensual marriages; a relatively high incidence of the abandonment of wives and children; a trend toward female- or mother-centered families, and consequently a much greater knowledge of maternal relatives; a strong predisposition to authoritarianism; lack of privacy; verbal emphasis upon family solidarity, which is only rarely achieved because of sibling rivalry; and competition for limited goods and maternal affection.

On the level of the individual the major characteristics are strong feelings of marginality, of helplessness, of dependence, and of inferiority. I found this to be true of slum dwellers in Mexico City and San Juan among families who do not constitute a distinct ethnic or racial group and who do not suffer from racial discrimination. In the United States, of course, the culture of poverty of the Negroes has the additional disadvantage of racial discrimination, but as I have already suggested, this additional disadvantage contains a great potential for revolutionary protest and organization that seems to be absent in the slums of Mexico City or among the poor whites in the South.

Other traits include high incidence of maternal deprivation, of orality, and of weak ego structure; confusion of sexual identification; lack of impulse control; strong present-time orientation, with relatively little ability to defer gratification and to plan for the future; sense of resignation and fatalism; widespread belief in male superiority; and high tolerance for psychological pathology of all sorts.

People with a culture of poverty are provincial and locally oriented and have very little sense of history. They know only their own troubles, their own local conditions, their own neighborhoods, their own way of life. Usually they do not have the knowledge, the vision, or the ideology to see the similarities between their problems and those of their counterparts elsewhere in the world. They are not class conscious although they are very sensitive indeed to status distinctions.

In considering the traits discussed above, the following propositions must be kept in mind. (1) The traits fall into a number of clusters and are functionally related within each cluster. (2) Many, but not all, of the traits of different clusters are also functionally related. For example, men who have low wages and suffer chronic unemployment develop a poor self-image, become irresponsible, abandon their wives and children, and take up with other women more frequently than do men with high incomes and steady jobs. (3) None of the traits, taken individually, is distinctive per se of the subculture of poverty. It is their conjunction, their function, and their patterning that define the subculture. (4) The subculture of poverty, as defined by these traits, is a statistical profile; that is, the frequency of distribution of the traits both singly and in clusters will be greater than in the rest of the population. In other words, more of the traits will occur in combination in families with a subculture of poverty than in stable working-class, middle-class, or upper-class families. Even within a single slum there will probably be a gradient from culture of poverty families to families without a culture of poverty. (5) The profiles of the subculture of poverty will probably differ in systematic ways with the difference in the national cultural contexts of which they are a part. It is expected that some new traits will become apparent with research in different nations.

I have not yet worked out a system of weighting each of the traits, but this could probably be done and a scale could be set up for many of the traits. Traits that reflect lack of participation in the institutions of the larger society or an outright rejection – in practice, if not in theory – would be the crucial traits; for example, illiteracy, provincialism, free unions, abandonment of women and children, lack of member-ship in voluntary associations beyond the extended family.

When the poor become class conscious or active members of trade-union organ-izations or when they adopt an internationalist outlook on the world, they are no longer part of the culture of poverty although they may still be desperately poor. Any movement – be it religious, pacifist, or revolutionary – that organizes and gives hope to the poor and effectively promotes solidarity and a sense of identification with larger groups destroys the psychological and social core of the culture of poverty. In this connection, I suspect that the civil-rights movement among the Negroes in the United States has done more to improve their self-image and self-respect than have their economic advances, although, without doubt, the two are mutually reinfor-cing. ... I have found very little revolutionary spirit or radical ideology among low-income Puerto Ricans. On the contrary, most of the families I studied were quite conservative politically, and about half of them were in favor of the Republican Statehood Party. It seems to me that the revolutionary potential of people with a culture of poverty will vary considerably according to the national context and the particular historical circumstances. In a country like Algeria, which was fighting for its independence, the lumpen proletariat was drawn into the struggle and became a vital force. However, in countries like Puerto Rico in which the movement for independence has very little mass support and in countries like Mexico that achieved their independence a long time ago and are now in their post-revolutionary period, the lumpen proletariat is not a leading source of rebellion or of revolutionary spirit.

In effect, we find that in primitive societies and in caste societies the culture of poverty does not develop. In socialist, fascist, and highly developed capitalist soci-eties with a welfare state, the culture of poverty tends to decline. I suspect that the culture of poverty flourishes in, and is generic to, the early free-enterprise stage of capitalism and that it is also endemic to colonialism.

It is important to distinguish between different profiles in the subculture of poverty, depending upon the national context in which these subcultures are found. If we think of the culture of poverty primarily in terms of integration in the larger society and a sense of identification with the great tradition of that society or with a new emerging revolutionary tradition, then we will not be surprised that some slum dwellers with a low *per capita* income may have moved further away from the core characteristics of the culture of poverty than others with a higher *per capita* income. For example, Puerto Rico has a much higher *per capita* income than Mexico, yet Mexicans have a deeper sense of personal and national identity. In Mexico even the poorest slum dweller has a much richer sense of the past and a deeper identification with the great Mexican tradition than do Puerto Ricans with their tradition. In both countries I presented urban slum dwellers with the names of national figures. In Mexico City quite a high percentage of the respondents, includ-ing those with little or no formal schooling, knew about Cuauhtémoc, Hidalgo, Father Morelos, Juárez, Díaz, Zapata, Carranza, and Cárdenas. In San Juan the respondents showed an abysmal ignorance of Puerto Rican historical figures. The names of Ramón Power, José de Diego, Baldorioty de Castro, Ramón Betances, Nemesio Canales, and Lloréns Torres rang no bell. For the lower-income Puerto Rican slum dweller, history begins and ends with Muñoz Rivera, his son Muñoz Marín, and *doña* Felisa Rincón!

I have listed fatalism and a low level of aspiration as key traits of the subculture of poverty. Here too, however, the national context makes a big difference. Certainly the level of aspiration of even the poorest sector of the population in a country like the United States with traditional ideology of upward mobility and democracy is much higher than in more backward countries like Ecuador and Peru, where both the ideology and the actual possibilities of upward mobility are extremely limited and where authoritarian values still persist in both the urban and the rural milieu.

Because of the advanced technology, the high level of literacy, the development of mass media, and the relatively high aspiration level of all sectors of the population, especially when compared with underdeveloped nations, I believe that although there is still a great deal of poverty in the United States (estimates range from 30 to 50 million people) there is relatively little of what I would call the culture of poverty. My rough guess would be that only about 20 percent of the population below the poverty line (from 6 to 10 million people) in the United States have characteristics that would justify classifying their way of life as that of a culture of poverty. Probably the largest sector within this group consists of very low-income Negroes, Mexicans, Puerto Ricans, American Indians, and southern poor whites. The relatively small number of people in the United States with a culture of poverty is a positive factor because it is much more difficult to eliminate the culture of poverty than to eliminate poverty per se.

Middle-class people – and this would certainly include most social scientists – tend to concentrate on the negative aspects of the culture of poverty. They tend to associate negative valences to such traits as present-time orientation and concrete versus abstract orientation. I do not intend to idealize or romanticize the culture of poverty. As someone has said, "It is easier to praise poverty than to live in it"; yet some of the positive aspects that may flow from these traits must not be overlooked. Living in the present may develop a capacity for spontaneity, for the enjoyment of the sensual, for the indulgence of impulse, which is often blunted in the middle-class, future-oriented man. Perhaps it is this reality of the moment that the existentialist writers are so desperately trying to recapture but that the culture of poverty experiences as natural, everyday phenomena. The frequent use of violence certainly provides a ready outlet for hostility so that people in the culture of poverty suffer less from repression than does the middle class.

In the traditional view, anthropologists have said that culture provides human beings with a design for living, with a ready-made set of solutions for human problems so that individuals in each generation do not have to begin all over again from scratch. That is, the core of culture is its positive adaptive function. I, too, have called attention to some of the adaptive mechanisms in the culture of poverty – for example, the low aspiration level helps to reduce frustration, the legitimization of short-range hedonism makes possible spontaneity and enjoyment. Indeed, it seems that in some ways the people with a culture of poverty suffer less from alienation than do those of the middle class. However, on the whole it seems to me that it is a thin, relatively superficial culture. There is a great deal of pathos, suffering, and emptiness among those who live in the culture of poverty. It does not provide much support or satisfaction, and its encouragement of mistrust tends to magnify helplessness and isolation. Indeed, the poverty of culture is one of the crucial aspects of the culture of poverty.

The concept of the culture of poverty provides a high level of generalization that, hopefully, will unify and explain a number of phenomena that have been viewed as distinctive characteristics of racial, national, or regional groups. For example, matrifocality, a high incidence of consensual unions, and a high percentage of households headed by women, which have been thought to be distinctive characteristics of Caribbean family organization or of Negro family life in the United States, turn out to be traits of the culture of poverty and are found among diverse peoples in many parts of the world and among peoples who have had no history of slavery.

The concept of a cross-societal subculture of poverty enables us to see that many of the problems we think of as distinctively our own or as distinctively Negro problems (or as those of any other special racial or ethnic group) also exist in countries where there are no distinct ethnic minority groups. This concept also suggests that the elimination of physical poverty per se may not eliminate the culture of poverty, which is a whole way of life.

What is the future of the culture of poverty? In considering this question, one must distinguish between those countries in which it represents a relatively small segment of the population and those in which it constitutes a very large one. Obviously, the solutions will differ in these two situations. In the United States, the major solution proposed by planners and social workers in dealing with multiple-problem families and the so-called hard core of poverty has been to attempt to raise slowly their level of living and to incorporate them into the middle class. Wherever possible, there has been some reliance upon psychiatric treatment.

In the underdeveloped countries, however, where great masses of people live in the culture of poverty, a social-work solution does not seem feasible.[5] Because of the magnitude of the problem, psychiatrists can hardly begin to cope with it. They have all they can do to care for their own growing middle class. In these countries the people with a culture of poverty may seek a more revolutionary solution. By creating basic structural changes in society, by redistributing wealth, by organizing the poor and giving them a sense of belonging, of power, and of leadership, revolutions frequently succeed in abolishing some of the basic characteristics of the culture of poverty even when they do not succeed in abolishing poverty itself.

Some of my readers have misunderstood the subculture of poverty model and have failed to grasp the importance of the distinction between poverty and the subculture of poverty. In making this distinction I have tried to document a broader generalization; namely, that it is a serious mistake to lump all poor people together, because the causes, the meaning, and the consequences of poverty vary considerably in different sociocultural contexts. There is nothing in the concept that puts the onus of poverty on the character of the poor. Nor does the concept in any way play down the exploitation and neglect suffered by the poor. Indeed, the subculture of poverty is part of the larger culture of capitalism, whose social and economic system channels wealth into the hands of a relatively small group and thereby makes for the growth of sharp class distinctions.

I would agree that the main reasons for the persistence of the subculture are no doubt the pressures that the larger society exerts over its members and the structure of the larger society itself. However, *this is not the only reason*. The subculture develops mechanisms that tend to perpetuate it, especially because of what happens to the world view, aspirations, and character of the children who grow up in it. For this reason, improved economic opportunities, though absolutely essential and of the highest priority, are not sufficient to alter basically or eliminate the subculture of poverty. Moreover, elimination is a process that will take more than a single generation, even under the best of circumstances, including a socialist revolution.

Some readers have thought that I was saying, "Being poor is terrible, but having a culture of poverty is not so bad." On the contrary, I am saying that it is easier to eliminate poverty than the culture of poverty. I am also suggesting that the poor in a precapitalistic caste-ridden society like India had some advantages over modern urban slum dwellers because the people were organized in castes and panchayats and this organization gave them some sense of identity and some strength and power. Perhaps Gandhi had the urban slums of the West in mind when he wrote that the caste system was one of the greatest inventions of mankind. Similarly, I have argued that the poor Jews of eastern Europe, with their strong tradition of literacy and community organization, were better off than people with the culture of poverty. On the other hand, I would argue that people with the culture of poverty, with their strong sense of resignation and fatalism, are less driven and less anxious than the striving lower middle class, who are still trying to make it in the face of the greatest odds.

[...]

NOTES

1. Although the term "subculture of poverty" is technically more accurate, I shall use "culture of poverty" as a shorter form.
2. Although the model presented here is concerned with conditions in contemporary urban slums, I find remarkable similarities between the culture of poverty and the way of life of Negro slaves in the antebellum South of the United States.
3. For discussion of these traits, see below, pp. 112–18.
4. *Compadrazgo* is a system of relationships and obligations between godparents (*padrinos*) and godchildren (*ahijados*) and between godparents and parents, who are *compadres*.
5. Indeed, it is doubtful how successful the social-work solution can be in the United States!

7 The Passing of Traditional Society (1958)

Daniel Lerner

The Passing of Traditional Society is an in-depth study of how people in the Middle East cope with the growing irrelevance of their traditional ways and adapt new forms of social organization. Daniel Lerner closely associates the process of "modernization" with "Westernization," by which he means adapting the secularization and rationalization characteristic of Western Europe and the USA. He also demonstrates how the pervasive tensions between traditional and modern are negotiated through the development of new personality traits such as "empathy" and the broadening of worldviews. Key motors of modernization for Lerner are media such as radio and television that bring new, incredibly different ideas from the far corners of the earth to all classes of people. Lerner also argues that in order to negotiate the new values and behaviors adapted during modernization, individuals need to be more flexible and be able to relate to a wide variety of people. Individuals learn this "empathy" through participation in modern social forms like the factory, cities, the schools, politics, and the media. Like many modernization theorists, Lerner sees imbalances in the different types of change as a major tension in the process of modernization.

... The source of Middle East unity is a thorny problem of scholarship, complicated by the recent efforts of ideologues to impose a definition that will be politically usable rather than historically valid. Scholars seem agreed that the current ideologies tend to obscure and evade some real issues.

The people of the area today are unified not by their common solutions but by their common problems: how to modernize traditional lifeways that no longer "work" to their own satisfaction. Some seek salvation in past pieties – the recourse to Islamic solidarity providing in this sense a parallel to the Crusades, which, in the name of orthodoxy, hastened the passing of medievalism and coming of modernity in the West. But, underlying the ideologies, there pervades the Middle East a sense that the old ways must go because they no longer satisfy the new wants. ...

Modernization, then, is the unifying principle in this study of the varied Middle East. The term is imposed by recent history. Earlier one spoke of Europeanization, to denote the common elements underlying French influence in Syria–Lebanon and British influence in Egypt and Jordan. More recently, following a century of educational and missionary activity, Americanization became a specific force and the common stimuli of the Atlantic civilization came to be called Westernization. Since

World War II, the continuing search for new ways has been coupled with repudiation of the Western aegis. Soviet and other modernizing models, as illustrated by India and Turkey, have become visible in the area. Any label that today localizes the process is bound to be parochial. For Middle Easterners more than ever want the modern package, but reject the label "made in U.S.A." (or, for that matter, "made in USSR"). We speak, nowadays, of modernization.

Whether from East or West, modernization poses the same basic challenge – the infusion of "a rationalist and positivist spirit" against which, scholars seem agreed, "Islam is absolutely defenseless."[1] The phasing and modality of the process have changed, however, in the past decade. Where Europeanization once penetrated only the upper level of Middle East society, affecting mainly leisure-class fashions, modernization today diffuses among a wider population and touches public institutions as well as private aspirations with its disquieting "positivist spirit." Central to this change is the shift in modes of communicating ideas and attitudes – for spreading among a large public vivid images of its own New Ways is what modernization distinctly does. Not the class media of books and travel, but the mass media of tabloids, radio and movies, are now the dominant modes. . . . To see why this is so – to comprehend what the Middle Eastern peoples are experiencing under the title of modernization – we remind ourselves of what, historically, happened in the West. For the sequence of current events in the Middle East can be understood as a deviation, in some measure a deliberate deformation, of the Western model.

This observational standpoint implies no ethnocentrism. As we shall show, the Western model of modernization exhibits certain components and sequences whose relevance is global. Everywhere, for example, increasing urbanization has tended to raise literacy; rising literacy has tended to increase media exposure; increasing media exposure has "gone with" wider economic participation (per capita income) and political participation (voting). The model evolved in the West is an historical fact. That the same basic model reappears in virtually all modernizing societies on all continents of the world, regardless of variations in race, color, creed, will be shown in this chapter. The point is that the secular process of social change, which brought modernization to the Western world, has more than antiquarian relevance to today's problems of the Middle East transition. Indeed, the lesson is that Middle Eastern modernizers will do well to study the historical sequence of Western growth.

Taking the Western model of modernization as a baseline is forced upon us, moreover, by the tacit assumptions and proclaimed goals which prevail among Middle East spokesmen. That some of these leaders, when convenient for diplomatic maneuver, denounce the West is politically important and explains why we have chosen to speak of "modernization" rather than "Westernization." Rather more important, Western society still provides the most developed model of societal attributes (power, wealth, skill, rationality) which Middle East spokesmen continue to advocate as their own goal. Their own declared policies and programs set our criteria of modernization. From the West came the stimuli which undermined traditional society in the Middle East; for reconstruction of a modern society that will operate efficiently in the world today, the West is still a useful model. What the West is, in this sense, the Middle East seeks to become.

But these societies-in-a-hurry have little patience with the historical *pace* of Western development; what happened in the West over centuries, some Middle

Easterners now seek to accomplish in years. Moreover, they want to do it their "own way. A complication of Middle East modernization is its own ethnocentrism – expressed politically in extreme nationalism, psychologically in passionate xenophobia. The hatred sown by anticolonialism is harvested in the rejection of every appearance of foreign tutelage. Wanted are modern institutions but not modern ideologies, modern power but not modern purposes, modern wealth but not modern wisdom, modern commodities but not modern cant. It is not clear, however, that modern ways and words can be so easily and so totally sundered. Underlying the variant ideological forms which modernization took in Europe, America, Russia, there have been certain behavioral and institutional compulsions common to all. These historical regularities some Middle East leaders now seek to obviate, trying instead new routes and risky by-passes. We alert ourselves to the novelty of these efforts by recapitulating briefly some essential elements in the modernization of the West.

I. The Mobile Personality: Empathy

People in the Western culture have become habituated to the sense of change and attuned to its various rhythms. Many generations ago, in the West, ordinary men found themselves unbound from their native soil and relatively free to move. Once they actually moved in large numbers, from farms to flats and from fields to factories, they became intimate with the idea of change by direct experience. This bore little resemblance to the migrant or crusading hordes of yore, driven by war or famine. This was movement by individuals, each having made a personal choice to seek elsewhere his own version of a better life.

Physical mobility so experienced naturally entrained social mobility, and gradually there grew institutions appropriate to the process. Those who gained heavily by changing their address soon wanted a convenient bank in the neighborhood to secure their treasure; also a law-and-police force to guard the neighborhood against disorder and devaluation; also a voice in prescribing standards of behavior for others.[2] So came into operation a "system" of bourgeois values that embraced social change as normal. Rules of the game had to be worked out for adjudicating conflicts over the direction and rate of change. Who was to gain, how, and how much? As the profits to be gained from mobility became evident to all, conflicts over access to the channels of opportunity became sharper. The process can be traced through the evolution of Western property and tax laws, whose major tendency is to protect the "haves" without disqualifying the "have-nots."[3] It was by protecting every man's *opportunity* to gain that the modern West turned decisively in the direction of social mobility.

Social institutions founded on voluntary participation by mobile individuals required a new array of skills and a new test of merit. Every person, according to the new democratic theory, was equally entitled to acquire the skills needed for shaping his own "future" in the Great Society. . . .

Thus the idea spread that personal mobility is itself a first-order value; the sense grew that social morality is essentially the ethics of social change. A man is what he may become; a society is its potential. These notions passed out of the realm of debate into the Western law and mores.

A mobile society has to encourage rationality, for the calculus of choice shapes individual behavior and conditions its rewards. People come to see the social future as manipulable rather than ordained and their personal prospects in terms of achievement rather than heritage. Rationality is purposive: ways of thinking and acting are instruments of intention (not articles of faith); men succeed or fail by the test of what they accomplish (not what they worship). So, whereas traditional man tended to reject innovation by saying "It has never been thus," the contemporary Westerner is more likely to ask "Does it work?" and try the new way without further ado.

The psychic gap between these two postures is vast. It took much interweaving through time, between ways of doing and ways of thinking, before men could work out a style of daily living with change that felt consistent and seamless. The experience of mobility through successive generations gradually evolved participant lifeways which feel "normal" today. Indeed, while past centuries established the public practices of the mobile society, it has been the work of the twentieth century to diffuse widely a *mobile sensibility* so adaptive to change that rearrangement of the self-system is its distinctive mode.

The mobile personality can be described in objective and technical fashion. Since this is what the book is largely about, it will do here to define its main feature and to suggest the main line of its secular evolution. The mobile person is distinguished by a high capacity for identification with new aspects of his environment; he comes equipped with the mechanisms needed to incorporate new demands upon himself that arise outside of his habitual experience. These mechanisms for enlarging a man's identity operate in two ways. *Projection* facilitates identification by assigning to the object certain preferred attributes of the self – others are "incorporated" because they are like me. (Distantiation or negative identification, in the Freudian sense, results when one projects onto others certain disliked attributes of the self.) *Introjection* enlarges identity by attributing to the self certain desirable attributes of the object – others are "incorporated" because I am like them or want to be like them. We shall use the word *empathy* as shorthand for both these mechanisms. ...

We are interested in empathy as the inner mechanism which enables newly mobile persons to *operate efficiently* in a changing world. Empathy, to simplify the matter, is the capacity to see oneself in the other fellow's situation. This is an indispensable skill for people moving out of traditional settings. Ability to empathize may make all the difference, for example, when the newly mobile persons are villagers who grew up knowing all the extant individuals, roles and relationships in their environment. Outside his village or tribe, each must meet new individuals, recognize new roles, and learn new relationships involving himself. ... Accordingly, we are interested in the mobile personality mainly as a social phenomenon with a history. Our concern is with the large historical movement, now becoming visible in the Middle East, of which an enlarged capacity for empathy is the distinctive psychic component. Our interest is to clarify the process whereby the high empathizer tends to become also the cash customer, the radio listener, the voter.[4]

It is a major hypothesis of this study that high empathic capacity is the predominant personal style only in modern society, which is distinctively industrial, urban, literate and *participant*. Traditional society is nonparticipant – it deploys people by kinship into communities isolated from each other and from a center; without an urban–rural division of labor, it develops few needs requiring economic interdependence; lacking the bonds of interdependence, people's horizons are limited by locale and their decisions involve only other *known* people in *known* situations. Hence, there is no need for a transpersonal common doctrine formulated in terms of shared secondary symbols – a national "ideology" which enables persons unknown to each other to engage in political controversy or achieve "consensus" by comparing their opinions. Modern society is participant in that it functions by "consensus" – individuals making personal decisions on public issues must concur often enough with other individuals they do not know to make possible a stable common governance. Among the marks of this historic achievement in social organization, which we call Participant Society, are that most people go through school, read newspapers, receive cash payments in jobs they are legally free to change, buy goods for cash in an open market, vote in elections which actually decide among competing candidates, and express opinions on many matters which are not their personal business.

Especially important, for the Participant Style, is the enormous proportion of people who are expected to "have opinions" on public matters – and the corollary expectation of these people that their opinions will matter. It is this subtly complicated structure of reciprocal expectation which sustains widespread empathy. Only in the lowest reaches of America's social hierarchy, for example, is it still discussed whether people *ought* to have opinions. ...

For, in any society, only when the accepted model of behavior is emulated by the population at large does it become the predominant personal style. The model of behavior developed by modern society is characterized by empathy, a high capacity for rearranging the self-system on short notice. Whereas the isolated communities of traditional society functioned well on the basis of a highly constrictive personality, the interdependent sectors of modern society require widespread participation. This in turn requires an expansive and adaptive self-system, ready to incorporate new roles and to identify personal values with public issues. This is why modernization of any society has involved the great characterological transformation we call psychic mobility. The latent statistical assertion involved here is this: In modern society *more* individuals exhibit *higher* empathic capacity than in any previous society.

2. The Mobility Multiplier: Mass Media

The historic increase of psychic mobility begins with the expansion of physical travel. Historians conventionally date the modern era from the Age of Exploration. ... Gradually the technical means of transporting live bodies improved and physical displacement became an experience lived through by millions of plain folk earlier bounden to some ancestral spot. Geographical mobility became, in this phase, the usual vehicle of social mobility. It remained for a later time to make vivid that each mobile soma of the earlier epoch housed a psyche, and to reconstruct transatlantic history in terms of psychic mobility. It is the contemporary historian who now distinctively perceives the mass immigration into America as a traumatic process of psychic encounter with the new and strange.[5] We accent the contemporaneity of the psychic dimension, because the moral injunction to "look shining at new styles of architecture" is something new in the world.[6]

The expansion of psychic mobility means that more people now command greater skill in imagining themselves as strange persons in strange situations, places, and times than did people in any previous historical epoch. In our time, indeed, the spread of empathy around the world is accelerating. The earlier increase of physical experience through transportation has been multiplied by the spread of *mediated* experience through mass communication. A generation before Columbus sailed to the New World, Gutenberg activated his printing press. The technical history of the popular arts suggests the sequence. The typical literary form of the modern epoch, the novel, is a conveyance of disciplined empathy. Where the poet once specialized in self-expression, the modern novelist reports his sustained imagination of the lives of others.[7] The process is carried further in the movies and in radio–television dramas. These have peopled the daily world of their audience with sustained, even intimate, experience of the lives of others. ...

Radio, film, and television climax the evolution set into motion by Gutenberg. The mass media opened to the large masses of mankind the infinite *vicarious* universe. Many more millions of persons in the world were to be affected directly, and perhaps more profoundly, by the communication media than by the transportation agencies. By obviating the physical displacement of travel, the media accented the psychic displacement of vicarious experience. For the imaginary universe not only involves more people, but it involves them in a different order of experience. There is a world of difference, we know, between "armchair travel" and actually "being there." What is the difference?

Physical experience of a new environment affronts the sensibility with new perceptions in their complex "natural" setting. The traveler in a strange land perceives simultaneously climate and clothing, body builds and skin textures, gait and speech, feeding and hygiene, work and play – in short, the ensemble of manners and morals that make a "way of life." A usual consequence for the traveler is that the "pattern of culture" among the strangers becomes confused, diverging from his prior stereotype of it and from his preferred model of reality.

Vicarious experience occurs in quite different conditions. Instead of the complexities that attend a "natural" environment, mediated experience exhibits the simplicity of "artificial" settings contrived by the creative communicator. Thus, while the traveler is apt to become bewildered by the profusion of strange sights and sounds, the receiver of communications is likely to be enjoying a composed and orchestrated version of the new reality. He has the benefit of more facile perception of the new experience as a "whole," with the concomitant advantage (which is sometimes illusory) of facile comprehension. The stimuli of perception, which shape understanding, have been simplified.

The simplification of stimuli, however, is accomplished at a certain cost. The displaced traveler's great pragmatic advantage is that he must take responsive action toward the stimuli presented by the new environment. However painful this may be – as when, to take a simple case, he has lost his way and must ask directions in a language of which his mastery is uncertain – overt action does help to discharge the traveler's interior tensions. But the passive audience for mediated communications has no such discharge channel. ...

Thus the mass media, by simplifying *perception* (what we "see") while greatly complicating *response* (what we "do"), have been great teachers of interior manipulation. They disciplined Western man in those empathic skills which spell modernity. They also portrayed for him the roles he might confront and elucidated the opinions he might need. Their continuing spread in our century is performing a similar function on a world scale. The Middle East already shows the marks of this historic encounter. As a young bureaucrat in Iran put it: "The movies are like a teacher to us, who tells us what to do and what not." The global network of mass media has already recruited enough new participants in all corners of the earth to make "the opinions of mankind" a real factor instead of a fine phrase in the arena of world politics. There now exists, and its scope accelerates at an extraordinary pace, a genuine "world public opinion." This has happened because millions of people, who never left their native heath, now are learning to imagine how life is organized in different lands and under different codes than their own. That this signifies a net increase in human imaginativeness, so construed, is the proposition under consideration.

3. The "System" of Modernity

A second proposition of this large historical order derives from the observation that modern media systems have flourished only in societies that are modern by other tests. That is, the media spread psychic mobility most efficiently among peoples who have achieved in some measure the antecedent conditions of geographic and social mobility. The converse of this proposition is also true: no modern society functions efficiently without a developed system of mass media. Our historical forays indicate that the conditions which define modernity form an interlocking "system." They grow conjointly, in the normal situation, or they become stunted severally.

It seems clear that people who live together in a common polity will develop patterned ways of distributing *information* along with other commodities. It is less obvious that these information flows will interact with the distribution of power, wealth, status at so many points as to form a system – and, moreover, a system so tightly interwoven that institutional variation in one sector will be accompanied by regular and determinate variation in the other sectors. Yet, just this degree of interaction between communication and social systems is what our historical exploration suggests. ... In media systems, the main flow of public information is operated by a corps of professional communicators, selected according to skill criteria, whose job it is to transmit mainly descriptive messages ("news") through impersonal media (print, radio, film) to relatively undifferentiated mass audiences. In oral systems, public information usually emanates from sources authorized to speak by their place in the social hierarchy, i.e., by status rather than skill criteria. Its contents are typically prescriptive rather than descriptive; news is less salient than "rules" which specify correct behavior toward imminent events directly involving the larger population, such as tax collections and labor drafts. (Oral and media systems also differ sharply in recreational content, as we shall see, but we here focus on informational content.) Even these prescriptive messages are normally transmitted via face-to-face oral channels (or via such point-to-point equivalents as letters) to the primary groups of kinship, worship, work and play.

Naturally, few societies in the world today give a perfect fit to either of these idealized sets of paired comparisons. America closely approximates the model of a media system, but people also speak to each other on public issues and the personal influence of the "opinion leader" is strong.[8] Conversely, Saudi Arabia corresponds to the oral system but operates its radio transmitters at Jidda. As we move around the world, subjecting our ideal types to empirical data, various elements in the patterns begin to shift. Most countries are in some phase of transition from one system to the other.

But two observations appear to hold for all countries, regardless of continent, culture, or creed. First the *direction* of change is always from oral to media system (no known case exhibiting change in the reverse direction). Secondly, the *degree* of change toward media system appears to correlate significantly with changes in other key sectors of the social system. If these observations are correct, then we are dealing with a "secular trend" of social change that is global in scope. What we have been calling the Western model of modernization is operating on a global scale. Moreover, since this means that other important changes must regularly accompany the development of a media system, there is some point in the frequent references to a "world communication revolution." We here consider the more moderate proposition that a communication system is both index and agent of change in a total social system. This avoids the genetic problem of causality, about which we can only speculate, in order to stress correlational hypotheses which can be tested. On this view, once the modernizing process is started, chicken and egg in fact "cause" each other to develop. ...

We subsume industrialization under our index of urbanization. This is a key variable in our "system," for it is with urbanization that the modernizing process historically has begun in Western societies. Our next task, having shown that literacy and media participation are highly correlated, was to establish their interdependence with urbanism. For the historical literature on this point, while allocating great influence to the growth of cities, is not clear on several important questions: if urbanization is a necessary condition of modernization (meaning that certain other changes can occur only in cities), then what are these other changes that regularly occurred in any society when urbanization occurred? If urbanization is necessary to start modernization, how much of it is necessary (what is the "critical minimum")? Is there a point at which modernization, once started, can sustain itself without much or any further urbanization (is there a "critical optimum" for urbanization)?

We formulated these questions, for testing, in three specific hypotheses: (1) that critical limits, minimum and optimum, can be established for urbanization within which literacy will increase directly as urban population grows in all countries; (2) that countries which have not reached the minimum limit of urbanization will also be predominantly illiterate; (3) that countries which have exceeded the optimum limit of urbanization will also be predominantly literate. To test these hypotheses, we classified all 73 countries according to the data on literacy provided by UNESCO. We then found the mean urbanization for all the countries in each literacy group ...

In all 22 countries less than 20 percent literate the mean proportion of population living in cities over 50,000 is only 7.4 percent. The "critical minimum" of urbanization appears to be between 7 and 17 percent of total population, for convenience one may say 10 percent. Only after a country reaches 10 percent of urbanization does its literacy rate begin to rise significantly. Thereafter urbanization and literacy increase together in a direct (monotonic) relationship, until they reach 25 percent, which appears to be the "critical optimum" of urbanization. Beyond this literacy continues to rise independently of the growth of cities. The surplus of 1.2 percent of urbanization ... is either insignificant, with only four countries, or else confirms the analysis. Between these limits of 10–25 percent, our findings indicate, the growth of cities and of literacy are closely interdependent. ...

The secular evolution of a participant society appears to involve a regular sequence of three phases. Urbanization comes first, for cities alone have developed the complex of skills and resources which characterize the modern industrial economy. Within this urban matrix develop both of the attributes which distinguish the next two phases – literacy and media growth. There is a close reciprocal relationship between these, for the literate develop the media which in turn spread literacy. But, historically, literacy performs the key function in the second phase. The capacity to read, at first acquired by relatively few people, equips them to perform the varied tasks required in the modernizing society. Not until the third phase, when the elaborate technology of industrial development is fairly well advanced, does a society begin to produce newspapers, radio networks, and motion pictures on a massive scale. This, in turn, accelerates the spread of literacy. Out of this interaction develop those institutions of participation (e.g., voting) which we find in all advanced modern societies. For countries in transition today, these high correlations suggest that literacy and media participation may be considered as a supply-and-demand reciprocal in a communication market whose locus, at least in its historical inception, can only be urban.

We shall later examine the idea that a common psychological mechanism underlies these phases – that it is the more empathic individuals who respond, in the first place, to the lure of cities, schools, media. Urban residence, schooling, media exposure then train and reinforce the empathic predisposition that was already present. On this view, the modern "style of life" can nowadays be acquired as a whole by individuals living in modernizing societies. This interpretation is quite plausible, but it does not clarify what happens to empathic individuals who are ready and able to modernize more rapidly and completely than their society permits. A large and important class of Middle Easterners are in this position today. Our data on 73 countries, distributed over all the continents of the earth, indicate that many millions of individuals everywhere are in the same position. This further suggests that the model of modernization follows an autonomous historical logic – that each phase tends to generate the next phase by some mechanism which operates independently of cultural or doctrinal variations. To understand the position of those millions who may be caught in some historical lag today, we look more closely at our three phases.

The first phase, then, is *urbanization*. It is the transfer of population from scattered hinterlands to urban centers that stimulates the needs and provides the conditions needed for "take-off" toward widespread participation. Only cities require a largely literate population to function properly – for the organization of urban life assumes enough literacy to read labels, sign checks, ride subways. ... The primitive social function of literacy, as of all skills, is to reduce waste of human effort. Its higher function is to train the skilled labor force with which cities develop the industrial complex that produces commodities for cash customers, including newspapers and radios and movies for media consumers. Cities produce the machine tools of modernization. Accordingly, increases of urbanization tend in every society to multiply national increases in literacy and media participation. By drawing people from their rural communities, cities create the demand for impersonal communication. By promoting literacy and media, cities supply this demand. Once the basic industrial plant is in operation, the development of a participant society passes into a subsequent phase. When voluntary urbanization exceeds 25 percent, thereby assuring the conditions of modern production, further urbanization no longer automatically guarantees equivalent increases in consumption. The need then shifts to modernizing the conditions which govern consumption.

Of this second phase, *literacy* is both the index and agent. To spread consumption of urban products beyond the city limits, literacy is an efficient instrument. The great symbol of this phase is the Sears-Roebuck catalogue. The mail-order house replaces the peddler only when enough people can read catalogues and write letters. In this sense literacy is also the basic skill required for operation of a media system. Only the literate produce the media contents which mainly the literate consume. Hence, once societies are about 25 percent urbanized, the highest correlation of media consumption is with literacy. ... by the time this second phase gets well under way, a different social system is in operation than that which governed behavior in a society that was under 10 percent urban and under 40 percent (roughly, less than half) literate. For, when most people in a society have become literate, they tend to generate all sorts of new desires and to develop the means of satisfying them.

It is this interplay of new desires and satisfactions which characterizes the third phase of modernization, namely *media participation*. Once people are equipped to handle the new experiences produced by mobility (via their move to the city), and to handle the new experiences conveyed by media (via their literacy), they now seek the satisfactions which integrate these skills. They discover, as did The Grocer in Balgat, the tingle of wondering "what will happen next" – the tingle which sounds the knell of traditional society, of routinized lifeways in which everyone *knew* what would happen next because it had to follow what came before. To satisfy this new desire requires the personal skill of empathy which, when spread among large numbers of persons, makes possible the social institution of media participation. This was the phase in which the West developed the "penny press," early symbol of the accelerating supply and demand for media products, which continues today with the pocket radio and the portable TV. It is characteristic of this phase, as the production–consumption reciprocal of media participation develops, that economists come to find production of radio sets a useful index of growth in total industrial production.[9]

For, rising media participation tends to raise participation in all sectors of the social system. In accelerating the spread of empathy, it also diffuses those other modern demands to which participant institutions have responded: in the consumer's economy via cash (and credit), in the public forum via opinion, in the representative polity via voting. ... [M]edia participation, in every country we have studied, exhibits a centripetal tendency. Those who read newspapers also tend to be the heaviest consumers of movies, broadcasts, and all other media products. Throughout the Middle East illiterate respondents said of their literate compatriots: "They live in another world." Thus literacy becomes the sociological pivot in the activation of psychic mobility, the publicly shared skill which binds modern man's varied daily round into a consistent participant lifestyle.

We come, then, to political participation. Democratic goverance comes late, historically, and typically appears as a crowning institution of the participant society. That the voting coefficient is so high indicates that these 54 countries have achieved stable growth at a high level of modernity. In these countries the urban literate tends to be also a newspaper reader, a cash customer and a voter. The modern "system" of self-sustaining growth operates across the land in these 54 countries – as their cities sprouted suburbs, as their urban districts grew into "urban regions," their national increase of literacy and participation kept pace. This capacity to incorporate continuing social change within the existing framework of institutions has become a distinctive structural feature of the developed modern societies. In a century that has reinstated revolution as a method of social change, they have managed to adapt their own accelerated growth mainly by nonviolent procedures. ...

4. The Hurdles of Modernization

When the underdeveloped lands of the world are tested by our model of modernity, the enormous hurdles in the path to modernization stand out more clearly. What the West accomplished gradually over three past centuries is not so easy for the East to achieve rapidly in the present century. ...

Whereas the modern nations have achieved "optimum" relations between urbanism, literacy, media participation, the traditional societies exhibit extremely variant "growth" patterns (deviations from the regression lines). Some are more urban than literate, others more media participant than urban.

In the Middle East, two recent trends account for much of this imbalance. One has been the accelerated postwar movement to the capital cities in each country. This is "urbanization" for census purposes, but it seriously revises the historic meaning of the term. In Cairo, for example, there is a huge floating population with no home but the city streets. They attend no schools, do no work, get no cash, buy no goods. It would be more accurate to tally these involuntary urbanites as "internal rural refugees," but until some such auditing change is made the Egyptian census will continue to show a huge and growing surplus of urban over literate population. The second postwar trend is the rapid diffusion of cheap (or free) radio receivers among the rural populations of the Middle East. This again is an alteration of the Western model, in which media participation reflected a market mechanism – radios produced privately for profit were bought individually for pleasure. Radios distributed gratis by government facilitate "social control" rather than "individual participation"; they also explain why most Arab countries show an excess of radio-listeners over urban literates.

Such events introduce a new stochastic factor into the historical model of modernization – one that is not accounted for by the model. Such a factor is the effort by new governments around the world to induce certain symbols of modernity by policy decisions, in a sequence which disregards the basic arrangement of lifeways out of which slowly evolved those modern institutions now so hastily symbolized. A stochastic factor may be a genuine innovation which will remake the model; or it may be a risk taken in ignorance of the model. The evidence now available suggests that, in the Middle East, we are usually dealing with the latter alternative.

An instance is the new global fashion to install some voting mechanism as a symbol of modern desires rather than as a functional agency of modern governance. Democracy has become a world fad, spread across national lines by symbolic *diffusion*, rather than an institutional outgrowth of needs internal to an increasingly participant society. As a result, some modernizing countries show extraordinarily high ("ahistorical") voting rates. Indeed, whereas voting correlates highly with the other variables in the modern countries, sharp deviations occur in Asia and the Middle East. Thus Egypt, in 1956, ordered its impoverished rural masses to "vote" in a single-option plebiscite, which gave Nasser the 97 percent endorsement common in such performances. These great "underdeveloped areas" have in common the historic poverty of their resources relative to the soaring heights of their current aspirations. They are inadequately urbanized, industrialized and literate, relative to their urge rapidly to install the symbols of modern participant society. ... [H]ow can these new societies-in-a-hurry hope to achieve stability while acquiring mobility? ... We turn then to a key problem of modernization in underdeveloped countries: How have they gone about diffusing the capacity for psychic mobility, along with other capacities that historically have equipped people for efficient functioning in participant society?

5. The Model of Transition

Our historical model provided suitable terms for describing the degree of modernization present in a given society at a given time. The indices of urbanization, literacy, media and political participation discriminated efficiently the relative positions in 1950 of very many countries on all the continents of the world. But the model was static to this point. A dynamic component was needed to show how a country *moved* from one phase to the next, why an urban person regularly *became* a literate and a radio listener and a voter. Such a dynamic component must connect institutional changes with alterations in the prevailing personal style.

We had already identified the characterological transformation that accompanies modernization as psychic mobility, with empathy as its mechanism. The questions now were: how can empathy be tested? How can the results of such testing be collated with the indices of participant behavior? What we needed to learn was whether a person who shows high empathy also exhibits the other attributes, and vice versa. Since empathy is an autonomous personality variable, it is not revealed by any census data, but must be elicited through psychological testing of individuals. At this point the Middle East survey supplied the missing link. The interviews contained a set of nine "projective questions" which we used to test each respondent's empathic capacity. ...

What these questions have in common is that they ask the respondent to imagine himself in a situation other than his real one. They are "role-playing" questions that require, for responsiveness, some capacity to empathize – to imagine what it must be like to be head of a government, editor of a newspaper, manager of a radio station, or even "people like yourself." The strenuousness of such demands upon persons untutored in empathic skills was underlined by the many respondents, in every country, who thought of suicide rather than imagine themselves in these exalted ranks. "My God! How can you say such a thing?" gasped the shepherd, when Tosun put such questions to him. ...

Our task was to devise a method to determine the degree of association between empathy, as tested by these questions, and the lifeways of modernity. The solution of this problem provided our theory of modernization with the dynamic component needed to analyze ongoing changes in the Middle East today. Our solution was to show, empirically, that persons who are urban, literate, participant, and empathic *differ* from persons who lack any of these attributes – and differ on a significant personal trait which is distinctive of the modern style. Such a trait is "having opinions" on public matters. Traditional man has habitually regarded public matters as none of his business. For the Modern man in a participant society, on the contrary, such matters are fraught with interest and importance. A broad range of opinions on public questions can be taken as a distinctive mark of modernity. ... The significant mode of participating, in any network of human communication, is by sharing a common interest in the messages it transmits – i.e., by having opinions about the matters which concern other participants. (Nonparticipation, conversely, consists of neither knowing nor caring about the messages relayed through a given network.) In a large public network, such as that of a nation, perfect participation is impossible – and perhaps undesirable. A network would hardly be manageable in which all citizens attended to all messages and expressed opinions on all public questions. There are determinate limits – maxima as well as minima – to the degree of participation appropriate for particular networks. The modernizing tendency is toward networks that can handle maximum participation, and concurrently to develop the participants needed to man these networks.

A person becomes a participant by learning to "have opinions" – further, the more numerous and varied the matters on which he has opinions, the more participant he is. To rank each respondent as a participant in the Middle Eastern opinion arena, we counted the number and variety of items in the questionnaire on which he expressed *some* opinion (i.e., did *not* say "I don't know" or "I have no opinion").

... The top opinion-holders ... typically were literate, urban, media participants, and high empathizers. Among illiterates, those living in cities tended to have more opinions ... than rurals. Among illiterate rurals, those with a significant measure of media exposure scored higher ... than those without such exposure. This left a group which – in terms of literacy, residence, media exposure – should have been homo-geneous in the opinion range, but in fact was not. Some of these individuals had significantly more opinions than the others. The only satisfactory way to account for this divergence was by our personality variable – empathy. For what distinguished these illiterate, rural, nonparticipant individuals ... from their peers ... was a keener interest in impersonal matters, a deeper desire to become participants of the opinion arena. They were marked less by their manifest ways than by their latent wants.

Once this was clear, our data fell beautifully into place. For the true Transitional is defined, dynamically, by what he wants to become. What differentiates him from his Traditional peers is a different *latent structure* of aptitudes and attitudes. ... The aptitude is *empathy* – he "sees" things the others do not see, "lives" in a world populated by imaginings alien to the constrictive world of the others. The attitude is *desire* – he wants *really* to see the things he has hitherto "seen" only in his mind's eye, *really* to live in the world he has "lived" in only vicariously. These are the sources of his deviant ways. When many individuals show deviation in this direction, then a transition is under way in their society. ...

Here we stress that the transition to participant society hinges upon the desire among individuals to participate. It grows as more and more individuals take leave of the constrictive traditional universe and nudge their psyche toward the expansive new land of heart's desire. The great gap is passed when a person begins to "have opinions" – particularly on matters which, according to his neighbors, "do not concern him." The empathic skill which makes this possible is not highly valued in the traditional community. There people are taught to handle the ego with minimum awareness of alternatives to current practices – in the technical sense, compulsively. The Constrictive Self is the approved personal style. Self-manipulation, continuous rearrangement of the self-system to incorporate new experience, is regarded as unworthy of any person with "good character."[10]

The classic case is The Grocer of Balgat, repudiated on all sides as he sought to incorporate the new identities of his vicarious experience. The Balgati feared his opinions and called him "infidel." Tosun found his role-playing distasteful and wrote of him: "Although he is on the same level with the other villagers ... he most evidently wishes to feel that he is closer to me than he is to them." The Transitionals, at various phases of modernization, are making their way toward an unclear future via a path replete with hard bumps and unsuspected detours. Their voyage entails a sustained commingling of joyous anticipations with lingering anxieties, sensuous euphoria with recurrent shame, guilt, and puzzlement. From their changes of pace and their shifts of direction we learn how they perceive the terrain, its pitfalls and its promises.

A deep problem of values is imbedded in the life histories of these men-in-motion. The moral issues of modernization often are reduced to this: *Should* they want what they want? Since they want what we have, Western responses to this question usually reflect only our own value-dilemmas. Rather more relevant is the judgment of Middle Easterners on what they have and what they want. If we resist the temptation to adjudicate conflicting preferences among others, at least long enough to see how they adjudicate these options themselves, then we have a sounder basis than our own conventional values for moral judgment.

For example: a very powerful finding of our study is that Middle Easterners who are modernizing consider themselves happier than do those who remain within traditional lifeways. This is in striking contrast with the impressions conveyed by some observers, often from highly modern settings themselves, who feel that the undermining of traditional ways by new desires must be a net loss. Among such observers the passing of cherished images of passive peasantry, noble nomads, brave Beduin evokes regrets. But these regrets are not felt by the modernizing peasants, nomads, Beduin themselves, or felt less disapprovingly by them than by the moderns who study them and love the familiar way they used to be. Thus Tosun, the bright young modern from Ankara, gave his sympathy to the miserable intimidated Shepherd but only his indignation to the ambitious outspoken Grocer. ... In the drama of modernization, those who have already incorporated the trends of the times (The Moderns) and those who have not yet been touched by them (The Traditionals) present a relatively static posture. The meaning of events is best clarified by those whom we perceive at the moment of "engagement" – a moment which occurs when an expansive Self, newly equipped with a functioning empathy, perceives connections between its private dilemmas and public issues. This is political consciousness, in the larger sense, and its acquisition distinguishes those who have been pierced by the present and in responding shape the future. The *Transitionals* are our key to the changing Middle East. What they are today is a passage from what they once were to what they are becoming. Their passage, writ large, is the passing of traditional society in the Middle East.

NOTES

1. G. E. von Grunebaum (ed.), *Unity and Variety in Muslim Civilization* (1955), p. 12.
2. Robert Park, *Human Communities* (1952).
3. S. Ratner, *American Taxation, Its History As A Social Force in Democracy* (1942).
4. This formulation approaches the typology on American society developed by David Riesman in *The Lonely Crowd* (1950). Cf. my article "Comfort and Fun: Morality in a Nice Society," *The American Scholar* (Spring 1958).
5. Oscar Handlin, *The Uprooted* (1952).
6. W. H. Auden, "Petition."
7. J. W. Beach, *The Twentieth Century Novel* (1932).
8. Elihu Katz and P. F. Lazarsfeld, *Personal Influence* (1955).
9. A. Bergson (ed.), *Soviet Economic Growth* (1953).
10. D. Lerner and D. Riesman, "Self and Society," *Explorations* (June 1955).

8 Making Men Modern: On the Causes and Consequences of Individual Change in Six Developing Countries (1969)

Alex Inkeles

Alex Inkeles (1920–) took general, qualitative assumptions about what makes people and societies modern and tested them empirically. In a bold Harvard University-directed project, Inkeles and a team of researchers studied 6,000 men in six poorer countries around the world to test hypotheses about what makes men "modern," and to find out if their definition of "modernity" held up in different cultural settings. They found exposure to "modernizing forces" such as formal school-based education and factory work led to changes in individuals' values and behaviors. For example, they found that men with these experiences were more open to other new experiences, were more likely to be involved with civic affairs, and were more willing to act independently from parental authority. As Professor Emeritus at Stanford University and a fellow at the Hoover Institution, Inkeles continues to study how personality traits at the individual level distinguish different cultures.

Since 1962 a group of my colleagues and I at Harvard University have been working to understand the impact on the individual of his participation in the process of modernization. In the pursuit of this goal we devised a complex and comprehensive questionnaire touching on a wide variety of life situations and intended to measure a substantial segment of the range of attitudes, values, and behaviors we conceive as particularly relevant to understanding the individual's participation in the roles typical for a modern industrial society. This questionnaire we then administered to some 6,000 young men in six developing countries: Argentina, Chile, India, Israel, Nigeria, and East Pakistan. All three of the continents containing the overwhelming majority of developing nations are represented. The sampled countries cover the range from the newest nations which have only recently won their independence to those with a long history of self-governance; from those only now emerging from tribal life to those with ancient high cultures, and from those furthest removed from, to those most intimately linked to, the European cultural and industrial social order. The men interviewed were selected to represent points on a presumed continuum of exposure to modernizing influences, the main groups being the cultivator of the land still rooted in his traditional rural community; the migrant from the countryside just arrived in the city but not yet integrated into urban industrial life; the urban but nonindustrial worker still pursuing a more or less traditional occupation, such as barber or carpenter, but now doing so in the urban environment even though outside the context of a modern large-scale organization; and the experienced industrial worker engaged in production using inanimate power and machinery within the context of a more or less modern productive enterprise. To these we have added sets of secondary school and university students who enjoy the presumed benefits of advanced education. Within and across these sample groups we exercised numerous controls in the selection of subjects and in the analysis of our data, both to understand the influence and to prevent the uncontrolled effects of sociocultural and biosocial factors such as age, sex, education, social origins, ethnic membership, past life experience, and the like.

Our interview included almost 300 entries. Some 160 of these elicited attitudes, values, opinions, and reports on the behavior of others and oneself, touching on almost every major aspect of daily life. The questionnaire included various tests of verbal ability, literacy, political information, intelligence, and psychic adjustment. In some cases it took four hours of interviewing to complete – a demanding experience for both interviewer and interviewee.

We completed our field work near the end of 1964, and since that time have been engaged in processing and then later analyzing the very substantial body of data we collected. At this time our analysis is sufficiently far advanced so that we can discern the main outlines of some of the conclusions we must draw. To present these within the rigorous limits of the time and space currently allotted for scholarly communications requires imposing a telegraphic style and forgoing the presentation of detailed evidence to support my arguments. Each of my conclusions will address itself to one of the main issues to which our research was directed. Each issue is presented in the form of a question to which I will assay an answer. The four main issues dealt with here should not be understood as being the only ones to which we addressed ourselves; neither should it be assumed that our data provide answers only to these questions.

1. *How far is there an empirically identifiable modern man, and what are his outstanding characteristics?* – Many social scientists have a conception of the modern man, but few have submitted this conception to an empirical test to ascertain whether this type really exists in nature and to determine how often he appears on the scene. Important exceptions may be found in the work of Kahl (1968), Dawson (1967), and Doob (1967). We too have our model of the modern man, a complex one including three components which we refer to as the analytic, the topical, and the behavioral models, all of which, we assumed, might well tap one general underlying common dimension of individual modernity.

We believe our evidence (presented in some detail in Smith and Inkeles 1966) shows unmistakably that there is a set of personal qualities which reliably cohere as a syndrome and which identify a type of man who may validly be described as fitting a reasonable theoretical conception of the modern man. Central to this syndrome are: (1) openness to new experience, both with people and with new ways of doing things such as attempting to control births; (2) the assertion of increasing independence from the authority of traditional figures like parents and priests and a shift of allegiance to leaders of government, public affairs, trade unions, cooperatives, and the like; (3) belief in the efficacy of science and medicine, and a general abandonment of passivity and fatalism in the face of life's difficulties; and (4) ambition for oneself and one's children to achieve high occupational and educational goals. Men who manifest these characteristics (5) like people to be on time and show an interest in carefully planning their affairs in advance. It is also part of this syndrome to (6) show strong interest and take an active part in civic and community affairs and local politics; and (7) to strive energetically to keep up with the news, and within this effort to prefer news of national and international import over items dealing with sports, religion, or purely local affairs.

This syndrome of modernity coheres empirically to meet the generally accepted standards for scale construction with reliabilities ranging from .754 to .873 in the six countries. Looking at the range of items which enters into the scale, one can see that it has a compelling face validity. In addition, the empirical outcome accords well with our original theoretical model and, indeed, with those of numerous other students of the problem. Evidently the modern man is not just a construct in the mind of sociological theorists. He exists and he can be identified with fair reliability within any population which can take our test.

To discover that there are indeed men in the world who fit our model of a modern man is comforting, but perhaps not startling. After all, we can probably somewhere find an example of almost any kind of man one might care to delineate. It is important to emphasize, therefore, that men manifesting the syndrome of attitudes, values, and ways of acting we have designated "modern" are not freaks. They are not even rare. On the contrary, there are very substantial numbers of them in all six of the countries we have studied.

Furthermore, we consider it to be of the utmost significance that the qualities which serve empirically to define a modern man do not differ substantially from occupation to occupation, or more critically, from culture to culture. In constructing our standard scales of modernity we utilized a pool of 119 attitude items. In each country these items were then ranked according to the size of the item-to-scale correlation, and the subset of items having the highest correlations was then selected as defining the modern man for the given country. Using this "coherence" method to construct the national modernity scales, we might have found a totally different set of items defining the syndrome of modernity in each of our six national samples. Indeed, if we used only the twenty items ranking highest in the item-to-scale correlations for each country, we could theoretically have come out with six totally different syndromes, one for each country, no one overlapping in the least with any other. The actual outcome of the analysis was totally different. The probability that even one item would come out in the top fifty in all six countries is approximately five in a thousand. We actually had ten items which were in the top fifty in all six countries, sixteen more in the top fifty in five countries, thirteen more which were in this set in four of the six countries. The probability that the same thirty-nine items would by chance be in the top fifty in four of the six countries is so infinitesimal as to make our results notable indeed.

This means that what defines man as modern in one country also defines him as modern in another. It argues for the actual psychic unity of mankind in a structural sense and the potential psychic unity of mankind in the factual sense. In speaking of the unity of mankind in terms of psychic structure, I mean that the nature of the human personality, its inner "rules" of organization, is evidently basically similar everywhere. That is, the association of the elements or components of personality do not – and I think in substantial degree *cannot* – vary randomly or even relatively freely. There is evidently a system of inner, or what might be called structural, constraints in the organization of the human personality which increase the probability that those individuals – whatever their culture – who have certain personality traits will also more likely have others which "go with" some particular basic personality system. So far as the future is concerned, moreover, I believe that this structural unity provides the essential basis for greater factual psychic unity of mankind. Such a factual unity, not merely of structure but of *content*, can be attained insofar as the forces which tend to shape men in syndromes such as that defining the modern man become more widely and uniformly diffused throughout the world. This point requires that we consider the second issue to which our research addressed itself.

2. *What are the influences which make a man modern? Can any significant changes be brought about in men who are already past the formative early years and have already reached adulthood as relatively traditional men?* – Education has often been identified as perhaps the most important of the influences moving men away from traditionalism toward modernity in developing countries. Our evidence does not challenge this well-established conclusion. Both in zero-order correlations and in the more complex multivariate regression analysis, the amount of formal schooling a man has had emerges as the single most powerful variable in determining his score on our measures. On the average, for every additional year a man spent in school he gains somewhere between two and three additional points on a scale of modernity scored from zero to 100.

Our modernity test is not mainly a test of what is usually learned in school, such as geography or arithmetic, but is rather a test of attitudes and values touching on basic aspects of a man's orientation to nature, to time, to fate, to politics, to women, and to God. If attending school brings about such substantial changes in these fundamental personal orientations, the school must be teaching a good deal more than is apparent in its syllabus on reading, writing, arithmetic, and even geography. The school is evidently also an important training ground for inculcating values. It teaches ways of orienting oneself toward others, and of conducting oneself, which could have important bearing on the performance of one's adult roles in the structure of modern society. These effects of the school, I believe, reside not mainly in its formal, explicit, self-conscious pedagogic activity, but rather are inherent in the school as an *organization*. The modernizing effects follow not from the school's curriculum, but rather from its informal, implicit, and often unconscious program for dealing with its young charges. The properties of the rational organization as a hidden pursuader – or, as I prefer to put it, as a silent and unobserved teacher – become most apparent when we consider the role of occupational experience in shaping the modern man.

We selected work in factories as the special focus of our attention in seeking to assess the effects of occupational experience in reshaping individuals according to the model of the modern man. Just as we view the school as communicating lessons beyond reading and arithmetic, so we thought of the factory as training men in more than the minimal lessons of technology and the skills necessary to industrial production. We conceived of the factory as an organization serving as a general school in attitudes, values, and ways of behaving which are more adaptive for life in a modern society. We reasoned that work in a factory should increase a man's sense of efficacy, make him less fearful of innovation, and impress on him the value of education as a general qualification for competence and advancement. Furthermore, we assumed that in subtle ways work in a factory might even deepen a man's mastery of arithmetic and broaden his knowledge of geography without the benefit of the formal lessons usually presented in the classroom. Indeed, the slogan for our project became, "The factory can be a school – a school for modernization."

Although our most sanguine hopes for the educational effects of the factory were not wholly fulfilled, the nature of a man's occupational experience does emerge as one of the strongest of the many types of variables we tested and is a quite respectable competitor to education in explaining a person's modernity. The correlation between time spent in factories and individual modernization scores is generally about 0.20. With the effects of education controlled, the factory workers generally score eight to ten points higher on the modernization scale than do the cultivators. There is little reason to interpret this difference as due to selection effects since separate controls show that new workers are not self- or preselected from the village on grounds of already being "modern" in personality or attitude. Nevertheless, we can apply a really stringent test by making our comparisons exclusively within the industrial labor force, pitting men with few years of industrial experience against those with many, for example, five or more. When this is done, factory experience continues to show a substantial impact on individual modernization, the gain generally being about one point per year on the overall measure of modernization (OM).

It is notable that even when we restrict ourselves to tests of verbal fluency and to tests of geographical and political information, the more experienced workers show comparable advantages over the less experienced. To choose but one of many available examples, in Chile among men of rural origin and low education (one to five years) – and therefore suffering a double disadvantage in background – the proportion who could correctly locate Moscow as being the Soviet Russian capital rose from a mere 1 percent among the newly recruited industrial workers to 39 percent among those with middle experience and to 52 percent among the men who had eight years or more in the factory. Even among those with the double advantage of higher education (six to seven years) and urban origins, the proportion correctly identifying Moscow decidedly rose along with increasing industrial experience, the percentages being 68, 81, and 92 for the three levels of industrial experience, respectively. ...

To cite these modernizing effects of the factory is not to minimize the greater absolute impact of schooling. Using a gross occupational categorization which pits cultivators against industrial workers, we find that the classroom still leads the workshop as a school of modernization in the ratio of 3:2. Using the stricter test which utilizes factory workers only, grouped by length of industrial experience, it turns out that every additional year in school produces three times as much increment in one's modernization score as does a year in the factory, that is, the ratio goes to

3:1. The school seems clearly to be the more efficient training ground for individual modernization. Nevertheless, we should keep in mind that the school has the pupil full time, and it produces no incidental by-products other than its pupils. By contrast, the main business of the factory is to manufacture goods, and the changes it brings about in men – not insubstantial, as we have seen – are produced at virtually zero marginal cost. These personality changes in men are therefore a kind of windfall profit to a society undergoing the modernization process. Indeed, on this basis we may quite legitimately reverse the thrust of the argument, no longer asking why the school does so much better than the factory, but rather demanding to know why the school, with its full time control over the pupil's formal learning, does not perform a lot *better* than it does relative to the factory. ...

Our experience with the factory enables us to answer the secondary question posed for this section. Since men generally enter the factory as more or less matured adults, the effects observed to follow upon work in it clearly are late socialization effects. Our results indicate that substantial changes can be made in a man's personality or character, at least in the sense of attitudes, values, and basic orientations, long after what are usually considered the most important formative years. The experience of factory work is, of course, not the only form which this late socialization takes. It may come in the form of travel or migration, by exposure to the media of mass communication, or through later life in the city for men who grew up in the countryside. We therefore combined our explanatory variables into two main sets, one representing *early* socialization experience – as in formal schooling – and the other reflecting *late* socialization experiences – as in one's adult occupation. ... In five countries the set of late socialization variables explained as much or more of the variance in modernization scores as did the combined early socialization variables, each set explaining between one-fourth and one-third of the variance.

In India the early socialization variables were decidedly more powerful – accounting for 52 percent as against 31 percent of the variance explained by the late socialization variables. But in absolute terms, the late experiences are still doing very well. All in all, we take this to be impressive evidence for the possibility of bringing about substantial and extensive changes in the postadolescent personality as a result of socialization in adult roles.

3. *Are there any behavioral consequences arising from the attitudinal modernization of the individual? Do modern men act differently from the traditional man?* – Many people who hear of our research into individual modernization respond to it by acknowledging that we may have discovered what modern man *says*, but they are more interested in knowing what he *does*. This view overlooks the fact that taking a stand on a value question is also an action, and one which is often a very significant one for the respondent. Our critics' comment also tends implicitly to underestimate the importance of a climate of expressed opinion as an influence on the action of others. And it probably assumes too arbitrarily that men use speech mainly to mislead rather than to express their true intentions. Nevertheless, the question is a legitimate one, and we addressed ourselves to it in our research. Although this part of our analysis is least advanced, we can offer some tentative conclusions on the basis of preliminary analysis.

We have the definite impression that the men we delineate as modern not only *talk* differently, they *act* differently. To explore this relationship we constructed a scale of modernization based exclusively on attitudinal questions, rigorously excluding those dealing with action rather than belief or feeling.[1] This measure of attitudinal modernity we then related to the behavioral measures in our survey. In all six countries we found action intimately related to attitude. At any given educational level, the man who was rated as modern on the attitudinal measure was also more likely to have joined voluntary organizations, to receive news from newspapers every day, to have talked to or written to an official about some public issue, and to have discussed politics with his wife. In many cases the proportion who claimed to have taken those actions was twice and even three times greater among those at the top as compared with those at the bottom of the scale of attitudinal modernity. ...

The particular behaviors we cited above are all "self-reported." The question inevitably arises as to whether then we are not merely testing attitudinal consistency – or merely consistency in response – rather than any strict correspondence between modernity of *attitude* and modernity of *behavior.* The answer is partly given by considering the relation of attitudinal modernity to our several tests of information. These questions did not deal with "mere" attitudes, but obliged the respondent to prove objectively whether he really knew something. Quite consistently the men who were more modern on the attitude measures validated their status as modern men by more often correctly identifying a movie camera, naming the office held by Nehru, and locating the city of Moscow. Men with the same education but with unequal modernity scores performed very differently on these tests, with those more modern in attitude scoring high on the tests of information two or more times as often as those classified as traditional in attitude. ...

We conducted a further and more exact check on the extent to which self-reported behavior is fact rather than fantasy by comparing what men claimed to do with objective tests of their actual performance. For example, we asked everyone whether or not he could read. Individuals certainly might have been tempted to exaggerate their qualifications. But later in the interview we administered a simple literacy test, asking our respondents to read a few lines from local newspaper stories we had graded for difficulty. In most settings less than 1 percent of the men who had claimed they could read failed the literacy test. They proved objectively to have been accurately and honestly reporting their reading ability. Similarly, men who claimed to use the mass media regularly were – as they should have been – better able to correctly identify individuals and places figuring prominently in world news. In Nigeria, for example, among experienced workers of low education, the proportion who could correctly identify de Gaulle as the president of the French Republic was 57 percent among those who claimed to pay only modest attention to the mass media, 83 percent among those who asserted they listened or read more often, and 93 percent among those who claimed to read a newspaper or listen to the radio almost every day. ... Clearly, the men who claim to have the attributes we score as modern give a better account of themselves on objective tests of performance. We may conclude not only that modern is as modern does, but also that modern *does* as modern *speaks.*

4. *Is the consequence of the individual modernization inevitably personal disorganization and psychic strain; or can men go through this process of rapid sociocultural change without deleterious consequences?* – Few ideas have been more popular among the social philosophers of the nineteenth and twentieth centuries than the belief that industrialization is a kind of plague which disrupts social organization, destroys cultural cohesion, and uniformly produces personal demoralization and

even disintegration. Much the same idea has been expressed by many anthropologists who fear – and often have witnessed – the destruction of indigenous cultures under the massive impact of their contact with the colossus represented by the European-based colonial empires. But neither the establishment of European industry in the nineteenth century, nor the culture crisis of small preliterate peoples overwhelmed by the tidal wave of colonial expansion may be adequate models for understanding the personal effects of industrialization and urbanization in developing nations.

To test the impact on personal adjustment resulting from contact with modernizing influences in our six developing countries, we administered the Psychosomatic Symptoms Test as part of our regular questionnaire. This test is widely acknowledged to be the best available instrument for cross-cultural assessment of psychic stress. Using groups carefully matched on all other variables, we successively tested the effect of education, migration from the countryside to the city, factory employment, urban residence, and contact with the mass media as these modernizing experiences might affect scores on the Psychosomatic Symptoms Test. No one of these presumably deleterious influences consistently produced statistically significant evidence of psychic stress as judged by the test. Those who moved to the city as against those who continued in the village, those with many years as compared to those with few years of experience in the factory, those with much contact with the mass media as against those with little exposure to radio, newspaper, and movies, show about the same number of psychosomatic symptoms.

In each of six countries, we tested fourteen different matched groups, comparing those who migrated with those who did not; men with more years in the factory with those with fewer, etc. Because some of these matches did not apply in certain countries, we were left with seventy-four more or less independent tests of the proposition that being more exposed to the experiences identified with the process of modernization produces more psychosomatic symptoms. Disregarding the size of the difference and considering only the sign of the correlation between exposure to modernization and psychosomatic symptoms as (+) or (−), it turns out that in thirty-four instances the results are in accord with the theory that modernization is psychologically upsetting, but in forty other matches the results are opposed to the theory. Very few of the differences in either direction, furthermore, were statistically significant. Indeed, the frequency of such statistically significant correlations was about what you would expect by chance. Of these significant differences, furthermore, only two supported the hypothesis while two contradicted it. This again suggests that only chance is at work here. We must conclude, therefore, that the theory which identifies contact with modernizing institutions and geographical and social mobility as certainly deleterious to psychic adjustment is not supported by the evidence. Indeed, it is cast in serious doubt. Whatever is producing the symptoms – and the test does everywhere yield a wide range of scores – it is something other than differential contact with the sources of modernization which is responsible.

Life does exact its toll. Those who have been long in the city and in industry but who have failed to rise in skill and earnings are somewhat more distressed. But this outcome can hardly be charged to the deleterious effects of contact with the modern world. Perhaps if we had studied the unemployed who came to the city with high hopes but failed to find work, we might have found them to have more psychosomatic symptoms. If we were faced with this finding, however, it would still be questionable whether the observed condition should be attributed to the effects of modernization. The fault would seem to lie equally in the inability of traditional agriculture to provide men with economic sustenance sufficient to hold them on the land.

We conclude, then, that modernizing institutions, per se, do not lead to greater psychic stress. We leave open the question whether the process of societal modernization in general increases social disorganization and then increases psychic tension for those experiencing such disorganization. But we are quite ready to affirm that extensive contact with the institutions introduced by modernization – such as the school, the city, the factory, and the mass media – is not in itself conducive to greater psychic stress.

Men change their societies. But the new social structures they have devised may in turn shape the men who live within the new social order. The idea that social structures influence the personal qualities of those who participate in them is, of course, as old as social science and may be found in the writings of the earliest social philosophers. Its most dramatic expression, relevant to us, was in the work of Marx, who enunciated the principle that men's consciousness is merely a reflection of their relation to the system of ownership of the means of production. The rigidity of Marx's determinism, and the counterdetermination of many people to preserve an image of man's spiritual independence and of the personal autonomy and integrity of the individual, generated profound resistance to these ideas. The idea that ownership or nonownership of the means of production determines consciousness is today not very compelling. To focus on ownership, however, is to concentrate on the impact of macrostructural forces in shaping men's attitudes and values at the expense of studying the significance of microstructural factors. Yet it may be that these microstructural features, such as are embedded in the locale and the nature of work, are prime sources of influences on men's attitudes and behavior.

In reviewing the results of our research on modernization, one must be struck by the exceptional stability with which variables such as education, factory experience, and urbanism maintain the absolute and relative strength of their impact on individual modernization despite the great variation in the culture of the men undergoing the experience and in the levels of development characterizing the countries in which they live. This is not to deny the ability of the macrostructural elements of the social order to exert a determining influence on men's life condition and their response to it. But such macrostructural forces can account for only one part of the variance in individual social behavior, a part whose relative weight we have not yet measured with the required precision. When we attain that precision we may find some confirmation of popular theories, but we are also certain to discover some of them to be contradicted by the data – just as we have in our study of microstructural factors. The resolution of the competition between these two theoretical perspectives cannot be attained by rhetoric. It requires systematic measurement and the confrontation of facts however far they are marshalled in the service of ideas. The facts *we* have gathered leave *us* in no doubt that microstructural forces have great power to shape attitudes, values, and behavior in regular ways at standard or constant rates within a wide variety of macrostructural settings.

NOTE

1. In the project identification system this scale is designated OM-1. It includes only seventy-nine items selected from the larger pool by a panel of expert judges on the grounds that (*a*) they dealt only with attitudes, not information, political orientation, or action, and (*b*) they clearly were appropriate to test the original theoretical conception of modernity as more or less "officially" defined by the project staff.

REFERENCES

Dawson, J. L. M. 1967. "Traditional versus Western Attitudes in Africa: The Construction, Validation and Application of a Measuring Device." *British Journal of Social and Clinical Psychology* 6(2): 81–96.

Doob, L. W. 1967. "Scales for Assaying Psychological Modernization in Africa." *Public Opinion Quarterly* 31:414–21.

Kahl, J. A. 1968. *The Measurement of Modernism, a Study of Values in Brazil and Mexico.* Austin and London: University of Texas Press.

Smith, David H., and Alex Inkeles. 1966. "The OM Scale: A Comparative Socio-Psychological Measure of Individual Modernity." *Sociometry* 29:353–77.

9 The Change to Change: Modernization, Development, and Politics (1971) and *Political Order in Changing Societies* (1968)

Samuel Huntington

Harvard political scientist Samuel Huntington emphasized the disruptive nature of modernization. In the first selection, "The Change to Change," Huntington outlines what he and others describe as the "Grand Process of Modernization." It is a process that occurs on many dimensions: it is an individual experience that changes societies; it happens in many different arenas (social, educational, economic, and political); it is an interrelated process; and although it is revolutionary in magnitude, it also is a very slow process that occurs in several stages. The second selection by Huntington, from his 1968 book *Political Order in Changing Societies*, suggests that a modern political system requires not only a high degree of political participation, but also a high level of political institutionalization and organization of politics. Huntington perceives these as the outcome of a process of political modernization that goes well beyond parties, elections, and leaders. Political stability in a modernized political system is only the end result of a multifaceted process of change that includes urbanization, education, a growing middle class, and economic development. The paradox of political modernization that Huntington identifies is that although the end result is a stable political system that allows for universal participation, getting to that point means that a society must pass through extremely disruptive and violent phases in the process. He sees political systems that emerge in developing countries as symptoms of the disruption caused by rapid development.

The Change to Change: Modernization, Development, and Politics

I. Political Science and Political Change

Change is a problem for social science. Sociologists, for instance, have regularly bemoaned their lack of knowledge concerning social change. ... Yet, as opposed to political scientists, the sociologists are relatively well off. Compared with past neglect of the theory of political change in political science, sociology is rich with works on the theory of social change. These more generalized treatments are supplemented by the extensive literature on group dynamics, planned change, organizational change, and the nature of innovation. Until very recently, in contrast, political theory in general has not attempted to deal directly with the problems of change. "Over the last seventy-five years," David Easton wrote in 1953, "political research has confined itself largely to the study of given conditions to the neglect of political change."[1] ...

II. The Context of Modernization

General theory of modernization

The new developments in comparative politics in the 1950s involved extension of the geographical scope of concern from Western Europe and related areas to the non-Western "developing" countries. It was no longer true that political scientists ignored change. Indeed, they seemed almost overwhelmed with the immensity of the changes taking place in the modernizing societies of Asia, Africa, and Latin America. The theory of modernization was embraced by political scientists, and comparative politics was looked at in the context of modernization. The concepts of modernity and tradition bid fair to replace many of the other typologies which had been dear to the hearts of political analysts: democracy, oligarchy, and dictatorship; liberalism and conservatism; totalitarianism and constitutionalism; socialism, communism, and capitalism; nationalism and internationalism. Obviously, these categories were still used. But by the late 1960s, for every discussion among political scientists in which the categories "constitutional" and "totalitarian" were employed, there must have been ten others in which the categories "modern" and "traditional" were used. ...

The essential difference between modern and traditional society, most theorists of modernization contend, lies in the greater control which modern man has over his natural and social environment. This control, in turn, is based on the expansion of scientific and technological knowledge. ... To virtually all theorists, these differences in the extent of man's control over his environment reflect differences in his fundamental attitudes toward and expectations from his environment. The contrast between modern man and traditional man is the source of the contrast between modern society and traditional society. Traditional man is passive and acquiescent; he expects continuity in nature and society and does not believe in the capacity of man to change or to control either. Modern man, in contrast, believes in both the possibility and the desirability of change, and has confidence in the ability of man to control change so as to accomplish his purposes.

At the intellectual level, modern society is characterized by the tremendous accumulation of knowledge about man's environment and by the diffusion of this knowledge through society by means of literacy, mass communications, and education. In contrast to traditional society, modern society also involves much better health, longer life expectancy, and higher rates of occupational and geographical mobility. It is predominantly urban rather than rural. Socially, the family and other primary groups having diffuse roles are supplanted or supplemented in modern society by consciously organized secondary associations having more specific functions. Economically, there is a diversification of activity as a few simple occupations give way to many complex ones; the level of occupational skill and the ratio of capital to labor are much higher than in traditional society. Agriculture declines in importance compared to commercial, industrial, and other nonagricultural activities, and commercial agriculture replaces subsistence agriculture. The geographical scope of economic activity is far greater in modern society than in traditional society, and there is a centralization of such activity at the national level, with the emergence of a national market, national sources of capital, and other national economic institutions. ...

The bridge across the Great Dichotomy between modern and traditional societies is the Grand Process of Modernization. The broad outlines and characteristics of this process are also generally agreed upon by scholars. Most writers on modernization implicitly or explicitly assign nine characteristics to the modernization process.

1. Modernization is a *revolutionary* process. This follows directly from the contrasts between modern and traditional society. The one differs fundamentally from the other, and the change from tradition to modernity consequently involves a radical and total change in patterns of human life. The shift from tradition to modernity, as Cyril Black says, is comparable to the changes from prehuman to human existence and from primitive to civilized societies. The changes in the eighteenth century, Reinhard Bendix echoes, were "comparable in magnitude only to the transformation of nomadic peoples into settled agriculturalists some 10,000 years earlier."[2]

2. Modernization is a *complex* process. It cannot be easily reduced to a single factor or to a single dimension. It involves changes in virtually all areas of human thought and behavior. At a minimum, its components include: industrialization, urbanization, social mobilization, differentiation, secularization, media expansion, increasing literacy and education, expansion of political participation.

3. Modernization is a *systemic* process. Changes in one factor are related to and affect changes in the other factors. Modernization, as Daniel Lerner has expressed it in an oft-quoted phrase, is "a process with some distinctive *quality* of its own, which would explain why modernity is felt as a *consistent whole* among people who live by its rules." The various elements of modernization have been highly associated together "because, in some historic sense, they *had to* go together."[3]

4. Modernization is a *global* process. Modernization originated in fifteenth- and sixteenth-century Europe, but it has now become a worldwide phenomenon. This is brought about primarily through the diffusion of modern ideas and techniques from the European center, but also in part through the endogenous development of non-Western societies. In any event, all societies were at one time traditional; all societies are now either modern or in the process of becoming modern.

5. Modernization is a *lengthy* process. The totality of the changes which modernization involves can only be worked out through time. Consequently, while modernization is revolutionary in the extent of the changes it brings about in traditional society, it is evolutionary in the amount of time required to bring

about those changes. Western societies required several centuries to modernize. The contemporary modernizing societies will do it in less time. Rates of modernization are, in this sense, accelerating, but the time required to move from tradition to modernity will still be measured in generations.

6. Modernization is a *phased* process. It is possible to distinguish different levels or phases of modernization through which all societies will move. Societies obviously begin in the traditional stage and end in the modern stage. The intervening transitional phase, however, can also be broken down into subphases. Societies consequently can be compared and ranked in terms of the extent to which they have moved down the road from tradition to modernity. While the leadership in the process and the more detailed patterns of modernization will differ from one society to another, all societies will move through essentially the same stages.

7. Modernization is a *homogenizing* process. Many different types of traditional societies exist; indeed, traditional societies, some argue, have little in common except their lack of modernity. Modern societies, on the other hand, share basic similarities. Modernization produces tendencies toward convergence among societies. Modernization involves movement "toward an interdependence among politically organized societies and toward an ultimate integration of societies." The "universal imperatives of modern ideas and institutions" may lead to a stage "at which the various societies are so homogeneous as to be capable of forming a world state. ..."[4]

8. Modernization is an *irreversible* process. While there may be temporary breakdowns and occasional reversals in elements of the modernizing process, modernization as a whole is an essentially secular trend. A society which has reached certain levels of urbanization, literacy, industrialization in one decade will not decline to substantially lower levels in the next decade. The rates of change will vary significantly from one society to another, but the direction of change will not.

9. Modernization is *a progressive* process. The traumas of modernization are many and profound, but in the long run modernization is not only inevitable, it is also desirable. The costs and the pains of the period of transition, particularly its early phases, are great, but the achievement of a modern social, political, and economic order is worth them. Modernization in the long run enhances human well-being, culturally and materially. ...

Political Order in Changing Societies

I. Political Order and Political Decay

The Political Gap

The most important political distinction among countries concerns not their form of government but their degree of government. The differences between democracy and dictatorship are less than the differences between those countries whose politics embodies consensus, community, legitimacy, organization, effectiveness, stability, and those countries whose politics is deficient in these qualities. Communist totalitarian states and Western liberal states both belong generally in the category of effective rather than debile political systems. The United States, Great Britain, and the Soviet Union have different forms of government, but in all three systems the government governs. Each country is a political community with an overwhelming consensus among the people on the legitimacy of the political system. In each country the citizens and their leaders share a vision of the public interest of the society and of the traditions and principles upon which the political community is based. All three countries have strong, adaptable, coherent political institutions: effective bureaucracies, well-organized political parties, a high degree of popular participation in public affairs, working systems of civilian control over the military, extensive activity by the government in the economy, and reasonably effective procedures for regulating succession and controlling political conflict. These governments command the loyalties of their citizens and thus have the capacity to tax resources, to conscript manpower, and to innovate and to execute policy. If the Politburo, the Cabinet, or the President makes a decision, the probability is high that it will be implemented through the government machinery.

In all these characteristics the political systems of the United States, Great Britain, and the Soviet Union differ significantly from the governments which exist in many, if not most, of the modernizing countries of Asia, Africa, and Latin America. These countries lack many things. They suffer real shortages of food, literacy, education, wealth, income, health, and productivity, but most of them have been recognized and efforts made to do something about them. Beyond and behind these shortages, however, there is a greater shortage: a shortage of political community and of effective, authoritative, legitimate government. ...

With a few notable exceptions, the political evolution of these countries after World War II was characterized by increasing ethnic and class conflict, recurring rioting and mob violence, frequent military coups d'état, the dominance of unstable personalistic leaders who often pursued disastrous economic and social policies, widespread and blatant corruption among cabinet ministers and civil servants, arbitrary infringement of the rights and liberties of citizens, declining standards of bureaucratic efficiency and performance, the pervasive alienation of urban political groups, the loss of authority by legislatures and courts, and the fragmentation and at times complete disintegration of broadly based political parties. ...

During the 1950s and 1960s the numerical incidence of political violence and disorder increased dramatically in most countries of the world. The year 1958, according to one calculation, witnessed some 28 prolonged guerrilla insurgencies, four military uprisings, and two conventional wars. Seven years later, in 1965, 42 prolonged insurgencies were underway; ten military revolts occurred; and five conventional conflicts were being fought. Political instability also increased significantly during the 1950s and 1960s. Violence and other destabilizing events were five times more frequent between 1955 and 1962 than they were between 1948 and 1954. Sixty-four of 84 countries were less stable in the latter period than in the earlier one.[5] Throughout Asia, Africa, and Latin America there was a decline in political order, an undermining of the authority, effectiveness, and legitimacy of government. There was a lack of civic morale and public spirit and of political institutions capable of giving meaning and direction to the public interest. Not political development but political decay dominated the scene. ...

What was responsible for this violence and instability? The primary thesis of this book is that it was in large part the product of rapid social change and the rapid mobilization of new groups into politics coupled with the slow development of political institutions. "Among the laws that rule human societies," de Tocqueville observed, "there is one which seems to be more precise and clear than all others. If men are to remain civilized or to become so, the art of associating together must grow and improve in the same ratio in which the equality of conditions is increased."[6] The political instability in Asia, Africa, and Latin America derives precisely from the failure to meet this condition: equality of political participation is growing much more rapidly than "the art of associating together." Social and economic change – urbanization, increases in literacy and education, industrialization, mass media expansion – extend political consciousness, multiply political demands, broaden political participation. These changes undermine traditional sources of political authority and traditional political institutions; they enormously complicate the problems of creating new bases of political association and new political institutions combining legitimacy and effectiveness. The rates of social mobilization and the expansion of political participation are high; the rates of political organization and institutionalization are low. The result is political instability and disorder. The primary problem of politics is the lag in the development of political institutions behind social and economic change.

For two decades after World War II American foreign policy failed to come to grips with this problem. The economic gap, in contrast to the political gap, was the target of sustained attention, analysis, and action. Aid programs and loan programs, the World Bank and regional banks, the UN and the OECD, consortia and combines, planners and politicians, all shared in a massive effort to do something about the problem of economic development. Who, however, was concerned with the political gap? American officials recognized that the United States had a primary interest in the creation of viable political regimes in modernizing countries. But few, if any, of all the activities of the American government affecting those countries were directly concerned with the promotion of political stability and the reduction of the political gap. How can this astonishing lacuna be explained?

It would appear to be rooted in two distinct aspects of the American historical experience. In confronting the modernizing countries the United States was handicapped by its happy history. In its development the United States was blessed with more than its fair share of economic plenty, social well-being, and political stability. This pleasant conjuncture of blessings led Americans to believe in the unity of goodness: to assume that all good things go together and that the achievement of one desirable social goal aids in the achievement of others. In American policy toward modernizing countries this experience was reflected in the belief that political stability would be the natural and inevitable result of the achievement of, first, economic development and then of social reform. Throughout the 1950s the prevailing assumption of American policy was that economic development – the elimination of poverty, disease, illiteracy – was necessary for political development and political stability. In American thinking the causal chain was: economic assistance promotes economic development, economic development promotes political stability. This dogma was enshrined in legislation and, perhaps more important, it was ingrained in the thinking of officials in AID and other agencies concerned with the foreign assistance programs.

If political decay and political instability were more rampant in Asia, Africa, and Latin America in 1965 than they were fifteen years earlier, it was in part because American policy reflected this erroneous dogma. For in fact, economic development and political stability are two independent goals and progress toward one has no necessary connection with progress toward the other. In some instances programs of economic development may promote political stability; in other instances they may seriously undermine such stability. So also, some forms of political stability may encourage economic growth; other forms may discourage it. India was one of the poorest countries in the world in the 1950s and had only a modest rate of economic growth. Yet through the Congress Party it achieved a high degree of political stability. Per capita incomes in Argentina and Venezuela were perhaps ten times that in India, and Venezuela had a phenomenal rate of economic growth. Yet for both countries stability remained an elusive goal.

With the Alliance for Progress in 1961, social reform – that is, the more equitable distribution of material and symbolic resources – joined economic development as a conscious and explicit goal of American policy toward modernizing countries. This development was, in part, a reaction to the Cuban Revolution, and it reflected the assumption among policymakers that land and tax reforms, housing projects, and welfare programs would reduce social tensions and deactivate the fuse to Fidelismo. Once again political stability was to be the by-product of the achievement of another socially desirable goal. In fact, of course, the relationship between social reform and political stability resembles that between economic development and political stability. In some circumstances reforms may reduce tensions and encourage peaceful rather than violent change. In other circumstances, however, reform may well exacerbate tensions, precipitate violence, and be a catalyst of rather than a substitute for revolution.

A second reason for American indifference to political development was the absence in the American historical experience of the need to found a political order. Americans, de Tocqueville said, were born equal and hence never had to worry about creating equality; they enjoyed the fruits of a democratic revolution without having suffered one. So also, America was born with a government, with political institutions and practices imported from seventeenth-century England. Hence Americans never had to worry about creating a government. This gap in historical experience made them peculiarly blind to the problems of creating effective authority in modernizing countries. When an American thinks about the problem of government-building, he directs himself not to the creation of authority and the accumulation of power but rather to the limitation of authority and the division of power. Asked to design a government, he comes up with a written constitution, bill of rights, separation of powers, checks and balances, federalism, regular elections, competitive parties – all excellent devices for limiting government. The Lockean American is so fundamentally anti-government that he identifies government with restrictions on government. Confronted with the need to design a political system which will maximize power and authority, he has no ready answer. His general formula is that governments should be based on free and fair elections.

In many modernizing societies this formula is irrelevant. Elections to be meaningful presuppose a certain level of political organization. The problem is not to hold elections but to create organizations. In many, if not most, modernizing countries elections serve only to enhance the power of disruptive and often reactionary social forces and to tear down the structure of public authority. "In framing a government which is to be administered by men over men," Madison warned in *The Federalist*, No. 51, "the great difficulty lies in this: you must first enable the government to control the governed; and in the next place oblige it to control itself." In many modernizing countries governments are still unable to perform the first function, much less the second. The primary problem is not liberty but the creation of a legitimate public order. Men may, of course, have order without liberty, but they cannot have liberty without order. Authority has to exist before it can be limited, and it is authority that is in scarce supply in those modernizing countries where government is at the mercy of alienated intellectuals, rambunctious colonels, and rioting students.

It is precisely this scarcity that communist and communist-type movements are often able to overcome. History shows conclusively that communist governments are no better than free governments in alleviating famine, improving health, expanding national product, creating industry, and maximizing welfare. But the one thing communist governments can do is to govern; they do provide effective authority. Their ideology furnishes a basis of legitimacy, and their party organization provides the institutional mechanism for mobilizing support and executing policy. ... The real challenge which the communists pose to modernizing countries is not that they are so good at overthrowing governments (which is easy), but that they are so good at making governments (which is a far more difficult task). They may not provide liberty, but they do provide authority; they do create governments that can govern. ...

Political Participation: Modernization and Political Decay

Modernization and Political Consciousness

... Those aspects of modernization most relevant to politics can be broadly grouped into two categories. First, social mobilization, in Deutsch's formulation, is the process by which "major clusters of old social, economic and psychological commitments are eroded or broken and people become available for new patterns of socialization and behavior."[7] It means a change in the attitudes, values, and expectations of people from those associated with the traditional world to those common to the modern world. It is a consequence of literacy, education, increased communications, mass media exposure, and urbanization. Secondly, economic development refers to the growth in the total economic activity and output of a society. It may be measured by per capita gross national product, level of industrialization, and level of individual welfare gauged by such indices as life expectancy, caloric intake, supply of hospitals and doctors. Social mobilization involves changes in the aspirations of individuals, groups, and societies; economic development involves changes in their capabilities. Modernization requires both. ... the most crucial aspects of political modernization can be roughly subsumed under three broad headings. First, political modernization involves the rationalization of authority, the replacement of a large number of traditional, religious, familial, and ethnic political authorities by a single secular, national political authority. This change implies that government is the product of man, not of nature or of God, and that a well-ordered society must have a determinate human source of final authority, obedience to whose positive law takes precedence over other obligations. Political modernization involves assertion of the external sovereignty of the nation-state against transnational influences and of the internal sovereignty of the national government against local and regional powers. It means national integration and the centralization or accumulation of power in recognized national lawmaking institutions.

Secondly, political modernization involves the differentiation of new political functions and the development of specialized structures to perform those functions. Areas of particular competence – legal, military, administrative, scientific – become separated from the political realm, and autonomous, specialized, but subordinate organs arise to discharge those tasks. Administrative hierarchies become more elaborate, more complex, more disciplined. Office and power are distributed more by achievement and less by ascription. Thirdly, political modernization involves increased participation in politics by social groups throughout society. Broadened participation in politics may enhance control of the people by the government, as in totalitarian states, or it may enhance control of the government by the people, as in some democratic ones. But in all modern states the citizens become directly involved in and affected by governmental affairs. Rationalized authority, differentiated structure, and mass participation thus distinguish modern polities from antecedent polities.

It is, however, a mistake to conclude that in practice modernization means the rationalization of authority, differentiation of structure, and expansion of political participation. A basic and frequently overlooked distinction exists between political modernization defined as movement from a traditional to a modern polity and political modernization defined as the political aspects and political effects of social, economic, and cultural modernization. The former posits the direction in which political change theoretically should move. The latter describes the political changes which actually occur in modernizing countries. The gap between the two is often vast. Modernization in practice always involves change in and usually the disintegration of a traditional political system, but it does not necessarily involve significant movement toward a modern political system. Yet the tendency has been to assume that what is true for the broader social processes of modernization is also true for political changes. Social modernization, in some degree, is a fact in Asia, Africa, Latin America: urbanization is rapid, literacy is slowly increasing; industrialization is being pushed; per capita gross national product is inching upward; mass media circulation is expanding. All these are facts. In contrast progress toward many of the other goals which writers have identified with political modernization – democracy, stability, structural differentiation, achievement patterns, national integration – often is dubious at best. Yet the tendency is to think that because social modernization is taking place, political modernization also must be taking place. ...

In actuality, only some of the tendencies frequently encompassed in the concept "political modernization" characterized the "modernizing" areas. Instead of a trend toward competitiveness and democracy, there was an "erosion of democracy" and a tendency to autocratic military regimes and one-party regimes.[8] Instead of stability, there were repeated coups and revolts. Instead of a unifying nationalism and nation-building, there were repeated ethnic conflicts and civil wars. Instead of institutional rationalization and differentiation, there was frequently a decay of the administrative organizations inherited from the colonial era and a weakening and disruption of the political organizations developed during the struggle for independence. Only the concept of political modernization as mobilization and participation appeared to be generally applicable to the "developing" world. Rationalization, integration, and differentiation, in contrast, seemed to have only a dim relation to reality.

More than by anything else, the modern state is distinguished from the traditional state by the broadened extent to which people participate in politics and are affected by politics in large-scale political units. ...

The disruptive effects of social and economic modernization on politics and political institutions take many forms. Social and economic changes necessarily disrupt traditional social and political groupings and undermine loyalty to traditional authorities. ... Modernization thus tends to produce alienation and anomie, normlessness generated by the conflict of old values and new. The new values undermine the old bases of association and of authority before new skills, motivations, and resources can be brought into existence to create new groupings.

The breakup of traditional institutions may lead to psychological disintegration and anomie, but these very conditions also create the need for new identifications and loyalties. The latter may take the form of reidentification with a group which existed in latent or actual form in traditional society or they may lead to identification with a new set of symbols or a new group which has itself evolved in the process of modernization. Industrialization, Marx argued, produces class consciousness first in the bourgeoisie and then in the proletariat. Marx focused on only one minor aspect of a much more general phenomenon. Industrialization is only one aspect of modernization and modernization induces not just class consciousness but new group consciousness of all kinds: in tribe, region, clan, religion, and caste, as well as in class, occupation, and association. Modernization means that all groups, old as well as new, traditional as well as modern, become increasingly aware of themselves as groups and of their interests and claims in relation to other groups. One of the most striking phenomena of modernization, indeed, is the increased consciousness, coherence, organization, and action which it produces in many social forces which existed on a much lower level of conscious identity and organization in traditional society. ... The same group consciousness, however, can also be a major obstacle to the creation of effective political institutions encompassing a broader spectrum of social forces. Along with group consciousness, group prejudice also "develops when there is intensive contact between different groups, such as has accompanied the movement toward more centralized political and social organizations."[9] And along with group prejudice comes group conflict. Ethnic or religious groups which had lived peacefully side by side in traditional society become aroused to violent conflict as a result of the interaction, the tensions, the inequalities generated by social and economic modernization. Modernization thus increases conflict among traditional groups, between traditional groups and modern ones, and among modern groups. The new elites based on Western or modern education come into conflict with the traditional elites whose authority rests on ascribed and inherited status. Within the modernized elites, antagonisms arise between politicians and bureaucrats, intellectuals and soldiers, labor leaders and businessmen. Many, if not most, of these conflicts at one time or another erupt into violence.

Modernization and Violence

[. . .]

The Gap Hypothesis.   Social mobilization is much more destabilizing than economic development. The gap between these two forms of change furnishes some measure of the impact of modernization on political stability. Urbanization, literacy, education, mass media, all expose the traditional man to new forms of life, new standards of enjoyment, new possibilities of satisfaction. These experiences break the cognitive and attitudinal barriers of the traditional culture and promote new levels of aspirations and wants. The ability of a transitional society to satisfy these new aspirations, however, increases much more slowly than the aspirations themselves. Consequently, a gap develops between aspiration and expectation, want formation and want satisfaction, or the aspirations function and the level-of-living function.[10] This gap generates social frustration and dissatisfaction. In practice, the extent of the gap provides a reasonable index to political instability.

The reasons for this relationship between social frustration and political instability are somewhat more complicated than they may appear on the surface. The relationship is, in large part, due to the absence of two potential intervening variables: opportunities for social and economic mobility and adaptable political institutions. . . . Consequently, the extent to which social frustration produces political participation depends in large part on the nature of the economic and social structure of the traditional society. Conceivably this frustration could be removed through social and economic mobility if the traditional society is sufficiently "open" to offer opportunities for such mobility. In part, this is precisely what occurs in rural areas, where outside opportunities for horizontal mobility (urbanization) contribute to the relative stability of the countryside in most modernizing countries. The few opportunities for vertical (occupational and income) mobility within the cities, in turn, contribute to their greater instability. Apart from urbanization, however, most modernizing countries have low levels of social-economic mobility. In relatively few societies are the traditional structures likely to encourage economic rather than political activity. Land and any other types of economic wealth in the traditional society are tightly held by a relatively small oligarchy or are controlled by foreign corporations and investors. The values of the traditional society often are hostile to entrepreneurial roles, and such roles consequently may be largely monopolized by an ethnic minority (Greeks and Armenians in the Ottoman Empire; Chinese in southeast Asia; Lebanese in Africa). In addition, the modern values and ideas which are introduced into the system often stress the primacy of government (socialism, the planned economy), and consequently may also lead mobilized individuals to shy away from entrepreneurial roles.

In these conditions, political participation becomes the road for advancement of the socially mobilized individual. Social frustration leads to demands on the government and the expansion of political participation to enforce those demands. The political backwardness of the country in terms of political institutionalization, moreover, makes it difficult if not impossible for the demands upon the government to be expressed through legitimate channels and to be moderated and aggregated within the political system. Hence the sharp increase in political participation gives rise to political instability. ...

Political instability in modernizing countries is thus in large part a function of the gap between aspirations and expectations produced by the escalation of aspirations which particularly occurs in the early phases of modernization. ... Modernization affects economic inequality and thus political instability in two ways. First, wealth and income are normally more unevenly distributed in poor countries than in economically developed countries.[11] In a traditional society this inequality is accepted as part of the natural pattern of life. Social mobilization, however, increases awareness of the inequality and presumably resentment of it. The influx of new ideas calls into question the legitimacy of the old distribution and suggests the feasibility and the desirability of a more equitable distribution of income. The obvious way of achieving a rapid change in income distribution is through government. Those who command the income, however, usually also command the government. Hence social mobilization turns the traditional economic inequality into a stimulus to rebellion.

Secondly, in the long run, economic development produces a more equitable distribution of income than existed in the traditional society. In the short run, however, the immediate impact of economic growth is often to exacerbate income inequalities. The gains of rapid economic growth are often concentrated in a few groups while the losses are diffused among many; as a result, the number of people getting poorer in the society may actually increase. Rapid growth often involves inflation; in inflation prices typically rise faster than wages with consequent tendencies toward a more unequal distribution of wealth. The impact of Western legal systems in non-Western societies often encourages the replacement of communal forms of land ownership with private ownership and thus tends to produce greater inequalities in land ownership than existed in the traditional society. In addition, in less developed societies the distribution of income in the more modern, non-agricultural sector is typically more unequal than it is in the agricultural. In rural India in 1950, for instance, 5 per cent of the families received 28.9 per cent of the income; but in urban India 5 per cent of the families received 61.5 per cent of the income.[12] Since the overall distribution of income is more equal in the less agricultural, developed nations, the distribution of income within the nonagricultural sector of an underdeveloped country is much more unequal than it is in the same sector in a developed country. ...

Economic development increases economic inequality at the same time that social mobilization decreases the legitimacy of that inequality. Both aspects of modernization combine to produce political instability.

NOTES

1. David Easton, *The Political System* (New York, 1953), p. 42.
2. Cyril E. Black, *The Dynamics of Modernization* (New York, 1966), pp. 1–5; Reinhard Bendix, "Tradition and Modernity Reconsidered," *Comparative Studies in Society and History*, IX (April 1967), 292–3.
3. Daniel Lerner, *The Passing of Traditional Society* (Glencoe, 1958), p. 438.
4. Black, *Dynamics of Modernization*, pp. 155, 174.
5. Wallace W. Conroe, "A Cross-National Analysis of the Impact of Modernization Upon Political Stability" (unpublished MA thesis, San Diego State College, 1965), pp. 52–4, 60–2; Ivo K. and Rosalind L. Feierabend, "Aggressive Behaviors Within Polities, 1948–1962: A Cross-National Study," *Journal of Conflict Resolution*, 10 (Sept. 1966), 253–4.
6. Alexis de Toqueville, *Democracy in America* (ed. Phillips Bradley, New York, Knopf, 1955), 2, 118.
7. Karl W. Deutsch, "Social Mobilization and Political Development," *American Political Science Review*, 55 (Sept. 1961), 494.
8. On the "erosion of democracy" and political instability, see Rupert Emerson, *From Empire to Nation* (Cambridge, Harvard University Press, 1960), ch. 5; and Michael Brecher, *The New States of Asia* (London, Oxford University Press, 1963), ch. 2.
9. Robert A. LeVine and Donald T. Campbell, "Report on Preliminary Results of Cross-Cultural Study of Ethnocentrism," *Carnegie Corporation of New York Quarterly* (Jan. 1966), 7.
10. These are terms employed by Deutsch, "Social Mobilization," pp. 493 ff.; James C. Davies, "Toward a Theory of Revolution," *American Sociological Review*, 27 (Feb. 1952), 5 ff.; Feierabend, "Aggressive Behaviors," pp. 256–62; Charles Wolf, *Foreign Aid: Theory and Practice in Southern Asia* (Princeton, Princeton University Press, 1960), pp. 296 ff.; and Manus Midlarsky and Raymond Tanter, "Toward a Theory of Political Instability in Latin America," *Journal of Peace Research*, 4 (1967), 271 ff.
11. See Simon Kuznets, "Qualitative Aspects of the Economic Growth of Nations: VIII. Distribution of Income by Size," *Economic Development and Cultural Change*, 11 (Jan. 1963), 68; UN Social Commission, *Preliminary Report on the World Social Situation* (New York, United Nations, 1952), pp. 132–3; Gunnar Myrdal, *An International Economy* (New York, Harper, 1956), p. 133.
12. Kuznets, "Qualitative Aspects," pp. 46–58.

Part III

Blaming the Victims? Dependency and World-Systems Theories Respond

10 The Development of Underdevelopment (1969)

Andre Gunder Frank

Andre Gunder Frank was born in Berlin in 1929, educated in the USA, and between 1963 and 1973 taught at universities in Brazil, Mexico, and Chile. While preceded by Chile-based United Nations ECLA scholars such as Raúl Prebisch, Paul Baran, and Fernando Henrique Cardoso, Gunder Frank was the first major dependency theorist to write in English. He brought back with him a succinct and controversial set of ideas that were an attractive foil to the dominant modernization perspective. Furthermore, the popularization of Gunder Frank's dependency theory was really the first time that Western theorists embraced an explanation of why poorer nations are poor that actually came from those poorer nations. Gunder Frank characterized the poverty of less developed nations and their dependence on wealthier nations as inescapable; his radical version of dependency theory claimed that relations of imperialism and domination trapped poor nations at the bottom of the global economy. According to Gunder Frank, at the same time that capitalism produces wealth and furthers development in the "core" countries, it creates poverty and underdevelopment in the "satellite" countries. This underdevelopment will not just go away with time or social change; their only recourse is to strongly protect their markets from the rich countries.

I

We cannot hope to formulate adequate development theory and policy for the majority of the world's population who suffer from underdevelopment without first learning how their past economic and social history gave rise to their present underdevelopment. Yet most historians study only the developed metropolitan countries and pay scant attention to the colonial and underdeveloped lands. For this reason most of our theoretical categories and guides to development policy have been distilled exclusively from the historical experience of the European and North American advanced capitalist nations.

Since the historical experience of the colonial and underdeveloped countries has demonstrably been quite different, available theory therefore fails to reflect the past of the underdeveloped part of the world entirely, and reflects the past of the world as a whole only in part. More important, our ignorance of the underdeveloped countries' history leads us to assume that their past and indeed their present resembles earlier stages of the history of the now developed countries. This ignorance and this assumption lead us into serious misconceptions about contemporary underdevelopment and development. Further, most studies of development and underdevelopment fail to take account of the economic and other relations between the metropolis and its economic colonies throughout the history of the world-wide expansion and development of the mercantilist and capitalist system. Consequently, most of our theory fails to explain the structure and development of the capitalist system as a whole and to account for its simultaneous generation of underdevelopment in some of its parts and of economic development in others.

It is generally held that economic development occurs in a succession of capitalist stages and that today's underdeveloped countries are still in a stage, sometimes depicted as an original stage of history, through which the now developed countries passed long ago. Yet even a modest acquaintance with history shows that under-development is not original or traditional and that neither the past nor the present of the underdeveloped countries resembles in any important respect the past of the now developed countries. The now developed countries were never *under*developed, though they may have been *un*developed. It is also widely believed that the con-temporary underdevelopment of a country can be understood as the product or reflection solely of its own economic, political, social, and cultural characteristics or structure. Yet historical research demonstrates that contemporary underdevelop-ment is in large part the historical product of past and continuing economic and other relations between the satellite underdeveloped and the now developed metro-politan countries. Furthermore, these relations are an essential part of the structure and development of the capitalist system on a world scale as a whole. A related and also largely erroneous view is that the development of these underdeveloped coun-tries and, within them of their most underdeveloped domestic areas, must and will be generated or stimulated by diffusing capital, institutions, values, etc., to them from the international and national capitalist metropoles. Historical perspective based on the underdeveloped countries' past experience suggests that on the contrary in the underdeveloped countries economic development can now occur only independently of most of these relations of diffusion.

Evident inequalities of income and differences in culture have led many observers to see "dual" societies and economies in the underdeveloped countries. Each of the two parts is supposed to have a history of its own, a structure, and a contemporary dynamic largely independent of the other. Supposedly, only one part of the economy and society has been importantly affected by intimate economic relations with the "outside" capitalist world; and that part, it is held, became modern, capitalist, and relatively developed precisely because of this contact. The other part is widely regarded as variously isolated, subsistence-based, feudal, or precapitalist, and there-fore more underdeveloped.

I believe on the contrary that the entire "dual society" thesis is false and that the policy recommendations to which it leads will, if acted upon, serve only to intensify and perpetuate the very conditions of underdevelopment they are supposedly designed to remedy.

A mounting body of evidence suggests, and I am confident that future historical research will confirm, that the expansion of the capitalist system over the past centuries effectively and entirely penetrated even the apparently most isolated sectors of the underdeveloped world. Therefore, the economic, political, social, and cultural institutions and relations we now observe there are the products of the historical development of the capitalist system no less than are the seemingly more modern or capitalist features of the national metropoles of these underdeveloped countries. Analogously to the relations between development and underdevelopment on the international level, the contemporary underdeveloped institutions of the so-called backward or feudal domestic areas of an underdeveloped country are no less the product of the single historical process of capitalist development than are the so-called capitalist institutions of the supposedly more progressive areas. In this paper I should like to sketch the kinds of evidence which support this thesis and at the same time indicate lines along which further study and research could fruitfully proceed.

II

The Secretary General of the Latin American Center for Research in the Social Sciences writes in that Center's journal: "The privileged position of the city has its origin in the colonial period. It was founded by the Conqueror to serve the same ends that it still serves today; to incorporate the indigenous population into the economy brought and developed by that Conqueror and his descendants. The regional city was an instrument of conquest and is still today an instrument of domination."[1] The Instituto Nacional Indigenista (National Indian Institute) of Mexico confirms this observation when it notes that "the mestizo population, in fact, always lives in a city, a center of an intercultural region, which acts as the metropolis of a zone of indigenous population and which maintains with the underdeveloped communities an intimate relation which links the center with the satellite communities."[2] The Institute goes on to point out that "between the mestizos who live in the nuclear city of the region and the Indians who live in the peasant hinterland there is in reality a closer economic and social interdependence than might at first glance appear" and that the provincial metropoles "by being centers of intercourse are also centers of exploitation."[3]

Thus these metropolis–satellite relations are not limited to the imperial or international level but penetrate and structure the very economic, political, and social life of the Latin American colonies and countries. Just as the colonial and national capital and its export sector become the satellite of the Iberian (and later of other) metropoles of the world economic system, this satellite immediately becomes a colonial and then a national metropolis with respect to the productive sectors and population of the interior. Furthermore, the provincial capitals, which thus are themselves satellites of the national metropolis – and through the latter of the world metropolis – are in turn provincial centers around which their own local satellites orbit. Thus, a whole chain of constellations of metropoles and satellites relates all parts of the whole system from its metropolitan center in Europe or the United States to the farthest outpost in the Latin American countryside.

When we examine this metropolis–satellite structure, we find that each of the satellites, including now-underdeveloped Spain and Portugal, serves as an instrument to suck capital or economic surplus out of its own satellites and to channel part of this surplus to the world metropolis of which all are satellites. Moreover, each national and local metropolis serves to impose and maintain the monopolistic structure and exploitative relationship of this system (as the Instituto Nacional Indigenista of Mexico calls it) as long as it serves the interests of the metropoles which take advantage of this global, national, and local structure to promote their own development and the enrichment of their ruling classes.

These are the principal and still surviving structural characteristics which were implanted in Latin America by the Conquest. Beyond examining the establishment of this colonial structure in its historical context, the proposed approach calls for study of the development – and underdevelopment – of these metropoles and satellites of Latin America throughout the following and still continuing historical process. In this way we can understand why there were and still are tendencies in the Latin American and world capitalist structure which seem to lead to the development of the metropolis and the underdevelopment of the satellite and why, particularly, the satellized national, regional, and local metropoles in Latin America find that their economic development is at best a limited or underdeveloped development.

III

That present underdevelopment of Latin America is the result of its centuries-long participation in the process of world capitalist development, I believe I have shown in my case studies of the economic and social histories of Chile and Brazil. My study of Chilean history suggests that the Conquest not only incorporated this country fully into the expansion and development of the world mercantile and later industrial capitalist system but that it also introduced the monopolistic metropolis–satellite structure and development of capitalism into the Chilean domestic economy and society itself. This structure then penetrated and permeated all of Chile very quickly. Since that time and in the course of world and Chilean history during the epochs of colonialism, free trade, imperialism, and the present, Chile has become increasingly marked by the economic, social, and political structure of satellite underdevelopment. This development of underdevelopment continues today, both in Chile's still increasing satellization by the world metropolis and through the ever more acute polarization of Chile's domestic economy.

The history of Brazil is perhaps the clearest case of both national and regional development of underdevelopment. The expansion of the world economy since the beginning of the sixteenth century successively converted the Northeast, the Minas Gerais interior, the North, and the Center-South (Rio de Janeiro, São Paulo, and Paraná) into export economies and incorporated them into the structure and development of the world capitalist system. Each of these regions experienced what may have appeared as economic development during the period of its respective golden age. But it was a satellite development which was neither self-generating nor self-perpetuating. As the market or the productivity of the first three regions declined, foreign and domestic economic interest in them waned; and they were left to develop the underdevelopment they live today. In the fourth region, the coffee economy experienced a similar though not yet quite as serious fate (though the development of a synthetic coffee substitute promises to deal it a mortal blow in the not too distant future). All of this historical evidence contradicts the generally accepted theses that Latin America suffers from a dual society or from the survival of feudal institutions and that these are important obstacles to its economic development.

IV

During the First World War, however, and even more during the Great Depression and the Second World War, São Paulo began to build up an industrial establishment which is the largest in Latin America today. The question arises whether this industrial development did or can break Brazil out of the cycle of satellite development and underdevelopment which has characterized its other regions and national history within the capitalist system so far. I believe that the answer is no. Domestically the evidence so far is fairly clear. The development of industry in São Paulo has not brought greater riches to the other regions of Brazil. Instead, it converted them into internal colonial satellites, de-capitalized them further, and consolidated or even deepened their underdevelopment. There is little evidence to suggest that this process is likely to be reversed in the foreseeable future except insofar as the provincial poor migrate and become the poor of the metropolitan cities. Externally, the evidence is that although the initial development of São Paulo's industry was relatively autonomous it is being increasingly satellized by the world capitalist metropolis and its future development possibilities are increasingly restricted. This development, my studies lead me to believe, also appears destined to limited or underdeveloped development as long as it takes place in the present economic, political, and social framework.

We must conclude, in short, that underdevelopment is not due to the survival of archaic institutions and the existence of capital shortage in regions that have remained isolated from the stream of world history. On the contrary, underdevelopment was and still is generated by the very same historical process which also generated economic development: the development of capitalism itself. This view, I am glad to say, is gaining adherents among students of Latin America and is proving its worth in shedding new light on the problems of the area and in affording a better perspective for the formulation of theory and policy.

V

The same historical and structural approach can also lead to better development theory and policy by generating a series of hypotheses about development and underdevelopment such as those I am testing in my current research. The hypotheses are derived from the empirical observation and theoretical assumption that within this world-embracing metropolis–satellite structure the metropoles tend to develop and the satellites to underdevelop. The first hypothesis has already been mentioned above: that in contrast to the development of the world metropolis which is no one's satellite, the development of the national and other subordinate metropoles is limited by their satellite status. It is perhaps more difficult to test this hypothesis than the following ones because part of its confirmation depends on the test of the other hypotheses. Nonetheless, this hypothesis appears to be generally confirmed by the non-autonomous and unsatisfactory economic and especially industrial development of Latin America's national metropoles, as documented in the studies already cited. The most important and at the same time most confirmatory examples are the metropolitan regions of Buenos Aires and São Paulo whose growth only began in the nineteenth century, was therefore largely untrammelled by any colonial heritage, but was and remains a satellite development largely dependent on the outside metropolis, first of Britain and then of the United States.

A second hypothesis is that the satellites experience their greatest economic development and especially their most classically capitalist industrial development if and when their ties to their metropolis are weakest. This hypothesis is almost diametrically opposed to the generally accepted thesis that development in the underdeveloped countries follows from the greatest degree of contact with and diffusion from the metropolitan developed countries. This hypothesis seems to be confirmed by two kinds of relative isolation that Latin America has experienced in the course of its history. One is the temporary isolation caused by the crises of war or depression in the world metropolis. Apart from minor ones, five periods of such major crises stand out and seem to confirm the hypothesis. These are: the European (and especially Spanish) Depression of the seventeenth century, the Napoleonic Wars, the First World War, the Depression of the 1930's, and the Second World War. It is clearly established and generally recognized that the most important recent industrial development – especially of Argentina, Brazil, and Mexico, but also of other countries such as Chile – has taken place precisely during the periods of the two World Wars and the intervening Depression. Thanks to the consequent loosening of trade and investment ties during these periods, the satellites initiated marked autonomous industrialization and growth. Historical research demonstrates that the same thing happened in Latin America during Europe's seventeenth-century depression. Manufacturing grew in the Latin American countries, and several of them such as Chile became exporters of manufactured goods. The Napoleonic Wars gave rise to independence movements in Latin America, and these should perhaps also be interpreted as confirming the development hypothesis in part.

The other kind of isolation which tends to confirm the second hypothesis is the geographic and economic isolation of regions which at one time were relatively weakly tied to and poorly integrated into the mercantilist and capitalist system. My preliminary research suggests that in Latin America it was these regions which initiated and experienced the most promising self-generating economic development of the classical industrial capitalist type. The most important regional cases probably are Tucumán and Asunción, as well as other cities such as Mendoza and Rosario, in the interior of Argentina and Paraguay during the end of the eighteenth and the beginning of the nineteenth centuries. Seventeenth- and eighteenth-century São Paulo, long before coffee was grown there, is another example. Perhaps Antioquia in Colombia and Puebla and Querétaro in Mexico are other examples. In its own way, Chile was also an example since, before the sea route around the Horn was opened, this country was relatively isolated at the end of the long voyage from Europe via Panama. All of these regions became manufacturing centers and even exporters, usually of textiles, during the periods preceding their effective incorporation as satellites into the colonial, national, and world capitalist system. . . .

VI

A corollary of the second hypothesis is that when the metropolis recovers from its crisis and re-establishes the trade and investment ties which fully re-incorporate the satellites into the system, or when the metropolis expands to incorporate previously isolated regions into the world-wide system, the previous development and industrialization of these regions is choked off or channelled into directions which are not self-perpetuating and promising. This happened after each of the five crises cited above. The renewed expansion of trade and the spread of economic liberalism in the eighteenth and nineteenth centuries choked off and reversed the manufacturing development which Latin America had experienced during the seventeenth century, and in some places at the beginning of the nineteenth. After the First World War, the new national industry of Brazil suffered serious consequences from American economic invasion. The increase in the growth rate of Gross National Product and particularly of industrialization throughout Latin America was again reversed and industry became increasingly satellized after the Second World War and especially after the post-Korean War recovery and expansion of the metropolis. Far from having become more developed since then, industrial sectors of Brazil and most conspicuously of Argentina have become structurally more and more underdeveloped and less and less able to generate continued industrialization and/or sustain development of the economy. This process, from which India also suffers, is reflected in a whole gamut of balance-of-payments, inflationary, and other economic and political difficulties, and promises to yield to no solution short of far-reaching structural change.

Our hypothesis suggests that fundamentally the same process occurred even more dramatically with the incorporation into the system of previously unsatellized regions. The expansion of Buenos Aires as a satellite of Great Britain and the introduction of free trade in the interest of the ruling groups of both metropoles destroyed the manufacturing and much of the remainder of the economic base of the previously relatively prosperous interior almost entirely. Manufacturing was destroyed by foreign competition, lands were taken and concentrated into latifundia by the rapaciously growing export economy, intraregional distribution of income became much more unequal, and the previously developing regions became simple satellites of Buenos Aires and through it of London. The provincial centers did not yield to satellization without a struggle. This metropolis–satellite conflict was much of the cause of the long political and armed struggle between the Unitarists in Buenos Aires and the Federalists in the provinces, and it may be said to have been the sole important cause of the War of the Triple Alliance in which Buenos Aires, Montevideo, and Rio de Janeiro, encouraged and helped by London, destroyed not only the autonomously developing economy of Paraguay but killed off nearly all of its population which was unwilling to give in. Though this is no doubt the most spectacular example which tends to confirm the hypothesis, I believe that historical research on the satellization of previously relatively independent yeoman-farming and incipient manufacturing regions such as the Caribbean islands will confirm it further. These regions did not have a chance against the forces of expanding and developing capitalism, and their own development had to be sacrificed to that of others. The economy and industry of Argentina, Brazil, and other countries which have experienced the effects of metropolitan recovery since the Second World War are today suffering much the same fate, if fortunately still in lesser degree.

VII

A third major hypothesis derived from the metropolis–satellite structure is that the regions which are the most underdeveloped and feudal-seeming today are the ones which had the closest ties to the metropolis in the past. They are the regions which were the greatest exporters of primary products to and the biggest sources of capital for the world metropolis and which were abandoned by the metropolis when for one reason or another business fell off. This hypothesis also contradicts the generally held thesis that the source of a region's underdevelopment is its isolation and its precapitalist institutions.

This hypothesis seems to be amply confirmed by the former super-satellite development and present ultra-underdevelopment of the once sugar-exporting West Indies, Northeastern Brazil, the ex-mining districts of Minas Gerais in Brazil, highland Peru, and Bolivia, and the central Mexican states of Guanajuato, Zacatecas, and others whose names were made world famous centuries ago by their silver. There surely are no major regions in Latin America which are today more cursed by underdevelopment and poverty; yet all of these regions, like Bengal in India, once provided the life blood of mercantile and industrial capitalist development – in the metropolis. These regions' participation in the development of the world capitalist system gave them, already in their golden age, the typical structure of underdevelopment of a capitalist export economy. When the market for their sugar or the wealth of their mines disappeared and the metropolis abandoned them to their own devices, the already existing economic, political, and social structure of these regions prohibited autonomous generation of economic development and left them no alternative but to turn in upon themselves and to degenerate into the ultra-underdevelopment we find there today.

VIII

These considerations suggest two further and related hypotheses. One is that the latifundium, irrespective of whether it appears as a plantation or a hacienda today, was typically born as a commercial enterprise which created for itself the institutions which permitted it to respond to increased demand in the world or national market by expanding the amount of its land, capital, and labor and to increase the supply of its products. The fifth hypothesis is that the latifundia which appear isolated, subsistence-based, and semi-feudal today saw the demand for their products or their productive capacity decline and that they are to be found principally in the above-named former agricultural and mining export regions whose economic activity declined in general. These two hypotheses run counter to the notions of most people, and even to the opinions of some historians and other students of the subject, according to whom the historical roots and socio-economic causes of Latin American latifundia and agrarian institutions are to be found in the transfer of feudal institutions from Europe and/or in economic depression.

The evidence to test these hypotheses is not open to easy general inspection and requires detailed analyses of many cases. Nonetheless, some important confirmatory evidence is available. The growth of the latifundium in nineteenth-century Argentina and Cuba is a clear case in support of the fourth hypothesis and can in no way be attributed to the transfer of feudal institutions during colonial times. The same is evidently the case of the postrevolutionary and contemporary resurgence of latifundia particularly in the North of Mexico, which produce for the American market, and of similar ones on the coast of Peru and the new coffee regions of Brazil. The conversion of previously yeoman-farming Caribbean islands, such as Barbados, into sugar-exporting economies at various times between the seventeenth and twentieth centuries and the resulting rise of the latifundia in these islands would seem to confirm the fourth hypothesis as well. In Chile, the rise of the latifundium and the creation of the institutions of servitude which later came to be called feudal occurred in the eighteenth century and have been conclusively shown to be the result of and response to the opening of a market for Chilean wheat in Lima.[4] Even the growth and consolidation of the latifundium in seventeenth-century Mexico – which most expert students have attributed to a depression of the economy caused by the decline of mining and a shortage of Indian labor and to a consequent turning in upon itself and ruralization of the economy – occurred at a time when urban population and demand were growing, food shortages became acute, food prices skyrocketed, and the profitability of other economic activities such as mining and foreign trade declined. All of these and other factors rendered hacienda agriculture more profitable. Thus, even this case would seem to confirm the hypothesis that the growth of the latifundium and its feudal-seeming conditions of servitude in Latin America has always been and still is the commercial response to increased demand and that it does not represent the transfer or survival of alien institutions that have remained beyond the reach of capitalist development. The emergence of latifundia, which today really are more or less (though not entirely) isolated, might then be attributed to the causes advanced in the fifth hypothesis – i.e., the decline of previously profitable agricultural enterprises whose capital was, and whose currently produced economic surplus still is, transferred elsewhere by owners and merchants who frequently are the same persons or families. Testing this hypothesis requires still more detailed analysis, some of which I have undertaken in a study on Brazilian agriculture.

IX

All of these hypotheses and studies suggest that the global extension and unity of the capitalist system, its monopoly structure and uneven development throughout its history, and the resulting persistence of commercial rather than industrial capitalism in the underdeveloped world (including its most industrially advanced countries) deserve much more attention in the study of economic development and cultural change than they have hitherto received. Though science and truth know no national boundaries, it is probably new generations of scientists from the underdeveloped countries themselves who most need to, and best can, devote the necessary attention to these problems and clarify the process of underdevelopment and development. It is their people who in the last analysis face the task of changing this no longer acceptable process and eliminating this miserable reality.

They will not be able to accomplish these goals by importing sterile stereotypes from the metropolis which do not correspond to their satellite economic reality and do not respond to their liberating political needs. To change their reality they must understand it. For this reason, I hope that better confirmation of these hypotheses and further pursuit of the proposed historical, holistic, and structural approach may help the peoples of the underdeveloped countries to understand the causes and eliminate the reality of their development of underdevelopment and their underdevelopment of development.

NOTES

1. *América Latina*, Año 6, No. 4 (Oct. – Dec. 1963), p. 8.
2. Instituto Nacional Indigenista, *Los centros coordinadores indigenistas* (Mexico City, 1962), p. 34.
3. *Ibid.*, pp. 33–4, 88.
4. Mario Góngora, *Origen de los "inquilinos" de Chile central* (Santiago: Editorial Universitaria, 1960); Jean Borde and Mario Góngora, *Evolución de la propriedad rural en el Valle del Puango* (Santiago: Instituto de Sociología de la Universidad de Chile); Sergio Sepúlveda, *El trigo chileno en el mercado mundial* (Santiago: Editorial Universitaria, 1959).

11 Dependency and Development in Latin America (1972)

Fernando Henrique Cardoso

After Brazil's military coup of 1964, Brazilian sociologist Fernando Henrique Cardoso was sent into exile in Chile. He returned to Brazil in the 1980s and, after serving as governor and senator, became Economic Minister and was elected President in 1995. While in exile in Chile he worked with other development theorists, including those in the United Nations' ECLA group. He took their economistic ideas in new social and political directions, with a more historical approach. Cardoso paid especially close attention to how elites in poorer nations have historically allied themselves with foreign interests to their benefit and to the detriment of the poorer masses in their countries. His historical analysis also shows how wealthier nations and wealthier people in poorer nations have used imperialist tactics to keep poorer countries producing cheaper things like minerals and food, so that these things are available to further economic development and industrialization in wealthier countries. Because he pays attention to the nuances within the economies and societies of poorer countries Cardoso, unlike many other "dependency theorists," is able to show how limited forms of development occur despite consistent subordination by wealthier nations. Believing that poorer nations must navigate toward what development they can within the global economy makes Cardoso an important intellectual and political leader of the more moderate "structuralist" group of dependency theorists.

The theory of imperialist capitalism, as is well known, has so far attained its most significant treatment in Lenin's works. This is not only because Lenin attempts to explain transformations of the capitalist economies that occurred during the last decade of the 19th century and the first decade of the 20th, but mainly because of the political and historical implications contained in his interpretations. In fact, the descriptive arguments of Lenin's theory of imperialism were borrowed from Hobson's analysis. Other writers had already presented evidence of the international expansion of the capitalist economies and nations. Nevertheless, Lenin, inspired by Marx's views, was able to bring together evidence to the effect that economic expansion is meaningless if we do not take into consideration the *political* and *historical* aspects with which economic factors are intimately related. From Lenin's perspective, imperialism is a new form of the capitalist mode of production. This new form cannot be considered as a *different* mode of economic organization, in so far as capital accumulation based on private ownership of the means of production and exploitation of the labour force remain the basic features of the system. But its significance is that of a new *stage* of capitalism. The historical "momentum" was a new one, with all the political consequences of that type of transformation: within the dominant capitalist classes, new sectors tried to impose their interests and ideologies; the State, the Army and all basic social and political institutions were redefined in order to assure expansion abroad. At the same time new types of liberation and social struggles came onto the historical scene – the colonial liberation movements and the fight against "trade unionism", the latter a struggle against an initial form of working-class compromise with the bourgeoisie made possible by the exploitation of the colonial world.

From that broad picture of a new historical stage of capitalist development Lenin inferred new political tasks, tactics and strategies for socialist revolution.

Lenin's Characterization of Imperialism

The main points of Lenin's characterization of imperialism that are essential to the present discussion can be summarized as follows:

a)   the capitalist economy in its "advanced stages" involves a concentration of capital and production (points that were well established by Marx in *Capital*) in such a way that the competitive market is replaced in its basic branches by a monopolistic one.

b)   this trend was historically accomplished through internal differentiation of capitalist functions, leading not only to the formation of a financial stratum among entrepreneurs but to the marked prominence of the banking system in the capitalist mode of production. Furthermore, the fusion of industrial capital with financial capital under the control of the latter turned out to be the decisive feature of the political and economic relations within capitalist classes, with all the practical consequences that such a system of relations has in terms of state organization, politics and ideology.

c)   capitalism thus reached its "ultimate stage of development" both internally and externally. Internally, control of the productive system by financiers turned the productive forces and the capital accumulation process toward the search for new possibilities for investment. The problem of "capital realization" became in this way an imperative necessity to permit the continuing of capitalist expansion. In addition there were internal limits that impeded the continuous reinvestment of new capital (impoverishment of the masses, a faster rate of capital growth than that of the internal market, and so on.) *External outlets* had to be found to ensure the continuity of capitalist advance and accumulation.

d)   the increased and increasing speed of the development of productive forces under monopolistic control also pushed the advanced capitalist countries toward the political control of foreign lands. The search for control over *raw materials* is yet another reason why capitalism in its monopolistic stage becomes expansionist.

In short, Lenin's explanations of why advanced capitalist economies were impelled toward the control of backward lands, was based on two main factors. One stressed movements of capital, the other outlined the productive process. Both were not only linked to each other but also related to the global transformation of the capitalist system that had led to the control of the productive system by financiers. It is not difficult to see that such modifications deeply affected state organization and functions as well as the relationships among nations, since a main thrust of capitalist development in the stage of imperialism was toward the territorial division of the world among the leading capitalist countries. This process guaranteed capital flows from the over-capitalized economies to backward countries and assured provision of raw materials in return.

Imperialism and Dependent Economies

From that perspective, the consequence of imperialism with respect to dependent economies and nations (or colonies) was the integration of the latter into the international market. Inequality among nations and economies resulted from imperialism's development to the extent that import of raw materials and export of manufactured goods were the bases of the imperialist-colonial relationship. The reproduction and amplification of inequality between advanced economies and dependent economies developed as a by-product of the very process of capitalist growth.

Certainly, Lenin was aware of particular types of interconnections, as in Argentina and other economies dependent on Great Britain, where local bourgeoisies controlled sectors of the productive system creating more complex patterns of exploitation. The same was true with respect to the political aspects of dependency in those countries where the state tried to defend the national bourgeoisie against imperialist pressures.

Nevertheless, from the theoretical point of view, as a mode of exploitation, imperialism should tend to restrict the economic growth of backward countries to mineral and agricultural sectors in order to assure raw materials for the advanced capitalist nations in their drive for further industrialization. For the same reasons the indigenous labour force could be kept at low wage and salary levels. By that means the dominant central economies were assured of cheap raw material prices. Consequently, in colonized or dependent nations, internal markets did not have any special strategic significance.

Of course, in terms of "capital realization", selling products abroad had importance. But even so, the main imperialistic tie in terms of direct capital investment was oriented toward the concession of loans to the dependent State or to private local entrepreneurs. In both cases, however, political and financial guarantees were assured by the State or the administration of the receiver country.

In short, imperialist profit was based on unequal trade and financial exploitation. The latter could be measured by the increasing indebtedness of exploited economies to the central economies. The former was evidenced through the different types of products exchanged, i.e. raw materials for manufactured goods. This process of exploitation of the indigenous labour force thus insured an unevenness in both types of economies. Moreover, technological advances in the industrial sectors of central economies provided a high level of exploitation, increasing the relative surplus value extracted through a continuously advancing technology of production (leading in turn to unevenness of the rate of organic composition of capital), while in the dominated economies the direct over-exploitation of labour prevailed in the productive system.

Politically, this type of economic expansion thus reinforced colonial links, through wars, repression and subjugation of peoples that previously were not only marginal to the international market, but were culturally independent and structurally did not have links with the Western world. Such were the African and Asian regions where nations, in spite of previous commercial–capitalist expansion, remained largely untouched in terms of their productive systems.

Latin America from the beginning was somewhat different in its links to the imperialist process. It is true that this process of colonialistic penetration obtained with respect to some countries (mainly the Caribbean nations). Yet throughout most of Latin America, the imperialistic upsurge occurred by way of a more complex process, through which Latin American countries kept their political independence, but slowly shifted from subordination to an earlier British influence to American predominance.

Ownership of the productive system was the site of the main differences. Some Latin American economies, even after imperialist predominance, were able to cope with the new situation by maintaining proprietorship of the local export economy in the hands of native bourgeoisies. Thus in some countries (such as Argentina, Brazil, Uruguay, Colombia, Chile), the export sector remained at least to some extent controlled by the local bourgeoisie and the links of dependence were based more on trade and financial relations than directly on the productive sectors. In some countries the internal financial system was itself mainly dominated by internal bankers, and financial dependence was based on international loans contracted, as noted above, by the State or under State guarantees.

In spite of numerous political and economic variations, Lenin's basic picture remained valid: the internal market of Latin American countries grew in a limited way during the period of the first imperialist expansion; the industrial sector was not significantly expanded; external financial dependence grew enormously; raw materials including foodstuffs constituted the basis of export economies.

At the same time not only were the majority of Latin American countries unable to keep control of the export sector, but some of the countries that had previously retained dominance of raw materials or food production, now lost that capacity (as in the Chilean mineral economy).

New Patterns of Capital Accumulation

In spite of the accuracy of Lenin's insights as measured against historical events during the first half of the century in many parts of the world, some important recent changes have deeply affected the pattern of relationship between imperialist and dependent nations. These changes demand a reappraisal of emergent structures and their main tendencies. Even if these modifications are not so deep as the shift that enabled Lenin to characterize a new stage of capitalism during the period of imperialist expansion, they are marked enough to warrant a major modification of the established analyses of capitalism and imperialism. Nevertheless, contemporary international capitalist expansion and control of dependent economies undoubtedly prove that this new pattern of economic relationships among nations remains imperialist. However, the main points of Lenin's characterization of imperialism and capitalism are no longer fully adequate to describe and explain the present forms of capital accumulation and external expansion.

With respect to changes that have occurred within the more advanced capitalist economies (chiefly the rise of monopoly capital and corporate enterprise) there are some consistent analyses. Baran and Sweezy's works, as well as those of Magdoff, Mandel and O'Connor, come to mind. These offer a comprehensive body of descriptive and explanatory material showing the differences between capitalism now and during Lenin's life.

In spite of some recent criticism, Baran and Sweezy argued convincingly (and Sweezy's article on "The Resurgence of Financial Control: Fact or Fancy?"[1] helps to affirm that conviction) that corporations operate as quasi-self-sufficient units of decision and action vis-à-vis capital accumulation. Hence previous notions of banking control over industry need to be rethought. Similarly, the conglomerate form of present big corporations and the multinational scope of the production and marketing adds considerable novelty to the capitalist form of production.[2]

These transformations (and we are only suggesting some of the principal ones which affect all processes of capitalist transformation) have led to important consequences that have been already analysed by the authors noted, as well as others. These writers stress, for instance, the increasing secular growth of profit rates under administered prices in a monopoly system. Of course, this is a central point in Marxian theory and in Lenin's analysis. Yet now important modifications, such as those mentioned, alter the type of political response that the capitalist system is able to produce in order to cope with the challenging situations created by its expansion.

It is equally necessary to approach the problem of surplus realization with a fresh perspective. In this connection some authors have considered the strengthened ties between militarist expansion and the reinforcement of military control over society, through a war economy, as the basic means of capital realization. As a second argument, but a still important factor, State expenditures in welfare are emphasized as alternative outlets for capital accumulation.

Though the adequacy of this analysis may be questioned, Marxist authors have carried out a fairly comprehensive *economic* reinterpretation of the mode of functioning of monopoly capitalism. The same is not true, however, when one considers the *political* aspects of the problem and especially the *politico-economic* consequences of monopoly capitalism in dependent economies. Let us start with the last aspect of the question.

New Forms of Economic Dependency

... [F]oreign investment in the new nations and in Latin America is moving rapidly away from oil, raw materials and agriculture and in the direction of the industrial sectors. Even where the bulk of assets continues to remain in the traditional sectors of imperialist investment, the rate of expansion of the industrial sector is rapid. This is true not only for Latin America but also for Africa and Asia.

The point is not only that multinational corporations are investing in the industrial sectors of dominated economies, instead of in the traditional agricultural and mineral sectors. Beyond that, even when "traditional" sectors of dependent economies, they are operating in technically and organizationally advanced modes, sometimes accepting local participation in their enterprises. Of course, these transformations do not mean that previous types of imperialistic investment, i.e. in oil or metals, are disappearing, even in the case of the most industrialized dependent economies, i.e., Argentina, Brazil and Mexico in Latin America. However, the dominant traits of imperialism in those countries, as the process of industrialization continues, cannot be adequately described and interpreted on the basis of frames of reference that posit the exchange of raw material for industrialized goods as the main feature of trade, and suppose virtually complete external ownership of the dependent economies' means of production.

Even the mineral sector (such as manganese in Brazil, copper in Chile during Frei's government, or petro-chemicals in various countries) is now being submitted to new patterns of economic ownership. The distinguishing feature of these new forms is the joint venture enterprise, comprising local state capital, private national capital and monopoly international investment (under foreign control in the last analysis).

As a consequence, in some dependent economies – among these, the so-called "developing countries" of Latin America – foreign investment no longer remains a simple zero-sum game of exploitation as was the pattern in classical imperialism. Strictly speaking – if we consider the purely economic indicators – it is not difficult to show that *development* and *monopoly penetration* in the industrial sectors of dependent economies are not incompatible. The idea that there occurs a kind of development of underdevelopment, apart from the play on words, is not helpful. In fact, *dependency, monopoly capitalism* and *development* are not contradictory terms: there occurs a kind of *dependent capitalist development* in the sectors of the Third World integrated into the new forms of monopolistic expansion.

As a result in countries like Argentina, Brazil, Mexico, South Africa, India, and some others, there is an internal structural fragmentation, connecting the most "advanced" parts of their economies to the international capitalist system. Separate although subordinated to these advanced sectors, the backward economic and social sectors of the dependent countries then play the role of "internal colonies". The gap between both will probably increase, creating a new type of dualism, quite different from the imaginary one sustained by some non-Marxist authors. The new structural "duality" corresponds to a kind of internal differentiation of the same unity. It results directly, of course, from capitalist expansion and is functional to that expansion, in so far as it helps to keep wages at a low level and diminishes political pressures inside the "modern" sector, since the social and economic position of those who belong to the latter is always better in comparative terms.

If this is true, to what extent is it possible to sustain the idea of *development* in tandem with dependence? The answer cannot be immediate. First of all I am suggesting that the present trend of imperialist investment allows some degree of local participation in the process of economic production. Let us indicate a crucial feature in which present and past forms of capitalism differ. During the previous type of imperialism, the market for goods produced in dependent economies by foreign enterprise was mostly, if not fully, the market of the advanced economies: oil, copper, coffee, iron bauxite, manganese, etc., were produced to be sold and consumed in the advanced capitalist countries. This explains why the internal market of dependent economies was irrelevant for the imperialist economies, excepting the modest portion of import goods consumed by the upper class in the dominated society.

Today for G.M. or Volkswagen, or General Electric, or Sears Roebuck, the Latin American market, if not the particular market in each country where those corporations are producing in Latin America, is the immediate goal in terms of profit. So, at least to some extent, a certain type of foreign investment needs some kind of internal prosperity. There are and there will be some parts of dependent societies, tied to the corporate system, internally and abroad, through shared interests.

On the other hand, and in spite of internal economic development, countries tied to international capitalism by that type of linkage remain economically dependent, insofar as the production of the means of production (technology) are concentrated in advanced capitalist economies (mainly in the US).

In terms of the Marxist scheme of capital reproduction, this means that sector I (the production of means of production) – the strategic part of the reproductive scheme – is virtually non-existent in dependent economies. Thus, from a broad perspective, the realization of capital accumulation *demands* a productive complementarity which does not exist within the country. In Lenin's interpretation the imperialist economies needed external expansion for the realization of capital accumulation. Conversely, within the dependent economies capital returns to the metropole in order to complete the cycle of capitalist reproduction. That is the reason why "technology" is so important. Its "material" aspect is less impressive than its significance as a form of maintenance of control and as a necessary step in the process of capital accumulation. Through technological advantage, corporations make secure their key roles in the global system of capital accumulation. Some degree of local prosperity is possible insofar as consumption goods locally produced by foreign investments can induce some dynamic effects in the dependent economies. But at the same time, the global process of capitalist development determines an interconnection between the sector of production of consumption goods and the capital goods sector, reproducing in this way the links of dependency.

One of the main factors which explained imperialist expansion in Lenin's theory was the search for capitalist investment. Now since foreign capital goes to the industrial sector of dependent economies in search of external markets, some considerable changes have occurred. First, in comparison with expanding assets of foreign corporations, the net amount of foreign capital actually invested in the dependent economies is decreasing: local savings and the reinvestment of profits realized in local markets provides resources for the growth of foreign assets with limited external flow of new capital. This is intimately related to the previously discussed process of expansion of the local market and it is also related to the mounting of "joint ventures" linking local capitalists and foreign enterprise.

Secondly, but no less important, statistics demonstrate that dependent economies during the period of monopolistic imperialist expansion are *exporting* capital to the dominant economies.

As a reaction against that process, some dependent countries have tried to limit exportable profits. Nevertheless, international corporations had the foresight to sense that the principal way to send returns abroad is through the payment of licenses, patents, royalties and related items. These institutional devices, together with the increasing indebtedness of the exploited nations vis-à-vis international agencies and banks (in fact controlled by the big imperialist countries), have altered the main forms of exploitation.

It is not the purpose of this presentation to discuss all the consequences of this for a monopoly capitalist economy. However, some repercussions of the new pattern of imperialism on the US and other central economies are obvious. If a real problem of capital realization exists under monopoly capitalism, the new form of dependency will increase the necessity to find new fields of application for the capital accumulated in the metropolitan economies. Witness the push toward more "technical obsolescence" administered by corporations. Military expenditures are another means of finding new outlets for capital.

Nevertheless, I am not considering the whole picture. In fact, some of these conclusions might change if the capital flows and trade interrelations among advanced capitalist economies were taken into consideration. Thus the preceding remarks are presented with the single aim of stressing that the present trend of capital export from the underdeveloped countries to the imperialist ones leads to a redefinition of the function of foreign expansion for capital realization.

The idea that the growth of capitalism depends on Third World exploitation requires some further elaboration. In fact, the main trends of the last decade show that Latin American participation in both the expansion of international trade and investment is decreasing. If we accept the distinction between two sectors of international trade – the Centre and the Periphery – one finds that the trade rate of growth was 7.9 per cent per year in the central economies and 4.8 per cent in the peripheral ones. As a consequence, exports of the peripheral economies which reached a peak in 1948 (32 per cent of the international trade) decreased to 26 per cent in 1958 and to 21 per cent in 1968 (below the 28 per cent of the pre-war period). In the Latin American case this participation decreased from 12 per cent in 1948 to 6 per cent in 1968. The same is happening with respect to the importance that the periphery has for US investments. The periphery absorbed 55 per cent of the total US direct investment in 1950 and only 40 per cent in 1968. Latin American participation in this process fell in the same period from 39 per cent to 20 per cent.

Of course, these data do not show the increase of "loans and aid" which – as was stressed before – has been of increasing importance in economic imperialism. However, the fact that the interrelations among the most advanced economies are growing cannot be utilized as an argument to infer the "end of imperialism". On the contrary, the more appropriate inference is that the relations between advanced capitalist countries and dependent nations lead rather to a "marginalization" of the latter within the global system of economic development (as Anibal Pinto has outlined).

Some Political Consequences

The new forms of dependency will undoubtedly give rise to novel political and social adaptations and reactions inside the dependent countries. If my analysis is correct, the above-mentioned process of fragmentation of interests will probably lead to an internal differentiation that in very schematic terms can be suggested as follows. Part of the "national bourgeoisie", (the principal one in terms of economic power – agrarian, commercial, industrial or financial) is the direct beneficiary, as a junior partner, of the foreign interest. I refer not only to the direct associates, but also to economic groups that benefit from the eventual atmosphere of prosperity derived from dependent development (as is easily demonstrated in Brazil or Mexico). The process goes further and not only part of the "middle class" (intellectuals, state bureaucracies, armies, etc.) are involved in the new system, but even part of the working class. Those employed by the "internationalized" sector structurally belong to it.

Of course, structural dependence does not mean immediate political co-option. Effective political integration of groups and persons depends on the political processes, movements, goals and alternatives that they face.

Nevertheless, as the process of internationalization of dependent nations progresses, it becomes difficult to perceive the political process in terms of a struggle between the Nation and the anti-Nation, the latter conceived as the Foreign Power of Imperialism. The anti-Nation will be inside the "Nation" – so to speak, among the local people in different social strata. Furthermore, to perceive that, in these terms, the Nation is an occupied one, is not an easy process: there are very few "others" in cultural and national terms physically representing the presence of "the enemy".

I do not wish to give the impression that I conceive the political process in a mechanistic way. Consequently, my intention is not to "derive" some political consequences from a structural economic analysis. Rather, the point is that most socialist interpretations of the Latin American political situation not only run in that direction but also assume the wrong structural point of departure.

Some more general remarks can be summarized thus:

a) Analysis which is based on the naive assumption that imperialism unifies the interests and reactions of dominated nations is a clear oversimplification of what is really occurring. It does not take into consideration the internal fragmentation of these countries and the attraction that development exerts in different social strata, and not only on the upper classes.

b) The term 'development of underdevelopment' (in A. G. Frank) summarizes another mistake. In fact, the assumption of a structural 'lack of dynamism' in dependent economies because of imperialism misinterprets the actual forms of economic imperialism and presents an imprecise political understanding of the situation. It is necessary to understand that in specific situations it is possible to expect *development* and *dependency*.

It would be wrong to generalize these processes to the entire Third World. They only occur when corporations reorganize the international division of labour and include parts of dependent economies in their plans of productive investment.

Thus the majority of the Third World is not necessarily involved in this specific structural situation. To assume the contrary will lead to political mistakes equivalent to those derived from, for instance, Debray's analysis of Latin America. Debray once accepted the view that imperialism homogenized all Latin American countries (with one or two exceptions) and assumed a frame of reference which stressed the old fashioned type of imperialist exploitation with its attendant reinforcement of oligarchic and landlord-based types of dominance.

Now, I am assuming that there are different forms of dependency in Latin America and that in some of them, development produces a shift in internal power, displacing the old oligarchical power groups and reinforcing more "modern" types of political control. In that sense, the present dictatorships in Latin America, even when militarily based, do not express, by virtue of pure structural constraints, a traditional and "anti-developmentalist" (I mean anti-modern capitalism) form of domination.

It is hardly necessary to repeat that from the left's point of view there are strong arguments to maintain its denunciation of both new forms of imperialism or dependency and political authoritarianism. But clearly, new political analyses are needed to explain the bureaucratic-technocratic form of authoritarian state which serves the interests of the internationalized bourgeoisie and their allies.

In this context, and in order to avoid a mechanistic approach, a correct orientation of the struggles against capitalist imperialism demands special attention to cultural problems and the different forms of alienation.

If the capitalist pattern of development in industrialized dependent countries pushes toward internal fragmentation and inequalities, values related to national integrity and social participation might be transformed into instruments of political struggle. To permit the State and bourgeois groups to command the banner of nationalism – conceived not only in terms of sovereignty but also of internal cohesion and progressive social integration – would be a mistake with deep consequences. I am not supporting the idea that the strategic (or revolutionary) side of dependent industrialized societies is the "marginalized sector". But denunciation of marginalization as a consequence of capitalist growth, and the organization of unstructured masses, are indispensable tasks of analysis and practical politics.

For this reason it is not very realistic to expect the national bourgeoisie to lead resistance against external penetration. Consequently, denunciation of the dependency perspective cannot rest on values associated with bourgeois nationalism. National integrity as cited above means primarily popular integration in the nation and the need to struggle against the particular form of development promoted by the large corporations.

In the same way that trade unionism may become a danger for workers in advanced capitalist societies, development is a real ideological pole of attraction for middle class *and workers'* sectors in Latin American countries. The answer to that attractive effect cannot be a purely ideological denial of economic progress, when it occurs. A reply must be based on values and political objectives that enlarge the awareness of the masses with respect to social inequalities and national dependency.

NOTES

1. See P. Sweezy, "The Resurgence of Financial Control: Fact or Fancy?," *Socialist Revolution*, 8:2:2 (Mar.–Apr. 1972), 157–92.
2. See H. Magdoff and P. Sweezy, "Notes on the Multinational Corporation," in Fann and Hodges, *Readings in U.S. Imperialism*, Boston, 1972, pp. 93–116.

12 The Dynamics of Rural Poverty in Latin America (1977)

Alain de Janvry and Carlos Garramón

Based on de Janvry's classic book about rural societies and rural land reforms, *The Agrarian Question*, this collaboration with Carlos Garramón is an important contribution to dependency theory because of its attention to the "disarticulation" of the economies and societies of poorer, more rural nations. Economists de Janvry and Garramón characterize these societies as disarticulated because they serve as sources of cheap goods and labor for wealthier areas and at the same time are not able to generate a significant internal market that might foster local development. This is because the labor force does not earn enough to buy locally produced goods. This means that rural poverty means little for either the national economy or international market and so it receives little attention from governments. Rural poverty helps maintain a situation of dependency and under-development because the poor can turn to subsistence production and family subsistence land when wages and the capitalist market cannot cover their needs for survival. And poverty begets poverty, as it becomes logical for rural poor people to have many children as their only chance for mobility and as a safeguard against the hard times and disabilities of old age. This cycle of poverty maintains an over-supply of workers in both the countryside and cities, which perpetually keeps wages brutally low.

The development and perpetuation of a functional dualism between the subsistence sector and the commodity-producing sector is an objective outcome of the laws of capital accumulation in the periphery of the world capitalist system. The necessity for this dualism derives from the drive of capitalists to maximise profits and thus maintain low wages. Its possibility arises from social disarticulation whereby labour's income does not participate in expanding the market for the modern sector. Through dualism, surplus value is increased not only by the orthodox means of central economies – principally increasing the productivity of work to reduce necessary labour embodied in wage goods – but, in addition, and dramatically more effectively, by collapsing the price of agricultural labour by an amount equal to the production of use-values by the worker's family in the subsistence plot. In this way, subsistence agriculture supplies cheap labour to commercial agriculture which, in turn, supplies cheap food to the urban sector where it sustains low wages. Socially disarticulated accumulation and functional dualism between capitalist and precapitalist modes perpetuate primitive accumulation in the modern sector based on surplus extraction from the peasant sector fundamentally via the labour market. This specific form of overexploitation of rural labour implies a particular dynamic in the use of labour and natural resources in subsistence agriculture. The pattern of rural poverty and the subjective contradictions of peripheral capitalism can thus largely be understood by identifying the antagonistic contradictions to which the subsistence economy is subject in adjusting to domination.

I. Accumulation on a World Scale and Primitive Accumulation

The laws of motion of capital in the centre-periphery structure, and their implications for the functionality of the subsistence sector in the periphery, can be derived from the concepts of oneness, heterogeneity (including disarticulation), and dominance:

1. Oneness of the process of capital accumulation on a world scale that is characterised by the necessary and contradictory relationship between production and circulation.
2. Heterogeneity of structures characterised by socially articulated centre economies and socially disarticulated peripheries. Social articulation is obtained when the modern sector is oriented at the production of wage-goods; and, hence the capacity to consume of the economic system develops through rising real wages in relationship to rising productivity of labour. The necessary relation between production and circulation thus implies a necessary relation between returns to capital and to labour and hence between rate of growth and distribution of income. Under social disarticulation, realisation is obtained either through the external sector (export enclaves including outward-oriented industry) or through partial consumption of the return to capital and rents (import-substitution industrialisation oriented towards the production of luxuries). The relationship between realisation and rising wages is lost. The rate of capital accumulation is maximised by minimising wages.
3. Dominance of centre over periphery whereby the centre historically moulds the structure of the periphery so that the contradictions of accumulation in the periphery create there the need for external relationships which, in turn, permit the centre to resolve its own contradictions.

In the centre, accumulation under articulation implies that the contradiction between capitalists and capital applies fully. "To each capitalist, the total mass of all workers, with the exception of his own workers, appear not as workers but as consumers" (Marx, 1973: 419). Moved by individual rationality, capital grows by striving to restrict the rise in real wages and thus permanently encounters a barrier in the sphere of circulation. The outcome is a cyclical tendency for the rate of profit to fall and the drive of capital to expand worldwide to compensate for this tendency. In the periphery, accumulation under disarticulation implies the emergence of four dominant objective contradictions. Diversion of part of the surplus value to create the capacity to consume for the modern sector implies a low rate of savings that severely curtails the rate of investment out of national income and a limited market size. Import substitution industrialisation implies increasing needs for imports of capital goods and technological knowledge, thus creating a structural deficit in the balance of payments that constrains industrial expansion. The reconciliation of capitalists and capital in striving for cheap labour creates the logic for cheap food. With modernisation of agriculture thus made unprofitable, food production stagnates. These four contradictions create in the periphery the need for external relationships with the centre, primarily calling on foreign capital and foreign food. Through their mutual needs, centre and periphery thus have an organic solidarity that establishes the laws of accumulation on a world scale.

Disarticulated accumulation leads to the emergence of markedly specific social relations of production in peripheral agriculture. These relations permit conceptualisation of the origin and dynamics of rural poverty in Latin America.

II. Social Relations of Production in the Rural Periphery

From the very beginning of Latin America's entry in the world mercantile and capitalist system, the logic of disarticulated accumulation has implied the establishment of social relations of production aimed at ensuring the availability of cheap labour. When labour is scarce, as in Latin America until the generalisation of marginality in the 1950s, two conditions must be satisfied for this purpose. One is the alienation of labour from access to the land through its monopolisation in order to reduce the opportunity cost of labour; the other is the imposition of social relations of production that prevent labour from capturing its own opportunity cost in the labour market.

Rapid appropriation of all the land through private property is a necessary condition to cheapen labour for both agriculture and industry. As Marx (1967: Chapter 25) states in his theory of colonisation, "the first condition of capitalist production is that land ownership be already taken away from the masses". This condition was met in Latin America. Monopolistic occupation of the land by a social group that thus became the traditional landed elite permitted cheap labour in the economy as it drastically curtailed the opportunity cost of scarce labour.

The value of labour can further be reduced by preventing it from realising this opportunity cost through imposition of precapitalist relations of production. This is, of course, essential when labour is scarce. ...

When a slave is a scarce good, his minimum salary is a fixed quantity, independent of his work. He cannot be overexploited, since the possibilities of replacing him are limited. Necessary conditions to allow for recovery from the wear due to his work efforts must be provided, including his support during periods of idleness, sickness, reproduction, etc. Only when the supply of slaves is highly elastic and at low price is overexploitation possible, with resulting early exhaustion through death or incapacitation. But this condition was never met in Latin America, where overexploitation of labour thus required, instead, "free" labour.

The superiority of free labour is that labour costs are thus transformed from being fixed to being variable. Wages are paid by employers only for time actually worked.

With a fully proletarianised labour force, however, the level of wages must be sufficient to cover the subsistence needs of the worker and his family.

Social relations of production do exist, however, which are more effective than proletarianisation for cheapening labour in the agricultural sector of the peripheral economy. According to the extent of surplus labour, these are "semiproletarian servile" labour or "semiproletarian free" labour.

With semiproletarian servile labour the worker receives in payment for his work the usufruct of a patch of land, some consumption goods, and a small amount of cash. For the employer, the cost of servile labour is less than the price of labour even for mere subsistence because the opportunity cost of the land given in usufruct to the worker is less than the value of production that the worker can generate on it through use of family labour. The cost incurred is thus less than the price of labour by an amount equal to the net between the value of production on the land plot and the opportunity of this plot for the landlord.[1] This difference can be very large. On the one hand, the land of the *latifundio* is extensively used and its opportunity cost consequently is low. On the other hand, the value of production per hectare in the serf's plot can be extremely high, since family labour has an opportunity cost of nearly zero as it is captive of the *latifundio*. That the price of labour may be maintained at the cost of subsistence – even when the workers' opportunity cost may be higher in the rest of the economy – results from a set of legal and traditional measures that are an integral part of the effectiveness of precapitalist relations of production in tying the labourer to the land. Relative to slavery, servitude already permits a better relating of labour costs to work effort. While the land plot is a fixed component of labour cost, the payments in kind and cash are directly related to the work effort. In periods of sickness, reproduction, or reduced labour needs, these costs need not be incurred.

The salaried labour of "free semiproletarians" settled in subsistence plots outside of the *latifundio* – the *minifundistas* – constitutes a source of labour which is still cheaper for the landlord than servile labour. In this case two advantages are secured: the possibilities of exploiting family labour in subsistence plots that have no cost for the employer and of paying the worker for his effective labour only when it is needed. On the average the price of labour will be the difference between the cost of subsistence for the worker and his family and the production of use values or petty commodities that can be obtained in the *minifundio*. Use of labour is now fully flexible since it will be paid only for work strictly necessary in conditions of needs that fluctuate between seasons and between years, according to the climate and the market.

Clearly, free semiproletarian labour can be used at this cost only when the whole economy enters into conditions of surplus labour, that is, once marginality is suffic-iently widespread. Servile relations of production, with labour tied to the land – what Engels called "the second slavery" – are hence an effective means of reducing the price of labour as long as there is labour scarcity in the economy. Once marginality is rampant, servitude loses economic rationality and free semiproletarian workers dominate.

The conditions of work will evolve from servile to free labour when correspond-ence ("homology") (Althusser and Balibar, 1970: 302) is established between rela-tions of possession and property. The worker must lose both possession of and property relations in the means of work in order for his labour to become a commodity. This law of transition derived from historical materialism is valid for the peripheral economy as well as the central economy. Only the objectives of proletarianisation differ.

In the central economy the freeing of labour serves a double purpose: it lowers the cost of labour by giving to the employer flexibility in hiring and firing and, simultaneously, it increases the size of the market. It implies the destruction of the subsistence economies and complete proletarianisation of the workers. In the periphery the cost of labour is also reduced through its freeing; but, due to social disarticulation, there is no rationality of market expansion through proletarianisation. Hence, whenever possible, as in agriculture, the subsistence economies will be maintained. This will permit the further lowering of labour costs, since it allows for the indirect exploitation of family labour occupied in the production of use values and petty commodities that cover part of the subsistence of the worker. There is proletarianisation of labour at the level of the employer in whose enterprise the worker loses both relations of possession and property; but there is semiproletarianisation of the worker who maintains relations of possession and, usually, property in his subsistence plot. Fierce competition among *minifundistas* on the labour market leads to a wage below subsistence that merely complements the gap between subsistence needs of the worker and his family and use-values produced in his plot.

The subsistence sector is, hence, characterised by noncapitalist relations of production and by simple reproduction. The structural dualism that exists under prevalence of the *latifundio* between the capitalist urban sector producing luxury goods and the precapitalist rural sector producing wage goods is thus preserved after externalisation of the *minifundio*. In this dual structure surplus extraction from commercial agriculture occurs through the product market via deterioration of the price of wage goods. Once the *minifundio* has been externalised, the agricultural sector itself is characterised by a functional dualism between the capitalist sector producing wage commodities and the noncapitalist sector producing use-values and petty commodities. Here, surplus extraction within agriculture occurs through the labour market via wages below subsistence. In the periphery, the freeing of labour thus permits increasing its level of exploitation. The capitalist agriculture-subsistence sector binomial is the structural reflection of the rationality of peripheral accumulation. It constitutes a functional system that symptomises and embodies the contradictions of peripheral capitalism.

III. Contradictions of the Subsistence Economy

The social division of labour between subsistence and commercial sectors implies a particular division of labour by sex and age in the latter. As domination over the subsistence sector increases, the struggle for survival induces an intense search for additional productive resources and for nontraditional factors in order to increase the productivity of labour. But this search is largely contradictory, as the very instruments of survival available to the *minifundista* are also factors of impoverishment either individually in the longer run (the ecological contradiction) or socially (the quantitative and qualitative demographic contradictions).

In the central economy an important number of women participate in the labour market. In the United States about two-fifths of the labour force is composed of women, and the wages they receive average three-fifths of male workers' earnings. Overexploitation of woman as a production agent thus exists in the central economy, but the principal aspect of her subordination to the needs of advanced capitalism is not there – it is in her role as a consumption agent. Continued accumulation in the centre is conditioned by sustained expansion of demand for industrial goods by the working classes. With men confined to the production of commodities for a major part of the day, the responsibility for managing consumption accrues to women. Female alienation under advanced capitalism principally originates in this forced function of transformer of commodities into use-values.

In the subsistence sector of the peripheral economy, by contrast, woman's subordination originates in her role as a production agent of use-values to cheapen semiproletarian labour, instead of one of consumption agent. The division of labour by sex which is primarily between production and consumption functions in the centre is here between production of commodities and production of use-values. Her overexploitation will commonly assume some of the most brutal forms as she cumulates an enormous amount of physically demanding tasks that have to be carried out under highly primitive conditions – cultivating the subsistence plot, elaborating food, rearing and feeding the children, tending the dwelling, going to the market, etc. As the CIDA (1966: 195) observes, "Intense work wears out to the point of exhaustion. At an early age, she appears old and weary." Children are of necessary assistance to her work, which is highly labour-intensive and which can be performed only by family labour, for only it can be overexploited to the necessary degree. In coincidence with her role, children are thus raised as production and protection agents and incorporated in the labour process of the *minifundio* at an early age.

The pattern of social division of labour by sex and age that results from the functional integration of the subsistence economy with the dominating commodity-producing sector is accompanied by ecological, demographic, and literacy contradictions that cumulatively deepen the development of underdevelopment in agriculture.

Grabbing of the land by commercial and plantation agriculture has limited subsistence agriculture to the least fertile and most easily destroyable lands. In addition, technological innovations have not been available for this type of agriculture: research has concentrated on cash crops or on food crops produced under commercial conditions. Virtually no research has been done for the production conditions that characterise subsistence agriculture: symbiotic cultivation (e.g., beans growing on cornstalks) instead of sequential cultivation (crop rotations); manual instead of mechanical cultivation; plant varieties and agronomic techniques allowing for high-risk aversion; use of plant residues for animal feeding or fuel; etc. Further, marginalisation from the institutions that distribute credit, information, and education implies that opportunities to improve yields that may exist have generally not been available to subsistence peasants. Unfertile land and backward technology thus result in low yields and low productivity.

The most immediately obvious contradiction into which increasing poverty forces subsistence agriculture is the destruction of productive natural resources. As poverty increases, more intensive use of available resources is necessary and the land is mined. Lower yields imply growing poverty which, in turn, force more mining of the land. The ecology is gradually destroyed in the subsistence sector and under-development progresses. In many areas of Latin America, destruction of the land is already complete.

Similarly, poverty in subsistence agriculture leads to increasing specialisation in the use of the land as activities shift from production of use-values for a safe and balanced diet to production of a reduced number of petty commodities in order to capitalise upon specific comparative advantages. As a result, exposure to both weather and market risks also increases.

A more insidious, although far more dramatic, contradiction into which subsistence agriculture is pushed by increasing poverty relates to population growth.

Clearly, the population explosion in the Third World has been identified as one of the most antagonistically contradictory aspects of underdevelopment. While numerous programmes of family planning have been implemented in the last decade, their impact has been remarkably insignificant. In large measure this is due to the failure of tailoring these programmes to the individual rationality of couples in the subsistence sector regarding family size. Here, too, a major contrast between centre and periphery needs to be established in the rationality of human fertility. Failure to conceptualise this contrast underlies severe misunderstandings of the population question and failure of population programmes.

Leibenstein (1957: 161) has identified three types of utility for which an additional child is wanted: (1) consumption utility, (2) work or income utility, and (3) security utility. The three functions that a child fulfils for his parents are referred to as consumption, production, and protection.

In the central economy children are essentially consumption items for their parents. For this reason, the Chicago School theory of fertility argues that the process of decision-making regarding family size is essentially the same as consumer rationality in the purchase of durable goods (see principally Becker [1960: 209–40] and Leibenstein [1974: 457–79]). Declining fertility, as income increases, would thus be due to two factors: (1) increasing substitution of children by other consumption goods and services and of quantity by quality of children and (2) increasing opportunity cost of time for parents that takes them away from childbearing and rearing. As a result, influences such as the rise in education of women; urbanisation; increases in the rights of women; decline of the extended family system; increases in socioeconomic and geographical mobility; and, of course, introduction of superior chemical and mechanical contraceptives that increase the efficiency of family planning are repeatedly found to be strong empirical determinants of the fall in fertility in developed economies. In the United States, family size has decreased steadily with economic progress to a size now compatible with zero population growth.

In the subsistence sector of the periphery, children are essential factors of production and protection. There, as Mamdani (1972: 14) correctly observed in contrast to conventional wisdom, "people are not poor because they have large families. Quite the contrary: they have large families because they are poor". Translated into economic terms, the logic of the argument is inescapable.

The point of departure is the well-evidenced observation that most couples, however primitive the conditions under which they live, are individually rational in adjusting the number of children they have to the economic, political, juridical, and ideological conditions under which they live. Among these conditions, the economic structure ultimately tends to be the major determinant of behaviour, especially at low-income levels. The degree of efficiency in applying this rationality to family size is conditioned by the use-effectiveness of the means of contraception available to individual couples. Family planning programmes often have succeeded merely in inducing those couples already practising birth control to switch to more efficient modern methods with only a minor overall effect on family size.

Individual economic rationality does not exist in the abstract – it is conditioned by the social position of the household relative to productive resources and to the social division of labour. It is also conditioned by the absolute income level relative to consumption and security needs of the couple. In subsistence agriculture, poverty implies pressure to seek control over additional productive resources. Since producing children often is the only means whereby *minifundistas* can secure access to additional resources, more children are raised to increase the labour-power applied to a fixed piece of land, in order not to fall below subsistence level. It is thus the farmers with least land that need most children.[2] As for tenants, the more hands a family can muster, the more land he can contract from the landlords. In this process all but the very young and the very old make some productive contribution to the economy of the household.

The crux of the economic rationality of meeting poverty in subsistence agriculture through increasing family size is ultimately twofold.

First, family labour can be overexploited to a far greater degree than labour hired outside the family unit. Since increasing poverty leads to the dual need of generating more productive resources and increasing the degree of overexploitation of labour, both inexorably imply having more children. But what are the conditions that permit overexploitation of family labour relative to hired labour? A first situation is that where labour available for hire is fully proletarianised. In this case the wage paid has to compensate the worker for production and reproduction of labour-power; that is, it must cover both his and his family's subsistence needs. Clearly, in this case, family labour is cheaper since only the survival cost of the labourer himself needs to be covered. But this is not the characteristic situation in rural Latin America, where labour is largely semiproletarian. In this case why, then, is family labour cheaper than labour available for hire that also has part of its production and reproduction covered in the subsistence economy? Anthropological information on the subsistence sector in Latin America is largely unavailable at the present time to provide an answer to this question. Existing knowledge, however, would suggest that the total claim of the family on the lives of its children until adulthood prohibits the existence of a labour market for rural children and, hence, alienates children from their own potential opportunity costs outside the family enterprise.

Second, children not only fulfil a role as production agents but serve also as protection agents. Here, children provide security to parents against health hazards, disability, and old age; against unemployment; and against structural and economic changes to which the work process has to be adjusted when parents may not have the needed flexibility to do so. In some cases a large family size is needed for sheer physical defence of scarce productive resources in a ferociously competitive environment ruled by the laws of survival. Because this function of protection can still largely be fulfilled by the child after he has left the family, optimal desired family size may be close to the biological maximum.

With fixed productive resources, the marginal return from children as production agents decreases with family size. Since older children – especially girls – are made responsible for the care of younger ones, the marginal cost of children is likely also to be with falling family size. Yet, economic rationality applied to children as production agents may still imply an optimum family size which is below biological maximum. As poverty increases, children will earlier be induced to capture their opportunity costs by migrating away from the family. And as the migration age decreases, procreation of more children is needed to maintain a constant stock of working children – a stock which itself has to increase with poverty. But this is not all. As children migrate, they cease to perform a production function but continue to ensure protection, as they can continue to provide material support to their parents if adversity strikes. Thus, while the private cost of a migrated child is zero, the return is by no means negligible. Through migration, optimum family size in the subsistence sector is brought yet closer to biological maximum. And the cost of additional children is shifted to society. The contradiction is complete. More poverty implies the private need for more children, and more children imply the social cost of more poverty.

The demographic contradiction reinforces the ecological contradiction at both private and social levels. The quantitative demographic contradiction is doubled by a qualitative one related to the capacity of body and mind of children raised in the subsistence sector. For children to perform their functions as production and protection agents, the costs of rearing, feeding, and educating them must be lower than the returns. With increasing poverty, these costs have to be cut and, simultaneously, the children's production function will tend to have dominance over their protection function as these two services are provided at successive points in time while the discount rate increases. Since children are used for menial and physical tasks in a traditional and routine environment, the returns from education are extremely low and quickly fall below cost. Even with free schooling, the cost of education is high, since it equals the forgone value of a child's contribution to production. Even when education is compulsory, large numbers of children in the subsistence sector do not attend school and remain illiterate, again as a result of strictly rational individual economic behaviour by parents. As these children later migrate, their absorption into the urban labour force will be among the ranks of the least qualified. At still higher levels of poverty, child nutrition will deteriorate and the ability to perform as a productive agent will also be curtailed.

Sheer individual economic rationality in reacting to poverty pressure in the subsistence economy thus leads to quantitative and qualitative demographic contradictions that bear antagonistically at both individual (in the long run) and social levels.

IV. Conclusion

The contradictions that characterise subsistence agriculture are the ultimate embodiment of the contradictions that derive from the process of accumulation in the centre-periphery binomial.

The objective needs for sustained capital accumulation under social articulation in the centre imply (1) market expansion in the centre and (2) cheapening of raw materials and of specific wage goods through imports from the periphery (commercial imperialism) and increased rate of profit on exported capital to the periphery (financial imperialism). While the first need is to develop the capacity to consume of the economic system, the second is to compensate for the downward pressure on the rate of profit that the contradiction between capitalists and capital implies.

In the centre, market expansion comes from increased real wages which in turn result from a dual set of forces. While, on the one hand, subjective forces materialise in political and trade union activity, on the other hand, objective forces that arise in the enormous productivity increase in agriculture and industry permit the collapse of the price of wage goods.

In the periphery, cheap exports of raw materials and of specific wage goods and high rates of profit result from suppressing (1) the value and price of the labour force (Emmanuel's [1972: 89] unequal exchange) and (2) the price of exportables (Braun's [1973] unequal trade). A lower value of the labour force in the periphery finds its objective logic in the laws of accumulation under social disarticulation (Amin's peripheral capitalism [1974]). Disarticulation implies dissociating labour's income from creating the capacity to consume of the modern sector which, instead, finds its demand abroad or in the consumption of surplus value. It allows for the exercise of subjective forces capable of compressing the workers' consumption baskets and of increasing the length of the working day. Direct action on the price of exportables is permitted by the global monopoly enjoyed by the centre in trade relations and backed by dependent bourgeoisies in the periphery. Reducing the price of the labour force results from international transmission – through free trade, over-valued exchange rates, and cheap food policies – of the collapse in food prices which originated in the centre through industrialisation of its agriculture. And cheap food, in turn, requires cheap agricultural labour in order to maintain the rate of profit and rents in commercial agriculture.

Cheap agricultural labour obtains via dualism that implies the functional integration through the labour market of commercial agriculture with a large noncapitalist subsistence sector. This integration permits wages to be collapsed below the subsistence wage by an amount equal to the production of use-values in peasant agriculture. It also implies a social division of labour by sex and age that is associated with dramatic ecological and demographic contradictions. And it constitutes the process through which rural poverty in Latin America is being created and perpetuated.

NOTES

1. For the serf, income (the price of labour) is equal to:

> Price of labour = payments in kind + payments in cash + value of production generated on land plot in usufruct.

For the landlord, the cost of labour is:

> Cost of labour = payments in kind + payments in cash + opportunity cost of land plot for the landlord
>
> = price of labour − (value of production of use values on plot − opportunity cost of plot).

2. This implies the existence of a negative relationship between farm size and desired family size. Because fertility declines with poverty (because of malnutrition, poor health and hygiene, and overwork) and infant mortality increases, actual completed family size is usually found to first increase with farm size and then decline in accordance with desired family size.

REFERENCES

Althusser, L. and Balibar, E., 1970, *Reading Capital*, New York: Pantheon Books.

Amin, S., 1974, *Accumulation on a World Scale*, New York: Monthly Review Press.

Becker, G., 1960, "An Economic Analysis of Fertility", in National Bureau of Economic Research, *Demographic Changes in Developed Countries*, Princeton: Princeton University Press.

Braun, O., 1973, *Comercio Internacional e Imperialismo*, Buenos Aires, Siglo XXI.

CIDA, 1966, *Tenencia de la Tierra y Desarrollo Socio-Economico del Sector Agricola*, Santiago, Chile.

Emmanuel, A., 1972, *Unequal Exchange: A Study of the Imperialism of Trade*, New York: Modern Reader.

Leibenstein, H., 1957, *Economic Backwardness and Economic Growth*, New York: John Wiley and Sons, Inc.

Leibenstein, H., 1974, "An Interpretation of the Economic Theory of Fertility: Promising Path or Blind Alley?", *Journal of Economic Literature*, XII: 2.

Mamdani, M., 1972, *The Myth of Population Control*, New York: Monthly Review Press.

Marx, K., 1973, *Grundrisse*, New York: Vintage Books.

Marx, K., 1967, *Capital, I*, New York: International Publishers.

13 The Rise and Future Demise of the World Capitalist System: Concepts for Comparative Analysis (1979)

Immanuel Wallerstein

Immanuel Wallerstein's (1930–) three-volume series *The Modern World System* launched a new field of social sciences called World Systems Theory. In it he claimed that one could no longer look at the histories of individual nations, but that a whole global system was evolving together. He described a hierarchy of wealthy "core" nations, poor "periphery" nations, and a middle group of "semi-periphery" nations which had some characteristics of each and which served to control and fragment the nations outside the core. His approach to the "socialist" nations was that they were merely "state capitalist," that is, their governments were acting as the owners, and trading in a world capitalist system where markets were determining prices. Founder of the Braudel Center at the State University of New York (SUNY) at Binghamton, Wallerstein presents an enduring challenge to development researchers to think globally, and he continues to advocate a radical breaking-down of disciplinary lines in the social sciences.

The growth within the capitalist world-economy of the industrial sector of production, the so-called "industrial revolution", was accompanied by a very strong current of thought which defined this change as both a process of organic development and of progress. There were those who considered these economic developments and the concomitant changes in social organization to be some penultimate stage of world development whose final working out was but a matter of time. These included such diverse thinkers as Saint-Simon, Comte, Hegel, Weber, Durkheim. And then there were the critics, most notably Marx, who argued, if you will, that the nineteenth-century present was only an antepenultimate stage of development, that the capitalist world was to know a cataclysmic political revolution which would then lead in the fullness of time to a final societal form, in this case the classless society.

One of the great strengths of Marxism was that, being an oppositional and hence critical doctrine, it called attention not merely to the contradictions of the system but to those of its ideologists, by appealing to the empirical evidence of historical reality which unmasked the irrelevancy of the models proposed for the explanation of the social world. The Marxist critics saw in abstracted models concrete rationalization, and they argued their case fundamentally by pointing to the failure of their opponents to analyze the social whole. As Lukács put it, "it is not the primacy of economic motives in historical explanation that constitutes the decisive difference between Marxism and bourgeois thought, but the point of view of totality".[1] ...

Shall we then turn to ... Marxism, to give us a better account of social reality? In principle yes; in practice there are many different, often contradictory, versions extant of "Marxism". But what is more fundamental is the fact that in many countries Marxism is now the official state doctrine. Marxism is no longer exclusively an oppositional doctrine as it was in the nineteenth century.

The social fate of official doctrines is that they suffer a constant social pressure towards dogmatism and apologia, difficult although by no means impossible to counteract, and that they thereby often fall into the same intellectual dead end of ahistorical model building. ...

Nothing illustrates the distortions of ahistorical models of social change better than the dilemmas to which the concept of stages gives rise. If we are to deal with social transformations over long historical time (Braudel's "the long term"), and if we are to give an explanation of both continuity and transformation, then we must logically divide the long term into segments in order to observe the structural changes from time A to time B. These segments are however not discrete but continuous in reality; *ergo* they are "stages" in the "development" of a social structure, a development which we determine however not *a priori* but *a posteriori*. That is, we cannot predict the future concretely, but we can predict the past.

The crucial issue when comparing "stages" is to determine the units of which the "stages" are synchronic portraits (or "ideal types", if you will). And the fundamental error of ahistorical social science (including ahistorical versions of Marxism) is to reify parts of the totality into such units and then to compare these reified structures.

For example, we may take modes of disposition of agricultural production, and term them subsistence cropping and cash cropping. We may then see these as entities which are "stages" of a development. We may talk about decisions of groups of peasants to shift from one to the other. We may describe other partial entities, such as states, as having within them two separate "economies", each based on a different mode of disposition of agricultural production. If we take each of these successive steps, all of which are false steps, we will end up with the misleading concept of the "dual economy" as have many liberal economists dealing with the so-called underdeveloped countries of the world. Still worse, we may reify a misreading of British history into a set of universal "stages" as Rostow does.

Marxist scholars have often fallen into exactly the same trap. If we take modes of payment of agricultural labor and contrast a "feudal" mode wherein the laborer is permitted to retain for subsistence a part of his agricultural production with a "capitalist" mode wherein the same laborer turns over the totality of his production to the landowner, receiving part of it back in the form of wages, we may then see these two modes as "stages" of a development. We may talk of the interests of "feudal" landowners in preventing the conversion of their mode of payment to a system of wages. We may then explain the fact that in the twentieth century a partial entity, say a state in Latin America, has not yet industrialized as the consequence of its being dominated by such landlords. If we take each of these successive steps, all of which are false steps, we will end up with the misleading concept of a "state dominated by feudal elements", as though such a thing could possibly exist in a capitalist world-economy. . . .

Not only does the misidentification of the entities to be compared lead us into false concepts, but it creates a non-problem: can stages be skipped? This question is only logically meaningful if we have "stages" that "coexist" within a single empirical framework. If within a capitalist world-economy, we define one state as feudal, a second as capitalist, and a third as socialist, then and only then can we pose the question: can a country "skip" from the feudal stage to the socialist stage of national development without "passing through capitalism"?

But if there is no such thing as "national development" (if by that we mean a natural history), and if the proper entity of comparison is the world system, then the problem of stage skipping is nonsense. If a stage can be skipped, it isn't a stage. And we know this *a posteriori*.

If we are to talk of stages, then – and we should talk of stages – it must be stages of social systems, that is, of totalities. And the only totalities that exist or have historically existed are minisystems and world-systems, and in the nineteenth and twentieth centuries there has been only one world-system in existence, the capitalist world-economy.

We take the defining characteristic of a social system to be the existence within it of a division of labor, such that the various sectors or areas within are dependent upon economic exchange with others for the smooth and continuous provisioning of the needs of the area. Such economic exchange can clearly exist without a common political structure and even more obviously without sharing the same culture.

A minisystem is an entity that has within it a complete division of labor, and a single cultural framework. Such systems are found only in very simple agricultural or hunting and gathering societies. Such minisystems no longer exist in the world. Furthermore, there were fewer in the past than is often asserted, since any such system that became tied to an empire by the payment of tribute as "protection costs"[2] ceased by that fact to be a "system", no longer having a self-contained division of labor. For such an area, the payment of tribute marked a shift, in Polanyi's language, from being a reciprocal economy to participating in a larger redistributive economy.[3]

Leaving aside the now defunct minisystems, the only kind of social system is a world-system, which we define quite simply as a unit with a single division of labor and multiple cultural systems. It follows logically that there can, however, be two varieties of such world-systems, one with a common political system and one without. We shall designate these respectively as world-empires and world-economies.

It turns out empirically that world-economies have historically been unstable structures leading either towards disintegration or conquest by one group and hence transformation into a world-empire. Examples of such world-empires emerging from world-economies are all the so-called great civilizations of premodern times, such as China, Egypt, Rome (each at appropriate periods of its history). On the other hand, the so-called nineteenth-century empires, such as Great Britain or

France, were not world-empires at all, but nation-states with colonial appendages operating within the framework of a world-economy.

World-empires were basically redistributive in economic form. No doubt they bred clusters of merchants who engaged in economic exchange (primarily long-distance trade), but such clusters, however large, were a minor part of the total economy and not fundamentally determinative of its fate. Such long-distance trade tended to be, as Polanyi argues, "administered trade" and not market trade, utilizing "ports of trade".

It was only with the emergence of the modern world-economy in sixteenth-century Europe that we saw the full development and economic predominance of market trade. This was the system called capitalism. Capitalism and a world-economy (that is, a single division of labor but multiple polities and cultures) are obverse sides of the same coin. One does not cause the other. We are merely defining the same indivisible phenomenon by different characteristics. . . .

On the "feudalism" debate, we take as a starting point Frank's concept of "the development of underdevelopment", that is, the view that the economic structures of contemporary underdeveloped countries is not the form which a "traditional" society takes upon contact with "developed" societies, not an earlier stage in the "transition" to industrialization. It is rather the result of being involved in the world-economy as a peripheral, raw material producing area, or as Frank puts it for Chile, "under-development . . . is the necessary product of four centuries of capitalism itself".[4]

This formulation runs counter to a large body of writing concerning the under-developed countries that was produced in the period 1950–70, a literature which sought the factors that explained "development" within non-systems such as "states" or "cultures" and, once having presumably discovered these factors, urged their reproduction in underdeveloped areas as the road to salvation.

Frank's theory also runs counter, as we have already noted, to the received orthodox version of Marxism that had long dominated Marxist parties and intellectual circles, for example in Latin America. This older "Marxist" view of Latin America as a set of feudal societies in a more or less prebourgeois stage of development has fallen before the critiques of Frank and many others as well as before the political reality symbolized by the Cuban revolution and all its many consequences. Recent analysis in Latin America has centered instead around the concept of "dependence".[5]

However, recently, Ernesto Laclau has made an attack on Frank which, while accepting the critique of dualist doctrines, refuses to accept the categorization of Latin American states as capitalist. Instead Laclau asserts that "the world capitalist system . . . includes, *at the level of its definition,* various modes of production". He accuses Frank of confusing the two concepts of the "capitalist mode of production" and "participation in a world capitalist economic system".[6]

Of course, if it's a matter of definition, then there can be no argument. But then the polemic is scarcely useful since it is reduced to a question of semantics. Furthermore, Laclau insists that the definition is not his but that of Marx, which is more debatable. . . .

There is . . . a substantive issue in this debate. It is in fact the same substantive issue that underlay the debate between Maurice Dobb and Paul Sweezy in the early 1950s about the "transition from feudalism to capitalism" that occurred in early modern

Europe.[7] The substantive issue, in my view, concerns the appropriate unit of analysis for the purpose of comparison. Basically, although neither Sweezy nor Frank is quite explicit on this point, and though Dobb and Laclau can both point to texts of Marx that seem clearly to indicate that they more faithfully follow Marx's argument, I believe both Sweezy and Frank better follow the spirit of Marx if not his letter[8] and that, leaving Marx quite out of the picture, they bring us nearer to an understanding of what actually happened and is happening than do their opponents.

What is the picture, both analytical and historical, that Laclau constructs? The heart of the problem revolves around the existence of free labor as the defining characteristic of a capitalist mode of production:

> The fundamental economic relationship of capitalism is constituted by the *free* [italics mine] labourer's sale of his labour-power, whose necessary precondition is the loss by the direct producer of ownership of the means of production ...[9] ...

There in a nutshell it is. Western Europe, at least England from the late seventeenth century on, had primarily landless, wage-earning laborers. In Latin America, then and to some extent still now, laborers were not proletarians, but slaves or "serfs". If proletariat, then capitalism. Of course. To be sure. But is England, or Mexico, or the West Indies a unit of analysis? Does each have a separate "mode of production"? Or is the unit (for the sixteenth–eighteenth centuries) the European world-economy, including England *and* Mexico, in which case what was the "mode of production" of this world-economy?

Before we argue our response to this question, let us turn to quite another debate, one between Mao Tse-Tung and Liu Shao-Chi in the 1960s concerning whether or not the Chinese People's Republic was a "socialist state". This is a debate that has a long background in the evolving thought of Marxist parties.

Marx, as has been often noted, said virtually nothing about the post-revolutionary political process. Engels spoke quite late in his writings of the "dictatorship of the proletariat". It was left to Lenin to elaborate a theory about such a "dictatorship", in his pamphlet *State and Revolution*, published in the last stages before the Bolshevik takeover of Russia, that is, in August 1917. The coming to power of the Bolsheviks led to a considerable debate as to the nature of the regime that had been established. Eventually a theoretical distinction emerged in Soviet thought between "socialism" and "communism" as two stages in historical development, one realizable in the present and one only in the future. In 1936 Stalin proclaimed that the USSR had become a socialist (but not yet a communist) state. Thus we now had firmly established *three* stages after bourgeois rule: a post-revolutionary government, a socialist state, and eventually communism. When, after the Second World War, various regimes dominated by the Communist Party were established in various east European states, these regimes were proclaimed to be "peoples' democracies", a new name then given to the post-revolutionary stage one. At later points, some of these countries, for example Czechoslovakia, asserted they had passed into stage two, that of becoming a socialist republic.

In 1961, the 22nd Congress of the CPSU invented a fourth stage, in between the former second and third stages: that of a socialist state which had become a "state of the whole people", a stage it was contended the USSR had at that point reached. The

Programme of the Congress asserted that "the state as an organization of the entire people will survive until the complete victory of communism".[10] One of its commentators defines the "intrinsic substance (and) chief distinctive feature" of this stage: "The state of the whole people is the first state in the world with no class struggle to contend with and, hence, with no class domination and no suppression."[11]

One of the earliest signs of a major disagreement in the 1950s between the Communist Party of the Soviet Union and the Chinese Communist Party was a theoretical debate that revolved around the question of the "gradual transition to Communism". Basically, the CPSU argued that different socialist states would proceed separately in effectuating such a transition whereas the CCP argued that all socialist states would proceed simultaneously.

As we can see, this last form of the debate about "stages" implicitly raised the issue of the unit of analysis, for in effect the CCP was arguing that "communism" was a characteristic not of nation-states but of the world-economy as a whole. This debate was transposed onto the internal Chinese scene by the ideological debate, now known to have deep and long-standing roots, that gave rise eventually to the Cultural Revolution.

One of the corollaries of these debates about "stages" was whether or not the class struggle continued in post-revolutionary states prior to the achievement of communism. The 22nd Congress of the CPSU in 1961 had argued that the USSR had become a state without an internal class struggle, there were no longer existing antagonistic classes within it. Without speaking of the USSR, Mao Tse-Tung in 1957 had asserted in China:

> The class struggle is by no means over ... It will continue to be long and tortuous, and at times will even become very acute ... Marxists are still a minority among the entire population as well as among the intellectuals. Therefore, Marxism must still develop through struggle ... Such struggles will never end. This is the law of development of truth and, naturally, of Marxism as well.[12]

If such struggles *never* end, then many of the facile generalizations about "stages" which "socialist" states are presumed to go through are thrown into question.

During the Cultural Revolution, it was asserted that Mao's report *On the Correct Handling of Contradiction Among the People* cited above, as well as one other, "entirely repudiated the 'theory of the dying out of the class struggle' advocated by Liu Shao-Chi ..."[13] Specifically, Mao argued that "the elimination of the system of ownership by the exploiting classes through socialist transformation is not equal to the disappearance of struggle in the political and ideological spheres".[14]

Indeed, this is the logic of a *cultural* revolution. Mao is asserting that even if there is the achievement of *political* power (dictatorship of the proletariat) and *economic* transformation (abolition of private ownership of the means of production), the revolution is still far from complete. Revolution is not an event but a process. This process Mao calls "socialist society" – in my view a somewhat confusing choice of words, but no matter – and "socialist society covers a fairly long historical period".[15] Furthermore, "there are classes and class struggle throughout the period of socialist society".[16] The Tenth Plenum of the 8th Central Committee of the CCP, meeting from 24 to 27 September 1962, in endorsing Mao's views, omitted the phrase "socialist society" and talked instead of "the historical period of proletarian revolution and proletarian dictatorship, ... the historical period of transition from capitalism to communism", which it said "will last scores of years or even longer" and during which "there is a class struggle between the proletariat and the bourgeosie and struggle between the socialist road and the capitalist road".[17]

We do not have directly Liu's counter arguments. We might however take as an expression of the alternative position a recent analysis published in the USSR on the relationship of the socialist system and world development. There it is asserted that at some unspecified point after the Second World War, "socialism outgrew the bounds of one country and became a world system ..."[18] It is further argued that: "Capitalism, emerging in the 16th century, became a world economic system only in the 19th century. It took the bourgeois revolutions 300 years to put an end to the power of the feudal elite. It took socialism 30 or 40 years to generate the forces for a new world system."[19] Finally, this book speaks of "capitalism's international division of labor"[20] and "international socialist cooperation of labor"[21] as two separate phenomena, drawing from this counterposition the policy conclusion: "Socialist unity has suffered a serious setback from the divisive course being pursued by the incumbent leadership of the Chinese People's Republic", and attributes this to "the great-power chauvinism of Mao Tse-Tung and his group".[22]

Note well the contrast between these two positions. Mao Tse-Tung is arguing for viewing "socialist society" as process rather than structure. Like Frank and Sweezy, and once again implicitly rather than explicitly, he is taking the world-system rather than the nation-state as the unit of analysis. The analysis by USSR scholars by contrast specifically argues the existence of *two* world-systems with two divisions of labor existing side by side, although the socialist system is acknowledged to be "divided". If divided politically, is it united economically? Hardly, one would think; in which case what is the substructural base to argue the existence of the system? Is it merely a moral imperative? And are then the Soviet scholars defending their concepts on the basis of Kantian metaphysics?

Let us see now if we can reinterpret the issues developed in these two debates within the framework of a general set of concepts that could be used to analyze the functioning of world-systems, and particularly of the historically specific capitalist world-economy that has existed for about four or five centuries now.

We must start with how one demonstrates the existence of a single division of labor. We can regard a division of labor as a grid which is substantially interdependent. Economic actors operate on some assumption (obviously seldom clear to any individual actor) that the totality of their essential needs – of sustenance, protection, and pleasure – will be met over a reasonable time span by a combination of their own productive activities and exchange in some form. The smallest grid that would substantially meet the expectations of the overwhelming majority of actors within those boundaries constitutes a single division of labor.

The reason why a small farming community whose only significant link to outsiders is the payment of annual tribute does not constitute such a single division of labor is that the assumptions of persons living in it concerning the provision of protection involve an "exchange" with other parts of the world-empire.

This concept of a grid of exchange relationships assumes, however, a distinction between *essential* exchanges and what might be called "luxury" exchanges. This is to be sure a distinction rooted in the social perceptions of the actors and hence in both their social organization and their culture. These perceptions can change. But this distinction is crucial if we are not to fall into the trap of identifying *every* exchange activity as evidence of the existence of a system. Members of a system (a minisystem or a world-system) can be linked in limited exchanges with elements located outside the system, in the "external arena" of the system. ...

We are, as you see, coming to the essential feature of a capitalist world-economy, which is production for sale in a market in which the object is to realize the maximum profit. In such a system production is constantly expanded as long as further production is profitable, and men constantly innovate new ways of producing things that will expand the profit margin. The classical economists tried to argue that such production for the market was somehow the "natural" state of man. But the combined writings of the anthropologists and the Marxists left few in doubt that such a mode of production (these days called "capitalism") was only one of several possible modes.

Since, however, the intellectual debate between the liberals and the Marxists took place in the era of the industrial revolution, there has tended to be a *de facto* confusion between industrialism and capitalism. This left the liberals after 1945 in the dilemma of explaining how a presumably non-capitalist society, the USSR, had industrialized. The most sophisticated response has been to conceive of "liberal capitalism" and "socialism" as two variants of an "industrial society", two variants destined to "converge". This argument has been trenchantly expounded by Raymond Aron.[23] But the same confusion left the Marxists, including Marx, with the problem of explaining what was the mode of production that predominated in Europe from the sixteenth to the eighteenth centuries, that is before the industrial revolution. Essentially, most Marxists have talked of a "transitional" stage, which is in fact a blurry non-concept with no operational indicators. This dilemma is heightened if the unit of analysis used is the state, in which case one has to explain why the transition has occurred at different rates and times in different countries.

Marx himself handled this by drawing a distinction between "merchant capitalism" and "industrial capitalism". This I believe is unfortunate teminology, since it leads to such conclusions as that of Maurice Dobb who says of this "transitional" period:

> But why speak of this as a stage of capitalism at all? The workers were generally not proletarianized: that is, they were not separated from the instruments of production, nor even in many cases from occupation of a plot of land. Production was scattered and decentralized and not concentrated. *The capitalist was still predominantly a merchant* [italics mine] who did not control production directly and did not impose his own discipline upon the work of artisan-craftsmen, who both laboured as individual (or family) units and retained a considerable measure of independence (if a dwindling one).[24]

One might well say: why indeed? Especially if one remembers how much emphasis Dobb places a few pages earlier on capitalism as a mode of *production* – how then can the capitalist be primarily a merchant? – on the concentration of such ownership in the hands of a few, and on the fact that capitalism is not synonymous with private ownership, capitalism being different from a system in which the owners are "small peasant producers or artisan-producers". Dobb argues that a defining feature of private ownership under capitalism is that some are "obliged to [work for those that own] since [they own] nothing and [have] no access to means of production [and hence] have no other means of livelihood".[25] Given this contradiction, the answer Dobb gives to his own question is in my view very weak: "While it is true that at this date the situation was transitional, and capital-to-wage-labour relations were still immaturely developed, the latter were already beginning to assume their characteristic features".[26]

If capitalism is a mode of production, production for profit in a market, then we ought, I should have thought, to look to whether or not such production was or was not occurring. It turns out in fact that it was, and in a very substantial form. Most of this production, however, was not industrial production. What was happening in Europe from the sixteenth to the eighteenth centuries is that over a large geographical area going from Poland in the northeast westwards and southwards throughout Europe and including large parts of the Western Hemisphere as well, there grew up a world-economy with a single division of labor within which there was a world market, for which men produced largely agricultural products for sale and profit. I would think the simplest thing to do would be to call this agricultural capitalism.

This then resolves the problems incurred by using the pervasiveness of *wage* labor as a defining characteristic of capitalism. An individual is no less a capitalist exploiting labor because the state assists him to pay his laborers low wages (including wages in kind) and denies these laborers the right to change employment. Slavery and so-called "second serfdom" are not to be regarded as anomalies in a capitalist system. Rather the so-called serf in Poland or the Indian on a Spanish *encomienda* in New Spain in this sixteenth-century world-economy were working for landlords who "paid" them (however euphemistic this term) for cash crop production. This is a relationship in which labor power is a commodity (how could it ever be more so than under slavery?), quite different from the relationship of a feudal serf to his lord in eleventh-century Burgundy, where the economy was not oriented to a world market, and where labor power was (therefore?) in no sense bought or sold.

Capitalism thus means labor as a commodity to be sure. But in the era of agricultural capitalism, wage labor is only one of the modes in which labor is recruited and recompensed in the labor market. Slavery, coerced cash-crop production (my name for the so-called "second feudalism"), sharecropping, and tenancy are all alternative modes. It would be too long to develop here the conditions under which differing regions of the world-economy tend to specialize in different agricultural products. I have done this elsewhere.[27]

What we must notice now is that this specialization occurs in specific and differing geographic regions of the world-economy. This regional specialization comes about by the attempts of actors in the market to avoid the normal operation of the market whenever it does not maximize their profit. The attempts of these actors to use non-market devices to ensure short-run profits makes them turn to the political entities which have in fact power to affect the market – the nation-states. ...

...In any case, the local capitalist classes – cash-crop landowners (often, even usually, nobility) and merchants – turned to the state, not only to liberate them from non-market constraints (as traditionally emphasized by liberal historiography) but to create new constraints on the new market, the market of the European world-economy.

By a series of accidents – historical, ecological, geographic – northwest Europe was better situated in the sixteenth century to diversify its agricultural specialization and add to it certain industries (such as textiles, shipbuilding, and metal wares) than were other parts of Europe. Northwest Europe emerged as the core area of this world-economy, specializing in agricultural production of higher skill levels, which favored (again for reasons too complex to develop) tenancy and wage labor as the modes of labor control. Eastern Europe and the Western Hemisphere became peripheral areas specializing in export of grains, bullion, wood, cotton, sugar – all of which favored the use of slavery and coerced cash-crop labor as the modes of labor control. Mediterranean Europe emerged as the semiperipheral area of this world-economy specializing in high-cost industrial products (for example, silks) and credit and specie transactions, which had as a consequence in the agricultural arena sharecropping as the mode of labor control and little export to other areas.

The three structural positions in a world-economy – core, periphery, and semiperiphery – had become stabilized by about 1640. How certain areas became one and not the other is a long story. The key fact is that given slightly different starting points, the interests of various local groups converged in northwest Europe, leading to the development of strong state mechanisms, and diverged sharply in the peripheral areas, leading to very weak ones. Once we get a difference in the strength of the state machineries, we get the operation of "unequal exchange"[28] which is enforced by strong states on weak ones, by core states on peripheral areas. Thus capitalism involves not only appropriation of the surplus value by an owner from a laborer, but an appropriation of surplus of the whole world-economy by core areas. And this was as true in the stage of agricultural capitalism as it is in the stage of industrial capitalism. . . .

Capitalism was from the beginning an affair of the world-economy and not of nation-states. It is a misreading of the situation to claim that it is only in the twentieth century that capitalism has become "world-wide", although this claim is frequently made in various writings, particularly by Marxists. . . . capital has never allowed its aspirations to be determined by national boundaries in a capitalist world-economy, and that the creation of "national" barriers – generically, mercantilism – has historically been a defensive mechanism of capitalists located in states which are one level below the high point of strength in the system.

. . . In the process a large number of countries create national economic barriers whose consequences often last beyond their initial objectives. At this later point in the process the very same capitalists who pressed their national governments to impose the restrictions now find these restrictions constraining. This is not an "internationalization" of "national" capital. This is simply a new political demand by certain sectors of the capitalist classes who have at all points in time sought to maximize their profits within the real economic market, that of the world-economy.

If this is so, then what meaning does it have to talk of structural positions within this economy and identify states as being in one of these positions? And why talk of three positions, inserting that of "semiperiphery" in between the widely used concepts of core and periphery? The state machineries of the core states were strengthened to meet the needs of capitalist landowners and their merchant allies. . . .

The strengthening of the state machineries in core areas has as its direct counter-part the decline of the state machineries in peripheral areas. ... In peripheral countries, the interests of the capitalist landowners lie in an opposite direction from those of the local commercial bourgeoisie. Their interests lie in maintaining an open economy to maximize their profit from world-market trade (no restrictions in exports and access to lower-cost industrial products from core countries) and in elimination of the commercial bourgeoisie in favor of outside merchants (who pose no local political threat). Thus, in terms of the state, the coalition which strengthened it in core countries was precisely absent.

The second reason, which has become ever more operative over the history of the modern world-system, is that the strength of the state machinery in core states is a function of the weakness of other state machineries. Hence intervention of outsiders via war, subversion, and diplomacy is the lot of peripheral states.

All this seems very obvious. I repeat it only in order to make clear two points. One cannot reasonably explain the strength of various state machineries at specific moments of the history of the modern world-system primarily in terms of a genetic-cultural line of argumentation, but rather in terms of the structural role a country plays in the world-economy at that moment in time. To be sure, the initial eligibility for a particular role is often decided by an accidental edge a particular country has, and the "accident" of which one is talking is no doubt located in part in past history, in part in current geography. But once this relatively minor accident is given, it is the operations of the world-market forces which accentuate the differences, institution-alize them, and make them impossible to surmount over the short run.

The second point we wish to make about the structural differences of core and periphery is that they are not comprehensible unless we realize that there is a third structural position: that of the semiperiphery. This is not the result merely of estab-lishing arbitrary cutting-points on a continuum of characteristics. ... The semiperi-phery is needed to make a capitalist world-economy run smoothly. Both kinds of world-system, the world-empire with a redistributive economy and the world-eco-nomy with a capitalist market economy, involve markedly unequal distribution of rewards. Thus, logically, there is immediately posed the question of how it is possible politically for such a system to persist. Why do not the majority who are exploited simply overwhelm the minority who draw disproportionate benefits? The most rapid glance at the historic record shows that these world-systems have been faced rather rarely by fundamental system-wide insurrection. While internal discontent has been eternal, it has usually taken quite long before the accumulation of the erosion of power has led to the decline of a world-system, and as often as not, an external force has been a major factor in this decline.

There have been three major mechanisms that have enabled world-systems to retain relative political stability (not in terms of the particular groups who will play the leading roles in the system, but in terms of systemic survival itself). One obviously is the concentration of military strength in the hands of the dominant forces. The modalities of this obviously vary with the technology, and there are to be sure political prerequisites for such a concentration, but nonetheless sheer force is no doubt a central consideration.

A second mechanism is the pervasiveness of an ideological commitment to the system as a whole. I do not mean what has often been termed the "legitimation" of a system, because that term has been used to imply that the lower strata of a system feel some affinity with or loyalty towards the rulers, and I doubt that this has ever been a significant factor in the survival of world-systems. I mean rather the degree to which the staff or cadres of the system (and I leave this term deliberately vague) feel that their own well-being is wrapped up in the survival of the system as such and the competence of its leaders. It is this staff which not only propagates the myths; it is they who believe them.

But neither force nor the ideological commitment of the staff would suffice were it not for the division of the majority into a larger lower stratum and a smaller middle stratum. Both the revolutionary call for polarization as a strategy of change and the liberal encomium to consensus as the basis of the liberal polity reflect this proposition. The import is far wider than its use in the analysis of contemporary political problems suggests. It is the normal condition of either kind of world-system to have a three-layered structure. When and if this ceases to be the case, the world-system disintegrates.

In a world-empire, the middle stratum is in fact accorded the role of maintaining the marginally desirable long-distance luxury trade, while the upper stratum concentrates its resources on controlling the military machinery which can collect the tribute, the crucial mode of redistributing surplus. By providing, however, for an access to a limited portion of the surplus to urbanized elements who alone, in premodern societies, could contribute political cohesiveness to isolated clusters of primary producers, the upper stratum effectively buys off the potential leadership of coordinated revolt. And by denying access to political rights for this commercial-urban middle stratum, it makes them constantly vulnerable to confiscatory measures whenever their economic profits become sufficiently swollen so that they might begin to create for themselves military strength.

In a world-economy, such "cultural" stratification is not so simple, because the absence of a single political system means the concentration of economic roles vertically rather than horizontally throughout the system. The solution then is to have three *kinds* of states, with pressures for cultural homogenization within each of them – thus, besides the upper stratum of core states and the lower stratum of peripheral states, there is a middle stratum of semiperipheral ones.

This semiperiphery is then assigned as it were a specific economic role, but the reason is less economic than political. That is to say, one might make a good case that the world-economy as an economy would function every bit as well without a semiperiphery. But it would be far less *politically* stable, for it would mean a polarized world-system. The existence of the third category means precisely that the upper stratum is not faced with the *unified* opposition of all the others because the *middle* stratum is both exploited and exploiter. It follows that the specific economic role is not all that important, and has thus changed through the various historical stages of the modern world-system. ...

Where then does class analysis fit in all of this? And what in such a formulation are nations, nationalities, peoples, ethnic groups? First of all, without arguing the point now, I would contend that all these latter terms denote variants of a single phenomenon which I will term "ethno-nations".

Both classes and ethnic groups, or status groups, or ethno-nations are phenomena of world-economies and much of the enormous confusion that has surrounded the concrete analysis of their functioning can be attributed quite simply to the fact that they have been analyzed as though they existed within the nation-states of this world-economy, instead of within the world-economy as a whole. This has been a Procrustean bed indeed.

The range of economic activities being far wider in the core than in the periphery, the range of syndical interest groups is far wider there.[29] Thus, it has been widely observed that there does not exist in many parts of the world today a proletariat of the kind which exists in, say, Europe or North America. But this is a confusing way to state the observation. Industrial activity being disproportionately concentrated in certain parts of the world-economy, industrial wage workers are to be found principally in certain geographic regions. Their interests as a syndical group are determined by their collective relationship to the world-economy. Their ability to influence the political functioning of this world-economy is shaped by the fact that they command larger percentages of the population in one sovereign entity than another. The form their organizations take have, in large part, been governed too by these political boundaries. The same might be said about industrial capitalists. Class analysis is perfectly capable of accounting for the political position of, let us say, French skilled workers if we look at their structural position and interests in the world-economy. Similarly with ethno-nations. The meaning of ethnic consciousness in a core area is considerably different from that of ethnic consciousness in a peripheral area precisely because of the different class position such ethnic groups have in the world-economy.

Political struggles of ethno-nations or segments of classes within national boundaries of course are the daily bread and butter of local politics. But their significance or consequences can only be fruitfully analyzed if one spells out the implications of their organizational activity or political demands for the functioning of the world-economy. . . .

The functioning then of a capitalist world-economy requires that groups pursue their economic interests within a single world market while seeking to distort this market for their benefit by organizing to exert influence on states, some of which are far more powerful than others but none of which controls the world market in its entirety. Of course, we shall find on closer inspection that there are periods where one state is relatively quite powerful and other periods where power is more diffuse and contested, permitting weaker states broader ranges of action. We can talk then of the relative tightness or looseness of the world-system as an important variable and seek to analyze why this dimension tends to be cyclical in nature, as it seems to have been for several hundred years.

We are now in a position to look at the historical evolution of this capitalist world-economy itself and analyze the degree to which it is fruitful to talk of distinct stages in its evolution as a system. The emergence of the European world-economy in the "long" sixteenth century (1450–1640) was made possible by an historical conjuncture: on those long-term trends which were the culmination of what has been sometimes described as the "crisis of feudalism" was superimposed a more immediate cyclical crisis plus climatic changes, all of which created a dilemma that could only be resolved by a geographic expansion of the division of labor. Furthermore, the balance of intersystem forces was such as to make this realizable. Thus a geographic expansion did take place in conjunction with a demographic expansion and an upward price rise. . . .

Each of the states or potential states within the European world-economy was quickly in the race to bureaucratize, to raise a standing army, to homogenize its culture, to diversify its economic activities. By 1640, those in north-west Europe had succeeded in establishing themselves as the core states; Spain and the northern Italian city-states declined into being semiperipheral; northeastern Europe and Iberian America had become the periphery. At this point, those in semiperipheral status had reached it by virtue of decline from a former more pre-eminent status.

It was the system-wide recession of 1650–1730 that consolidated the European world-economy and opened stage two of the modern world-economy. For the recession forced retrenchment, and the decline in relative surplus allowed room for only one core state to survive. The mode of struggle was mercantilism ... In this struggle England first ousted the Netherlands from its commercial primacy and then resisted successfully France's attempt to catch up. As England began to speed up the process of industrialization after 1760, there was one last attempt of those capitalist forces located in France to break the imminent British hegemony. This attempt was expressed first in the French Revolution's replacement of the cadres of the regime and then in Napoleon's continental blockade. But it failed.

Stage three of the capitalist world-economy begins then, a stage of industrial rather than of agricultural capitalism. Henceforth, industrial production is no longer a minor aspect of the world market but comprises an ever larger percentage of world gross production – and even more important, of world gross surplus. This involves a whole series of consequences for the world-system.

First of all, it led to the further geographic expansion of the European world-economy to include now the whole of the globe. This was in part the result of its technological feasibility both in terms of improved military firepower and improved shipping facilities which made regular trade sufficiently inexpensive to be viable. But, in addition, industrial production *required* access to raw materials of a nature and in a quantity such that the needs could not be supplied within the former boundaries. At first, however, the search for new markets was not a primary consideration in the geographic expansion since the new markets were more readily available within the old boundaries, as we shall see.

The geographic expansion of the European world-economy meant the elimination of other world-systems as well as the absorption of the remaining minisystems. The most important world-system up to then outside of the European world-economy, Russia, entered in semiperipheral status, the consequence of the strength of its state machinery (including its army) and the degree of industrialization already achieved in the eighteenth century. The independences in the Latin American countries did nothing to change their peripheral status. They merely eliminated the last vestiges of Spain's semiperipheral role and ended pockets of noninvolvement in the world-economy in the interior of Latin America. Asia and Africa were absorbed into the periphery in the nineteenth century, although Japan, because of the combination of the strength of its state machinery, the poverty of its resource base (which led to a certain disinterest on the part of world capitalist forces), and its geographic remoteness from the core areas, was able quickly to graduate into semiperipheral status. ...

The creation of vast new areas as the periphery of the expanded world-economy made possible a shift in the role of some other areas. Specifically, both the United

States and Germany (as it came into being) combined formerly peripheral and semiperipheral regions. The manufacturing sector in each was able to gain political ascendancy, as the peripheral subregions became less economically crucial to the world-economy. Mercantilism now became the major tool of semiperipheral countries seeking to become core countries, thus still performing a function analogous to that of the mercantilist drives of the late seventeenth and eighteenth centuries in England and France. To be sure, the struggle of semiperipheral countries to "industrialize" varied in the degree to which it succeeded in the period before the First World War: all the way in the United States, only partially in Germany, not at all in Russia.

The internal structure of core states also changed fundamentally under industrial capitalism. For a core area, industrialism involved divesting itself of substantially all agricultural activities (except that in the twentieth century further mechanization was to create a new form of working the land that was so highly mechanized as to warrant the appellation industrial). Thus whereas, in the period 1700–40, England not only was Europe's leading industrial exporter but was also Europe's leading agricultural exporter – this was at a high point in the economy-wide recession – by 1900, less than 10 percent of England's population were engaged in agricultural pursuits.

At first under industrial capitalism, the core exchanged manufactured products against the periphery's agricultural products – hence, Britain from 1815 to 1873 as the "workshop of the world". Even to those semiperipheral countries that had some manufacture (France, Germany, Belgium, the US), Britain in this period supplied about half their needs in manufactured goods. As, however, the mercantilist practices of this latter group both cut Britain off from outlets and even created competition for Britain in sales to peripheral areas, a competition which led to the late nineteenth-century "scramble for Africa", the world division of labor was reallocated to ensure a new special role for the core: less the provision of the manufactures, more the provision of the machines to make the manufactures as well as the provision of infrastructure (especially, in this period, railroads).

The rise of manufacturing created for the first time under capitalism a large-scale urban proletariat. And in consequence for the first time there arose what Michels has called the "anti-capitalist mass spirit",[30] which was translated into concrete organizational forms (trade unions, socialist parties). This development intruded a new factor as threatening to the stability of the states and of the capitalist forces now so securely in control of them as the earlier centrifugal thrusts of regional anti-capitalist landed elements had been in the seventeenth century.

At the same time that the bourgeoisies of the core countries were faced by this threat to the internal stability of their state structures, they were simultaneously faced with the economic crisis of the latter third of the nineteenth century resulting from the more rapid increase of agricultural production (and indeed of light manufactures) than the expansion of a potential market for these goods. Some of the surplus would have to be redistributed to someone to allow these goods to be bought and the economic machinery to return to smooth operation. By expanding the purchasing power of the industrial proletariat of the core countries, the world-economy was unburdened simultaneously of two problems: the bottleneck of demand, and the unsettling "class conflict" of the core states – hence, the social liberalism or welfare-state ideology that arose just at that point in time.

The First World War was, as men of the time observed, the end of an era; and the Russian Revolution of October 1917 the beginning of a new one – our stage four. This stage was to be sure a stage of revolutionary turmoil but it also was, in a seeming paradox, the stage of the *consolidation* of the industrial capitalist world-economy. The Russian Revolution was essentially that of a semiperipheral country whose internal balance of forces had been such that as of the late nineteenth century it began on a decline towards a peripheral status. ... The Revolution brought to power a group of state managers who reversed each one of these trends by using the classic technique of mercantilist semiwithdrawal from the world-economy. In the process of doing this, the now USSR mobilized considerable popular support, especially in the urban sector. At the end of the Second World War, Russia was reinstated as a very strong member of the semiperiphery and could begin to seek full core status. ...

It was the Second World War that enabled the United States for a brief period (1945–65) to attain the same level of primacy as Britain had in the first part of the nineteenth century. United States growth in this period was spectacular and created a great need for expanded market outlets. The Cold War closure denied not only the USSR but eastern Europe to US exports. And the Chinese Revolution meant that this region, which had been destined for much exploitative activity, was also cut off. Three alternative areas were available and each was pursued with assiduity. First, western Europe had to be rapidly "reconstructed", and it was the Marshall Plan which thus allowed this area to play a primary role in the expansion of world productivity. Secondly, Latin America became the reserve of US investment from which now Britain and Germany were completely cut off. Thirdly, southern Asia, the Middle East and Africa had to be decolonized. On the one hand, this was necessary in order to reduce the share of the surplus taken by the western European inter-mediaries, as Canning covertly supported the Latin American revolutionaries against Spain in the 1820s.[31] But also, these countries had to be decolonized in order to mobilize productive potential in a way that had never been achieved in the colonial era. Colonial rule after all had been an *inferior* mode of relationship of core and periphery, one occasioned by the strenuous late-nineteenth-century conflict among industrial states but one no longer desirable from the point of view of the new hegemonic power.[32]

But a world capitalist economy does not permit true imperium. Charles V could not succeed in his dream of world-empire. The Pax Britannica stimulated its own demise. So too did the Pax Americana. ...

Such a decline in US state hegemony has actually *increased* the freedom of action of capitalist enterprises, the larger of which have now taken the form of multi-national corporations which are able to maneuver against state bureaucracies when-ever the national politicians become too responsive to internal worker pressures. Whether some effective links can be established between multinational corporations, presently limited to operating in certain areas, and the USSR remains to be seen, but it is by no means impossible.

This brings us back to one of the questions with which we opened this paper, the seemingly esoteric debate between Liu Shao-Chi and Mao Tse-Tung as to whether China was, as Liu argued, a socialist state, or whether, as Mao argued, socialism was a *process* involving continued and continual class struggle. No doubt to those to whom the terminology is foreign the discussion seems abstrusely theological. The issue, however, as we said, is real. If the Russian Revolution emerged as a reaction to the threatened further decline of Russia's structural position in the world-economy, and if fifty years later one can talk of the USSR as entering the status of a core power in a *capitalist* world-economy, what then is the meaning of the various so-called socialist revolutions that have occurred on a third of the world's surface? First let us notice that it has been neither Thailand nor Liberia nor Paraguay that has had a "socialist revolution" but Russia, China and Cuba. That is to say, these revolutions have occurred in countries that, in terms of their internal economic structures in the pre-revolutionary period, had a certain minimum strength in terms of skilled personnel, some manufacturing, and other factors which made it plausible that, within the framework of a capitalist world-economy, such a country could alter its role in the world division of labor within a reasonable period (say 30–50 years) by the use of the technique of mercantilist semi-withdrawal. (This may not be all that plausible for Cuba, but we shall see.) Of course, other countries in the geographic regions and military orbit of these revolutionary forces had changes of regime without in any way having these characteristics (for example, Mongolia or Albania). It is also to be noted that many of the countries where similar forces are strong or where considerable counterforce is required to keep them from emerging also share this status of minimum strength. I think of Chile or Brazil or Egypt – or indeed Italy.

Are we not seeing the emergence of a political structure for *semiperipheral* nations adapted to stage four of the capitalist world-system? The fact that all enterprises are nationalized in these countries does not make the participation of these enterprises in the world-economy one that does not conform to the mode of operation of a capitalist market system: seeking increased efficiency of production in order to realize a maximum price on sales, thus achieving a more favorable allocation of the surplus of the world-economy. If tomorrow US Steel became a worker's collective in which all employees without exception received an identical share of the profits and all stockholders are expropriated without compensation, would US Steel thereby cease to be a capitalist enterprise operating in a capitalist world-economy?

What then have been the consequences for the world-system of the emergence of many states in which there is no private ownership of the basic means of production? To some extent, this has meant an internal reallocation of consumption. It has certainly undermined the ideological justification in world capitalism, both by showing the political vulnerability of capitalist entrepreneurs and by demonstrating that private ownership is irrelevant to the rapid expansion of industrial productivity. But to the extent that it has raised the ability of the new semiperipheral areas to enjoy a larger share of the world surplus, it has once again depolarized the world, recreating the triad of strata that has been a fundamental element in the survival of the world-system.

Finally, in the peripheral areas of the world-economy, both the continued economic expansion of the core (even though the core is seeing some reallocation of surplus internal to it) and the new strength of the semiperiphery has led to a further weakening of the political and hence economic position of the peripheral areas. The pundits note that "the gap is getting wider", but thus far no one has succeeded in doing much about it, and it is not clear that there are very many in whose interests it would be to do so. Far from a strengthening of state authority, in many parts of the world we are witnessing the same kind of deterioration Poland knew in the sixteenth century, a deterioration of which the frequency of military coups is only one of many signposts. And all of this leads us to conclude that stage four has been the stage of the *consolidation* of the capitalist world-economy.

Consolidation, however, does not mean the absence of contradictions and does not mean the likelihood of long-term survival. ...

There are two fundamental contradictions, it seems to me, involved in the workings of the capitalist world-system. In the first place, there is the contradiction to which the nineteenth-century Marxian corpus pointed, which I would phrase as follows: whereas in the short run the maximization of profit requires maximizing the withdrawal of surplus from immediate consumption of the majority, in the long run the continued production of surplus requires a mass demand which can only be created by redistributing the surplus withdrawn. Since these two considerations move in opposite directions (a "contradiction"), the system has constant crises which in the long run both weaken it and make the game for those with privilege less worth playing.

The second fundamental contradiction, to which Mao's concept of socialism as process points, is the following: whenever the tenants of privilege seek to coopt an oppositional movement by including them in a minor share of the privilege, they may no doubt eliminate opponents in the short run; but they also up the ante for the next oppositional movement created in the next crisis of the world-economy. Thus the cost of "cooption" rises ever higher and the advantages of cooption seem ever less worthwhile.

There are today no socialist systems in the world-economy any more than there are feudal systems because there is only *one* world-system. It is a world-economy and it is by definition capitalist in form. Socialism involves the creation of a new kind of *world*-system, neither a redistributive world-empire nor a capitalist world-economy but a socialist world-government. I don't see this projection as being in the least utopian but I also don't feel its institution is imminent. It will be the outcome of a long struggle in forms that may be familiar and perhaps in very few forms, that will take place in *all* the areas of the world-economy (Mao's continual "class struggle"). Governments may be in the hands of persons, groups or movements sympathetic to this transformation but *states* as such are neither progressive nor reactionary. It is movements and forces that deserve such evaluative judgment.

NOTES

1. George Lukács, "The Marxism of Rosa Luxemburg", in *History and Class Consciousness* (London: Merlin Press, 1968), p. 27.
2. See Frederic Lane's discussion of "protection costs" which is reprinted in part 3 of *Venice and History* (Baltimore: Johns Hopkins Press, 1966). For the specific discussion of tribute, see pp. 389–90, 416–20.
3. See Karl Polanyi, "The Economy as Instituted Process", in Karl Polanyi, Conrad M. Arsenberg and Harry W. Pearson (eds), *Trade and Market in the Early Empire* (Glencoe: Free Press, 1957), pp. 243–70.
4. Andre Gunder Frank, "The Myth of Feudalism", in *Capitalism and Under-development in Latin America* (New York: Monthly Review Press, 1967), p. 3.

5. See Theotonio Dos Santos, *La Nueva Dependencia* (Buenos Aires: s/ediciones, 1968).
6. Ernesto Laclau, "Feudalism and Capitalism in Latin America", *New Left Review*, 67 (May–June 1971), 37–8.
7. The debate begins with Maurice Dobb, *Studies in the Development of Capitalism* (London: Routledge and Kegan Paul, 1946). Paul Sweezy criticized Dobb in "The Transition from Feudalism to Capitalism", *Science and Society*, 14: 2 (Spring 1950), 134–57, with a "Reply" by Dobb in the same issue. From that point on many others got into the debate in various parts of the world. I have reviewed and discussed this debate *in extenso* in *The Modern World-System: Capitalist Agriculture and the Origins of the European World-Economy in the Sixteenth Century* (New York: Academic Press, 1974), ch. 1.
8. It would take us into a long discursus to defend the proposition that, like all great thinkers, there was the Marx who was the prisoner of his social location and the Marx, the genius, who could on occasion see from a wider vantage point. The former Marx generalized from British history. The latter Marx is the one who has inspired a critical conceptual framework of social reality. W. W. Rostow incidentally seeks to refute the former Marx by offering an alternative generalization from British history. He ignores the latter and more significant Marx. See *The Stages of Economic Growth: A Non-Communist Manifesto* (Cambridge: University Press, 1960).
9. Laclau, "Feudalism and Capitalism", pp. 25, 30.
10. Cited in F. Burlatsky, *The State and Communism* (Moscow: Progress Publishers, n.d. [1961]), p. 95.
11. Ibid., p. 97.
12. Mao Tse-Tung, *On The Correct Handling of Contradictions Among The People*, 7th edn, revised translation (Peking: Foreign Languages Press, 1966), pp. 37–8.
13. *Long Live The Invincible Thought of Mao Tse-Tung!*, undated pamphlet, issued between 1967 and 1969, translated in *Current Background*, 884 (18 July 1969), 14.
14. This is the position taken by Mao Tse-Tung in his speech to the Work Conference of the Central Committee at Peitaiho in August 1962, as reported in the pamphlet, *Long Live...*, p. 20. Mao's position was subsequently endorsed at the 10th Plenum of the 8th CCP Central Committee in September 1962, a session this same pamphlet describes as "a great turning point in the violent struggle between the proletarian headquarters and the bourgeois headquarters in China". *Ibid.*, p. 21.
15. Remarks made by Mao at 10th Plenum, cited in *ibid.*, p. 20.
16. Mao Tse-Tung, "Talk on the Question of Democratic Centralism", 30 January 1962, in *Current Background*, 891 (8 October 1969), 39.
17. "Communiqué of the 10th Plenary Session of the 8th Central Committee of the Chinese Communist Party", *Current Background*, 691 (5 October 1962), 3.
18. Yuri Sdobnikov (ed.), *Socialism and Capitalism: Score and Prospects* (Moscow: Progress Publications, 1971), p. 20.
19. Ibid., p. 21.
20. Ibid., p. 26.
21. Ibid., p. 24.
22. Ibid., p. 25.
23. Say Raymond Aron, *Dix-huit leçons de la société industrielle* (Paris: Ed. Gallimard, 1962).
24. Maurice Dobb, *Capitalism Yesterday and Today* (London: Lawrence and Wishart, 1958), p. 21.
25. Ibid., pp. 6–7.
26. Ibid., p. 21.
27. See my *The Modern World-System*, ch. 2.
28. See Arghiri Emmanuel, *Unequal Exchange* (New York: Monthly Review Press, 1972).

29. "Range" in this sentence means the number of different occupations in which a significant proportion of the population is engaged. Thus peripheral society typically is overwhelmingly agricultural. A core society typically has its occupations well-distributed over all of Colin Clark's three sectors. If one shifted the connotation of range to talk of style of life, consumption patterns, even income distribution quite possibly one might reverse the correlation. In a typical peripheral society, the differences between a subsistence farmer and an urban professional are probably far greater than those which could be found in a typical core state.
30. Robert Michels, "The Origins of the Anti-Capitalist Mass Spirit", in *Man in Contemporary Society* (New York: Columbia University Press, 1955), vol. 1, pp. 740–65.
31. See William W. Kaufman, *British Policy and the Independence of Latin America, 1804–28* (New Haven: Yale University Press, 1951).
32. Cf. Catherine Coquery-Vidrovitch, "De l'impérialisme britannique à l'impérialisme contemporaine – l'avatar colonial", *L'Homme et la société*, 18 (October-December 1970), 61–90.

14 The Effects of International Economic Dependence on Development and Inequality: A Cross-National Study (1975)

Christopher Chase-Dunn

Johns Hopkins University sociologist Christopher Chase-Dunn pioneered quantitative approaches to dependency and world-system analysis. Chase-Dunn took the same data utilized by World Bank analysts and showed that countries were hurt, not helped, by the presence of large transnational firms investing in their countries. The point has been much debated since, with many qualifications. But the original piece presented here is important because it helped open up a new direction in the field of development, and one which allowed these researchers to survive as political scientists and sociologists in US universities, where the "right journals" favored quantitative work. Fernando Henrique Cardoso critiqued World Systems Theory precisely for the oversimplification and depoliticization that came with the "Americanization" of dependency theory into "World Systems Theory." But Chase-Dunn's work answered critiques of dependency and world systems approaches that said they offered no testable hypotheses and were therefore more historical than scientific. His more recent work has included the influential book *Global Formation* and studies of economic interactions between prehistoric societies.

... Dependency theorists claim that international economic dependence produces the "development of underdevelopment" in peripheral areas of the world economy. At the same time, the core-periphery distinction has led to revisions in the theory of capitalist development which focus on the world-system, rather than national societies, as the relevant unit of analysis. In combination these two ideas imply that while Marx's law of uneven development and pauperization may have been wrong for the core nations, it is correct for the world economy as a whole and for the peripheral nations in particular. The growing gap between core and periphery and the gross inequalities within peripheral countries suggest that this is indeed the case.

However, the hypothesis that dependence retards development has not been adequately tested by formal comparative research. Case studies have found evidence both contradictory and supportive of this hypothesis, as have the few previous comparative studies which have been done. The related hypothesis that dependence increases inequality within peripheral countries has not been subjected to comparative test. This paper reports the results of a longitudinal comparative study of the effects of two kinds of international economic dependence on economic development and a cross-sectional test of the effects of dependence on income inequality.

International Economic Dependence

International power-dependence relations range from direct military force, through formal political subjugation (colonialism), to more subtle economic forms of power and influence such as foreign investment, foreign aid and trade relations based on a vertical division of labor. Although it is clear that these different forms are functionally interrelated, the focus of this research is on the more subtle neo-colonial types of economic dependence which predominated in the period studied – the *Pax Americana* from 1950 to 1970.

International economic dependence itself varies from direct penetration to indirect dependence resulting from location in a larger structure. The most direct economic penetration by core nations of peripheral areas is through private investment by transnational corporations which directly own and control the process of production. Less direct influence is exercised by foreign aid programs and credit agencies. Indirect economic dependence results from a nation's location in a restricted position in the world trade network or its specialization in a marginal role in the international division of labor.

This research examines the economic effects of two specific types of dependence: investment dependence and debt dependence. These two types of economic dependence are positively correlated (.63) and they may have similar effects on economic development and income inequality.

Theoretical Approaches to Dependence and Development

Uneven Development and International Power-Dependence Relations

Myrdal (1957) points out that capitalist development unleashes market forces which create both "spread" effects by which growth in one area or sector creates development in other areas and "backwash" effects which drain resources out of the hinterland and concentrate them. In the developed nations (comprising what Wallerstein [1974a] calls the "core" of the world-system), class struggle and political processes have strengthened spread effects resulting in a more even distribution of development. In the periphery, however, backwash effects have been dominant, resulting in the concentration of development in the core and in enclaves attached to the core. At the level of the world-system as a whole, uneven development remains the dominant trend.

The operation of control structures between core-states and peripheral areas may reinforce this uneven development. Direct colonial control of peripheral areas has been replaced by the neo-colonial mechanisms of direct foreign investment and credit. It is my hypothesis that, other things equal, penetration by external control structures has a negative effect on economic development through the mechanisms reviewed below. The period studied in this research, 1950 to 1970, was a period of world economic expansion in which almost all national economies were growing (Meyer et al., 1975). The hypothesis is, then, that dependent nations grow less than others.

Before discussing theories which predict or imply hypotheses about dependence effects on development, it is necessary to clarify three possible misunderstandings. First, what many theorists understand to be simply resource flows between largely unconnected societies are considered by other theorists to be control structures which link superordinate to subordinate units in the same interactive system. These radically different ways of perceiving the same reality lead to completely different predictions about the consequences of such relations.

The second problem in discussing different theoretical approaches is that some theorists propose very long-run structural mechanisms by which dependence may affect development while others propose short-term effects. Both long-run and short-term hypotheses are reviewed because the research design used in this study is germane to both.

Third, some theories deal with the effects of international power-dependence relations in general, others deal specifically with investment and debt dependence. Again both types are discussed as the research is relevant to both, although more directly to the latter...

The Theory of Imperialism   Marx (1967) saw the historical relationship between the centers of capitalist development and the hinterlands of the world in terms of the notion of primitive accumulation. Part of the impetus for the emergence and domination of the capitalist mode of production was the appropriation by European powers of the wealth of Africa, Asia and the Americas. Marx thought that the domination of the capitalist mode of production would spread throughout the world economy battering down all Chinese walls with the cheap prices of its commodities. Colonialism would destroy the pre-capitalist mode of production and each nation would develop the way England had.

Lenin (1965) introduced the concept of imperialism into the Marxist analysis of capitalist development. He pointed out that the exploitation of peripheral areas was an important dimension of capitalist development rather than a passing phase. Lenin saw monopoly capitalism as needing to export capital and to appropriate raw materials and markets in the periphery. He predicted inter-imperialist wars resulting from the division and redivision of the periphery by the advanced capitalist powers. Lenin expected that the original centers of capitalist development in Europe would become decadent and that the source of industrial strength would move to the periphery.

Dependency Theory.   The persistence of underdevelopment in the periphery led to the reexamination of the theory of imperialism and monopoly capitalism by Baran (1956). Baran put forth the theory that penetration of the periphery by core-capitalism actually creates obstacles to development. Later Frank (1969) was to term this idea the "development of underdevelopment," implying that the poverty of the periphery is an ongoing modern process not a primordial state. The literature on the mechanisms by which interaction between core and periphery has retarded the latter has grown greatly in recent years. Dependency theory deals with three main topics: exploitation, structural distortion and suppression of autonomous policies.

a. Exploitation of the Periphery by the Core

Capitalist development on a world scale involves competition among different actors (capitals and states) for shares of the economic surplus. New resources are created, but at any point in time the amount of extant surplus is finite. Frank (1969) argues that penetration of the periphery by foreign investment drains surplus from the periphery to the core through the repatriation of profits and interest. This backwash effect accumulates capital in the core and underdevelops the periphery. Amin (1974) contends that this "decapitalization" results from a continuing process of primitive accumulation in which political and military force backs up economic advantage in core-periphery relations.

Emmanuel (1972) contends that exploitation is hidden in the prices at which commodities from the periphery are exchanged for commodities from the core. This "unequal exchange" stems from the different wage structures in the core and the periphery. In the periphery, a worker must work, say, two hours to produce what is exchanged for a product which a core worker produces in one hour – and at the same level of productivity. Thus, the market prices of core-periphery exchange contain a transfer of value to the core.

Some theorists argue that unequal exchange and uneven development will occur in any system of interaction in which the distribution of power is unequal (Baumgartner et al., 1975). This happens because more powerful actors will use their power to determine outcomes to their advantage. This approach seems to apply to any situation in which the welfare of the less powerful is not heavily protected by social or political institutions. Certainly the world economy is such a system. If foreign investment and credit are control structures between superordinate and subordinate actors in a competitive system, they should cause uneven development.

Thus, exploitation of the periphery by the core is hypothesized to occur by means of decapitalization, unequal exchange and subordination to external controls in a competitive system. These mechanisms are thought to retard the development of the periphery.

b. Structural Distortion of the Peripheral Economy

A number of dependency theorists argue that the economic structure which emerges in the periphery as a result of the world division of labor is distorted in such a way as to create obstacles to development (Amin, 1974; DosSantos, 1970). An outward oriented economy specializing in the production of raw materials for export does not develop a differentiated internal structure. Frank (1969) observes that the infrastructure created by colonialism and foreign investment is oriented toward the ports of exit. Railroads, roads, telegraph lines, etc. all function to carry raw materials out of the country and return processed goods. This retards the integration of the national economy by linking the different areas and sectors of the peripheral countries with the external world rather than with one another (Ehrensaft, 1971). The multiplier effect, by which demand in one sector or area of a country creates demand in another, is weak because externally oriented linkages soon transfer demand to the international economy (Singer, 1971). ...

Prebisch (1950) maintains that any national economy which remains undifferentiated will suffer from the vicissitudes of the international market, and that this is especially true of those specialized in the production of raw materials because the terms of trade for these commodities decline relative to manufactured goods and capital equipment produced in the core. Also, as there is more fluctuation in price for raw materials in the world market, instability makes economic planning (private or public) more difficult.

In addition Griffin and Enos (1970) argue that dependence on foreign credit reduces the domestic marginal propensity to save and thus negatively affects economic growth by lowering domestic capital formation.

Beckford's (1971) analysis of the role of transnational corporations in plantation economies suggests that the short-term impact of these corporations increases national income and opens new areas of production, but the long-run institutional and structural effect is to distort the use of resources in the peripheral economy. Transnational corporations greatly affect land use, labor markets and the allocation of investments. Beckford maintains that the logic by which these corporations operate is derived from the scope of the enterprise as a whole, including processing and marketing operations in the core. Thus, they influence the allocation of resources in the periphery from this point of view, using market imperfections (monopoly power in sales and consumption) to guard against the risks of natural or political disaster. Their interest in maintaining relatively cheap labor, low taxes and the freedom to maneuver is often inconsistent with the balanced development of the peripheral country in which they produce. The distortion of resource use patterns creates what Beckford calls a state of dynamic underdevelopment. Thus dependence is hypothesized to distort the economic structure of the periphery in the following ways: specialization in raw material production (low differentiation); outward-oriented infrastructure (low integration); the creation of resource use patterns which retard economic development.

c. Suppression of Autonomous Policies in the Periphery

Some dependency theorists have argued that dependence retards development through its suppression of autonomous policies in government and business which would mobilize balanced development (Johnson, 1972). Baran (1956) contends that dependence distorts the development of a national bourgeoisie. Merchants, with their stake in the export of raw materials and the import of manufactured goods, combine with landed classes (which have similar interests) to prevent the emergence of a domestic manufacturing or industrial bourgeoisie. They do this by politically preventing the introduction of tariffs which would protect infant industries against the competition of already developed producers in the core-states. Frank (1969) sees this process in the history of Latin American development. Civil wars occurring around 1830 in most of the newly independent republics involved the issue of autonomous versus external orientation. In each case, the forces of "free trade" and external orientation triumphed. Wallerstein (1972) makes a similar case for the peripheralization of Poland in the sixteenth-century European "world-economy."

Other theorists maintain that strong links between elites in the periphery and core elites form what Galtung (1971) calls a "bridgehead" of interests and connections. The external orientation of these "liaison elites" and the fact that their power and interests are based on connections with the core-states means that they suppress policies and leaders seeking to mobilize balanced autonomous development. According to Hayter (1971), international and transnational agencies which lend to peripheral countries (development banks and private banks) stand behind the operations of transnational companies in maintaining "a good climate for foreign investment."

Sunkel (1973) claims that the connections of ruling groups in the dependent periphery with core-states and transnational corporations create a political structure which keeps wages low and concentrates development in the international sector. The links between the core and elites in the periphery increase income inequality by (1) raising the incomes of elites and (2) keeping the wages of workers low. The power of the elites in dependent peripheral countries is backed by their alliances with the core, so they are able to suppress demands for higher wages and income redistribution. Thus dependence creates a political situation which retards development by linking elites in the periphery to the interests of the core. This prevents the emergence of autonomous forces seeking to mobilize balanced development and maintains extreme inequalities in the periphery.

Theoretical Approaches Which Hypothesize Positive Effects of Dependence on Development

Most neo-classical economists and modernization theorists in sociology see that dependence as resource flows or the diffusion of modernity from advanced to backward societies. The notion that foreign investment and credit constitute a form of domination is seen as paranoid and reactive and as a remnant of the unfortunate colonial past (Viner, 1952). . . .

Neo-Classical International Economics.   In neo-classical international economics, the flow of capital from advanced to less-developed nations is understood to be a main engine of economic growth. Capital is capital and its investment should lead to increased production in the enterprise into which it is channeled, as well as economic growth in other sectors due to increased demand. Unrestricted international flow of capital to areas where it will bring the highest return will result in the maximization of growth for the system as a whole and presumably also for the peripheral areas to which the capital flows. The benefits of foreign investment will spread due to incomes created by new employment and the "trickle-down" effect caused by increased demand for land, labor and materials (Schelling, 1958). The input of foreign aid should result in growth for the same reasons and also because it supplements local savings and makes greater investment possible (Chenery and Strout, 1966). The use of aid funds to build public works and infrastructure should have positive effects on later growth.

The theory of comparative advantage holds that specialization in the production of raw materials (one of the correlates of dependence) will not have negative effects on growth if it is more economical to exchange raw materials for manufactured goods than to produce the imported goods domestically. Ricardo (1933) put forward the theory of comparative advantage to show why it was mutually advantageous for nations to trade. The example he used was the exchange of English linen for Portuguese wine. The theory holds that "whether or not one of two regions is absolutely more efficient in the production of every good than is the other, if each specializes in the products in which it has a comparative advantage (greatest relative efficiency), trade will be mutually profitable to both regions" (Samuelson, 1964). This is in direct contradiction to the idea of "structural distortion" discussed above.

Modernization Theory   Most sociologists who study development and modernization focus almost exclusively on processes internal to national societies (Eisenstadt, 1966; Stanley, 1972; Smelser, 1963). The exceptions to this are those theorists who discuss borrowing or diffusion of modern traits from advanced to premodern societies. ... Parsons (1971)... focusing on diffusion, claims that

> ...the "imperialist" phase of Western society's relationship with the rest of the world was transitional. The trend toward modernization has now become world-wide. In particular, the elites of most nonmodern societies accept crucial aspects of the values of modernity, especially economic development, education, political independence, and some form of "democracy."

Modernization theorists also emphasize the transfer of advanced technology, modern rational organizational forms, labor habits complementary to industrial production and "modern" attitudes toward the self, the family and the society which facilitate economic development (Moore and Feldman, 1960). This approach implies that a country which is penetrated by direct foreign investment (has located within it subsidiaries of modern transnational corporations) should develop more than a country that is not so penetrated. Similarly, foreign aid which brings technical assistance and advice regarding fiscal and development policies should also facilitate economic growth.

Summary of Propositions

Dependency theorists predict a negative effect of dependence on economic growth and a positive effect on income inequality. Neo-classical economic theories and modernization theories predict a positive effect for economic growth and a negative effect on income inequality. The dependency literature reviewed above discusses mechanisms by which international power-dependence relations in general have effects on development. The following propositions relate specifically to the types of dependence studied in this research – investment and debt dependence.

Mechanisms by which investment and debt dependence negatively effect economic growth:

(a) Exploitation by the core drains resources from the periphery which are needed for its development. Profits on foreign investment and interest on credit transfer value from the periphery to the core and retard the development of the periphery.

(b) Externally oriented production and penetration by transnational corporations distort the economic structure of the periphery. Differentiation and integration of national economies are obstructed and a pattern of resource use is created which maintains a state of dynamic underdevelopment.

(c) Links between elites in the core and the dependent periphery act to suppress autonomous mobilization of national development.

Mechanisms by which foreign investment and credit positively effect economic growth:

(a) Foreign capital creates production directly in the enterprise in which it is invested and generates demand for other inputs which contribute to economic growth.

(b) Foreign credit finances public infrastructure needed for development.

(c) Diffusion of technology, work habits, modern organizational forms, modern attitudes and consumption preferences stimulate economic development.

Mechanisms by which investment and debt dependence affect income inequalities within dependent countries:

(a) Positive effect – In peripheral countries penetrated by external control structures, the ruling groups are able to obtain a large share of the national income and to prevent income redistribution because their power is backed up by alliances with the core.

(b) Negative effect – Foreign investment and credit expand the wage-earning working class and the salaried middle class which enlarges the middle of the income distribution and lowers overall inequality.

Let us turn now to a comparative test of dependence effects on economic development. This enables us to estimate whether aggregate effects are positive or negative, but does not differentiate between all the mechanisms hypothesized above. Any estimated aggregate effect may be the resultant of the simultaneous operation of different mechanisms, but findings which are consistently negative will direct further attention to dependency theory.

Research Design

Panel Regression Analysis

Panel regression analysis is a flexible statistical method for testing causal propositions which allows the introduction of multiple independent variables and, because it employs data at different points in time, reduces the likelihood of false inferences due to reciprocal causality. The dependent variable is measured at both the first and the second point in time (in this study, 1950 and 1970). The independent variables are measured at the earlier time point. The dependent variable at the later time point (t) is regressed on itself at the early time point (t−1) and on the independent variables at t−1.

This provides an estimate of the effect of the independent variable which is "independent" of variance in the dependent variable at t−1. It is an estimate of the effect which the independent variable has on the dependent variable over the period of time between the two measurements. The length of time between the two measurements is referred to as the "lag," and the t−1 measurement of the dependent variable is called the "lagged dependent variable." The basic equation for this panel model is:

$$Y_t = a + bY_{t-1} + bX_{i(t-1)} + U_t$$

where Y_t = dependent variable

$\quad Y_{t-1}$ = lagged dependent variable

$\qquad a$ = constant

$\qquad b$ = unstandardized regression coefficient

$\quad X_{i(t-1)}$ = measure of economic dependence

$\qquad U_t$ = disturbances affecting Y_t but unrelated to other variables in the equation.

If it is hypothesized that a variable not in the equation is causing a spurious estimate of the effect of the independent variable, it can be controlled by including it in the equation. Failure to include such a variable may lead to faulty inferences.

Weighting of Variables

Measures of dependence used in the tables reported below have been weighted by population size (per capita) rather than on economic size (per GNP) of the nation in order to make a conservative test of the hypothesis of a negative effect of dependence on development. Weighting with population size rather than economic size should bias the estimate toward the positive if there is an artifact due to ratio measures having common terms.

Sample of Nations

The theoretical literature on dependence effects focuses on less-developed countries and so our sample of nations consists of those with less than $406 per capita GNP in 1955. This excludes the richest nations from the analysis while leaving enough cases to allow meaningful regression estimates. Thus we are comparing poor, dependent nations with poor independent or isolated nations. A parallel analysis including the rich nations is reported in Chase-Dunn (1975). The results are very similar to those presented below.

Measurement

The research design employed in this study requires that data be gathered at two points in time – 1950 and 1970. A great quantity of comparable data have been produced over the last twenty-five years by international organizations. Secondary analysis of these data require that a fit be made between the information available and the theoretical variables of interest.

Measurement of International Economic Dependence

Investment dependence per capita – the penetration of a nation by direct private foreign capital investment – is measured by employing an item from the International Monetary Fund Balance of Payments Yearbook: (1950–55) "Debits on investment income" in US dollars. It reports all profits made by foreign direct investment in the "host" country (regardless of whether or not they are repatriated). The average debits on investment income are computed for the period from 1950 to 1955 (to smooth out short-term variation) and divided by the population. This variable, due to its badly skewed distribution, is converted to a logarithmic scale to make it suitable for use in linear regression analysis. ....

Debt dependence per capita – the dependence of a nation on foreign credit – is measured by the total "external public debt," which is composed of loans to the government and government-guaranteed loans (IBRD, World Bank, 1971). The per capita distribution of this variable is not badly skewed, so it is unnecessary to convert it to a logarithmic scale. Since these data are not available before 1965, we are forced to use a shorter time lag for our panel regression estimates.

Measurement of Economic Development

We use three conventional measures of aggregate economic development:

(1) Log Gross National Product per capita for 1950 and 1970 (IBRD, 1971; 1973). This measure and the measure of kilowatt hours have been converted to a logarithmic scale because of the extreme right-skewness of the unlogged distributions.

(2) Log kilowatt hours of electricity consumed per capita for 1950 and 1965 (Taylor and Hudson, 1971).

(3) The percentage of the male labor force not employed in agriculture for 1950 and 1960. These data, based on national censuses, are reported by the International Labour Organization (ILO, 1971).

Measures of Other Causal Variables

There are two additional variables introduced into the equations estimating the effects of dependence on aggregate economic development. They are hypothesized to be related to both dependence and development and so they must be included in a model estimating the effect of dependence on development.

(1) Domestic Capital Formation – a measure of local savings, domestic capital formation as a percentage of Gross Domestic Product.[1] It is found for 1960 in Taylor and Hudson (1971).

(2) Specialization in mining – the percentage of Gross Domestic Product produced in the mining sector shows the extent to which a national economy is specialized in the production of mineral raw materials. It is found in data presented by the World Bank for 1955 (IBRD, 1971).

Measure of Income Inequality

Data on income inequality are not available for different time points so panel analysis which uses it as a dependent variable is not possible.

Individual and household income inequality – a Gini index computed from the distribution of national income to quintiles of the population, from the poorest 20 percent to the richest 5 percent. It has been gathered by Adelman and Morris (1971) and improved by Paukert (1973) resulting in 58 cases available for around 1965.

Results

First, let us consider the cross-sectional correlations between debt dependence, investment dependence and economic development. The correlation between investment dependence and debt dependence is .63 indicating that they are somewhat different aspects of economic dependence. ...

Both investment dependence and debt dependence are positively correlated with measures of economic development in the sample of poor nations. This is because a number of very poor nations are not dependent on foreign investment and credit, that is, they are relatively isolated from neo-colonial control structures. Foreign capital tends to flow where there is already greater economic activity; thus the correlation between dependence and development is positive. ... Similarly, debt dependence is higher among more developed peripheral countries because credit is extended on the basis of economic potential. Previous research has interpreted these positive cross-sectional correlations as evidence that dependence facilitates development. Panel analysis enables us to separate the reciprocal effects of dependence and development, that is, to estimate the effect of dependence on development separately from the effect of development on dependence.

Effects of Investment Dependence on Economic Development

Let us look now at the panel regression estimates of investment dependence effects on three measures of economic development in Table 1. The lags differ between dependent variables so it is difficult to compare the size of the effects. The direction (positive or negative) is the main question.

The regression coefficients estimating the effects of investment dependence are negative for all three measures of economic development (betas = $-.22$; $-.12$; $-.02$) indicating that investment dependence retards development. For GNP per capita and kilowatt hours of electricity per capita, the estimates are statistically significant at the .05 level. The estimated effect on the percentage of the labor force in

Table I Panel Regression Estimates of Effect of Investment Dependence on Economic Development

Y_t		Log GNP per capita 1970			Log kilowatt hours per capita 1965			% Non-agricultural labor force 1960		
		b	S.E.b	Beta	b	S.E.b	Beta	b	S.E.b	Beta
Constant	$-.17$				1.13			-6.7		
Y_{t-1}		1.32	.13	.99	.78	.05	.97	1.02	.03	.98
Investment Dependence 1950–55		$-.097$	.045	$-.22^*$	$-.087$	.041	$-.12^*$	-1.62	2.27	$-.02$
Cases			N = 38			N = 31			N = 46	

Y_t = Dependent Variable   S.E.b = Standard Error of b
Y_{t-1} = Lagged Dependent Variable, 1950   * = P < .05

non-agricultural production is small and not statistically significant, but this measure of occupational structure changes slowly and there is only a ten-year lag, as data are not yet available for 1970.

Beckford's (1971) contention that foreign investment has immediate positive effects, but long-run negative effects on development is supported by the finding that longer lags with the same dependent variables produce larger negative estimates (Chase-Dunn, 1975).

The stability terms in the panel regressions (the estimates for Y_{t-1}) are always large and thus significance levels are not indicated for these coefficients in the tables. The amount of variance in the dependent variable accounted for by panel regression analysis is always very high (above .70), so no measure of explained variance is reported.

The estimated effect on Log Kilowatt Hours in Table 1 is for a fifteen-year lag (1950–1965). Data are available for 1970 on this variable, but for fewer cases. The estimate using the 1970 measure of Kilowatt Hours is also negative (beta = −.15).

The model examined in Table 1 assumes that other variables are not interacting with investment dependence and economic development. However, specialization in mining and capital formation may interact with investment dependence and economic development to change the effects shown in Table 1. Therefore, there is a need to introduce these two variables into the model.

First, we know that core-states need to acquire raw materials, so foreign investment is attracted to countries with substantial mineral resources. This means that the effect of having mineral resources is confounded with the effect of investment dependence in Table 1.

In Table 2 we introduce another independent variable, the specialization of a nation in mining, including the production of oil and other minerals. The correlation between investment dependence and specialization in mining is .40, which supports the idea that foreign investment is drawn to areas with mineral resources. Table 2 shows the estimated effects on three measures of economic development of both investment dependence and specialization in mining.

Table 2 Panel Regression Estimates of Effects of Investment Dependence and Specialization in Mining on Economic Development

Y_t	Log GNP per capita 1970			Log kilowatt hours per capita 1965			% Non-agricultural labor force 1960		
	b	S.E.b	Beta	b	S.E.b	Beta	b	S.E.b	Beta
Constant	−.39			1.27			−13.7		
Y_{t-1}	1.50	.16	1.05	.76	.04	.98	1.07	.06	.99
% GNP in mining 1950	.120	.046	.28**	.099	.039	.17**	.89	1.01	.05
Investment Dependence 1950–55	−.187	.059	−.41**	−.145	.044	−.22**	−2.27	1.15	−.12*
Cases	N = 25			N = 24			N = 25		

Y_t = Dependent Variable   S.E.b. = Standard error of b
Y_{t-1} = Lagged Dependent Variable, 1950   * = P < .05   ** = P < .01

The estimates of investment dependence effects are all more negative and statistically significant in Table 2 than in Table 1. Thus, the hypothesis that investment dependence has negative effects on development is strongly supported. The effects of specialization in mining are positive on all three dependent variables and are statistically significant at the .01 level except for the effect on the percentage of the labor force in non-agricultural production. These results provide support for the contention that mineral resources facilitate economic development.

Second, it may be that investment dependence is related to the ability to generate local savings. If domestic savings for new investment are low, foreign capital may flow in to take up the available opportunities. At the same time the low propensity to save and invest may be related to other difficulties within a peripheral economy which retard economic development. If this were so it would produce a spurious negative estimate of the effect of investment dependence on economic development when domestic capital formation is not included in the model.

Table 3 shows the results of including a measure of domestic capital formation in an equation estimating the effect of investment dependence on development. Due to lack of data in 1950 on domestic capital formation, a shorter time lag for the dependent variable is used in Table 3. (The longer lag with fewer cases produces results very similar to those shown in Table 3.) The shorter time lag reduces the size of the estimated effect of investment dependence, but Table 3 presents the estimate both with and without domestic capital formation. It can be seen by comparing the estimates that the inclusion of domestic capital formation reduces the negative estimate of the investment dependence effect only slightly. This means that investment dependence has negative effects independent of its relationship with domestic capital formation.

The effect of domestic capital formation is positive on both GNP per capita and Kilowatt Hours per capita, although only the first estimate is statistically significant.
. . .

Effects of Debt Dependence on Economic Development

Data on external public debt are not available for most poor countries before 1965. A short-lag panel analysis can be made between 1965 and 1970, however.

Table 4 contains the results of an analysis which includes debt dependence and domestic capital formation as independent variables. Domestic capital formation is included because it may be related to the tendency to contract foreign debt and because it is known to effect economic development. The estimated effects of debt dependence are both negative, but only the effect on kilowatt hours is statistically significant. This is weak evidence that debt dependence has negative effects, but fairly strong evidence that it does not have positive effects.

The estimated effect of domestic capital formation, which was significant with the longer lag in Table 3, is not significant in Table 4 for either dependent variable.

Effects of Debt and Investment Dependence on Inequality

Dependence is thought to affect development in part through its effects on the class structure of the peripheral countries. It is hypothesized that liaison elites in

Table 3 Panel Regression Estimates of Effects of Investment Dependence and Domestic Capital Formation on Economic Development

A. Without Domestic Capital Formation in the equation:

Y_t		Log GNP per capita 1970				Log kilowatt hours per capita 1965		
		b	S.E.b	Beta		b	S.E.b	Beta
Constant	−24				.19			
Y_{t-1}		1.18	.07	.97		.95	.02	.99
Investment Dependence 1956–60		−.052	.027	−.12*		.034	.018	−.04

B. With Domestic Capital Formation in the equation:

Y_t		Log GNP per capita 1970				Log kilowatt hours per capita 1965		
		b	S.E.b	Beta		b	S.E.b	Beta
Constant	−.16				.19			
Y_{t-1}		1.09	.08	.89		.94	.03	.98
Domestic Capital Formation 1960		.89	.35	.16**		.25	.29	.03
Investment Dependence 1956–60		−.044	−.024	−.11*		−.031	.019	−.04
Cases		N = 28				N = 28		

Y_t = Dependent Variable   S.E.b = Standard Error of b
Y_{t-1} = Lagged Dependent Variable, 1960   * = P < .05   ** = P < .01
Cases are those for which data are available on both Domestic Capital Formation and Investment Dependence.

Table 4 Panel Regression Estimates of Effects of Debt Dependence and Domestic Capital Formation on Economic Development

Y_t		Log GNP per capita 1970				Log Kilowatt Hours per capita 1970		
		b	S.E.b.	Beta		b	S.E.b.	Beta
Constant	−.03				−.06			
Y_{t-1}		1.09	.07	.99		1.19	.14	1.03
Domestic Capital Formation 1960		.004	.27	.001		−.49	1.09	−.05
Debt Dependence 1965		−.007	.007	−.05		−.059	.028	−.22*
Cases		N = 33				N = 26		

Y_t = Dependent Variable   * = P < .05
y_{t-1} = Lagged Dependent Variable, 1965   S.E.b = Standard Error of b

dependent countries are supported by external power and thus the distribution of resources is very unequal. Only cross-sectional data on income inequality are available and they are not gathered at exactly the same time point for each case (Paukert, 1973). Even so, given the theoretical relevance of the proposition that dependence effects on development are connected with effects on inequality, a preliminary test of the effect on inequality is justified. Table 5 contains the results of the cross-sectional analysis of the effects of investment and debt dependence on income inequality in peripheral countries. Included as dependent variables in both equations are specialization in mining and economic development – both thought to be related to dependence and inequality.

The estimates of the dependence effects are both positive but not statistically significant (although nearly so at the .05 level). This is weak support for the hypothesis that dependence maintains income inequality in peripheral countries.[2]

Summary of Results

The hypothesis that investment dependence retards economic development is strongly supported by Tables 1, 2 and 3. Further investigation of dependence effects on growth in different economic sectors indicates that there are negative effects on production in agriculture and manufacturing, but that investment dependence has a *positive* effect on production in mining (Chase-Dunn, 1975). This suggests that

Table 5 Cross-sectional Regression Estimates of the Effects of Investment and Debt Dependence, Economic Development and Specialization in Mining on Income Inequality

A. Investment Dependence

Y		Gini Index of inequality of distribution of national income among individuals and households		
		b	S.E.b	Beta
Constant	38.59			
Log GNP per capita		−3.28	7.6	−.09
Specialization in Mining		.014	.018	.17
Investment Dependence		6.11	3.84	.44
		N = 31	$r^2 = .27$	

B. Debt Dependence

Y		Income inequality		
		b	S.E.b	Beta
Constant	45.62			
Log GNP per capita		−1.19	7.12	−.04
Specialization in Mining		.021	.018	.22
Debt		.011	.008	.31
		N = 30	$r^2 = .18$	

dependence effects are not uniform and that further research should be done to determine the loci of effects on development.

It is shown that debt dependence definitely does not facilitate economic development, and there is weak evidence that it retards it. It may require a longer time lag for the negative effects of debt dependence to become measurable by cross-national research. This question can be settled as more complete data are collected.

Table 5 provides some support for the hypothesis that dependence causes the unequal distribution of income. It should be added that the estimated effect of investment dependence on the income share received by the top five percent of the population is positive, while effects on the income received by the bottom three quintiles of the population are negative. This is further evidence that dependence provides support for elites in the periphery and keeps wages low relative to the income of elites.

Theoretical Implications

The findings reported above indicate that dependency theory must be taken seriously as an explanation for uneven development in the world economy. Power-dependence relations between core and periphery operate to reproduce the inequalities between national societies. In a competitive world economy, subjection to external controls is a disadvantage which retards relative development. This is shown to be true for direct penetration by investment dependence and is also true of indirect forms of dependence resulting from restricted location in the international trade network. ...

The finding of a negative effect of investment dependence on economic development means that foreign capital must be seen as a form of control as well as a flow of resources. The structural and institutional context in which this economic flow is imbedded produce effects which are opposite those of domestic capital investment. The proposed mechanisms by which dependence retards development are not directly tested herein, and further research focusing specifically on intervening variables needs to be done. The most plausible explanation for the short-term effects of dependence is that proposed by Beckford (1971). Nations which are subjected to external controls cannot appropriate their own surplus capital for investment in balanced development. Transnational corporations operate to further their own growth, but not the development of the countries in which they are located. These corporations use their political and economic influence to keep labor costs and taxes low and to maintain the conditions for their continued profitable operation.

The preliminary finding that dependence maintains income inequalities suggests that one way in which dependence retards development is by linking national elites in the periphery to the interests of the transnational corporations and the international economy. Thus political and economic forces which attempt to mobilize balanced national development are suppressed.

We know that a great deal of foreign investment in peripheral countries goes into the extraction of mineral raw materials. Therefore the finding that investment dependence increases production in the mining sector (Chase-Dunn, 1975) suggests that foreign investment has positive effects on the enterprise in which it is invested. In combination with the finding of negative effects on aggregate economic development, this suggests that foreign investment combines positive direct effects on the enterprise in which it is invested with negative effects on the rest of the national economy, resulting in overall negative effects.

In the light of these findings, oppositional movements and national policies in the periphery which stress self-reliance and careful control over inputs from the core must be seen as other than reactive ignorance. . . .

One solution to the problem of dependence would appear to be the control of inputs from the core to assure compatibility with balanced development (Morley, 1975). A number of nations have made laws regulating foreign investment in an attempt to gain the benefits without the costs, e.g., Japan, Mexico, India and Yugoslavia. This strategy is difficult in a competitive world in which the transnational corporations have the upper hand. The larger scale on which transnational corporations operate gives them the advantage over small peripheral countries (Moran, 1973). The Balkanization of the periphery which is the legacy of the colonial empires makes solidarity among peripheral nations difficult. Competition for foreign investment, rather than concerted regulation of it, has been the main tendency.

Regional agreements to regulate core inputs such as the Andean group may be a good strategy for the periphery (Girvan, 1973). The example of the Organization of Petroleum Exporting Countries indicates that effective coordination of policies between peripheral states is possible, and this alternative may be more realizable with the economic downturn which began in 1967. A world-wide contraction of production with increasing competition between core-states has compromised the hegemony which the United States enjoyed during the *Pax Americana*. Increasing economic competition and political pluralism in the world-system, with more of a balance between competing core-states, may create opportunities for peripheral solidarity which have not heretofore existed.

We have already seen manifestations of such solidarity in the OPEC and other producers' combinations, the growth of regional trade, investment and development agreements and the rise of economic nationalism in many peripheral nations. This growing awareness of the core-periphery contradiction and the effects of dependence may be the beginning of a political process which eventually will modify the grossly uneven development of the world economy. . . .

NOTES

1. Gross Domestic Product is GNP plus net factor payments to abroad. It includes income which returns to non-nationals, including profit and interest on foreign investment and loans (O'Loughlin, 1971).
2. The possibility that this result is due to reciprocal causation – a positive effect of inequality on investment dependence due to low wages or the policies of liaison elites – is partly ruled out by a panel analysis which includes income inequality as an independent variable. An estimate of the effect of inequality on investment dependence was computed by regressing investment dependence in 1966 on income inequality in 1965 while controlling for investment dependence in 1955. This revealed no effect of inequality on investment dependence, although this is not a conclusive result because of the time at which inequality is measured.

If it may be assumed that inequality is fairly stable over this time period, this result rules out the hypothesis of a reciprocal effect which would account for the cross-sectional relationship shown in Table 5. This is additional support for the hypothesis that dependence causes inequality.

REFERENCES

Adelman, Irma and C. T. Morris, 1971, "Anatomy of patterns of income distribution in developing countries." Final research report, US Agency for International Development, CSD–2236.

Amin, Samir, 1974, *Accumulation on a World Scale*. New York: Monthly Review Press.

Baran, Paul, 1956, *The Political Economy of Growth*. New York: Monthly Review Press.

Baumgartner, Tom, Walter Buckley, and Tom R. Burns, 1975, "Toward a systems theory of unequal exchange, uneven development and dependency relations." Paper prepared for the Third International Congress of Cybernetics and Systems, Bucharest.

Beckford, George, 1971, *Persistent Poverty: Underdevelopment in Plantation Regions of the World*. New York: Oxford University Press.

Chase-Dunn, Christopher, 1975, "International economic dependence in the world system." Ph.D. dissertation, Stanford University.

Chenery, H. B. and A. M. Strout, 1966, "Foreign assistance and economic development." *American Economic Review* 56: 144–51.

Dos Santos, Teotonio, 1970, "The structure of dependence." Papers and Proceedings, *American Economic Review* 60: 231–6.

Ehrensaft, Philip, 1971, "Semi-industrial capitalism in the Third World." *Africa Today* 18:40–67.

Eisenstadt, S. N., 1966, *Modernization: Protest and Change*. Englewood Cliffs, NJ: Prentice-Hall.

Emmanuel, Arghiri, 1972, *Unequal Exchange: A Study of the Imperialism of Trade*. New York: Monthly Review Press.

Frank, Andre Gunder, 1969, *Latin America: Underdevelopment or Revolution*. New York: Monthly Review Press.

Galtung, Johan, 1971, "A structural theory of imperialism." *Journal of Peace Research*: 8:61–77.

Girvan, Norman, 1973, "The development of dependency economics in the Caribbean and Latin America." *Social and Economic Studies* 22:1–33.

Griffin, Keith B. and J. L. Enos, 1970, "Foreign assistance: objectives and consequences." *Economic Development and Cultural Change* 18:313–27.

Hayter, Teresa, 1971, *Aid as Imperialism*. Baltimore: Penguin.

IBRD (International Bank for Reconstruction and Development), 1971, *World Tables*. Washington, DC. 1973, *World Economic Atlas*. Washington, DC.

ILO (International Labour Organization), 1971, Labour Force Projections. Parts 1–5, ILO, Geneva.

IMF (International Monetary Fund), 1950–1955, *Balance of Payments Yearbook*. Washington, DC.

Johnson, Dale L., 1972, "Dependence and the international system." in J. D. Cockcroft, A. G. Frank and D. L. Johnson (eds.), *Dependence and Underdevelopment*. New York: Anchor.

Kaufman, Robert R., Daniel S. Geller and Harry I. Chernotsky, 1975, "A preliminary test of the theory of dependency." *Comparative Politics* 7:303–31.

Lenin, V. I., 1965, *Imperialism: The Highest Stage of Capitalism*. Peking: Foreign Language Press.

Marx, Karl, 1967, *Capital*, Vol. 1. New York: International Publishers.

Meyer, John W., John Boli-Bennett and Christopher Chase-Dunn, 1975, "Convergence and divergence in development." *Annual Review of Sociology*.

Moore, Wilbert and David Feldman, 1960, *Labor Commitment and Social Change in Developing Areas*. New York: Social Science Research Council.

Moran, Theodore H., 1973, "Transnational strategies of protection and defense by multinational corporations." *International Organization* 27:273–301.

Morley, Samuel A., 1975, "What to do about foreign direct investment: a host country perspective." *Studies in Comparative International Development* 10:45–66.

Myrdal, Gunnar, 1957, *Rich Nations and Poor*. New York: Harper and Row.

O'Loughlin, Carleen, 1971, *National Economic Accounting*. Oxford: Pergamon.

Parsons, Talcott, 1971, *The System of Modern Societies*. Englewood Cliffs, NJ: Prentice-Hall.

Paukert, Felix, 1973, "Income distribution at different levels of development." *International Labor Review* 108:97–125.

Prebisch, Raul, 1950, *The Economic Development of Latin America and its Principal Problems*. New York: United Nations Department of Social and Economic Affairs.

Ricardo, David, 1933, *Principles of Political Economy and Taxation*. London: Dent.

Samuelson, Paul A., 1964, *Economics*, 6th ed. New York: McGraw-Hill.

Schelling, Thomas C., 1958, *International Economics*. Boston: Allyn and Bacon.

Singer, Hans, 1971, "The distribution of gains between investing and borrowing countries." in Geo. Dalton (ed.), *Economic Development and Social Change*. Garden City, NY: Natural History Press.

Smelser, Neil E., 1963, "Mechanisms of change and adjustment to change." in B. F. Hoselitz and W. E. Moore (eds.), *Industrialization and Society*. Paris: UNESCO/Mouton.

Stanley, Manfred (ed.), 1972, *Social Development*. New York: Basic Books.

Sunkel, Osvaldo, 1973, "Transnational capitalism and national disintegration in Latin America." *Social and Economic Studies* 22: 132–76.

Taylor, Charles C. and M. C. Hudson, 1971, *World Handbook of Political and Social Indicators II*. Inter-University Consortium for Political Research, University of Michigan.

Viner, Jacob, 1952, "America's aims and the progress of underdeveloped areas." in B. F. Hoselitz (ed.), *The Progress of Underdeveloped Areas*. Chicago: University of Chicago Press.

Wallerstein, Immanuel, 1972, "Three paths to national development in 16th century Europe." *Studies in Comparative International Development* 8:95–101.

1974, *The Modern World System*. New York: Academic Press.

15 Rethinking Development Theory: Insights from East Asia and Latin America (1994)

Gary Gereffi

After earlier research on the pharmaceutical industry in Brazil, Duke University sociologist Gary Gereffi (1948–) pioneered what has become known as "the commodity chain approach." He argued that poor countries were able to develop only so far because they were selling their goods on unfavorable terms, for example, in contracting arrangements, where US firms like Nike carried out the marketing of shoes produced cheaply in Korea or China. In this chapter, first published in 1989, Gereffi points out the differences and similarities in the trajectories of Latin American and Asian developing nations, comparing Brazil and Mexico with Korea and Taiwan. He examines the question of why East Asian countries were able to maintain growth in the 1970s and 1980s when other nations endured the effects of a global recession. His work is useful in tracing the stages of policies taken by nations in the two regions, showing how production for export (Asia) or internal markets (Latin America) was based on and later influenced many aspects of the nation's social structure, such as income distribution or politics.

Introduction

The sociology of development has evolved by formulating paradigms and comparative generalizations that incorporate the experience of particularly dynamic sets of societies in the world system. In recent years, the main challenge for development studies has shifted to East Asia. The reasons why are rather easy to understand.

Japan and its regional neighbors South Korea, Taiwan, Hong Kong, and Singapore have made the most impressive economic strides of any nations in the world in the postwar era. They registered record economic growth rates not only during the prosperous 1960s when international trade and investment were expanding worldwide, but they also have managed to sustain their dynamism throughout the 1970s and 1980s in the face of severe oil price hikes, a global recession, and rising protectionism in their major export markets. This rapid economic growth, furthermore, has been accompanied by a relatively egalitarian distribution of income. Small wonder that development specialists are intrigued by the East Asian experience as they try to understand how these high-growth economies operate and why they have been so resilient.

This interest in East Asia has sparked a rejuvenation of cross-regional research on development issues. Latin America is a prime candidate for comparison with East Asia. The two regions are the most industrialized in the developing world, with Mexico, Brazil, and Argentina being the Latin American analogues of East Asia's "Four Tigers" (South Korea, Taiwan, Hong Kong, and Singapore). In the 1980s, however, Latin American nations found it difficult to maintain their previous levels of growth, as they confronted mountainous external debts, chronic inflation, shortages of investment capital, and the growing social and economic marginalization of large segments of their population.

The highly industrialized countries in East Asia and Latin America have been a fertile spawning ground for a variety of theories and concepts dealing with Third World development. However, the weight of the evidence used in support of these approaches typically has been quite uneven across the two regions. The theories and concepts often are biased because they reflect events in only some of the East Asian and Latin American nations, leading them to misrepresent the reality of the others.

This essay is an effort to rethink some of the key suppositions of development theory and to identify the fallacies that have been generated by a selective reading of the evidence from East Asia and Latin America. Although the East Asian and Latin American nations by no means cover the entire spectrum of development possibilities in the Third World, they are a good base from which to build solid comparative generalizations because they embody different routes to industrial success. This suggests that there are a number of alternative paths of national development.

The first part of this essay outlines several theoretical perspectives on development that highlight key features of the East Asian and Latin American experiences. While these perspectives offer some important insights, each one is flawed by attempts to generalize beyond the cases that gave rise to the insight itself. These misperceptions are dealt with in the remainder of the study, which presents cross-regional evidence from East Asia and Latin America leading to a reformulation and synthesis of some of these earlier approaches.

Theoretical Perspectives on East Asian and Latin American Development: Perceptions and Misconceptions

The development theories related to East Asia and Latin America are at several different levels of generality, including new trends in the global economy, distinct conceptual categories used to describe and analyze the highly industrialized nations in the two regions, and the roles of domestic institutions and sociocultural factors that shape the process of national development. The literature on *the new international division of labor* traces the recent surge of manufactured exports from the Third World to the emergence of a global manufacturing system based on labor-intensive export platforms established by transnational corporations in low-wage areas. This new international division of labor was created in order to exploit reserve armies of labor on a world scale by using the advanced transport and communication technologies that permit the spatial segmentation of the production process (Fröbel et al., 1981).

An extension of this approach, the *globalization of production* perspective, argues that the shift of manufacturing capacity toward decentralized production sites is occurring in both the advanced and the developing countries, and it reflects the increasingly centralized control and coordination by transnational corporations (TNCs) of these decentralized production units. This has fostered both greater international interdependence and enhanced TNC leverage over national governments and domestic labor (Gordon, 1988).

The most widely used term in referring to the high-growth, diversified economies of East Asia and Latin America is *newly industrializing countries* (or NICs). The expression was coined in the mid-1970s by the advanced capitalist nations, which were concerned that a number of developing countries were significantly expanding their world share in the production and export of manufactured goods. (See OECD, 1979. The NICs included are South Korea, Taiwan, Hong Kong, Singapore, Brazil, Mexico, Spain, Portugal, Greece, and Yugoslavia.) The specter of "other Japans" was a worry to the slumping Western industrial economies, giving rise in some circles to strident calls for protectionism.

Once the economic trends in the NICs became well established, the World Bank and prominent neoclassical economists in a variety of other institutions began to offer unambiguous policy prescriptions regarding the *development strategies* of these Third World nations. They argued that the outward-oriented development strategies of the East Asian NICs led to better economic performance in terms of exports, economic growth, and employment than did the inward-oriented development strategies of the Latin American NICs (see Balassa, 1981: 1–26; Balassa et al., 1986; World Bank, 1983: chap. 5). The clear implication was that the East Asian NICs should serve as a model to be emulated by the rest of the developing world.

World-systems theory employs the concept of *semiperipheral countries* to identify an intermediate stratum between core and peripheral nations that promotes the stability and legitimacy of the three-tiered world economy. The countries within the semiperipheral zone, which includes the East Asian and Latin American NICs, supposedly have the capacity to resist peripheralization but not the capability to move into the upper tier (Wallerstein, 1974; Arrighi and Drangel, 1986).

Dependency theory uses the term *dependent development* to indicate that structural dependency on foreign capital and external markets in rapidly industrializing Third World nations like the Latin American and East Asian NICs constrains and distorts, but is not incompatible with, capitalist economic development (Evans, 1979; Cardoso and Faletto, 1979; Gold, 1981; Lim, 1985). This was a striking departure from earlier "stagnationist" views that claimed dependency could only lead to underdevelopment and revolution (see Gereffi, 1983: chap. I, for an overview of this debate).

Some political scientists argue that one of the key institutional features of successful late industrializers is the rise of a *developmental state* oriented to selective but substantial intervention in their economies in order to promote rapid capital accumulation and industrial progress. In Latin America as well as East Asia, the state has tended to be strong, centralized, authoritarian (often under military control), and actively involved in economic affairs (O'Donnell, 1973; Collier, 1979; Johnson,

1987; Wade, 1990). This literature raises the question of whether a developmental state is a prerequisite for capitalist industrialization on the periphery.

The rapid growth of the East Asian NICs has refocused attention on the role of *cultural factors* in national development. Various writers have recently argued that Confucianism confers certain advantages over other traditions in the quest for economic development. Because Confucian beliefs place a high value on hard work, loyalty, respect for authority, and punctuality, these characteristics are thought to have facilitated the national consensus around high-speed economic growth evident in Japan and the East Asian NICs since the 1950s and 1960s. This culturally derived capacity for cooperation led political elites, industrial leaders, workers, and other citizens to agree on the primacy of economic objectives for the society as a whole and on the means to achieve those objectives (Johnson, 1983:6–10; see also the chapters by Lucien Pye, Gordon Redding, and Siu-lun Wong in Berger and Hsiao, 1988). In Latin America, a divergent set of cultural norms based upon an Ibero-Catholic heritage has been identified as impeding the economic advancement of the region (see Valenzuela and Valenzuela, 1978, for a review of this approach).

Each of these theoretical perspectives contains valuable observations about the development of the East Asian and Latin American NICs. Recent comparative research, however, suggests that some of these prior generalizations may be too sweeping. They often fit one region or time period reasonably well but falter when their scope is expanded. To facilitate efforts at reformulating the earlier theoretical approaches, I will highlight the fallacies or misperceptions embedded in each of these perspectives.

1. The early discussions of the new international division of labor place an undue emphasis on labor-intensive, assembly-oriented export production in the NICs, which in retrospect characterizes only the initial phase of their export efforts. Since the 1970s, both the East Asian and the Latin American NICs have moved toward more technology- and skill-intensive exports focusing on high-value-added products. Furthermore, these newer export industries are not "export enclaves" but instead promote high levels of integration with a well-developed local industrial base.

2. The globalization of production approach correctly highlights the emergence of a decentralized global manufacturing system in which production capacity is dispersed to an unprecedented number of developing as well as industrialized countries. However, this does not rest solely on a base of increasingly centralized and coordinated control by TNCs. Local private firms are the main exporters in many of the Third World nations today, but their ability to effectively capture the economic surplus in these export industries tends to be restricted by the kinds of subcontracting relationships in which they are enmeshed.

3. The East Asian and Latin American NICs are not really "newly" industrializing, nor have they developed in response to the same kinds of global dynamics. Because these NICs originated in the mid-1970s as a defensive reaction by OECD (Organization for Economic Cooperation and Development) countries to increasing Third World exports, many studies of the NICs tend to focus too narrowly on manufactured exports and implicitly or explicitly marginalize the opportunities for countries that have a rich endowment of natural resources. To

understand the emergence of the NICs we need to adopt a broader historical and world-systems perspective that is sensitive to different kinds of economic capabilities in Third World nations.

4. The contrast between the outward-oriented and inward-oriented development strategies of the East Asian and Latin American NICs, respectively, is overdrawn. Each of the countries in the two regions has pursued a combination of inward- and outward-oriented strategies. Furthermore, it is this mix of development strategies that helps us understand how industrial diversification has led to enhanced export flexibility and competitiveness in both sets of NICs in the 1980s.

5. The semiperipheral zone encompasses an extremely diverse range of countries. In order to understand the actual roles played by semiperipheral nations in the world economy today, we need to disaggregate this concept and focus on the specific characteristics of the NICs in different geographical regions like East Asia and Latin America.

6. Dependent development is applicable to the NICs in East Asia as well as Latin America. The nature and consequences of dependency are quite different in the two regions, however. Dependency in the East Asian NICs is a product of their heavy reliance on foreign aid and foreign trade, while dependency in the Latin American NICs is an outgrowth of their extensive involvement with trans-national corporations and transnational banks. The developmental consequences of these different types of dependency turn, in large degree, on the ability of the state to convert these external linkages to national advantage. Successful "dependency management" depends on the historical timing of these efforts as well as institutional factors.

7. While there is a substantial degree of state intervention in the economies of the Latin American and East Asian NICs (with the exception of Hong Kong), the developmental state is not a singular phenomenon in the two regions. The objectives, social bases, and policy instruments of the state are quite different in each country, with major implications for the exercise of state autonomy in areas like industrial policy.

8. Simplistic cultural arguments run into a variety of problems. First, regions are not culturally homogeneous; this is particularly true of East Asia. In Taiwan and South Korea, for example, Taoism and Buddhism as well as Confucianism have important followings, and there is a significant Christian minority in some East Asian countries like South Korea. More importantly in terms of the timing of high-speed growth, both the Confucian and Ibero-Catholic traditions have existed for centuries. In both regions, but especially in East Asia, however, the dynamic shifts in economic performance have occurred primarily in recent decades. A more sophisticated cultural interpretation would see culture as historically situated, emergent, and mediated through institutions (see Swidler, 1986). The impact of cultural variables probably is most important in outlining an acceptable range of solutions to development problems, rather than in determining specific economic outcomes.

The following sections of this essay address some of these themes in greater detail. In closing, I will outline the elements for a new theoretical synthesis, with some suggestions for future research.

The NICs in Historical and World-Systems Contexts

The East Asian and Latin American NICs are a very heterogeneous group, with major differences in population size, land area, resource endowments, cultural legacies, political regimes, social structures, per capita income, and economic policies. Nonetheless, these nations tend to have several dynamic features in common that lead them to be widely perceived as industrial "success stories": rapid and generally sustained economic growth, based on a sharp increase in the manufacturing sector's share of total output and employment; a growing diversification of industrial production that permits each nation to make ever broader ranges of manufactured goods; and a fast expansion of exports with an emphasis on manufacturers.

The Latin American and East Asian NICs are at relatively advanced levels of industrial development. They are all upper-middle- or upper-income countries by World Bank standards, although the average gross national product (GNP) per capita in 1990 was considerably higher in the East Asian nations: Hong Kong, $11,490; Singapore, $11,160; Taiwan, $7,680; South Korea, $5,400; Brazil, $2,680; Mexico, $2,490; and Argentina, $2,370. However, while the East Asian NICs grew rapidly during the 1980s, the Latin American NICs suffered an absolute as well as a relative decline. The 1981 GNP per capita figures highlight both trends (see Table 1). The Latin American NICs had similar or, in the case of Argentina, substantially lower per capita incomes in 1990 than nine years earlier. The East Asian NICs, on the other hand, doubled or tripled their average incomes in the 1980s.

Manufacturing has been a cornerstone of development for the Latin American and East Asian NICs, while the role of agriculture has declined in these economies since 1965. The manufacturing sector's share of gross domestic product (GDP) in 1990 was 18 percent in Hong Kong; it ranged between 23 percent and 29 percent in Mexico, Brazil, and Singapore; and it reached peak levels of 31 to 35 percent in South Korea, Taiwan, and Argentina (see Table 1). The prominence of manufacturing activities in the NICs is much higher than in the United States (17 percent) and comparable to many of the other advanced industrial economies, including Japan (29 percent). In all of the core nations, and Hong Kong as well, the service sector now is the most dynamic sector of the economy.

The East Asian and Latin American NICs have launched major export drives since 1980. By 1990, the East Asian NICs had clearly established themselves as the Third World's premier exporters. Taiwan and South Korea topped the list in 1990 with $67 and $65 billion in exports, respectively, followed by Singapore with an export total (including re-exports) of nearly $53 billion. Hong Kong, Brazil, and Mexico occupied a second tier with exports in the $27 to $31 billion range, while Argentina ($12 billion) lagged well behind the rest of the pack (see Table 2). The East Asian "super-exporters" thus tended to surge well ahead of the other NICs in export volume.

The NICs also vary considerably in the priority given to external trade. The East Asian nations are export-led economies in which exports in 1990 accounted for 43 percent and 27 percent of GDP in Taiwan and South Korea, respectively, and for 100 percent or more of GDP in the entrepôt city states of Hong Kong and Singapore

Table 1 The East Asian and Latin American NICs: Basic Indicators

Country	Population (millions, mid-1990)	Area (thousands of square kilometers)	GDP (US$ billions)		GNP per capita		Distribution of Gross Domestic Product (percent)							
							Agriculture		Industry		Manufacturing[a]		Services, etc.	
			1980	1990	1981	1990	1990	Δ1965–90	1990	Δ1965–90	1990	Δ1965–90	1990	Δ1965–90
South Korea	42.8	99	58.3	236.4	1,700[b]	5,400	9	–29	45	+20	31	+13	46	+9
Taiwan	20.4	36	41.5	156.4	2,560[b]	7,680[b]	4	–19	42	+12	34	+12	54	+7
Hong Kong	5.8	1	20.2	59.7	5,100[b]	11,490	0[c]	–2[d]	26[c]	–14[d]	18[c]	–6[d]	73[c]	+15[d]
Singapore	3.0	1	10.5	34.6	5,240[b]	11,160[b]	0	–3	37	+13	29	+14	63	–11
Brazil	150.4	8,512	210.7	414.1	2,220[b]	2,680	10	–9	39	+6	26	0	51	+3
Mexico	86.2	1,958	166.7	237.8	2,250[b]	2,490	9	–5	30	+3	23	+3	61	+2
Argentina	32.3	2,767	130.9	93.3	2,560[b]	2,370	13	–4	41	–1	35[c]	+2[d]	45	+3

Sources: World Bank (1982:115 for 1980 GDP; 1983:149 for 1981 GDP per capita; and 1992:223).

[a] Because manufacturing is generally the most dynamic part of the industrial sector, its share of GDP is shown separately.

[b] Data refer to GDP per capita.

[c] 1989.

[d] 1965–89.

Δ1965–90 = percentage change in sectoral distribution of GDP, 1965 to 1990.

Table 2 Exports by the East Asian and Latin American NICs, 1965 to 1990

| Country | Exports (US$ billions) | | Exports/GDP (percentage) | | Percentage Share of Exports | | | | | | | |
| | | | | | Primary Commodities | | Textiles and Clothing | | Machinery and Transport Equipment | | Other Manufactures | |
	1980	1990	1980	1990	1990	Δ1965–90	1990	Δ1965–90	1990	Δ1965–90	1990	Δ1965–90
South Korea	17.5	64.8	30	27	7	−33	22	−5	37	+34	35	+6
Taiwan	19.8	67.0	48	43	8	−22	15	−10	36	+21	42	+13
Hong Kong	19.7[a]	29.0	97[a]	49	4	−2	39	−13	23	+16	34	−1
Singapore	19.4[a]	52.6[a]	185[a]	152[a]	27	−38	5	−1	48	+38	20	+2
Brazil	20.1	31.2	10	8	47	−45	3	+2	18	+16	32	+26
Mexico	15.3	26.7	9	11	56	−28	2	−1	25	+24	17	+5
Argentina	8.0	12.4	6	13	65	−29	3	+3	7	+6	26	+21

Sources: World Bank (1982:115, 125; 1992:223, 245, 249).
[a] Includes substantial re-exports.
Δ1965–90 = change in percentage share of exports, 1965 to 1990.

when their re-exports are included. This compares with export/GDP ratios of only 8 percent to 13 percent in the much larger Latin American NICs (Table 2). To put these figures in a broader perspective, Japan, which often is seen as a model for its East Asian neighbors, had an export/GDP ratio of 10 percent in 1990, while the export ratio for the United States was only 7 percent. The East Asian NICs, partly because of their smaller size, thus are far more dependent on external trade than are their Latin American counterparts or Japan.

In exports as in production, manufactures are the chief source of growth in the NICs. While the role of primary commodity exports decreased sharply in all these economies between 1965 and 1990, manufactured items in 1990 constituted well over 90 percent of all exports in the East Asian NICs (except Singapore, where petroleum refining is highly significant) and for between one-third and one-half of the export total in the Latin American NICs (see Table 2).

The maturity or sophistication of a country's industrial structure can be measured by the complexity of the products it exports. Here again, the East Asian NICs are relatively advanced. In Singapore and South Korea, overseas sales of machinery and transport equipment, which utilize capital- and skill-intensive technology, grew by 38 and 34 percent, respectively, from 1965 to 1990 as a share of total merchandise exports. Taiwan's exports in this sector increased by 21 percent and Hong Kong's by 16 percent. In Latin America, Mexico (24 percent) and Brazil (16 percent) also made machinery and transport equipment a dynamic export base, while both Brazil and Argentina achieved solid export gains in the "other manufactures" category (see Table 2). Textiles and clothing, the most important export sector in the East Asian NICs in the 1960s, actually shrank as a proportion of total exports in these four nations during the past 25 years, reflecting their transition from traditional to more advanced forms of manufacturing.

The economic growth of the Latin American and East Asian NICs has occurred at different historical phases and in different rhythms. Furthermore, changes in the world system profoundly shaped the patterns of industrialization in the developing world.

The phrase *newly industrializing countries* actually is a misnomer when applied to Argentina, Brazil, and Mexico, since they established their first major wave of import-substituting industries in the 1930s and 1940s in response to the international economic dislocations caused by the Great Depression and World War II. In fact, the process of industrial growth in the larger Latin American countries already was well under way in the interwar period. The deterioration of the terms of trade for agricultural exports began in the 1920s, reflecting falling demand and rising supplies of agricultural goods throughout the industrialized nations and the adoption of protectionism in many countries of Continental Europe. This led to the demise of the primary product export model and served as an incentive for import-substituting industrialization (see Thorp, 1984; Cortes Conde and Hunt, 1985). Instead of representing a sudden mutation, then, the 1929 crisis brought into high relief trends that originated in the years immediately after World War I.

In Latin America, "the world slump of 1929–33 cut the purchasing power of the continent's exports by 60 percent, and ended the possibility of much borrowing abroad. Most countries were obliged to suspend the convertibility of their currencies, cut imports radically and take measures to stimulate the production of domestic substitutes" (Harris, 1987: 17). While the manufacturing output of the advanced countries declined precipitously during the 1930s, World War II production demands actually had an expansive impact on the Third World countries that helped supply the bellicose powers (Gordon, 1988: 34–5).

The postwar economic expansion of the United States as the hegemonic leader of the capitalist world economy was fueled by a decade of reconstruction in Europe and Asia. The revitalization of direct foreign investment (DFI) and international trade laid the groundwork for a new international division of labor, based on increasingly complex networks of industrial production and sourcing, and new forms of geographical specialization (Fröbel et al., 1981).

The Latin American NICs sought to deepen their industrialization in the mid-1950s by opening their doors to new waves of DFI from the United States, Western Europe, and eventually Japan. Whereas foreign investors in Latin America traditionally had concentrated on export-oriented projects in mining, oil, and agriculture, postwar DFI emphasized import-substituting investments in advanced manufacturing industries like automobiles, chemicals, machinery, and pharmaceuticals whose output was destined primarily for the relatively large domestic markets in Latin America.

The East Asian NICs followed a contrasting sequence. They did not begin their rapid economic growth until the mid-1960s, after an extended period of colonization by Japan prior to 1945 and with a heavy infusion of American aid during the next two decades. Hong Kong, Singapore, South Korea, and Taiwan pursued policies of outward-oriented industrialization in the 1960s in order to generate foreign exchange via manufactured exports. During this initial phase of export expansion, the rapid growth of the East Asian NICs was founded on light, labor-intensive industries like textiles, garments, and electronic equipment. In subsequent phases, however, South Korea, Taiwan, and Singapore achieved success in much heavier industries like steel, petrochemicals, shipbuilding, vehicle manufacture, and computers that were less well suited to their original factor endowments (i.e., limited raw materials, unskilled labor, and small markets). The East Asian NICs thus were motivated by the principle of dynamic competitive advantage rather than by their static comparative advantage in cheap, disciplined labor.

The emergence and evolution of the NICs has been a product of cyclical shifts in the world economy. When the conditions that made import substitution a viable and appealing option for many countries changed, there was increased general interest in export promotion. The turn outward by the East Asian NICs in the 1960s foreshadowed similar efforts in the following decades by a wide range of developing nations, including the Latin American NICs. To gain a better picture of the dynamic relationship between these patterns of inward- and outward-oriented industrialization, we need to examine more closely the paths of industrialization followed by the Latin American and East Asian NICs.

The Dynamic Interplay of Inward- and Outward-Oriented Industrialization

Based on a broad historical view of industrialization in the Latin American and East Asian NICs, one can identify five main phases of industrial development. Three of these are outward looking: a commodity export phase, and primary and secondary export-oriented industrialization (EOI). The other two are inward looking: primary and secondary import-substituting industrialization (ISI). The subtypes within the outward and inward approaches are distinguished by the kinds of products involved in each.

In the commodity export phase, the output typically is unrefined or semiprocessed raw materials (agricultural goods, minerals, oil, etc.). Primary ISI entails the shift from imports to the local manufacture of basic consumer goods, and in almost all countries the key industries during this phase are textiles, clothing, footwear, and food processing. Secondary ISI involves using domestic production to substitute for imports of a variety of capital- and technology-intensive manufactures: consumer durables (e.g., automobiles), intermediate goods (e.g., petrochemicals and steel), and capital goods (e.g., heavy machinery).

Both phases of EOI involve manufactured exports. In primary EOI these tend to be labor-intensive products, while secondary EOI includes higher-value-added items that are skill intensive and require a more fully developed local industrial base.

Following this schema, the principal sequences of industrial development in Mexico, Brazil, South Korea, and Taiwan are outlined in Figure I. For convenience, I use the phrase *paths of industrialization* to refer to these economic outcomes. The varied role of government policies, incentives, and explicit development strategies in bringing about these industrial shifts is an important but separate issue that I will not address here. (This topic is analyzed in Cheng and Haggard, 1987; Cheng, 1990; Kaufman, 1990; and Wade, 1990.)

Each of the two regional pairs of NICs has followed a distinctive industrial trajectory that includes the ISI and EOI ideal types mentioned above, plus a "mixed" phase in the most recent period. An analysis of these trajectories, as shown in Figure I, suggests the following conclusions (see Gereffi and Wyman, 1989).

First, the contrast often made between the Latin American and the East Asian NICs as representing inward- and outward-oriented industrial paths, respectively, is

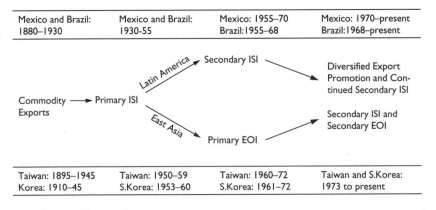

Figure I   Paths of Industrialization in Latin America and East Asia: Commonalities, Divergence, and Convergence

oversimplified. While this distinction is appropriate for some periods, a historical perspective shows that each of these NICs has pursued both inward- and outward-oriented approaches.

Every nation, with the exception of Britain at the time of the Industrial Revolution, went through an initial stage of ISI in which protection was extended to incipient manufacturing industries producing for domestic markets. Even Hong Kong, the most laissez-faire of the NICs, benefited from a period of "disguised ISI" on the Chinese mainland. Refugees to Hong Kong from the mainland included a significant segment of the Shanghai capitalist class and a huge supply of politically unorganized labor, and they brought with them technical know-how, skills, and even machinery (Haggard and Cheng, 1987: 106–10). Furthermore, each of the NICs subsequently has combined both advanced ISI and different types of EOI in order to avoid the inherent limitations of an exclusive reliance on domestic or external markets, and also to facilitate the industrial diversification and upgrading that are required for these nations to remain competitive in the world economy. Rather than being mutually exclusive alternatives, the ISI and EOI development paths in fact have been complementary and interactive (Gereffi and Wyman, 1990).

Second, the early phases of industrialization – commodity exports and primary ISI – were common to all of the Latin American and East Asian NICs, although the timing and specific products involved varied considerably. The subsequent divergence in the regional sequences stems from the ways in which each country responded to the basic problems associated with the continuation of primary ISI. These problems included balance of payments pressures, rapidly rising inflation, high levels of dependence on intermediate and capital goods imports, and low levels of manufactured exports.

Third, the duration and timing of these development patterns vary by region. Primary ISI began earlier, lasted longer, and was more populist in Latin America than in East Asia. Timing helps explain these sequences because the opportunities and constraints that shape development choices are constantly shifting. The East Asian NICs began their accelerated export of manufactured products during a period of extraordinary dynamism in the world economy. The two decades that preceded the global economic crisis of the 1970s saw unprecedented annual growth rates of world industrial production (approximately 5.6 percent) and world trade (around 7.3 percent), relatively low inflation and high employment rates in the industrialized countries, and stable international monetary arrangements. The expansion of world trade was fastest between 1960 and 1973, when the average annual growth rate of exports reached almost 9 percent.

Starting in 1973, however, the international economy entered a troublesome phase. From 1973 to the end of the decade, the annual growth in world trade fell to 4.5 percent as manufactured exports from the developing countries encountered stiffer protectionist measures in the industrialized markets. These new trends were among the factors that led the East Asian NICs to modify their EOI approach in the 1970s (see Cheng and Haggard, 1987).

Fourth, the development trajectories of the Latin American and East Asian NICs show some signs of convergence in the 1970s and 1980s. To support this convergence thesis, it is necessary to distinguish two subphases during the most recent period. In the 1970s Mexico and Brazil began to expand both their commodity exports (oil, soybeans, minerals, etc.) and their manufactured exports, as well as to accelerate their foreign borrowing, in order to acquire enough foreign exchange to finance the imports necessary for furthering secondary ISI. This "diversified exports" approach, which became even more prominent in the 1980s in the face of sharply curtailed foreign borrowing, was an important addition to Mexico's and Brazil's earlier emphasis on industrial deepening.

South Korea and Taiwan, on the other hand, emphasized heavy and chemical industrialization from 1973 to 1979, with a focus on steel, automobiles, shipbuilding, and petrochemicals. The objective of heavy and chemical industrialization in East Asia was twofold: to develop national production capability in these sectors, justified by national security as well as import substitution considerations, and to lay the groundwork for more diversified exports in the future. China's reentry into the international community, ushered in by its détente with the United States in the early 1970s, not only made South Korea's and Taiwan's domestic defense concerns more credible, but China also presented a long-term threat to labor-intensive industries in the region. South Korea and Taiwan have used the secondary ISI industries established during the 1970s as a base for launching a far more variegated array of technology- and skill-intensive manufactured exports in the 1980s (Gereffi, 1989).

It is clear that neither inward-oriented nor outward-oriented paths of industrialization are self-sufficient models of development. Both are susceptible to systemic constraints or vulnerabilities such as recurring balance of payments problems, persistent inflation, and the disruption of key trading relationships (see Gereffi, 1990b). However, the NICs in each region have adapted or switched their development trajectories in response to these problems, and thus they succeeded in moving to a more diversified pattern of export growth in the 1980s.

Dependent Development in Latin America and East Asia

Dependency theory has been flawed by its historically close association with the development of the Latin American NICs. The "dependent development" literature drew heavily on the experience of Latin American nations, and it looked at the problems of Third World development with an eye toward investment and debt dependency. Therefore it has been claimed that dependency theory has little, if any, relevance to the East Asian NICs (Amsden, 1979; Barrett and Whyte, 1982; Berger, 1986). In fact, the East Asian NICs have experienced two distinct kinds of dependency: the dependency on American aid in the 1950s, and trade dependency, again largely on the United States, since the 1960s. The internal and external consequences of each kind of dependency are quite different.

To approach the issue of dependent development in a cross-regional setting, the concept of transnational economic linkages (TNELs) is quite useful. There are four main TNELs: foreign aid, foreign trade, direct foreign investment, and foreign loans. They affect development strategies and outcomes in several ways (see Gereffi and Wyman, 1989).

First, they represent economic resources that may be used, singly or in diverse combinations and sequences, to finance development. For example, DFI sustained secondary ISI in Latin America, much as massive foreign aid flows made primary ISI possible in East Asia.

Second, the availability of these resources is conditioned by factors beyond as well as within the control of nation states. Factors beyond the control of individual countries include global economic conditions (e.g., trends in world trade) as well as geopolitical pressures that help channel capital toward some countries and away from others. National policies regarding domestic wage levels, foreign investment, and the degree of political stability in a country, on the other hand, can also shape the performance of TNELs.

Third, the destination and use of TNELs in a country directly affect the power of domestic actors. It matters, for example, whether these economic resources are used to finance luxury imports for the wealthy or irrigation systems and public transport-ation for the masses, just as it matters whether the presence of these resources strengthens or weakens agrarian elites vis-à-vis the peasantry or the industrial bourgeoisie rather than the urban working class.

Table 3 identifies the relative importance of each of the TNELs in Brazil, Mexico, South Korea, and Taiwan during the different phases of industrialization discussed earlier. The high, medium, and low weights in Table 3 are based on estimates of the relative significance of the TNELs in each economy, compared with other developing countries at similar stages in their industrialization process.

There is considerable variation among the NICs in the role played by TNELs. First, the salience of TNELs varies markedly over time within each region, since each phase of the industrial trajectories of the Latin American and East Asian NICs is associated with a different mix of external resources used to finance development. In East Asia, for example, primary ISI relied on a great deal of foreign aid and little export trade; conversely, the subsequent phase of primary EOI was defined by extensive exports and virtually no foreign aid.

Second, the salience of TNELs also varies between the two regions within the same phase of industrialization. For example, both regions went through a period of primary ISI, but the dynamics were quite different. In East Asia primary ISI was financed by massive amounts of foreign economic assistance, whereas in Latin America the same phase tended to be carried out by local industrialists with the support of the state and with limited participation by transnational corporations. It is widely acknowledged that the South Korean and Taiwanese economies could not have survived the 1950s without American assistance. Between 1951 and 1965, $1.5 billion in economic aid and $2.5 billion in military aid were sent to Taiwan by the United States. South Korea received a similar amount of U.S. aid in the 1953–61 period, with $2.6 billion earmarked for economic assistance and $1.6 billion for military expenditures. Aid financed 40 percent of fixed investment in Taiwan and 80 percent in South Korea. Concessional capital flows were used to purchase 70 percent of the imports coming into South Korea, as well as to pay 90 percent of the balance of trade deficit in Taiwan (Jacoby, 1966; Cole, 1980).

Third, the contrast with regard to TNELs is sharpest during the 1960s, when Latin America's secondary ISI is juxtaposed with East Asia's primary EOI. The former phase relied heavily on DFI and external loans but was oriented toward supplying local markets; the latter phase depended on access to overseas markets but was implemented in large part by domestic entrepreneurs who drew mainly on local

Table 3 The Structure of Dependent Development in Latin America and East Asia

Transitional Economic Linkages	Development Strategies, Brazil and Mexico				Development Strategies, South Korea and Taiwan			
	Commodity Exports	Primary ISI	Secondary ISI	Diversified Exports and Secondary ISI	Commodity Exports	Primary ISI	Primary EOI	Secondary ISI and EOI
Foreign aid	Low	Low	Medium	Low	Low	High	Medium	Medium
Foreign trade	High	Low	Low (exports) Medium (imports)	Medium (imports) High (exports)	High	Low (exports) Medium (imports)	High	High
Direct foreign investment	Medium (Brazil) High (Mexico)	Low	High	Medium	Medium	Low	Low (S. Korea) Medium (Taiwan)	Medium (S. Korea) High (Taiwan)
Foreign borrowing	Medium	Low	Medium	High	Low	Low	Low (Taiwan) Medium (S. Korea)	Medium (Taiwan) High (S. Korea)

Source: Gereffi and Wyman (1989).

financial resources (this was especially true in Taiwan, whereas in South Korea local capitalists became heavily indebted to foreign creditors in the 1970s).

Fourth and finally, Latin America and East Asia differ in terms of the overall weight that TNELs have had in the two regions. Historically DFI and foreign loans represented the most important external economic resources for the Latin American NICs; in contrast, export trade and foreign aid have been the key forms of East Asian linkage to the international economy. A main reason why dependency has been such a thorny issue for the Latin American countries is that DFI tends to create greater frictions than other types of foreign capital in Third World countries (see Stallings, 1990). In the East Asian NICs, on the other hand, trade dependency on the United States has been declining since the early 1970s, and their export profile has become more diversified (Barrett and Chin, 1987), thus reducing but not eliminating some of the deleterious consequences of export partner and product concentration.

The dependency perspective can be enriched by dealing more explicitly with issues of dependency management. This approach focuses attention on the capacity of domestic institutions to use external economic resources productively and selectively to serve local interests. A key to understanding the success of the East Asian NICs' export strategy, for example, is the performance of locally owned exporting firms that aggressively sought and exploited opportunities for profitable overseas sales. These local exporters established close ties with foreign buyers, who assisted in matters of product design and technology transfer. The adaptation of available modern technology has enabled the East Asian NICs to move from conventional labor-intensive exports like textiles, clothing, and footwear to heavier and high-technology industries like transportation equipment, electrical machinery, and computer components. Joint-venture research projects, as well as locally owned companies, have been set up in South Korea and Taiwan to give these countries greater flexibility in developing their own production and technological capabilities (Schive, 1990). The success of both primary and secondary EOI in the East Asian NICs thus is explained in large part by the ability of domestic firms to manage effectively their dependency relationships in the areas of international trade and investment.

The Emergent Global Manufacturing System: Toward a Theoretical Synthesis

This comparative overview of industrialization in the East Asian and Latin American NICs provides the elements for a new synthesis in development theory. This theoretical synthesis is based on a modified world-systems perspective, in which my focus is the changing parameters for mobility by the NICs in the emergent global manufacturing system.

I will discuss three related themes to illustrate the direction this approach might take: (1) the declining significance of industrialization, (2) the position of core and peripheral capital in contemporary commodity chains and export/marketing networks, and (3) a framework for differentiating the roles of the NICs in the world economy. My concluding remarks will address issues for future research on this topic.

The Declining Significance of Industrialization

Since the 1950s, the gap between developed and developing countries has been narrowing in terms of industrialization. Industry as a share of GDP has increased substantially in the vast majority of Third World nations, not only in absolute terms but also relative to that of the core countries (see Harris, 1987). By the late 1970s, the NICs as a whole not only caught up with but overtook the core countries in terms of their degree of industrialization (Arrighi and Drangel, 1986: 54–5).

By 1986, all of the NICs in Latin America and East Asia, with the exception of Hong Kong, had industry/GDP ratios that exceeded the industrial market countries' average level of 35 percent. The same pattern holds true for manufacturing, which is generally the most dynamic part of the industrial sector. The manufacturing/GDP ratio in 1990 for the United States, for example, was 17 percent, which was lower than that of any of the seven Latin American and East Asian NICs (see Table 1).

While industry and manufacturing as a share of GDP are on the decline in the most developed nations of the world economy, this trend is counterbalanced by the core's emphasis on the service sector and on the most productive, high-value-added segments of manufacturing. Ironically, as more and more countries in the world are becoming industrialized, industrialization itself is losing the key status it once had as an ultimate hallmark of national development.

These observations lead to two basic conclusions about the theoretical status of industrialization in the contemporary world economy. First, *industrialization* and *development* are not synonymous. This is apparent in the disparate social and economic consequences of industrial growth in the Latin American and East Asian NICs over the past couple of decades. Despite similarly high levels of industrialization in the NICs from both regions, the East Asian nations have performed significantly better than their Latin American counterparts in terms of standard indicators of development such as GNP per capita, income distribution, literacy, health, and education (see Gereffi and Fonda, 1992).

Second, just as industrialization cannot be equated with development, neither does it guarantee proximity to core status in the world system. Although the NICs are now more industrialized than most of the core countries, this achievement generally has not led to a substantial change in the relative position of the NICs in the hierarchy of nations in the world economy. Arrighi and Drangel (1986: 44), who measured upward and downward mobility in the world system over the past fifty years in terms of national changes in per capita GNP, found that 95 percent of the states classified in one of the three world-system zones (core, semiperiphery, and periphery) in 1938–50 were in the same zone in 1975–83. Among the few exceptional cases of upward mobility in the world system were Japan and Italy, which moved from the semiperiphery to the core, and South Korea and Taiwan, which moved from the periphery to the semiperiphery.

Therefore, while industrialization may be a necessary condition for core status in the world system, it no longer is sufficient. Mobility from the semiperiphery to the core, or from the periphery to the semiperiphery, should not be defined simply in terms of a country's degree of industrialization, but rather by a nation's success in upgrading its mix of economic activities toward technology- and skill-intensive products and techniques with higher levels of local value added. Continued innovations by the most developed countries tend to make core status an ever receding frontier.

Commodity Chains and Export/Marketing Networks

In the global manufacturing system of today, production of a single good commonly spans several countries, with each nation performing tasks in which it has a cost advantage. This is true for traditional manufactures, such as garments and footwear, as well as for modern products, like automobiles and computers (Gereffi, 1989). To analyze the implications of this globalization of production for specific sets of countries like the East Asian and Latin American NICs, it is helpful to utilize the concept of commodity chains.

A "commodity chain," as defined by Hopkins and Wallerstein (1986: 159), refers to "a network of labor and production processes whose end result is a finished commodity." To delineate the anatomy of the chain, one typically starts with the final production operation for a consumable good and moves sequentially backward until one reaches the raw material inputs. However, the complexity of commodity chains for the kinds of export-oriented manufacturing industries that the NICs are predominant in today requires us to extend the model proposed by Hopkins and Wallerstein in several ways (see Gereffi and Korzeniewicz, 1994).

First, the dynamic growth of the NICs has revolved around their success in expanding their production and exports of a wide range of consumer products destined mainly for core-country markets. This means that it is extremely important to include forward as well as backward linkages from the production stage in the commodity chain. Most commodity chains are composed of four major segments: (1) raw material supply, (2) production, (3) exporting, and (4) marketing and retailing. In the footwear industry, for example, a full commodity chain takes us across the entire spectrum of activities in the world economy: the agro-extractive sector (cattle for leather, and crude oil as the basis for plastic and synthetic rubber inputs), the industrial sector (footwear manufacturing), and the service sector (the activities associated with the export, marketing, and retailing of shoes). Commodity chains in most other manufacturing industries today are similar in their broad scope.

Second, the extension of commodity chains beyond production to include the flow of products to the final consumer is essential for our ability to detect where economic surplus is concentrated in a global industry. The comparative advantage of the NICs lies primarily at the production stage because of the low labor costs in these countries relative to the core and their high productivity relative to the periphery. An important corollary of this fact, however, is that the distribution and retail marketing segments of these commodity chains tend to be more profitable than manufacturing per se. Furthermore, the economic surplus that accrues to distributors and retailers in core countries generally is much higher when production is done overseas rather than domestically.

The distributors' margins in the footwear industry in the United States, for example, averaged 50 percent in the mid-1970s but were closer to 60 percent for imported goods (Gereffi and Korzeniewicz, 1990: 54–5). Product differentiation by means of heavily advertised brand names (e.g., Nike, Reebok, or Florsheim in shoes) and the use of diverse retail outlets allow core-country firms rather than those in the semiperiphery to capture the lion's share of economic rents in a diverse range of consumer goods industries.

For semiperipheral countries to ascend in the world economy, they will have to find new ways to move to the most profitable end of commodity chains. This requires a fundamental shift from manufacturing in the semiperiphery to marketing in the core, a daunting task that will require new patterns of investment in research and development, advertising, and retail distribution by the NICs.

Differentiating the Roles of the NICs in the World Economy

The foregoing analysis of the Latin American and East Asian NICs allows us to identify a differentiated set of roles that semiperipheral nations play in the world economy. These roles reflect the mix of core-peripheral economic activities in the NICs, as well as the significance of core and peripheral capital in carrying out these development efforts. These roles are not mutually exclusive, and their importance for a given country or set of countries may undergo fairly dramatic shifts over time. From the perspective of world-systems theory, it is essential to note that these roles in the world economy are largely determined by domestic conditions, such as the pattern of economic, social, and political organization within the NICs.

This framework focuses on export production in the NICs, since this is the best indicator of a country's international competitive advantage. The NICs can be characterized in terms of at least four basic types of economic roles: (1) the commodity-export role, (2) the export-platform role, (3) the specification-contracting role, and (4) the component-supplier role.

The *commodity-export role* is of prime importance for the Latin American NICs, where natural resources account for two-thirds or more of total exports, and also for Singapore, which processes and re-exports a large volume of petroleum-related products (see Table 2). Peripheral capital controls most of these natural-resource industries at the production stage in Latin America, with the petroleum and mining industries usually being run by state-owned enterprises, while the agricultural and livestock industries generally are owned by local capital. In Singapore, by contrast, TNCs are the proprietors of most of the petroleum-related industries. These commodity exports are sent to a wide range of nations, with the predominant share going to core countries. The export and distribution networks are usually controlled by core capital.

The *export-platform role* corresponds to those nations that have foreign-owned, labor-intensive assembly of manufactured goods in export-processing zones. These zones offer special incentives to foreign capital and tend to attract firms in a common set of industries: garments, footwear, and electronics. Virtually all of the East Asian and Latin American NICs have engaged in this form of labor-intensive production, although its significance tends to wane as wage rates rise and countries become more developed. In Taiwan and South Korea, export-processing zones have been on the decline during the past two decades, largely because labor costs have been rapidly increasing. These nations have been trying to upgrade their mix of export activities by moving toward more skill- and technology-intensive products. The export-platform role in Asia is now being occupied by low-wage countries like China, the Philippines, Thailand, Indonesia, and Malaysia.

In Latin America, on the other hand, export-platform industries are on the upswing because the wage levels in most countries of the region are considerably below those of the East Asian NICs, and recent currency devaluations in the Latin American NICs make the price of their exports more competitive internationally. The export platforms in Latin America also have the advantage of geographical proximity to the most important core-country markets in comparison with Asian export platforms. Mexico's *maquiladora* industry, which was set up in 1965 as an integral part of Mexico's Northern Border Industrialization Program, is probably the largest and most dynamic of these export areas. The *maquiladora* industry doubled its foreign exchange earnings from 1982 ($850 million) to 1987 ($1.6 billion). In the latter year, *maquila* exports were Mexico's second largest source of foreign exchange, surpassed only by crude oil exports (see Carrillo-Huerta and Urquidi, 1989). There are similar zones in Brazil, Colombia, Central America, and the Caribbean. Core capital controls the production, export, and marketing stages of the commodity chains for these consumer goods. The main contribution of peripheral nations is cheap labor.

The *specification-contracting role* refers to the production of finished consumer goods by locally owned firms, where the output is distributed and marketed by core capital or its agents. This is the major niche filled by the East Asian NICs in the contemporary world economy. In 1980, three of the East Asian NICs (Hong Kong, Taiwan, and South Korea) accounted for 72 percent of all finished consumer goods exported by the Third World to OECD countries; other Asian countries supplied another 19 percent, while just 7 percent came from Latin America and the Caribbean. The United States was the leading market for these products, with 46 percent of the total (Keesing, 1983: 338–9). In East Asia, peripheral capital controls the production stage of the finished consumer-goods commodity chains (see Haggard and Cheng, 1987; Gereffi, 1990a), while core capital tends to control the more profitable export, distribution, and retail marketing stages. While the international subcontracting of finished consumer goods is growing in Latin America, it tends to be subordinated to the export-platform and component-supplier forms of production.

The *component-supplier role* refers to the production of component parts in capital- and technology-intensive industries in the periphery, for export and usually final assembly in the core country. This has been the major niche for the manufactured exports of the Latin American NICs during the past two decades. Brazil and Mexico have been important production sites for vertically integrated exports by TNCs to core-country markets, especially the United States, since the late 1960s. This is most notable in certain industries like motor vehicles, computers, and pharmaceuticals (see Newfarmer, 1985). American, European, and Japanese automotive TNCs, for example, have advanced manufacturing facilities in Mexico and Brazil for the production of engines, auto parts, and even completed vehicles for the US and European markets.

In Latin America, the manufacturing stage of the commodity chain in component-supplier production typically is owned and run by core capital, sometimes in conjunction with a local partner. The export, distribution, and marketing of the manufactured items are handled by the TNC. A major advantage of this production arrangement is that it is most likely to result in a significant transfer of technology from the core nations.

In East Asia there are two variants of the component-supplier role. The first is similar to the Latin American arrangement in which foreign subsidiaries manufacture parts or subunits in East Asia for products like television sets, radios, sporting goods, and consumer appliances that are assembled and marketed in the country of destination (most often the United States).

The second variant of the component-supplier role involves production of components by East Asian firms for sale to diversified buyers on the world market. This is illustrated in the semiconductor industry. South Korean companies have focused almost exclusively on the mass production of powerful memory chips, the single largest segment of the semiconductor industry, which are sold as inputs to a wide range of domestic and international manufacturers of electronic equipment. Taiwan, on the other hand, has targeted the highest-value-added segment of the semiconductor market: tailor-made "designer chips" that perform special tasks in toys, video games, and other machines. Taiwan was reported to have forty chip-design houses that specialize in finding export niches and then developing products for them (*Far Eastern Economic Review*, 1988).

Taiwan, with its technological prowess, is acquiring the flexibility to move into the high-value-added field of product innovation. However, without their own internationally recognized company brand names, a substantial advertising budget, and appropriate marketing and retail networks, Taiwan's ingenious producers will find it difficult to break free of the international subcontracting role. South Korea probably has more potential to enter core-country markets successfully because the *jaebols* have the capital and technology to set up overseas production facilities and marketing networks. Thus South Korea's leading auto manufacturer, Hyundai Motor Company, has become one of the top importers into both Canada and the United States since the mid-1980s (see Gereffi, 1990a).

This typology of the different roles that the Latin American and East Asian NICs play in the world economy shows that the standard development literature has presented an oversimplified picture of the semiperiphery. The East Asian NICs have been most successful in the areas of international subcontracting and component supply, with secondary and declining importance given to the export-platform role emphasized in "the new international division of labor" literature. The Latin American NICs, on the other hand, have a different kind of relationship to the world economy. They are prominent in the commodity-export, export-platform, and component-supplier forms of production, but they lag far behind the East Asian NICs in the international-subcontracting type of manufactured exports.

Although each of these roles has certain advantages and disadvantages in terms of mobility in the world system, the prospects for the NICs can only be understood by looking at the interacting sets of roles in which these nations are enmeshed. If development theory is to be relevant for the 1990s, it will have to become flexible enough to incorporate both increased specialization at the commodity and geographical levels, along with new patterns of regional and global integration.

Directions for Future Research

The theoretical synthesis outlined above suggests several promising areas for research on the varied performance of the NICs in the world economy. In order to better understand why some nations have developed more rapidly or extensively than others, and what the latter can learn from the former, we need to focus on several interrelated levels of analysis: the global or world system level, policies and institutions at the national level, and the social bases of competitiveness at the local level.

The global manufacturing system that has emerged in the last couple of decades and the related expansion in export activity by the NICs has led to new patterns of diversification and specialization in the contemporary export-oriented, network-centered world economy. While the diversification of the NICs' exports toward nontraditional, capital- and technology-intensive manufactured goods is now a clear trend (see Table 2), less well recognized is the tendency of the NICs to develop higher levels of specialization in their national export profiles. There is evidence of increasing heterogeneity in the export profiles of the NICs *within* East Asia and Latin America, for example, which leads us to question the assumption that there are homogeneous regional models of industrial development (see Gereffi, 1989; Gereffi and Fonda, 1992). How and why did these patterns of export specialization emerge during the past several decades? How did the East Asian NICs construct such effective export networks for consumer goods in the 1960s? What are the lessons to be derived by other countries that wish to expand their manufactured exports today?

Commodity chains are an important analytical tool that can be used to address some of these questions (see Gereffi and Korzeniewicz, 1994). Detailed studies of commodity chains in diverse industries are required in order to detect the mix of core-peripheral activities at each node of the chain, and also to identify the strategies different nations are pursuing to move upward or conversely to resist peripheralization in the world system (Arrighi and Drangel, 1986). The recent success of Korean automobiles, semiconductors, and home appliances; Taiwanese computers and sporting goods; and Mexican beer in the US market indicates that it is possible for firms in the NICs to capture significant shares of core-country markets, even in technology- and advertising-intensive industries. (See Newfarmer, 1985, for a related approach applying industrial organization economics to a variety of internationally oriented manufacturing industries in Latin America.) Comparative research on commodity chains is needed to illuminate the conditions under which domestic producers in the NICs can capture higher levels of economic surplus through integrated production and marketing strategies at the global level.

National differences in government policies, economic organization, and social structure are important determinants of how the NICs have responded to opportunities and constraints in the world economy. Industrial policy in each of the NICs, for example, has been influenced by varied patterns of ownership in terms of the relative importance of foreign-owned corporations, state enterprises, and local private companies (Gereffi, 1990a). Intraregional differences are often as striking as cross-regional ones. Whereas South Korea's concentrated industrial structure composed of locally owned conglomerates and proletarian industrial communities predisposes it to a "mass-production model" of economic growth, Taiwan's myriad array of smaller firms and its more fragmented labor force leads to a "flexible-specialization model" of permanent innovation that attempts to accommodate change rather than control it (this theme is suggested but not developed in Sabel, 1986, and Deyo, 1990).

The social basis of competitiveness in the NICs focuses our attention on how economic activity is embedded in structures of social relations in modern industrial societies (Granovetter, 1985). Effective production, export, and marketing networks are rooted in cooperative as well as competitive relationships that draw upon ethnicity, kinship, gender, class, and other social ties. Japan, South Korea, and Taiwan, for example, have very different principles of social organization that affect their approach to domestic expansion as well as their orientation to world markets (see Hamilton et al., 1987; Hamilton and Biggart, 1988). Research on the informal sector has highlighted how complex patterns of social embeddedness underlie efficient production arrangements that cut across social strata and realign the relations between employers, workers, and government in a wide range of nations (see Portes et al., 1989). These issues have become especially salient for many export-oriented industries in which global competitiveness requires rapid and flexible adaptations to changing conditions in the world economy.

Development theory needs to incorporate and integrate the global, national, and local levels of analysis if we are to understand the challenges and choices that confront industrializing nations. The false dilemma of outward- versus inward-oriented development must be replaced by a more comprehensive approach that sees countries as occupying differentiated roles in the world economy requiring a combination of export industries as well as those producing for domestic markets. A multidisciplinary view of development issues offers the best hope for a theory that is responsive to concrete problems and can also provide the basis for useful generalizations.

REFERENCES

Amsden, Alice H., 1979, "Taiwan's economic history: A case of étatisme and a challenge to dependency theory." *Modern China* 5:341–80.

Arrighi, Giovanni, and Jessica Drangel, 1986, "The stratification of the world economy: An exploration of the semiperipheral zone." *Review* 10:9–74.

Balassa, Bela, 1981, *The Newly Industrializing Countries in the World Economy*. New York: Pergamon Press.

Balassa, Bela, Gerardo M. Bueno, Pedro-Pablo Kuczynski, and Mario Henrique Simonsen, 1986, *Toward Renewed Economic Growth in Latin America*. Washington, DC: Institute of International Economics.

Barrett, Richard E., and Soomi Chin, 1987, "Export-oriented industrializing states in the capitalist world system: Similarities and differences." In *The Political Economy of the New Asian Industrialism*, edited by Frederic C. Deyo, 23–43. Ithaca, NY: Cornell University Press.

Barrett, Richard E., and Martin King Whyte, 1982, "Dependency theory and Taiwan: Analysis of a deviant case." *American Journal of Sociology* 87:1064–89.

Berger, Peter L., 1986, *The Capitalist Revolution*. New York: Basic Books.

Berger, Peter L., and Hsin-Huang Michael Hsiao, eds., 1988, *In Search of an East Asian Development Model*. New Brunswick, NJ: Transaction Books.

Cardoso, Fernando Henrique, and Enzo Faletto, 1979, *Dependency and Development in Latin America*. Berkeley: University of California Press.

Carrillo-Huerta, Mario, and Victor L. Urquidi, 1989, "Trade deriving from the international division of production: Maquila and post-maquila in Mexico." Unpublished manuscript, El Colegio de Mexico, Mexico City.

CEPD (Council for Economic Planning and Development), 1991, *Taiwan Statistical Data Book, 1991*. Taipei: CEPD.

Cheng, Tun-jen, 1990, "Political regimes and development strategies: South Korea and Taiwan." In *Manufacturing Miracles: Paths of Industrialization in Latin America and East Asia*, edited by Gary Gereffi and Donald Wyman, 139–78. Princeton, NJ: Princeton University Press.

Cheng, Tun-jen, and Stephan Haggard, 1987, *Newly Industrializing Asia in Transition: Policy Reform and American Response*. Berkeley: Institute of International Studies, University of California.

Cole, David C., 1980, "Foreign assistance and Korean development." In *The Korean Economy – Issues of Development*, edited by David C. Cole, Youngil Lim, and Paul W. Kuznets, 1–29. Berkeley: Institute of East Asian Studies, University of California.

Collier, David, ed., 1979, *The New Authoritarianism in Latin America*. Princeton, NJ: Princeton University Press.

Cortes Conde, Roberto, and Shane J. Hunt, eds., 1985, *The Latin American Economies: Growth and the Export Sector, 1880–1930*. New York: Holmes and Meier.

Deyo, Frederic C., 1990, "Economic policy and the popular sector." In *Manufacturing Miracles: Paths of Industrialization in Latin America and East Asia*, edited by Gary Gereffi and Donald Wyman, 179–204. Princeton, NJ: Princeton University Press.

Evans, Peter, 1979, *Dependent Development: The Alliance of Multinationals, State and Local Capital in Brazil*. Princeton, NJ: Princeton University Press.

Far Eastern Economic Review, 1988, "Sizzling hot chips: Asia is the source of the semiconductor industry's spectacular growth." August 18, pp. 80–6.

Fröbel, Folker, Jurgen Heinrichs, and Otto Kreye, 1981, *The New International Division of Labor*. New York: Cambridge University Press.

Gereffi, Gary, 1983, *The Pharmaceutical Industry and Dependency in the Third World*. Princeton, NJ: Princeton University Press.

——, —— 1989, "Development strategies and the global factory." *Annals of the American Academy of Political and Social Science* 505:92–104.

——, —— 1990a, "Big business and the state." In *Manufacturing Miracles: Paths of Industrialization in Latin America and East Asia*, edited by Gary Gereffi and Donald Wyman, 90–109. Princeton, NJ: Princeton University Press.

——, —— 1990b, "International economics and domestic policies." In *Economy and Society: Overviews in Economic Sociology*, edited by Alberto Martinelli and Neil J. Smelser, 231–58. Newbury Park, Calif.: Sage.

Gereffi, Gary, and Stephanie Fonda, 1992, "Regional paths of development." *Annual Review of Sociology* 18:419–48.

Gereffi, Gary, and Miguel Korzeniewicz, 1990, "Commodity chains and footwear exports in the semiperiphery." In *Semiperipheral States in the World-Economy*, edited by William Martin, 45–68. Westport, CT: Greenwood Press.

Gereffi, Gary, and Miguel Korzeniewicz, eds., 1994, *Commodity Chains and Global Capitalism*. Westport, Conn.: Greenwood Press.

Gereffi, Gary, and Donald Wyman, 1989, "Determinants of development strategies in Latin America and East Asia." In *Pacific Dynamics: The International Politics of Industrial Change*, edited by Stephan Haggard and Chung-in Moon, 23–52. Boulder, Colo.: Westview Press.

Gereffi, Gary, and Donald Wyman, eds., 1990, *Manufacturing Miracles: Paths of Industrialization in Latin America and East Asia*. Princeton, NJ: Princeton University Press.

Gold, Thomas B., 1981, "Dependent development in Taiwan." Ph.D. diss., Harvard University, Cambridge, Mass.

Gordon, David M., 1988, "The global economy: New edifice or crumbling foundations?" *New Left Review* 168:24–64.

Granovetter, Mark, 1985, "Economic action and social structure: The problem of embeddedness." *American Journal of Sociology* 91:481–510.

Haggard, Stephan, and Tunjen Cheng, 1987, "State and foreign capital in the East Asian NICs." In *The Political Economy of the New Asian Industrialism*, edited by Frederic C. Deyo, 84–135. Ithaca, NY: Cornell University Press.

Hamilton, Gary G., and Nicole Woolsey Biggart, 1988, "Market, culture, and authority: A comparative analysis of management and organization in the Far East." *American Journal of Sociology* 94 (Special Supplement): S52–S94.

Hamilton, Gary G., Marco Orru, and Nicole Woolsey Biggart, 1987, "Enterprise groups in East Asia: An organizational analysis." *Financial Economic Review* (Tokyo) 161:78–106.

Harris, Nigel, 1987, *The End of the Third World: Newly Industrializing Countries and the Decline of an Ideology*. New York: Viking Penguin.

Hopkins, Terence K., and Immanuel Wallerstein, 1986, "Commodity chains in the world-economy prior to 1800." *Review* 10:157–70.

IMF (International Monetary Fund), 1986, *International Financial Statistics Yearbook 1986*. Washington, DC: IMF.

Jacoby, Neil H., 1966, *U.S. Aid to Taiwan*. New York: Praeger.

Johnson, Chalmers, 1983, "The 'internationalization' of the Japanese economy." *California Management Review* 25:5–26.

——, —— 1987, "Political institutions and economic performance: The government–business relationship in Japan, South Korea, and Taiwan." In *The Political Economy of the New Asian Industrialism*, edited by Frederic C. Deyo, 136–64. Ithaca, NY: Cornell University Press.

Kaufman, Robert, 1990, "How societies change development strategies or keep them: Reflections on the Latin American experience in the 1930s and the post-war world." In *Manufacturing Miracles: Paths of Industrialization in Latin America and East Asia*, edited by Gary Gereffi and Donald Wyman, 110–38. Princeton, NJ: Princeton University Press.

Keesing, Donald B., 1983, "Linking up to distant markets: South to North exports of manufactured consumer goods." *American Economic Review* 73:338–42.

Lim, Hyun-Chin, 1985, *Dependent Development in Korea, 1963–1979*. Seoul: Seoul National University Press.

Newfarmer, Richard, 1985, *Profits, Progress and Poverty: Case Studies of International Industries in Latin America*. Notre Dame, Ind.: University of Notre Dame Press.

O'Donnell, Guillermo, 1973, *Modernization and Bureaucratic Authoritarianism: Studies in South American Politics*. Berkeley: Institute of International Studies, University of California.

OECD (Organization for Economic Cooperation and Development), 1979, *The Impact of the Newly Industrializing Countries on Production and Trade in Manufactures*. Paris: OECD.

Portes, Alejandro, Manuel Castells, and Lauren A. Benton, eds., 1989, *The Informal Economy: Studies in Advanced and Less Developed Countries*. Baltimore: Johns Hopkins University Press.

Sabel, Charles F., 1986, "Changing models of economic efficiency and their implications for industrialization in the Third World." In *Development, Democracy, and the Art of Trespassing*, edited by Alejandro Foxley, Michael S. McPherson, and Guillermo O'Donnell, 27–55. Notre Dame, Ind.: University of Notre Dame Press.

Schive, Chi, 1990, "The next stage of industrialization in Taiwan and South Korea." In *Manufacturing Miracles: Paths of Industrialization in Latin America and East Asia*, edited by Gary Gereffi and Donald Wyman, 267–91. Princeton, NJ: Princeton University Press.

Stallings, Barbara, 1990, "The role of foreign capital and economic development." In *Manufacturing Miracles: Paths of Industrialization in Latin America and East Asia*, edited by Gary Gereffi and Donald Wyman, 55–89. Princeton, NJ: Princeton University Press.

Swidler, Ann, 1986, "Culture in action: Symbols and strategies." *American Sociological Review* 51:273–86.

Thorp, Rosemary, ed., 1984, *Latin America in the 1930's: The Role of the Periphery in the World Crisis*. Oxford: Macmillan.

Valenzuela, J. Samuel, and Arturo Valenzuela, 1978, "Modernization and dependency: Alternative perspectives in the study of Latin American underdevelopment." *Comparative Politics* 10:535–57.

Wade, Robert, 1990, "Industrial policy in East Asia – Does it lead or follow the market?" In *Manufacturing Miracles: Paths of Industrialization in Latin America and East Asia*, edited by Gary Gereffi and Donald Wyman, 231–66. Princeton, NJ: Princeton University Press.

Wallerstein, Immanuel, 1974, "Dependence in an interdependent world: The limited possibilities of transformation within the capitalist world economy." *African Studies Review* 17:1–26.

World Bank, 1982, *World Development Report 1982*. New York: Oxford University Press.

—— —— 1983, *World Development Report 1983*. New York: Oxford University Press.

—— —— 1992, *World Development Report 1992*. New York: Oxford University Press.

Part IV

Attempts to Understand Globalization and its Social Effects

16 The New International Division of Labor in the World Economy (1980)

Folker Fröbel, Jürgen Heinrichs, and Otto Kreye

This landmark book coined the phrase "new international division of labor," spurring a new literature that showed how the closing of factories in the wealthy nations (which took off in the 1970s) was linked to the opening of sweatshops in the periphery. Fröbel's, Heinrichs's, and Kreye's book examined how firms relocated their factories to areas of low wages, devastating economies in regions where labor unions and worker protections were strong. The book forcefully argues that workers in both regions were being impoverished by the change, and was popular because it addressed workers' fears and the difficulty of resolving the situation without concern for workers in the poor nations. It also was among the first to consider the role of gender in the choice of locations and workers by the transnational firms, who often sought out young, single women because they tended to work long hours in poor conditions without complaining or organizing. Desperate for income and aware that they could easily be replaced by millions of other job-seekers, these women were often treated as "disposable" by factory owners. *The New International Division of Labor in the World Economy* marks the beginning of the globalization literature, because it shows how new ways of organizing the production process globally has different social effects in different places, but which all are linked.

Two fundamental issues confront corporate management in 1977. They are:
- the probability that the post-war era of unusual rapid economic expansion is over, and
- the probability that the post-war era of unprecedented world economic and political cooperation is coming to an end.

The world's departure from these patterns could force companies into the most radical and painful reassessments of their plans and strategies in living memory . . . Growth, translated into improved living conditions, has . . . become one of the basic expectations of all the world's citizens, including the poorest. These assumptions clearly must now be challenged. The recent world recession will, hopefully, prove to have been merely an extremely severe one, but 1977 may reveal the recession as the sign-off of an exceptional period in world economic history. Within many nations, the tensions from a prolonged era of no or low growth could ultimately prove explosive ... The turmoil within and between nations resulting from the frustration of mass expectations would, in many instances, bring revolution and war to the fore.[1]

A blueprint for a new economic era published today outlines profound changes in life-styles that will be needed over the next five years to put capitalist societies back on the track for sustained economic growth. The most significant change is a shift away from the consumer-oriented growth that has marked the post-war period to a model more akin to the Communist bloc countries with the emphasis on improving and expanding plant and equipment. This shift would be achieved in part through a reduction in real wages and limits on the growth of living standards. One of the major tools to effect these changes would be a sustained level of unemployment well over post-war norms although below the record level seen in the just ended recession .... The author of this blueprint is the secretariat of the Organisation for Economic Cooperation and Development, the economic clearing house for the 24 largest industrialised states outside the Communist bloc. ... [The OECD notes] "that it would be tempting to consider a more favourable scenario. ... Unfortunately, there are few grounds for believing that this is a realistic alternative unless economic policies prove much more effective than in the past."[2]

1.1 The Phenomenon

Business International is one of the world's largest business consultancy firms. The OECD is the supranational institution which was established by the Western industrialised countries for the purpose of observing and coordinating their economies. What is the empirical evidence of recent changes in the world economy which has induced these two institutions to proffer such gloomy forecasts?

In the Western *industrialised countries* the rate of unemployment has reached its highest level for many years. In 1975 the official rate of unemployment, which always understates the real volume of unemployment, averaged 5 percent for the OECD countries (USA = 8.5 percent, Japan = 1.9 percent, Federal Germany = 4.7 percent) and has remained at this high level with no indications that it will decrease. The number of people in OECD countries officially registered as unemployed has hovered around the fifteen million mark since 1975 and there is no reason to suppose that it will fall in the immediate future.

An increasing number of the industrial branches of the OECD countries are reporting declining output, overcapacities, short-time working and mass redundancies. For example, the garment, textile and synthetic fibres industries in the most highly industrialised countries have, almost without exception, drastically cut back the production of their respective products at the traditional manufacturing sites as production there is becoming increasingly less competitive in the world market. Employees in many branches of industry are threatened with redundancy and the devaluation of their professional skills – victims of spreading automation and, in particular, of the recent leap forward in the rationalisation of the production process made possible by technical developments in the electrical engineering industry, especially the shift from electro-mechanical to electronic components in the production both of consumer goods and components to be used in other sectors of the economy.

Domestic investment in the largest industrialised countries (USA, Japan, Federal Germany, France, United Kingdom) has not only been stagnating but has even fallen in Japan and Federal Germany as a proportion of gross national product in the first half of the 1970s. In the face of the decreasing profitability of domestic investments, companies in the OECD countries have expanded and justified their policy of investment directed towards rationalisation on the grounds that they cannot expect any change in the current trends for the foreseeable future. In many countries the increase in the share of domestic investment which has been directed towards rationalisation schemes over recent years has resulted in a substantial loss of local jobs, without any reduction in productive capacity.

By contrast, *foreign* investments originating from the Western industrialised countries have been steadily increasing for a number of years. An ever-increasing share of these investments is flowing into the developing countries. Foreign investment for the purpose of industrial relocation is gaining in importance, both that undertaken in industrialised countries, as well as in developing countries.

Stagnating output, short-time working and mass redundancies in numerous countries do not, however, necessarily reflect the fates of individual companies. On the contrary, many companies, both large and small, from the industrialised countries are expanding their investments, production capacities and employment abroad, especially in developing countries, whilst their investments, production capacities and employment at home are stagnating or even declining.

The primacy given to investment for rationalisation instead of for expansion in the Western industrialised countries implies increased "mobility" for workers. More and more workers are losing not only their jobs but also their acquired profession as a result of rationalisation schemes. They are thrown onto the labour market where, because they lack relevant qualifications or training, they are obliged to sell their labour-power as unskilled or semiskilled workers at considerably worse terms than before. Given the rapid changes in the specifications and qualifications demanded of the labour-force by current economic developments and the concurrent increase in occupational "mobility", it is hardly surprising that the rationale and usefulness of professional training is becoming more and more questionable, and that companies are increasingly cutting back on comprehensive programmes of industrial training. More and more workers are being forced to make rapid and psychologically exhausting adjustments to the changing demands of the labour market – changes which are both abrupt and more or less unforeseeable.

In addition, the Western industrialised countries are experiencing a long-term fiscal crisis of the state. High unemployment and short-time working have forced the state to increase its expenditure, while at the same time the state's tax receipts have fallen because high unemployment has reduced the revenue from personal taxation and the threat or reality of industrial relocation has reduced the ability of the state to tax private companies. It is becoming more and more difficult to provide adequate funds for public pension and health programmes. Outlays on social services are being cut, while at the same time higher social security contributions and taxes threaten employees with a decrease in real incomes. On the other hand, the state has been compelled to provide grants, loans and tax concessions to private business on an increasing scale, hoping that this will stimulate domestic investment, reduce the rate of unemployment, and thus avert the danger of potentially explosive social tensions. This policy of curbing real wages and of promoting the so-called growth industries by official massive backing from the state has nonetheless so far failed to yield any noticeable success in making domestic industrial sites attractive again. "The horses have been led to the water, but are refusing to drink."

These economic, social and political problems in each of the Western industrialised countries are occurring in the context of world-wide higher turnovers and profits by individual companies. The annual reports of most large companies show that, even in the years of the world recession, these companies have been operating very successfully.

A remarkable contrast then exists between the success of individual private companies and the failure of the economic policies of the industrialised countries to attain their declared principal policy aim, namely the reduction in unemployment. The panacea of the last few decades, high rates of growth in gross national product, no longer appears to be available. In fact, whether the extensive elimination of unemployment is seriously the prime objective of the economic policies of the industrial nations is far from certain when one considers the OECD "scenario" cited at the beginning of this chapter. One cannot avoid the question: Are the politicians simply incapable, or have the structures of national economies recently undergone such profound changes that the present problem of chronic unemployment is simply so much more intractable than formerly? We shall return to this question later.

The number of un- and underemployed in the *developing countries* is even greater: they constitute an enormous mass of people who are either not at all or only partially integrated as productive labour into the so-called modern sector. This reservoir of potential labour amounts to hundreds of millions of workers. It is an oversimplification to say that it is the traditionally bad living conditions in underdeveloped countries which produced an ever-increasing flow of people seeking work and incomes from the countryside into the cities, the potential sites of the industry which can grant these things. Paradoxically the cause must be looked for in the modernisation of agriculture which can only attain its declared goal of increasing food production by the destruction of small subsistence farming, the traditional modest basis of survival for large sections of the rural population who are then forced to migrate to the cities where they are not usually able to obtain an income sufficient to provide them with a decent living.

The contemporary slums and similar poverty-stricken districts of the underdeveloped countries' cities are overcrowded with these landless rural immigrants. (By 1970 population statistics from at least ten cities in the so-called Third World showed that more than a million people in each of them were living in such areas.) Transformed into proletarianised wage workers they are forced to seek employment regardless of the level of remuneration and under the most inhuman conditions merely to ensure their sheer physical survival. They constitute a nearly inexhaustible source of the cheapest and most exploitable labour in the underdeveloped countries.

This vast industrial reserve army of extremely cheap labour feeds a process of industrialisation which can be observed in many contemporary developing countries. But this process of industrialisation rarely absorbs any significant proportion of the local labour-force. It is oriented to production for export, as the purchasing power of the mass of the local population is too low to constitute an effective demand on the local market for the products of the country's own industry. The markets supplied by the industrialisation of the developing countries are therefore predominantly over-seas, primarily in the traditional industrial countries.

This process of export-oriented industrialisation in developing countries is not only highly dependent on foreign companies but also extremely fragmented. Only very rarely do developing countries end up with the establishment of reasonably complex industrial branches (e.g. textile and garment industry in some cases complemented by synthetic fibre production). And even in the very few developing countries where such centres of partial industrialisation have been established there are no signs that they are being supplemented by a wider industrial complex which would enable them to free themselves eventually from their dependency on the already industrialised countries for imports of capital- and other goods, and for the maintenance of their industrial installations.

However, in the overwhelming majority of developing countries not even the beginnings of this partial industrialisation process can be observed, that is, a process which would at least serve to develop a few individual branches of industry. Instead, industrial production is confined to a few highly specialised manufacturing processes: inputs are imported from outside the country, are worked on by the local labour-force in "world market factories" (for example, sewing, soldering, assembling and testing) and are then exported in their processed form. In other words, these world market factories are industrial enclaves with no connection to the local economy except for their utilisation of extremely cheap labour and occasionally some local inputs (energy, water and services for example), and are isolated from the local economy in almost all other respects. The labour-force recruited for production in these industrial enclaves is equipped with the necessary training in a period that rarely lasts for more than a few weeks, is exploited for a time-span which is optimal for the companies, and is then replaced by a newly recruited and freshly trained labour-force. Under such conditions there is no such thing as a skilled labour-force, or, at best, the skills which the workers do acquire are very minimal. Likewise there is no observable transfer of technology, despite the euphoric claims made by firms which relocate their manufacturing processes in the developing countries. The technology which is employed in these world market factories is not only in most cases quite simple, but also dependent on the expertise of foreign specialists and managers. This technology is often quite useless for the development of any form of industrialisation which would serve the basic needs of the local population.

So far export-oriented industrialisation has failed to achieve any improvement in the social conditions of the mass of the populations of the developing countries, not even as far as their most fundamental needs such as food, clothing, health, habitation and education are concerned. Nor can any improvement be expected in the foreseeable future. Quite the opposite – the social tensions and struggles between the tiny privileged minority which benefits from export-oriented industrialisation, and the vast majority of the population which derives no benefits from it will intensify in the future. It is such predictable developments as these which have occasioned Business International to take account of war and revolution in many countries. The increasing militarisation of the so-called Third World is a clear indication that increasingly overt and repressive force is needed to prevent the violent eruption of social tensions. South Africa, Chile and Thailand are but three especially well-known examples of military repression – but there are very many others. The "preventive counter-revolution", to use an expression coined by Herbert Marcuse, is well under way in most parts of the so-called Third World (and not only there).

After decades and centuries of the underdevelopment of the so-called developing countries the recent export-oriented industrialisation of these countries offers but faint hope that living standards and conditions of the mass of their populations will undergo any substantial improvements in the foreseeable future. Moreover there is no reason to assume that the main goal of the policies pursued by the governments of many developing countries is, in fact, the improvement of the material conditions of the mass of their populations. But even in those developing countries whose governments appear to be actively pursuing this goal, little progress can be discerned, except in very rare instances. Again, are the politicians of these developing countries simply incapable, or are the economic and social structures of the developing countries – the stark contrast between élite and masses, and debilitating economic dependency – so rigid that the goal of improving the living standards of the masses of the populations is unattainable under present circumstances? We shall come back to this question also.

Even the most superficial description of the *world economy* in the 1970s cannot be confined to a consideration of the situation of the industrialised countries on one hand, and of the developing countries on the other, each looked at in artificial isolation. (The "socialist" countries will be taken into account in our study only inasmuch as they are also integrated into the world market.) The world economy is not simply the sum total of national economies, each of which functions essentially according to its own laws of motion, with only marginal interconnections, such as those established by external trade. These national economies are, rather, organic elements of one all-embracing system, namely a world economy which is in fact a single world-wide capitalist system. As our cursory survey has already shown, the structural changes in individual national economies are interrelated within this single world economy and mutually determine one another.

The most striking manifestation of the world economy is international trade. Well over 15 percent of all commodities and services which are produced every year in Western industrialised and developing countries enter international trade, and this percentage has been steadily increasing for at least the last fifteen years. Recognition of this fact is a first step towards understanding the increase of world-wide economic interpenetration.

The industrialised countries handle 70 percent of international trade and the developing countries only 20 percent. Seventy per cent of exports from both developing and industrialised countries are destined for industrialised countries and only 20 percent for the developing countries. In other words, whereas the foreign trade of the industrialised countries is mostly with each other, the foreign trade of the developing countries is mostly with the industrialised countries, and not their fellow developing countries. Recognition of this fact is a first step towards understanding the economic dependency of the developing countries on the industrialised countries.

The developing countries' exports to the industrialised countries still consist overwhelmingly of raw materials, whereas the vast bulk of the exports of the industrialised countries to the developing countries are still manufactures. In recent years, however, there has been a marked, slow but steady increase in manufactures exported from developing countries as a proportion of total world exports of manufactured goods. Recognition of this fact is a first important step towards understanding a potential change in the structure not only of world trade, but also, and more importantly, of the world economy itself. This change is especially evident in the rapid expansion of textile and garment exports from the developing countries to the industrialised countries.

International trade and world-wide industrial production, however, provide only a very superficial picture of the increasing interpenetration of national economies. World trade is increasingly becoming a flow of commodities between the plants of the same company spread throughout the world, or at least a flow between companies and their partners in subcontracting agreements. (For instance company A in Federal Germany delivers semiprocessed products for further manufacturing to a subcontractor B abroad; the finished manufactures are subsequently re-imported into Federal Germany.) In this case, foreign trade is not just simply an exchange of commodities between two national economies, but more precisely, a concrete manifestation of the international division of labour, consciously planned and utilised by individual companies.

One, albeit incomplete, expression of this international division of labour, which has been organised by private companies in pursuit of their own profit maximisation, is foreign investment. Figures for Federal German investment show that in recent years investment abroad by Federal German companies has exceeded investment by foreign companies in Federal Germany. Taken together with the fact that investment policy in Federal Germany has concentrated on rationalisation schemes for a number of years, this would suggest that Federal Germany has now apparently become less "interesting" as a site for the expansion of industrial production. (Figures on the development of industrial assets of Federal German companies, including the re-invested profits, both at home and abroad would, in all probability, if available, demonstrate this phenomenon even more clearly.)

However, perhaps the clearest expression of the structural changes in the world economy which can be observed in the mid-1970s is the relocation of production. One form of this relocation (among other equally important ones) is the closing down of certain types of manufacturing operations in undertakings in the industrial nations and the subsequent installation of these parts of the production process in the foreign subsidiaries of the same company. The Federal German textile and garment industries represent one of the best-known examples of such relocations. Trousers for the Federal German market are no longer produced for example in Mönchengladbach, but in the Tunisian subsidiary of the same Federal German company. The process of relocation is also gaining momentum in other branches of industry. Injection pumps which were formerly made for the Federal German market by a Federal German company in Stuttgart, are now manufactured partly to the same end by the same company at a site in India. Television sets are produced on the same basis by another company in Taiwan; car radio equipment in Malaysia, car engines in Brazil, watches in Hong Kong, electronic components in Singapore and Malaysia all fall into the same category.

The Federal German worker rendered unemployed by the relocation of production has been replaced by a newly hired worker in a foreign subsidiary of "his" or "her" company.

1.2 Main Tendencies in the Contemporary World Economy

The question which we began with was the following: What has happened in the world economy to have occasioned the forecasts published by the OECD and Business International? To answer this we started with an outline of the economic situation of both the industrialised and the developing countries and we were occasionally obliged to resort to the vague term "the rest of the world". We have tried, however, to correct some of the misleading implications of this initial proce-dure by subsequent reference to some of the mutual relations and dependencies between the economies of the industrialised countries and the developing countries, which make up one world economy. We have chosen this descriptive procedure by way of introduction in order not to have to use more information, where possible, than is already available to any newspaper reader who is interested in political and economic matters.

Our next step is to undertake a *systematic presentation of essentially the same observable facts* and to show how they can only be understood as an *expression of the development of a single world economy.* (In Chapter 2 we try to explain the development of the world economy over the last five centuries showing how this development can only be understood as a necessary expression of the development of a *capitalist* world system.)

The origins of the present-day world economy are to be found in the sixteenth century. Its genesis was inextricably connected with the simultaneous emergence of a regional division of labour which affected the whole world. Different forms of the organisation of labour were used in different regions of the world (or introduced from outside the region itself) for different types of production. The following represent some characteristic examples:

From the Sixteenth Century to the Eighteenth Century

(a)   Independent crafts and domestic labour (the putting-out system) formed the basis in Western Europe of manufactures such as textiles and metals, ship-building and arms production. Wage labour was also already used in individual large-scale manufacturing enterprises.

(b)   Forced or slave labour formed the basis of silver mining in Peru and Mexico, and also of sugar plantations established by European colonial masters in Brazil and the West Indies. Serf labour formed the basis of grain production in Eastern Europe; the "second serfdom", a reversal in the trend towards the disintegration of landlord/serf relations, was utilised and even intensified owing to the demand for corn from Western Europe.

Eighteenth and Nineteenth Centuries

(a)   Wage labour supplanted other forms of labour as the basis of the industrial revolution, which spread from England where cotton manufacturing, the steam engine and railways were developed.

(b)   Slave labour became the basis of raw cotton production in the West Indies and in the Southern United States; India's indigenous cotton manufacturing which had initially been stimulated by world trade was destroyed; China and Japan were "opened up" for world trade (the Opium Wars etc.).

First Half of the Twentieth Century

(a)   Wage labour formed the basis of manufacturing in Europe, USA and Japan.

(b)   A peculiar form of wage labour (which will be discussed below) formed the basis of the extraction and production of raw materials in the enclaves of Latin America, Africa and Asia (coffee in Brazil, saltpetre and copper in Chile, gold and diamonds in South Africa). These were primarily for export onto the world market. A partial industrialisation process was established in a small number of developing countries through a policy of import-substitution.

The regions of Latin America, Africa and Asia have therefore been integrated for centuries into the developing world economy chiefly as producers of agricultural and mineral raw materials, sometimes as the suppliers of a labour-force (e.g. African slaves). This integration was enforced wherever it was feasible and necessary by the military, technological and economic superiority which the West European nations and rulers developed after the sixteenth century.

Some countries of the so-called Third World have, under certain very specific conditions, experienced a weak process of industrialisation based on a policy of import-substitution: for instance, parts of Latin America during the partial disintegration of the world economy between 1930 and 1945. During this period it was possible for a modest local industry to develop in some underdeveloped countries for the purpose of supplying a very restricted domestic market. This development was possible only behind a barrier of selective import restrictions and was facilitated by the preoccupation of the most powerful industrialised nations with their "own" problems during this period, a preoccupation which prevented them from intervening in the so-called Third World. This modest profitable local industry, however, very quickly reached the limits of local effective demand, and since it was non-competitive on the world market, receded into stagnation almost everywhere after the Second World War, and even in some cases, such as Argentina, collapsed into agony.

Our earlier descriptive sketch of some typical aspects of the contemporary world economy has already indicated that the old or "classical" international division of labour is now open for replacement. The decisive evidence for this hypothesis is the fact that developing countries have increasingly become sites for manufacturing – producing manufactured goods which are competitive on the world market. The three case studies presented in this book provide extensive documentation of this world market oriented production of manufactures which is now being established and developed on new industrial sites, especially those in the developing countries.

This world market oriented industrialisation which is emerging today in many developing countries is not the result of positive decisions made by individual governments or companies. Industry only locates itself at those sites where production will yield a certain profit, sites which have been determined by five centuries of development of the world economy. In the "classical" international division of labour which developed over this period, industrial sites for manufacturing basically only existed in Western Europe, and later in the USA and Japan. Since it is evident that the developing countries are now providing sites for the profitable manufacture of industrial products destined for the world market to an ever-increasing extent, we quickly come up against the question: What changes are responsible for this development?

Three preconditions taken together seem to be decisive for this new development.

Firstly, a practically inexhaustible reservoir of disposable labour has come into existence in the developing countries over the last few centuries. This labour-force is extremely cheap; it can be mobilised for production for practically the whole of the year, and all hours of the day, on shift work, night work and Sunday work; in many cases it can reach levels of labour productivity comparable with those of similar processes in the developed countries after a short period of training; companies can afford to exhaust the labour-force by overwork as it can easily be replaced, and they can also select their employees very specifically according to age, sex, skill, discipline and other relevant factors as there is an oversupply of people who are forced to take any job which is available.

Secondly, the division and subdivision of the production process is now so advanced that most of these fragmented operations can be carried out with minimal levels of skill easily learnt within a very short time.

Thirdly, the development of techniques of transport and communication has created the possibility, in many cases, of the complete or partial production of goods at any site in the world – a possibility no longer ruled out by technical, organisational and cost factors.

The coincidence of these three preconditions (which are supplemented by other, less important ones) has brought into existence a world market for labour and a real world industrial reserve army of workers, together with a world market for production sites. Workers in the already industrialised countries are now placed on a world-wide labour market and forced to compete for their jobs with their fellow workers in the developing countries. Today, with the development of a world-wide market in production sites, the traditional industrialised and the developing countries have to compete against one another to attract industry to their sites.

In other words, for the first time in the history of the 500-year-old world economy, the profitable production of manufactures for the world market has finally become possible to a significant and increasing extent, not only in the industrialised countries, but also now in the developing countries. Furthermore, commodity production is being increasingly subdivided into fragments which can be assigned to whichever part of the world can provide the most profitable combination of capital and labour.

The term which we shall use to designate this qualitatively new development in the world economy is the *new international division of labour*.

Of those countries which were able to supply vast reserve armies of potential industrial workers and to offer these workers' labour-power at a low price, the first to attract the relocation of parts of the production process were countries with close geographical and commercial links to existing industrial centres. The first shifts of US industry were to Western Europe and to countries "south of the border"; West European companies transferred production to other regions in Europe, such as Eire, Greece, Portugal and the south of Italy; Japanese industry moved into South Korea and Taiwan. At the same time, industrial firms recruited labour from countries with high rates of unemployment and drew it in to the traditional sites of industrial production. Hence the appearance of *Gastarbeiter* in Western Europe, and Mexican and Puerto Rican immigrant workers in the USA.

Since then, sites for relocated manufacturing are not only being supplied in the border areas of Western Europe, Central America, North Africa, and South East Asia, but increasingly in Eastern Europe, South America, Central Africa and South Asia. The transfer of production to places with cheap labour not only affects the more or less labour-intensive production processes but also processes which are heavily dependent on raw materials and energy, and those which are a source of environmental pollution, given that the new sites can also offer favourable conditions as far as other factors of production are concerned. It has even affected capital-intensive production processes, contrary to the unsubstantiated prejudices of a number of international economists. Not only are investments, production capacities and output expanded and developed at these new sites, but existing facilities at the traditional sites which have become obsolete in terms of profitability are closed down.

This means that any company, almost irrespective of its size, which wishes to survive is now forced to initiate a transnational reorganisation of production to adapt to these qualitatively new conditions.

By far the most important means by which companies have secured their continued survival in the past has been through "investment in rationalisation" – the installation of more efficient machinery and a reduction in the size and skills of the labour-force. This device alone (along with other "classical" devices) is no longer adequate. The development of the world economy has increasingly created conditions (forcing the development of the new international division of labour) in which the survival of more and more companies can only be assured through the relocation of production to new industrial sites, where labour-power is cheap to buy, abundant and well-disciplined; in short, through the transnational reorganisation of production.

1.3 Selected Case Studies

Until now we have tried to locate the tendency towards a new international division of labour as an aspect of the continued development of world economy, an economy which can only be understood as a single, integrated system. In Chapter 2 we shall try to explain this growing tendency as the necessary expression of the operation of the world capitalist system – the valorisation of capital. Though this theoretical insight into the nature of the development of the world economy must be our starting point, it is not in itself sufficient to deduce in specific terms the extent to which the tendency towards a new international division of labour has already become a reality. Actual empirical research is needed to answer this question.

Three case studies were selected out of a long list of possible studies: these were based both on considerations of the availability of the relevant information, and our own research capabilities. They were:

I   The structural changes in the Federal German textile and garment industries which have been determined by economic developments occurring in the world economy.
II   Production and employment of foreign labour abroad (outside the EEC) by Federal German manufacturing industry, excluding the textile and garment industry.
III   New industrial sites for world market oriented production in developing countries: free production zones.

The first of these three case studies was an in-depth investigation of the most important structural changes in one branch of industrial production. The second analysed the world-wide redistribution of production sites for all manufacturing industry (with the exclusion of the textile and garment industries) of one important industrialised country. The third examined the establishment of new industries in underdeveloped countries with reference to specific examples. Each case study attempted to arrive at a complete coverage of the subject under investigation, and was not merely a study of either random or specifically selected samples.

The data collected in these case studies is systematically presented and interpreted to provide information about the structure of the world labour market and the world market in production sites, the redistribution of industrial sites and the conditions and consequences associated with these phenomena. Each of these case studies in fact represents only a small part of the global process. But taken together they provide adequate information to allow an empirical assessment and elucidation of the fundamental forms in which the new international division of labour is appearing, and the determining forces which are shaping it.

Detailed evidence is provided of the new industrial sites and the number of people at work in them, along with details of wage differentials and differences, and variations in other important working conditions. The study includes the world-wide reorganisation of production illustrated by an investigation into the industrial branches of one important industrialised country, and world market oriented manufacturing in the underdeveloped countries. The closing down of production at the traditional sites and the connected relocation of production and structural changes in world trade are also examined. We discuss the relationship between rationalisation and the decision to relocate production, both of which are instruments companies employ to guarantee their competitiveness. Two examples are taken here: the textile and garment industry, and the production of electronic components.

We also attempt to provide some answers to other questions which were not the main focus of our empirical research, which means that our answers in these areas are only partial or provisional in nature. This applies, for example, to the effects of new technologies on the transnational organisation of production, effects on the size and structure of total employment in individual countries, and changes in the distribution of skills among the work-force at different industrial sites. By "skill structure" or "distribution of skills" we refer to the occupational skills or technical qualifications available in an economy regardless of whether the bearers of these skills are in employment or not. We use the term "pattern of employment" to indicate the types of jobs, defined in terms of their skill requirements, which are available to the holders of different types of skill, regardless of whether these jobs are occupied or exist as unfilled vacancies. These jobs and vacancies constitute the social demand for labour-power: workers' skills and qualifications the supply. Whether the worker is able to find a buyer on the labour market is a circumstance which is dependent on the structure of available employment on the one hand, and the previous pattern of training on the other.

We can only allude to, but not elaborate on, the social and political consequences of the findings in our study. These include changes in the international structure of the dependency of national economies on one another, and the reproduction of the world-wide industrial reserve army. For these, and other topics, further empirical research is needed.

The results of our empirical studies are presented in Parts I, II and III. Some of the results are presented in summary form immediately below. If read without being placed in the context of our later more extensive presentation they may lead to distorted interpretations. The figures mentioned in this summary should therefore only be taken as approximate indications of the extent to which the new inter-national division of labour has already developed.

Case Study I is a survey of 214 textile and 185 garment companies from Federal Germany. In 1974 these companies accounted for roughly 60 percent of turnover and employment in the Federal German textile industry and 40 percent in the Federal German garment industry. In each of these samples about a hundred companies had *subsidiaries* producing abroad by 1974/75. These figures do not include production abroad by a quite significant number of nominally independent foreign producers, in particular through subcontracting and export-processing cooperation agreements with Eastern European and East Asian firms. These figures should be compared with those of other studies which identified about thirty firms from each industry in 1966, and forty firms from each in 1970 producing either in wholly or partly owned subsidiaries abroad.

A breakdown of our findings by region shows that in 1974 foreign production in the subsidiaries of the companies covered by our case study was concentrated in the industrialised countries (chiefly, the EEC countries, Austria and Switzerland) on the one hand, with a share of 50–60 percent, and in certain of the developing countries on the other hand (the textile industry in Africa and the Mediterranean countries, and the garment industry in the Mediterranean countries and Asia). The concentration of production in these regions is confirmed statistically regardless of whether we look at the number of foreign subsidiaries or the number of employees.

The following figures are the numbers of employees in the foreign subsidiaries of the Federal German textile and garment industries. In the textile industry, the numbers of employed increased from 8000 in 1966 to 14,200 in 1970 and finally to 29,500 in 1974: these are minimum estimates. In the garment industry, the equivalent figures are 15,000, 24,800 and 31,000. The sizes of the labour-force employed in foreign subsidiaries as a proportion of these industries' domestic employment in the Federal Republic of Germany are as follows: in the textile industry, 1.5 percent in 1966, 2.8 percent in 1970 and 7.5 percent in 1974/75; in the garment industry, 3.7 percent in 1966, 6.5 percent in 1970 and 10.0 percent in 1974/75. Foreign employment in Federal German subsidiaries in the "low wage countries' as proportion of the total foreign labour employed by Federal German subsidiaries abroad in the textile and garment industries has increased from approximately 25 percent in 1966 to approximately 45 percent by 1974/75.

A breakdown of employment abroad by sex and age group reveals that the subsidiaries of Federal German garment companies in the "low wage countries" employ an extremely high percentage of young female workers. Roughly 43 percent of the employed are younger than twenty, and more than 90 percent are female.

If one includes *subcontracting arrangements* with foreign firms, then the Federal German textile and garment industries are employing at least 69,000 workers in subsidiaries and subcontracted firms abroad, and very probably significantly more; a figure of over 80,000 employees for the Federal German textile and garment industry abroad is not an improbable estimate for 1974/75.

In short, the foreign employment of the Federal German textile and garment industries has more than doubled between 1966 and 1974/75, whereas domestic employment has decreased by roughly a quarter over the same period. An estimate for 1977 would show that for every hundred workers employed by the Federal German textile and garment industries in Federal Germany itself, there are more than ten foreign workers employed abroad.

In 1974/75, some 30,000 employees in the foreign production facilities of the Federal German textile and garment industry were producing either exclusively or predominantly for the Federal German market. This is an indication of the extent to which companies have relocated production for the domestic market from production sites in Federal Germany to sites abroad.

The case study analyses in some detail the following indicators of the new international division of labour in the sphere of the textile and garment industries: the drastically increased negative balance of trade in textiles and clothing of Federal Germany; the structural unemployment in the traditional industrial centres which has been caused by this development in the world economy; the export-oriented industrialisation of the developing countries; the corresponding relocations of production as industry is moved from sites in the "centre" to the "periphery"; and the increasing subdivision of the production process into fragmented routines which can be distributed throughout the world. The growing significance of these factors over the last ten to fifteen years in the sphere of the textile and garment industries provides incontrovertible evidence of the fact that the economic pressure of the world-wide labour market and the world market for industrial sites is forcing companies to undertake a global reorganisation of their own production processes. Rationalisation schemes, both at home and abroad, and industrial relocation abroad (especially to "low wage countries") go hand in hand.

What this process means for those it directly affects is, first and foremost, unemployment and the devaluation of skills for workers in the traditional industrial countries, and the subjection of the populations of the developing countries to inhuman working conditions, with no hope for improvement in the foreseeable future. Furthermore, the inevitable development of this process means that in the years to come working people will be threatened even more drastically than in the past with the degradation and rigid discipline which reduces them to the status of mere appendages of the machine.

Case Study II surveys 602 Federal German manufacturing companies (excluding the textile and garment industries) which have had at least one subsidiary producing abroad (outside the EEC) between 1961 and 1976. The sum total of these subsidiaries (Federal German formal share-in-capital between 25 percent and 100 percent) of these companies producing outside the EEC is 1760. Of these companies, 339 have one subsidiary abroad, 528 companies have up to four subsidiaries abroad, and twelve companies have twenty or more. These subsidiaries are located in a total of seventy-seven countries, with Brazil, Spain, the USA and Austria each accounting for more than a hundred. Of the 602 companies in our survey, 335 have 709 subsidiaries in industrialised countries, and 444 have 1051 subsidiaries in developing countries.

It was possible to collect employment figures for 1178 of the 1760 subsidiaries surveyed; in 1975 these subsidiaries employed 560,788 persons. If the EEC countries and the textile and garment industries are included, our estimate of the total employment abroad by Federal German manufacturing companies amounts to 1.5 million workers. That is, the number of workers directly employed by Federal German manufacturing companies in foreign countries amounts to 20 percent of the total domestic labour-force in Federal German manufacturing industry. This figure, which is based on quite conservative estimates, is considerably higher than any other estimate published to date.

Foreign production is fairly well distributed over the different branches of industry. The mechanical engineering branch has the highest number of companies involved in production abroad, the chemicals industry has the most subsidiaries, and the electrical engineering industry has the most employees abroad. The data collected shows that nearly all branches of Federal German industry participate to a significant degree in production abroad and industrial relocation.

Between 1961 and 1976 the number of foreign subsidiaries belonging to the companies surveyed in this case study increased fourfold, with much of this increase first starting at the end of the 1960s. The increase in the number of employees abroad has been even more striking since many existing foreign subsidiaries have expanded their production and employment during the period of time under investigation. Complete data is available for a subsample of the companies surveyed, and reveals that the number of employees employed abroad by these companies increased five-fold between 1961 and 1974.

The above figures represent only a fraction of all foreign production by Federal German industry. This is due not so much to lack of information on the companies producing abroad but more significantly to our operational definition of what constitutes Federal German production abroad, i.e. production where the Federal German share in the subsidiaries' capital was at least 25 percent, which therefore excludes instances of Federal German foreign production where the direct holding is low or non-existent. However, it is possible for Federal German industry to use foreign production facilities without any direct capital participation, as evidenced by such cooperative arrangements as international subcontracting, management, supply and licence agreements. Our case study does not provide statistical data on the extent of this type of foreign production, and it is difficult to estimate how widespread it is. In some parts of the world, at least, this type of foreign production is more important than that controlled through direct capital holdings (e.g. in Eastern Europe and India).

These complexities must be taken into account in estimating the amount of industrial relocation. The procedure must start not only with individual companies and take note of all changes in industrial sites for the totality of production organised by those companies, but must add to this processes of relocation at the level of whole branches of industry which are not organised by domestic companies alone; for example, if domestic production in a given company is cut back or shut down completely because the product is now obtained from non-Federal German companies producing abroad. An assessment of the tendencies towards the relocation of industry throughout the world, and hence of the structural changes in the world economy and its subeconomies, can only be obtained by a global estimate of the redistribution of industrial sites.

The results of case study II (the study of industry in one major industrial country) testify to the changed conditions for the world-wide valorisation of capital which are forcing industrial undertakings, regardless of size and industrial branch, to reorganise their production. In an increasing number of cases, this reorganisation involves the relocation of production abroad. To conclude: the new international division of labour is manifested in the changing world distribution of, in this case, Federal German production facilities. The high level of structural unemployment in Federal Germany is an inevitable result of the transfer of industrial employment elsewhere in the world.

Case Study III is based on data embracing 103 countries in Asia, Africa and Latin America. Whereas in the mid-1960s manufacturing for the markets of the industrialised countries was virtually non-existent in the underdeveloped countries, ten years later, there were literally thousands of factories in production in the underdeveloped countries producing goods almost exclusively for the markets of the industrialised countries. Such factories existed in at least thirty-nine underdeveloped countries; fifteen of these countries were in Asia, eight in Africa and sixteen in Latin America. This spread of industrial production in the so-called Third World is tied up with the creation of a new type of industrial site – the free production zone – and with the creation of a new type of factory – the world market factory.

Free production zones are industrial areas which are separated off from the rest of the country, located at places where labour is cheap and designated as sites for world market oriented industry; world market factories are factories which are built on these sites, but can also be situated elsewhere, and intended for the industrial utilisation of the available labour and the processing of goods destined essentially for the markets of the industrialised countries. In 1975, seventy-nine free production zones were in operation in twenty-five underdeveloped countries; eleven of these countries were in Asia, five in Africa and nine in Latin America.

As far as the structure of production at these sites is concerned, nearly all branches of manufacturing industry are represented. On the other hand, as far as individual zones and countries are concerned, there is a tendency for the development of industrial mono-structures. In 1975 the bulk of production was accounted for by the products of the textiles and garment industry on one hand, and those of the electrical engineering industry on the other. Production in world market factories is highly vertically integrated into the transnational operations of the individual companies and involves non-complex production operations; as regards the processing of each product or product group, the production process is largely confined to part operations: the manufacturing of parts, assembling of parts, or final assembly. Only in the case of a few product groups, and in a few countries, can one identify anything resembling complex manufacture; textiles and garments are one example.

The employment structure in free production zones and world market factories is extremely unbalanced. Given a virtually unlimited supply of unemployed labour, world market factories at the free production zones, or other sites, select one specific type of worker, chiefly women from the younger age groups. The criteria used for the selection of workers are quite unambiguous: the labour which is employed is that which demands the least remuneration, provides the maximum amount of energy (i.e. fresh labour which can be expected to work at a high intensity) and which is predominantly unskilled or semiskilled.

The case study attempts to provide an answer to the question as to whether the aims of development policy, which are allegedly linked with world market oriented industrialisation, are being attained. These are: reduction in unemployment, training of skilled personnel, access to modern technology, and increases in the foreign currency earned by the country concerned. The historical record up to now and the foreseeable future both indicate that the answer to this question is an unequivocal "no".

NOTES

1. Business International Corporation, *Business International – Weekly Report to Managers of Worldwide Operations*, 7 January 1977, p. 1.
2. "Changes in West life-styles expected. OECD sees tough capitalist road ahead," *Herald Tribune*, 28 July 1976; cf. OECD, *Economic Outlook*, 19 July 1976, Special Supplement, "A growth scenario to 1980".

17 Globalization: Myths and Realities (1996)

Philip McMichael

Australian Philip McMichael's research has focused on rural development and food dependency in the Third World. His book *Development and Social Change* broadens his discussion beyond the rural scope, but is uniquely strong in the globalization literature in discussing the role of agriculture. In his book and this article from the journal *Rural Sociology*, McMichael argues that a new phase of globalization has meant "a qualitative shift" in the way our societies are organized. Namely, local people and their governments no longer have control over the key decisions that will shape their lives. Rather, they must always worry about how their actions are being seen by international investors and huge international financial institutions like the IMF and World Bank. This is because they are heavily in debt or need future access to loans, and to continue to be able to make their payments they need to keep good "credit ratings." Many indebted nations (the list includes almost the whole world, but especially the poor nations) have been forced to cut food, housing, and medical aid to the poor, housing assistance, and to take away trade protections for their home industries. In examining the case of the Zapatista rebellion in Chiapas, Mexico, McMichael sees the possibilities of strong local resistance to the crushing demands of global capitalism.

Introduction

The late 20th century offers rural sociology a unique opportunity for revitalization in the crisis of the development paradigm – the modernist project associated with nation-building. The development paradigm subordinated rural populations, and hence rural studies, to the higher authority of industrialism. Development theorists extrapolated from the example of modern states, whose rural populations had diminished drastically as agriculture industrialized. Remaining rural populations, across the world, were cast essentially as "unlimited supplies of labor" for an industrial future (Lewis 1954). In this way, rural issues were marginalized in the social scientific agenda. But marginalization has not eliminated them; if anything, it has magnified their significance. The consequences of agro-industrialism – land-lessness, hyper-urbanization, and environmental deterioration – reveal the short-comings of the development paradigm's underlying belief in inexorable technological progress. Sustainability has become the new catchword.

The rising concern with sustainability reveals the limits of the development paradigm in guaranteeing the survival of the human species and the natural world. In

addition, the growing unsustainability of the institutions of the development paradigm confounds this crisis, as globalization undermines social protections. This
argument is based on the following premises: First, development is perhaps the
"master" concept of the social sciences, and has been understood as an evolutionary
movement bringing rising standards of living – a logical outcome of human rationality, as revealed in the European experience; second, the development project was a
political strategy to institute nationally managed economic growth as a replicable
pattern across the expanding system of states in the post-World War II world order;
third, the paradigm of developmentalism offered a broadly acceptable interpretation
of how to organize states and international institutions around the goal of maximizing national welfare via technological advances in industry and agriculture; fourth,
this paradigm has collapsed with the puncturing of the illusion of development in the
1980s debt crisis, the management of which dismantled development institutions;
and fifth, debt management instituted a new organizing principle of "globalization"
as an alternative institutional framework, with the underlying message that nation-
states no longer "develop;" rather, they position themselves in the global economy.

This paradigmatic shift resonates globally. It registers in the demise of welfarist
regimes in the First World, of socialist regimes of central planning in the Second
World, and of the Third World as a political collectivity of post-colonial states. All
are subsumed within the big tent of globalism, which displaces simultaneously their
institutional and ideological legacies. In a general reversal of thinking, the present is
no longer the logical development of the past; rather it is increasingly the hostage of
the future: a future defined by globalists as one of inexorable efficiency.

In this essay, I elaborate this interpretation of the origins of post-developmentalism, and then consider some consequences for rural sociology. In particular, the
connection between local, rural processes and globalization needs clarification.
Globalization tends to be understood as a process of economic integration –
observed through local prisms, or "grounded" in local terms, giving a local face to
processes of globalization. But these processes (such as proliferating commodity
chains or transnational firm expansion) are routinely taken as given contexts, to be
observed on the "ground," where agency and culture enter in. An alternative
approach is first to ground globalization as a historical project, and, as such, to
problematize it as a set of institutional and ideological relations constructed by
powerful social forces (e.g., managers of international agencies, states and firms,
academic ideologues). Local processes, and local expressions of globalization,[1] are
then situated in an historically concrete, rather than an abstract context.

Globalization

Global exchanges predate the capitalist era. Why should they only now take on the
appearance of being the governing force of the late-20th century world? Advocates
of globalization claim, for example, that "the world's needs and desires have been
irrevocably homogenized," and technology "drives consumers relentlessly towards
the same common goals – alleviation of life's burdens and the expansion of discre-
tionary time and spending power" (Levitt 1983: 99). Global economic integration is
an empirical fact, but it is hardly the only reality. About 80 percent of the more than

five billion people in the world live outside global consumer networks (Barnet and Cavanagh 1994: 383).

Nevertheless, globalization has become consequential by virtue of its institutional force within the state system, and from there it reaches out to subject populations. Its most palpable impact has been through the worldwide process of restructuring of states and economies, bringing diverse populations and regions into the realm of a common dynamic. This dynamic is not simply a quantitative extension of commodity relations. It is, rather, a qualitative shift in the mode of social organization that marks a historic transition in the capitalist world order.

Arrighi (1994) links this shift to the onset of "financialization" – a contagious preference for liquid rather than fixed capital on the part of private and institutional investors under specific historical conditions (usually associated with the decline of a hegemonic state). Most recently, the (relative) decline of the United States is pegged to the rise of offshore money markets in the 1970s (discussed below). These currency markets stimulated the rise of unregulated financial institutions alongside of traditional (nationally regulated) banking systems. Heightened mobility of capital has privileged, and rewarded, financial speculation at the expense of fixed investment. Arrighi characterizes this as the subordination of the "territorial" principle to the "capitalist" principle. It marks a new stage of competition among states and firms in an unstable, post-hegemonic world order. When the center of accumulation (the US home market) erodes, speculation on an unknown financial future heightens.

As money capital decoupled from productive capital, financiers consolidated power and reshaped modern political and economic institutions in the 1980s, including farming (Bienefield 1989; Marsden and Whatmore 1994). Growing financial securitization (i.e., trading in securities, including debt) heightened the authority of debt security rating institutions, which meant in effect that all firms and states found their credit ratings subject to a global "information standard" (Sinclair 1994). Corporate downsizing and relocation, and state restructuring programs, in the service of credit-worthiness, have rippled across the global social landscape.

The new power of financial institutions has been at the expense of the sovereignty of state monetary authorities. In 1992, the former Chairman of Citicorp described the 200,000 currency traders across the world, as conducting "a kind of global plebiscite on the monetary and fiscal policies of the governments using currency. [This system] is far more draconian than any previous arrangement, such as the gold standard of the Bretton Woods system, since there is no way for a nation to opt out" (quoted in Brecher and Costello 1994: 30). In other words, precisely because of the non-territorial character of financialization, all states are constrained to manage their finances according to global criteria.

Under these circumstances, state organizations transmitted the effects of financial restructuring through the relatively circumscribed institutions of the "formal" economy and beyond, where communities depend on "informal" markets, subsidies, public lands, and casual employment on the fringes of the "formal" economy. In order to justify, or discount, the divisive consequences of restructuring – notably the social concentration of resources and the fragmentation of previously coherent social systems (e.g., economic arrangements, social protections, communities) – globalization advocates appeal to a higher good, namely, efficiency, and stress the importance of discipline in the global economy. Since some of these advocates are policymakers, they claim the discipline is imposed by the debt managers. ...

In short, as the rationale for recent restructuring of states and economies, "globalization" is an historically specific project of global economic (financial) management. Prosecuted by a powerful global elite of financiers, international and national bureaucrats, and corporate leaders, the globalist project grows out of the dissolution of the development project.

The Development Project

The development project was a postwar construct through which the world capitalist economy was stabilized. Like any social construct, the institutions of market economy are historically specific. Just as early capitalism emerged within distinct political frameworks – pre-19th century mercantilism (trade organized to enlarge national wealth), 19th century liberalism (free trade imperialism to enlarge capitalist markets) – so mid-20th century capitalism was organized within the framework of the (now universal) nation-state system (McMichael 1987). The completed nation-state system *combined* the principles of mercantilist and liberal organization into a new international regime of "embedded liberalism" (Ruggie 1982). This regime subordinated trade to systems of national economic management, anchored in strategic economic sectors like steel and farming. Together, international and national institutions regulated monetary and wage relations to stabilize national capitalisms within a liberal trade regime. Its extension to the so-called Third World, as the decolonization process unfolded, generated the paradigm of "developmentalism."

Under the project of developmentalism, states were responsible for managing national economic growth, with trade as a stimulus. How individual states accomplished this was generally their own concern, giving rise to a clear range of national political-economies (e.g., Japanese state capitalism, German corporatism, and US liberal capitalism underwritten by military spending). The macroeconomic goal was to consolidate national welfare, through a context of stable monetary relations. Again, with rich variation, this principle of nationally-managed economic growth was the adopted form of political economy in the multiplicity of new states that formed during this period. Economic Commission for Latin America (ECLA) prescriptions for import-substitution industrialization dovetailed with the green revolution (providing essentially urban wage foods) to shape national economic growth in Third World countries.

Development was a universal project, also inspiring accelerated industrialization in the Second World. It took its cue from the European experience, understood as superior economic performance and/or living standards vis-à-vis the non-European world. It was an ideal that we know, at least from hindsight, was unrealizable. But development was not just an ideal (as idealized history, and prescription). It was thoroughly institutionalized in the post-war world.

The institutionalization of development, as the central postwar project, required a stable international monetary regime and a uniform political entity such as the nation-state. It was a matter of historical choice. When pan-Africanists demanded territorial federations during the decolonization movement, they were overridden by the European powers and their fellow nationalists – both groups seeing in the nation-state form a vehicle for stable accumulation of wealth and extraction of economic resources on the national and the international scale (see Davidson 1992).

The monetary regime, instituted through the Bretton Woods agreements in 1944, established the principle of fixed exchange rates and mechanisms whereby the IMF could maintain stable currency exchange by extending short-term loans to those states with payments imbalances (Block 1977). National economies, geared to stabilizing the wage relation through rising investment (in mass production) and state subsidies (to promote full employment and rising consumption), were supported by a stable trade environment. This formula, despite its uneven implementation, is often characterized as a mix of Keynesian/Fordist political-economy (Harvey 1989).

Alongside of this multilateral arrangement were the geopolitical realities of the Cold War. The United States, in particular, deployed Marshall aid to redistribute dollars to capital-poor regions of the world (from Europe, through East Asia to Africa). This established the dollar as the international reserve currency and pro-moted freedom of enterprise, which became the litmus test of the so-called free world (Arrighi 1982). Export credits, extended to Marshall Plan recipients, facilitated the transfer of American technology. In turn, the World Bank (along with other such multilateral financial assistance institutions) disbursed long-term loan funds to encourage the habit of developmentalism (Rich 1994).

Without further elaboration, the point remains that in the mid-20th century the foundations of capitalism were reformulated through a massive restructuring of the world order. In other words, not only is "restructuring" not unique to the late-20th century, but it has an essential institutional dimension. In the postwar era, it com-bined forms of international (monetary relations) with national (wage relation) regulation. Developmentalism emerged within this institutional framework. First World (and Cold War) planners perceived their goal as raising and protecting living standards, and to this end pursued massive (military and economic) assistance programs. Developmentalism thus instrumentalized the nation-state, and bilateral and multilateral institutions, as its appropriate vehicles and agents.

Developmentalism was, indeed, a project originating in the stabilization of world capitalism after the inter-war crisis and in the context of the Cold War. It was a constructed order, even though planners presented development in ideal terms: as an evolutionary progression along a linear trajectory of modernization. In this respect, not only would each state replicate the modernity of the First World (with the US at the apex), but there were expectations that the development gap between First and Third Worlds would be progressively closed. Despite some apparent successes (e.g., the newly industrializing countries of East Asia and some Latin American states for a time), the development gap across these world divisions remained. The development project was unsuccessful in its own universalist terms. Its failure is both cause and consequence of the rise of an new, alternative project: the globalization project.

The Globalization Project

As suggested, globalization is not specific to our era. But globalization as a view of ordering the world is. It is a historical project, just as the development project was.

The development project was a view of ordering the world, but it was understood, institutionalized, and embraced as a process to be replicated in nation-states. Post-war capitalism was stabilized through national economic management. Altern-atively, the globalization project seeks to stabilize capitalism through global economic management – this time along the lines of specialization, rather than replication. Specialization differentiates states and regions (and includes margin-alization), whereas replication was a universalist project (in the sense that all nation-states were expected to follow and realize the ideal Western path). Many of the same institutions obtain (e.g., states, multilaterals, banks, aid institutions, even non-governmental organizations). But they operate in a transformed world. Their character, role and significance in the world order are different.

The concept of a "globalization project" allows an analogous, and related, view of a particular institutional form of capitalism. It replaced the development project as an organizing principle, growing out of the dissolution of that project. Its enuncia-tion as a vision by new global elites is quite distinct from the developmentalist vision elaborated in the postwar world. The developmentalist elites were essentially state managers who shared an interest in stabilizing the world capitalist order, one in which First World working classes, and colonial and post-colonial populist move-ments were demanding inclusion. ...

The elites associated with the globalization project are a different kettle of fish. In addition to state managers (those embracing liberalization), there are the new financial and transnational corporate elites combined with the managers of newly-empowered multilateral institutions like the IMF, the World Bank and the World Trade Organization. As proponents of globalization – formed through the conjunc-tion of the Trilateral Commission (a 1970s global think-tank), debt crisis manage-ment and Uruguay Round negotiations regarding global trade and investment regulation – these elites constitute what is arguably an incipient global ruling class.

Global Integration Trends

The globalization project grew out of the development project because development-alism included specific international relations. In particular, the US emphasis on the principle of freedom of enterprise, and the use of bilateral measures (i.e., dollar credits and investment and market guarantees) to underwrite this, encouraged transnational economic integration. ...

As this transnational dimension extended to firms from Europe and Japan and some Third World countries, a series of global exchanges began to overlay national economies. In the late 1960s and 1970s, Third World newly industrializing countries (NICs) actively participated in these global exchanges through a strategy of export-oriented industrialization (EOI). Under these circumstances, the World Bank in its 1980 *World Development Report* redefined development as "participation in the world market" (Hoogvelt 1987: 58). Symbolically this marked the demise of the development regime as a global economy emerged alongside of declining national economies. This is not to say, however, that all consumers and producers were now "global," but that the global economy itself became consequential in reshaping the conditions under which states made economic policy.

Transnational economic integration depended ultimately on the role of the dollar as a reserve international currency. Postwar disbursements of the dollar, via export credits and foreign investment, allowed an offshore dollar market to form, beyond the reach of national banking and currency controls – the origins of financialization. This "Eurodollar" market promoted the rise of transnational corporate activity, and especially the rise of global banks. But as the offshore capital market expanded (from $3 billion in 1960, to $75 billion in 1970, and eventually to over $1 trillion in 1984), it undercut the Bretton Woods monetary regime (Strange 1994: 107). This occurred as mounting pressure on the dollar from offshore holdings forced President Nixon to end the gold-dollar standard and declare the dollar non-convertible in 1971 – initiating a destabilizing shift from fixed to floating currency exchange rates. The foundational monetary relations of the development project unraveled.

In the 1970s, Third World developmentalist states and global banks entered into a loan binge, where unsecured funds flowed into extravagant public developmentalist projects sponsored by Third World states bent on pursuing the goal of catch-up with the First World. In this sense, borrowing amplified the central purpose of the development project: industrialization. The debt-based development of the 1970s coincided with First World profitability declines and recession. Under these circumstances, the Third World, especially the newly industrializing countries, became the engine of growth for the global economy. The stimulus of a substantial decentralization of industrial investment encouraged a "new international division of labor" to form as First World firms relocated unskilled production offshore and sold components and products on the world market (Fröbel, Heinrichs and Kreye 1979).

By the end of the 1970s, debt became a liability rather than a vehicle of development. Monetarism had gained legitimacy as a mechanism of restructuring the balance of power within First World states, putting labor and social programs on the defensive. When the US Federal Reserve Board reduced the money supply in 1980 to stem the fall in the value of the dollar, lending to Third World countries slowed, and came on shorter terms. By 1986, Third World debt totalled $1 trillion, and even though it was only half of that of the US national debt in that year, it was now a debt crisis. Third World countries were devoting new loans entirely to servicing previous loans, whereas the US (given its sheer global power) was able to continue the fiction of a paper dollar standard.

The Debt Regime

The debt crisis marked the reversal of the development project. Debt management served to reconstruct global, and hence national, monetary relations. The IMF assumed a de facto role of banker to the world, determining, with the World Bank, conditions by which states could renegotiate their outstanding loans and/or service their debt. These conditions were universally imposed and adopted, as states privatized public assets, slashed social budgets, cut wages, devalued national currencies, and promoted exporting. In short, the goals of the development project of nationally-managed economic growth with a view to enhancing national welfare yielded to a new principle: globally-managed economic growth with a view to sustaining the integrity of the global financial system and the conditions for transnational corporate capitalism.

Structural adjustment measures were adopted across the so-called "three worlds," and those states that did not formally undergo structural adjustment have done so informally in order to compete in the global economy. The conditions of the 1980s debt crisis suggested that developmentalism was an illusion (Arrighi 1990), ending the Second and Third Worlds as geo-political categories. Commentators spoke of the "lost decade" for the Third World, and political and economic liberalization spread across the socialist world (Friedmann 1998; Harris 1987). The definition of development was further refined to encompass a comprehensive policy of economic liberalization – especially privatization of public functions and the application of market principles to the administration of wages, prices, trade and investment.

Structural adjustment programs allowed the multilateral institutions combined with state managers and financial classes to reformulate the role of the state. States found they were under pressure to pursue credit-worthiness and competitiveness in the global economy by downgrading their national priorities – especially welfare enhancement and sustaining political constituencies supportive of national economic integration around an industrial base. Boosting export production and offering attractive conditions for foreign investment became the new priorities alongside an extraordinary roll-back of public investment in the former Third World, as privatization increased tenfold across the decade (Crook 1993: 16). Shrinking the state reduced its capacity as a national institution at the same time as it privileged the financial and trade ministries that survived and managed the cuts in other ministries, such as education, agriculture, health and social services. This means that state agencies that support and regulate economic and social sectors affecting the lives of the majority of the citizenry, especially poorer classes, have lost resources. And they have lost them to agencies more concerned with the sectors that connect with global enterprise. Hence global-economic criteria cast a shadow over the social criteria that defined the national project.

In structurally adjusting countries on a case-by-case basis but with a standard package of adjustments, this debt regime transformed the discourse of development in two distinct ways. First, the conditions imposed on debtors for renewal of credit enabled the debt managers to reframe the national project. It was no longer a question of pursuing the goals of the development project; rather, wholesale restructuring (to compete in the global economy) was necessary to guarantee repayment of debt. Indeed, the World Bank's traditional focus on project loans yielded to a new focus in the 1980s on policy loans, that is, loans linked to policies of liberalization. Second, austerity measures, privatization and export expansion renewed the global economy (or the global financial system) rather than individual national economies. Austerity measures lowered wages to encourage foreign investment, privatization ensured renewal of the principle of the global freedom of enterprise, and export expansion sustained the flow of products to the wealthier zones of the global economy.

Each measure potentially undermined the coherence and sovereignty of national economies. Lowered wages reduced local purchasing power. Wage-earners had to tighten their belts, which meant that the market for locally produced goods contracted. Privatization of public enterprises reduced the capacity of states. This meant they were no longer in a position to enter into joint ventures with private firms, using this to set production priorities. Reduction in public expenditure generally reduced states' capacity for coordination of national economic and social programs. As parts of national economies became embedded more deeply in global enterprise, they weakened as nationally-coordinated units themselves, and strengthened the reach of the global economy. This was not unique to the 1980s, but the mechanisms of the debt regime institutionalized the power and authority of global management within states' very organizations and procedures, as illustrated in the following case study.

The Mexican Dress Rehearsal for NAFTA

Perhaps the most dramatic case of state restructuring in recent years is that of the Mexican dress rehearsal for the implementation of NAFTA in the 1990s. The Mexican state sponsored agro-industrialization in the form of irrigated commercial agriculture through the postwar development era, at the same time regulating a basic grains sector. Despite the agro-industrial priority, President Echeverría's 1971 revision of the agrarian reform code, under pressure from *campesinos* (peasants and farmworkers) for greater participation, renewed financial and institutional support for the *ejido* sector (community controlled land holdings deriving from the Mexican Revolution of 1910). Basic grain prices were subsidized and various forms of agricultural credit assisted the small farm sector. In other words, the state managed an extensive rural social system based on *campesino* agriculture supplying foods to domestic markets, alongside a profitable commercial agribusiness sector. But the government supported the *campesino* sector with multilateral loans, rather than a national progressive tax.

When Mexico's oil prices fell in 1981, the debt financing of the basic grains sector could no longer continue, and the Mexican crisis triggered the so-called debt crisis. The national food security system (i.e., grain production and distribution scheme) that had begun the previous year under the López Portillo government was scrapped. Between 1980 and 1991, Mexico negotiated 13 adjustment loans with the World Bank, and six agreements with the IMF. The World Bank proposed an agricultural Structural Adjustment Loan in 1986 to assist in the elimination of imported food subsidies, privatization of rural parastatal agencies, the liberalization of trade and domestic food prices, "sound" public investment, and cutbacks in the size of the agricultural ministry (McMichael and Myhre 1991).

These were the conditions of multilateral loans, and the Mexican government's submission to them (eschewing joining a Latin American debtor's cartel) became the model of restructuring. Rural social services were subordinated to economic criteria which focused on expanding agro-industrial exports to service the debt and thereby assist in stabilizing the global financial system. In 1991, a follow-up sectoral adjustment loan for Mexican agriculture further liberalized food importing, privatized state-owned monopolies and eliminated price guarantees on corn – a drastic step. The social repercussions were sufficiently severe that the World Bank subsequently supported the government's Pronasol and Procampo programs, which offered financial assistance to poor rural producers (Barry 1995: 36, 43–4, 144).

Through a decade of liberal reforms mandated by the global managers and pursued by the Mexican government to maintain its credit-worthiness, the state abandoned its role as manager and regulator of the enormous agricultural sector. It shed agencies, and withdrew its financial support from the *campesinos*, at the same time as funds shifted into expanding agro-exports. This overall priority shift prepared the ground for NAFTA. During the debates preceding the signing of NAFTA, the opposition candidate, Cuauhtémoc Cárdenas, argued that "exploitation of cheap labor, energy, raw materials, technological dependency, and lax environmental protection should not be the premises upon which Mexico establishes links with the United States, Canada, and the world economy" (quoted in Resource Center 1993: 2).

As a result of this drastic shrinking of state involvement in the rural sector, the percentage of *campesinos* with access to official credit fell from 50 to less than 20 percent at the end of the 1980s. Under these conditions, *campesino* organizations have mobilized to create new and locally controlled credit systems to replace the vacuum left by the state. Their dilemma is that this vacuum compels them to negotiate with the National Banking Commission, which regulates credit arrangements and which is increasingly geared to the new principles of global competitiveness – clearly quite distinct from the principles on which *campesino* communities run (Myhre 1994). In sum, when states restructure, they may improve their financial standing and their export sectors, but the majority of citizens and poorer classes find their protections shorn away in the rush to participate in the world market.

Global Economic Management

The globalization project is not simply an external imposition on states from global agencies. State managers collaborate in the restructuring of state organs under the dictates of the new rules of the multilateral agencies to improve the efficiency of the economic enterprise under their jurisdiction. The South Commission noted that the "most powerful countries in the North have become a de facto board of management for the world economy, protecting their interests and imposing their will on the South" (South Centre 1993: 3). While this is a Third Worldist perspective – as it is not Northern countries, but instead regulators and business executives from the North and the South that do the managing – it does draw attention to the new project of managing the world economy as a singular entity.

Not only has the globalist regime-in-the-making actively reorganized states, but this reorganization has been profoundly unrepresentative. Bureaucrats in global agencies exert a growing influence as makers or custodians of the new market rules – this much is clear from the imposition of liberalization measures on indebted states with little or no scrutiny by the citizens of those states. And this practice is to be extended in the newly created World Trade Organization (WTO), which has independent jurisdiction and oversees trade in manufactures, agriculture, services, investment, and intellectual property protection. The WTO has global governing power insofar as its rules are binding on all members, and it has the potential to overrule state and local powers regulating environment, product and food safety. Its staff are unelected bureaucrats, who have no constituency to answer to other than an abstract set of free trade rules and their proponents. Proceedings are secret, denying citizen participation.

Through the WTO, global managers assume extraordinary powers to manage the web of global economic relations overlaying states, at the expense of those state organizations, including their democratic achievements. What is remarkable is that the reach of real economic globalization itself is so limited in terms of the populations it includes, and yet its impact is so extensive. The impact is extensive precisely because states have been absorbed into the project. Just as nation-states were the ideal vehicle of the development project, so restructured states convey the globalization project to their populations. A similar configuration of undemocratic power defines numerous free trade agreements (e.g., NAFTA, APEC, the European Union) springing up as global regionalist arrangements and reflecting what Stephen Gill (1992) has termed "the internationalization of political authority."

The internationalization of political authority includes both the centralization of power in multilateral institutions to set global rules and the internalization of those rules in national policymaking, as our discussion of Mexico suggests. The definition of an international regime – adherence to internationally agreed upon rules through multilateral consent – is thereby refined to include the actual determination, or at least implementation, of those rules by global agencies. In other words, the potential global regime is only formally multilateral, as states lose capacity as sovereign rule makers.

The centralization of state power in global institutions means, in effect, the ability to shape state administrative priorities. This tendency is exemplified by the World Bank's new lending criteria. The World Bank's 1992 *World Development Report* stated that, "Good governance, for the World Bank, is synonymous with sound development management" (George and Sabelli 1994: 150). As the most influential development agency in the world, the World Bank now insists on shaping governments rather than simply economic trajectories – a practice it refined during the 1980s by way of its Structural Adjustment Loans (Cahn 1993).

The globalization project represents a new institutional form for stabilizing capitalism. It is emerging out of the contradictions of the development project that came to a head in the 1980s. Although it could be said that the Third World was a proving ground, this new project of economic management is thoroughly global, as all states submit to the new market rules. In addition, the restructuring of the former Third World has a recursive effect, as it has accelerated the movement of refugees from south to north and driven down wages across the world, in what is termed the "race to the bottom" (Brecher and Costello 1994). Both of these trends are spawning a politics of racial intolerance as employment conditions decline, dividing labor and civilian populations in states across the world. First World national politics, for example, are increasingly framed in exclusive, or "status," terms, rather than the inclusive citizenship terms associated with social democracy.

Restructuring the Wage Relation

In this shift we can see the restructuring of the wage relation along global lines. Certainly states still manage the wage relation, but the conditions under which they do so are increasingly globally defined. Labor protections, achieved over decades of political struggle and compromise and providing the social foundation for the welfare state, are steadily eroded under the new dictates of global market efficiency – just as labor organization itself has steadily eroded since the onslaught of monetarism in the 1970s.

Returning to the NAFTA example, free trade has a "harmonizing" effect on policies regarding levels of wages and social services, which means reducing the differential towards the minimal standard, typically found in the lower cost regions. This is known as "downward leveling." Consider the recent process of "harmonization" from the US side. Industries that shift to Mexico are those in which women are disproportionately employed, such as apparel, consumer electronics, and food processing. Many of these women entered the workforce in the late 1970s and 1980s, because families could no longer get by on a single wage. Once their already low-wage jobs move south, the possibility of regaining equivalent work lessens. The pressure on family livelihood increases. This only adds to the general downward pressure on the US wage, as Mexico's cheaper labor comes on line. ...

In the global economy, product cycles are unstable, as consumer fashions and sourcing sites change relentlessly. The loss of jobs is not simply an economic transfer from one nation to another; more fundamentally, it represents the "hollowing out" of a nation's economic base, and the erosion of social institutions that stabilize the conditions of employment and habitat associated with those jobs. A century of institution-building in labor markets, in corporate/union relations, and in communities, can disappear overnight when the winds of the market are allowed to blow across national boundaries. Those who have work find they are often working longer hours to make ends meet. Wage labor as we know it is undergoing a profound transformation, signalled by the increasingly unstable terms on which people are hired across the world, and the growing range of forms of labor in industry and agriculture – from stable cores of wage work through contract- and piece-work to new forms of indentured, slave and child labor – incorporated into global commodity chains under the conditions of restructuring of the global economy.

Globalization is ultimately an institutional transformation. It has no single face, as institutions and institutional change vary across the world. Former categories like the Three Worlds, and "core" and "periphery," lose their salience, as chains of commodity production and exchange operate above, below, and across national and regional boundaries, generating their own time-compressed spatial relations as the velocity of economic transactions intensifies (Mittelman 1995). State organizations restructure accordingly, complemented by emerging global and regional institutions.

Elsewhere, I have suggested that globalization is a formative and contradictory process with no clear structural imperative (McMichael 1994). Its only unifying dimension, I would argue, is the political project of restructuring to secure or stabilize market conditions for corporate expansion on a world scale. Following the Third World "lost decade" of the 1980s, this has been pursued with draconian effect in Eastern Europe since the collapse of the Berlin Wall (Gowan 1995). Financial regulation is ad hoc – managed politically through the multilateral institutions, meetings of the powerful Group of Seven (G-7) states, and macro-regional free trade agreements.

The global regulation of monetary relations, however fragile, is necessary under circumstances where nation-states have lost the ability to regulate their own currency values, and vast amounts of currency cross national borders daily. At the national level, states continue to regulate wage relations, but increasingly under global, rather than national, terms – which often means under the terms of the firms that organize commodity complexes. This "global wage relation" combines a mosaic of quite different forms of labor (paid and unpaid) contributing to the global production and circulation of value under increasingly casual, insecure, globally competitive conditions.

In short, the extensive transition in economic and political arrangements that we term "restructuring" has its roots in the displacement of the development project (the management of national economic growth and welfare) by the globalization project (the management of global economic growth and the global commons). It is not simply a quantitative economic trend; rather it involves substantive changes in institutional and ideological relations – generating the new paradigm of "post-developmentalism."

The World of Post-Developmentalism: The Possibilities of Localism

The post-developmentalist paradigm is shared by globalists and anti-globalists alike, because of the differentiating effects of global integration. The erosion of state capacities to manage national economic growth and welfare disorganizes class coalitions formed around developmentalism, including the dismantling of public patronage systems. The series of IMF food riots in the last two decades attests to this (Walton & Seddon 1994). As states decentralize, the opportunity for local political renewal presents itself, often quite compellingly. As global integration intensifies, the currents of multiculturalism swirl faster. Under these conditions, which include the juxtaposition of ethnically distinct labor forces and communities, the politics of identity tends to substitute for the civic (universalist) politics of nation-building. Also, regions and communities see self-determination as more than a political goal. It extends to the idea of cultural renewal, which includes recovering local knowledges. ...

The new forms of imagination embody what Wolfgang Sachs (1992: 112) terms "cosmopolitan localism," that is, the assertion of diverse localism as a universal right. Cosmopolitan localism questions the assumption of uniformity in the global project. It is by definition part of the contradictory dynamics of globalization, often being a protective response where communities try to avoid the marginalization or disruption of unpredictable global markets. Such questioning also asserts the need to respect alternative cultural traditions as a matter of global survival. Finally, it is a question of preserving or asserting human and democratic rights within broader settings, whether a world community or individual national arenas.

The Chiapas Rebellion

The most potent recent example of cosmopolitan localism was the 1994 peasant revolt in Mexico's southern state of Chiapas. Chiapas is a region in which small peasant farms are surrounded by huge cattle ranches and coffee plantations. A third of the unresolved land reforms in the Mexican agrarian reform department, going back more than half a century, are here. To alleviate this situation, the government allowed landless *campesinos* to colonize the Lacandon jungle and produce subsistence crops, coffee, and cattle. Coffee, cattle, and corn prices all fell during the 1980s, but *campesinos* were prohibited from logging despite the fact that timber companies continued the practice (Fox 1994). The revolt, therefore, had these deepening class inequities as its foundation. But the source of these deepening inequities transcended the region.

The January 1, 1994 revolt was timed to symbolize the conjunction of these inequities with another set of inequities, this time on a macro-regional scale. The revolt coincided with the day of implementation of the North American Free Trade Agreement (NAFTA). To the Chiapas rebels, NAFTA completed the undermining of the revolutionary heritage in the Mexican national Constitution of 1917. In particular, under this constitution, communal lands (*ejido*) were protected from alienation. In 1992, under the pretext of structural adjustment policies and the promise of NAFTA, the Mexican government began opening these lands for sale to Mexican and foreign agribusinesses. In addition, the terms of the NAFTA included a provision to deregulate commodity markets – especially for maize, the staple peasant food. Not only was the government deciding the fate of local communities such as those in Chiapas; it was also proceeding without representation from those communities.

The *Zapatistas* perceive the Mexican state as the chief agent exploiting the region's cultural and natural wealth, especially through dismantling the communal tradition of the Mexican national state symbolized in the infamous reform of Article 27 of the Constitution. The Article now privileges private (foreign) investment in land over the traditional rights of *campesinos* to petition for land redistribution within the frame-work of the *ejido* (Indian community land held in common). The *Zapatistas* argue that this reform, along with NAFTA liberalizations, seriously threatens the Mexican smallholder and the basic grains sector. They understand that the US "comparative advantage" in maize production (6.9 US tons vs 1.7 Mexican tons per hectare, including infrastructural disparities) would swamp Mexican producers, especially since under NAFTA the Mexican government has agreed to phase out guaranteed prices for staples such as maize and beans (Harvey 1994: 14). Herman Daly, former World Bank senior economist, warned: "US corn subsidized by depleting topsoil, aquifers, oil wells and the federal treasury can be freely imported [to Mexico, and] it is likely that NAFTA will ruin Mexican peasants" (quoted in Chomsky 1994: 180).

The *Zapatistas'* demands for inclusion in the political process signify the movement for local political renewal. This addresses the absence of free and fair elections in Chiapas (and elsewhere in Mexico), adequate political representation of *campesino* interests (as against those of Chiapas planters and ranchers), and the elimination of violence and authoritarianism in local government. The Ejército Zapatista de Liberación Nacional (EZLN) demands included a formal challenge to a centuries-old pattern of *caciquismo* (local strongman tradition) in which federal government initiatives have been routinely thwarted by local, too often venal, political and economic interests.

The Chiapas revolt has had a clear demonstration effect, as communities throughout Mexico have since mobilized around similar demands, especially as they face common pressures, such as market reforms. In challenging local patronage politics, the *Zapatistas* elevated national demands for inclusion of *campesino* organizations in political decisions regarding rural reforms. These include equity demands for small farmers as well as farm workers. They also advanced the cause of local and/ or indigenous development projects that sustain local ecologies and cultures (Fox 1994: 18; Harvey 1994: 36–7). Nevertheless, aside from demanding indigenous co-governors, the rebellion assumed a pan-Mayan identity rather than a specific ethnic identity.

The Chiapas rebellion is distinguished by the texture of its political action. Timed to coincide with the implementation of NAFTA, it wove together a powerful and symbolic critique of the politics of globalization. This critique had two objectives: first, opposing the involvement of national elites and governments in implementing neo-liberal (economic) reforms on a global or regional scale (which undo the institutionalized social entitlements associated with political liberalism); and second, asserting a new political agenda of renewal of a politics of rights that goes beyond individual (property) rights to human, and therefore, community rights. The push for regional autonomy challenged local class inequalities, and demanded the empowerment of *campesino* communities. These communities have created a "fabric of co-operation," woven from the various threads of local groupings. They substitute fluid organizational patterns for the bureaucratic organizational forms associated with modernist politics – such as political parties, trade unions, and hierarchical state structures (Cleaver 1994: 150). In that sense they express an emerging post-developmentalist politics.

In addition, the timing of this revolt to coincide with NAFTA's implementation implicitly addressed the broader movement to reform global economic rules, via the GATT Uruguay Round. While the revolt contributes to long-term resistance to a global economic regime, it has already destabilized the monetary system, as evidenced in the Mexican *peso* crisis of December 1994. Impatient with economic and political instabilities in Mexico, a sudden outflow of capital depressed the *peso*, creating the *tequila effect*, which rippled through regional money markets. In the space of a decade, a second Mexican bailout was necessary, to the tune of more than $40 billion.

In June of 1995, the G–7 powers created a worldwide emergency fund to bail out states on the verge of national bankruptcy. . . . In this way, the *Zapatista* uprising has indirectly contributed to new initiatives to stabilize global monetary relations. Global and local processes are thoroughly intertwined. This contradictory and unpredictable dynamic, rather than some trend or scenario of progressive homogenization of the world's social landscape, is the essence of "globalization." . . .

Unless we specify the historical relations in our concepts they remain abstract. "Levels," or units of analysis cannot be taken as empirically given. Social units are self-evident in neither space nor time: they form relationally. In this sense, the opposition of local and global analysis is a false opposition, as each template is a condition of the other. On their own, conceived in non-relational terms, global and local "units" can only exist as reified levels of analysis. Global relations are inconceivable without local "faces" (e.g., states, micro-regions, communities), just as the "local" has no meaning without context (whether it is a community with exchange relations beyond its boundaries or a community resisting the reach of states and markets). The very definitions of "global" or "local" are not only mutually conditioning, they continually change. For this reason, the use of "local" and/or "global" terms of reference needs problematizing. This essay has attempted this in regard to the concept of globalization and its expression, through restructuring processes, in local contexts. . . .

. . . [P]ost-developmentalism is not simply a new phase of capitalism or social organization – it is the consequence of an active project of globalization, involving a drastic restructuring of political and economic relations. Rather than concede the process of economic globalization as inevitable context, we are better served by problematizing it. . . .

In this essay, I used the Mexican case to illustrate the mutual conditioning of local and global relations. This case demonstrates that it is difficult to isolate local relations, as "localism" expresses itself precisely in historical, and therefore, global terms. Arguably, this is likely to be the case, one way or another, with most local entities, since their boundaries are ultimately social rather than geographical. In other words, it is not the entity itself so much as the entity in its relational field that concretizes restructuring. And in order to concretize, we need to have some understanding of the way in which relational fields are constructed historically.

As a broad relational field, developmentalism was constructed as a transnational project designed to integrate the postwar world, and is now undergoing dramatic revision via globalization. I conceptualize this project as the global reconstitution of the monetary and wage relations of capitalism across the state system. As such, it provides a fluid institutional context within which particular cases and entities can be examined. That is, while it does interpret the broad shift in organizing principles in the world economy, it can only initiate, rather than prefigure, analysis of particular cases and entities that negotiate this relational field.

NOTE

1. The term "local expressions" is shorthand for the process by which local communities negotiate their social context, which includes global relations as embedded in institutions that condition local communities.

REFERENCES

Arrighi, Giovanni. 1982. "A Crisis of Hegemony." Pp. 55–109 in *Dynamics of Global Crisis*, edited by S. Amin, G. Arrighi, A. G. Frank, and I. Wallerstein. New York: Monthly Review.

——, ——. 1990. "The Developmentalist Illusion: A Reconceptualization of the Semiperiphery." Pp. 18–25 in *Semiperipheral States in the World Economy*, edited by W.G. Martin. Westport, CT: Greenwood.

——, ——. 1994. *The Long Twentieth Century: Money, Power, and the Origins of Our Times*. London: Verso.

Barnet, Richard J. and John Cavanagh. 1994. *Global Dreams: Imperial Corporations and the New World Order*. New York, NY: Touchstone.

Barry, Tom. 1995. *Zapata's Revenge: Free Trade and the Farm Crisis in Mexico*. Boston, MA: South End.

Bienefeld, Manfred. 1989. "The Lessons of History." *Monthly Review* 3: 9–41.

Block, Fred L. 1977. *The Origins of International Economic Disorder: A Study of United States International Monetary Policy from World War II to the Present*. Berkeley & Los Angeles, CA: University of California Press.

Brecher, Jeremy, and Tim Costello. 1994. *Global Village or Global Pillage: Economic Reconstruction From the Bottom Up*. Boston, MA: South End.

Cahn, Jonathan. 1993. "Challenging the New Imperial Authority: the World Bank and the Democratization of Development." *Harvard Human Rights Journal* 6: 159–94.

Chomsky, Noam. 1994. *World Orders Old and New*. New York, NY: Columbia University Press.

Cleaver, Harry. 1977. "Food, Famine and the International Crisis." *Zerowork* 2:7–70.

——, ——. 1994. "The Chiapas Uprising." *Studies in Political Economy* 44: 141–57.

Crook, Clive. 1993. "New Ways to Grow. A Survey of World Finance." *The Economist*. Special Supplement. 25 September.

Davidson, Basil. 1992. *The Black Man's Burden: Africa and the Curse of the Nation-State*. New York: Random House.

Fox, Jonathan. 1994. "The Challenge of Democracy." *Akwe:kon* 11(2): 13–19.

Friedmann, Harriet. 1998. "Warsaw Pact Socialism: Detente and Economic Tensions in the Soviet Bloc." In *Rethinking the Cold War: Essays on Its Dynamic, Meaning and Morality*, edited by Allen Hunt. Philadelphia, PA: Temple University Press.

Fröbel, Folker, Jürgen Heinrichs and Otto Kreye. 1979. *The New International Division of Labor*. New York: Cambridge University Press.

George, Susan and Fabrizio Sabelli. 1994. *Faith and Credit: The World Bank's Secular Empire*. Boulder, CO: Westview Press.

Gill, Stephen. 1992. "Economic Globalization and the Internationalization of Authority: Limits and Contradictions." *Geoforum* 23: 269–83.

Gowan, Peter. 1995. "Neo-Liberal Theory and Practice for Eastern Europe." *New Left Review* 213: 3–60.

Harris, Nigel. 1987. *The End of the Third World: Newly Industrializing Countries and the Decline of an Ideology*. Harmondsworth: Penguin.

Harvey, David. 1989. *The Condition of Postmodernity*. Oxford: Basil Blackwell.

Harvey, Neil. 1994. *Rebellion in Chiapas: Rural Reforms, Campesino Radicalism, and the Limits to Salinismo*. San Diego, CA: Center for US-Mexican Studies.

Hoogvelt, Ankie M. M. 1987. *The Third World in Global Development*. London: Macmillan.

Levitt, Theodore. 1983. "The Globalization of Markets." *Harvard Business Review* 61(3): 92–102.

Lewis, W. Arthur. 1954. "Economic Development with Unlimited Supplies of Labor." *Manchester School of Economics and Social Studies* 22: 139–91.

Marsden, Terry, and Sarah Whatmore. 1994. "Finance Capital and Food System Restructuring: Global Dynamics and their National Incorporation." Pp. 107–28 in *The Global Restructuring of Agro-Food Systems*, edited by P. McMichael. Ithaca, NY: Cornell University Press.

McMichael, Philip. 1987. "State Formation and the Construction of a World Market." Pp. 187–237 in *Political Power and Social Theory*, Vol. 6, edited by M. Zeitlin. Greenwich, CT: JAI.

——, ——. 1994. "Global Restructuring: Some Lines of Inquiry." Pp. 277–300 in *The Global Restructuring of Agro-Food Systems*, edited by P. McMichael. Ithaca, NY: Cornell University Press.

McMichael, Philip and David Myhre. 1991. "Global Regulation vs. the Nation-State: Agro-Food Systems and the New Politics of Capital." *Capital and Class* 43: 83–106.

Mittelman, James H. 1995. "Rethinking the International Division of Labour in the Context of Globalisation." *Third World Quarterly* 16(2): 273–95.

Myhre, David. 1994. "The Politics of Globalization in Rural Mexico: Campesino Initiatives to Restructure the Agricultural Credit System." Pp. 145–69 in *The Global Restructuring of Agro-Food Systems*, edited by P. McMichael. Ithaca, NY: Cornell University Press.

Resource Center. 1993. "Free Trade: The Ifs, Ands, and Buts." *Resource Center Bulletin*, pp. 31–2.

Rich, Bruce. 1994. *Mortgaging the Earth: The World Bank, Environmental Impoverishment and the Crisis of Development*. Boston, MA: Beacon.

Ruggie, John Gerard. 1982. "International Regimes, Transactions and Change: Embedded Liberalism in the Post-War Economic Order." *International Organization* 36: 397–415.

Sachs, Wolfgang. 1992. "One World." pp. 102–15 in *The Development Dictionary*, edited by W. Sachs. London: Zed.

Sinclair, Timothy J. 1994. "Passing Judgement: Credit Rating Processes as Regulatory Mechanisms of Governance in the Emerging World Order." *Review of International Political Economy* 1: 133–59.

South Centre. 1993. *Facing the Challenge: Responses to the Report of the South Commission*. London: Zed.

Strange, Susan. 1994. *States and Markets*. London, New York: Pinter.

Walton, John, and David Seddon. 1994. *Free Markets and Food Riots: The Politics of Global Adjustment*. Oxford: Blackwell.

18 Capitalism: The Factory of Fragmentation (1992)

David Harvey

Geographer David Harvey (1935–) has taught at the universities of Oxford and Johns Hopkins. His initial work centered around geographical methods and is represented by his classic work, *Explanation in Geography*. Later he co-founded *Antipode*, a journal of radical geography. His shift toward a neo-Marxist approach is reflected in his books *Limits to Capital* and *The Condition of Postmodernity*, which have had substantial impact beyond the field of geography. Essentially a critic of the postmodern idea that there is no one single reality or truth, Harvey here argues that capitalism must be examined carefully and that we cannot discard historical materialist analysis (the study of how people use money to make money). An important contribution of this small piece is Harvey's point that while based on simple rules, global capitalism creates great diversity in people's experiences. With the electronic media, faster air transit and better communications, time and space have been "compressed," and this has created crises of identity where people don't know who they are or where they belong. These identity crises can lead to the rise of racism, ethnic conflict, and isolationism, Harvey warns. But he also sees capitalism's inherent tendencies to create crises as a great opportunity to envision a new, socialist society.

The drive for capital accumulation is the central motif in the narrative of historical-geographical transformation of the Western world in recent times and seems set to engulf the whole world into the 21st century. For the last 300 years it has been the fundamental force at work in reshaping the world's politics, economy and environment. This process of using money to make more money is not the only process at work, of course, but it is hard to make any sense of social changes these last 300 years without looking closely at it.

Contemporary historical materialism attempts to isolate the fundamental processes of capital accumulation that generate social, economic and political change and, through a careful study of them, get some understanding of the whys and hows of those changes. The focus is on *processes*, rather than on things and events. It's a bit like watching a potter at work on a wheel: the process may be simple to describe, but the outcomes can be infinitely varied in shape and size.

However, to say there is a simple process at work is not to say that everything ends up looking exactly the same, that events are easily predictable or that everything can be explained by reference to it alone. The drive for capital accumulation has helped create cities as diverse as Los Angeles, Edmonton, Atlanta and Boston, and transformed out of almost all recognition (though in quite different ways) ancient cities like Athens, Rome, Paris and London. It has likewise led to a restless search for new product lines, new technologies, new lifestyles, new ways to move around, new places to colonize – an infinite variety of stratagems that reflect a boundless human ingenuity for coming up with new ways to make a profit. Capitalism has, in short, always thrived on the production of difference.

Yet the rules that govern the game of capital accumulation are relatively simple and knowable. Capitalism is always about growth, no matter what the ecological, social or geopolitical consequences (indeed, we define "crisis" as low growth); it is always about technological and lifestyle changes ("progress" is inevitable); and it is always conflictual (class and other forms of struggle abound).

Above all, capitalism generates a lot of insecurity: it is always unstable and crisis prone. The history of capitalist crisis formation and resolution is, I maintain, fundamental to understanding our history. Understanding the rules of capital accumulation helps us understand why our history and our geography take the forms they do.

The Worship of Fragments

In *The Condition of Postmodernity* I tried to put this style of thinking to work in explaining recent changes in economy and culture in the advanced capitalist world. I noticed that postmodern thought tended to deny anything systematic or general in history, and to jumble together images and thoughts as if criteria of coherence did not matter: it emphasized separation, fragmentation, ephemerality, difference and what is often now called "otherness" (a strange term that is mainly used to indicate that I have no right to speak *for* or even, perhaps, *about* others or that when I do speak about them I "construct" them in my own image).

Furthermore, some postmodern theorists argued that the world was not knowable because there was no sure way of establishing truth and that even pretending to know or, worse still, holding to some version of "universal truth" lay at the root of gulags, holocausts and other social disasters. The best that we could hope for, they said, was to let things flourish in their multiple and different ways, look for alliances where possible, but always avoid peddling supposed universal solutions or pretending there were general, knowable truths. This sort of thinking carried over into architecture, the arts, popular culture, new life styles and gender politics.

Now, there is much that is refreshing about all of this, particularly the emphasis upon heterogeneity, diversity, multiple overlapping concerns of gender, class, ecology, etc. But I just could not see why the sort of heterogeneity that postmodernism celebrates was in any way inconsistent with thinking the world was knowable through an appreciation, of, for example, processes of capital accumulation, which not only thrive upon but actively produce social difference and heterogeneity.

The Postmodern Phoenix

Since this shift in cultural sensibility paralleled some quite radical changes in the organization of capitalism after the capitalist crisis in 1973–5, it even seemed plausible to argue that postmodernism itself was a product of the process of capital accumulation.

After 1973, for example, we find that working-class politics went on the defensive as unemployment and job insecurity rose, economic growth slackened, real wages stagnated, and all sorts of substitutes for real productive activity took over to compensate for wave after wave of deindustrialization. Merger manias, credit binges and all the other excesses of the 1980s, which we are now paying for, were the only vital activity at a time of gradual dismantling of the welfare state and the rise of laissez-faire and very conservative politics. Strong appeal to individualism, greed and entrepreneurial spirit characterized the Reagan–Thatcher years. Furthermore, the crisis of 1973 set in motion a frantic search for new products, new technologies, new lifestyles and new cultural gimmicks that could turn a profit. And these years also saw a radical reorganization of international power relations, with Europe and Japan challenging a dominant US power in economic and financial markets.

This general shift from old-style capital accumulation to a new style, I call the shift from Fordism (mass assembly line, mass political organization and welfare state interventions) to flexible accumulation (the pursuit of niche markets, decentralization coupled with spatial dispersal of production, withdrawal of the nation-state from interventionist policies coupled with deregulation and privatization). It seemed to me quite plausible to argue, therefore, that capitalism, in undergoing this transition, had produced the conditions for the rise of postmodern ways of thinking and operating.

Time–Space Compression

But it is always dangerous to treat simultaneity as causation, so I set about looking for some sort of link between the two trends. The link I believed worked best was the one between time and space. Capital accumulation has always been about speed-up (consider the history of technological innovations in production processes, marketing, money exchanges) and revolutions in transport and communications (the railroad and telegraph, radio and automobile, jet transport and telecommunications), which have the effect of reducing spatial barriers.

The experience of time and space has periodically been radically transformed. We see a particularly strong example of this kind of radical transformation since around 1970: the impact of telecommunications, jet cargo transport, containerization of road, rail and ocean transport, the development of futures markets, electronic banking and computerized production systems. We have recently been going through a strong phase of what I call "time–space compression": the world suddenly feels much smaller, and the time-horizons over which we can think about social action become much shorter.

Our sense of who we are, where we belong and what our obligations encompass – in short, our *identity* – is profoundly affected by our sense of location in space and time. In other words, we broadly locate our identity in terms of space (I belong *here*) and time (this is *my biography, my history*). Crises of identity (Where is my place in this world? What future can I have?) arise out of strong phases of time–space compression. Moreover, I think it plausible to argue that the most recent phase has so shaken up our sense of who and what we are that there had to be some kind of crisis of representation in general, a crisis that is manifest in the contemporary world primarily by postmodern ways of thinking.

Embracing ephemerality as a desired quality in cultural production, for example, matches the rapid shifts in fashion and production designs and techniques that evolved as part of the response to the crisis of accumulation that developed after 1973.

Interestingly, when we look back on other phases of rapid time–space compression – the period after 1848 in Europe, the period just before and during the First World War, for example – we find similar phases of rapid change in the arts and in cultural activities. From this I conclude that it is possible to arrive at a *general* interpretation of the rise of postmodernism and its relation to the new experience of space and time that new forms of capital accumulation have produced.

But, again, I want to enter a caveat: this is not to say that everything is simply deterministic. I repeat, capitalism thrives on and produces heterogeneity and difference, though only within certain bounds.

Niche Markets

There is nothing about postmodernism in general that inhibits the further development of capital accumulation. Indeed, the postmodern turn has proved a perfect vehicle for the development of new fields and forms of profit-making.

Fragmentation and ephemerality, for example, open up abundant opportunities to explore quick-changing niche markets for new products. But this does not mean that there has been any radical inversion of the historical materialist view of reality, an inversion where culture, not economics, has become the driving force of history. I think such a view misinterprets rather than misrepresents what is happening.

Marx held that production of any sort requires the prior exercise of the human imagination; it is always about the mobilization of human desires, purposes and intentions to a given end. The problem under industrial capitalism is that most people are denied access to this process: a select few do the imagining and designing, make all the decisions and set up technologies that regulate the worker's actions, so that for the mass of the population the full play of human creativity is denied.

That is a profoundly alienating situation, and much of history recounts attempts to respond to this alienation. The rich and the privileged, themselves not enamored of industrialism, countered alienation by developing a distinctive field of *culture* – think of romanticism and the cultivation of aesthetic pleasures and values – as a kind of protected zone for creative activities outside of the crass materialism of industrial capitalism.

Workers likewise developed their own creative pleasures when they could: hunting, gardening, tinkering with cars. These activities, which went under the general name of "culture," high or low, were not so much superstructural as compensatory for what industrial capitalism denied to the mass of the people in the work place.

Over time, those compensatory pleasures have gradually become absorbed into the processes of capital accumulation and turned into new spheres for making profit. As industrial capitalism became less and less profitable – at least in the US and Britain – so these new spheres of profit-making became much more important, particularly after 1945 and even more so after the crisis of 1973–5.

So, there is a sense in which culture no longer trails other forms of economic activity but has moved into the vanguard – not as a protected zone of non-economic activity, however, but as an arena of fierce competition for profit-making. The accumulation of market niches, of diverse preferences and the promotion of new heterogeneous life-styles, all occur within the orbit of capital accumulation.

The latter, furthermore, has had the effect of breaking down distinctions between high and low culture – it commercializes aesthetics – at the same time as it has thrived, as it always does, on the production of diversity, heterogeneity and differ-ence. What we generally think of as "culture" has become a primary field of entrepreneurial and capitalistic activity.

Through the Postmodern Door

The picture I have so far painted probably looks very pessimistic, with capital accumulation, market materialism and entrepreneurial greed ruling the roost. So let me look now at the opportunities and dangers that attach to this postmodern condition.

I notice, first of all, that capitalism has not solved its crisis tendencies and that capital accumulation, economic growth and sustained development into the foresee-able future are, if anything, more remote now than they were 20 years ago. When the fundamental irrationality of capitalism becomes plainer for all to see – as in the present depression on both sides of the Atlantic – the conditions are set up in which some kind of new direction has to be taken (if only throwing the ruling party out of power).

Secondly, the frantic promotion of cultural heterogeneity and difference over the past 20 years has opened up all kinds of new spaces for the exploration of different lifestyles, different preferences and a more generalized debate about human potential-ities and the sources of their frustration. This is the positive side of what much of postmodernism stands for: it produces openings for a critique of dominant values, including those that directly attach to the rules of capital accumulation, and there-fore all kinds of opportunities for radical politics. The corollary is that contemporary radical politics has as much to do with culture as with traditional problems of class struggle in production.

But here we encounter as many dangers as opportunities. The crisis of identity provoked by time–space compression can lead to the acceptance of exclusionary religious doctrines (the promise of eternity in a world of rapid change) or exclu-sionary territorial practices (maintaining the security and position of the home, the locality, the nation against external and international pressures). The rise of fascist and exclusionary sentiments across Europe and the progress of the Buchanan cam-paign in the US provide good examples. The refusal to accept that there are some basic processes at work and that knowable truths can be established can all too easily lead to head-in-the-sand politics ("I will pursue my particular political interest and to hell with all the rest").

The fetishism of the image at the expense of any concern for the social reality of daily life can divert our gaze, our politics, our sensitivities away from the material world of experience and into the seemingly endless and intricate webs of representations. And while it is true that the "personal is political," we don't have to look much further than the present presidential campaign to see how that principle can be abused. Above all, the promotion of cultural activities as a primary field of capital accumulation promotes a commodified and prepackaged form of aesthetics at the expense of concerns for ethics, social justice, fairness, and the local and international issues of exploitation of both nature and human nature.

So postmodernism opens a door to radical politics but for the most part has refused to pass through it. To pass to a thoroughly radical critique of contemporary capitalism, which is plainly languishing not only economically but culturally and spiritually, requires that we grapple with the central processes of capital accumulation that are so radical in their implications for our lives. Capitalism has transformed the face of the earth at an accelerating pace these last 300 years. It cannot possibly continue on that trajectory for another 300 years. Someone, somewhere, has to think about what kind of social system should replace it. There seems no alternative except to build some kind of socialist politics that will have as its central motif the question: What could life be about if capital accumulation no longer dominated? That question deserves the close attention of everyone.

19 Has Globalization Gone Too Far? (1997)

Dani Rodrik

Dani Rodrik is an expert on globalization with the Institute for International Economics and Professor of International Political Economy at Harvard University. Rodrik, who takes a position differing from those of many of the other authors in this volume, believes that the negative opinions about globalization represent merely the complaints of those who have lost out in the process, such as labor unions, retired people, and environmentalists. In a recent interview on the *Boston Review* webpage, he said: "globalization has become a bogeyman – a topic about which it is futile to expect to have a rational conversation." Politicians and employers are making the situation worse for workers, Rodrik says, by using globalization as an excuse to take advantage of workers' perceived vulnerability. However, Rodrik's goal in this book is to move both polarized sides to the middle and forge a more useful debate and policies to address them. In the end he maintains that free trade and streamlined governments are the best policies for nations to deal with globalization.

Labor strikes in France at the end of 1995, which were aimed at reversing the French government's efforts to bring its budget in line with the Maastricht criteria, threw the country into its worst crisis since 1968. Around the same time in the United States, a prominent Republican was running a vigorous campaign for the presidency on a plank of economic nationalism, promising to erect trade barriers and tougher restrictions on immigration. In the countries of Eastern Europe and in Russia, former communists have won most of the parliamentary elections held since the fall of the Berlin Wall, and communist candidate Gennady Zyuganov garnered 40 percent of the vote in the second round of the Russian presidential election held in July 1996.

These apparently disparate developments have one common element: the international integration of markets for goods, services, and capital is pressuring societies to alter their traditional practices, and in return broad segments of these societies are putting up a fight. The pressures for change are tangible and affect all societies: In Japan, large corporations have started to dismantle the postwar practice of lifetime employment, one of Japan's most distinctive social institutions. In Germany, the federal government has been fighting union opposition to cuts on pension benefits aimed at improving competitiveness and balancing the budget. In South Korea, trade unions have gone on nationwide strikes to protest new legislation making it easier for firms to lay off workers. Developing countries in Latin America have been competing with each other in opening up to trade, deregulating their economies, and privatizing public enterprises. Ask business executives or government officials why these changes are necessary, and you will hear the same mantra repeatedly: "We need to remain (or become) competitive in a global economy."

The opposition to these changes is no less tangible and sometimes makes for strange bedfellows. Labor unions decrying unfair competition from underage workers overseas and environmentalists are joined by billionaire businessmen Ross Perot and Sir James Goldsmith in railing against the North American Free Trade Agreement (NAFTA) and the World Trade Organization (WTO). In the United States, perhaps the most free-market-oriented of advanced industrial societies, the philosophical foundations of the classical liberal state have come under attack not only from traditional protectionists but also from the new communitarian movement, which emphasizes moral and civic virtue and is inherently suspicious of the expansion of markets.

The process that has come to be called "globalization" is exposing a deep fault line between groups who have the skills and mobility to flourish in global markets and those who either don't have these advantages or perceive the expansion of unregulated markets as inimical to social stability and deeply held norms. The result is severe tension between the market and social groups such as workers, pensioners, and environmentalists, with governments stuck in the middle.

This book argues that the most serious challenge for the world economy in the years ahead lies in making globalization compatible with domestic social and political stability – or to put it even more directly, in ensuring that international economic integration does not contribute to domestic social *dis*integration.

Attuned to the anxieties of their voters, politicians in the advanced industrial countries are well aware that all is not well with globalization. The Lyon summit of the Group of Seven, held in June 1996, gave the issue central billing: its communiqué was titled "Making a Success of Globalization for the Benefit of All." The communiqué opened with a discussion of globalization – its challenges as well as its benefits. The leaders recognized that globalization raises difficulties for certain groups, and they wrote:

> In an increasingly interdependent world we must all recognize that we have an interest in spreading the benefits of economic growth as widely as possible and in diminishing the risk either of excluding individuals or groups in our own economies or of excluding certain countries or regions from the benefits of globalization.

But how are these objectives to be met?

An adequate policy response requires an understanding of the sources of the tensions generated by globalization. Without such an understanding, the reactions are likely to be of two kinds. One is of the knee-jerk type, with proposed cures worse than the disease. Such certainly is the case with blanket protectionism à la Patrick Buchanan or the abolition of the WTO à la Sir James Goldsmith. Indeed, much of what passes as analysis (followed by condemnation) of international trade is based on faulty logic and misleading empirics. To paraphrase Paul Samuelson, there is no better proof that the principle of comparative advantage is the only proposition in economics that is at once true *and* nontrivial than the long history of misunderstanding that has attached to the consequences of trade. The problems, while real, are more subtle than the terminology that has come to dominate the debate, such as "low-wage competition," or "leveling the playing field," or "race to the bottom." Consequently, they require nuanced and imaginative solutions.

The other possible response, and the one that perhaps best characterizes the attitude of much of the economics and policy community, is to downplay the problem. Economists' standard approach to globalization is to emphasize the benefits of the free flow of goods, capital, and ideas and to overlook the social tensions that may result. A common view is that the complaints of nongovernmental organizations or labor advocates represent nothing but old protectionist wine in new bottles. Recent research on trade and wages gives strength to this view: the available empirical evidence suggests that trade has played a somewhat minor role in generating the labor-market ills of the advanced industrial countries – that is, in increasing income inequality in the United States and unemployment in Europe.

While I share the idea that much of the opposition to trade is based on faulty premises, I also believe that economists have tended to take an excessively narrow view of the issues. To understand the impact of globalization on domestic social arrangements, we have to go beyond the question of what trade does to the skill premium. And even if we focus more narrowly on labor-market outcomes, there are additional channels, which have not yet come under close empirical scrutiny, through which increased economic integration works to the disadvantage of labor, and particularly of unskilled labor. This book attempts to offer such a broadened perspective. As we shall see, this perspective leads to a less benign outlook than the one economists commonly adopt. One side benefit, therefore, is that it serves to reduce the yawning gap that separates the views of most economists from the gut instincts of many laypeople.

Sources of Tension

I focus on three sources of tension between the global market and social stability and offer a brief overview of them here.

First, reduced barriers to trade and investment accentuate the asymmetry between groups that can cross international borders (either directly or indirectly, say through outsourcing) and those that cannot. In the first category are owners of capital, highly skilled workers, and many professionals, who are free to take their resources where they are most in demand. Unskilled and semiskilled workers and most middle managers belong in the second category. Putting the same point in more technical terms, globalization makes the demand for the services of individuals in the second category *more elastic* – that is, the services of large segments of the working population can be more easily substituted by the services of other people across national boundaries. Globalization therefore fundamentally transforms the employment relationship.

The fact that "workers" can be more easily substituted for each other across national boundaries undermines what many conceive to be a postwar social bargain between workers and employers, under which the former would receive a steady increase in wages and benefits in return for labor peace. This is because increased substitutability results in the following concrete consequences:

- Workers now have to pay a larger share of the cost of improvements in work conditions and benefits (that is, they bear a greater incidence of nonwage costs).
- They have to incur greater instability in earnings and hours worked in response to shocks to labor demand or labor productivity (that is, volatility and insecurity increase).
- Their bargaining power erodes, so they receive lower wages and benefits whenever bargaining is an element in setting the terms of employment.

These considerations have received insufficient attention in the recent academic literature on trade and wages, which has focused on the downward shift in demand for unskilled workers rather than the increase in the elasticity of that demand.

Second, globalization engenders conflicts within and between nations over domestic norms and the social institutions that embody them. As the technology for manufactured goods becomes standardized and diffused internationally, nations with very different sets of values, norms, institutions, and collective preferences begin to compete head on in markets for similar goods. And the spread of globalization creates opportunities for trade between countries at very different levels of development.

This is of no consequence under traditional multilateral trade policy of the WTO and the General Agreement on Tariffs and Trade (GATT): the "process" or "technology" through which goods are produced is immaterial, and so are the social institutions of the trading partners. Differences in national practices are treated just like differences in factor endowments or any other determinant of comparative advantage. However, introspection and empirical evidence both reveal that most people attach values to processes as well as outcomes. This is reflected in the norms that shape and constrain the domestic environment in which goods and services are produced – for example, workplace practices, legal rules, and social safety nets.

Trade becomes contentious when it unleashes forces that undermine the norms implicit in domestic practices. Many residents of advanced industrial countries are uncomfortable with the weakening of domestic institutions through the forces of trade, as when, for example, child labor in Honduras displaces workers in South Carolina or when pension benefits are cut in Europe in response to the requirements of the Maastricht treaty. This sense of unease is one way of interpreting the demands for "fair trade." Much of the discussion surrounding the "new" issues in trade policy – that is, labor standards, environment, competition policy, corruption – can be cast in this light of procedural fairness.

We cannot understand what is happening in these new areas until we take individual preferences for processes and the social arrangements that embody them seriously. In particular, by doing so we can start to make sense of people's uneasiness about the consequences of international economic integration and avoid the trap of automatically branding all concerned groups as self-interested protectionists. Indeed, since trade policy almost always has redistributive consequences (among sectors, income groups, and individuals), one cannot produce a principled defense of free trade without confronting the question of the fairness and legitimacy of the practices that generate these consequences. By the same token, one should not expect broad popular support for trade when trade involves exchanges that clash with (and erode) prevailing domestic social arrangements.

Third, globalization has made it exceedingly difficult for governments to provide social insurance – one of their central functions and one that has helped maintain social cohesion and domestic political support for ongoing liberalization throughout the postwar period. In essence, governments have used their fiscal powers to insulate domestic groups from excessive market risks, particularly those having an external origin. In fact, there is a striking correlation between an economy's exposure to foreign trade and the size of its welfare state. It is in the most open countries, such as Sweden, Denmark, and the Netherlands, that spending on income transfers has expanded the most. This is not to say that the government is the sole, or the best, provider of social insurance. The extended family, religious groups, and local communities often play similar roles. My point is that it is a hallmark of the postwar period that governments in the advanced countries have been expected to provide such insurance.

At the present, however, international economic integration is taking place against the background of receding governments and diminished social obligations. The welfare state has been under attack for two decades. Moreover, the increasing mobility of capital has rendered an important segment of the tax base footloose, leaving governments with the unappetizing option of increasing tax rates disproportionately on labor income. Yet the need for social insurance for the vast majority of the population that remains internationally immobile has not diminished. If anything, this need has become greater as a consequence of increased integration. The question therefore is how the tension between globalization and the pressures for socialization of risk can be eased. If the tension is not managed intelligently and creatively, the danger is that the domestic consensus in favor of open markets will ultimately erode to the point where a generalized resurgence of protectionism becomes a serious possibility.

Each of these arguments points to an important weakness in the manner in which advanced societies are handling – or are equipped to handle – the consequences of globalization. Collectively, they point to what is perhaps the greatest risk of all, namely that the cumulative consequence of the tensions mentioned above will be the solidifying of a new set of class divisions – between those who prosper in the globalized economy and those who do not, between those who share its values and those who would rather not, and between those who can diversify away its risks and those who cannot. This is not a pleasing prospect, even for individuals on the winning side of the divide who have little empathy for the other side. Social disintegration is not a spectator sport – those on the sidelines also get splashed with mud from the field. Ultimately, the deepening of social fissures can harm all.

Globalization: Now and Then

This is not the first time we have experienced a truly global market. By many measures, the world economy was possibly even more integrated at the height of the gold standard in the late 19th century than it is now. ... In the United States and Europe, trade volumes peaked before World War I and then collapsed during the interwar years. Trade surged again after 1950, but none of the ... regions is significantly more open by this measure now than it was under the late gold standard. Japan, in fact, has a lower share of exports in GDP now than it did during the interwar period.

Other measures of global economic integration tell a similar story. As railways and steamships lowered transport costs and Europe moved toward free trade during the late 19th century, a dramatic convergence in commodity prices took place (Williamson 1996). Labor flows were considerably higher then as well, as millions of immigrants made their way from the old world to the new. In the United States, immigration was responsible for 24 percent of the expansion of the labor force during the 40 years before World War I (Williamson 1996, appendix table 1). As for capital mobility, the share of net capital outflows in GNP was much higher in the United Kingdom during the classical gold standard than it has been since.

Does this earlier period of globalization hold any lessons for our current situation? It well might. There is some evidence, for example, that trade and migration had significant consequences for income distribution. According to Jeffrey Williamson, "[G]lobalization ... accounted for more than half of the rising inequality in rich, labor-scarce countries [e.g., the United States, Argentina, and Australia] and for a little more than a quarter of the falling inequality in poor, labor-abundant countries [e.g., Sweden, Denmark, and Ireland]" in the period before World War I (1996, 19). Equally to the point are the political consequences of these changes:

> There is a literature almost a century old that argues that immigration hurt American labor and accounted for much of the rise in inequality from the 1890s to World War I, so much so that a labor-sympathetic Congress passed immigration quotas. There is a literature even older that argues that a New World grain invasion eroded land rents in Europe, so much so that landowner-dominated Continental Parliaments raised tariffs to help protect them from the impact of globalization. (Williamson 1996, 1)

Williamson (1996, 20) concludes that "the inequality trends which globalization produced are at least partly responsible for the interwar retreat from globalization [which appeared] first in the rich industrial trading partners."

Moreover, there are some key differences that make today's global economy more contentious. First, restrictions on immigration were not as common during the 19th century, and consequently labor's international mobility was more comparable to that of capital. Consequently, the asymmetry between mobile capital (physical and human) and immobile "natural" labor, which characterizes the present situation, is a relatively recent phenomenon. Second, there was little head-on international competition in identical or similar products during the previous century, and most trade consisted of the exchange of noncompeting products, such as primary products for manufactured goods. The aggregate trade ratios do not reflect the "vast increase in the exposure of tradable goods industries to international competition" that is now taking place compared with the situation in the 1890s (Irwin 1996, 42). Third, and perhaps most important, governments had not yet been called on to perform social-welfare functions on a large scale, such as ensuring adequate levels of employment, establishing social safety nets, providing medical and social insurance, and caring for the poor. This shift in the perceived role of government is also a relatively recent transformation, one that makes life in an interdependent economy considerably more difficult for today's policymakers.

At any rate, the lesson from history seems to be that continued globalization cannot be taken for granted. If its consequences are not managed wisely and creatively, a retreat from openness becomes a distinct possibility.

Implications

So has international economic integration gone too far? Not if policymakers act wisely and imaginatively.

We need to be upfront about the irreversibility of the many changes that have occurred in the global economy. Advances in communications and transportation mean that large segments of national economies are much more exposed to international trade and capital flows than they have ever been, regardless of what policymakers choose to do. There is only limited scope for government policy to make a difference. In addition, a serious retreat into protectionism would hurt the many groups that benefit from trade and would result in the same kind of social conflicts that globalization itself generates. We have to recognize that erecting trade barriers will help in only a limited set of circumstances and that trade policies will rarely be the best response to the problems that will be discussed here. Transfer and social insurance programs will generally dominate. In short, the genie cannot be stuffed back into the bottle, even if it were desirable to do so. We will need more imaginative and more subtle responses. I will suggest some guidelines in the concluding chapter.

Even so, my primary purpose in this book is not prescriptive; it is to broaden the debate on the consequences of globalization by probing deeper into some of the dimensions that have received insufficient attention and ultimately recasting the debate so as to facilitate a more productive dialogue between opposing groups and interests. It is only through greater understanding of what is at stake that we can hope to develop appropriate public policies.

One final introductory note. I hope the reader will soon realize that this book is not a one-sided brief *against* globalization. Indeed, the major benefit of clarifying and adding rigor to some of the arguments against trade is that it helps us draw a distinction between objections that are valid (or at least logically coherent) and objections that aren't. From this perspective, what I end up doing, at least on occasion, is strengthening the arsenal of arguments in favor of free trade. If this book is viewed as controversial, it will have done its job; I have failed if it is perceived as polemical.

The chapters that follow will elaborate on the three sources of tension between globalization and society identified above and will review the relevant empirical evidence. The objectives will be to cast the debate in terms that both sides – economists and populists alike – can join, marshal evidence on the likely significance of the tension in question, and where there is evidence for serious concern, open the debate on possible remedies.

REFERENCES

Irwin, Douglas A., "The United States in a New Global Economy? A Century's Perspective," *American Economic Review*, V: 86 (1996), 41–6.

Williamson, Jeffrey G., "Globalization, Convergence, and History," *Journal of Economic History*, V: 56 (1996), 277–306.

20 Gender, Industrialization, Transnational Corporations and Development: An Overview of Trends and Patterns (1995)

Kathryn B. Ward and Jean Larson Pyle

Since the days of Marx, Weber, and Durkheim more than a century ago, enormous intellectual effort has gone into analyzing social change and development. Yet not until the 1980s and 1990s has there been systematic analysis about women and the importance of gender. Kathryn B. Ward, author of *Women Workers and Global Restructuring* (1990) and Jean Larson Pyle, Associate Professor of Economics at University of Massachusetts, Lowell, review the literature about women and development, and they offer their own gendered analysis of development, in the age of the "global economy." Ward and Pyle argue that gender is crucial for several reasons. First, globalization affects women differently because state policies, and those of transnational companies, can both incorporate and limit women. Second, women influence the process of globalization through their different needs to participate in the labor force and how their availability to work determines corporations' choices about location and hiring strategies. Furthermore, Ward and Pyle point out the critical differences between paid and unpaid work, the informal economy, family relations of work, and household survival strategies. They also acknowledge how the intertwining of class, race, and gender shapes economic roles, often in different ways in different parts of the world.

The literature on women's industrial labor and its relation to informal and household work can be understood only in the larger context of changes in the world economy that have significantly affected women's economic roles. Global restructuring in the latter part of the 1980s was characterized by three trends. First, there was a movement toward market-based economies, in particular, export-oriented strategies, at the behest of international financial institutions such as the World Bank and International Monetary Fund (Mitter 1986). Second, the rapid globalization of productive and marketing activities by transnational corporations from many countries was accompanied by substantial informalization and subcontracting of work arrangements beyond state regulation (Portes et al. 1989), or what Harvey (1989) labels "flexible accumulation." Finally, various economic crises, involving periodic recessions, debt, and the environment, have occurred. As a consequence of all these changes, industrial and family-based economies now exist side by side in a mixture of factory organization and subcontracting to family sweatshops that maintains men's control over women workers (Harvey 1989).

Several themes are clear in this portion of the women-in-development literature. First, in the six years of research between 1986 and 1992, we find many similarities and some instructive differences regarding the use of women's labor and the effects of employment in export-led development and transnational corporations' production networks. As wages have risen in some areas, transnationals have cut labor costs by various combinations of relocating production to another tier of low-wage countries, increasing the use of subcontracting and/or homework (home-based assembly), or restructuring work through automation (Heyzer 1988; Elson 1989; Harvey 1989; Portes et al. 1989; Kamel 1990; Pyle and Dawson 1990). These trends reveal the growing relationship of industrial work to the informal sector and the household. Second, we note an implicit and explicit need for theoretical and empirical redefinition of "work" to capture the reality that, particularly for women, daily work often takes place in the three spheres of the formal and informal sectors and the household (Mitter 1986; Benería and Roldán 1987; Ward 1990b; Benería 1991; Hossfeld forthcoming). Third, women's resistance to unequal situations and their efforts to empower themselves involve many diverse strategies and encompass struggles in all three spheres.

Furthermore, we see the importance of the intertwining of class, race or ethnicity, and gender in shaping women's economic roles. State policy, independently or in conjunction with transnationals, plays a critical role here because it can be used to incorporate women or limit their access to opportunities. If drawn into the development process, women, people of color, and/or poor people are often restricted in their choices, and their activism is suppressed by state policy. Because of the importance of the intersection of gender, race, and class with the state, it is clear that new theoretical frameworks and praxis must be developed to incorporate these factors.

Women and Industrialization

In the early 1980s women-in-development scholars debated whether employment in transnationals was beneficial for women or if they were being exploited in yet another way, as low-wage workers, employed at most for a few years, and working under unhealthy conditions (for a review of this earlier literature, see Lim 1985; Tiano 1987; Ward 1988b; Joel 1989, 1990). Few references to this controversy have been made since then. Linda Lim (1985, 1990) continued to argue that such employment is an advantage to women, while others maintained that the net impact of such employment on women was unfavorable (Ward 1988b, 1990a).

Instead, from the mid-1980s onward, we find that this dichotomous debate has largely been replaced by analyses acknowledging the contradictions and dynamics of women's employment in transnational corporations. This newer view recognizes that transnationals have some positive and many adverse effects on women, which evolve over time because of changes in corporate strategy, state policy, geographical location, and/or worker resistance.

Although employment in transnational firms is a small proportion of women's work in the global economy, it remains a critical component for several reasons. First, women's work in these firms constitutes a growing proportion of women's work in currently developing countries (Ward 1988b; Benería 1989; Lim 1990) due to the primacy placed on the export-oriented industrial growth strategies involving transnationals by international development and financial institutions. As a result, transnationals now arise from a wider range of countries, including Japan and the newly industrializing countries (NICs) in Asia. Second, export-oriented transnational firms constitute a dynamic sector in which continual change (automation, increased use of subcontracting and homework, and movement into new tiers of countries) affects rapidly expanding numbers of women. Finally, researchers increasingly recognize the direct links of formal sector transnational employment to the many women working in the informal sector and the household.

Since the mid-1980s much research has examined women's experiences in transnational corporations and in the informalized layers of subcontracting and homework they are establishing. Such production networks span both the currently developing and the industrialized countries. In reviewing these studies, we find similarities across regions as well as unique local patterns. On the one hand, the new research has increased our understanding of the parallels that exist globally in the importance of women's labor to transnational corporations' production networks in industries such as electronics, garments/textiles, shoes/footwear, toys, plastics, and consumer products and the way gender, class, and ethnicity interact in shaping the composition of the workforce. Similarities also exist in the sometimes contradictory yet largely negative effects of transnational employment on women and how these effects persist or change over time as corporations relocate to lower-wage countries, increase their layers of subcontracting and homework, or automate. On the other hand, this research has shown how the effect of transnationals on women is mediated by preexisting cultural patterns of male dominance, state policies, and workers' resistance that can vary across countries. As a consequence, profiles of women's labor-force participation differ among some countries.

Importance of Women's Labor in Transnational Corporations

Women are employed in transnational corporations in many areas of the world: Pacific Asia, Latin America, a few areas of Africa, and throughout industrialized countries. Important differences exist by region.

Several groups of Pacific Asian countries have pursued export-oriented growth by attracting transnationals in a wide range of labor-intensive industries. Research confirms that women workers are critical to the existence of these industries throughout this region (Heyzer 1986, 1988, 1989). Since the 1960s, in the newly industrializing countries of South Korea, Taiwan, Hong Kong, and Singapore, women have provided the needed supply of low-cost labor for the remarkably rapid economic growth this region has experienced (Li 1985; Gallin 1990). The

Philippines, Malaysia, Indonesia, and Thailand have relied on female workers since the 1970s; state development agencies in Thailand and Malaysia still actively advertise their availability to attract foreign investors (Pyle and Dawson 1990). In the latest group of Asian countries to establish export processing zones during the 1980s, such as Sri Lanka, Bangladesh, and areas of China and India, there is heavy reliance on the labor of women and often children (Rosa 1987; Sultana 1990). In addition, export processing zones are being planned for other developing countries as diverse as Iran, Vietnam, and Mongolia.

New studies on women's employment in transnational corporations in Latin America center on the *maquiladoras* along the United States border with Mexico and on those industries located in Mexico City, Costa Rica, Peru, Colombia, Brazil, and the Caribbean (Benería and Roldán 1987; Humphrey 1987; Peña 1987; Ruiz and Tiano 1987; Young 1987; Ríos 1990; Scott 1990; Tiano 1990; Truelove 1990; Yelvington 1993). The free trade zones along the Mexican border and in the Caribbean produce mostly garments and electronics and hire predominantly women (Gereffi 1990). In contrast to *maquiladora* production, small sweater-making workshops have expanded in rural Mexico (Wilson 1991). These backstreet shops or homesites rely extensively on women's labor. In addition, the Caribbean is the initial offshore location for newer service industry jobs in banking, airline reservations, and telemarketing (Anderson 1989; Freeman 1989; Kamel 1990).

In a few areas of Africa transnational firms employ women assembly workers. In South Africa they have used mostly black men as workers, leaving women to work as domestics (Cock 1988). Although black women were finally allowed to become factory workers, they were the last group to be employed, and a very small percentage of them work in transnationals (Seidman 1985; for a history of women cannery workers, see Berger 1990). Mauritius established the first export-oriented free trade zone on the African continent. This zone focused on textiles and garment industries and hired female workers (Hein 1986; Rosa 1987). Proximity to Europe and well-behaved workforces have made North African countries attractive sites for production. In clothing factories established in Morocco, female labor was also preferred (Joekes 1987).

Transnational corporations have also set up operations in several countries in the western European semiperiphery, such as Greece, Spain, and the Republic of Ireland. The European textile and clothing industry has developed extensive links via coproduction or subcontracting with firms in eastern Europe and northern Africa that employ mostly women (Redclift and Mingione 1985; Mitter 1986; Elson 1989; Hadjicostandi 1990; Pyle 1990a, b). Many of these firms, such as Benetton, are marketing ventures that coordinate subcontracted production activities of family- and sweatshop-based industries (Harvey 1989).

State policies in this region have differentially affected workforce gender composition. For example, in Greece state-sponsored transnational garment manufacturing generally has employed women and structured production to take place both in the factory and at home under a piece-rate system (Hadjicostandi 1990). By contrast, the government of the Republic of Ireland designed its export-oriented development strategy to attract corporations that would employ primarily men and used discriminatory state employment and policies on family/reproductive rights to limit women's employment (Pyle 1990b).

In the United States transnational corporations operate in the same types of industries (i.e., garments and electronics) as in developing countries (Safa 1986; Lamphere 1987; Rosen 1987; Fernández Kelly and Garcia 1988, 1992; Fernández Kelly 1989; Hossfeld 1990, forthcoming; Kamel 1990). Contrary to the widespread impression that electronics and garments are declining industries, total employment in the apparel industry in the United States is greater than in the automotive, steel, and electronics industries combined (Fernández Kelly 1989).

Patterns in the composition of the labor force evolve in relation to the hiring preferences of the transnational corporations, labor shortages, state policies, and preexisting relations of male domination as well as ethnicity and class. Although the workforces in electronics consist largely of young, single women, some variation has occurred over time, and married women are employed by textiles/garment and electronics firms in countries such as Thailand and the Philippines (Lim 1990). In Ciudad Juárez, Mexico, when *maquila* employers increased job benefits to attract more workers, the proportion of men increased; but in other cities where employers did not increase benefits, this pattern did not occur (Catanzarite and Strober 1993). In Pacific Asia the state has been active in shaping the workforce via family policies and family planning programs that manipulate fertility rates either to increase the current supply of women workers or to augment the future labor supply. In Thailand and the Philippines cultural traditions have permitted women wider economic roles, whereas in Taiwan and Japan patriarchal norms have restricted women's employment in the formal sector to the period before marriage (Carney and O'Kelly 1990; Gallin 1990).

Ethnicity, class, and gender also shape the structure of the transnational corporation workforce. For example, in Taiwan in the late 1970s managers and union leaders in factories were predominantly mainland Chinese military men, whereas the workers were native Taiwanese, largely women (Arrigo 1985). Similarly, in Malaysia native Malay women are more likely to be found in assembly work than Chinese women (Salih and Young 1989). Such patterns also occur in Mexico and Latin America (Fernández Kelly and Garcia 1988, 1992; Zavella 1988; Fernández Kelly 1989). For example, Kevin Yelvington's (1993) research in Trinidad reveals that line workers are women, predominantly black, while floor supervisors are men, mainly white. Annie Phizacklea's (1990) research on the small-firm sector of the fashion industry of the United Kingdom found that production relations are conditioned by class, gender, and ethnicity. Last, in Los Angeles the labor force in garment manufacture is largely female, 91 percent of whom are minority, chiefly Hispanic (Fernández Kelly 1989).

Effects of Employment in Transnational Corporations on Women

Literature from the late 1980s and early 1990s on the effects of employment in transnational corporations on women supports two major points. First, this type of work has contradictory effects on women; positive aspects can exist even in the presence of widespread adverse impacts. Because of this recognition, the earlier dichotomous discussion regarding whether such employment was beneficial or disadvantageous for women has been replaced by a more complex analysis. Second, corporate strategies in the late 1980s increasingly involved cost-cutting measures such as relocation of production to lower-wage countries, increased use of subcontracting/homework, and/or automation, each of which has definite effects on women workers.

Female factory workers often consider transnational corporation employment a favorable option initially, because it provides them immediate earned income, material benefits, and more independence from their families than existing alternatives (Agarwal 1988; Salaff 1988). Some women in the newly industrializing countries have experienced improved working conditions and absolute wage levels over time due to worker resistance and organization. Lim (1990) argues that although wages are low in these corporations relative to industrialized countries and working conditions more adverse, in many areas transnational firms offer conditions and pay that are relatively better than those of other local employers.

On the other hand, most research since 1985 shows that, over time, women working in transnationals encounter a variety of adverse effects: occupational segregation and lack of advancement possibilities, job insecurity or loss, wages relatively lower than men's, and a variety of oppressive working conditions. Women occupy low positions on occupational ladders, and there is an absence of opportunities to gain skills and advance in the job hierarchy (Humphrey 1987). These jobs are often precarious, and in recessions, enterprises employing predominantly women are the most likely to cut back or close. For example, South Korean women remain a peripheral workforce (Phongpaichit 1988).

Relative male/female wage differentials have persisted over time and appear to be substantially due to discrimination, even in newly industrializing countries such as Taiwan and South Korea (Gannicott 1986; Amsden 1989). Subsistence or lower wage levels often prevail, and transnational corporations may rely on households to support low-wage workers. For example, in Indonesia corporations have located production in rural areas because they can pay the young women they employ less than subsistence wages since they live with their families (Mather 1985; Wolf 1990b, 1993). Cynthia Truelove (1990) argues that agribusiness transnationals in the coffee industry established rural mini-*maquiladoras* in Colombia, employing women at below-subsistence wages to produce shoes and garments for export. The year-round work of women subsidizes the wages of male agricultural workers, who are employed only seasonally.

In parts of Latin America employment in transnational corporations has little impact either on high unemployment rates for women and men or on subsistence wages, even for women with extensive labor histories (Tiano 1990; for an exception, see Catanzarite and Strober 1993). Many Latin American women display ambivalent feelings toward this type of work, because although they need money for household survival, this form of economic activity contradicts women's cultural roles (Young 1987; Tiano 1990). Transnationals in Mexico have capitalized on these contradictions to reduce unionization of Mexican women to less than 10 percent and thereby remove a source of upward pressure on wages (Kamel 1990).

Moreover, conditions of employment are often oppressive with long hours, forced overtime, increased production quotas or speedups, poor working conditions or housing, stress, and harassment from management and the state. These conditions lead to deterioration of workers' health and often to high turnover, which has been particularly documented for Asia. Although conditions may have improved in some newly industrializing countries, adverse impacts persist throughout most of the region (Rosa 1987; Agarwal 1988; Heyzer 1989; Pyle and Dawson 1990; Sultana 1990). As a result, workers continue to resist and unionize (Ong 1987; Mai 1989; Kamel 1990). In the latest group of Asian countries to attract foreign investment, for example, Bangladesh and Sri Lanka, conditions are the worst. Furthermore, in Pacific Asia the state has always been active in controlling the workforce in transnational corporations, often at the cost of democratic movements and human rights (Agarwal 1988; Heyzer and Kean 1988; Enloe 1989). Lourdes Arrigo (1985) examines parallels between Taiwan and South Korea, the Philippines and Malaysia in terms of military dictatorships that maintained a stable economic climate for foreign investment.

In regard to the second major effect of employment in transnationals, each of the corporate cost-cutting strategies used throughout the world in the latter part of the 1980s – including relocation to lower-wage countries, development of extensive networks of subcontracting and homework, and automation – has had distinctly negative effects on women workers. As corporations relocate to lower-wage countries, women in the original country lose jobs. For example, wages in Caribbean countries are higher than in Mexico or in some Asian countries (Massiah 1989; Griffith 1990; Yelvington 1993), and employment can be shifted. Relocation is particularly disadvantageous for the original women workers if they are in low-skill jobs in a country that is restructuring its export-led economy toward higher technology products, such as South Korea (Hyo-chae 1988), or if they are in areas such as the Caribbean (or even the United States) where slow growth means few alternative job opportunities. In addition, as corporations move production into new tiers of countries, as has occurred in Asia, these firms and their local networks commonly adopt the same exploitative practices they formerly used in other countries.

Subcontracting to local factories and homework (home-based assembly) have increased throughout the world from Mexico, the United States, and Europe to Taiwan, China, Bangladesh, and India (Arrigo 1985; Benería and Roldán 1987; Harvey 1989; Standing 1989; Sultana 1990). These extended production networks cut costs because corporations can pay lower wages than in factories, bypass provision of benefits, and avoid protective legislation. These workers are unlikely to unionize and their employment can be immediately terminated in an economic downturn. The women involved are often married or heads of households, and such work is their only option for combining home duties with participation in the wage economy. At the lowest level of the subcontracting pyramid in Taiwan, for example, mothers and children assemble components at home at piece rates about half the hourly wage for factory work (Arrigo 1985). In Mauritius transnational corporations locate factories throughout the country to avoid unionization efforts and to use homeworkers (Hein 1986).

Automation of existing industries or accompanying the restructuring of an economy toward more technologically complex industries has differential gender effects on employment, because it tends to reduce the number of lower-skill jobs that are primarily female. Governments in Taiwan and South Korea are deliberately altering the structure of industries in export processing zones by shifting to higher technology, automation, heavier industries, and men workers (Hyo-chae 1988; Gereffi 1990). Kamal Salih and Mei Ling Young's study of the semiconductor industry in Malaysia (1989) reveals that, although there was net growth in employment in this industry from 1977 to 1984, the proportion of women decreased. This trend is also expected to occur in the garment industry when it automates (Elson 1989).

Redefinitions of Work

Global restructuring, industrialization, and transnational corporations are increasingly linked to the growing informal sector and to unwaged work in the household, both because of these corporations' burgeoning networks of subcontracting and homework and because people are forced to find informal sector work and/or increase household subsistence activities in times of economic crisis and retrenchment. This recognition reinforces the longstanding theme in women-in-development literature that much of the work women do takes place in the informal sector and household and often is omitted from statistics on labor force participation. Because women predominate in the work done in these sectors, formal labor force data present a particularly inadequate profile of women's economic contributions (Bene-ría 1989, 1991) and of economies that include a variety of activities such as large factories, informal sectors, and ethnic enclaves (Harvey 1989).

As a consequence, much of the research on women and work since 1984 has emphasized the need to redefine "work" (Mies 1986; Standing 1989; Ward 1990b, 1993; Benería 1991; Hossfeld forthcoming). Women's and men's work must incorporate all three dimensions – paid labor in the formal sector, paid informal labor, and unpaid labor in the household – and should be analyzed along a continuum from formal to informal to household work, as described by Kathryn Ward (1990b). Parts of this work continuum have been suggested by others, but none has incorporated all three dimensions (Bruce and Dwyer 1987; Stichter and Parpart 1988a, 1990; Grown and Sebstad 1989; Collins and Gimenez 1990; Nash 1990). Benería (1991) reviews the widespread efforts – conceptual, methodological, and empirical – since the mid-1970s to correct the underestimation of women's work in subsistence production, unaccounted paid work, domestic production, and volunteer work.

The majority of the world's women work in two to three of these categories, a situation Karen Hossfeld (forthcoming) has aptly called "the triple shift." For example, Joycelin Massiah (1989) describes the sixteen-hour-a-day triple shift activities of women in the Caribbean, and Noeleen Heyzer (1989) provides a detailed account for Asian women. The boundaries of the triple shift are fluid for women and relatively rigid for men (Ward 1990b). Men define work as something that takes place outside the household (Hossfeld forthcoming) and rarely engage in household labor (Hochschild 1989), whereas women's work spans all three sectors. Hossfeld (forthcoming) found that, in the Silicon Valley, women worked up to fifteen hours a day in various combinations of the triple shift, while men were often unemployed and worked far fewer hours. Caren A. Grown and Jennefer Sebstad (1989) found that poor women may spend up to sixty hours per week in unpaid household labor.

Informal Sector

Informal sector work is heterogeneous, encompassing entrepreneurial activities and wage labor that is unregulated by the state. This sector includes subcontracted industrial and service work, retail activities (street vendors), domestic service, the sex trade, and agricultural work. Although predicted to disappear over time with the expansion of the capitalist world system (Chase-Dunn 1989), the informal sector and women's participation in it have expanded dramatically (Harvey 1989). Whether this sector is part of the logic of late capitalism or represents another mode of economic organization has been debated (Harvey 1989; Portes et al. 1989; Ward 1993), but for the most part, researchers have ignored significant gender differences in informal sector activities.

Women and men enter the informal sector for different reasons. For men, the informal sector often produces more income than the formal sector and provides upward mobility during economic restructuring (Schmink 1986; Brydon and Chant 1989; Ward 1990b). In Latin America and Africa urban men make up 60 to 75 percent of the informal sector business owners and operators (Grown and Sebstad 1989). Men often become subcontractors, controlling the labor of women home-workers.

For women, informal sector work is usually a strategy for economic survival used in addition to formal paid labor and household subsistence activities (Schmink 1986; Benería and Roldán 1987). This is particularly the case for female heads of house-holds, who constitute an average of one-third of the world's households and as many as one-half in some countries (Nash 1988b; Bruce 1989; Moser 1989). In addition, many women seek to avoid the contradictory pulls of economic necessity, childcare and household duties, and patriarchal ideologies against women working outside the home by engaging in informal sector work in the home. The money earned may give them some power within the household (Mizan 1992).

Ethnic and gender differences are pronounced in the informal sector. For example, in the Miami garment industry most manufacturers are Jewish, the subcontractors are 90 percent Cuban men, and the workers are 95 percent Cuban women (Fernández Kelly and Garcia 1992). In addition, immigrants are central to the informaliza-tion strategy throughout the world, where they labor in subcontracting networks at manufacturing or service tasks, as domestics, or in the sex trade (Enloe 1989; Kamel 1990). Immigrants often are economically vulnerable and located in low-paid service and assembly work (Sassen 1988), although differences among immigrant groups exist. Fernández Kelly and Garcia (1988, 1992) find that women immigrants from Cuba who worked in ethnic enclaves were able to earn more than the economically vulnerable Mexican women working in garment assembly plants in Los Angeles. Cuban women's work facilitated the economic mobility and wealth of Cuban men.

Women's participation in the informal sector globally is higher than their formal participation rates and is expanding throughout the world in both rural and urban areas (Redclift and Mingione 1985; Sen and Grown 1987; Sassen 1988; Boris and Daniels 1989; Enloe 1989; Grown and Sebstad 1989; Truelove 1990; Fernández Kelly and Garcia 1992). For example, by 1980 in Chile, Brazil, and Costa Rica, about three-quarters of informal employees were women (Tokman 1989). Women in the informal sectors are marginalized, however, through job segregation and by wages that are only 45 to 74 percent of men's earnings (Scott 1986; Tokman 1989).

Women's informal industrial work takes place in clandestine assembly shops that evade protective, immigration, and wage legislation or in the household where subcontractors drop off electronic parts, garment pieces, jewelry, or envelopes for home processing. A new informal service industry involves clerical or telemarketing services subcontracted to women's homes, where workers input insurance information, airline ticket data, and medical texts at piece rates or subminimum wages (Applebaum 1987; Boris and Daniels 1989; Freeman 1989). Informal retail service activities, such as hawking produce, prepared food, or cigarettes in the streets, are also common.

Domestic service, a female occupation involving childcare, food preparation, housecleaning, and shopping, is an important component of women's informal sector work internationally and often supports the formal sector work of other women. This work is shaped by class, race, gender, and international political issues, particularly when many women domestic workers from South Asia, North Africa, and the Middle East migrate to other countries (Gowen 1988; Enloe 1989). By hiring domestic workers, middle- and upper-class women around the world can resolve conflicts with male partners over housework and childcare and engage in formal sector work (Byerly 1986; Rollins 1985; Ruiz 1987; Cock 1988; Anderson 1989; De Melo 1989; Enloe 1989; Gimenez 1990).

Many domestic workers experience particularly exploitative working conditions because their work falls outside state regulation (Chaney and Garcia Castro 1989). A hierarchy exists within the occupation (Enloe 1989). Nannies and *au pairs* (frequently white Europeans) have relatively more power than maids (often women of color or immigrant women who may be fleeing political persecution or economies plagued by underdevelopment and debt crises). The latter are more economically vulnerable and often subject to sexual harassment by men in employers' households, as documented for Filipinas in Hong Kong, Singapore, Japan, and the Middle East, and for African American and immigrant women in the United States (Rollins 1985; Gowen 1988; Paguio 1988; Heyzer 1989). At the same time, in contrast to the historical experience of industrialized countries, many currently developing countries such as Bangladesh, the Philippines, and Sri Lanka have become dependent on the wages that their migrant domestic workers remit to their home countries (Heyzer 1989).

A type of informal sector work increasingly mentioned in the late 1980s is the international sex trade, which uses patterns of racism and sexism in the prostitution of women and children in Asia (Heyzer 1986; Mies 1986; Enloe 1989; Truong 1990), the Caribbean (Levy and Lerch 1991), and Africa (Brydon and Chant 1989). These women and children often come from impoverished families in rural areas, and the numbers involved are substantial. Benería (1989), citing Thanh-dam Truong (1990), notes that in Bangkok the number of prostitutes is equivalent to 10 percent of the workers in transnational corporations. The sex trade is linked to international business investments and transnationals, the United States' military bases, and male patrons from currently developed countries. International financial institutions and some countries see the promotion of this industry as a solution to the debt crisis (Enloe 1989). Ironically, the governments of these countries play a central role in promoting this form of women's informal labor while simultaneously extolling the virtues of women factory workers (Enloe 1989).

Informalization and global restructuring also affect agricultural work. Capitalists retain flexibility during labor-intensive harvest and food-processing periods, when women and men are used in a mixture of industrial and agricultural activities to ensure that families do not migrate during slack times (Aguiar 1986; Enloe 1989; Heyzer 1989; Truelove 1990). Cynthia Enloe (1989) describes the shifting gender and race division of labor and informalization on sugar and banana planta- tions in Central America that seasonally employ women and use race to allocate jobs.

Many women homeworkers, other informal workers, and entrepreneurs report dissatisfaction with the arrangements because of low wages, little control over the work processes, health risks, long hours, and overhead costs (Leung 1986; Boris and Daniels 1989; Enloe 1989; Narotzky 1990). For example, Ximena Bunster, Elsa Chaney, and Ellan Young (1985) and Linda North (1988) describe the struggles of Peruvian market women who work eighteen to twenty hours a day. In Africa and Latin America women's informal businesses have lower sales revenues, asset bases, and profit margins than men's (Grown and Sebstad 1989; Jiggins 1989). M. Patricia Fernández Kelly and Anna Garcia (1988) found similar conditions for women entrepreneurs in Los Angeles. Janice Jiggins (1989), however, describes how some Sub-Saharan African women entrepreneurs have moved from survival activities to more prosperous growth-oriented enterprises. As in formal factory work, the empowerment of women is a complex process. Women homeworkers and entrepre- neurs benefit immediately by the wages earned in informal sector work. In the long run, though, many women work in isolated, hazardous conditions and continue to exist at the survival level rather than experience economic mobility (Jiggins 1989; Massiah 1989).

Household Labor

As discussed above, women's household labor is integrally linked to formal and informal sector work, since the majority of women worldwide pursue some combi- nation of these types of work to sustain their families. Transnational firms are increasingly intertwined with women and households when they subcontract assem- bly work as paid homework and when they pay low wages, because women's work in the household subsidizes the actual cost of family maintenance. Such relationships with transnationals intensify women's workloads. If the totality of women's work lives is not examined, this fact is obscured.

The literature since the mid-1980s has reinforced and extended research showing that women's unpaid labor in the household and agriculture is critical. As producers and consumers, women provide food, clothing, and energy and maintain the family in time-consuming activities. For poor households in many countries, such work contributes at least half the household subsistence (J. L. Collins 1990; Narotzky 1990; Stichter 1990). Women's household labor is intensified in times of economic crisis and global restructuring (Friedmann 1990).

Another major development in scholarship regarding women's roles in the house- hold is the movement beyond earlier research that treated household members as having a unity of interests (Smith, Wallerstein, and Evers 1984). New studies show how the roles of individuals in the household vary by gender, race, and class (Bruce and Dwyer 1987; Acker 1988; Lever 1988; Stichter and Parpart 1988b, 1990; Blumberg 1989; Bruce 1989; Fernández Kelly 1989; Collins and Gimenez 1990; Wolf 1990a, b, 1993; Amott and Matthaei 1991; Mizan 1992).

For example, women contribute far more of their earnings and unpaid labor to the household, in some cases up to 100 percent, whereas men may use most earnings for personal consumption. This is illustrated in rural Spain (Narotzky 1990) and in Mexico City, where male partners often do not pool money or information with spouses (Benería and Roldán 1987). In some cases, poor and minority men share fewer resources and devote less money and effort to the household than more economically advantaged men do (Blumberg 1989; Hochschild 1989). To maintain status and power within the household, men may devalue women's economic contributions or resort to domestic violence.

Resistance

The new scholarship on women's industrial labor and its connections to the informal and household sectors reveals broader dimensions of women's resistance to their subordinate positions than had formerly been recognized (Dill 1986, 1988; Bookman and Morgen 1988; Ward 1988a; Westwood and Bhachu 1988; P. H. Collins 1990; Talwar 1990). In the past many labor unions viewed women workers as unorganizable. Earlier accounts depicted women as passive victims of the consequences of development, transnational corporations, and various types of marginalization.

New research has illustrated the need to examine forms of resistance other than large-scale social movements or union activities. Like the commonalities noted in women's experiences in transnational employment and the informal sector around the world, similarities exist among women's resistance strategies. Bettina Aptheker (1989: 173–4) proposes examining women's daily resistance: "To see women's resistance is to also see the accumulated effects of daily, arduous, creative, sometimes ingenious labors, performed over time, sometimes over generations." She suggests that since much resistance is based on the need to survive, survival itself is a form of resistance. Resistance strategies fall into three categories: (1) making use of traditional structured organizations along with spontaneous daily resistance in the formal workplace, (2) household transformation, and (3) the act of survival itself, which may involve various combinations of activities in the formal, informal, and household sectors. Contradictions may be inherent in these strategies.

Despite barriers placed by governments and corporations, women workers in both developed and developing countries organize and strike for better wages and working conditions and against plant closures. Women workers are among the most militant union members, particularly in South Korea, the Philippines, and South Africa. Increasing international connections between women workers and unions in different countries facilitate communication of ways to support workers and strikes and to fight runaway plants, de-skilling, low wages, and other transnational corporation tactics (Arrigo 1985; Byerly 1986; Rosa 1987; Jayakody and Goonatilake 1988; Pineda-Ofreneo and Del Rosario 1988; Elson 1989; Enloe 1989; Heyzer 1989; Mai 1989; Berger 1990; Kamel 1990).

This resistance takes place daily at the computer terminals, on the shopfloor, and at other worksites around the world (Byerly 1986; Bookman and Morgen 1988; Zavella 1988). In Barbados women workers entering data for airlines reprogram their computers to record higher than actual output (Freeman 1989). Women workers in the United States' Silicon Valley use managers' racist and sexist biases to acquire more power and control over their working conditions on the shopfloor. For example, women workers may tell their male managers that they need frequent "hormone" or menstrual rest breaks (Hossfeld 1990). Sallie Westwood (1985) and Westwood and Parminder Bhachu (1988) show how immigrant women workers in England have used a variety of strategies such as wedding and baby showers to control interaction on the shopfloor. Devon Peña (1987) describes the "turtle" or slowdown strategy of workers in Mexican *maquiladoras*. Finally, Malaysian women factory workers have sought control over their work by spirit possession (Ong 1987).

Self-employed and informal sector workers are also organizing (Sen and Grown 1987; Bhatt 1989). In India the success of the Self-Employed Women's Association (SEWA) demonstrates how previously isolated women in the informal sector can achieve some power over their work situation. Loan groups based on the Grameen Bank model provide supportive contexts for women's education, economic development, and empowerment vis-à-vis men in the household (Mizan 1992; Blumberg 1995). Nash (1988a) describes how market women in Lima, Peru, organize *comedores populares*, or communal kitchens, to ease household burdens. Migrant domestic workers in Europe organize to counter the increasing growth of transnational cleaning corporations (Gowen 1988).

New research indicates that for women around the world, some combination of work in the formal, informal, or household sector is a survival strategy and one way to resist marginalization from low-wage employment. For example, homemakers whose households' survival is threatened by the debt crisis take to the streets in alliances with unions and formal sector workers to challenge austerity programs in Latin America (Nash 1988a, 1988b, 1995; North 1988) or governmental violence (Bunster-Burrotto 1986). Bonnie Thornton Dill (1986, 1988) argues that survival itself is resistance and discusses how women of color in the United States pass skills along to their children, ensuring their survival and resisting negative socioeconomic forces (see also P. H. Collins 1990).

Aptheker (1989) describes how household relationships can be transformed by women's resistance activities. In the United States Barbara Kingsolver (1989) describes permanent transformations of gender relationships in households after Chicana and Mexicana family members and workers formed their own support organizations during the Arizona copper mine strike in 1983.

This resistance, however, contains ambivalence as women seek to reconcile the cultural and religious contradictions among their work, resistance, and the structures of male dominance in which they live (Bookman and Morgen 1988; North 1988; Freeman 1989; Hossfeld 1990; Ward 1990b). As Fernández Kelly and Garcia (1992) note, some women rationalize their need to work without questioning their particular cultural ideology.

Often women's resistance only temporarily mediates their immediate, individual situation without generating changes in the structures or institutions that control their labor. Although the triple shift strategy may ensure survival, it can reinforce the global economy that made such a strategy necessary. As a consequence, large numbers of women remain exhausted in a survival mode, and only a privileged handful experience economic mobility via this strategy.

Conclusion

Significant developments since the mid-1980s in the literature on women's role in industrialization and its relation to the informal and household sectors have added immeasurably to our understanding of women's subordinate roles. They have provided an invaluable foundation of knowledge for developing more relevant theoretical frameworks and building political and economic strategies to improve women's positions in developing and developed countries. Clearly, much theoretical, empirical, and political work is needed. This literature review and the trends we highlight starkly reveal the need for theoretical models that incorporate gender, class, ethnicity, the changing strategies of transnational corporations, the totality of work, and the role of the state in analyzing women's roles in economic development. Our review also shows that theories focusing only on work in the formal capitalist sector with little consideration of gender are simply inadequate (Mies 1986; Benería 1991; Ward 1993).

Accordingly, much more empirical research is needed. First, longitudinal and cross-national studies must be made at the firm and industry level to examine women's job histories, wage trends, differences in working conditions, and the range of economic choices women working in transnationals have in selecting employment. For example, more information is needed on the length of time women spend in such employment. Estimates from the 1970s speculated that women in electronics worked an average of only two years. If this trend remains, then any benefits for women of employment in transnationals would be short-lived. The relationship between layoffs by gender and business cycles also should be more thoroughly examined.

Changes in wages for women, at an absolute level and relative to men, should be studied to determine the effects on education levels, work experience, uninterrupted work history, support from the household, and discrimination. In addition, working conditions can be more closely examined to ascertain differences within a country between transnationals and indigenous firms or between different firms in the same industry internationally. Interviews can be conducted to provide more information regarding structural constraints versus personal choice and the economic options these women had when selecting transnational jobs. This type of information must be collected for those directly employed in such firms as well as for those working in extended subcontracting networks. Data can be gathered regarding what proportion of women's work lives are spent in factories compared with other types of work in the formal, informal, and household sectors.

Second, researchers can extend examination of women's and men's multifaceted experiences of work along the continuum of formal, informal, and household labor. More comparative and longitudinal research is needed to document commonalities and differences in women's experiences in these three sectors and the racial and class patterns that prevail. These proposed comparative work histories would require a movement away from reliance on formal labor force statistics to a combination of macrostudies and microsurveys of time use that incorporate gender, race, and class. Innumerable aspects of this work continuum can be examined. For example, ties among women's work in factories, informal assembly, and participation in the sex trade constitute an important area for new research.

Third, scholars and organizers must more fully study and understand all forms of women's resistance and the contradictions that may accompany them, recognizing that the increasing informalization of work makes effective organizing difficult. As David Harvey notes in regard to women workers (1989, 153), "struggling against capitalist exploitation in the factory is very different from struggling against a father or uncle who organizes family labour into a highly disciplined and competitive sweatshop that works to order for multinational capital." Women workers and community groups can develop new organizing strategies that encompass women's everyday acts of resistance as well as unionization. For example, local-based groups such as SEWA or the Grameen Bank projects can empower women workers relative to their immediate environment and families. In addition, researchers must more extensively analyze the international connections between gender and work in developing and industrialized countries, identifying the many parallels that exist as well as the differences. Women's groups can work toward cross-national coordination of and support for strikes and contract negotiations (Kamel 1990). Thus, scholars and activists can formulate effective strategies for change that empower women workers while facilitating socioeconomic development.

Finally, in conjunction with these dimensions of analysis, future research must more systematically and completely study the role of state policy and the intertwining of gender, race, and class. With respect to state policy, for example, scholars can examine, via case studies or comparative analyses, how the state determines the conditions of women's work by attracting investments on the basis of gender; by weakening state regulations to attract investment, thereby creating hazardous working conditions or informalizing work processes; by using police or military power to suppress workers' resistance activities; by promoting and using women workers in the tourist or sex trade; or by influencing fertility patterns with labor-supply objectives in mind. In many cases, states have sought short-run development without looking at the long-run socioeconomic and political costs of competing with other states for transnational corporations' investment. Understanding the way the state shapes women's economic lives is critical for the development of strategies for effective change.

Scholars and activists should build on these predominant themes in the women-in-development literature to create a new theoretical framework and to extend empirical research. In so doing, they will establish a solid basis for understanding women's roles in economic development and for innovating strategies that more efficiently and equitably incorporate women into this process, thus eradicating their subordinate status.

REFERENCES

Acker, Joan. 1988. "Class, Gender, and the Relations of Production." *Signs: Journal of Women in Culture and Society* 13: 473–97.

Agarwal, Bina, ed. 1988. *Structures of Patriarchy*. London: Zed.

Aguiar, Neuma. 1986. "Research Guidelines: How to Study Work in Latin America." In *Women and Change in Latin America*, ed. June Nash and Helen Safa, 22–34. South Hadley, Mass.: Bergin and Garvey.

Amott, Teresa, and Julie Matthaei. 1991. *Race, Gender, and Work: A Multicultural Economic History of Women in the United States.* Boston: South End Press.

Amsden, Alice H. 1989. *Asia's Next Giant: South Korea and Late Industrialization.* New York: Oxford University Press.

Anderson, Patricia. 1989. "Domestics and Their Employers." *Connexions* 30: 20–1.

Applebaum, Eileen. 1987. "Restructuring Work." In *Computer Chips and Paper Clips: Technology and Women's Employment*, vol. 2, ed. Heidi Hartmann, 268–312. Washington, DC: National Academy Press.

Aptheker, Bettina. 1989. *Tapestries of Life.* Amherst: University of Massachusetts Press.

Arrigo, Lourdes. 1985. "Economic and Political Control of Women Workers in Multinational Electronics Factories in Taiwan." *Contemporary Marxism* 11: 77–95.

Benería, Lourdes. 1989. "Gender and the Global Economy." In *Instability and Change in the World Economy*, ed. Arthur MacEwan and William K. Tabb, 241–58. New York: Monthly Review.

——,——. 1991. "Accounting for Women's Work: Assessing the Progress of Two Decades." Paper presented at UNRISD, Meeting on Social Development Indicators, Rabat, Morocco, April.

Benería, Lourdes, and Martha Roldán. 1987. *The Crossroads of Class and Gender: Industrial Homework, Subcontracting, and Household Dynamics in Mexico City.* Chicago: University of Chicago Press.

Berger, Iris. 1990. "Gender, Race, and Political Empowerment: South African Canning Workers, 1940–1960." *Gender & Society* 4 (3): 398–420.

Bhatt, Ela. 1989. "Toward Empowerment." *World Development* 17: 1059–65.

Blumberg, Rae Lesser. 1995. "Gender, Microenterprise, Performance, and Power: Case Studies from the Dominican Republic, Ecuador, Guatemala, and Swaziland." In *Women in the Latin American Development Process*, ed. Christine E. Bose and Edna Acosta-Bele'n, 194–226. Philadelphia: Temple University Press.

——,——. 1989. "Toward a Feminist Theory of Development." In *Feminism and Sociological Theory*, ed. Ruth Wallace, 161–99. Beverly Hills, Calif.: Sage.

Bookman, Ann, and Sandra Morgen, eds. 1988. *Women and the Politics of Empowerment.* Philadephia: Temple University Press.

Boris, Eileen, and Cynthia R. Daniels, eds. 1989. *Homework: Historical and Contemporary Perspectives on Paid Labor at Home.* Urbana: University of Illinois Press.

Bruce, Judith. 1989. "Homes Divided." *World Development* 17: 979–91.

Bruce, Judith, and Daisy Dwyer, eds. 1987. *A Home Divided: Women and Income in the Third World.* Stanford: Stanford University Press.

Brydon, Lynne, and Sylvia Chant. 1989. *Women in the Third World.* New Brunswick, NJ: Rutgers University Press.

Bunster, Ximena, Elsa M. Chaney, and Ellan Young. 1985. *Sellers and Servants: Working Women in Lima, Peru.* New York: Praeger.

Bunster-Burrotto, Ximena. 1986. "Surviving beyond Fear: Women and Torture in Latin America." In *Women and Change in Latin America*, ed. June Nash and Helen I. Safa, 297–325. South Hadley, Mass.: Bergin and Garvey.

Byerly, Virginia. 1986. *Hard Times Cotton Mill Girl.* Ithaca, NY: ILR Press.

Carney, Larry, and Charlotte O'Kelly. 1990. "Women's Work and Women's Place in the Japanese Economic Miracle." In *Women Workers and Global Restructuring*, ed. Kathryn Ward, 113–45. Ithaca, NY: ILR Press.

Catanzarite, Lisa, and Myra Strober. 1993. "Gender Recomposition of the Maquiladora Workforce." *Industrial Relations.* 32: 133–47.

Chaney, Elsa, and Mary Garcia Castro, eds. 1989. *Muchachas No More: Household Workers in Latin America and the Caribbean.* Philadelphia: Temple University Press.

Chase-Dunn, Christopher. 1989. *Global Formations*. Cambridge, Mass.: Basil Blackwell.

Clark, Roger, Thomas W. Ramsbey, and Emily S. Alder. 1991. "Culture, Gender, and Labor Force Participation: A Cross-National Study." *Gender & Society* 5 (1): 47–66.

Cock, Jacklynn. 1988. "Trapped Workers: The Case of Domestic Servants in South Africa." In *Patriarchy and Class: African Women in the Home and the Workforce*, ed. Sharon Stichter and Jane L. Parpart, 205–19. Boulder, Colo.: Westview.

Collins, Jane L. 1990. "Unwaged Labor in Comparative Perspective." In *Work without Wages*, ed. Jane L. Collins and Martha Gimenez, 3–24. Albany: State University of New York Press.

Collins, Jane L., and Martha Gimenez, eds. 1990. *Work without Wages*. Albany: State University of New York Press.

Collins, Patricia Hill. 1990. *Black Feminist Thought*. Boston: Allen and Unwin.

De Melo, Hildete Pereira. 1989. "Feminists and Domestic Workers in Rio de Janeiro." In *Muchachas No More: Household Workers in Latin America and the Caribbean*, ed. Elsa M. Chaney and Mary Garcia Castro, 245–67. Philadelphia: Temple University Press.

Dill, Bonnie Thornton. 1986. *Our Mothers' Grief: Racial Ethnic Women and the Maintenance of Family*. Research Paper no. 4. Memphis: Center for Research on Women, Memphis State University.

———, ———. 1988. "'Making Your Job Good Yourself': Domestic Service and the Construction of Personal Dignity." In *Women and the Politics of Empowerment*, ed. Ann Bookman and Sandra Morgen, 33–52. Philadelphia: Temple University Press.

Elson, Diane. 1989. "The Cutting Edge: Women's Employment and Multinationals in the EEC Textiles and Clothing Industry." In *Women's Employment and Multinationals in Europe*, ed. Diane Elson and Ruth Pearson, 80–110. London: Macmillan.

Enloe, Cynthia. 1989. *Bananas, Beaches, and Bases: Making Feminist Sense of International Politics*. Berkeley: University of California Press.

Fernández Kelly, M. Patricia. 1989. "Broadening the Scope: Gender and International Economic Development." *Sociological Forum* 4: 11–35.

Fernández Kelly, M. Patricia, and Anna Garcia. 1988. "Economic Restructuring in the United States." In *Women and Work #3*, ed. Barbara Gutek, Laurie Larwood, and Ann Stromberg, 49–65. Beverly Hills, Calif.: Sage.

———, ———, ———. 1992. "Power Surrendered, Power Restored: The Politics of Home and Work among Hispanic Women in Southern California and Southern Florida." In *Women and Politics in America*, ed. Louise Tilly and Patricia Guerin, 130–49. New York: Russell Sage.

Freeman, Carla. 1989. "High-Tech and High Heels: Barbadian Women in the Off-Shore Information Industry." Paper presented at the 15th Annual Conference of the Caribbean Studies Association, Trinidad and Tobago.

Friedmann, Harriet. 1990. "Family Wheat Farms and Third World Debts." In *Work without Wages*, ed. Joan L. Collins and Martha Gimenez, 193–214. Albany: State University of New York Press.

Gallin, Rita. 1990. "Women and the Export Industry in Taiwan: The Muting of Class Consciousness." In *Women Workers and Global Restructuring*, ed. Kathryn Ward, 179–92. Ithaca, NY: ILR Press.

Gannicott, Kenneth. 1986. "Women, Wages, and Discrimination: Some Evidence from Taiwan." *Economic Development and Cultural Change* 34: 721–30.

Gereffi, Gary. 1990. "Rethinking Development Theory: Insights from East Asia and Latin America." *Sociological Forum* 4: 505–35.

Gimenez, Martha E. 1990. "The Dialectics of Waged and Unwaged Work." In *Work without Wages*, ed. Jane L. Collins and Martha Gimenez, 25–46. Albany: State University of New York Press.

Gowen, Susan. 1988. "Invisible Workers." *Isis: International Women's Journal* 17: 34–6.

Griffith, Winston H. 1990. "CARICOM Countries and the Caribbean Basin Initiative." *Latin American Perspectives* 17: 33–54.

Grown, Caren A., and Jennefer Sebstad. 1989. "Introduction." *World Development* 17: 937–52.

Hadjicostandi, Joanna. 1990. "'Facon': Women's Formal and Informal Work in the Garment Industry in Kavala, Greece." In *Women Workers and Global Restructuring*, ed. Kathryn Ward, 64–81. Ithaca, NY: ILR Press.

Harvey, David. 1989. *The Condition of Post-Modernity*. Oxford: Basil Blackwell.

Hein, Catherine. 1986. "The Feminization of Industrial Employment in Mauritius: A Case of Sex Segregation." In *Sex Inequalities in Urban Employment in the Third World*, ed. Catherine Hein, 277–311. New York: St. Martin's Press.

Heyzer, Noeleen. 1986. *Working Women in South-East Asia*. Milton Keynes, England: Open University Press.

——,——. ed. 1988. *Daughters in Industry: Work, Skills, and Consciousness of Women Workers in Asia*. Kuala Lumpur, Malaysia: Asian and Pacific Development Centre.

——,——. 1989. "Asian Women Wage Earners." *World Development* 17: 1109–24.

Heyzer, Noeleen, and Tan Boon Kean. 1988. "Work, Skills, and Consciousness of Women Workers in Asia." In *Daughters in Industry: Work, Skills, and Consciousness of Women Workers in Asia*, ed. Noeleen Heyzer, 3–32. Kuala Lumpur, Malaysia: Asian and Pacific Development Centre.

Hochschild, Arlie. 1989. *The Second Shift*. New York: Viking.

Hossfeld, Karen. 1990. "'Their Logic against Them': Contradictions in Sex, Race, and Class in Silicon Valley." In *Women Workers and Global Restructuring*, ed. Kathryn Ward, 149–78. Ithaca, NY: ILR Press.

——,——. Forthcoming. *Small, Foreign, and Female: Immigrant Women Workers in Silicon Valley*. Berkeley: University of California Press.

Humphrey, John. 1987. *Gender and Work in the Third World: Sexual Division in Brazilian Industry*. London: Tavistock.

Hyo-chae, Lee. 1988. "The Changing Profile of Women Workers in South Korea." In *Daughters in Industry: Work, Skills, and Consciousness of Women Workers in Asia*, ed. Noeleen Heyzer, 329–55. Kuala Lumpur, Malaysia: Asian and Pacific Development Centre.

Jayakody, Soma, and Hema Goonatilake. 1988. "Industrial Action by Women Workers in Sri Lanka." In *Daughters in Industry: Work, Skills, and Consciousness of Women Workers in Asia*, ed. Noeleen Heyzer, 292–307. Kuala Lumpur, Malaysia: Asian and Pacific Development Centre.

Jiggins, Janice. 1989. "How Poor Women Earn Income in Sub-Saharan Africa and What Works against Them." *World Development* 17: 953–63.

Joekes, Susan. 1987. *Women in the World Economy*. New York: Oxford University Press.

Joel, Susan. 1989. "An Assessment of the Integration/Exploitation Framework for Understanding Women in the International Division of Labor." Master's thesis, Michigan State University, East Lansing.

——,——. 1990. "Female Factory Workers in Less Developed Countries: A Bibliography." *Women in International Development Working Paper*. East Lansing: Office of Women in Development, Michigan State University.

Kamel, Rachel. 1990. *The Global Factory: Analysis and Action for a New Economic Era*. Philadelphia: American Friends Service Committee/Omega Press.

Kingsolver, Barbara. 1989. *Holding the Line*. Ithaca, NY: ILR Press.

Lamphere, Louise. 1987. *From Working Daughters to Working Mothers*. Ithaca, NY: Cornell University Press.

Leung, Trini W. Y. 1986. "The Dark Side of Industrialization." *Multinational Monitor* 7: 22–30.

Lever, Alison. 1988. "Capital, Gender, and Skill: Women Homeworkers in Rural Spain." *Feminist Review* 30: 3–24.

Levy, Diane E., and Patricia B. Lerch. 1991. "Tourism as a Factor in Development." *Gender & Society* 5 (1): 67–85.

Li, K. T. 1985. "Contributions of Women in the Labor Force to Economic Development in Taiwan, the Republic of China." *Industry of Free China* (August): 1–8.

Lim, Linda. 1985. *Women Workers in Multinational Enterprises in Developing Countries.* Geneva: International Labor Office.

———,———. 1990. "Women's Work in Export Factories: The Politics of a Cause." In *Persistent Inequalities: Women and World Development*, ed. Irene Tinker, 101–19. New York: Oxford University Press.

Mai, Kimori. 1989. "Malaysia's Workers: Jolting the Electronics Industry." *Multinational Monitor* 10: 11–13.

Massiah, Joycelin. 1989. "Women's Lives and Livelihoods: A View from the Commonwealth Caribbean." *World Development* 17: 965–77.

Mather, Celia. 1985. "'Rather than Make Trouble, It's Better Just to Leave.'" In *Women, Work, and Ideology in the Third World*, ed. Helen Afshar, 153–80. London: Tavistock.

Mies, Maria. 1986. *Patriarchy and Accumulation on a World Scale: Women in the International Division of Labour.* London: Zed.

Mitter, Swasti. 1986. *Common Fate, Common Bond: Women in the Global Economy.* London: Pluto Press.

Mizan, Ainon. 1992. "Rural Women's Economic Participation and Decision-Making Power in the Family: A Study on Grameen Bank in Bangladesh." Ph.D. dissertation, Southern Illinois University at Carbondale.

Moser, Carol. 1989. "Gender Planning in the Third World: Meeting Practical and Strategic Gender Needs." *World Development* 17 (Nov.): 1799–1826.

Narotzky, Susana. 1990. "'Not to Be a Burden': Ideologies of the Domestic Group and Women's Work in Rural Catalonia." In *Work without Wages*, ed. Jane L. Collins and Martha Gimenez, 70–88. Albany: State University of New York Press.

Nash, June. 1988a. "The Mobilization of Women in the Bolivian Debt Crisis." In *Women and Work #3*, ed. Barbara Gutek, Laurie Larwood, and Ann Stromberg, 67–86. Beverly Hills, Calif.: Sage.

———,———. 1988b. "Cultural Parameters of Sexism and Racism in the International Division of Labor." In *Racism, Sexism, and the World System*, ed. Joan Smith, Jane Collins, Terrence Hopkins, and Akbar Muhammad, 11–36. Westport, Conn.: Greenwood.

———,———. 1990. "Latin American Women in the World Capitalist Crisis." *Gender & Society* 4 (3): 338–52.

North, Linda. 1988. "The Women Poor of Peru." *Isis: International Women's Journal* 17: 12–14.

Ong, Aihwa. 1987. *Spirits of Resistance and Capitalist Discipline: Factory Women in Malaysia.* Albany: State University of New York Press.

Paguio, B. 1988. "No Bed of Roses for Filipinas Abroad." *Isis: International Women's Journal* 17: 37, 42.

Peña, Devon. 1987. "*Tortuosidad*: Shop Floor Struggles of Female *Maquiladora* Workers." In *Women on the U.S.-Mexico Border: Responses to Change*, ed. Vicki L. Ruiz and Susan Tiano, 129–54. Boston: Allen and Unwin.

Phizacklea, Annie. 1990. *Unpacking the Fashion Industry: Gender, Racism, and Class in Production.* London: Routledge.

Phongpaichit, Pasuk. 1988. "Two Roads to the Factory: Industrialisation Strategies and Women's Employment in Southeast Asia." In *Structures of Patriarchy*, ed. Bina Agarwal, 151–63. London: Zed.

Pineda-Ofreneo, Rosalinda, and Rosario Del Rosario. 1988. "Filipino Women Workers in Strike Actions." In *Daughters in Industry: Work, Skills, and Consciousness of Women*

Workers in Asia, ed. Noleen Heyzer, 308–26. Kuala Lumpur, Malaysia: Asian and Pacific Development Centre.

Portes, Alejandro, Manuel Castells, and Lauren Benton, eds. 1989. *The Informal Economy: Studies in Advanced and Less Developed Countries*. Baltimore: Johns Hopkins University Press.

Pyle, Jean Larson. 1990a. "Export-Led Development and the Underemployment of Women: The Impact of Discriminatory Development Policy in the Republic of Ireland." In *Women Workers and Global Restructuring*, ed. Kathryn Ward, 85–112. Ithaca, NY: ILR Press.

———,———. 1990b. *The State and Women in the Economy: Lessons from Sex Discrimination in the Republic of Ireland*. Albany: State University of New York Press.

Pyle, Jean Larson, and Leslie Dawson. 1990. "The Impact of Multinational Technology Transfer on Female Workforces in Asia." *Columbia Journal of World Business* 25 (4): 40–8.

Redclift, Nanneke, and Enzo Mingione, eds. 1985. *Beyond Employment: Household, Gender, and Subsistence*. Oxford: Basil Blackwell.

Ríos, Palmira N. 1990. "Export-Oriented Industrialization and the Demand for Female Labor: Puerto Rican Women in the Manufacturing Sector, 1952–1980." *Gender & Society* 4 (3): 321–37.

Rollins, Judith. 1985. *Between Women: Domestics and Their Employers*. Philadelphia: Temple University Press.

Rosa, Kumudhini. 1987. "Organizing Women Workers in the Free Trade Zone, Sri Lanka." In *Third World, Second Sex*, ed. Miranda Davies, 159–64. London: Zed.

Rosen, Ellen. 1987. *Bitter Choices: Blue-Collar Women In and Out of Work*. Chicago: University of Chicago Press.

Ruiz, Vicki L. 1987. "By the Day or the Week: Mexicana Domestic Workers in El Paso." In *Women on the U.S.-Mexico Border: Responses to Change*, ed. Vicki L. Ruiz and Susan Tiano, 61–76. Boston: Allen and Unwin.

Ruiz, Vicki L., and Susan Tiano, eds. 1987. *Women on the U.S.- Mexico Border: Responses to Change*. Boston: Allen and Unwin.

Safa, Helen. 1986. "Runaway Shops and Female Employment." In *Women's Work: Development and the Division of Labor by Gender*, ed. Eleanor B. Leacock and Helen I. Safa, 58–71. South Hadley, Mass.: Bergin and Garvey.

Salaff, Janet W. 1988. *State and Family in Singapore: Restructuring an Industrial Society*. Ithaca, NY: Cornell University Press.

Salih, Kamal, and Mei Ling Young. 1989. "Changing Conditions of Labour in the Semiconductor Industry in Malaysia." *Labour and Society* 14: 59–80.

Sassen, Saskia. 1988. *Mobility of Labor and Capital*. Cambridge: Cambridge University Press.

Schmink, Marianne. 1986. "Women and Urban Industrial Development in Brazil." In *Women and Change in Latin America*, ed. June Nash and Helen Safa, 136–64. South Hadley, Mass.: Bergin and Garvey.

Scott, Alison MacEwen. 1986. "Women and Industrialisation: Examining the 'Female Marginalisation' Thesis." *Journal of Development Studies* 22: 649–80.

———,———. 1990. "Patterns of Patriarchy in the Peruvian Working Class." In *Women, Employment, and the Family in the International Division of Labour*, ed. Sharon Stichter and Jane L. Parpart, 198–220. Philadelphia: Temple University Press.

Seidman, Ann. 1985. *The Roots of Crisis in Southern Africa*. Trenton, NJ: Africa World Press.

Sen, Gita, and Caren Grown. 1987. *Development, Crises, and Alternative Visions*. New York: New Feminist Library.

Smith, Joan, Immanuel Wallerstein, and Hans Evers, eds. 1984. *Households and the World Economy*. Beverly Hills, Calif.: Sage.

Standing, Guy. 1989. "Global Feminization through Flexible Labor." *World Development* 17 (7): 1077–95.

Stichter, Sharon. 1990. "Women, Employment, and the Family: Current Debates." In *Women, Employment, and the Family in the International Division of Labour,* ed. Sharon Stichter and Jane L. Parpart, 11–71. Philadelphia: Temple University Press.

Stichter, Sharon, and Jane L. Parpart. 1988a. "Introduction: Towards a Materialist Perspective on African Women." In *Patriarchy and Class: African Women in the Home and the Workforce,* ed. Sharon Stichter and Jane L. Parpart, 1–26. Boulder, Colo.: Westview.

——,——,——. eds. 1988b. *Patriarchy and Class: African Women in the Home and the Workforce.* Boulder, Colo.: Westview.

——,——,——. eds. 1990. *Women, Employment, and the Family in the International Division of Labour.* Philadelphia: Temple University Press.

Sultana, Hazera. 1990. "The Violation of Garment Workers' Human Rights." *SAMACHAR* 3: 3–7.

Talwar Oldenburg, Veena. 1990. "Lifestyle as Resistance: The Case of the Courtesans of Lucknow, India." *Feminist Studies* 16 (2): 259–87.

Tiano, Susan. 1987. "Gender, Work, and World Capitalism." In *Analyzing Gender,* ed. Beth Hess and Myra Marx Ferree, 216–43. Beverly Hills, Calif.: Sage.

——,——. 1990. "*Maquiladora* Women: A New Category of Workers?" In *Women Workers and Global Restructuring,* ed. Kathryn Ward, 193–223. Ithaca, NY: ILR Press.

Tinker, Irene, ed. 1990. *Persistent Inequalities: Women and World Development.* New York: Oxford University Press.

Tokman, Victor E. 1989. "Policies for a Heterogeneous Informal Sector in Latin America." *World Development* 17: 1067–76.

Truelove, Cynthia. 1990. "Disguised Industrial Proletarians in Rural Latin America." In *Women Workers and Global Restructuring,* ed. Kathryn Ward, 48–63. Ithaca, NY: ILR Press.

Truong, Thanh-dam. 1990. *Sex, Money, and Morality: Prostitution and Tourism in Southeast Asia.* London: Zed.

Ward, Kathryn. 1984.

——,——. 1988a. "Female Resistance to Marginalization: The Igbo Women's War of 1929." In *Racism and Sexism in the World System,* ed. Joan Smith, 121–36. Westport, Conn.: Greenwood.

——,——. 1988b. "Women in the Global Economy." In *Women and Work #3,* ed. Barbara Gutek, Laurie Larwood, and Ann Stromberg, 17–48. Beverly Hills, Calif.: Sage.

——,——. ed. 1990a. *Women Workers and Global Restructuring.* Ithaca, NY: ILR Press.

——,——. 1990b. "Introduction and Overview." In *Women Workers and Global Restructuring,* ed. Kathryn Ward, 1–24. Ithaca, NY: ILR Press.

——,——. 1993. "Reconceptualizing World System Theory to Include Women." In *Theory on Gender/Feminism on Theory,* ed. Paula England, 43–68. Hawthorne, NY: Aldine.

Westwood, Sallie. 1985. *All Day, Every Day: Factory and Family in the Making of Women's Lives.* Champaign: University of Illinois Press.

Westwood, Sallie, and Parminder Bhachu. 1988. *Enterprising Women: Ethnicity, Economy, and Gender Relations.* London: Routledge.

Wilson, Fiona. 1991. *Sweaters: Gender, Class, and Workshop-Based Industry in Mexico.* New York: St. Martin's Press.

Wolf, Diane. 1990a. "Linking Women's Labor with the Global Economy: Factory Workers and Their Families in Rural Java." In *Women Workers and Global Restructuring,* ed. Kathryn Ward, 25–47. Ithaca, NY: ILR Press.

——,——. 1990b. "Daughters, Decisions, and Domination: An Empirical and Conceptual Critique of Household Strategies." *Development and Change* 21: 43–74.

——,——. 1993. *Factory Daughters, Their Families, and Rural Industrialization in Central Java.* Berkeley: University of California Press.

Yelvington, Kevin A. 1993. "Gender and Ethnicity at Work in a Trinidadian Factory." In *Women and Change in the Caribbean: A Pan-Caribbean Perspective*, ed. Janet Momsen, 263–77. London: Methuen.

Young, Gay. 1987. "Gender Identification and Working-Class Solidarity among *Maquila* Workers in Ciudad Juárez." In *Women on the U.S.-Mexico Border: Responses to Change*, ed. Vicki L. Ruiz and Susan Tiano, 105–28. Boston: Allen and Unwin.

Zavella, Patricia. 1988. "The Politics of Race and Gender: Organizing Chicana Cannery Workers in Northern California." In *Women and the Politics of Empowerment*, ed. Ann Bookman and Sandra Morgen, 202–24. Philadelphia: Temple University Press.

21 Development after Ecology (1995)

Bob Sutcliffe

Bob Sutcliffe is professor at the Institute for the Study of Development and the International Economy (Hegoa), at the University of the Basque Country, Bilbao, Spain. Sutcliffe here blasts the development community for ignoring the mountains of evidence that indicate that global development itself is impossible, since it would be ecologically unsustainable. He argues that the core assumptions of development are all incorrect: that it will not solve the human welfare needs of the majority, that nations do not develop as a unit, and that the obstacles are not only human. Sutcliffe argues that development is in reality going in the wrong direction: the underdeveloped countries would be much better models for sustainable societies than the developed ones. Despite the strength of ecological arguments such as Sutcliffe's and the persistence of environmental concerns since 1970, the mainstream literature on development continues to nearly entirely ignore these fundamental concerns. An opportunity to redirect development has been lost with the hijacking and watering-down of the term "sustainability."

... Today the echoes of that great debate have become fainter. What became of it? Why did it recede? Part of the answer is that the world threw up facts and problems which seemed important but which could not be easily explained or answered by either side in the great debate. The growth of the NICs seemingly violated the expectations of the rejectionists and helped to throw their paradigm into crisis. And the accumulation of development disasters, especially in Africa, along with the reverses associated with the debt crisis and worsening terms of trade seemed to confound the optimism of the proponents of mutual benefit. But, with the benefit of hindsight, we can also see that there was another reason that the debate receded: although at the time it had seemed to be based on profound disagreement, there was much more common ground than appeared. In debates, things on which both sides agree don't seem to be important at the time and so are ignored. Yet they may in the end turn out to be more significant than the matters which are debated. And so, in my view, it proved with the great development debate.

What was it that all the sides agreed on? First, there was an idea of what development would be like. It was, roughly speaking, thought to be similar to the situation which existed in the developed countries, which of course is why they were so called. Development was a place on the conceptual map somewhere between the

United States, Western Europe and Japan. These countries might not be perfect but no one questioned most aspects of their (especially economic) characteristics: industrialization, the use of modern, highly productive technology, high levels of employment of productive workers working with machines for about eight hours a day, high average standards of living, efficiency, punctuality, longevity, the elimination of most deaths from infectious diseases ... the familiar list can be long.

The second shared idea was that there was a close or even automatic connection between these economic aspects of development (especially rising production and productivity) and the meeting of basic needs and human welfare. Some held that development would after a time automatically equalize benefits, others believed that the state might have to intervene, still others thought that the best that the poor could expect was what trickled down from the rich. But all believed that national material riches (development) would or could result in greater human welfare. In other words, they believed that development was desirable.

The third issue they all seemed to agree on was that the idea of development applied first and foremost to countries or nations. That is why the characteristics of development already listed refer basically to the structure of national economies. It also explains why the predominant attitude to human welfare was that it was a sub-product of national development.

The fourth clause of the tacit accords was that, if there were obstacles to the universalization of development, then these were social, economic and political (domestic or international) but not natural. It seldom occurred to any participant in the great debate that universal development to European/Japanese/United States levels might not be materially possible. If everyone had some conception (sometimes implicit) of the relation between development and welfare almost no one thought about the connection between development and the physical environment.

The fifth clause is closely related to the fourth. Universal development was implicitly expected to produce an equalization between countries. This would be through a levelling up. So equalization did not imply redistribution (i.e. those at the top being brought down so that those at the bottom could gain). The famous aid target of 0.7 per cent of GNP was the most daring redistribution that anyone proposed. And the rejectors of mutual benefit in general saw deliberate redistribution through aid as a fraud or a poisoned chalice.

The sixth accord was that development was seen as a permanent state. There was a kind of socio-economic ratchet and countries were not expected to revert to underdevelopment once development had been attained.

Not everyone who was interested in development and underdevelopment thought that the great debate over mutual benefit was the most important one. Some people didn't hold the six shared assumptions and so tried to launch different debates. But for a long time they were regarded as fairly marginal to the real issues; the time for their ideas was still to come.

Doubts About the Destination and the Validity of the Map

... It is in this context that the environment makes its first appearance. An important facet of this many-sided destinational critique of development arose out of the sudden growth in awareness of the effect of human activities on the environment and the resulting impact on the conditions of human existence. Development produces pollution of many kinds and this means that any benefits of development can be partly or wholly offset by worse conditions of life. Many of these disadvantages (air and water quality, for instance) were only too obvious; others (like the health effects of asbestos, electric fields, nuclear power, noise, diet) were revealed by scientific research. In this sense growing ecological awareness was no more than one more strand in the critique of the desirability of the previously unquestioned development destination.

Environmental consciousness and research, however, also gave rise to a different concern which often appears to transcend the others, not because it is intrinsically more important but because it portends happenings which would make the other debates redundant. In the early 1970s many people began to foretell the imminent exhaustion of the material resources on which development had been based (Meadows and others 1972); later came the predictions of climatic and other changes resulting from actually existing development which would at best shortly inflict profound changes on the physical conditions of human life and might at worst rapidly make it impossible, through the overuse of resources or the overproduction of wastes. Here the concern is not merely that development has undesirable side-effects on human life but rather that it, and in particular its generalization, might make human life impossible.

The influence of environmental questions in the development debate is new. Until very recently authoritative texts on development appeared which made no reference to it. And, once incorporated into the debate, it produced very varying reactions regarding its practical and methodological importance. Even for those who regard environmental questions as important in development there are some who see them as factors which must be taken account of within a basically unchanged, if slightly more complicated, methodology (for example, Mikesell 1992 and Pierce, Barbier and Markandya 1990) and others who see them as demanding a drastic methodological change. Some see the environmental problem as confirming the need for rapid economic growth (World Bank 1992) while others see it as demanding a cessation of growth and a radical reorganization of human social life (Daly 1991, Trainer 1985 and 1989).

Thus the great debate about the route to development, which displaced debates about the appropriate vehicle, has itself been to a great extent displaced by two different ones about, respectively, the desirability and the possibility of the previously posited destination. From now on I will refer to these as being about the welfare critique and the environmental critique. The welfare critique asks if a destination of development different from the one normally posited would not be better. The environmental critique questions whether the normally posited destination actually exists if it is pursued by all. In other words it argues that the current state of the world, or at least the state towards which it is heading, is materially unsustainable. ...

Common Features of Existing Development Critiques

These two critiques of actually existing development (the welfare critique and the environmental critique) have a number of important features in common. In the first place, both of them, in different ways, see actually existing development as a partly contradictory process. The proponents of the welfare critique question the assumed positive relation between development and welfare and even suggest that actually existing development may produce negative consequences for human welfare and thus be undesirable.

The environmental critique embodies an even sharper notion of the contradictory nature of actually existing development. It sees the possibility or probability that such development will undermine its own material base and so become impossible to maintain. So, a phenomenon whose global generalization was previously regarded, almost axiomatically, as both desirable and possible is seen as neither: attempting to produce something regarded as good produces something else which is to a significant extent bad and which progressively destroys the chance of producing anything at all.

The second common feature of the welfare and environmental critiques, largely a by-product of the first, is their rejection of the most commonly used indicators of development, especially the national product (GNP) or national income. As a measure of welfare or development this concept has received so many criticisms during its history that it is really surprising that it continues to be economists' most successful export to the rest of the world. Nonetheless, national income and national product continue to be the most commonly employed economic statistics: a remarkable violation of the economists' principle of the virtues of the market!

The proponents of the welfare critique point out two drawbacks to using the well-known measures of national income or product as indicators of economic welfare. First, they assign equal value to a dollar's worth of production of arms or untruthful advertising on the one hand as to a dollar's worth of medicines or literature on the other. This means that there is a relative undervaluation of those activities which contribute to human welfare. Second, they value a dollar of income of a millionaire on a par with a dollar of income of a poor person when the latter is obviously "worth" more.

The proponents of the environmental critique also make two main criticisms of the calculation of the national income or product. The first refers to its way of dealing with pollution and its ill effects. Nothing is subtracted from the figure for national income to take into account the "negative externalities" of pollution. (Hence, assuming these are greater than positive externalities, the national income is overestimated). Even more absurd, if action is taken to rectify the bad effects of pollution (for example, expenditure on cleaning up a river polluted by industrial waste) such expenditures appear as positive in the national income figures. In other words it is possible for the *cost* of contamination to appear as a *benefit* in the national income, not only once but in some cases twice!

The second criticism refers to the conversion of the national income or product figures from "gross" value to "net" value in order to take into account the part of the capital stock which is used up in the production process; but the capital considered here is only capital created by human investment and, wrongly, does not include the natural resources used up (see Daly 1988). These criticisms, like those from the side of the welfare critique, lead to the conclusion that the national income or product figures tend to overvalue enormously what is really "produced" by human economies and what is really "earned" by their participants.

The two critiques coincide on a third point. Both reject the idea, one of the main characteristics of earlier development thinking, that development is a process in which the "underdeveloped" progressively approach the state of the "developed". This coincidence leads to a fourth: both see development not so much as a problem of some countries (underdeveloped ones) which the developed countries have overcome but rather as a problem for the world. The environmental critique emphasizes global interdependence, while the welfare critique draws attention to deficiencies in meeting needs in both rich and poor countries.

A fifth point which the critiques have in common is their concern with distribution and equity – between rich and poor, both within and between nations (welfare) and between present and future, or between generations (environmental), a point to which I will return later.

Finally the critiques share a sixth characteristic that they are not at all new. Every one of the arguments mentioned up to now was present in economic debates more than a century ago. The modern critique of development is as much a revivalist as an original phenomenon.

There is a parallel between the beginning of the great debate about mutual benefit and these new development debates which has aided their impact. Rejectors of mutual benefit argued that the previous debates about development policy were all but irrelevant if they took place in the context of an unequal global socio-economic environment which prevented development. Those who advocated major social change as a necessary preliminary to development, therefore, seemed to be positing something more basic as the main discussion. Economic policy debates seemed trivial in comparison with the choice between capitalism and socialism. Now, similarly, both the welfare and the environmental critiques of development appear to define a problem which is in some way logically prior to the question of the socio-economic system. If humans do not benefit from it, and if it is materially impossible, it hardly seems to matter under what social system generalized development takes place. If such a line of thinking helps to explain the present interest in these issues, they are not, as I shall reassert later, soluble in isolation from the question of the socio-economic and political system. ...

The Importance of Redistribution

Defined as they have been here, both critical concepts (human and sustainable development) involve an improvement in the relative access to resources of excluded groups: the poor in the case of human development; future generations (and perhaps other species) in the case of sustainable development. Human development without attention to sustainability improves distribution in the present at the cost of worsening the distribution between present and future (the unborn subsidize the poor). At the same time sustainability without human development means maintaining the material levels of the over-endowed and reducing the levels of the poor, thus worsening distribution in the present (the poor subsidize the unborn and the rich).

There is a way out of this ugly contradiction: redistribution in the present. If the negative environmental impact of human activity, for which the rich of today are primarily responsible, is mitigated then any given improvement in the situation of the poor becomes more sustainable. To put the same point in another way: if negative environmental impacts are reduced then it will be more difficult to implement human development unless the rich (nations, classes and individuals) of today accept a disproportionate decline in their use of resources and production of wastes.

The conflict between the poor of today and the unborn exists to the extent that a real reduction in the negative environmental impact of the rich of today is not contemplated. Thus, human development is in danger of being unsustainable unless there is redistribution; and sustainable development is in danger of being anti-human unless it is accompanied by redistribution.

Looked at in this way, the two concepts of development and the two forms of redistribution which they imply are seen to be mutually reinforcing. Present and future justice demands that they be pursued simultaneously. They entail different (but not necessarily contradictory) kinds of changes. But they have one major common implication: to pursue both together demands a considerable reduction in the use of resources and production of pollutants by the people, classes and nations which are now rich and over-endowed. It is the same people at the same time who are wastefully using the resources needed both by today's deprived and by the unborn. If the waste continues then either human development or sustainable development or both will not be possible, or at the very least will be more difficult.

The general desire for development, about which such disillusion has been generated, should then be replaced by one not for human development nor sustainable development alone but for sustainable human development in which both kinds of redistribution are effected. Large scale redistribution of the use of resources in the world seems to be a necessary condition for sustainable human development.

The historical moment when increasing numbers of people are reaching such conclusions has, ironically, coincided with a period of triumph for the ideology of the free market which tends to produce contrary effects. The recent ascendency of free market ideologies is perversely associated with the rise of environmentalist and welfare concerns. The "all power to the free market" faction in the old debates about the route to development has held together because they argue that the new questions really make no difference. Since for them free capitalist enterprise maximizes growth and income, and that people on the whole in a market system get what they want, questions about the persistence of deprivation or the environmental depletion and pollution are not bothersome. This convenient aspect of their doctrines is certainly not the only reason for their remarkable spread during the 1980s; but, given the disarray and confusion which the new debates produced among their former opponents, it probably made a contribution.

Related to the neo-liberal counter-revolution is a growing disillusion with mechanisms of redistribution in the world. The amount of international aid, except from a few countries, and for purposes which benefit the economy of the donor, is in decline. Welfare state measures which were established, and which really redistributed income when countries were poorer than they are now, are, by some wonderland logic, threatened because, now that those countries are richer, it is said that they can no longer afford them. There has been little sign of major redistribution of income between countries. During the two decades from 1970 to 1989, according to Gini coefficients, overall world inequality either remained the same or worsened, depending on the method of conversion used. According to all methods, East Asia increased its share of the world's product faster than its share of the population while Africa's share of population increased while its share of world product decreased as did its absolute level of income per head. There is evidence of a major redistribution towards the rich in a number of developed countries (in Britain the post-tax personal income of the richest 20 per cent of the population has doubled as a multiple of that of the poorest 20 per cent since 1979 (Sandford 1993 quoting HM Treasury)) as well as in some underdeveloped ones, especially in Latin America (World Bank 1993). In the absence of major political change, therefore, we must at present acknowledge that the times are not very propitious for the major redistribution necessary as a concomitant of sustainable human development.

It is, of course, very difficult to quantify the amounts by which pollution and resource depletion need to fall and so the degree of redistribution which is necessary. But in some areas research which enables us to make more reliable calculations is accumulating rapidly. The enormous data base on carbon emissions produced by the Carbon Dioxide Information Analysis Center in the United States has been widely used to spell out the dimensions of the problem. . . . Some climatologists have argued that to stabilize CO_2 concentrations in the atmosphere it will be necessary to reduce the average level of per head emissions to about the current level of India . . . . If such an aim is deemed to be necessary then the transformation in the lifestyles of rich countries (and in the way in which poor countries try to change theirs) will be profound, for many people, perhaps, unthinkably so.

Such data as these have had the effect of presenting in a very dramatic way the scale of the task and also the relative division of current responsibility for the problem. If it is the moral duty of the polluter to change then such figures as these can perform an important political role in weakening the bargaining power of the great polluters. The battle over international redistribution will be in part a battle over indicators and their interpretation (Agarwal and Narain 1991 and World Resources Institute 1992).

Rescuing the Baby

If inequality and how to end it are questions central to the achievement of sustainable human development, we must go beyond defining concepts and attempt to give them concrete meaning. We must look to the causes of the persistence of inequalities. That surely means that we must go back to the debates about development which the new concerns have partially ousted. The rejectors of "mutual benefit" analysed the obstacles on the route to development. Although the debates about destination have questioned their concept of development, the same or related obstacles also stand in the way on the road to sustainable human development; many of the arguments of the rejectors of mutual benefit are still valid in relation to redefined objectives.

An essential part of most rejectionist analyses of the world was that various mechanisms in the world economy produced a systematic transfer of value from poor countries to rich countries (through unequal exchange and the false invoicing of exports and imports by multinational companies, the repatriation of profits, the service of the debt and so on). In so far as this transfer of value exists (and each item has provoked controversy) it constitutes a perverse redistribution of income which can only worsen the conditions for achieving sustained human development. Regardless of one's assessment of the overall argument there is no doubt that the transfer of resources from poor to rich has on some counts risen in recent years. The two most notable items here are the enormous service of the debt since the early 1980s (Sutcliffe 1993a) and the sharp adverse movement in the terms of trade of primary products since the mid-1970s (Maizels 1992).

These events can only have had negative environmental impacts in the poorer countries. Not only do they drain resources which can in principle be used for constructive purposes, including environmental improvement, but they also tend to produce a race to acquire foreign exchange either to pay debt service or to compensate for declining export earnings. This race can lead to the development of new environmentally unsound activities such as the production of some commercial agricultural export crops or overfelling of tropical forests for timber exports; and they may discourage necessary protective investments (Cruz and Repetto 1992). They also lead to a desperate desire to reduce costs and to become more competitive which among other things may encourage a lax (cheap) environmental protection regime. And they have probably led to overexploitation of some non-renewable resources resulting in the excessive rundown of reserves and lower prices which might disguise situations of shortage (Bunker and O'Hearn 1992). This is an argument against those economists who argue that price signals will control any tendency towards the excessive depletion of non-renewable resources.

Integral to some rejectionist accounts of the world has been the notion of unequal exchange through which, it is argued, rich developed countries have in the long run received imports from poor countries at prices below their values. Hardly ever has this argument taken into account the considerations now commonly raised by ecological economists that the extraction of non-renewable resources has always taken place at a cost far below its real cost since the natural stock of the material is not valued. In this sense the ecological argument vastly strengthens the argument for the existence of unequal exchange since poor countries have for centuries depleted their non-renewable resources, largely for export to the developed countries, and in so doing have literally given away a part of their patrimony (Martinez Alier 1987).

Thus ecological arguments strengthen some aspects of the rejectionist (or, if you like, dependency theory) analysis of the world; and at least important parts of this analysis remain, therefore, a necessary foundation for understanding the obstacles to sustainable human development. If development needs to be redefined, then so equally does underdevelopment. We are now witnessing a rapid accumulation of writings which in effect demonstrate how environmental and welfare deterioration have been and are in many cases the consequences of inequalities in the international distribution of wealth and power. The development of underdevelopment has also been the development of unsustainability. Hence the new debate should not be allowed to displace completely the old one. In the rush to reexamine dependency theory and criticize some of its undoubted limitations, the baby of rejectionism should not be thrown out with the bathwater of actual existing development.

Where in the World is Development?

I have argued that the tacit accords with which development was approached have been shattered by the persistence of extreme mass privation in an ever more developed world and by growing evidence of the environmental destructiveness of actually existing development. Out of a response to these two contradictions of the process a different concept of sustainable human development is being constructed which suggests directions of change which are radically different from the directions suggested by more traditional concepts of development.

The old map of development is now difficult to use when choosing the direction in which to proceed. Some of the environmentalist critiques of actually existing development imply that it is difficult to know exactly where we are on the map, concretely how close we are to an ecological precipice. If the starting point is in part indefinable, the destination is also in many ways mysterious. But we can say that a more rational concept of development directed towards equalizing welfare and sustainability will be radically different from every one of the five shared assumptions of the tacit accords mentioned earlier.

1. The present nature of the developed countries is not an appropriate destination. Their level of resource use and the volume of contamination which they produce are the main generators of the global environmental crisis. Despite their prodigal use of resources they are unable to meet the human needs of large sections of their populations. The globalization of the characteristics of developed countries would surely make the planet uninhabitable.

   In terms of the level of the use of resources per head a destination appropriate for the whole world must be much closer to the existing situation in most underdeveloped countries than in developed ones. ...

   Current underdeveloped country levels of consumption, if generalized, would evidently be dramatically more sustainable that those of developed countries. There are other respects, too, in which underdeveloped countries often, if by no means always, offer a better model than developed ones: for instance, the persistence in some places of more sustainable forms of agricultural production[1] and healthier vegetable-based diets which are less costly in resources; there are some examples where common rights are better maintained; and others where mechanisms of social solidarity and redistribution are more intact.

   Actually existing development has been so far from sustainable human development that such a destination is likely to be at least as distant from the present location of the developed countries as from the underdeveloped ones. Development in this sense is something which has not yet occurred anywhere and which is, therefore, a valid objective in both developed and underdeveloped countries.

2. The traditional concept of development tended to assume that welfare would be a by-product. This becomes less convincing by the day. Improving human welfare on a permanent and secure basis seems to demand that it is clearly defined and is made into a primary objective of development, again in both developed and underdeveloped countries. Economic and productive change then becomes a by-product of the pursuit of welfare improvement.

3. The new critiques of development undermine in various ways the idea that the appropriate unit of development is a country or nation. In so far as development is the fulfilment of social need it has many appropriate units: the individual, the family, the village, the city, the social group identified by ethnic origin, sex, sexuality, age and so on. While it is appropriate that the government of states

assume important tasks in promoting human development, neither the power of the state nor the average material level within a country are appropriate indicators of development. Sustainability also imposes duties on national governments but it also points to other needed levels of analysis. The notion of sustainability can be applied locally, globally and anywhere in between (Jacobs 1991: 96–8). Perhaps the most resolute decisions in approaching sustainability need to be taken globally; some actions of a single nation state may be pointless unless they are part of general enforceable international agreements. And the same applies to local in relation to national decisions .... Sustainability, to make sense, requires action and change at all these levels together.

4. The old development debate assumed that in some way or other universal development according to the old model was possible. It now seems clear that it is not. The implication of this is that as long as the developed countries maintain their unglobalizable way of life they will in both open and hidden ways prevent development elsewhere.

5. The fifth shared assumption of the debate must therefore be abandoned along with the fourth: that equalization of development levels could occur without a major reduction in the resources used by the rich and developed. If sustainability makes it clear that such a redistribution must take place, the abandonment of the second shared assumption suggests that to reduce resource use and pollution is not necessarily to reduce the level of fulfilment of welfare, though it may involve reduced material production and reduced GDP ....

Even in the absence of such a redistribution, it still makes sense for the people of underdeveloped countries to try to construct forms of sustainable human development. They can at least make gains in relation to welfare and local sustainability. But they can hardly be expected to make material sacrifices in order to contribute to global sustainability when this is continually undermined by the ways of life of part of the population of the rich developed countries.

Who Wants Development? The Problem of the Driver

The extreme degrees of material inequality which exist in the world today, both between and within nations, is both a strength and weakness of the quest for sustainable human development. It is a strength because it means that there is scope for a considerable amount of redistribution of resources, as a result of which simultaneously a very small minority lose part of what they have, the deprived majority may have more of what they need, and the overall amount of resources used may be reduced, thus allowing more for the use of future generations. The weakness is that it is the very same minority which monopolizes most of the political and military power and the economic wealth which it uses to maintain its share.

There seems no sign that this minority, any more than any other in history, will voluntarily relinquish its privileges. So it seems impossible to imagine that the world can go far towards sustainable human development without destroying the power and removing the wealth of this minority. Sustainable human development is thus a task demanding radical mass political action. If we think of vehicles and routes, of maps and destinations we are in danger of reducing the problem of development to a technocratic one. While it is important to know the relationship between actuality and objective possibility, in other words to have a sense of destination, there remain the questions of the vehicle and the route (the appropriate socio-economic systems and policies) and perhaps above all the question of the driver (how a development process is managed and directed politically). These questions are closely related. The idea of human development logically requires popular participation, democracy, equity and justice both as part of the destination and part of the conditions for the journey. In other words development is not just the destination; it is also the process of reaching it.

If that is clear for the human part of sustainable human development it may also be true in a different way for the sustainable part. Part of the cause of unsustainability is the exclusion of the majority from taking a full and informed part in decisions about economic activities. The environmental knowledge of people who live and produce in very "underdeveloped conditions" and their ability to live in a complex symbiosis with the environment is often very remarkable and contrasts with the ignorance and hostility to the environment often produced by development.

The political basis of the concept of sustainable human development which I have tried to outline in this chapter must appear to be a surrealistic alliance between those who are excluded from the benefits of actually existing development: unborn generations and the living poor and disposessed. But surreal does not necessarily mean illogical. The only hope for a radical redistribution towards the future is a radical redistribution away from the rich in the present. If greater equality in the present is one of the traditional concerns of red politics, greater equality between generations is an essential characteristic of the new green politics. But not all reds are yet green; nor do all greens look as if they will become reds. The future of sustainable human development depends on a more thorough mixing of colours.

NOTE

1. World Resources Institute 1992, p. 36, for a summary of various studies which reach this conclusion.

REFERENCES

Agarwal, Anil and Narain, S. (1991) *Global Warming in an Unequal World: a case study of environmental colonialism*. Centre for Science and Environment, Delhi.

Bunker, S.G. and O'Hearn, D. (1992) *Raw materials access strategies – US and Japan*: Draft, University of Wisconsin.

Cruz, W. and Repetto, R. (1992) *Structural adjustment and sustainable development in the Philippines*. World Resources Institute, New York.

Daly, H.E. (1988) "On sustainable development and national accounts" in D. Collard, D. Pearce and D. Ulph (eds) *Economics, Growth and Sustainable Environments: essays in memory of Richard Lecomber*. Macmillan, London pp 41–56.

Daly, H.E. (1991) *Steady-state economics* (2nd ed). Island Press, Washington DC.

Jacobs, M. (1991) *The Green Economy*. Pluto Press, London.

Maizels, A. (1992) *Commodities in Crisis*. Oxford University Press, Oxford.

Martinez Alier, J. (1987) *Ecological Economics: energy, environment and society*. Basil Blackwell, Oxford.

Meadows, D.H. et al (1972) *Limits to growth*. Universe Books, New York.

Mikesell, R. (1992) *Economic development and the environment: a comparison of sustainable development with conventional development economics*. Mansell, London and New York.

Pearce, D., Barbier, E. and Markandya, A. (1990) *Sustainable development: economics and the environment in the Third World*. Edward Elgar, London.

Sandford, C. (1993) "How Lamont can square the circle." *Financial Times*, 11 March 1993.

Sutcliffe, B. (1993a) *The burden of Third World debt*. Kingston University Apex Centre, Kingston upon Thames.

Trainer, T. (1985) *Abandon affluence*. Zed, London.

Trainer, T. (1989) *Developed to death: rethinking Third World development*. Green Print, London.

World Bank (1992) *World Development Report: Development and the environment*. Oxford University Press, Oxford and New York.

World Bank (1993) *Poverty and Income Distribution in Latin America: the story of the 1980s*. World Bank Human Resources Division, Washington DC.

World Resources Institute (1992) *World Resources 1992–93*. Oxford University Press, New York and Oxford.

22 Social Movements and Global Capitalism (1995)

Leslie Sklair

Lecturer at the London School of Economics and author of *Sociology of the Global System*, Leslie Sklair here argues that "globalizing capitalism has all but defeated labor." Therefore, he says, we need to pay much more attention to other social movements, such as women's groups, neighborhood organizations, environmentalists, lesbian and gay groups, civil rights groups, and the peace movement. However, these groups all have difficulty targeting the sources of their problems. Sklair argues that consumerism, as part of modernization, has completely replaced other ideologies (belief systems) and has distracted the attention of all people from the real damages they are suffering as a result of globalization. He observes that new social movements only organize successfully against local opponents, but need to link with other movements around the world to successfully counter the global capitalist elite. Sklair proposes the unusual suggestion that one useful strategy to counter the trap of modernization and globalization is to fight consumerism.

Introduction

This paper begins with some ground-clearing work, namely a brief and selective review of recent contributions to the literatures on "social movements" and "globalisation". The central argument is that while capitalism is increasingly organised on a global basis, effective opposition to capitalist practices tends to be manifest locally.

The traditional response of the labour movement to global capitalism has been to try to forge links between workers' organisations internationally. As is being argued increasingly by those of all anti-capitalist persuasions, this strategy, despite some notable successes, has generally failed. Most of the debate has focused on whether this is due to some sea-change in workers' consciousness or is more of an organisational question. The argument here is that a key issue is the globalisation of capitalism in the economic, political and culture-ideology spheres, and that important theoretical and substantive questions for social movements research are the extent to which the characteristic institutional expressions of this globalisation – transnational corporations, transnational capitalist classes and the culture-ideology of consumerism – can be resisted locally. The *local* is defined in terms of sub-global communities that can be meaningfully represented through collective action. The *global* and the *local*, in this context, are not exclusively geographical terms but have organisational and representational dimensions.

Theory and Research on Social Movements

Social movements, under a variety of labels, have always been of interest to socio-logists. The literature, unsurprisingly, is enormous and it is significant that "social movements research" which used to be rather marginal is now being drawn into the centre of social theory, particularly under the rubric of "New Social Movements" (NSMs). For example, two recent books Eder (1993) and Ray (1993), in rather different ways, convincingly argue this position in terms of a "new politics of class" and "critical theory" respectively. The argument that, even when they are not apparently interested in seizing state power, New Social Movements can still be as sociologically interesting as, say, revolutionary movements has in some ways liber-ated the study of them.

The idea of New Social Movements has proved extremely useful both methodo-logically and ideologically. Methodologically, it points to the unmistakable novelty of the practices (for example, the use of credit card donations and the media for mobilisation) and the appeal of some of the most prominent social movements of recent decades, notably the women's and environmental movements. Ideologically, NSM theory and research also provide ammunition for those who proclaim that the working class as a revolutionary force organised through the labour (and/or trade union) movement is finally dead. From the first publication of Herbert Marcuse's *One-Dimensional Man* in 1964 to the project of Touraine (1981; and Touraine *et al.* 1987), and before and after, this thesis has had many adherents. Whether from Marcuse's impressionistic eloquence or from Touraine's empirical research-based analysis, the central idea is the same: the working class cannot hope to defeat national or global capitalism and, even more seriously, NSM "weaken working class consciousness and erode its self-confidence, rather than providing new sources of energy for it" (Touraine *et al.* 1987: 224).

Three books of the 1990s, far removed geographically, rather different in sub-stance, but not so far removed theoretically, take up these issues fruitfully. Each in its own way illuminates the issue of the relationship of the NSMs and the labour movement in very concrete terms and connects this with the opposition between what can be identified as "organisation" models and "disruption" models of social movements and resistances to capitalism. Gail Omvedt's *Reinventing Revolution: New Social Movements and the Socialist Tradition in India* (1993) is a major study which points out that the notable Indian social movements since the 1970s have not been traditional Marxist class ones, but movements of women, low castes, peasants, farmers, tribals, ethnic groups. None of them, Omvedt argues, has effected much change, but they have tended to be movements of groups either ignored or exploited by traditional Marxism or exploited in new ways (for example, environmentally). So, while Marxism has traditionally been a historical materialism of the proletariat, what is needed, she argues, is an historical materialism of all oppressed groups and their varying forms of oppression. With an impressive degree of clarity, Omvedt attempts this for the anti-caste, women's, farmers' and environmental movements in

India and argues that New Social Movements are best defined as movements that redefine spheres of exploitation (especially economic exploitation) which are not properly addressed by traditional Marxism: thus the choice of the four NSMs at the centre of her book. Conflicts between toilers and those who directly employ them play a relatively small role in Indian NSMs. Wage struggles are not central, more important are encroachments on state or landlord lands and peasant struggles for community control; job reservation for anti-caste groups; women's struggles against male property rights; higher prices for farmers. These struggles and the disruptions they produce are directed as much against state agencies as against capitalists. The inescapable conclusion of this analysis is that Marxism definitely needs to be rethought and the idea of revolution needs to be reinvented. Central to this rethinking and reinvention is that NSMs are not necessarily aiming to seize state power, but use many tactics to achieve many shorter-term ends. Indeed, this argument can be expanded to suggest that the actual revolutionary consequences of such movements can far exceed the rhetorical revolutionary utterances of most movements dedicated to seizing state power.

Verity Burgmann's *Power and Protest: Movements for Change in Australian Society* (1993) is a study of five key NSMs in Australia: the black (aborigine), women's, lesbian and gay, peace and green movements. Despite the large differences (only two of the movements overlap) there are some surprising parallels with Omvedt's book. Burgmann argues that NSMs tend to represent the better off among the disadvantaged, and that NSMs frequently lose control of the ways their demands are conceded. As all these movements take place in capitalist societies, albeit of different types, class relations mediate what is possible: "It is for this reason that the support of the labour movement, with its ability seriously to contest the power relations based on class, offers the best potential means for more substantial gains to be achieved by the movements for change" (1993: 263). But the labour movement has to change too, and modified for the Indian case, this is also Omvedt's conclusion. The problem is how to forge links of solidarity between people as workers and as more or less oppressed in other social spheres. Research such as that reported in Hayter and Harvey (1993) on the relationships between workers at Cowley in Oxford and local community groups shows exactly how difficult this can be.

The title of Brecher and Costello's contribution to this debate, *Building Bridges: The Emerging Grassroots Coalition of Labor and Community* (1990), at least names the question. The new social alliance, they argue, is unheralded nationally in the USA because it is being built at the grassroots, where the mass media have little interest: "These coalitions have generally been created without the dominance of a single unifying organization, program, or leader. Rather they have been constructed by active efforts of mutual outreach – by 'bridge building'" (1990: 9). Most surprising is the participation of unionists, evidence of some breakdown in the traditional separation of labour from social movements. The array of projects and movements described in this collection is certainly impressive, though it is difficult to work through the very disparate causes that lie behind these social movements in order to see the wood for the trees.

The evidence arrayed in these books, and others like them, suggest that NSM theory needs to rethink the dichotomy between *labour movement* and *new social movement*. This is necessary because insufficient attention has been paid to two factors, namely the organisational question and the changing nature of global capitalism, the globalisation question. For the first of these Piven and Cloward (1979) propose an uncompromising proposition. Fundamentally, they argue that the success of a movement depends not on its organisational prowess but on its ability to disrupt, so collective defiance is the key to social movements. The reason why movements fail is to be found in the capacity of the authorities to divert their disruptive force into normal politics, usually with the collaboration of the movement organisers. This is, of course, not an entirely novel thesis. At least since Michels's *Political Parties* (first published in 1911), the idea that the workers' leaders would be likely to subordinate revolutionary goals to bureaucratic means has been a commonplace. Acknowledging the difficulty of retaining revolutionary goals within a capitalist or a Stalinist communist society while actually improving the lot of those whose interests the movement is intended to serve, might soften some of the moral outrage felt about such leaders, but it does little to solve the problem of the successes and failures of social movements. Burgmann puts this in an oblique but significant way: "The relative purity and incorruptibility of the leaders of new social movements attests not to their moral superiority but to their relative powerlessness ... You cannot sell out if you have nothing to sell ... The corruptibility of the labour movement is evidence of its real political power, for good or evil" (1993: 264). And when NSMs are seen to have power, they too can sell out.

While their approach has been criticised on a variety of grounds (for example, by Castells 1983), Piven and Cloward have elaborated a theoretically coherent and empirically researchable set of theses on this very problem. So, we can see how the militants of the workers' movements, the civil rights movement and the national (and local) welfare rights organisation (whom Piven and Cloward so evocatively document), each in their own ways, tried, succeeded, or failed to establish, different connections in their struggles against "the system". Touraine, in his influential studies of the workers' movement, and Piven/Cloward make one essentially similar point, which might be seen as a defining moment for the problem of social movements in its totality. Piven and Cloward write: "*people cannot defy institutions to which they have no access, and to which they make no contribution*" (1979: 23, italics in original); Touraine and his colleagues write: "As well as finding increasing difficulty in self-definition, the working class actor is also finding it increasingly hard to identify his [sic] adversary" (Touraine *et al.* 1987: 109). On the surface these *appear* to be opposing rather than similar points, Piven and Cloward arguing that people cannot defy institutions that exclude them, Touraine arguing that workers no longer know whom to oppose. But they are, in reality, mirror images of the same dilemma, which can be identified as the local and the global. The dilemma is that the only chance that people in social movements have to succeed is by disrupting the local agencies with which they come into direct contact in their daily lives, rather than the more global institutions whose interests these agencies are serving directly, or, more often, indirectly, while workers are often confused about whom (which representation of capital) to oppose when their interests (conditions of labour, livelihoods) are threatened. Increasingly, as capitalism globalises, subordinate groups find difficulty in identifying their adversaries.

Now neither Touraine nor Piven and Cloward says anything like this; neither mentions local-global issues. The implication in their works is that labour and other types of social movements are national not global. There have been few, if any, examples of successful movements against the global capitalist system, which is not very surprising. As Tilly and others have argued, most social movements have developed in relation to the nation state. If we are, indeed, entering a phase of global capitalism we might expect this to change. The next section outlines one conception of globalisation with a view to clarifying how global capitalism works, and to begin to construct the argument that while contemporary capitalism is organised globally, it can only be resisted locally.

Global System Theory

Globalisation is a relatively new idea in sociology, though in other disciplines like international business studies and international relations, it has been common for some time. The central feature of the idea of globalisation is that many contemporary problems cannot be adequately studied at the level of nation states, that is, in terms of *international* relations, but need to be theorised in terms of *global* (*transnational*) processes, beyond the level of the nation state. Globalisation researchers have focused on two new phenomena that have become significant in the last few decades: (i) qualitative and quantitative changes in the transnational corporations (TNCs) through processes such as the globalisation of capital and production; and (ii) transformations in the technological base and subsequent global scope of the mass media. For these reasons, it is increasingly important to analyse the world economy and society *globally* as well as nationally. There are several different competing models of globalisation theory and research, for example, the world-system, global culture, globalisation of space-time, globo-local and world society approaches. Here I shall focus on my own contribution, global system theory.

Global system theory is based on the concept of transnational practices, practices that cross state boundaries but do not necessarily originate with state agencies or actors. Analytically, they operate in three spheres, the economic, the political, and the cultural-ideological. The whole is what I mean by "the global system". The global system, at the end of the twentieth century is not synonymous with global capitalism, but the dominant forces of global capitalism are the dominant forces in the global system. The building blocks of the theory are the *transnational corporation*, the characteristic institutional form of economic transnational practices, a still-evolving *transnational capitalist class* in the political sphere, and in the culture-ideology sphere, the *culture-ideology of consumerism*.

In the economic sphere, the global capitalist system offers a limited place to the wage earning masses in most countries. The workers, the direct producers of goods and services, have occupational choices that are generally free within the range offered by the class structures in national capitalisms. The inclusion of the subordinate classes in the political sphere is very partial. To put it bluntly, the global capitalist system has very little need of the subordinate classes in this sphere. In parliamentary democracies the parties must be able to mobilise the masses to vote every so often, but in most countries voting is not compulsory and mass political participation is usually discouraged. In non-democratic capitalist polities even these minimal conditions are absent.

The culture-ideology sphere is, however, entirely different. Here, the aim of global capitalists is total inclusion of all classes, and especially the subordinate classes insofar as the bourgeoisie can be considered already included. The cultural-ideological project of global capitalism is to persuade people to consume above their "biological needs" in order to perpetuate the accumulation of capital for private profit, in other words, to ensure that the global capitalist system goes on for ever. The culture-ideology of consumerism proclaims, literally, that the meaning of life is to be found in the things we possess. To consume, therefore, is to be fully alive, and to remain fully alive we must continuously consume. The notions of men and women as economic or political beings are discarded by global capitalism, quite logically, as the system does not even pretend to satisfy everyone in the economic or political spheres. People are primarily consumers. The point of economic activity for "ordinary members" of the global capitalist system is to provide the resources for consumption, and the point of political activity is to ensure that the conditions for consuming are maintained.

Pro-capitalist global system movements are, therefore, those that support the transnational corporations, serve the interests of the transnational capitalist class and promote the culture-ideology of consumerism. Anti-capitalist global system movements, consequently, are those that challenge the TNCs in the economic sphere, oppose the transnational capitalist class and its local affiliates in the political sphere, and promote cultures and ideologies antagonistic to capitalist consumerism. In the next section the argument is advanced that movements working in all three spheres for the global capitalist system are very successful both at the global and the local levels, while movements working against global capitalism have been singularly unsuccessful globally, though their prospects of challenging global capitalism locally and making this count globally, globalising disruptions, seem more realistic.

Disrupting the TNCs

The characteristic institutional focus of transnational economic practices is the transnational corporation. Therefore, challenging global capitalism in the economic sphere involves disrupting the TNCs' capacity to accumulate profits at the expense of their workforces, their consumers and the communities which are affected by their activities. These are the truly global contexts of the TNCs, the places where their raw materials come from, where these raw materials are processed, the places through which they are transported, where the components are made and assembled, where the final consumer goods are manufactured, and sold, and used, and eventually disposed of. As is well known, an important part of economic globalisation today is the increasing dispersal of the manufacturing process into many discrete phases carried out in many different places. Being no longer so dependent on the production of one factory and one workforce gives capital a distinct advantage, particularly against the strike weapon which once gave tremendous negative power to the working class. Global production chains can be disrupted by strategically planned stoppages, but this generally acts more as an irritation than as a real weapon of labour against capital. By the nature of the case, the international division of labour builds flexibility into the system so that not only can capital migrate anywhere in the world to find the cheapest source of labour but also few workforces can any longer decisively "hold capital to ransom" by withdrawing their labour. At the level of the production process, as many have argued, globalising capital has all but defeated labour. In this respect, at least, the global organisation of the TNCs will invariably be too powerful for the local organisation of labour.

But what of the global organisation of labour? The traditional response of the labour movement to global capitalist hegemony has been to try to forge international links between workers in different countries. This strategy, despite some notable successes, has generally failed and it is not difficult to understand why it has failed (see, for example, Cohen 1987). Where the TNCs have been disrupted, to the extent that their hegemony has been weakened and even, in some cases, they have been forced to change their ways and compensate those who have grievances against them, it has usually been due to local campaigns of disruption and counter-information against TNC malpractices which have attracted world-wide publicity. There are sufficient cases (like the Distillers' Company thalidomide tragedy, Union Carbide's Bhopal disaster, various oil companies' environmental catastrophes, ongoing campaigns against Nestle's infant formula, logging companies, etc.) to suggest that such single-issue social movements do have genuine disruptive effects in curbing the worst excesses of profiteering TNCs. Omvedt argues this starkly: "Bhopal was the major disaster that revealed for the whole world the murderous nature of the multinational companies and of the capitalist 'development' that was the major ideological base of postindependence third world regimes" (1993: 149). The knowledge that workers, citizens, church and other concerned groups all around the world are monitoring their activities, clearly encourages some TNCs to act more responsibly than they otherwise might be doing. The fact that it takes constant monitoring and public exposure of wrongdoing to force some corporations to act responsibly helps transform local disruptions of TNC activities into global challenges to capitalist hegemony.

Disrupting the Transnational Capitalist Class

The transnational capitalist class (TCC) is transnational in the double sense that its members have global rather than, or in addition to, local perspectives; and it typically contains people from many countries who operate internationally as a normal part of their working lives. The transnational capitalist class can be conceptualised in terms of the following four fractions:

(i) TNC executives and their local affiliates;
(ii) globalising state bureaucrats;
(iii) capitalist-inspired politicians and professionals;
(iv) consumerist elites (merchants, media).

This class sees its mission as organising the conditions under which its interests and the interests of the system can be furthered in the global and local context. The concept of the transnational capitalist class implies that there is one central *transna-tional* capitalist class that makes system-wide decisions, and that it connects with the TCC in each locality, region and country. While the four fractions are distinguishable analytic categories with different functions for the global capitalist system, the people in them often move from one category to another (sometimes described as the "revolving door" between government and business).

Each of the four fractions of the TCC tends to be represented, to a greater or lesser extent, in movements and campaigns on behalf of the interests of the global capitalist system. *TNC executives and their affiliates* typically organise themselves into local, national, international and global trade and industry associations all over the world. Chambers of commerce, Lions, Kiwanis and similar organisations are also prime sites for the study of how TNC executives and their local affiliates work "in the community" on behalf of the capitalist global project. The political activities of "civil servants" provide ample evidence of the role of *globalising state bureaucrats* in pro-capitalist movements all around the world, notably in many countries officially hostile to global capitalism in previous decades. This is not to say that all bureaucrats in all governments are entirely and wholeheartedly in favour of the global capitalist project – far from it – indeed, this conception of the global system theorises the transition from a capitalism that is circumscribed by national interests to one in which globalising bureaucrats and politicians in national governments increasingly begin to see their interests best served by a more open adherence to the practices of global capitalism, and in more open alliance with the TNCs. Substantial lobbying efforts by governments on behalf of regional trade agreements, for example, is a particularly important marker of this transition.

The role of *capitalist-inspired politicians and professionals* is also illustrated by the case of regional trade agreements. Capitalist-inspired politicians either simply line up behind their governments in the voting lobbies or, sometimes, take more active parts in promoting such initiatives. The PR people and professional lobbyists, business and trade consultants of all shapes and sizes, legal personnel and others flock to the global capitalist banner. It can be argued that such people will sing any tune they are paid to sing and this is, largely, true. But it cannot be denied that the big money tends to be mainly behind one tune. That is why it is such an important test case for the argument about the transnational capitalist class. On many issues big (transnational) business sings many tunes, but on "free trade" the fundamental interests of global capitalism are clear and relatively single-minded. To this extent, the transnational capitalist class all over the world is united.

Consumerist elites (merchants and media) are frequently active in social move-ments for global capitalism. Most merchants and media, unsurprisingly, back global capitalism with more or less enthusiasm. The major retailing chains naturally sup-port every move that looks likely to increase mass markets anywhere in the world. The mass media, while giving some space and time to oppositional arguments, generally present the viewpoints of the transnational capitalist class in prime-time, general news presentation, features and editorial matter. The mass media extend and deepen the "global reach" of the transnational capitalist class.

Apart from communist and revolutionary socialist parties and movements dedic-ated to the seizure of state power, there is a long and varied history of social movements against the capitalist class. Representatives of big business have rarely been popular, even among those who work for them. Piott (1985), in his informative study of popular resistance to the rise of big business in the US Midwest in the decades around the turn of the twentieth century, usefully labels it "The Anti-Monopoly Persuasion". For the anti-monopolists of the late nineteenth century, banks, land and railroad trusts represented a new anti-democratic America, symbolising outside interests threatening local communities. In his analysis of the St. Louis streetcar strike of 1900, Piott comments: "The strike developed a cross-class sense of community consciousness ... People in roles as consumers, housewives, workers, taxpayers, citizens, and merchants united against the streetcar monopoly" (1985: 70). Similar anti-monopoly movements against the beef trusts and Standard Oil led to a nation-wide movement against the "robber barons". The "anti-monopoly persuasion" still exists, but with the decisive difference that it now has to combat a genuinely global adversary whose capacities, mobility and flexibility are unprecedented in human history.

Disrupting Consumerism

It is now almost a commonplace to label contemporary society, east or west, north or south, rich or poor, "consumerist". Nothing and no one seems immune from commodification, commercialisation, being bought and sold. Ordinary so-called "counter-cultures" are regularly incorporated into the consumer culture and pose little threat. Indeed, by offering both real and illusory variety and choice, they are a source of great strength to the global capitalist system and of personal enrichment for those able to enjoy the abundance of cultural forms undeniably available. The celebrations of the twentieth anniversary of the student revolts of the 1960s became media events and were relentlessly commercially exploited, with the willing and presumably lucrative participation of many of those who had then been (and still are) dedicated to the overthrow of the capitalist system. Consumerist appropriations of the bicentennial of the French and American revolutions are other interesting examples. We shall have to wait for the year 2017 to see what the culture-ideology of consumerism makes of the Bolshevik revolution!

The only counter-cultures that do present threats to global capitalist consumerism at present, now that Stalinist communism is thoroughly discredited and has lost most of its institutional supports, are religious (particularly Islamic) fundamentalism (see, for example, Ray 1993: Chapters 6 and 7) and environmental movements (see, for example, Burgmann 1993; Eder 1993; Omvedt 1993). Religious fundamentalism, with a few isolated exceptions, does not challenge consumerism on a global scale. Environmental movements, in some forms, could certainly challenge the culture-ideology of consumerism, but evidence from the Earth Summit in Rio in 1992 suggests that at least some of its main representatives appear to be in the process of being incorporated, and those that refuse incorporation are being marginalised. The "greening of the corporation", in both its genuine and its false manifestations, is well under way but it is the corporations not the "Greens" who are firmly in control of the process (Sklair 1994).

The logic of this argument is clearly under-consumptionist. Capitalists in the twentieth century have the capacity to produce consumer goods in historically unprecedented quantities and varieties, but capitalist relations of production tend to inhibit the level of consumption of these goods by the masses on a global scale. The cycles of boom and slump are periods of high consumer spending followed by overproduction of goods which causes business failures, unemployment, a drop in consumer spending and, thus, underconsumption. While not wishing to become embroiled in the technicalities of this debate, I shall simply note that the point of the concept of the "culture-ideology of consumerism" is precisely that, under capitalism, the masses cannot be relied upon to keep buying – obviously when they have neither spare cash nor access to credit, and less obviously when they do have spare cash and access to credit. The creation of a culture-ideology of consumerism, therefore, is bound up with the self imposed necessity that capitalism must be ever-expanding on a global scale. This expansion crucially depends on selling more and more goods and services to people whose "basic needs" (a somewhat ideological term) have already been comfortably met as well as to those whose "basic needs" are unmet.

This suggests that the culture-ideology of consumerism may serve different functions for different social groups and even for different societies. Clearly, the culture-ideology of consumerism is superfluous to explain why people who are hungry or cold eat or clothe themselves, while it does help to explain snacking or "grazing" on food and drinks that are demonstrably unhealthy and why people go into debt to buy many sets of clothes, expensive cars, etc. Even more challenging is the enigma of why poor people, in poor and rich countries, apparently defy economic rationality by purchasing relatively expensive global brands in order to forge some sense of identity with what we can only call in a rather crude sense "symbols of modernity" (or even "symbols of postmodernity").

The implications of the spread of the "culture-ideology of consumerism" and the economic and political institutions on which it is built, from its heartlands in the First World and the other places where tiny privileged minorities have adopted it, to the rest of the world, is a social change of truly global significance. In order to understand fully what has been happening in the "neo-liberalizing" West, let alone eastern Europe and China in recent years, my contention is that it is important to theorise about the "culture-ideology of consumerism", its role in confusing the issue of the satisfaction of basic needs, and the difficulty of mobilising against global capitalism on the basis of anti-consumerist ideology. Any attack on capitalist consumerism is an attack on the very centre of global capitalism. In the context of environmental movements, some nervous members of transnational capitalist classes around the world are quite correct when they label consumer movement activists (particularly those propagating "green" ideology) as "subversive".

One example of an anti-consumerist social movement, small in scale but large in potential significance, is the Seikatsu Club in Japan, based on the idea of consumer self-sufficiency through cooperatives. This is a consumers' co-operative which started out in a small way in 1965 by organising collective purchases of milk to offset price rises imposed by the few companies that dominated the market. As of March 1992, the Club had over 200,000 members in thousands of small local units making purchases of over 66 billion yen (about US$700 million) annually, a political network with representatives on local city councils, 27 workers' collectives (mostly small food businesses), investments in suppliers' enterprises, and a social movement research centre. One telling statistic is that while the volume of waste per day in the average Tokyo household is 560 grams, in Seikatsu households it is only 210 grams. Every three years an intensive review of all purchases is carried out to distinguish between real needs and pseudo-needs (sic) which are foisted on consumers by those interested only in profits. Therefore, "co-operative purchase is a way to deny the capitalistic system of consumption" (Seikatsu 1992: 21). While possibly the best organised and the most ideologically coherent of such movements, there are many others all over the world.

Some may consider this a rather "sublime" example of a social movement against capitalist consumerism, so let me briefly allude to the "ridiculous", namely reclaiming the shopping mall as public space! In his absorbing study of the "Magic of the Mall", Goss points out that shopping is the second most important leisure time activity in the USA (after watching TV, and much of TV promotes shopping anyway): "Shopping has become the dominant mode of contemporary public life" (1993: 18). While this is true at present only for parts of the First World and perhaps some privileged elites elsewhere, the rest of world appears to be following rapidly. The study of shopping malls, therefore, is important. The idea of the mall signals a third, public, space after home and work/school, to see and be seen. Malls are not just places to buy and sell but are increasingly taking on other functions (for example, educational, cultural, child care) very much oriented to the middle classes. They aim to provide safe, secure environments for "normal" consumers, but are reluctant to provide genuine public services like drinking fountains, public toilets, telephones, etc. where deviants or non-shoppers can congregate. Goss reports that the average length of time spent in shopping centre trips in the USA has increased from 20 minutes in 1960 to nearly three hours in the 1990s, no doubt facilitated by the omnipresent grazing opportunities in the fast food outlets. Art and museums are now being brought into the mall directly: the first US National Endowment for the Arts grant to a private corporation went for art projects in malls.

Having established the centrality of the mall in the USA and, by implication, the future of the world, Goss poses the interesting question: how can the mall be reclaimed for the people? He suggests that citizens could: (i) expose commodity fetishism, and force advertisers and retailers to become more honest; (ii) resist the economic and spatial logic of malls by helping community groups struggle against redevelopment; (iii) open up the mall as a genuine public space; (iv) organise tactical occupations of spaces; (v) subvert the systems of signification. Goss is clearly ambivalent about consumerism and about malls, and he is not alone. The merit of his approach is that it hints of the possibility of an opposition to capitalist consumerism that does not entail hair-shirts and a life totally bereft of all the consumer goods that make life "better" for ordinary people today all over the world. Those who are guilty about their excessive consumerism are more likely to be so because of environmental reasons than because they believe that their consumption patterns somehow subvert or destroy meaning in their lives. Victory in the struggle for a decent standard of living (that changes over time) clearly does not have a simple connection to resistance to capitalist consumerism.

Conclusions

The burden of my argument has been that while capitalism increasingly organises globally, the resistances to global capitalism can only be effective where they can disrupt its smooth running (accumulation of private profits) locally and can find ways of globalising these disruptions. No social movement appears even remotely likely to overthrow the three fundamental institutional supports of global capitalism that have been identified, namely the TNCs, the transnational capitalist class and the culture-ideology of consumerism. Nevertheless, in each of these spheres there are resistances expressed by social movements. The TNCs, if we are to believe their own propaganda, are continuously beset by opposition, boycott, legal challenge and moral outrage from the consumers of their products and by disruptions from their workers. The transnational capitalist class often finds itself opposed by vocal coalitions when it tries to impose its will in new ways. There are many ways to be ambivalent about the culture-ideology of consumerism, some of which the "Green" movement has successfully exploited. In an informative compendium, Ekins (1992) describes the winners of the Right Livelihoods Awards from 1980–90 (known to some as a sort of "Alternative Nobel Prize") and their social movements, some very well-known (like the Sarvodaya Shramadama Movement in Sri Lanka), some much less well-known (like the Six S Association/NAAM Movement in Burkino Faso), all trying to escape from the domination of the global capitalist system and experiment with alternative ways of living (see also Wignaraja 1993). The irony is that so many of these social movements actually rely on funding from foreign agencies to grow.

Opposing capitalism locally, from households, communities, cities, all the way up to the level of the nation state has always been practically difficult but, at least, organisationally and ideologically manageable. In most capitalist societies, social movements for what has come to be known as social democracy, have united those who are hostile to capitalism, those who struggle to alleviate the worst consequences of capitalism and those who simply want to ensure that capitalism works with more social efficiency than the so-called "free market" allows. This has inevitably meant that anti-capitalists (principally socialists) of many kinds have seen no alternative to using capitalist practices to achieve anti-capitalist ends, whether locally or nationally. The implication of the foregoing argument is that the transition from social democracy to democratic socialism is one that can only be achieved through social movements that target global capitalism through its three main institutional supports, the TNCs, the transnational capitalist class and the culture-ideology of consumerism (see Sklair 1995: especially ch. 9). These three supports manifest themselves both globally and locally, but they can only be effectively challenged locally by those who are prepared to disrupt their anti-social practices.

The issue of democracy is central to the practice and the prospects of social movements against capitalism, local and global. The rule of law, freedom of association and expression, freely contested elections, as minimum conditions and however imperfectly sustained, are as necessary in the long run for mass-market based, global consumerist capitalism as they are for alternative social systems. As markets for many types of consumer goods become saturated in the First World, TNCs have been visibly expanding their activities to the new Second and Third Worlds. This shift has contradictory effects: it gives the institutions of global capitalism previously unimagined actual and potential powers to extend and target their global reach, while at the same time it makes these institutions peculiarly vulnerable to challenge and disruptions on a global scale. To conclude where I began, to be effective social movements against global capitalism will need to find new forms that do not reproduce the failures of Piven and Cloward's "poor people's movements" but rather reproduce their successes. This will mean disrupting capitalism locally and finding ways of globalising these disruptions, while seizing the opportunities to transform it that democracy provides.

REFERENCES

Brecher, J. and Costello, T. 1990. *Building Bridges: The Emerging Grassroots Coalition of Labor and Community*. New York: Monthly Review Press.

Burgmann, V. 1993. *Power and Protest: Movements for Change in Australian Society*. St Leonards, NSW: Allen Unwin.

Castells, M. 1983. *The City and the Grassroots: A Cross-Cultural Theory of Urban Social Movements*. Berkeley and Los Angeles: University of California Press.

Eder, K. 1993. *The New Politics of Class: Social Movements and Cultural Dynamics in Advanced Societies*. London: Sage.

Ekins, P. 1992. *A New World Order: Grassroots Movements for Global Change*. London: Routledge.

Goss, J. 1993. "The 'Magic of the Mall': An Analysis of Form, Function, and Meaning in the Contemporary Retail Built Environment". *Annals of the Association of American Geographers* 83: 18–47.

Hayter, T. and Harvey, D. (eds.) 1993. *The Factory and the City: The Story of the Cowley Automobile Workers in Oxford*. London: Mansell.

Omvedt, G. 1993. *Reinventing Revolution: New Social Movements and the Socialist Tradition in India*. Armonk: M. E. Sharpe.

Piott, S. 1985. *The Anti-Monopoly Persuasion. Popular Resistance to the Rise of Big Business in the Midwest*. Westport: Greenwood Press.

Piven, F. and Cloward, R. 1979. *Poor People's Movements: Why They Succeed, How They Fail*. New York: Vintage.

Ray, L. 1993. *Rethinking Critical Theory: Emancipation in the Age of Global Social Movements*. London: Sage.

Seikatsu Club Consumers' Co-operative. 1992. *Co-operative Action based on "Han"*. Tokyo: Seikatsu Club.

Sklair, L. 1994. "Global Sociology and Global Environmental Change", in M. Redclift and T. Benton (eds.), *Social Theory and the Global Environment*. London: Routledge.

Sklair, L. 1995. *Sociology of the Global System*, second edition. London: Harvester.

Touraine, A. 1981. *The Voice and the Eye: An Analysis of Social Movements*. Cambridge: Cambridge University Press.

Touraine, A., Wieviorka, M. and Dubet, F. 1987. *The Workers' Movement*. Cambridge: Cambridge University Press.

Wignaraja, P. (ed.) 1993. *New Social Movements in the South: Empowering the People*. London: Zed.

23 Neoliberalism and the Sociology of Development: Emerging Trends and Unanticipated Facts (1997)

Alejandro Portes

Cuban-born Alejandro Portes now teaches at Princeton University and is a recent president of the American Sociological Association. His work has been influential in the areas of migration and immigrant communities, urban development, and the informal economy, as well as the topic dealt with here, the impact of the global economy on local processes. In this piece Portes reviews the debate over development, noticing the irony that most discussion is no longer about reducing poverty or inequality, but rather concerns itself only with how nations can become better competitors in the global economy and protect their currencies and stock markets. Portes also critiques neoliberal (free-trade, laissez-faire) policy and its academic supporters for their lack of academic rigor. He also critiques World Systems Theory for failing to engage in practical debates over development. Portes discusses how the new global economy has produced unexpected roles for family and informal labor; individuals and families act globally as corporations, migrating and creating transnational trading groups.

As we approach the end of the century, indeed the millennium, an issue that has preoccupied social scientists and policymakers during the last 50 years has taken an unexpected turn. The issue is the persistent economic and social inequalities between countries of the advanced world and many countries of the formerly colonial and semi-colonial third world. The unexpected turn is the shift away from efforts – stemming from different theoretical perspectives – to reduce these inequalities and toward the recognition of their permanence, indeed functionality for the operation and growth of the global economy. In this transformed context, the sociology of development, concerned as it was with the mechanisms that reproduced inequality and the means to overcome them, seems to have lost much of its raison d'être. This loss of ground is abetted by the dominance of a market-oriented approach to the question of national development and the willingness of governments to follow the policy dictates of international finance organizations based on that perspective.

...the last 25 years have witnessed an acceleration of the flows of information, technology, trade, and labor on a universal scale binding ever more closely the populations of disparate regions. The collapse of the socialist states of Eastern Europe also supported Wallerstein's contention that socialism, as it unfolded in the former Soviet bloc, was not a counter-system at all. Instead it represented a bold, but ultimately failed strategy to gain ascendance within the global capitalist system (Hopkins and Wallerstein 1977; Chase-Dunn 1982). Above all, this last quarter-century has been marked by a new phase of intense competition between multinationals based in various advanced countries and the rise of novel strategies of capital accumulation linked to space-bridging technologies (Sassen 1988; Castells and Portes 1989; Fernández-Kelly 1983).

In contrast to prescriptions stemming from dependency theory, which dictated a partial withdrawal from the world economy, the priority for less developed countries today is to insert themselves in the commodity chains and circles of global finance in order to avoid economic and political marginalization. The pursuit of national "competitiveness" within an increasingly bound global economy is consonant with the world-system approach and places this perspective in a theoretically privileged position to analyze current trends. Yet by its resolute focus on long-term historical evolution, this school has failed to capitalize on that advantage. The postulate of a single universal unit of analysis is a major weakness since the level at which most development problems, dilemmas, and decisions take place is the intermediate one of nations and communities seeking to cope with the constraints of their particular situations. Hence, paradoxically, the sociological perspective that came closest to prediction of present trends has become marginal to specific policy strategies designed to cope with them.

By refusing to budge from the level of global generalization, world-system theorists remain outside these concrete policy debates, and their influence has weakened the sociology of development. To recapture the lost terrain and place the sociological study of development squarely in the midst of present realities, we must abandon modernization-versus-dependency debates and move beyond sweeping historical statements. For this task, it is necessary to take advantage of insights from other bodies of theory. Such a shift includes greater attention to factors of a domestic order, including characteristics of states, the relationships of states with classes in civil society, population size, and density. It is at this level that recent developments in economic sociology are promising since they offer a way of overcoming the limitations of past theories and engaging currently fashionable macroeconomic models of national growth. To understand how this alternative perspective can elucidate current development issues, I now complement the preceding theoretical review with an outline of the events that led to the present dominance of a market-oriented approach.

What Changed?

As in other areas of inquiry, theorizing in the field of national development reflects and interacts with events in the real world. The modernization and dependency schools arose and competed in a context possessing several distinct characteristics. First, the United States was regarded as the uncontested center of technological innovation and capitalist accumulation. Depending on one's perspective, North

American hegemony was described either as the source of beneficial influences promoting innovation and change in less developed countries or as the root cause of their stagnation. Second, there was the relatively recent experience at the time of countries like Germany and Japan, whose successful industrialization could be reasonably imputed to a strategy of import substitution. Given theoretical form by economists of the German Historical School, particularly Friedrich List (1885), these experiences proved an inspiration to those in Latin America and elsewhere who sought an autonomous path to development (Prebisch 1950; Amin 1974).

Third, the presence of the Soviet bloc provided not only a political counterweight but an ideological alternative to the West, as communist countries privileged the role of the state in promoting the growth of national economies. Compared with this radical alternative, the model of import-substitution industrialization as a way out of dependency offered a reasonable, eclectic path. Still capitalist in orientation, this path sought to nurture infant industries behind tariff barriers and with vigorous state support, much as Germany and then Japan had done. The same global context featuring a stable hierarchy of a single hegemonic country, an intermediate layer of mostly European nations, and a vast sector of impoverished colonial and semi-colonial lands served as inspiration for the concept of a single world-system (O'Brien 1975; Kahl 1976; Portes and Walton 1981: Ch. 1).

Beginning in the 1970s and accelerating thereafter, this context began to change with the commercial challenge posed by a resurgent Japan, then Western Europe, and finally the newly industrialized Asian countries. The challenge was neither military nor scientific, but focused on the efficient application of known technologies to the production of manufactured goods with an increasing value-added component. Japan, in particular, excelled in this strategy based on large, solidary business groups, their close coordination with state agencies, and a highly skilled and disciplined labor force (Arrighi 1994). The challenge took the United States by surprise, as it had focused up to that point on two related strategies: first, the containment and eventual neutralization of Soviet military power through massive investments in military-oriented scientific and technological innovation; second, the stabilization of domestic class relations through the incorporation of organized labor into the country's institutional framework and the creation of a well-paid, secure industrial working class (Edwards, Reich, and Gordon 1975; Edwards 1979; O'Connor 1973).

Large US industrial corporations could agree to the demands of their workers and, in the process, create a large blue-collar "middle class" because oligopolistic control of markets allowed them to transfer higher wages and other costs into prices. The same privileged control of markets allowed these firms to focus on expansion via advertising and cosmetic product changes, rather than make actual improvements in product quality. The end result of these twin processes was the growth of a vast industrial complex producing high-quality military goods under monopoly conditions, an oligopolistic sector of mass-produced medium- and low-quality goods for the domestic and export markets, and the rise of a "primary" industrial working class associated with both sectors and deriving material benefits from their interest in labor stability. The bifurcation of the American working class into this protected "primary" sector and a "secondary" fringe of workers subject to the vagaries of the market was belatedly recognized by labor economists (Piore and Sabel 1984; Gordon 1972). Their discovery came just about the time when this structure had started to disintegrate.

The entry of Japan as global competitor did more than provide a credible challenge to US multinationals. It fundamentally altered the way in which advanced countries thought about managing their economies and third world countries sought to develop theirs. The proliferation of international industrial competitors, led by Japanese companies but including an increasing number of European and other Asian players, simultaneously challenged the ideas of demand-driven economic growth based on sustained market expansion in developed countries and of state-led import-substitution development in peripheral ones. In both regions of the world economy, the principal loser was, and continues to be, the organized segment of the working class.

In the United States, the increasing threat of foreign competition led a number of large corporations to jettison the social pact on which the "primary" sector of the labor market had been built. The Keynesian notion that the expansion of this sector of well-paid jobs fueled growth through sustained increases in consumer demand was abandoned because it became obvious that much of that demand was now satisfied by more efficient foreign producers (Sassen 1988; Gereffi and Korzeniewicz 1994; Hill and Fujita 1995). There are different schools of thought about the factors that led to the demise of entire industrial districts in the United States and the consequent savaging of its protected industrial work force, but they all agree that the initial cause was the shock of foreign competition and the rapid loss of market share (Bluestone and Harrison 1982; McKenzie 1984; Jaffee 1986; Storper and Walker 1989).

Earlier arguments about deindustrialization being due to higher comparative costs gave way under scrutiny to the view that its core determinants were grounded precisely in the past successes of American corporations with vertically integrated plants producing goods under conditions of oligopoly. A protected industrial working class was simply part of this complex in which products were mass-marketed and priced without serious regard for external competitors. As Romo and Schwartz (1995: 888) put it:

> ...the loss of market share in most industries (including auto, steel, photocopiers, and agricultural implements) derived largely from the failure of U.S. firms to match product innovations and adopt new production methodologies. ... They were offering an inferior product at higher prices because their technology and production systems were behind the times.

Caught in this bind, many North American corporations resorted to the "spatial fix" (Harvey 1982), shifting production to low-wage areas to compensate, at least temporarily, for their inferior production technologies. In the process, they left behind much of their "primary" working class and the formerly prosperous communities built around it. The onslaught of Japanese corporations so deeply impressed a number of Western analysts that some have been led to declare the end of US hegemony and the beginning of a "new era" of capitalism. For Arrighi (1994: 335), for example:

> The speed and extent of the Japanese acquisition of a larger share of the world's income and liquidity have no parallel in the contemporary world-economy. They put the Japanese capitalist class in a category of its own as the true heir of the Genoese, the

Dutch, the British, and the U.S. capitalist classes at the time of their respective great leaps forward as new leaders of systemic processes of capital accumulation.

In peripheral countries, such as those of Latin America, an incipient industrial working class created behind barriers of import substitution, suffered a similar fate, as one country after another sought to emulate the economic successes of the "Asian tigers" and, in the process, yielded to pressures of international finance organizations to open up their economies (Balassa et al. 1986; Williamson 1994). The bankruptcy of many domestic firms unable to withstand foreign competition shrank the protected industrial working class, while the labor victories of earlier times came under relentless pressure as so many barriers to external "competitiveness." In some countries, like Chile, labor standards and minimum wages were drastically curtailed by military regimes. In others, governments sought to bypass their own labor legislation through the expedient of "special" export zones where these covenants did not apply. The process may be summarized as follows:

> ... if Mexico refused to let the U.S. runaway industries in the border region circumvent the contracts obtained by the Mexican unions, these industries would simply move elsewhere, and the process of industrialization would stop. ... [N]ewly industrialized countries informalize themselves *vis-à-vis* their competitors as well as *vis-à-vis* their own formal laws, so as to obtain a competitive advantage for their production relative to more regulated areas of the world economy. (Castells and Portes 1989: 29)

In every region of the international capitalist system – advanced and peripheral alike – processes of industrial downsizing, restructuring, and relocation have been justified by the threat and demands of global competition. Although some sectors of the "primary" working class have put up a spirited defense of their privileges, the threat of additional plant closings and foreign relocations has generally allowed companies to keep their shrunken work forces in line. A relatively secure and well-paid working class ceased to be the norm or at least the goal in both advanced and peripheral countries, giving way instead to a mix of "flexible" production arrangements, subcontracting to low-cost nonunion firms, and a quantum leap in the number of people employed in "special" export zones (Bluestone and Harrison 1982; Piore and Sabel 1984; Sassen 1989; Itzigsohn 1994).

For our purposes, the central point is that conditions created by the new global competition in industrial goods and later in financial services became increasingly incompatible with the theories that had previously dominated economic thinking, that is, Keynesianism in the centers and anti-dependency import substitution in the periphery. By the same token, these conditions helped resurrect older economic theories. The remarkable comeback of the neoclassical approach to development was hastened by its fit with the new economic realities and by the vigorous actions of its supporters to further that convergence. Plant closings and relocations abroad may have been anathema to advocates of a national "industrial policy," but were perfectly compatible with a theory that regarded protected work forces as a constraint on market competition. Removal of state subsidies and tariff barriers may have adversely affected the standard of living of workers and the growth prospects of certain industrial sectors in the periphery, but they were needed medicine in order to get the prices "right" (Williamson 1994). Foreign competition may devastate the primary labor market in the advanced countries, but it benefited their consumers through access to cheaper goods.

In the mid-1980s, a team of conservative economists, led by the World Bank's Bela Balassa, produced the equivalent of a capitalist manifesto for bringing growth to third world countries, particularly those of Latin America. The document went through the orthodox litany of complaints against import-substitution policies and proclaimed the path to development to be marked by a radically new model: unilaterally lifting tariff barriers, abolishing consumer subsidies, getting the state out of economic micro-management, and encouraging foreign capital inflow in all its forms (Balassa et al. 1986). Heavily promoted by the World Bank and the US Agency for International Development, this neoclassical manifesto was circulated widely in Latin America, providing the rationale and inspiration for a growing band of "liberal" reformers. In Latin America, the term "liberal" is used in an opposite sense to what is customary in North American political discourse. Latin liberals are the equivalent of US conservatives, insofar as they preach market solutions to social and economic problems and a drastically reduced role for the state. This use of the term corresponds to its original meaning, associated with the British School and its classical defense of free trade (Bruton 1960).

By the end of the 1980s, the demise of the Soviet bloc gave the final push toward the consolidation of neoclassical theory as the dominant, indeed the only major approach to national development. With the most state-centric of growth strategies (those of the former communist states) thoroughly discredited, the road was clear for the global expansion of capitalism and, along with it, the hegemony of the most market-oriented theoretical school. In Latin America, the formal implementation of this perspective was dubbed "neoliberal" adjustment and consisted of seven basic steps: (1) unilateral opening to foreign trade; (2) extensive privatization of state enterprises; (3) deregulation of goods, services, and labor markets; (4) liberalization of the capital market, with extensive privatization of pension funds; (5) fiscal adjustment, based on drastic reduction of public outlays; (6) restructuring and downscaling of state-supported social programs, focusing on compensatory schemes for the neediest groups; and (7) the end of "industrial policy" and any other form of state capitalism and concentration on macroeconomic management (Diaz 1996).

Along with these formal economic steps, neoliberalism also brought about socio-cultural changes of a more diffuse, but equally important character: (1) reevaluation of capitalist profitmaking as desirable and congruent with national interests; (2) concomitant devaluation of organized labor and protected industry as "rental havens" inimical to economic efficiency; (3) support of foreign investment as necessary for sustained growth; (4) renewed faith in the market, via trickle-down effects, for the reduction of social inequality; and (5) reorientation of the sources of national pride away from resistance to foreign hegemony and toward skilled reinsertion into the circles of global trade (Castells and Laserna 1989; Evans 1995; McMichael 1995).

The diffusion of these value orientations along with the economic program they fostered left little space for a reconceptualization of development in terms other than success in the marketplace. Yet implementation of neoliberal adjustment policies in a number of third world countries has produced unexpected consequences, some of them inimical to the original development goals. These trends point to the limitations of the current hegemonic model and the need for an alternative theoretical perspective.

What Went Wrong?

Although promoted everywhere by international finance organizations and applied uniformly in third world countries, the neoliberal program has ended up having disparate outcomes. The stampede of prices has been controlled in all countries that underwent this economic treatment. In other respects, however, the results have been indecisive and, at times, contrary to those expected. Neither individuals nor institutions have reacted uniformly to the application of these policies; hence predictions about the behavior of such economic categories as "entrepreneurs," "consumers," and "savers" have often failed to materialize.

This section examines several instances of these predictive difficulties as examples of a much broader theme, namely the limitations of an exclusive market approach to national development. To anticipate the core of the argument: the assumptions of rational self-interest and unrestricted pursuit of gain that underlie neoliberal adjustment policies neglect the historical context in which the policies are implemented. The specific characteristics of such contexts and the forms in which they mold institutional behavior interact with formal policies to yield a wide variety of results. The analysis of such differing outcomes requires a conceptual apparatus emphasizing the embeddedness of economic action in social structures, including political and demographic factors, and the roles of class and networks in guiding collective strategies. This is the theoretical realm of economic sociology.

The Hidden Social Bases of Neoliberal Success and Failure

A dispassionate account of the application of neoclassical thinking to national development reveals both successes and failures. In Latin America, Chile and increasingly Peru under President Fujimori are hailed as examples of what neoliberal programs can accomplish. But in nearby Ecuador and Bolivia, efforts to spur the economy through similar policies have become bogged down or yielded mixed results. In Argentina, seven years of neoliberal adjustment under Domingo Cavallo, an economic minister heavily backed by the International Monetary Fund, yielded very low inflation, but an erratic record of growth with increasing external indebtedness (Filgueira 1996; ECLAC 1990; *Latin American Weekly Report* 1996a).

The signal failure of the new "model" is arguably Mexico, where a policy of unilateral external opening and rapid privatizations under the Salinas administration culminated in an overvalued currency that sent the country spinning into depression. The Mexican crisis nearly toppled the delicate hemispheric economic balance, and its ratchet effect was avoided only by a heavy injection of capital and loan guarantees by the US Treasury. Such interventionist action by the United States runs directly against neoclassical prescriptions enjoining state interference in the free operation of markets.

Whenever such incidents occur, supporters of neoliberal adjustment blame them on its imperfect application or argue for more time for its effects to take hold. But these justifications only beg the question. If the neoliberal model is properly applied only where it yields success and is improperly applied where it produces failure, the argument becomes hopelessly circular. Similarly, the plea for more time can become open ended and render impossible the falsification of any prediction. In Mexico's case, international finance agencies and other advocates of neoliberal adjustment were hailing its successes until the very moment in which it came crashing down, thus revealing the "imperfections" of its application. In Argentina, repeated predictions by economic minister Cavallo about the end of the fiscal deficit and the arrival of sustained growth came to naught, thus expanding indefinitely the time horizon for the predicted benefits to materialize.

A more appropriate course of action is to examine what factors are missing from the neoclassical analysis of determinants of development so that outcomes may be predicted more accurately rather than explained away. My initial argument about the significance of the socio-historical context in which policies are applied may now be fleshed out by specifying some of these key contextual factors at a broad level of generality. They can be summarized in the following hypothesis, the first of several I will advance in the remainder of this article:

1. Results of any comprehensive economic development program will depend on the internal characteristics of the state and its external relationship with the class structure of civil society.

This broad proposition can be further specified by identifying those characteristics and relationships. To do so properly, however, it is necessary to illustrate the dynamics at play with some concrete examples. For the sake of brevity, I use only two cases – one (Chile) generally regarded as a success story of neoliberal adjustment, the other (Mexico) as one of its main failures.

Chile.   In Chile, a country of 14 million people, the neoliberal approach to development was implemented by an authoritarian state in the wake of a military coup. It is now commonplace to note the paradox that an economic ideology that hails free markets and freedom of choice could only be imposed on Chilean society by force of arms (Foxley 1983). Less obvious are two equally important points: that Chile's neoliberal experiment did not so much "free" markets as create them from scratch using the resources of the state; and that the process was greatly aided by the policies pursued by the two previous governments, including that of the socialist–communist alliance.

Chilean neoliberalism was launched by a technocratic elite, trained in North American universities and enjoying the support of the military regime under General Pinochet. The first "orthodox" application of the model started with the economic shock of April 1975, which culminated in the economic crisis of 1982–83. During the latter years, unemployment in Chile reached 19.1 percent, quintupling the figure at the time of the 1973 coup, while gross national product remained stagnant. Critics of the regime were quick to sound the death knell of the neoliberal experiment, while even supporters called for realistic modifications to the rigid orthodoxy of the "Chicago boys" (Meller 1981; Foxley 1981, 1983).

That first decade of military government gradually destroyed the social order linked to the prior model of development. The technocrats in charge of the economy survived the debacles provoked by their theories, not only because of vigorous military repression against the working class and the peasantry, but also because other more powerful contenders, such as landowners and industrialists, had been greatly weakened by the policies of previous administrations. The Christian Democratic land reform, conducted under President Eduardo Frei, helped transform the old rural order, neutralizing the power of the landed oligarchy. The wave of nationalizations of industrial plants under the Allende administration undermined the industrial bourgeoisie created by import-substitution policies, while placing in the hands of the state an amount of economic power far outweighing that of any private economic actor (Valenzuela 1978; Diaz 1996; Puryear 1994).

Chilean technocrats were hence in the privileged position of being simultaneously immune from the pressures of civil society and possessing the resources to recreate Chilean capitalism in their own image. They did not restore property to former landowners or align themselves too closely with the old import-substitution industrialists. Instead, they used the political influence created by the policies of the previous administrations to foster a new commercial farming class in the countryside and a new financial and industrial entrepreneurial class in the cities. Land markets, financial markets, and inter-firm competition were not so much regulated by the Chilean government as created by it in the process of divesting itself of the massive resources it controlled.

Chile's technocratic elite could sustain setbacks and failures that would have discredited their leadership had they occurred under democratic conditions. As the technocrats learned the practical limits of their theories and shifted to a more realistic stance, they used the privatization of state enterprises to create new entrepreneurial groups and then selectively protected them along lines reminiscent of the old import-substitution model. This second eclectic phase of economic policy followed the crisis of 1982–83 and yielded much better results. By the time the military regime left power in 1989, key economic indicators had rebounded and a period of sustained growth with low inflation had commenced (Piñera 1994). The trend continued under two successive Christian Democratic administrations, which did not so much embrace neoliberalism as pursue its adaptation to Chilean realities. ...

For our purposes, the key lesson from the Chilean case is the unique historical context inherited by the new technocratic elite. As Chilean sociologist Alvaro Diaz (1996: 8) puts it:

> Christian Democracy and especially the Chilean left empowered the state and, by destroying the old oligarchic regime, cleared the terrain for neo-liberal elites to initiate their radical reform program in a fashion that they could never have done by themselves, since it would have destroyed their own bases of political support.

Mexico. The socio-historical context in Mexico, a larger and more complex country of some 90 million, was notably different from that of Chile. The Mexican state was not much less autocratic than Chile's at the time of application of the neoliberal model. But while the latter based its claim to power on maintaining social distance from civil society and repressing its opposition, in Mexico the state sought to perpetuate its hegemony by embracing the entire society through complex patronage networks. The Mexican regime, born of a revolutionary uprising against an aristocratic dictatorship, paid close attention to grassroots demands and swiftly coopted or repressed dissidents (Camp 1993; Centeno 1994).

Mexican corporatism is a system of interest representation that integrates individuals into the state via mass organizations that channel their demands and have the ear of the authorities. Power is heavily concentrated in the executive branch, especially around the president, but the ruling Institutional Revolutionary Party (PRI) has been able to mediate between the executive and various sectors of civil society. ... As a result, a system of patronage and reciprocity exchanges based on personal connections became institutionalized as the modus operandi of both the PRI and the Mexican state. ...

This structure of power was buttressed by a model of development based on protection of domestic industry and involvement of the state in all sectors of this vast country via publicly owned corporations. This import-substitution model gave the Mexican government the leverage required to maintain a system of legitimacy based on selective concessions and patronage, but it also strained its resources. During the 1970s, the government was able to maintain the status quo through heavy foreign borrowing backed by newly discovered oil reserves. A drop in the price of oil in the early 1980s, however, exposed the underlying financial vulnerability of the Mexican economy, forcing authorities to declare a unilateral moratorium on debt repayment (Camp 1993; Ayala and Duran 1986).

The debt squeeze of 1982 plunged the Mexican economy into its deepest recession since the 1930s and created the conditions for a quick shift in economic policy. Under urgent prodding from the US government and the International Monetary Fund (IMF), the incoming administration of President Miguel de la Madrid took the first steps along the neoliberal path (Manning 1996). The difference vis-à-vis Chile at this economic conjuncture is noteworthy. While the Pinochet dictatorship abolished all vestiges of Chilean populism, the de la Madrid government initiated its neoliberal experiment while burdened with the commitments and constraints of an entrenched corporatist system. Mexico's size did not make things easier, as it multiplied the forms in which this imbrication of state and civil society manifested itself.

The problem was rendered acute by the contradiction between the goals of neoliberal policy and the prior social pacts on which the legitimacy of the regime rested. The new policy aimed at "getting the state out of the economy" by reducing tariff protection for domestic capital, cutting consumption subsidies for the middle and lower classes, and dismantling employment opportunities in state-owned firms. These were precisely the pillars on which the regime's political strategy of inclusion and cooptation depended. Not surprisingly, affected sectors, inside and outside the government, resisted. Unlike the case of Chile, their numbers and capacity for mobilization were both larger and intact so that they were able to mount an effective counterattack, protecting their interest and undermining the economic model (Centeno 1994; Manning 1996).

Predictably, the neoliberal blitz of the de la Madrid administration stalled. While the government had some successes in reducing inflation and the budget deficit, capital flight continued and negative trade balances and economic stagnation persisted, exacerbated by the effects of a major earthquake in 1985. The incoming administration of President Salinas de Gortari retained the neoliberal model, taking aggressive steps to privatize state enterprises, reduce consumption subsidies, and enforce tax collection. The signing of the North American Free Trade Agreement (NAFTA) became the cornerstone of Mexican economic policy, as the government sought to leave import substitution behind and rely on flows of external capital investment under the new free trade regime. The technocrats managing the new model showed themselves willing to pay the price through decimation of Mexican industry, rising levels of unemployment and poverty, and growing opposition within the governing party (Cordoba 1994). Their hopes were for a swift payoff of the new policies through economic growth so as to provide a new basis of legitimacy for the government and the "modern" sectors of the PRI.

But again the imbrication of government and party with organized sectors of civil society meant a much-reduced space for technocratic initiative. Corruption and reciprocity deals between government officials and entrenched private interests continued unabated. Further, Mexican technocrats did not have the freedom of their Chilean counterparts to recognize major policy errors, recover, and change course. Instead, the model had to "show results" and do so in a relatively short period (Cook, Middlebrook, and Horcasitas 1994). For this reason and to protect foreign investor confidence on which success so heavily depended, Mexican authorities supported an overvalued currency, exacerbating the trade deficit and the lack of competitiveness of national exports. This desperate effort, which, not incidentally, led to the sacrifice of hard currency reserves, proved futile. Just as in 1982, but for different reasons, the financial house of cards gave way, forcing a sudden and sharp devaluation. The 1994 devaluation sent the Mexican economy into a tailspin with consequences worse than those suffered 12 years earlier.

... While signs of economic recovery have been detected since then, the events leading to this major policy failure suffice to illustrate a central theoretical point. The contrasting neoliberal experiences of Mexico and Chile show unequivocally how social and historical factors interact with the application of a uniform policy package to produce different outcomes. The size of the country, the composition of its population, its class structure, and the character of the state all play significant roles in the process. It is possible, on the basis of these and similar experiences elsewhere, to advance a second theoretical proposition about the role of contextual factors in national development:

2. The greater the power of the state relative to civil society and the weaker the ties of reciprocity and patronage linking state managers with private economic actors, the more coherent the application of adjustment policies and the greater the chances for success of the neoliberal or any other development model.

Evans (1995) refers to the joint operation of both factors – relative state power and freedom from entanglements with rent-seeking private groups – as indicators of the relative "autonomy" of the state. In Chile, this archetype was fulfilled by the military and technocrats, who were able to remove themselves from the pressures of former elite sectors in a relatively uniform society (Piñera 1994). In Mexico, similar tendencies of technocratic innovation confronted the powerful opposition of a complex system of political patronage. The Mexican debt crisis of 1982 forced the enactment of drastic austerity measures. But their implementation, as well as the subsequent introduction of an aggressive neoliberal model under President Salinas, was resisted by the corporatist structure created under prior governments and not dismantled after the crisis. The Mexican case furnishes the basis for a third proposition that complements the previous one:

3. The stronger the civil class structure and the greater the organizational resources of its various sectors vis-à-vis the state, the greater the difficulty in implementing adjustment models at variance with established economic interests and institutionalized practice.

Failed Promises: Equality Via Trickle-Down Effects

Since its classic formulation by W. Arthur Lewis, the orthodox economic doctrine on national development has emphasized that the "social" payoff of adjustment programs in the form of reduced poverty and inequality must flow from the market rather than through state intervention. Lewis's theory was grounded in a hydraulic analogy where labor flowed from a stagnant traditional sector to a dynamic modern one. If no artificial constraints were imposed on this flow through state-enforced wage rates and work protections, development was expected eventually to dry up the pool of underemployed labor, at which point wages would start to rise (Lewis 1959; Bairoch 1973).

This model is compatible with the famous Kuznets curve describing the relationship between economic development and income inequality. Inequality rises in the earlier stages of development (when the traditional sector is being disrupted and labor is abundant) and shrinks at later stages (when the labor oversupply starts to disappear and wages increase) (Kuznets 1955). Historical and contemporary studies based on the Kuznets model have verified the predicted trend, but have also registered exceptions (Nielsen and Alderson 1995). These exceptional cases are important insofar as they point to other factors affecting the evolution of income inequality. Similarly, Lewis's model, though an article of faith among orthodox economists, has been shown to register many anomalies.

The empirical literature shows that social and political forces, not all of them having to do with the state imposition of artificially high wages, can retard or derail the labor absorption process. Firms balk at the expected consequences of a shrinking labor supply and use their political and economic power to maintain its price artificially low. South Africa and several countries of Southeast Asia provide telling examples (Wolpe 1975; Deyo 1989; You 1988). In Latin America, the experience of two decades of policies designed to free markets has not been encouraging. Uruguayan sociologist Carlos Filgueira (1996: 13) summarizes the experience as follows:

> After more than 15 years of experimentation with policies of structural adjustment and stabilization along the width and length of the continent, the expected economic results are questionable and the social effects have been decidedly negative. ... For 19 Latin American countries, the percentage of persons under the poverty line reached 46 percent of the total in 1990. This figure is superior to that registered in 1970, 1980, and 1986. In particular, the 1980s were the decade where the problems of poverty and inequality increased with notable regularity.

It could be argued that these 15 years represent the initial period of sustained development when inequality increases as markets are deregulated. A closer look at individual country experiences, however, indicates wide disparities in the evolution of poverty and inequality:

> The most recent data available show that income inequality between 1980 and 1992/94 continued to increase in six of the twelve Latin American countries for which there is information. The largest increase of the Gini coefficient occurred in the three largest countries of the region – Argentina, Mexico, and Brazil. Colombia improved notably its income distribution between 1980 and 1986 and remained stable afterwards, while Uruguay continued a regular and continuous process of decline of inequality. (Filgueira 1996: 15)

The impact of neoliberal adjustment on unemployment rates presents the same mixed picture. Overall, Lewis's prediction of rapid labor absorption with market liberalization failed to materialize, but again the record shows significant variation. As of mid-1996, Argentina, one of the most faithful followers of economic orthodoxy, had an official unemployment rate of 16 percent, up 10 percentage points from five years earlier and more than double the rate when the neoliberal model began to be implemented. Four other countries registered unemployment rates exceeding 10 percent, the figures having increased or remained stagnant during the 1990s. At the other end, four countries – three of them in Central America – registered declines in unemployment of 2 to 3 percentage points during the same period (*Latin American Weekly Report* 1996c).

In Chile, the country where unemployment declined most and where trickle-down effects appeared to have the best chance to materialize, the figures indicate a paradoxical result. . . . both employment and real wages rose substantially between 1983 and 1995. Yet inequality failed to diminish because the income level of the highest decile rose still faster. As a result, Chile continued to have one of the most unequal income distributions in the hemisphere. Its Gini coefficient of .479 for 1994 was only slightly below that of Brazil, the country with the most unequal income distribution in the region and probably in the world (ECLAC 1995: Table 11; Filgueira 1996: 16).

A second, more subtle consequence of the lifting of state labor protections and the advent of free markets is the rise of exploitative practices in the work place. Chile is again a telling example, as the benefits of economic growth – employment and higher wages – have been accompanied by job insecurity and the increasing subjection of workers to arbitrary authority:

> Chilean law does not protect workers – especially women, the young, and the aged – against recessions, rationalization, and productive re-organizations. Nor does it protect them against authoritarian bosses who continue to exist in most Chilean enterprises and who have led to an increase in the intensity of work and the probability of work accidents in many of them. (Diaz 1996: 25)

Recent research on other countries raises a further complication, as it calls into question not only the consequences of labor transfers from the traditional to the modern sector, but the direction of that transfer itself. In particular, where the modern sector is comprised of labor-intensive firms facing stiff external competition, there is every incentive to drive wages and work conditions down. In these instances, many workers find traditional activities preferable to the harsh work and low pay in the "modern" sector. This is the case in the Dominican Republic, where conditions in the newly established export zones are so poor as to trigger a sizable return flow of labor toward informal self-employment. In his comparative study of labor markets in the Caribbean, Itzigsohn (1994: 257–8) reports this reversal:

> . . . the relaxation of laws which provide protection to workers leads, when carried to an extreme, to a complete blurring of the lines between the formal and informal economies; informal enterprise has acquired renewed importance, if not as an avenue of social mobility, at least as a source of whatever standards of living are achievable for many people in peripheral cities.

The informal economy is generally defined in the literature as a refuge for those unable to find jobs in the modern sector of the economy. In Latin America, this was standard usage during the period of import-substitution industrialization (Portes and Schauffler 1993; Perez-Sainz 1991; Tokman 1982). It is ironic that the advent of neoliberalism has reversed the prior relationship between the two sectors, turning informality into a refuge against the depredations of the free market. Neoclassical theory lacks the conceptual apparatus to approach these realities and, for this reason, tends to explain them away. The alternative perspective stemming from sociological theories of the economy is useful here as a source of a different family of testable propositions. For the case at hand, this reconceptualization of labor transfers leads to the following hypothesis:

4. In situations of labor oversupply, removal of state-enforced protections tends to drive the price of labor to a minimum. Workers in these situations compensate for the low remuneration of their human capital with the mobilization of their social capital – the ability to command scarce resources by virtue of membership in networks of kin and friendship. The economic opportunities that such networks make available are commonly situated in the informal economy, thus leading to a reversed labor flow toward this sector.

Escaping Trickle-Down: The Transnationalization of Labor

As they sought to break the barriers of foreign trade in the interest of a nascent industrial bourgeoisie, British political economists of the early nineteenth century envisioned a world in which commodities and capital flowed freely across national borders, but labor stayed put. This vision stemmed, in part, from the realities of the time in which mass labor migrations across national borders were exceptional and, in part, from the legacy of mercantilism. Indeed, for David Ricardo and other prominent representatives of the classical school, the battle to open Britain to cheap foreign grain was based on the need to lower the costs of reproduction of a largely immobile urban proletariat, thus making British industrial goods more competitive abroad (Dobb 1981; Letiche 1960).

Although the size and origins of international labor migrations have changed dramatically since that time, orthodox economic theory has remained firmly grounded on three postulates stemming from the classical period: (1) labor, for the most part, is immobile; (2) when migrations occur, they follow capital in search of employment; and (3) migrations are composed mostly of propertyless workers looking for higher wages. These postulates form the theoretical core for the analysis of labor displacements in terms of the push-pull framework where individuals stay or move on the basis of a rational calculus of interest, determined by the prior movement of capital. Brinley Thomas's classic study of trans-Atlantic migration, for example, posited a lagged correlation between these two movements (Thomas 1973: Part III).

The same postulates underlie the application of neoliberal adjustment policies in Latin America and other third world countries at present. Opening these economies to foreign capital is expected to increase local employment opportunities, drawing labor toward them and reducing incentives for outmigration. Those who continue to emigrate will be, for the most part, propertyless workers attracted by higher wages abroad. Some of these expectations are borne out by the recent empirical literature, but others are not.

Those who emigrate are seldom the poorest of the poor, and several studies indicate growing participation of professionals and entrepreneurs in these flows. Further, immigrants do not always go where labor demand exists, but where their co-nationals concentrate. A sizable number do not engage in wage labor at all, but move quickly into self-employment. Finally, there is no evidence that application of the neoliberal model has reduced the incentives for emigration, and, in countries like Mexico and the Dominican Republic, it has increased it (Acevedo and Espenshade 1992; Goldring 1992; Guarnizo 1994). In general, the origins and forms of contemporary international migration correspond poorly to predictions based on an exclusively individualistic calculus of costs and benefits and on orthodox expectations about the dynamics of capital and labor movements.

It is possible to construct an alternative explanation of international migration from an economic sociology perspective. Instead of isolated workers chasing capital at home and abroad, we have a more complex situation in which social networks are mobilized to cope with the new constraints and opportunities created by the neoliberal model. As was mentioned previously, the types of jobs generated by new export industries created under the stimulus of this model are frequently so unappealing that many workers opt for informal self-employment. Others adapt by moving abroad. Such a decision can seldom be implemented alone, however, but must be embedded in a web of family and community resources. This is the reason why groups of kin, not isolated individuals, tend to migrate and why migrants often select destinations not according to where labor demand exists, but according to where their networks are located (Massey and Espinosa 1996; Portes and Bach 1985; Tilly 1990).

... outmigration from less developed countries is a far more complex process than that depicted by economic push-pull theories and that its novel features are invariably embedded in the social and cultural context of immigrant communities. As multinational corporations break down barriers across countries in their quest for profits, they also open spaces that allow common people to seek new avenues to improve their precarious condition and avoid dead-end employment.

Immigrants turned into transnational entrepreneurs, like former employees of special export zones transformed into informal traders, provide evidence against predictions of a steady trickle-down effect. These workers have not waited for its dubious benefits to materialize, but have confronted the conditions foisted on them by globalization and neoliberalism with their personal and social resources. Their experiences can be summarized in the following final proposition:

5 Capital's search for cheap industrial labor in the third world does not lead to a uniform process of labor absorption. The more labor market conditions are stacked against peripheral workers, the more these groups will mobilize their social capital in search of alternatives. Economic globalization itself opens up new opportunities appropriated by immigrant entrepreneurs through mobilization of their networks. The growth of transnational enterprise is a direct outcome of this process.

Conclusion

I have reviewed theoretical perspectives in the sociology of development and sketched the concatenation of events in the global economy that led to the resurrection and hegemony of a market-oriented approach to economic development. This approach, which informs a standard set of policy measures applied in a number of countries, possesses considerable merit. Not the least of these is the coherent set of expectations about the behavior of individual economic actors and the possibility of submitting these predictions to empirical scrutiny. Yet many adherents of these ideas tend to dismiss their predictive failures or to explain them away in circular fashion. The outcome is a new form of scholasticism where facts are made to fit the theory rather than vice versa, with potentially serious practical consequences.

Both at the level of macro-structural results and at the level of effects on labor absorption and social equity, application of the neoliberal model confronts a series of contingencies that are not generally interpretable within the conceptual framework that inspires it. These alternative factors range from the character of the state apparatus and its relations with different sectors of civil society, to the size and composition of the population and the density of social networks among its less privileged sectors. Such forces determine variations in the outcomes of a uniform neoliberal policy package applied in different national contexts, and unexpected responses by the groups most directly affected.

The analysis of these forces and their effects belongs properly to the realm of the sociology of development. Incorporation of conceptual innovations coming from more general sociological theories of the economy should help this field produce fine-tuned descriptions of the political, demographic, and social conditions limiting the application of models of development and of the likely reaction of different sectors of the population. Without this type of work and its diffusion within policy-making circles, it is probable that neoliberal adjustment policies will continue to generate "surprises" and that the fulfillment of the developmental goals of sustained growth and social equity will become anything but certain.

By the same token, absent this type of work, the non-economic social sciences will remain confined to the margins of development policy debates, where they currently stand and where they do not properly belong. A renewed emphasis on the practical significance of demographic trends, social structures, and institutions should provide a much-needed corrective to the individualistic bias of the dominant paradigm.

REFERENCES

Acevedo, Dolores and Thomas J. Espenshade. 1992. "Implications of a North American Free Trade Agreement for Mexican migration into the United States," *Population and Development Review* 18: 729–44.

Amin, Samir. 1974. *Accumulation on a World Scale: A Critique of the Theory of Underdevelopment*. New York: Monthly Review Press.

Arrighi, Giovanni. 1994. *The Long Twentieth Century*. London: Verso Books.

Ayala, Jose and Clemente R. Duran. 1986. "Development and crisis in Mexico: A structuralist approach," in J. Hartlyn and S. A. Morley (eds.), *Latin American Political Economy, Financial Crisis and Political Change*, pp. 243–64. Boulder: Westview Press.

Bairoch, Paul. 1973. *Urban Unemployment in Developing Countries: The Nature of the Problem and Proposals for Its Solution*. Geneva: International Labour Office.

Balassa, Bela, Gerardo M. Bueno, Pedro-Pablo Kuczynsky, and Mario H. Simonsen. 1986. *Toward Renewed Economic Growth in Latin America*. Washington, DC: Institute for International Economics.

Bluestone, Barry and Bennett Harrison. 1982. *The Deindustrialization of America*. New York: Basic Books.

Bruton, Henry J. 1960. "Contemporary theorizing on economic growth," in B. F. Hoselitz et al. (eds.), *Theories of Economic Growth*, pp. 239–98. New York: Free Press.

Camp, Roderic A. 1993. *Politics in Mexico*. New York: Oxford University Press.

Castells, Manuel and Roberto Laserna. 1989. "The new dependency: Technological change and socio-economic restructuring in Latin America," *Sociological Forum* 4: 535–60.

Castells, Manuel and Alejandro Portes. 1989. "World underneath: The origins, dynamics, and effects of the informal economy," in A. Portes, M. Castells, and L. A. Benton (eds.), *The Informal Economy: Studies in Advanced and Less Developed Countries*, pp. 11–37. Baltimore: Johns Hopkins University Press.

Centeno, Miguel A. 1994. *Democracy within Reason: Technocratic Revolution in Mexico*. University Park: Pennsylvania State University Press.

Chase-Dunn, Christopher. 1982. *Socialist States in the World-System*. Beverly Hills: Sage.

Coleman, James S. 1988. "Social capital in the creation of human capital," *American Journal of Sociology* 94: S95–S121.

Cook, Maria Lorena, Kevin J. Middlebrook, and Juan M. Horcasitas. 1994. "The politics of economic restructuring in Mexico: Actors, sequencing, and coalition change," in M. L. Cook, K. J. Middlebrook, and J. M. Horcasitas (eds.), *The Politics of Economic Restructuring: State–Society Relations and Regime Change in Mexico*, pp. 3–52. San Diego: Center for U.S.–Mexican Studies.

Cordoba, Jose. 1994. "Mexico," in J. Williamson (ed.), *The Political Economy of Policy Reform*, pp. 232–84. Washington, DC: Institute for International Economics.

Deyo, Frederic C. 1989. *Beneath the Miracle: Labor Subordination in the New Asian Industrialism*. Berkeley: University of California Press.

Diaz, Alvaro. 1996. "Chile: Hacia el pos-Neoliberalismo?" paper presented at the Conference on Responses of Civil Society to Neo-Liberal Adjustment, University of Texas at Austin, April.

Dobb, Maurice. 1981. *Studies in the Development of Capitalism*. New York: International Publishers.

ECLAC (Economic Commission for Latin America and the Caribbean). 1990. *Crecimiento con Equidad*. Santiago de Chile: United Nations.

——. 1995. *Panorama Social de América Latina*. Santiago de Chile: United Nations.

Edwards, Richard C. 1979. *Contested Terrain: The Transformation of the Workplace in the Twentieth Century.* New York: Basic Books.

Edwards, Richard C., Michael Reich, and David M. Gordon. 1975. *Labor Market Segmentation.* Lexington: D. C. Heath.

Evans, Peter. 1979. *Dependent Development: The Alliance of Multinational, State, and Local Capital in Brazil.* Princeton: Princeton University Press.

——, ——. 1995. *Embedded Autonomy: States and Industrial Transformation.* Princeton: Princeton University Press.

Fernández-Kelly, M. Patricia. 1983. *For We Are Sold, I and My People: Women and Industry in Mexico's Frontier.* Albany: State University of New York Press.

Filgueira, Carlos. 1996. "Estado y sociedad civil: Políticas de ajuste estructural y estabilización en América Latina," paper presented at the Conference on Responses of Civil Society to Neo-Liberal Adjustment, University of Texas at Austin, April.

Foxley, Alejandro. 1981. "La economía chilena: Algunos temas del futuro," *Estudios CIEPLAN,* no. 6 (December): 177–88.

——, ——. 1983. *Latin American Experiments in Neo-Conservative Economics.* Berkeley: University of California Press.

Gereffi, Gary and Miguel Korzeniewicz. 1994. *Commodity Chains and Global Capitalism.* Westport: Praeger.

Gold, Thomas B. 1986. *State and Society in the Taiwan Miracle.* Armonk: M. E. Sharpe.

Goldring, Luin. 1992. "La Migración Mexico–EUA y la transnacionalización del espacio político y social: Perspectivas desde el Mexico rural," *Estudios Sociológicos* 29: 315–40.

Gordon, David. 1972. *Theories of Poverty and Unemployment.* Lexington: D. C. Heath.

Guarnizo, Luis E. 1994. "Los 'Dominican Yorkers': The making of a binational society," *Annals of the American Academy of Political and Social Science* 533: 70–86.

Harvey, David. 1982. *Limits to Capital.* Chicago: University of Chicago Press.

Hill, Richard C. and Kuniko Fujita. 1995. "Product cycles and international divisions of labor: Contrasts between the United States and Japan," in D. A. Smith and J. Borocz (eds.), *A New World Order? Global Transformations in the Late Twentieth Century,* pp. 91–108. Westport: Praeger.

Hopkins, Terence K. and Immanuel Wallerstein. 1977. "Patterns of development in the modern world-system," *Review* 1: 111–45.

Itzigsohn, José A. 1994. "The informal economy in Santo Domingo and San Jose: A comparative study," Ph.D dissertation, Department of Sociology, Johns Hopkins University.

Jaffee, David. 1986. "The political economy of job loss in the United States, 1970–1980," *Social Problems* 33: 297–318.

Kahl, Joseph A. 1976. "The new sociology in Latin America," in J. A. Kahl, *Modernization, Exploitation, and Dependency in Latin America,* pp. 1–22. New Brunswick: Transaction Books.

Kuznets, Simon. 1955. *Economic Growth and Structure.* New York: W. W. Norton.

Kyle, David. 1995. "The transnational peasant: The social structures of economic migration from the Ecuadoran Andes," Ph.D. dissertation, Department of Sociology, Johns Hopkins University.

Latin American Weekly Report. 1996a. "Credibility gap on Cavallo's forecasts," WR–96–24 (27 June): 284.

——. 1996b. "No 'boat-rocking' is the unspoken slogan as Cavallo is finally ditched," WR–96–30 (8 August): 349.

——. 1996c. "Unemployment: The regional picture," WR–96–18 (16 May): 212.

——. 1997. "Convertibility pact now in doubt: The crisis that led to the downfall of Bucarám," WR–97–07 (11 February): 77.

Letiche, J. M. 1960. "Adam Smith and David Ricardo on economic growth," in B. F. Hoselitz et al. (eds.), *Theories of Economic Growth*, pp. 65–88. New York: Free Press.

Lewis, W. Arthur. 1959. *The Theory of Economic Growth*. London: Allen and Unwin.

Light, Ivan and Edna Bonacich. 1988. *Immigrant Entrepreneurs: Koreans in Los Angeles 1965–1982*. Berkeley: University of California Press.

List, Friedrich. 1885. *The National System of Political Economy*. New York: Augustus Kelley.

Lomnitz, Larissa. 1982. "Horizontal and vertical relations and the social structure of urban Mexico," *Latin American Research Review* 17: 51–74.

Mahler, Sarah. 1995. *Dreaming in American*. Princeton: Princeton University Press.

Manning, Susan K. 1996. "Politics and economic change in Mexico: Neoliberalism, the state, and civil society," paper presented at the Conference on Responses of Civil Society to Neo-Liberal Adjustment, University of Texas at Austin, April.

Massey, Douglas S. and Kristin E. Espinosa. 1996. "What's driving Mexico–U.S. Migration? A theoretical, empirical, and policy analysis," paper presented at the Conference on Becoming American/America Becoming, Social Science Research Council, Sanibel Island, January.

McKenzie, Robert E. 1984. *Fugitive Industry: The Economics and Politics of Deindustrialization*. San Francisco: Ballinger.

McMichael, Philip. 1995. "The new colonialism: Global regulation and the restructuring of the state system," in D. A. Smith and J. Borocz (eds.), *A New World Order? Global Transformations in the Late Twentieth Century*, pp. 37–55. Westport: Praeger.

Meller, Patricio. 1981. "Problemas y opciones del modelo económico," *Estudios CIEPLAN*, no. 6 (December): 189–94.

Nielsen, François and Arthur S. Alderson. 1995. "Income inequality, development, and dualism: Results from an unbalanced cross-national panel," *American Sociological Review* 60 (October): 674–701.

O'Brien, Philip J. 1975. "A critique of Latin American theories of dependency," in I. Oxaal, T. Barnett, and D. Booth (eds.), *Beyond the Sociology of Development: Economy and Society in Latin America and Africa*, pp. 7–27. London: Routledge and Kegan Paul.

O'Connor, James. 1973. *The Fiscal Crisis of the State*. New York: St. Martin's Press.

Perez-Sainz, Juan Pablo. 1991. *Informalidad Urbana en América Latina*. Caracas: Nueva Sociedad.

Piñera, José. 1994. "Chile," in J. Williamson (ed.), *The Political Economy of Policy Reform*, pp. 225–31. Washington, DC: Institute for International Economics.

Piore, Michael J. and Charles F. Sabel. 1984. *The Second Industrial Divide*. New York: Basic Books.

Portes, Alejandro and John Walton. 1981. *Labor, Class, and the International System*. New York: Academic Press.

Portes, Alejandro and Robert L. Bach. 1985. *Latin Journey: Cuban and Mexican Immigrants in the United States*. Berkeley: University of California Press.

Portes, Alejandro and Douglas Kincaid. 1989. "Sociology and development in the 1990s: Critical challenges and empirical trends," *Sociological Forum* 4 (December): 479–503.

Portes, Alejandro and Richard Schauffler. 1993. "Competing perspectives on the Latin American informal sector," *Population and Development Review* 19: 33–60.

Prebisch, Raúl. 1950. *The Economic Development of Latin America and Its Principal Problems*. New York: United Nations.

——, ——. 1964. *The Economic Development of Latin America in the Post-War Period*. New York: United Nations.

——, ——. 1986. "Notes on trade from the standpoint of the periphery," *CEPAL Review* 28 (April): 203–16.

Puryear, Jeffrey M. 1994. *Thinking Politics: Intellectuals and Democracy in Chile, 1973–1988*. Baltimore: Johns Hopkins University Press.

Romo, Frank P. and Michael Schwartz. 1995. "The structural embeddedness of business decisions: The migration of manufacturing plants in New York State, 1960 to 1985," *American Sociological Review* 60 (December): 874–907.

Sassen, Saskia. 1988. *The Mobility of Labor and Capital: A Study in International Investment and Labor Flow.* New York: Cambridge University Press.

——, ——. 1989. "New York City's informal economy," in A. Portes, M. Castells and L. A. Benton (eds.), *The Informal Economy: Studies in Advanced and Less Developed Countries,* pp. 60–77. Baltimore: Johns Hopkins University Press.

Smith, Robert. 1992. "New York in Mixteca: Mixteca in New York," *NACLA Report on the Americas* 26(1).

——, ——. 1995. "Los ausentes siempre presentes: The imaging, making, and politics of a transnational community between Ticuani, Mexico and New York City," Ph.D. dissertation, Department of Political Science, Columbia University.

Storper, Michael and Richard Walker. 1989. *The Capitalist Imperative: Territory, Technology, and Industrial Growth.* New York: Basil Blackwell.

Thomas, Brinley. 1973. *Migration and Economic Growth: A Study of Great Britain and the Atlantic Economy.* Cambridge: Cambridge University Press.

Tilly, Charles. 1990. "Transplanted networks," in V. Yans-McLaughlin (ed.), *Immigration Reconsidered: History, Sociology, and Politics,* pp. 79–95. New York: Oxford University Press.

Tokman, Victor E. 1982. "Unequal development and the absorption of labour: Latin America, 1950–1980," *CEPAL Review* 17: 121–33.

Valenzuela, Arturo. 1978. *The Breakdown of Democratic Regimes: Chile.* Baltimore: Johns Hopkins University Press.

Wallerstein, Immanuel. 1974. *The Modern World-System: Capitalist Agriculture and the Origins of the European World-Economy in the Sixteenth Century.* New York: Academic Press.

——. 1991. *Geopolitics and Geoculture: Essays on the Changing World-System.* Cambridge: Cambridge University Press.

Waters, Mary C. 1994. "West Indian immigrants, African Americans, and whites in the workplace: Different perspectives on American race relations," paper presented at the meeting of the American Sociological Association, Los Angeles (August).

Williamson, John (ed.). 1994. *The Political Economy of Policy Reform.* Washington, DC: Institute for International Economics.

Wolpe, Harold. 1975. "The theory of internal colonialism: The South African case," in I. Oxaal, T. Barnett, and D. Booth (eds.), *Beyond the Sociology of Development: Economy and Society in Latin America and Africa,* pp. 252–79. London: Routledge and Kegan Paul.

You, Jong-il. 1988. "South Korea," in S. Herzenberg and J. F. Perez-Lopez (eds.), *Labor Standards and Development in the Global Economy,* pp. 97–121. Washington, DC: US Department of Labor.

Zhou, Min and Carl L. Bankston. 1995. "Entrepreneurship," in I. Natividad (ed.), *Asian American Almanac,* pp. 511–28. Columbus, OH: Gale Research.

First-Hand Resources on Development: Web Sites of Development Agencies and Groups

AD2000 and Beyond Movement
www.ad2000.org

CARE Development Facts
www.care.org/world/devfact.html

Corporate Watch
www.corpwatch.org

Development Alternatives with Women for a New Era (DAWN)
www.dawn.org.fj/

Global Exchange
www.globalexchange.org/

The Globalization and the MAI Information Centre
www.islandnet.com/~ncfs/maisite/homepage.html

Hoover Institute
www-hoover.stanford.edu/

Institute for Food and Development Policy (Food First)
www.foodfirst.org/

Institute for International Economics
www.iie.com/

Inter-American Development Bank
www.iadb.org/

The International Centre for Human Rights and Democratic Development
www.ichrdd.ca/

International Development Network: Sources
www.idn.org

International Institute for Sustainable Development
www.iisd1.iisd.ca/

International Labour Organization
www.ilo.org/

International Monetary Fund
www.imf.org/

Overseas Development Council
www.odc.org/

Pan-American Health Organization
www.paho.org/

Rainforest Action Network
www.ran.org

Sustainable Development and the Americas
www.txinfinet.com/mader/ecotravel/sustain.html

UNICEF
www.unicef.org

United Nations Development Programme
www.undp.org/

United Nations
www.un.org/

US Agency for International Development
www.info.usaid.gov

UT-LANIC: Latin American Resources
www.lanic.utexas.edula/region/development/

The World Bank
www.worldbank.org/

World Health Organization
www.who.org/

World Resources Institute
www.wri.org/

World Trade Organization
www.wto.org/

World Wildlife Fund
www.wwf.org

Further Reading

Readers particularly interested in one or a series of the readings in this book would be well advised to seek out the original documents from which they are drawn. Beyond those, we suggest some general discussions of development and some specific texts for each section of the reader. This list is by no means exhaustive; these are pieces we believe are especially clear and approachable, and many are readings we had to cut from this volume.

General Perspectives on Development

Allahar, Anton L. 1995. *Sociology and the Periphery: Theories and Issues*. Toronto: Garamond.

Brohman, John. 1996. *Popular Development*. Cambridge, MA: Basil Blackwell.

Evans, Peter B. and John D. Stephens. 1988. "Development and the World Economy," in *Handbook of Sociology*, ed. Neil J. Smelser. Newbury Park, CA: Sage Publications, pp. 739–73.

Gereffi, Gary. 1994. "The International Economy and Economic Development," in *The Handbook of Economic Sociology*, ed. Neil J. Smelser and Richard Swedberg. Princeton, NJ: Princeton University Press, pp. 206–33.

Harrison, David. 1988. *The Sociology of Modernization and Development*. London: Routledge.

Klaren, Peter F. and Thomas J. Bossert. 1986. *Promise of Development: Theories of Change in Latin America*. Boulder, CO: Westview Press.

Larrain, Jorge. 1989. *Theories of Development: Capitalism, Colonialism and Dependency*. Malden, MA: Basil Blackwell.

McMichael, Philip. 1996. *Development and Social Change*. Thousand Oaks, CA: Pine Forge Press.

Portes, Alejandro and John Walton. 1981. *Labor, Class and the International System*. New York: Academic Press.

Preston, P. W. 1996. *Development Theory: An Introduction*. Cambridge, MA: Basil Blackwell.

Sklair, Leslie. 1991. *Sociology of the Global System*. Baltimore, MD: Johns Hopkins University Press.

Classics

Adam Smith. 1776. *The Wealth of Nations*.

Calhoun, Calhoun. Forthcoming. *Classic Sociological Theory*. Cambridge, MA: Basil Blackwell.

Ricardo, David. 1891. *Principles of Political Economy and Taxation*. London: G. Bell and Sons.

Simmel, Georg. 1950. *The Sociology of Georg Simmel*, ed. and trans. Kurt Wolff. New York: Free Press.

Tönnies, Ferdinand. 1963. *Community & Society (Gemeinschaft und Gesellschaft)*, trans. and ed. Charles P. Loomis. New York: Harper and Row.

Modernization

Germani, Gino. 1975. "Stages of Modernization in Latin America," in *Latin America: The Dynamics of Social Change*, ed. Stefan A. Halper and John R. Sterling. New York: St. Martin's Press, pp. 1–43.

Hirschman, Albert. O. 1958. *The Strategy of Economic Development*. New Haven, CT: Yale University Press.

Hoselitz, Bert F. 1960. *Sociological Aspects of Economic Growth*. Glencoe, IL: The Free Press.

Kuznets, Simon. 1954. "Economic Growth and Income Inequality," *American Economic Review*, 45: 1–28.

McClelland, D. C. 1961. *The Achieving Society*. New York: Free Press.

Rustow, Dankwart. 1967. *World of Nations: Problems of Political Modernization*. Washington, DC: Brookings Institution.

Structuralism, Dependency, and World Systems

Amin, Samir. 1976. *Unequal Development*. London: Monthly Review Press.

Baran, Paul. 1957. *The Political Economy of Growth*. New York: Monthly Review Press.

Boserup, Ester. 1970. *Women's Role in Economic Development*. New York: St. Martin's Press.

Dos Santos, Theotonio. 1970. "The Structure of Dependence," *American Economic Review*, 60 (2): 231–6.

Evans, Peter B. 1979. *Dependent Development: The Alliance of Multinational, State, and Local Capital in Brazil*. Princeton, NJ: Princeton University Press.

Furtado, Celso. 1970. *Economic Development of Latin America*. London: Cambridge University Press.

Kay, Cristobal. 1989. *Latin American Theories of Development and Underdevelopment*. London: Routledge.

Prebisch, Raúl. 1950. *The Economic Development of Latin America and its Problems*. New York: United Nations.

Shannon, Thomas R. 1996. *An Introduction to the World-System Perspective*, 2nd edn. Boulder, CO: Westview Press.

Globalization

Amsden, Alice. 1990. "Third World Industrialization: 'Global Fordism' or a New Model," *New Left Review*, 182: 5–31.

Belassa, Bela, Gerardo M. Bueno, Pedro-Pablo Kuczynski, and Mario Henrique Simonsen. 1986. *Toward Renewed Economic Growth in Latin America*. Washington, DC: Institute for International Economics.

Dicken, Peter. 1992. *Global Shift: The Internationalization of Economic Activity*. New York: Guilford.

Gordon, David M., Richard Edwards, and Michael Reich. 1982. *Segmented Work, Divided Workers: The Historical Transformation of Labor in the United States*. New York: Cambridge University Press.

Harvey, David. 1989. *The Condition of Postmodernity*. Cambridge, MA: Basil Blackwell.

Long, Norman. 1990. "From Paradigm Lost to Paradigm Regained? The Case for an Actor-oriented Sociology of Development", *European Review of Latin American and Caribbean Studies*, 49 (December): 3–24.

Mingione, Enzo. 1991. *Fragmented Societies: A Sociology of Economic Life Beyond the Market Paradigm*. Oxford: Basil Blackwell.

Roberts, J. Timmons. 1996. "Global Restructuring and the Environment in Latin America," in *Latin America and the World Economy*, ed. Roberto P. Korzeniewicz and William C. Smith. Westport, CT: Greenwood Press, pp. 187–210.

Tinker, Irene, ed. 1990. *Persistent Inequalities: Women and World Development*. New York: Oxford University Press.

Trainer, Ted. 1989. *Developed to Death: Rethinking Third World Development*. London: Green Point.

UNRISD. 1997. *States of Disarray: The Social Effects of Globalization*. Geneva: UNRISD.

Walton, John and David Seddon. 1994. *Free Markets & Food Riots: The Politics of Global Adjustment*. Cambridge, MA: Blackwell.

Index